The *Routledge Companion to Non-Market Strategy* field and identifies a rich set of research opportunities for improving our understanding of the non-market environment, for developing new insights to improve strategy formulation and selection, and for empirically evaluating the effectiveness of strategies for enhancing a firm's performance and legitimacy.

Foreword from David P. Baron, University of Stanford, USA

The authors of this volume have an exciting project: dragging the strategy discipline beyond the clichés of market competition towards full recognition of regulators, family networks, not-for-profits, pressure groups, and state-owned enterprises as crucial actors in the contemporary environment. They advance a view in which markets are much more complex than traditionally seen.

Richard Whittington, Professor, University of Oxford, UK

A comprehensive, thorough, and contemporary examination of the field of non-market strategy. Each chapter is written by the leading figures of the discipline, and provides a complete and authoritative overview of the state of knowledge on some of the most central questions and debates. The whole spectrum of non-market activities is covered in this Companion – from corporate political activities and social responsibility, to climate change. No other non-market strategy book covers the same range of topics in this depth. This superb book is indispensable for any scholar or student of non-market strategy.

Kamel Mellahi, Professor, University of Warwick, UK

The Routledge Companion to Non-Market Strategy

It is commonplace for today's transnational enterprises to undertake political, social, and environmental risk analysis when choosing foreign markets and creating entry strategies. Despite this, non-market elements of corporate strategy are less well researched than the traditional market-based perspectives.

Providing comprehensive and leading-edge overviews of current scholarship, this Companion surveys the current state of the field and provides a basis for improving our understanding of the non-market environment, encouraging new insights to improve strategies for enhancing a firm's performance and legitimacy.

With a foreword by David Baron, the international team of contributors includes Jean-Philippe Bonardi, Bennet Zelner, and Jonathan Doh, who combine to create a book that is essential reading for students and researchers in business, management, and politics, including those interested in business regulation, environmental policy, political risk, and corporate social responsibility.

Thomas C. Lawton is Professor of Strategy and International Management at the Open University Business School, UK, and Visiting Professor at the Tuck School of Business, Dartmouth, USA.

Tazeeb S. Rajwani is Senior Lecturer in Strategic Management at Cranfield School of Management, UK.

Routledge Companions in Business, Management and Accounting

Routledge Companions in Business, Management and Accounting are prestige reference works providing an overview of a whole subject area or sub-discipline. These books survey the state of the discipline, including emerging and cutting-edge areas. Providing a comprehensive, up-to-date, definitive work of reference, each Routledge Companion can be cited as an authoritative source on the subject.

A key aspect of these Routledge Companions is their international scope and relevance. Edited by an array of highly regarded scholars, these volumes also benefit from teams of contributors who reflect an international range of perspectives.

Individually, Routledge Companions in Business, Management and Accounting provide an impactful one-stop-shop resource for each theme covered. Collectively, they represent a comprehensive learning and research resource for researchers, postgraduate students and practitioners.

Published titles in this series include:

The Routledge Companion to Non-Market Strategy

Edited by Thomas C. Lawton and Tazeeb S. Rajwani

LONDON AND NEW YORK

First published 2015
by Routledge

2 Park Square, Milton Park, Abingdon, Oxfordshire OX14 4RN
711 Third Avenue, New York, NY 10017

Routledge is an imprint of the Taylor & Francis Group, an informa business

First issued in paperback 2018

British Library Cataloguing in Publication Data
A catalogue record for this book is available from the British Library

Library of Congress Cataloging in Publication Data
The Routledge companion to non-market strategy / edited by Thomas
C. Lawton, Tazeeb Rajwani.
   pages cm. – (Routledge companions in business, management and
   accounting)
   Includes bibliographical references and index.
   1. International business enterprises–Management. 2. Comparative
   management. 3. Strategic planning. I. Lawton, Thomas C., editor.
   II. Rajwani, Tazeeb, editor.
   HD62.4.R6956 2015
   658.4'012–dc23   2014039642

ISBN: 978-0-415-71231-6 (hbk)
ISBN: 978-1-138-36323-6 (pbk)

Typeset in Bembo
by Sunrise Setting Ltd, Paignton, UK

For Thomas, to Eileen and James
For Tazeeb, to Sultan and Zarina

Contents

Contents

SECTION D
Non-market context and challenges

Illustrations

Figures

Tables

Exhibits

Contributors

Yusaf H. Akbar is Associate Professor in Management at the Central European University, Hungary.

David Bach is Senior Lecturer in Global Business and Politics at Yale School of Management, USA.

Paul R. Baines is Professor of Political Marketing at Cranfield University School of Management, UK.

Rodrigo Bandeira-de-Mello is Professor of Strategic Management at FGV EAESP, Brazil.

David Baron is David S. and Ann M. Barlow Professor of Political Economy and Strategy, Emeritus, at the Graduate School of Business, Stanford University, USA.

Jean-Philippe Bonardi is Professor of Strategy in the Faculty of Business and Economics, University of Lausanne, Switzerland.

Ariel A. Casarin is Associate Professor, Escuela de Negocios, Universidad Adolfo Ibáñez, Chile.

Izzet Sidki Darendeli is a doctoral candidate in Strategic Management at Fox School of Business, Temple University, USA.

Jonathan P. Doh is the Herbert G. Rammrath Endowed Chair in International Business at Villanova University School of Business, USA.

Sinziana Dorobantu is Assistant Professor of Management and Organizations at Stern Business School, New York University, USA.

Gabriel Eweje is Associate Professor in Business and Sustainability at the School of Management, Massey University, New Zealand.

Susan Feinberg is Associate Professor of Strategic Management at Fox School of Business, Temple University, USA.

Jedrzej George Frynas is Professor of CSR and Strategic Management at Middlesex University Business School, UK.

Abby Ghobadian is Professor of Organisational Performance and Head of the School of Leadership, Organisations and Behaviour at Henley Business School, University of Reading, UK.

Thomas Graf holds a Ph.D. in Strategic Management from IE Business School, Spain.

Thomas A. Hemphill is Associate Professor of Strategy, Innovation and Public Policy at the University of Michigan-Flint, USA.

T.L. Hill is Associate Professor in Strategic Management at Fox School of Business, Temple University, USA.

Carola Hillenbrand is Professor of Organisational Psychology at Henley Business School, University of Reading, UK.

Contributors

Anna John is Lecturer in Strategic Management at the Open University Business School, UK.

Allison F. Kingsley is Assistant Professor of Management in the School of Business Administration, University of Vermont, USA.

Maciej Kisilowski is Assistant Professor at the Central European University, Hungary.

Carl Joachim Kock is Professor of Strategy at IE Business School, Spain.

Thomas C. Lawton is Professor of Strategy and International Management at the Open University Business School, UK, and Visiting Professor at the Tuck School of Business, Dartmouth, USA.

Benjamin Littell is Research Fellow at Villanova University School of Business, USA.

Steven McGuire is Professor of Management and Director of the School of Management and Business, University of Aberystwyth, UK.

Ishva Minefee is a doctoral candidate in the College of Business, University of Illinois at Urbana-Champaign, USA.

Kevin Money is Associate Professor of Reputation at Henley Business School, University of Reading, UK.

Jennifer Oetzel is Associate Professor at the Kogod School of Business, American University, USA.

Chang Hoon Oh is Associate Professor of International Business at the Beedie School of Business, Simon Fraser University, Canada.

Nitha Palakshappa is Senior Lecturer in the School of Communication, Journalism and Marketing, Massey University, New Zealand.

Susan E. Perkins is Assistant Professor of Management and Organizations at the Kellogg School of Management, Northwestern University, USA.

Tazeeb S. Rajwani is Senior Lecturer in Strategic Management at Cranfield School of Management, UK.

Jorge E. Rivera is Professor of Strategic Management and Public Policy in the School of Business, George Washington University, USA.

Gabriele Suder is Principal Fellow at Melbourne School of Business and Director of International Relations, University of Melbourne, Australia.

Peter Tashman is Assistant Professor of Management in the School of Business Administration, Portland State University, USA.

Richard G. Vanden Bergh is Associate Professor of Strategic Management, School of Business Administration, University of Vermont, USA.

Howard Viney is Senior Lecturer in Strategic Management at the Open University Business School, UK.

George O. White III is Assistant Professor of Management and International Business at Old Dominion University, USA.

Monika Winn is Professor of Business Strategy and Sustainability at the Peter B. Gustavson School of Business, University of Victoria, Canada.

Bennet A. Zelner is Associate Professor of Business and Public Policy at the Robert H. Smith School of Business, University of Maryland, USA.

Acknowledgments

We first wish to thank friends and colleagues in the non-market strategy community for their inspiration and support in the development of this book. Many have contributed to this *Companion*, and to each and every one we extend our sincere gratitude. Without their enthusiasm and commitment, this project would not have come to fruition.

We want to thank our editorial team at Routledge, particularly Terry Clague and Sinéad Waldron, for their unfailing encouragement and patience. We are grateful for their professionalism and guidance throughout this project.

Our thanks to the Open University and to Cranfield University for their ongoing support and facilitation of this research and of our work on non-market strategy more broadly. We appreciate and acknowledge the financial backing of our respective institutions to attend the Academy of Management, Academy of International Business and Strategic Management Society conferences to share our research and to build momentum for this book.

Last but not least, a special thank you to our wives, Katalin and Carly, as without their love and support this process would have been a longer and more arduous journey.

Thomas would like to dedicate this book to his parents, Eileen and James, and Tazeeb wishes to dedicate the book to his parents, Sultan and Zarina. Our endeavors would not have been possible without their faith, generosity and wisdom in developing us as reflective human beings.

Thomas C. Lawton and
Tazeeb S. Rajwani

Foreword

Over the past 25 years, non-market strategy has flourished as a field of scholarly inquiry and has become an increasingly important component of the strategy arsenal of most firms. Yet it is not new. Firms in regulated industries and state-owned firms have long interacted with government, as have firms in resource-extraction industries. In many countries, particularly in Asia, family-controlled holding companies have maintained long-established political ties with governments. Direct social pressure was also a factor for some firms, as evidenced by the boycott of Nestlé over the marketing of infant formula in developing countries and the anti-apartheid campaigns against Western firms operating in South Africa. Scholars and their textbooks naturally focused on market failures and government intervention in markets, political strategies for regulated firms, and firms' responsibilities to their stakeholders.

In the 1970s the importance of non-market strategy increased sharply due to the wave of social regulation that focused on the environment, occupational and product safety, and other social issues that cut across industry lines. Many firms that had operated largely free of government regulation found themselves having to deal with complex regulations that forced changes in their operating practices and strategies. Also, in many countries, the participation of government in the economy expanded. Firms began to recognize that they needed to participate in public policy processes rather than have policy developed in response to opposing interest groups. The importance of non-market strategy also increased as a result of the deregulation and privatization movements. Scholars turned their attention away from the evaluation of market failures and government intervention and towards the strategies of firms participating in developing the rules of the game that governed market competition and shaped the non-market environment in which they operated. Some firms that thought they were free from these forces found their competitors working to shape the rules to their own advantage and were forced to participate to protect their interests.

By the early 1990s firms had sharpened their non-market strategies and slowed the pace of new government regulation. Some critics of business turned their attention from influencing government to directly targeting companies through, for example, naming and shaming campaigns. The non-market strategies of activist non-governmental organizations (NGOs) proved successful in many instances, and, particularly after Greenpeace's success in stopping Shell from disposing of the obsolete Brent Spar oil platform in the North Atlantic, direct pressure on firms both intensified and broadened. Firms facing criticism of and attacks on their market strategies began to develop non-market strategies to deal with the pressure they faced. Some firms, however, were too powerful to challenge with campaigns, and activists and NGOs innovated by targeting their supply and distribution chains. This exposed a much larger set of firms to social pressure and broadened the importance of non-market strategy. Firms responded by self-regulating. This self-regulation was often called corporate social responsibility (CSR), but its motivation was different from the earlier version that focused on responsibilities to stakeholders. Some firms discovered that this strategic social responsibility could also be used in marketing and reputation-building. For these firms, non-market strategy was naturally integrated with their market strategy. Non-market strategy had evolved from being a necessary response of industries to government regulation to being an integral component of value creation and preservation.

Researchers followed these developments, providing frameworks to help understand which non-market strategies were successful in which settings. Strategies that were effective in countries where the rules of the game were clear, however, were often ineffective where those rules were unclear or at times arbitrary. Effective non-market strategies, for example in emerging markets, had to address new forms of political risk and an often country-specific set of challenges. Corruption and lax enforcement of regulations complicated the market and non-market landscapes these firms faced. The wave of outsourcing and globalization exposed more firms to the challenges of operating in emerging markets.

Most research on non-market strategy focuses on established firms, yet innovation often begins with entrepreneurs who have new ideas for value creation. Some entrepreneurial firms are able to operate without a non-market strategy or to free-ride on the efforts of others, but many others face non-market issues early in their lives. Uber, for example, immediately faced regulations governing taxi and livery service, and those regulations varied not only by country but even by city. Moreover, in some local markets interest groups, including taxi drivers and in some countries public transportation workers, organized protests and worked for more stringent regulations to limit Uber's penetration of their markets. Similarly, Tesla faced a host of local regulations on the marketing of its automobiles, and well-organized auto dealers sought to erect new barriers. Internet-based firms faced challenges ranging from user privacy protection to censorship and taxation. Amazon and Airbnb initially were able to avoid collecting sales and value-added taxes, but non-market forces developed to require collection, reducing their competitive advantage over traditional retailers and hotels. The study of non-market strategy for entrepreneurial firms is still in its infancy, providing many research opportunities.

Non-market strategies can be thought of as serving one or more of five purposes. One is rent seeking, as when wind and solar power companies seek to continue their generous subsidization. More important are strategies directed at unlocking opportunities, as when firms seek to open markets closed by a government or to deregulate an industry dominated by government-controlled firms. Third, and more frequently, non-market strategies are used to defend against rivals and critics seeking to restrict a firm's opportunities or operations, to forestall social pressure directed by activists and NGOs, and to forestall initiatives of governments seeking to impose additional responsibilities on firms. Fourth, non-market strategy may be used to attract customers with preferences for environmental protection, social justice, or the protection of rights. Fifth, non-market strategies are used to create value by strengthening reputations, building trust, and enhancing legitimacy. Self-regulation, the acceptance of social responsibilities, forthrightness, and relationship-building are often components of these strategies.

Scholars from a variety of disciplinary backgrounds have been attracted to non-market strategy, and naturally they have developed quite different approaches to the field. This diversity has enriched the field but also left it disjointed. The absence of consensus and consolidation means that the opportunities for innovative research remain almost unlimited.

David P. Baron

The Routledge Companion to Non-Market Strategy presents the current state of the art in the field and identifies a rich set of research opportunities for improving our understanding of the non-market environment, for developing new insights to improve strategy formulation and selection, and for empirically evaluating the effectiveness of strategies for enhancing a firm's performance and legitimacy.

David P. Baron

Section A

Theoretical lenses on non-market strategy

Introduction

The evolution of non-market strategy in theory and practice

Thomas C. Lawton and Tazeeb S. Rajwani

The late Kenneth Waltz, father of the neorealist approach to international relations, first suggested that a bipolar world is more stable,[1] arguing that a world dominated by two great powers is less prone to large-scale conflict.[2] The end of the Cold War heralded the dissolution of this system and the emergence of a unipolar world dominated by the United States. Susan Strange's notion of structural power[3] seemed to support this thesis, since, during the 1990s, the US had the authority to shape and determine the structure of the global political economy. This power manifests as the ability to control the four key pillars of the world economy: security, production, finance, and knowledge.

As the twenty-first century has progressed, we have witnessed cracks appearing in this new world order. In addition to the financial burden and psychological strain that being a lone superpower places on a nation, other countries have been challenging the US for regional and global authority and influence. At a global level, the rise of China and the resurgence of Russia have tested the limits of US power, both economically and politically. At a regional level, countries like Brazil and India increasingly challenge the US's role as global hegemon. Although not all commentators agree, many believe that the world has entered an era of multipolarity, with no one center of gravity, and with power diffused amongst numerous countries.

The increased volatility and uncertainty heralded by a multipolar world economy, together with the challenges and opportunities of the post-recession/financial crisis era, ensure that non-market variables have become ever more important contextual inputs for corporate strategy decisions and actions. For international strategy, the influence and impact of non-market forces increases exponentially. For instance, it is commonplace for transnational enterprises to undertake political, regulatory, cultural, and social risk analysis when selecting foreign investment opportunities and devising entry strategies (Lawton, Doh, and Rajwani, 2014).

The challenge for academics, students, and practitioners alike is how to conceptualize, theorize, and manage non-market strategy. This book will explore key factors that constitute how, at a senior management level, firms anticipate, preempt, and respond to actors, influences, and actions emanating from the political/regulatory and cultural/social arenas.

The start – and often end – point for many strategic management courses is a discussion of PESTEL (political, economic, social, technological, environmental, and legal) variables. Usually described as "analysis," PESTEL is little more than an extensive list of factors that may or may not impact upon a company's strategy making and competitive advantage. As a consequence of this knowledge and know-how lacuna, interest in non-market strategy within the strategic management research and consulting communities has been increasing steadily. In particular, research on corporate political activity and corporate social responsibility has burgeoned, as have efforts to align both with market strategy principles and processes (Lawton, Doh, and Rajwani, 2014). With this in mind, our *Companion* tries to capture the state of knowledge in non-market strategy and offer a comprehensive guide to students and academics on the theoretical underpinnings, conceptual classifications, and thematic emphases of non-market strategy research.

The twenty-three chapters in this volume are organized in four thematic sections. All sections are essentially multidisciplinary in approach, but offer a distinct focus on strategic management. Disciplines drawn upon include economics, law, political science, public policy, sociology, psychology, and management. The structure is intended to reflect the increasing diversity of contemporary research on non-market strategy.

Each chapter provides an overview of current knowledge, identifying issues and discussing relevant debates. This is particularly the case in Sections A and B, whereas the chapters in Sections C and D tend to delve deeper into specific aspects, applications, or outcomes of non-market strategy. Most chapters also indicate future directions for research in the area. Some authors use qualitative approaches, while others use quantitative data points to extend or test theory in the non-market field. Some develop conceptual models and theories drawing on other studies to understand better this ever-expanding field.

Themes of the *Companion*

In preparing this book, we reviewed the dominant intellectual paradigms in non-market strategy research (Doh, Lawton, and Rajwani, 2012). Many of the authors identified in our review were invited to contribute to the *Companion* book. We established that the most comprehensive and intellectually useful way to subdivide the book was as follows:

- first, the *theoretical approaches* to the study and conceptualization of the non-market field;
- second, the disciplinary and intellectual *foundations and structures* of non-market research;
- third, engagement with stakeholders and practice and the *impact and performance* of non-market strategy; and
- fourth, the *context and challenges* of different countries and regions of the world, as well as the constraints and possible opportunities imposed by climate change, regional trade agreements, nonprofits, and other increasingly relevant non-market phenomena.

There is inevitably some overlap between sections and chapters, but this serves to reinforce the most important aspects of contemporary non-market strategy. The final set of chapters provides a wide-ranging analysis of non-market strategy in theory and practice across the globe.

Our contributors comprise both senior and emerging scholars from advanced and emerging economies. They are based in business and management and law schools, economics, sociology, and political science departments. The diversity of background and approach nonetheless coalesces around the centrality of the non-market to corporate strategy decisions and practices in the modern world economy. The result is a book that provides the reader with a holistic perspective on how to think about and approach non-market strategy.

We next discuss each section and chapter in brief, providing an overview of this *Companion*.

Section A: Theoretical lenses on non-market strategy

Political knowledge and the resource-based view of the firm

In Chapter 2, Bonardi and Vanden Bergh combine insights from the literature on knowledge and political markets to develop a unique typology of political knowledge into two dimensions, using the degree of institution-specificity and the degree of firm-specificity of political knowledge. Using this typology, the authors consider a resource-based view of non-market activities to think about the *types* of political knowledge that are valuable for firms or how they are learned or acquired.

An institutional perspective on non-market strategies for a world in flux

In Chapter 3, Feinberg, Hill, and Darendeli reconcile evidence from the economics and finance literature with ideas from the neo-institutional and corporate political activity (CPA) literature to examine relationships between firms' connections, non-market strategies, and outcomes during periods of institutional change. These approaches provide complementary points of view regarding the ways in which institutions shape firms and their non-market strategies. These diverse bodies of literature also provide insight into how firms' non-market strategies shape the institutional context for firm advantage. Finally, the authors focus on what happens, what works, and what questions are raised when institutions are in flux.

How regulatory uncertainty drives integrated market and non-market strategy

In this chapter, Kingsley and Vanden Bergh draw on the literature addressing political markets and multinational political risk to explain the drivers of regulatory uncertainty and the implications for firms' non-market strategies. They analyze both the demand and supply sides of the political market. On the demand side of the political market, they first introduce how the ideology and policy preference alignment of rival demanders affects regulatory uncertainty. On the supply side of the political market, they focus on how the concept of political constraints also affects regulatory uncertainty. They bring these two sides of the political market together, arguing that a specific regulatory context allows a focal firm to predict the level of regulatory uncertainty it will face if it makes an investment.

A politics and public policy approach

In Chapter 5, Bach outlines a politics and public policy approach to non-market strategy. The author explores how normal business operations in the presence of market failures link the firm's market- and non-market environments and thereby make strategic non-market management a managerial imperative. Once business operations have stretched into the non-market environment, as they frequently and inevitably do, the firm becomes a political actor alongside a multitude of other interest groups with varying degrees of organization vying for political power and influence. Failure to adjust to and account for these differences is the primary cause of countless corporate non-market failures.

The uneasy interplay between non-market strategy and international relations

In Chapter 6, McGuire explores the political science literature and the struggle to integrate the study of the firm into a broader understanding of power. Political science has been accused of lacking a theory of the firm, instead bundling the firm as a political actor into a more general theory of interest groups. Yet firms are, somewhat paradoxically, considered to be *primes inter pares* among interest groups for their capacity to mobilize resources in support of policy preferences. The sub-discipline of international relations has even less "space" for considering firms, and leaves the cross-border activities of firms to management studies. However, the growth of private regulatory regimes and an increasing appreciation of the impact of commercial activity on states and societies have produced a new effort to integrate the formally separate worlds of politics and business more fully.

Section B: Non-market foundations and structure

Corporate social responsibility

In Chapter 7, Doh and Littell trace the growth and development of CSR as a concept in practice and scholarship, noting differing perspectives on the antecedents and objectives of CSR in corporations. They focus especially on "strategic" views of CSR and their connection to non-market strategy. They describe company-specific and collective approaches to CSR and their relationship to non-market strategic objectives, as well as outlining non-market mechanisms and providing suggestions for future research.

Corporate political activity

In this chapter, John, Rajwani, and Lawton review various studies on corporate political activity (CPA) in firms and develop a framework that integrates and details the existing research in the non-market field. Using a systematic approach to review the CPA literature, the authors look at three domains within CPA that require more investigation – resources and capabilities, institutional focus, and political environment focus – and discuss the contributions of each to our understanding of CPA in the pursuit or defense of competitive advantage. The chapter also suggests that the internationalization of business and the rise of developing economies present scholars with the challenge of understanding CPA in more varied institutional settings.

Non-market strategies in legal arenas

In this chapter, Casarin discusses and elaborates on how legal arenas offer firms strategic options to sustain and create realizable value in relation to other players in the value chain. While politics plays a large role in judicial domains, the author narrows the focus to firms' non-market strategic behavior in legal arenas to give attention mainly to judicial actors and policy-makers. Moreover, this chapter examines how non-market strategies are used in legal arenas, and therefore it gives some attention to the law and economics of litigation. Also, the empirical review mostly focuses on the direct effects of firms' actions in legal environments, and indirectly looks at reputational, relational, and financial impacts that firms might experience when disputing issues in legal domains.

Culture and international investment

In Chapter 10, Mello addresses an empirical gap in the culture-based explanation for the internationalization of Brazilian multinationals. In particular, he specifies the political nature of the phenomena that affect the location of foreign direct investment (FDI) in culturally distant places. The author shows that not all firms in a given country are equally capable of jumping cultural distance, but those that are more closely connected to the home governments are more likely to cope with cultural distance. This argument also contributes towards specifying the value of political connections with home governments.

Managing business–government relationships through organizational advocacy

In Chapter 11, Viney and Baines discuss and exemplify a typology of different levels of relationship engagement (LRE) based upon the non-market strategic options available to an organization. They discuss how managers with responsibility for government relations can use their typology to tailor an appropriate and contingent non-market strategy which complements and aligns with the overall strategic direction of their organization. The typology is not intended as sequential, but rather it can develop a strategic approach that may involve the enacting of several options simultaneously or systematically plan for engagement as opportunities or threats emerge from decisions taken by governments or regulators.

Section C: Non-market impact and performance

Environmental performance and non-market strategy: the impact of inter-organizational ties

In the first chapter of Section C, Graf and Kock show that firms respond to non-market pressures in different ways, leading to rather heterogeneous efforts in terms of reducing or avoiding waste or developing environmentally friendly or even enhanced products or service ideas. Building on the existing literature, the authors propose that all these efforts also differ depending on the interaction with different stakeholders. They provide an overview of the key issues uncovered by environmental management studies, particularly emphasizing the impact of market versus non-market stakeholders. Thereafter, they highlight the potential impact of inter-organizational linkages, such as alliances or director interlocks, on a firm's environmental management. Finally, they explore the potentially important effects of these linkages.

Corporate responsibility and stakeholder relationship impact

In Chapter 13, Hillenbrand, Money, and Ghobadian provide two important contributions. First, they develop a theoretical model of how corporate responsibility (CR) impacts customer and employee relationships. Second, they foster empirical research with actual stakeholders. Their model is then empirically tested with customers and employees of a service organization in the UK that has implemented a range of CR-related activities into its business operations. This chapter differs notably from existing CR frameworks in that it operationalizes the impact of CR activities of firms at the level of customer and employee experiences of such activities. CR-related experiences are differentiated into experiences that impact individuals themselves ("self-related" CR experiences) and those that impact other stakeholders ("others-related" CR experiences). A theoretical model is developed that places both sets of CR-related experiences as exogenous variables in the model. The authors also find evidence that CR experiences drive the development of beliefs and trust independently and in the presence of "self-related" CR experiences.

Strategic CSR, value creation, and competitive advantage

In his chapter, Frynas investigates the links between strategic CSR, value creation, and competitive advantage by summarizing key ideas and theoretical frameworks. The chapter starts with a definition of strategic CSR. Then the key theoretical perspectives on CSR and the main papers on the organizational benefits of strategic CSR are summarized. Thereafter, the chapter explores innovation, which is regarded as a key potential benefit of strategic CSR. Two case vignettes are used to illustrate the application of Barney's VRIO framework and to explore the link between strategic CSR, value creation, and sustainable competitive advantage. The chapter ends with a brief discussion and directions for future research.

Managing non-market risk: is it possible to manage the seemingly unmanageable?

The focus of Oetzel and Hoon Oh's chapter is on discontinuous non-market risk. They review what major non-market discontinuities are, how they can be characterized, and what factors influence the likelihood that these discontinuities will affect businesses, and explore the range of strategic responses available to managers. An important contribution of this chapter is the discussion of innovative strategic responses that some firms have adopted to address non-market discontinuities. Rather than emphasizing risk avoidance strategies, the strategies introduced highlight situations and host-country and risk-specific conditions in which it might be appropriate for firms to engage in risk mitigation directly or indirectly at its source, or in enhancing the resiliency of firms and the communities and regions in which they operate.

States, markets, and the undulating governance of the global electric power supply industry: scholarship meets practice

In Chapter 16, Dorobantu and Zelner trace non-market strategy patterns through a historical analysis of the global electric power supply industry. Much of the research has looked at infrastructure industries such as telecommunications, water, sanitation, and gas, from which the appropriate balance between market and state governance has long been debated in both intellectual circles and policy arenas. Hence, the history of infrastructure industries and the fundamental transformations they have undergone can be written around the search for the answer to one of the most vexing questions about the state's role in the economy: when and how should governments intervene in markets in which the economics of existing technologies "naturally" limit competition, harming social welfare? This chapter explores this question with reference to non-market strategies.

Section D: Non-market context and challenges

Corporate climate change adaptation: an emerging non-market strategy in an uncertain world

In the first chapter of Section D, Tashman, Winn, and Rivera draw attention to the importance of non-market strategies for managing climate-change-related phenomena, specifically through the lens of corporate climate change adaptation (CCCA). The area of climate change lacks a common organizing framework that scholars can use to structure their approach to identifying, framing, and studying important questions. For this reason, this chapter develops one such framework around the diversity of exposure pathways through which climate-change-related pressures may affect the firm, and then proposes how this framework might be used as a basis for future research. Thus, the authors build a framework around categories reflecting the firm's exposure in its biophysical, industrial–economic, and institutional environments, which include political, social, and technological forces related to climate change.

Stakeholder collaboration as a catalyst for development: company–NPO partnerships in New Zealand

In Chapter 18, Eweje and Palakshappa examine collaboration between business and nonprofits for community development in New Zealand. The increasing demands on corporations to provide community development programs and assistance in the communities in which they operate have resulted in numerous collaborations designed to meet locally defined social and economic goals. Firm–nonprofit collaboration is becoming increasingly important as corporations grow in size and influence, and, in turn, public pressure intensifies for them to address pressing social and environmental concerns through non-market alternatives.

Regional trade agreements: non-market strategy in the context of business regionalization

In this chapter, Suder explores regionalization and its influence on corporate internationalization strategy. The form that regionalization takes is driven by political and regulatory actors in close proximity to firms' home markets or extending those markets; they shape business context and they are shaped by them at the same time. Hence, the regional nature of the world economy – determined in part by, or overlapping with, regional trade agreements (RTAs) – necessitates a regional strategy that includes non-market action. This non-market strategy is increasingly multi-layered, multi-venued (national, regional, and international), and multi-networked in scale and scope, and alters the internationalization knowledge available to the firm. With this in mind, the author provides an overview of such networks and their impact on non-market strategy, and subsequently links non-market strategy in RTAs to performance gains in corporate internationalization.

Wholly owned foreign subsidiary government relation-based strategies in the Philippines: regulatory distance and performance implications

White and Hemphill's chapter examines which dimensions of qualitative and quantitative performance are enhanced through wholly owned foreign subsidiary (WOFS) government relation-based strategy deployment in the Philippines, and how regulatory distance moderates these relationships. Their analysis, conducted on 181 WOFSs in the Philippines, suggests that government relation-based strategies (GRBSs) are positively related to different dimensions of qualitative performance, but negatively related to certain dimensions of quantitative performance. They also find that the relationship between GRBSs and qualitative and quantitative performance is moderated by regulatory distance.

Non-market strategy in Eastern Europe and Central Asia

In Chapter 21, Akbar and Kisilowski focus on specific non-market strategic decisions and initiatives taken by managers. Their research reflects a broader academic interest in managerial influence within the processes of strategy process. Academics in this tradition have generally questioned the descriptive and prescriptive usefulness of the classic definition of strategy as a top-down approach. This choice of level of granularity of their analysis proves helpful in demonstrating some important characteristics of non-market strategies in the wider Eastern European and Central Asian region. These specificities are evident precisely when non-market strategies are examined through the prism of concrete decisions and types of initiatives rather than broader strategy narratives. Thus, the authors explore initiatives that depend on the level of political–economic development of a given country. Non-market initiatives also vary based on whether they represent a proactive or reactive choice and by the level of non-market risks.

Jeitinho Brasileiro: adopting non-market strategies in Brazil

In the book's penultimate chapter, Perkins and Minefee explore non-market strategy in Brazil, providing both a context for market dynamics and case examples of the institutional voids that require the most navigation. The authors expose the expropriation risks present in this complex corporate, legal, social, and political environment and show how foreign firms could benefit by developing a *jeitinho Brasileiro*, a Portuguese term used throughout this chapter which means "the Brazilian way of doing things." They argue that with the implementation of culturally informed non-market strategies, a foreign investor has the opportunity to navigate successfully through the tendentious institutional environment for which Brazil has become infamous.

Conclusion: where next for non-market strategy?

In the final chapter, we summarize and consolidate the key contributions of the *Routledge Companion to Non-market Strategy*. We also explore new and emergent streams of research in non-market strategy scholarship. Finally, we look at nascent research opportunities and thematics and raise some broad non-market challenges touched on by various contributors to this *Companion*.

Notes

1 Waltz, K. N. 1964. The stability of a bipolar world. *Daedalus*, 93(3): 881–909.
2 Waltz, K. N. 1979. *Theory of International Politics*. Reading, MA: Addison-Wesley.
3 Strange, S. 1988. *States and Markets*. London: Pinter.

Bibliography

Doh, J., Lawton, T., and Rajwani, T. 2012. Advancing non-market strategy research: institutional perspectives in a changing world. *Academy of Management Perspectives*, 26(3): 22–39.

Hillman, A. J. and Hitt, M. A. 1999. Corporate political strategy formulation: a model of approach, participation, and strategy decisions. *The Academy of Management Review*, 24(4): 825–42.

Lawton, T. C., Doh, J. P., and Rajwani, T. 2014. *Aligning for Advantage: Competitive Strategies for the Political and Social Arenas*. Oxford: Oxford University Press.

2

Political knowledge and the resource-based view of the firm

Jean-Philippe Bonardi and Richard G. Vanden Bergh

Why does the propensity to engage in the political process vary across firms? Existing research on corporate political strategy emphasizes the role of external or industry-level factors in explaining such differences – the concentration of firms within an industry, the costs of collective action (Olson, 1965; Stigler, 1971; Grier, Munger, and Roberts, 1994), the existence of industry associations (Weymouth, 2010), the degree of public procurement (Masters and Keim, 1985), and the attractiveness of political markets, including the extent of interest group rivalry (Bonardi, Hillman, and Keim, 2005). To explain firm-level variations, however, recent literature has explored the idea that firms acquire or develop specific non-market resources or capabilities, which anchor their political activities (Dahan, 2005; Oliver and Holzinger, 2008; Holburn and Zelner, 2010; Bonardi, 2011).

Among other political assets, this literature stresses the importance of political knowledge in order to navigate non-market environments of a different nature. As suggested by Holburn and Zelner (2010: 1292):

> The capacity to choose the right resources ex ante (Makadok, 2001) – to identify key local political actors and their preferences – represents an especially important component of political capabilities for MNEs [multinational enterprises] entering new host countries. MNEs suffer a liability of foreignness (Zaheer, 1995) relative to domestic competitors and interest groups as a result of local actors' superior jurisdiction-specific political resources, including detailed knowledge of the identities and preferences of key local political actors and, in many cases, direct ties to these actors.

Other literature also supports the idea that political knowledge is critical to what firms do, including the literature on political connections (Faccio, 2006) and political lobbying (Kersh, 1986). Little is known, however, about what political knowledge really is. While there is a growing literature that explores the fit between integrated market and non-market strategies and the characteristics of the political market (e.g., Baron, 1995b; de Figueiredo, 2009; Kingsley, Vanden Bergh, and Bonardi, 2012), researchers have only implicitly addressed the importance of political knowledge as a component of integrated strategy. From our reading of the literature, we found that no scholars have developed a deeper understanding of political knowledge, the tradeoffs associated with developing it, and how it affects the design of integrated strategy.

In this paper we contribute to the political strategy literature[1] by focusing on the role of organizational knowledge about the political environment in explaining firm-level differences in political engagement. Organizational knowledge enables firms to employ, manipulate, and transform various organizational resources effectively into desired outputs (Nonaka, 1991). It may be embedded explicitly or tacitly in entities such as tools, tasks, technologies, and people. When replication or transmission is difficult, internally generated organizational knowledge can serve as the basis for sustained competitive advantage and superior performance in the market place (Nelson and Winter, 1982). Several previous studies and case-study evidence suggest that firms can develop knowledge of their political environment through experience in dealing with local governments, stakeholders, and political actors in a jurisdiction (Suarez, 1998). However, as far as we are aware, no research has provided a framework to think about the *types* of political knowledge that are valuable for firms or how they are learned or acquired. This is one purpose of our paper.

As an illustration, consider the example of a "big box" retail chain store, such as Walmart or Target, which wishes to obtain local municipal council approval to open a store in a new city. What types of political knowledge does a firm need to obtain such approval? And how can that knowledge be acquired? At the most basic level firms need to understand the institutional process through which permitting decisions are made: how to initiate an application; what documentation to submit; voting rules on relevant committees and the full council; appeals mechanisms; and so forth. Since retail developments can elicit varying degrees of local opposition, firms must also assess the likely nature and intensity of organized stakeholder action, such as from labor unions, small business associations, and competitors, all of which may exert influence, either positive or negative, on the council. In addition, knowledge of the general preferences of individual councilors and city staff towards new retail sites will enable firms to assess the unconditional probability of obtaining a favorable decision. Knowledge of councilor preferences regarding the specific application at hand is also important as market and non-market conditions can be heterogeneous even in a single municipality. Especially critical, however, is knowing how to bargain effectively with or obtain the support of pivotal decision-makers (Krehbiel, 1998; Holburn and Vanden Bergh, 2004). Gaining political support, through formal and informal mechanisms, requires knowledge of the value that politicians place on additional assets that the firm can provide – such as employment guarantees, local sourcing commitments, funding of charities or community projects, or electoral campaign contributions – as well as the cost to the firm of making such offers. Identifying and crafting mutually beneficial "trades" can be a lengthy process of discovery and negotiation as each deal is idiosyncratic. In the case of the opening of a new Target store in Harlem, New York, one observer noted that:

> the preparations were extreme: nearly 10 years of calculated philanthropy and schmoozing across Harlem, an effort that Minneapolis-based Target has characterized as smart community relations but critics suggested was akin to bribery. Long before the ribbon-cutting, Target had wooed notable Harlem residents with dinner parties, struck deals to carry exclusive gear designed by neighborhood luminaries, and sponsored prominent charitable projects and events, including the refurbishing of a school library and the sprucing up of a rundown lot near the store on 117th Street.

> (Clifford, 2010)

In this chapter we combine insights from the literature on knowledge (Hayek, 1945; Dosi and Marengo, 2007) and from the literature on political markets (Bonardi, Holburn and Vanden Bergh, 2006) to develop a unique typology of political knowledge that simplifies the situation above into two main dimensions – the degree of institution-specificity and the degree of firm-specificity of political knowledge – on which we elaborate below. Armed with this typology, we consider two questions that are central to developing a resource-based view of firms' non-market activities. First, we consider governance mechanism choices: when firms want to develop one type of political knowledge or another, which governance mechanism should they consider? Second, we look at how the different kinds of political knowledge could or should lead to some form of competitive advantage in political arenas. This question is far from obvious, because it is often unclear whether firms should develop political knowledge to generate a competitive advantage. In what follows, we consider these two questions in turn.

Political knowledge

A now relatively large literature in management shows the importance of knowledge in a firm's strategy, either as a source of competitive advantage (Miller and Shamsie, 1996) or as a fundamental determinant of its existence (Kogut and Zander, 1992; Grant, 1996). Knowledge that has been accumulated in the past leads an individual or an organization to select a different view of the causal relationships that determine how events happen (knowledge of what) and of what should be done (knowledge of how), than what would have otherwise been selected (Dosi, Faillo, and Marengo, 2008). This knowledge may then be translated into formal or informal organizational routines and structures. Organizations cope with individuals' rational limitations by building structures that guide behaviors (Simon, 1961; Cyert and March, 1992). Crossan, Lane, and White (1999) detail how new knowledge is originally accumulated with new insights or ideas identified by individuals within an organization, how this knowledge is shared, given inter-subjective meaning, adopted for action, and finally embodied in the creation of an organizational routine.

Why knowledge should play an important role in political environments

Miller and Shamsie (1996) show how knowledge, as it allows managers to coordinate or re-coordinate various assets within a firm, is particularly important for firms in changing and unpredictable environments. Similarly, Dosi and Marengo (2007: 494) argue that problems "may occur in circumstances whereby agents have an imperfect understanding of the world in which they operate due to (a) a lack of information, (b) an imprecise knowledge of its structure, (c) mastery of only a limited repertoire of actions in order to cope with whatever problem they face." These situations typically exist in political environments. Participation in political processes is plagued with uncertainties and transaction costs (North, 1990; Dixit, 1998). For example, the policy preferences of politicians (Mayhew, 1974; Keim and Zeithaml, 1986), the nature of interest group competition (Wilson, 1980), and the efficacy of political tactics (Bonardi, Holburn, and Vanden Bergh, 2006) are each subject to uncertainty. Thus, one would expect firms to value political knowledge and to seek means to develop or acquire it.

In spite of this importance, research on the role of knowledge in political environments is limited to a handful of articles. Oliver and Holzinger (2008) suggest that firms develop political knowledge and dynamic capabilities to manage their political and regulatory environment strategically. Examples of this can be found in historical and longitudinal case studies of corporate lobbying. Suarez (1998), for instance, showed that US pharmaceutical and electronic companies lobbying on a similar issue over the 1976–93 period consistently behaved in reference to what they knew in the previous period. Martin (1995), studying healthcare debates in the 1990s, found similar patterns, stressing the role of regional and national associations as a repository of what firms knew in political arenas through their past experiences. Vogel (1983), in his study of the politicization of the corporate environment, also suggests that firms develop knowledge based on their interaction with the opponents that frequently defeat them in political arenas, such as environmental and consumer groups. However, what this political knowledge is actually about – or how there might be different types of knowledge that might be more or less useful, dependent on the environment – remains unclear.

A related stream of research examines how firms can benefit from political knowledge acquired through political connections (Hillman, 2005). Firms that establish close ties with elected politicians – through appointing politically connected board members or senior management – tend to benefit from higher stock prices (Hillman and Hitt, 1999), easier access to capital, lower tax rates, larger market shares (Faccio, 2007), broader diversification opportunities (Mahmood and Mitchell, 2004), and even improved chances of securing government bailouts (Faccio, Masulis, and McConnell, 2006). Again, the literature suggests that political knowledge can be important for firms, but why and when this is the case remain unexplained. In other words, the concept of political knowledge is still a black box, and a theoretical framework is needed to start opening it. We provide such a framework by focusing on some of the key characteristics for why political knowledge might matter for firms. This will help us identify different types of political knowledge, which will facilitate a discussion of when these different types can be important and how they can be obtained.

Four types of political knowledge

Following the retail example outlined above, we argue that firms' political knowledge can be considered along two dimensions: institution-specificity and firm-specificity. At the theoretical level, the framework we develop is based on two sets of insights. First, it draws on the literature on organizational knowledge, which suggests that some knowledge components are generalizable to multiple circumstances, but also that other components are very local: that is, they are conditional on specific conditions regarding time and space (Hayek, 1945). In the case of political environments, specific conditions consist of the types of institutional environments in which an individual or a firm operates. Institutions differ not only in terms of formal rules but also in informal rules, such as norms and non-written practices, that can take time to learn (North, 1994). These considerations drive the first dimension of our framework – the degree of institution-specificity of political knowledge – on which we elaborate below.

The second dimension of our framework is rooted in the literature on political markets, which argues that public policy-making can be modeled as the outcome of interactions between demanders (firms, interest groups, activists, etc.) and suppliers (politicians, regulators, courts) (Buchanan and Tullock, 1962; Stigler, 1971). From this perspective, firms that develop corporate political strategies provide assets of value to policy-makers (e.g., campaign resources, policy information, credit claiming opportunities, etc.) (Hillman and Hitt, 1999; Bonardi, Hillman, and Keim, 2005). Salient knowledge includes information about how to gain access to influential politicians and regulators, and also knowledge of the value of the firms' assets to policy-makers (Bonardi, 2008). Firms might also decide to commit some of their economic assets to political means, a practice referred to as "asset freezing" in the literature (Bonardi and Urbitztondo, 2013), if it has knowledge about the fact that these economic assets could be highly valued by policy-makers. Investment in high-visibility green technologies, keeping under-performing plants operating, and so on are examples of political behaviors based on economic assets that might have value for some policy-makers. The political value of a firm's assets and business depends on the idiosyncratic preferences of policy-makers, and it is subject to considerable uncertainty. But such knowledge might be discovered. This is the basis for the second key dimension in our framework – the degree of firm-specificity of political knowledge.

The degree of institution-specificity of political knowledge

Political knowledge can be either more generic or, conversely, more tailored to a specific institutional environment. Knowledge of the principles of how to organize a grass-roots campaign or how to cultivate interest group coalitions, for instance, is common from one jurisdiction to another. The existing theoretical and empirical literature supports this idea. Holburn and Zelner (2010) argue that firms develop generalizable political knowledge when they deal with their home governments and institutional environments, which can be redeployed in other institutional areas. This implies that part of the political knowledge that firms possess is of a generic nature and can be leveraged in multiple jurisdictions.

On the other hand, part of what firms learn in a political environment is naturally institution-specific. Baron (2001), for instance, details the different information structures that determine the nature of the policy-making game in various institutional settings. The legislative process, for instance, operates differently in presidential and parliamentary countries (Holburn and Vanden Bergh, 2008). Understanding how to navigate policy-making in a jurisdiction additionally requires an appreciation of the policy preferences of different parties, including those in formal positions of authority as well as stakeholders, organized interest groups, and other constituents who may be affected by policy outcomes. Firms may find well-organized, hostile opponents to their preferred policies in some environments, or more supportive actors in others, both of which can change due to political elections and/or demographic trends (Keim and Zeithaml, 1986). Gathering information on policy positions and patterns of alliances or coalitions between parties enables firms to determine whether opportunities exist to initiate or lobby for favorable policy changes and the optimal method for effecting change.

The degree of firm-specificity of political knowledge

By firm-specific, we mean knowledge of the political value attributed to the firm's business assets, operating practices, and strategy. While firms create value for consumers in the market place, they also create benefits – and potentially costs, too – for politicians in their jurisdiction, for example through the creation of local jobs, the augmentation of labor force skills and enhanced taxation revenues, or their attitude towards the natural environment, each of which can affect politicians' future electoral prospects. Walmart and Target likely have a deep understanding of the firm-specific political impact of locating a store in a new neighborhood and of how to adjust their market-based strategies to achieve political objectives.

The literature on the integration of market and non-market strategy stresses that what distinguishes a firm from its competitors in the market place is a critical aspect of the design and success of a successful and meaningful political action (Baron, 1995a and 1995b). In that spirit, Bonardi (2008) underlines the importance of leveraging firms' specific technologies and assets as a way to influence public policies. Judging political value, however, can be a difficult exercise, particularly for firms that are inexperienced in a jurisdiction, as the following quote illustrates:

> BHP Billiton Ltd. said it was withdrawing its hostile $38.6-billion offer for Potash Corp., but company officials took the unusual step of outlining why they felt Ottawa's decision was wrong. The Australian company laid out what it called "unparalleled" promises it made on jobs and investment, including commitments to spend $370-million on infrastructure in two provinces, to give five-year employment guarantees at Potash Corp.'s Canadian mines and to move 200 jobs from outside the country to Saskatchewan and Vancouver.
>
> (Bouw, Kiladze, and Chase, 2010)

The four types of political knowledge

Considering these two dimensions simultaneously, we obtain four types of a firm's political knowledge, as represented in Figure 2.1.[2] First, with a low degree of institutional and firm-specificity, is *generic political knowledge*, such as a framework for assessing generic political decision-making processes; this may be applied in any jurisdiction. Second, *institution-specific political knowledge* consists of a high degree of institution-specific knowledge, such as the knowledge of pivotal politicians' policy preferences on a given topic (Vanden Bergh and Holburn, 2007), or the rules and procedures governing agency decision-making (de Figueiredo and Vanden Bergh, 2004).

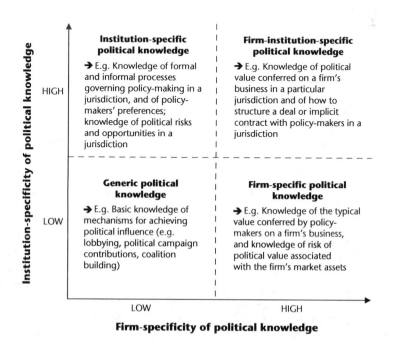

Figure 2.1 Typology of political knowledge

Third, *firm-specific political knowledge* reflects an understanding of the political value of the firm's assets or operating practices in any political environment, for instance the value attributed to local sourcing practices or to paying above minimum-level wages. These will have value in any political environment. Many firms might develop firm-specific political knowledge as a precautionary mechanism in case a more integrated market and non-market strategy becomes necessary, for instance if a new regulation affecting one specific firm (instead of the whole industry) could be put in place. Fourth, *firm-institution-specific political knowledge* consists of the knowledge of the value of such firm activities in a particular juris-diction and reflects the idiosyncratic preferences of local politicians, regulators, and stake-holders. This type of political knowledge is the one a firm will need when directly challenged in a particular political market.

Note that firms will often combine these different types of knowledge in the context of their political strategies, and that they might have more or less of each of these types of knowledge at any single moment.

Governance mechanisms regarding political knowledge

Since firms differ in their need for political knowledge as a component of their integrated strategy, they also organize and develop political knowledge in different ways. In this section, we explore the mechanisms that firms can utilize to develop the political knowledge type they need. Our logic here is that firms can get political knowledge through two complemen-tary mechanisms: first, by choosing between market-based solutions and integrated solutions or, to use Williamson's term, hierarchy (Williamson, 1975); second, by learning political knowledge, either experientially (Suarez, 1998) or by observing others (i.e., vicariously) (Haunschild, 1993). We examine these two mechanisms in turn, then explore how they might interact to develop the different kinds of political knowledge identified above.

Market versus hierarchy to acquire political knowledge

Firms may acquire political knowledge in the market place for instance by hiring lobbyists or consultants who have political ties or knowledge of policy-making in a jurisdiction (Kersh, 1986). However, there are limits to using market contracts as a method for obtain-ing such expertise (de Figueiredo and Kim, 2003; de Figueiredo and Tiller, 2001). The challenge for external consultants in brokering "trades" or agreements with political actors is that effectively doing so may require deep knowledge of the firm's market-based assets, resources, capabilities, and market strategy in some contexts. For instance, while a lobbyist may understand the political value that a legislator places on the construction of a corporate headquarters or new manufacturing facility in the legislator's jurisdiction, he or she is less likely to appreciate the organizational implications or additional cost to the firm of locating there rather than in the optimal location from a market-based calculation. Similarly, accurately valuing potential public policy alternatives depends on the lobbyist understanding the full cost and revenue implications for the firm as well as for its compet-itive position relative to other firms. Such information asymmetries between a lobbyist and the firm regarding the firm's market-based assets and strategy make it difficult for an external lobbyist to identify mutually beneficial trades with politicians. Contracting for lobbying services thus becomes a challenge when performance may not be easily meas-ured *ex post* or specified *ex ante*.

Experiential versus vicarious learning to develop political knowledge

Previous work suggests that learning is an important mechanism to acquire knowledge in political environments (North, 1990). As indicated by Bonardi, Holburn, and Vanden Bergh (2006), Dean and Brown (1995) and Suarez (1998), one key mechanism there is experiential learning, in which firms learn by doing. Another mechanism, however, is also likely to play an important role: vicarious learning (Levitt and March, 1988). Vicarious learning, which implies that firms learn from the experiences of others, has received much attention from organizational theorists and economists in the study of knowledge spillovers (Thornton and Thompson, 2001). There is now robust evidence of such vicarious learning, especially under conditions of uncertainty, across many different contexts (Lant and Mezias, 1992; Haunschild, 1993; Haveman, 1993; Greve, 1996, 1998; Haunschild and Miner, 1997; Baum, Xiao, and Usher, 2000; Greve and Taylor, 2000; McKendrick, 2001; Beckman and Haunschild, 2002; Haunschild and Sullivan, 2002). When facing high uncertainty, as is the case in political environments, firms are more likely to learn from the actions of other firms (e.g., Mezias and Lant, 1994; Haunschild and Miner, 1997; Mezias and Eisner, 1997), which should indicate that vicarious learning should play an important role in developing political knowledge.

How firms can develop the four different kinds of political knowledge

In this section, we relate our typology of the different kinds of political knowledge (see Figure 2.1) to the two knowledge acquisition mechanisms identified above. At the bottom left of our typology, generic political knowledge is mostly explicit and publicly observable. Short-term contracts with external lobbying firms are probably enough to acquire this type of knowledge. Firms that view generic political knowledge as optimal do not need to develop large-scale internal resources. For those firms that do decide to develop generic political knowledge internally, they will be able to develop this type of political knowledge through vicarious observation of other firms or interest groups in the political markets. As firms observe others engaging in political and regulatory arenas, they are likely to learn about the basic public policy process and how to operate in the political environment. As suggested by Kim and Miner (2007), firms learn much by observing others struggle, make mistakes, and fail.

On the other hand, firms will likely acquire and/or develop institution-specific political knowledge as part of their integrated strategy, which might require some degree of experiential learning. However, firms have outside options there. Becoming an active member of a trade association and/or long-term contracts with external lobbyists are solutions for institution-specific knowledge because policy-makers change and it is important to update the knowledge over time. Firms' ability to seize some market opportunities might depend on it. However, firms do not need to share sensitive information about their market investments with policy-makers in order to influence policy outcomes. To the extent that other firms in an industry are affected by policy, trade association membership may be the best option. Otherwise the firm may need to develop longer-term contracts with external lobbyists.

For those firms that choose to develop institution-specific political knowledge internally, vicarious learning in a firm's local jurisdiction will be critical. Interactions between other firms and policy-makers in a jurisdiction reveal cues or signals about different aspects of the policy environment: for instance, the willingness of elected politicians to sponsor or resist reform proposals; policy positions of elected and appointed officials on contentious issues; and the degree of organization of supportive or hostile stakeholders. While some aspects of the policy environment may be difficult to observe, others are revealed only during periods of engagement between firms and governments. Firms may initiate policy reviews through administrative filings or else trigger public discourse on policy issues in the media and government arenas. Participation by firms, interest groups, and policy-makers in regulatory or judicial hearings is another source of information pertinent to a jurisdiction. Policy-making processes thus reveal information to firms that provides benefit in terms of configuring political strategies and reducing uncertainties about possible policy outcomes.

As a firm develops greater levels of firm-specific political knowledge as a component of its integrated strategy, a tighter linkage between the firm's market strategy and its non-market influence efforts will be required. This type of knowledge has to be developed internally, and a specific organization has to be put in place in order to achieve this. However, in the case of firm-specific political knowledge (the bottom-right quadrant in Figure 2.1), much of this political knowledge is likely to be developed vicariously as it does not apply to a specific institutional environment. Experiential knowledge is less critical there.

The situation is different for firm-institution-specific political knowledge (upper-right quadrant in Figure 2.1). Many aspects of what a firm can leverage in its negotiations with policy-makers relate to the political value of the firm's assets and practices. As a further example, a firm's decision to move specific operations off-shore may create economic value for the firm but result in negative political value due to local job losses. In a specific institutional environment, the managers responsible for off-shoring may not understand how much political value this might have and for whom. As this example makes clear, some of the unknown and unobservable components of political knowledge are in fact related to firm-specific factors that the firm can leverage in a political context. Because of this, it is difficult to learn firm-institution-specific knowledge vicariously. Instead, a firm learns through its own experience which of its assets and technologies (or other characteristics) are valuable in the context of a political negotiation.

Our general argument about the governance of political knowledge is depicted in Figure 2.2, which builds on Figure 2.1 but concentrates on the mechanisms available for firms to develop the different kinds of political knowledge. Going from left to right in Figure 2.2, firms tend to integrate more the political function and develop their own political or regulatory affairs department (instead of building their non-market strategies on political knowledge acquired through external contracting). Going from the bottom left to the top right, firms also rely less and less on vicarious learning and more and more on experiential learning to acquire the political knowledge they need.

Political knowledge and competitive advantage

From the perspective of the resource-based view, the type of political knowledge that is the most likely to create a sustainable competitive advantage for a firm is the one that is the most difficult to imitate or replicate (Wernerfelt, 1984; Keim and Zeithaml, 1986; Barney, 1991). Our framework would then suggest that firm-institution-specific political knowledge should be the type that will most likely generate a sustainable competitive advantage in a given political environment. However, one has to consider important tradeoffs associated with developing the various types of political knowledge before concluding that the only value-enhancing type is firm-institution-specific political knowledge. Since corporate political activities are generally complementary activities that have to be integrated with firms' market strategies (Baron, 1995b; de Figueiredo, 2009), firms might not always find it

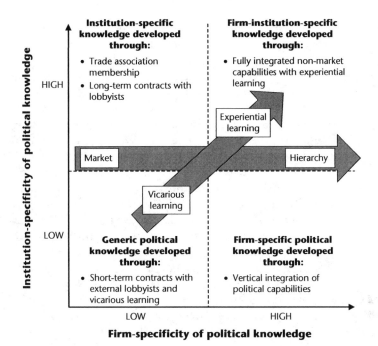

Figure 2.2 Optimal governance structure for acquisition and development of political knowledge

value enhancing to develop firm–institution-specific political knowledge. The other types of political knowledge might, in fact, be optimal from a resource-based view and an integrated strategy perspective.

We argue that the contribution of each type of political knowledge towards a firm's competitive advantage depends upon two factors. First, the level of control that government has over the profit opportunities of the firm will determine the frequency with which a firm needs to interact with policy-makers. Baron (1995b) argues that the level of government control is positively correlated with the frequency of interaction with the government and that this degree of control varies across industries. For example, for firms developing video-game technology, the degree of government control is low. By contrast, firms developing medical technologies face much greater government control over their profit opportunities. Second, firms must consider the degree of rivalry from interest groups present in the political market. A number of scholars have demonstrated that the degree of interest group rivalry varies across political markets (Wilson, 1980; Bonardi, Hillman, and Keim, 2005). For example, an electric utility firm with operations in multiple political markets can face little interest group rivalry in one political market but intense interest group rivalry in another (Fremeth, Holburn, and Spiller, 2014).

Within a given political market environment, firms differ on these two dimensions. Some subset of all firms faces a low level of government control. For firms that face a low level of government control, a smaller subset will face intense interest group rivalry while others face minimal rivalry. Similarly, for the set of firms that faces a high level of government control, a subset will face high degrees of interest group rivalry while the others will face low levels of rivalry in the political market. We argue that a firm's optimal choice over which type of political knowledge to acquire or develop is directly related to the characteristics of the political environment, as described by these two dimensions.

Consider a firm where the level of government control over profit opportunities is low and they face limited interest group rivalry. In this political market, the firm's integrated strategy will be heavily weighted toward their market strategy, with little to zero weight placed on non-market components. The opportunity costs of investing in the development and acquisition of political knowledge are high, relative to the limited benefits. Policy change affecting the firm is unlikely and thus the benefit of understanding the details of the public policy-making process is limited. Rival interest groups are not actively seeking to change policy in directions that hurt the firm. In these markets there is limited to no benefit in the firm understanding how politicians and/or their constituents respond to firm investments. In many respects, any interaction with the government in this type of political market can be viewed by the firm as a simple cost of implementing its market strategy. As such, it is likely optimal for the firm to place little weight on its non-market assets and to acquire mostly generic political knowledge as and when needed.

Firms that face greater levels of government control are more likely to adopt institution-specific political knowledge as opposed to generic political knowledge. This hypothesis is fairly intuitive. As the level of control by government increases so too does the frequency of interaction between the government and the firm (Baron, 1995b). Thus, the incremental benefit to the firm of developing institution-specific knowledge is more likely to outweigh the added cost of developing institution-specific relative to maintaining only generic political knowledge.

As the level of interest group rivalry in the political market increases, we posit that firms are more likely to develop firm-specific political knowledge. Active rival interest groups, whether advocacy groups or other firms within an industry, will present arguments that emphasize how policy change affects the stakeholders of the rival interest group as well as the constituents of policy-makers. For a firm to counteract a rival interest group, it will need capabilities to understand and articulate how policy affects the value of its own assets, its own stakeholders, etc. Furthermore, the firm will need to articulate how these value changes affect the political prospects of the policy-makers. To develop this deeper understanding will be costly to the firm relative to maintaining generic knowledge. However, the benefits of this firm-specific knowledge are more likely to outweigh the costs when interest group rivalry increases. At low levels of rivalry the firm does not need to incur the costs of developing this knowledge because it does not need to counteract opposing attempts to influence the policy outcome.

When interest group rivalry is high but government control over market opportunities is low, then firms might concentrate on acquiring firm-specific political knowledge. This might be mainly for precautionary reasons – in case the government decides to regulate a particular activity that was not regulated previously and in which the firm is involved. On the other hand, when both interest group rivalry and government control over market opportunities are high, firms need to develop firm-institution-specific political knowledge, as it will be critical to maintain an edge over rival interest groups in a jurisdiction in which a particular government body has decided to push forward a certain policy. As these two factors increase in importance so too does the weight the firm must place on its non-market strategy in developing an integrated strategy for sustainable competitive advantage.

In Figure 2.3, we capture our main hypotheses about the relationship between characteristics of the political market and the firm's optimal choice of political knowledge type.

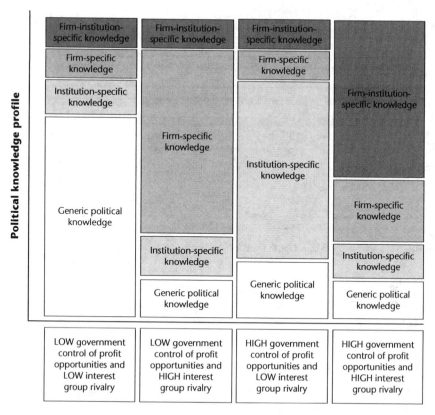

Figure 2.3 Optimal choice of political knowledge type

Figure 2.3 assumes that every firm has, to a certain degree, all four kinds of political knowledge, but that the knowledge needed depends on the competitive situation the firm is facing. Boxes characterizing political knowledge represent how important each kind of political knowledge is (so, with low government control of profit opportunities and low interest group rivalry, the most important type of political knowledge to develop or acquire is generic political knowledge; the others are much less valuable in that case). Note that Figure 2.3 does not say anything about how much political knowledge a firm needs *overall*, just how much of each type is likely to be needed in each situation (which we call the firm's "political profile").

Conclusion and discussion

This chapter is the first attempt to develop a conceptual framework of different types of political knowledge and of how they can be developed or acquired by organizations. Whereas most of the existing literature in management, economics, and political science focuses on factors related to industry characteristics or to firm size in explaining organizations' decisions to engage in political activities, our work suggests that political knowledge should also be considered as an important factor. Our approach has several implications for future research on firms' non-market strategies, as is discussed below.

One of the contributions of our chapter is to explain why firms differ in their abilities to manage their political environments and hence in their levels of political engagement

(Boddewyn and Brewer, 1994; Dean and Brown, 1995; Oliver and Holzinger, 2008). Unlike research in the competitive strategy field on how and why firms develop or acquire heterogeneous technological and market-based capabilities, relatively few studies have addressed the same regarding non-market strategy. Even though we do not explicitly articulate a theory of firms' idiosyncratic non-market capabilities, we believe that it provides some useful pieces in order to do so. Our analysis implies that a firm's non-market capabilities originate in the different types of political knowledge identified earlier. Since these four types of political knowledge have different characteristics in terms of imitability or replicability, they also have different implications in terms of competitive advantage in a political environment. In particular, firm-institution-specific knowledge is by far the hardest to imitate and therefore the one that will most likely create an advantage over non-market competitors.

However, we also point out that political knowledge is not always there to generate a competitive advantage in a political environment, but rather to complement market capabilities that will generate an overall competitive advantage for the firm. Instead of focusing squarely on the imitability or the replicability of knowledge as in the market version of the resource-based view, it is therefore critical to look at the knowledge profile that the firm needs to put in place in order to propose an effective integrated strategy (Baron, 1995b; Bonardi, 2004; Kingsley, Vanden Bergh, and Bonardi, 2012).

Our paper also brings new insights to the question of whether non-market capabilities can be developed internally within organizations or whether they can be acquired by contracting for lobbyists or government relations experts (de Figueiredo and Kim, 2003). Our framework suggests that generic and institution-specific knowledge can be obtained from external sources. However, for firm-institution-specific political knowledge, there are significant transaction costs associated with contracting for their acquisition in the market place. Unlike in competitive goods and services markets, where numerous transactions enable firms readily to understand consumers' willingness to pay, the infrequency of transactions and/or negotiations in the political realm creates uncertainty for firms about the political value of their businesses. Political preferences vary from jurisdiction to jurisdiction, and can change over time with the election cycle. Policy-makers may also deliberately obscure their true policy positions from public view due to perceived election ramifications, further complicating the task of organizations that seek favorable policy decisions.

Contracting for political services under such conditions of uncertainty and asymmetric information becomes challenging. Instead, we argue here that firms' direct experiences in political processes and bargaining can uncover hidden information about the value that politicians and regulators place on the firm's business and assets in their jurisdiction. Direct interaction between firms and policy-makers thus allows for firms to learn firm-institution-specific political knowledge that would otherwise be unobtainable through external lobbyists. In this sense, we point to organizational experience in a jurisdiction as a major mechanism for the development of idiosyncratic political capabilities (Dean and Brown, 1995).

Returning to our earlier example of Target opening a store in Harlem, it was not sufficient for the firm simply to rely on its prior (and extensive) experience elsewhere in opening new retail premises to shape its approach for gaining permit approval in Harlem. The firm likely understood that it would face opposition from a variety of stakeholders; but a bigger uncertainty at the outset would be the creation of offsetting benefits in the community to gain the necessary level of political support in the council. Establishing an organizational presence in the community to explore potential factors and approaches over an extended time period was one way for the firm to develop the requisite firm-institution-specific political knowledge.

Relatedly, our analysis sheds light on why empirical studies have found a positive correlation between political connections of firms' senior executives or board members and measures of firm performance, such as stock price movements, access to capital, and so on (Hillman, 2005; Faccio, 2006; Faccio, Masulis, and McConnell, 2006). Connections and relationships with policy-makers can provide access to a firm, but this may be insufficient for creating value. Instead, we argue that as politically connected executives develop deep knowledge over time about a firm's operations and business, they become better able to identify the political value of the firm's business and hence to recognize opportunities for mutually beneficial policy "deals" with government and other stakeholders. Future research could test this thesis by examining how the impact of board level or executive political connections on firm performance evolves with the tenure of such executives.

We also believe our chapter can provide new avenues for research in international business. One of these avenues relates to the study of how non-market capabilities developed in one institutional area can be redeployed to other institutional arenas in the context of foreign markets entry. Holburn and Zelner (2010), for instance, find support for the idea that there are indeed non-market capabilities that can be redeployed across international markets. The framework developed in our paper suggests that these redeployable non-market capabilities are based in generic political knowledge and firm-specific political knowledge. On the other hand, we argue that there are also important aspects of firms' non-market capabilities that cannot be redeployed in foreign countries, especially institution-specific and firm-institution-specific political knowledge. Future research should try to identify the full implications of these differences on firms' internationalization decisions.

Notes

1 For recent surveys of the corporate political activity literature, see Hillman et al. (2004) and Lawton et al. (2013). De Figueiredo (2009) provides a survey of literature addressing integrated market and non-market strategy.
2 We recognize that each dimension is most likely continuous in nature. However, for simplicity and to begin the research conversation, we employ a discrete characterization for each, resulting in a two-by-two framework.

References

Barney, J. 1991. Firm resources and sustained competitive advantage. *Journal of Management*, 17: 99–120.
Baron, D. 1995a. Integrated market and non-market strategies in client and interest group politics. *Business and Politics*, 1(1): 7–34.
— 1995b. Integrated strategy: Market and non-market components. *California Management Review*, 37: 47–65.
— 2001. Theories of strategic non-market participation: Majority-rule and executive institutions. *Journal of Economics and Management Strategy*, 10(1): 46–89.
Baum, J. A., Xiao Li, S., and Usher, J. 2000. Making the next move: How experiential and vicarious learning shape the locations of chains' acquisitions. *Administrative Science Quarterly*, 45(4): 766–801.
Beckman, C. and Haunschild, P. 2002. Network learning: The effects of partners' heterogeneity of experience on corporate acquisitions. *Administrative Science Quarterly*, 47(1): 92–124.
Boddewyn, J. and Brewer, T. 1994. International-business political behavior: New theoretical directions. *Academy of Management Review*, 19(1): 119–43.

Bonardi, J. P. 2004. Global and political strategies in deregulated industries: The asymmetric behaviors of former monopolies. *Strategic Management Journal*, 25: 101–20.

— 2008. The limits to firms' non-market activity. *European Management Review*, 5: 165–74.

— 2011. Corporate political resources and the resource-based view of the firm. *Strategic Organization*, 9(3): 247–55.

Bonardi, J. P. and Urbitztondo, S. 2013. Asset freezing, corporate political resources and the Tullock paradox. *Business and Politics*, 15(3): 275–93.

Bonardi, J. P., Hillman, A., and Keim, G. 2005. The attractiveness of political markets: Implications for firm strategy. *Academy of Management Review*, 30: 397–413.

Bonardi, J. P., Holburn, G., and Vanden Bergh, R. 2006. Non-market strategy performance: Evidence from US electric utilities. *Academy of Management Journal*, 49(6): 1209–28.

Bouw, B., Kiladze, T., and Chase, S. 2010. Ottawa firm on takeover; Australian miner BHP walks away. *The Globe and Mail*, November 14.

Buchanan, J. and Tullock, G. 1962. *The Calculus of Consent: Logical Foundations of Constitutional Democracy*. Ann Arbor: University of Michigan Press.

Clifford, S. 2010. The fruits of Target's wooing. *The New York Times*, August 13.

Crossan, M., Lane, H., and White, R. 1999. An organizational learning framework: From intuition to institution. *Academy of Management Review*, 24(3): 522–37.

Cyert, R. and March, J. 1992. *A Behavioral Theory of the Firm*. Second edition. Oxford: Blackwell.

Dahan, N. 2005. A contribution to the conceptualization of political resources utilized in corporate political action. *Journal of Public Affairs*, 5(1): 43–54.

de Figueiredo, J. M. 2009. Integrated political strategy. *Advances in Strategic Management*, 26: 459–86.

de Figueiredo, J. M. and Kim, J. J. 2003. When do firms hire lobbyists? The organization of lobbying at the Federal Communications Commission. *Industrial and Corporate Change*, 23(6): 883–900.

de Figueiredo, J. M. and Tiller, E. H. 2001. The structure and conduct of lobbying: An empirical analysis of corporate lobbying at the federal communications commission. *Journal of Economics and Management Strategy*, 10(1): 91–122.

de Figueiredo, R. J. and Vanden Bergh, R. G. 2004. The political economy of state level administrative procedure acts. *Journal of Law and Economics*, 47(2): 569–88.

Dean, T. and Brown, R. 1995. Pollution regulation as a barrier to new firm entry: Initial evidence and implications for future research. *Academy of Management Journal*, 38: 288–303.

Dixit, A. 1998. *The Making of Economic Policy: A Transaction Cost Politics Perspective*. Boston, MA: The MIT Press.

Dosi, G. and Marengo, L. 2007. On the evolutionary and behavioural theories of organizations: A tentative roadmap. *Organization Science*, 18(3): 491–502.

Dosi, G., Faillo, M., and Marengo, L. 2008. Organizational capabilities, patterns of knowledge accumulation and governance structures in business firms: An introduction. *Organization Studies*, 29(8–9): 1165–85.

Faccio, M. 2006. Politically connected firms. *American Economic Review*, 96(1): 369–86.

— 2007. The characteristics of politically connected firms. Working paper. Vanderbilt University.

Faccio, M., Masulis, R., and McConnell, J. 2006. Political connections and corporate bailouts. *Journal of Finance*, 61(6): 2597–635.

Fremeth, A., Holburn, G., and Spiller, P. 2014. The impact of consumer advocates on regulatory policy in the electric utility sector. *Public Choice*, 161: 157–81.

Grant, R. 1996. Towards a knowledge-based theory of the firm. *Strategic Management Journal*, 17: 109–22.

Greve, H. R. 1996. Patterns of competition: The diffusion of a market position in radio broadcasting. *Administrative Science Quarterly*, 41: 29–60.

— 1998. Managerial cognition and the mimetic adoption of market positions: What you see is what you do. *Strategic Management Journal*, 19: 967–88.

Greve, H. R. and Taylor, A. 2000. Innovations as catalysts for organizational change: Shifts in organizational cognition and search. *Administrative Science Quarterly*, 45(1): 54–80.

Grier, K. B., Munger, M. C., and Roberts, B. E. 1994. The determinants of industry political activity, 1978–1986. *American Political Science Review*, 88(04): 911–26.

Haunschild, P. 1993. Interorganizational imitation: The impact of interlocks on corporate acquisition activity. *Administrative Science Quarterly*, 38: 564–92.

Haunschild, P. and Miner, A. 1997. Modes of interorganizational imitation: The effects of outcome salience and uncertainty. *Administrative Science Quarterly*, 42(3): 472–500.

Haunschild, P. and Sullivan, B. 2002. Learning from complexity: Effects of prior accidents and incidents on airlines' learning. *Administrative Science Quarterly*, 47(4): 609–43.

Haveman, H. A. 1993. Follow the leader: Mimetic isomorphism and entry into new markets. *Administrative Science Quarterly*, 38: 593–627.

Hayek, F. 1945. The use of knowledge in society. *American Economic Review*, 35(4): 519–30.

Hillman, A. 2005. Politicians on the board of directors: Do connections affect the bottom line? *Journal of Management*, 31: 1–18.

Hillman, A. and Hitt, M. 1999. Corporate political strategy formulation: A model of approach, participation and strategy decisions. *Academy of Management Review*, 24(4): 825–42.

Hillman, A. J., Keim, G. D., and Schuler, D. 2004. Corporate political activity: A review and research agenda. *Journal of Management*, 30(6): 837–57.

Holburn, G. and Vanden Bergh, R. 2004. Influencing agencies through pivotal political institutions. *Journal of Law, Economics and Organization*, 20(2): 458–83.

— 2008. Making friends in hostile environments: Political strategy in regulated industries. *Academy of Management Review*, 33(2): 521–40.

Holburn, G. and Zelner, B. 2010. Political capabilities, policy risk and international investment strategy: Evidence from the global electric power industry. *Strategic Management Journal*, 31: 1290–315.

Keim, G. and Zeithaml, C. 1986. Corporate political strategy and legislative decision making: A review and contingency approach. *Academy of Management Review*, 11(4): 828–43.

Kersh, R. 1986. Corporate lobbyists as political actors: A view from the field. In A. J. Cigler and B. A. Loomis (eds.), *Interest Group Politics*: 225–47. Washington, DC: CQ Press.

Kim, J. Y. and Miner, A. S. 2007. Vicarious learning from the failure or near-failure of others: Evidence from the US commercial banking industry. *Academy of Management Journal*, 50(2): 687–714.

Kingsley, A. K., Vanden Bergh, R. G., and Bonardi, J. P. 2012. Political markets and regulatory uncertainty: Insights and implications for integrated strategy. *Academy of Management Perspectives*, 26(3): 52–67.

Kogut, B. and Zander, U. 1992. Knowledge of the firm, combinative capabilities, and the replication of technology. *Organization Science*, 3(3): 383–97.

Krehbiel, K. 1998. *Pivotal Politics: A Theory of US Lawmaking*. Chicago: University of Chicago Press.

Lant, T. and Mezias, S. 1992. An organizational learning model of convergence and reorientation. *Organization Science*, 3(1): 47–71.

Lawton, T., McGuire, S., and Rajwani, T. 2013. Corporate political activity: A literature review and research agenda. *International Journal of Management Reviews*, 15(1): 86–105.

Levitt, B. and March, J. G. 1988. Organizational learning. *Annual Review of Sociology*, 14: 319–40.

Mahmood, I. and Mitchell, W. 2004. Two faces: Effects of business groups on innovation in emerging economies. *Management Science*, 50: 1348–65.

Makadok, R. 2001. Toward a synthesis of the resource-based and dynamic-capability views of rent creation. *Strategic Management Journal*, 22(5): 387–401.

Martin, C. J. 1995. Nature or nurture? Sources of firm preference for national health reform. *American Political Science Review*, 89: 898–913.

Masters, M. F. and Keim, G. D. 1985. Determinants of PAC participation among large corporations. *Journal of Politics*, 47: 1158–73.

Mayhew, D. R. 1974. *Congress: The Electoral Connection*. New Haven, CT: Yale University Press.

McKendrick, D. 2001. Global strategy and population level learning: The case of hard disk drives. *Strategic Management Journal*, 22: 307–34.

Mezias, S. and Eisner, B. 1997. Competition, imitation and innovation: An organizational learning approach. *Advances in Strategic Management*, 14: 261–94.

Mezias, S. and Lant, T. 1994. Mimetic learning and the evolution of organizational populations. In J. Baum and J. Singh (eds.), *Evolutionary Dynamics of Organizations*: 179–93. Oxford: Oxford University Press.

Miller, D. and Shamsie, J. 1996. The resource-based view of the firm in two environments: The Hollywood film studio from 1936 to 1965. *Academy of Management Journal*, 39(3): 519–43.

Nelson, R. R. and Winter, S. G. 1982. *An Evolutionary Theory of Economic Change*. Cambridge: Belknap Press.

Nonaka, I. 1991. The knowledge creating company. *Harvard Business Review*, 69: 96–104.

North, D. 1990. A transaction cost theory of politics. *Journal of Theoretical Politics*, 2(4): 355–67.

— 1994. Economic performance through time. *American Economic Review*, 84(3): 359–68.

Oliver, C. and Holzinger, I. 2008. The effectiveness of strategic political management: A dynamic capabilities framework. *Academy of Management Review*, 33(2): 496–520.

Olson, M. 1965. *The Logic of Collective Action*. Cambridge: Cambridge University Press.

Simon, H. 1961. *Administrative Behavior*. Second edition. New York: Macmillan.

Stigler, G. 1971. The theory of economic regulation. *Bell Journal of Economics and Management Science*, 2: 3–21.

Suarez, S. L. 1998. Lesson learned: Explaining the political behavior of business. *Polity*, 31(1): 161–78.

Thornton, R. and Thompson, P. 2001. Learning from experience and learning from others: An exploration of learning and spillovers in wartime shipbuilding. *American Economic Review*, 91(5): 1350–68.

Vanden Bergh, R. and Holburn, G. 2007. Targeting corporate political strategy: Theory and evidence from the US accounting industry. *Business and Politics*, 9(2): article 1. DOI: 10.2202/1469-3569.1202.

Vogel, D. 1983. The power of business in America: A reappraisal. *British Journal of Political Science*, 13(1983): 19–43.

Wernerfelt, B. 1984. A resource-based view of the firm. *Strategic Management Journal*, 5(2): 171–80.

Weymouth, S. 2010. Oligopolists rule: The microeconomic determinants of lobbying and political influence. Working paper. Department of Political Science, University of California, San Diego.

Williamson, O. 1975. *Markets and Hierarchies*. New York: Free Press.

Wilson, J. Q. 1980. The politics of regulation. In J. Q. Wilson (ed.), *The Politics of Regulation*: 319–36. New York: Basic Books.

Zaheer, S. 1995. Overcoming the liability of foreignness. *Academy of Management Review*, 38(2): 341–63.

3

An institutional perspective on non-market strategies for a world in flux

Susan Feinberg, T. L. Hill, and Izzet Sidki Darendeli

The rationale behind firms' non-market strategies is that the political, legal, social, and cultural context can affect firms' ability to succeed in the market place. In this chapter, we reconcile evidence from the economics and finance literature with ideas from the neo-institutional and corporate political activity (CPA) literature to examine relationships between firms' connections, non-market strategies, and outcomes during periods of institutional change. These approaches provide complementary points of view regarding the ways in which institutions shape firms and their non-market strategies. Importantly, these diverse bodies of literature also provide insight into how firms' non-market strategies shape the institutional context for firm advantage. To highlight the interplay between non-market strategy and institutions, we focus on what happens, what works, and what questions are raised when institutions are in flux.

To some degree, institutions are always changing, driven, in part, by the non-market strategies of firms. During periods of intense institutional transition, such as abrupt regime change, the relationships between institutions, firms, and non-market strategies become particularly salient (Peng, 2003). When the tide turns and institutions change, insiders can become outsiders and connections can become liabilities. Advantages gained from years of relationship- and legitimacy-building can disappear altogether (Siegel, 2007). When the institutional context shifts, the value of firms' non-market connections changes and the appropriateness and effectiveness of firms' non-market strategies also changes. This then raises the question of how firms might build successful non-market strategies that are robust to, or even thrive on, institutional change.

To think about how non-market strategies can cope with constant change, one must first understand the effect of institutional change on a firm's position and connections within a given institutional context. Accordingly, this chapter begins with a brief discussion of the ways in which firms are nested within, constrained by, and act upon institutions. We then dive more deeply into the links between social and political connections; firms' political activities and strategies; and institutions. Finally, we discuss the ways in which political connections and corporate political activity interact during periods of institutional change. We examine this relationship in three increasingly uncertain contexts: during institutional change that does not threaten the established institutional order; during institutional change that does threaten the established institutional order (e.g., sweeping market reforms such as trade and capital market liberalization); and during periods of intense political and institutional volatility.

The examination of routine institutional change in stable institutional environments draws attention to the underlying mechanisms linking firms to institutions, and through which non-market strategies must act. Similarly, the focus on institutional change that threatens to change an established order underscores the self-reinforcing nature of institutional arrangements, and consequently the resistance to change that is commonly observed. In environments characterized by intense institutional volatility, firm survival often requires developing sensitivity to the subtlest signals and developing the ability to adjust rapidly, even while trying to influence the evolving institutional context. At the extreme, the challenge of coping with abrupt regime change highlights the importance of hedging beyond the formal institutional realm, often by building connections with sources of power and influence located in the social sector.

The institutional context of firm action

There is broad agreement that firms are nested within political, legal, social, and cultural institutions and that these institutions shape firm strategy (Peng, Wang, and Jiang, 2008). However, there is no single theory or literature stream that explores this phenomenon. Just within the management literature, there are at least three approaches to these questions (Doh, Lawton, and Rajwani, 2012). The first approach concentrates on the effect of institutions on firms and vice versa; the second approach explores the mechanisms through which institutions constrain firms; and the third emphasizes comparisons between institutional systems and their effects on firms and firm strategies. Within the economics and finance traditions, different data, methods, and underlying theoretical paradigms are used to raise similar questions about the impact of institutions on firms, the ways in which firms can affect institutions, and variation in firm behavior across institutional contexts. Part of our goal is to reconcile these disparate literatures with their often complementary insights.

Figure 3.1 summarizes the realm in which non-market strategies operate and illustrates the nesting of firms and non-governmental organizations (NGOs) within institutional frameworks. Most importantly, it highlights the role of bi-directional connections (the vertical lines) between

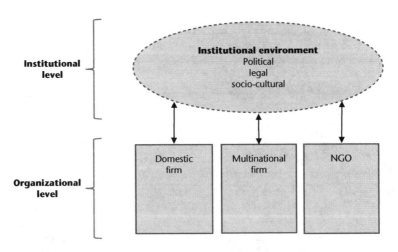

Figure 3.1 The bi-directional connections between institutions and organizations

institutions and organizations. In this section, we discuss in general terms how institutions shape organizations and vice versa.

Institutions shape organizations

Drawing in part on North's (1990) work on the nature, structure, and evolution of national institutions, scholars in economics and finance ask questions about economic growth and efficiency, and how these are affected by different types of institutions and levels of institutional development (e.g., Levine, 1997; Morck, Stangeland, and Yeung, 1998; Rajan and Zingales, 1998). By looking at how different institutional arrangements affect the behavior of firms, scholars can gain insight into why some economies grow more robustly than others. For example, Rajan and Zingales (1998) find that industries that rely more heavily on external finance grow relatively faster in countries that have well-developed financial market institutions than they do in countries that start with comparatively weak financial market institutions. Demirguc-Kunt and Maksimovic (1996) find that firms with access to more developed stock markets to raise funds grow at faster rates than those without access to these markets. Interestingly, firms with weak home-market institutions may be able to escape this constraint if they can access better-quality institutions in foreign markets. In general, the effects of institutional context on firm choices and firm performance are especially pronounced in emerging markets because of the potential for institutional volatility (Makino, Isobe, and Chan, 2004).

The management literature has a similar, if smaller, stream of research into the relationship between national institutions and firm choices and performance. For example, Hillman and Keim (1995) argue that the focus of corporate political activity will tend to shift from executive to legislative branch depending upon whether a democracy is corporatist or pluralist. In a similar vein, Bonardi, Holburn, and Vanden Bergh (2006) show that the structure of a firm's regulatory context, the political rivalries that emanate from that context, and a firm's ability to cope with the context and rivalries together determine the effectiveness of its non-market strategy.

Recent new institutionalism literature focuses on how institutions shape firms' perspectives, actions, and outcomes. According to this literature, firms achieve legitimacy by fitting into the formal and informal rules, norms, and cognitive categories that comprise institutional logics (Scott, 2008). Institutional logics shape the interests, identities, assumptions, and attention of individual executives and organizations (Thornton, 2004). In turn, executives and organizations that take actions consistent with the prevailing institutional logics achieve legitimacy in the market place (Biggart and Guillén, 1999). This results in clusters of firms that look and act the same. Kogut, Walker, and Anand (2002: 175) argue that observed international coherence in firm (diversification) strategy is "the etching on a space of technical possibilities left by the confluence of actors and institutions."

What is generally missing from this literature is detailed work on the mechanisms through which formal and informal political, social, and cultural forces shape business arrangements and conceptual frameworks (Aldrich and Fiol, 1994), which in turn enable and constrain market and non-market strategies (Peng et al., 2008). An emerging stream of literature focuses on the agency of actors embedded within institutions and the role of these actors in driving institutional change (Greenwood and Suddaby, 2006; Hirsch and Lounsbury, 1997). Through the development of new policies, organizational forms, and institutional logics, actors embedded within institutions can bring about institutional change (Patriotta, Gond, and Schultz, 2011; Thornton, Ocasio, and Lounsbury, 2012). For example, Lounsbury (2007) examines how competition between two traditions of practice and their supporting logics drove the evolution of structures in the US mutual funds industry. Another driver of institutional change is friction between institutions. Such frictions can result from the actions of non-business stakeholder groups that challenge existing arrangements and contribute to the building of new ones (Zhang and Luo, 2013). One example is the role of student environmental action committees in the evolution of recycling on college campuses, and of the recycling industry more generally (Lounsbury, 2001).

Organizations shape institutions

A great deal of research in both the management and economics fields has explored how firms strive to improve their performance by positioning themselves within the broader institutional context and by shaping that context when they can. A well-established stream in the international business literature shows that firms can – and do – improve their performance by scanning, anticipating, and influencing the political environment in host countries (Alon, Gurumoorthy, Mitchell, and Steen, 2006; Boddewyn and Brewer, 1994; Eden and Lenway, 2001; Oliver and Holzinger, 2008). In so doing, global firms conform to rules, norms, and belief systems of the actors in a host country. But they also actively engage in manipulating practice and symbols to try to affect both perceptions of what is legitimate and their fit within those perceptions (Bitektine, 2011; Kostova, Roth, and Dacin, 2008).

For example, Dahan, Doh, and Guay (2006) describe how firms work in concert with others in policy networks to create a predictable institutional context in which to operate. Vasudeva, Zaheer, and Hernandez (2013) argue that firms use their boundary-spanning scope both to derive advantage from variation in institutional arrangements and to try to shape institutional arrangements to their liking. An analogous example in the economics and finance literature is the use of cross-listing by emerging market firms as a form of institutional "rental" (Siegel, 2007). Siegel (2005) argues that because many emerging-market firms come from weak institutional environments, they have difficulty signaling their quality, which prevents them from accessing cheap external resources. By cross-listing and adhering to strict developed-market reporting requirements, firms span national boundaries to "borrow" developed institutions and credibly enhance their global reputation (Siegel, 2009).

The pervasive role of connections

A fundamental assumption underlying research on the relationship between institutions and firms is that both can form and leverage "boundary-spanning personal and institutional linkages between firms and the constituent parts of public authorities" (Sun, Mellahi, and Wright, 2012: 68). Such connections carry symbolic and material advantages (Delmas and Montes-Sancho, 2010; Thornton and Ocasio, 2008). Connections intermediate firms' interactions with all institutions, and in the following sections we discuss the links between connections, firms' non-market strategies, and institutions. We then discuss the effect of institutional change on the value of firms' connections.

Connections and non-market strategy

To gain a better understanding of the ways in which institutions interact with firms' non-market strategies, we distinguish between the ways in which firms are connected and why; the implications of these connections for the types of non-market strategies firms can successfully pursue; and the kinds of benefits firms can gain from their non-market strategies.

We begin by describing the links between connections and non-market strategy, as informed by two related but distinct streams of literature – the management literature on corporate political activity (CPA); and the economics/finance literature on political connections. We focus specifically on firms' *political* connections with the implicit assumption that these connections can bring firms direct financial advantage and can facilitate advantageous institutional change.

Firms' political connections arise from three main sources. First, connections between managers and politicians can arise from "exogenous" sources, such as attending similar schools (Bertrand, Kramarz, Schoar, and Thesmar, 2006; Cohen, Frazzini, and Malloy, 2010); family relationships (Morck et al., 1998); party membership (Li, Meng, Wang, and Zhou, 2008); business group ties (e.g., Khanna and Palepu, 2000); and geographic ties to politicians (Faccio and Parsley, 2009). Johnson and Mitton (2003: 353) provide a great example from a study of Malaysian political economy:

> the connection of firms to individual politicians appears to have been based primarily on chance personal histories. Early friendships with rising politicians, such as Mahathir and Anwar, have been an effective way to build firms in Malaysia over the past 20 years. In other words, the personal relationships between individuals in our dataset largely predate associations of these individuals with particular firms and so political connections were not determined by the nature of the firms themselves.

Second, connections can be formed as a natural result of what businesses do. For example, heavily regulated firms and firms that work as government contractors develop ongoing associations with government actors at a variety of different levels (e.g., Birnbaum, 1985).

Third, political connections arise endogenously as part of a firm's corporate political strategy. This can involve hiring former politicians or including them on corporate boards (Lester, Hillman, Zardkoohi, and Cannella, 2008); placing firm executives in political positions (Goldman, Rocholl, and So, 2009; Hillman, Zardkoohi, and Bierman, 1999); and making campaign contributions, PAC contributions (donations to "political action committees" that bundle donations and, in turn, donate to candidates or campaigns), or other monetary gifts (Cooper, Gulen, and Ovtchinnikov, 2010; Stratmann, 1991).

Some scholars have tried to link firms' political strategies with their political connections. For example, Hillman and Hitt (1999) make the distinction between relational and transactional approaches to political strategy. The relational approach to political strategy has to do with the "development of social capital that is embedded in a continued exchange relationship between parties" (Hillman and Hitt, 1999: 829). When firms use a relational approach to political strategy, they develop and maintain close links to important connections as a matter of priority. In contrast, the transactional approach to political strategy is more issue-driven and involves developing and communicating with connections on an as-needed basis. Conceptually, however, the distinction is hard to maintain, since firms no doubt use their "relational" position with connections to lobby for particular "transactional" favors, such as preferred policies, subsidies, and so on, while firms that engage in repeated "transactional" approaches will likely develop "relational" interactions with those political actors with whom they have often engaged on issues. To us, this conundrum highlights the complex links between political strategy and political connections: political strategies are embedded in relationships, even as relationships facilitate strategies.

In general, the management literature has tended to focus more on the question of what firms do with their connections, while the economics and finance literature has tended to focus more on the connections themselves and the value firms derive from those connections

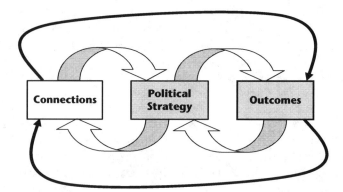

Figure 3.2 Interactive relationship between connections, political strategy, and outcomes

in a variety of contexts. Combining the economics and finance literature's emphasis on the ties themselves and the strategy literature's emphasis on the intentional formation and manipulation of ties suggests a more complex relationship between firms' political connections, political strategies, and outcomes than is implied in either literature alone. Figure 3.2 shows a stylized set of relationships between firms' connections, the implications of these connections for political strategies, and the kinds of outcomes firms can gain from their political strategies.

The dense web of relational and structural ties that exist prior to the formation of any given political strategy are critical to the kinds of political strategies firms devise. Conversely, firms' political strategies may necessitate the development of new connections to politicians at various levels of government. "Since political institutions are among the most difficult environmental dependencies to control, firms may seek to co-opt political stakeholders by developing personal and organizational linkages so that potentially hostile elements of environmental uncertainties can be neutralized" (Sun et al., 2012: 70–1). In this way, strategy also influences political connections.

Firms' connections can lead to direct outcomes, such as trade or capital market restrictions (Morck et al., 1998). Similarly, outcomes have a feedback loop to connections, implying that firms may need to "compensate" connections in some fashion for bestowing them with favors (e.g., Nee, 1989). Positive or negative outcomes provide feedback to firms with regard to the value of their connections. Firms may react to disappointing outcomes by developing different connections or trying to reform or redirect existing connections. Outcomes also have a bi-directional relationship with firm strategy, suggesting that strategies may be reinforced or reconsidered in light of their ability to generate positive outcomes.

Finally, changes in the value of these connections affects the outcomes firms receive as well as their political strategies and tactics. In the next section, we discuss these relationships further in the context of different types of institutional change.

Institutional change, connections, and political strategy

There are two primary mechanisms through which changes in institutions affect firms' non-market strategies. First, institutional changes can affect the *value of firms' political connections.* For example, when politicians, regimes, or parties to whom firms are closely connected change, these connections often lose their ability to extract benefits for firms (Fisman, 2001; Johnson and Mitton, 2003). At the extreme, political connections can become liabilities when a new government comes into power (Leuz and Oberholzer-Gee, 2006; Siegel, 2007).

Institutional change can also affect firms' political strategies by *limiting the ability of connections to distribute benefits to favored firms*. For instance, when countries experience severe economic shocks, the ability of policy-makers to provide direct subsidies to firms is severely curtailed. Johnson and Mitton (2003) and Leuz and Oberholzer-Gee (2006) find that at the initial onset of the Asian economic crisis, the most politically connected firms suffered disproportionately relative to less connected firms. These results suggest that the crisis reduced the expected value of government subsidies to politically connected firms. In a similar vein, Morck et al. (1998) posit that trade liberalization and capital market liberalization can help level the playing field between entrenched family-controlled firms, entrepreneur-controlled firms, and widely held firms.

At the most general level, these mechanisms imply that when institutional change affects the value of a firm's political connections, then the firm's strategy should adjust either to foster new and more productive connections or to forgo connections entirely. Being so responsive requires active monitoring and management of a firm's myriad ties. In this regard, Sun et al. (2012) begin to specify the non-market factors that affect the value and usefulness of a firm's connections, including the portfolio of ties maintained, the nature of the ties themselves (e.g., ownership versus non-controlling), the political or social fortunes of the counterparty, and the bargaining-power balance between the firm and its counterparties. In addition, we suggest that the speed and size of the institutional changes at hand will prove critical. A political strategy that works well to cope with routine policy change in an orderly and stable institutional environment might not work so well if the institutional environment itself is shifting (as in liberalization). Even more challenging is designing and implementing a political strategy that is effective during periods of extreme institutional volatility, or, worse, regime change. In the following sub-sections, we consider the role and value of connections – and the implications for strategy – of policy change in a stable institutional environment, when there are gradual shifts in the institutional context, and when institutional volatility reigns.

The role and value of connections during political change that does not threaten the institutional order

A large and robust literature finds that, in stable institutional environments with orderly changes in power, the value of politically connected firms is significantly enhanced by favorable political outcomes. In general, the finance and economics literature has shown that connected firms are given superior access to finance (Claessens, Feijen, and Laeven, 2008; Morck et al., 1998), favoritism with regard to government contracts (Amore and Bennedsen, 2013; Goldman, Rocholl, and So, 2013), and favorable regulatory and other policies (Morck et al., 1998). In a cross-country study, Faccio (2006) finds substantial increases in firm value when large shareholders or officers of firms enter politics, and when politicians to whom firms are connected are appointed as ministers or elected to parliament. Knight (2006) found significant positive returns to firms associated with either Bush or Gore in reaction to news that the candidate to whom they were connected had a higher probability of winning the presidential election. In a similar vein, Goldman et al. (2009) found the value of firms connected to the Republican Party increased after Bush won the 2000 presidential election.

In fascinating recent research, Braggion and Moore (2013) document that in Victorian Britain firms with board members elected or reelected to the House of Commons experienced a significant increase in value. However, the benefits were not the same for all connected firms. The authors find that only "new-tech" firms – that is, younger firms associated with the second Industrial Revolution – experienced significant increases in value, while established "old-tech" firms experienced no impact. The authors attribute this result to the fact that new-tech firms needed connections to gain legitimacy and, more importantly, access to financial resources.

The use of connections as a means to confer legitimacy and access to capital still operates today, as Powell, White, Koput, and Owen-Smith (2005) describe in their study of the dynamics of the establishment of biotechnology as a recognizable, network-based industry. Such research showing that connections have a differential effect on new-tech and old-tech firms points to a need for research to open up the black box of the association between connections and firm value. For example, Khwaja and Mian (2005: 1373) use a very detailed dataset on loans made to firms, electoral data, and information on firms' political connections to shed some light on the mechanisms underlying their findings that politically connected firms receive greater preferential treatment from government banks when either the politicians or the political parties to which the firms are connected win an election.

> These results offer a particular mechanism of political rent seeking consistent with the institutional environment of Pakistan's banking and political system. Politically powerful firms obtain rents from government banks by exercising their political influence on bank employees. The more powerful and successful a politician is, the greater is his ability to influence government banks. This influence stems from the organizational design of government banks that enables politicians to threaten bank officers with transfers and removals, or reward them with appointments and promotions.

Similarly, Hillman et al. (1999) find significant increases in firm value stemming from personal service in elected or appointed policy positions by managers or board members of firms. However, they acknowledge the problems inherent in uncovering underlying mechanisms: "Given [the use of event study] methodology, we cannot determine what underlies the change in performance, whether it be reduced uncertainty, reduced transaction/information costs, increased legitimacy or prestige, etc., and we cannot generalize beyond these sample appointments" (Hillman et al., 1999: 79). We view the potential to uncover these underlying mechanisms as one of the most important avenues for future research.

One promising approach to teasing out the underlying mechanisms would be the use of social network analysis to map the pattern of political and social ties that connect political and corporate actors and then to trace the flow of information and resources through those ties. For example, Jäger (2013) finds that French and German executives' relative centrality in social and political networks is strongly associated with their motivation and ability to support the introduction of the euro, while Mahon, Heugens, and Lamertz (2004) show how network density and centrality affect the management of issues and coalitions. The tracing of informational and resource flows through various kinds of networks would contribute significantly to our understanding of *how* political and social connections affect both firm performance and institutional arrangements.

The role and value of connections during political change that threatens the institutional order

Policies aimed at liberalizing trade, capital markets, and other components of the institutional environment pose great threats to connected firms in that they level the playing field for non-connected firms (Morck et al., 1998; Siegel, 2007). The degree and scope of liberalization matters because superficial *cosmetic* liberalization can actually increase the favoritism granted to connected firms (Siegel, 2007). However, *real* liberalization can negatively affect connected firms in two ways. First, if liberalization includes appointing technocrats to positions once held by politicians or cronies, then the *policy change will directly affect the value of firms' political connections* by removing them from various branches of government. Second, even if no personnel or organizational changes are made, *liberalization should affect the ability of firms' connections to grant favors*. For example, increased transparency and rule of law makes it more difficult to divert government contracts to favored (but less efficient) firms. Similarly, greater transparency limits the ability of politicians to give connected firms direct subsidies and preferential access to finance (Gelos and Werner, 2002). In contrast, when more cosmetic liberalization occurs but institutional uncertainties, weak property rights, and/or inadequate rule of law persist, the value of firms' connections may not change at all, or could even increase (e.g., Bian and Logan, 1996; Luo and Chung, 2005; Park and Luo, 2001). In such situations, the failure to enact meaningful policy and institutional change means that politicians and cronies to whom firms are connected retain their ability to channel benefits to connected firms.

Liberalization, or any thoroughgoing institutional change, is often contested precisely because the stakes are high for politicians and executives alike. During periods of institutional change, connected firms and politicians can be expected to defend the status quo. For example, Morck, Wolfenzon, and Yeung (2005: 657) argue that, because connected firms often receive preferential access to finance in countries with weak financial market institutions and a lack of transparency (Claessens et al., 2008; Faccio et al., 2006; Morck et al., 1998), these firm have a particular interest in hindering the liberalization of capital markets: "to preserve their privileged positions under the *status quo* . . . elites might invest in political connections to stymie the institutional development of capital markets and to erect a variety of entry barriers."

Well-connected elites are likely to fight liberalization because preferential access to finance affects the financial and operating strategies of connected firms. For example, politically connected firms tend to be much more leveraged than non-connected firms (Faccio, 2006) and are less likely to raise money on foreign financial markets, despite their larger size (Leuz and Oberholzer-Gee, 2006). If connected firms benefit from cheap and easy access to capital in the home market, taking on more debt involves less risk of bankruptcy, especially since politically connected firms are also more likely to be bailed out when experiencing financial distress (Faccio et al., 2006). Similarly, there is no need for connected firms to incur the added costs and more stringent reporting standards required in countries with more developed financial markets if they have ample access to cheap financing at home. Indeed, Chaney, Faccio, and Parsley (2011) find that connected companies disclose lower-quality accounting information than non-connected firms. In well-functioning capital markets, firms that disclose lower-quality accounting information face a higher cost of capital, but connected firms are not penalized in this way. For all these reasons, connected firms become dependent upon their connections to continue to maintain favorable policies, and they support their connections with gifts, donations, and bribes (Guthrie, 1998), channeling resources to corrupt politicians and strengthening their grip on power.

Using the example of capital market institutions, Figure 3.3 sketches these interactions and illustrates self-reinforcing mechanisms that provide an explanation for why and how institutional arrangements tend to persist, and why they are so difficult to change. This cycle of influence suggests that institutions are in many ways generated endogenously by interactions between the players that shape institutions.

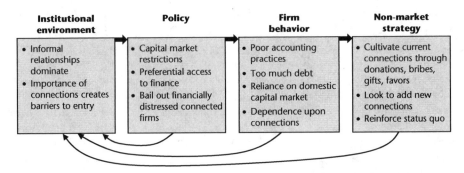

Figure 3.3 The self-reinforcing process that links capital market institutions, policy, and firm behavior through connections

In environments with weak institutions and rule of law, investments in political connections are particularly valuable (Park and Luo, 2001). The use of these connections, in itself, is likely to weaken the institutional environment further and discourage transparency. Connected firms will pursue policies that bring net benefits, such as trade protection and capital market restrictions, and the existence of these policies will affect firms' operations. In the case of capital market restrictions, connected firms can receive preferential access to finance which enables them to rely exclusively on the domestic market for financing (Faccio, 2010). Restricted domestic capital markets reduce firm growth and discourage transparency (Morck et al., 1998), further weakening institutional development. And so the circle turns, and the system of power relationships reinforces itself (see also Djelic, Nooteboom, and Whitley, 2005).

Not surprisingly, such a system is likely to resist change imposed from the outside, often by using political and legal means (Schuler, Rehbein, and Cramer, 2002). For example, Feinberg, Magelssen, and Smith (2014) document an interesting example of widespread resistance to liberalization that took place in India in the context of an IMF bailout in 1991. As part of the bailout, the International Monetary Fund (IMF) required India to lower its import tariffs dramatically from an average of 85 percent (Bown and Tovar, 2011). Facing a strict deadline and wanting to avoid the emergence of political opposition (Topalova, 2008), the Indian government chose to implement reform rapidly. By 1997, tariffs had fallen to an average of 25 percent, significantly increasing the competition faced by inefficient domestic firms. Rather than submit quietly to these changes, leading politically connected firms set off a wave of antidumping complaints in an effort to roll back the tariff reform.

Despite such opposition, institutional arrangements do change, sometimes radically, and during periods of change these same reinforcing mechanisms may, at some point, accelerate rather than resist such change. Thus, in the context of Chinese agricultural reforms, Nee (1989) hypothesizes that as market exchange replaces the redistributive mechanisms in state socialism, political capital will lose value relative to market capital. Nee finds several fascinating effects of "real" agricultural liberalization. First, the transition from redistributive to market coordination shifts sources of power and privilege to producers relative to redistributors. Second, this shift stimulates the growth of private markets. Third, as markets grow, incentives and opportunity structures change, giving entrepreneurs a path to prosperity and social mobility. Fourth, the rapid economic growth in China placated the elites. Although their relative power declined due to the loss in value of their connections, "the greater affluence produced by markets reinforce[d] the sense that the benefits of economic reform [were] widely distributed" (Nee, 1989: 678). Finally, by 1998, market reform had combined with economic growth to reduce the value of firms' political connections in China, leading firms to substitute legal mechanisms for *guanxi practice* – the reliance on connections (or *guanxi*) to "carry out procedures and go around the law" (Guthrie, 1998: 254). A Chinese manager interviewed in Guthrie's study comments:

> When people rely on "guanxi practice" for procedural matters . . . as they did in the past, society becomes very messy . . . In the old system, if you wanted to get procedures done, you had to make sure you knew people in the right places, you had to try getting procedures passed by relying on the people you knew. You had to talk to many people, and the process always took a long time. It wasn't always certain you would know the right people to get procedures taken care of. But now it's all very clear. You just follow the laws and make sure that you follow all of them closely. Things happen much more quickly today.
>
> *(Guthrie, 1998: 254)*

As Figure 3.3 and these examples illustrate, institutional arrangements seem to be endogenous and self-reinforcing, in the sense that they are created and maintained by the very firms, politicians, and other interest groups who are embedded in the institutional web. Given this, we suggest that new research should explore the nature and consequences of the various feedback loops between connected firms and their behavior; government actors at different levels and the policies they put in place; and the institutional environment in which these interactions take place.

Furthermore, an analysis of these relationships in the context of institutional change would help shed light on the mechanisms underlying observed relationships between political connections, firm strategy, and outcomes. For example, do firms change their approach to political connections (e.g., relational and transactional) after successful or unsuccessful efforts to influence policy? Do firms reaffirm their commitment to existing connections or redouble their efforts to forge new ones in light of the outcomes of their political activity? What kinds of favors come from different kinds of connections and how does this influence firms' political strategy? Is there a qualitative difference between the kinds of favors firms can get from connections that arise from chance preexisting relationships versus connections that are cultivated as part of an overall political strategy? What kinds of quid pro quo do firms' connections demand in return for granting favorable policies? What, if any, effect does the demand for quid pro quo have on firms' political strategies and their future approach to dealing with connections?

The role and value of connections in a volatile political and institutional environment

During periods of intense and sustained volatility, uncertainty about institutional change affects firms' political strategies by making *political sensitivity and responsiveness* central to company survival. In contexts characterized by institutional voids (Khanna, Palepu, and Sinha, 2005) governments exercise extreme and volatile control over regulation, resources, information, and the license to operate. In management research, the dominant prescription has been for firms in such environments to develop deep personal and organizational relationships with leading governmental figures and entities (Cuervo-Cazurra, 2006; Sun, Mellahi, and Thun, 2010). For example, embedding a firm within the local power structure has been shown to mitigate various political and contractual risks, to improve learning about the local system, and to improve access to resources, information, and political favors (Frynas, Mellahi, and Pigman, 2006; Peng and Luo, 2000; Peng et al., 2008). Similarly, Peng and collaborators have shown that in difficult and changeable environments, managers still find a way to succeed, often relying on network-based growth strategies (Peng, 1997; Peng and Heath, 1996; Peng and Zhou, 2005). Sometimes, firms can succeed by exploiting their complex family and social connections to politicians to monitor and buffer changes in the institutional environment and firms that are successful in unstable institutional environments may be those that are attuned to every nuance of the political wind (Farashahi and Hafsi, 2009). These firms cultivate deep relations with specific constituencies and interact often and assertively with the government to try to create a more predictable context. Thus, in unstable contexts, executives find themselves in the unfamiliar role of political analysts and diplomats trying to discern which political faction will prevail, which set of rules will dominate, and how to engage politically (Chen, Ding, and Kim, 2010; Getz and Oetzel, 2009; Jallat and Shultz, 2011; Margolis and Walsh, 2003).

Becoming so closely attuned to the political wind demands a tremendous investment in understanding the local political situation and behavioral norms, and then, when possible, building effective means of influence within this context (Bonardi et al., 2006; Frynas et al., 2006; Lawton and Rajwani, 2011). However, the experience of firms and individual managers can reduce the difficulties and costs of managing political and regulatory uncertainty (Bonardi et al., 2006; Henisz and Delios, 2004). Indeed, firms that have grown up in unstable home countries show a greater willingness to enter and a greater ability to survive in similarly uncertain contexts, at least in part because of political sensitivity and adaptability (Cuervo-Cazurra and Genc, 2008; Holburn and Zelner, 2010).

In many instances, the reliance on personal connections to affect government is associated with cronyism and corruption (Bunkanwanicha and Wiwattanakantang, 2009; Johnson and Mitton, 2003; Morck et al., 1998). These conditions may be reinforced by culture (Khatri, Tsang, and Begley, 2006; Mauro, 1995) and the personal interests of powerful families and groups (Fisman, 2001; Morck et al., 1998; Wood and Frynas, 2006). In the context of institutional volatility, relying on political ties heightens the risk of becoming dependent on, and beholden to, political actors within the larger network (Sun et al., 2010), who may arbitrarily increase their demands for support (Kivleniece and Quelin, 2012) or be thrown out of office when the political regime changes.

Indeed, the most significant risk to firms that have invested in political ties in uncertain environments is the potential for the entire political context to shift. In such cases, the value of firms' political connections can evaporate completely. In the extreme, connections to old regimes can become liabilities when a new government comes into power and attempts to turn the tables on the previous regime (Leuz and Oberholzer-Gee, 2006; Siegel, 2007). Experience in Iran (1977), Central Asia (1991), Indonesia (1998), and during the Arab Spring has shown how quickly countries can shift from stability to chaos as power flows from unexpected sources to upset the established order (Fisman, 2001; Sun et al., 2010).

While firms can sometimes help to resolve even violent conflict (e.g., by facilitating negotiations; Getz and Oetzel, 2009), they run the very real risk that close association with the government will be devastating if their political patrons suffer a setback (Leuz and Oberholzer-Gee, 2006; Siegel, 2007). For example, in the context of a hotly contested Malaysian election after the imposition of capital controls, Johnson and Mitton (2003) find that connections to Mahatir (the winner) accounted for 20 percent of the increase in firm value, and connections to Anwar (the loser) were associated with a 6.3 percent decrease in firm value. Similarly, Fisman (2001) provides early evidence that the threat of regime change is particularly damaging to politically connected firms. Examining how share prices of politically connected and non-connected Indonesian firms reacted to rumors of Suharto's ill health, Fisman concludes that political connections are a large source of value for a relatively small group of entrenched and powerful firms. More dramatic still are examples of the complete collapse of firms associated with regimes that are deposed during a revolution (Getz and Oetzel, 2009).

As in all political situations, however, there may be more nuance than meets the eye, even during abrupt regime change. A recent case study of how Turkish multinational construction firms navigated the collapse of the Gaddafi regime (Darendeli and Hill, 2013) suggests that the firms that had developed relations with regionally powerful families outside of Gaddafi's circle and those associated with public-benefit projects, such as universities and hospitals, were protected from looting and allowed to continue their work, even if they had also benefited from close ties with the Gaddafi regime. Investment in connections to non-governmental sources of power and corporate social responsibility (CSR)-type efforts proved to be an effective hedge against the consequences of being associated with an overthrown dictator.

This example points to sources of legitimacy and countervailing power embedded in the social sector as a way to establish and maintain legitimacy, even in the face of extreme institutional volatility (Ramamurti and Doh, 2004). Actors in this sector have successfully pushed for institutional change that affects both business and political interests. For example, "the many codes, standards, and norms developed to encourage industries to adopt better environmental, labor and human rights practices are primarily a result of institutional pressure from social movements and actors" (Doh et al., 2012: 35). Looking outside the political realm broadens the list of influential actors with whom firms can form meaningful connections to include advocacy groups, consumers, labor, nonprofits, and the media (Dacin, Oliver, and Roy, 2007). Further, directing non-market strategies toward civil society actors has been shown to have a positive impact on the success of firms' overseas operations (Tashman and Marano, 2009; Vachani, Doh, and Teegen, 2009) and to help heal rifts after conflicts (Getz and Oetzel, 2009). Similarly, local non-governmental organizations (NGOs) can provide firms with access to countries, markets, or social strata that might otherwise be unattainable (Boddewyn and Doh, 2011; London and Hart, 2004).

Conclusion

We began this chapter by asking how firms might build successful non-market strategies that are robust to, or even thrive on, change. We tried to craft an answer by examining a diverse literature as it relates to situations in which political change is routine and does not threaten the established institutional order; situations in which political change does indeed threaten the established institutional order; and situations in which both the political and institutional contexts are volatile and uncertain. Throughout, we focused on the role of boundary-spanning interpersonal ties that connect firms to institutions and through which influence and resources flow.

Our exploration of the role and value of connections during change that does not threaten institutional arrangements served to highlight the formation, role, and bi-directionality of flows through connections. The key idea is that connections, strategy, and outcomes reinforce each other – that the formation, maintenance, use, and value of connections comprise a process that is constantly in motion and in need of continual attention. We suggest that scholars focus further attention on understanding this process and that social network analysis tools could be useful in this regard.

Our exploration of the role and value of connections during change that does threaten institutional arrangements generated a mechanism of self-reinforcing feedback loops that, ironically, helps to explain why institutional arrangements are so resistant to change. This model also suggests that institutional arrangements are largely endogenous in the sense of being created through the interplay of firms and other actors embedded within a given institutional context.

Our exploration of the role and value of connections in a volatile institutional environment focused on potential sources of power and influence outside of the political realm, and we highlighted the role of civil society as a source of legitimacy and countervailing power. There is a growing body of literature that suggests that it would be useful for scholars and managers alike to turn their attention to the active management and deployment of connections in the social sector, perhaps using the social movement literature as a guide.

More philosophically, we hope that this chapter reinforces two points: that connections are central to non-market strategy; and that change is the norm, even in seemingly slow-moving institutional environments. As social beings, we bring our interpersonal ties to everything we do, and contribute to the formation, reinforcement, or dissolution of ties through every interaction. It is perhaps not surprising that such ties are central to non-market strategies, and that they extend not just to the political institutions but to social institutions and indeed throughout markets. It also seems likely to us that personal connections and associated informal institutions will remain important parts of the institutional landscape in varying forms and combinations.

Similarly, while institutions may well be endogenously generated and resistant to change, they do change, and constantly, in response both to exogenous shocks and to the agency of interconnected actors nested within them. Change is the usual state and so requires a more process-oriented approach to research and theory, as well as real engagement in whether the direction of change is somehow positive or negative in its impact on diverse actors. Whether the effect of institutional change is positive or negative has important ramifications for society at large. When institutions encourage efficient and high-quality firms to grow, invest, and innovate, the resultant economic growth can bring widespread benefits.

References

Aldrich, H. E. and Fiol, C. M. 1994. Fools rush in? The institutional context of industry creation. *Academy of Management Review*, 19(4): 645–70.

Alon, I., Gurumoorthy, R., Mitchell, M. C., and Steen, T. 2006. Managing micropolitical risk: A cross-sector examination. *Thunderbird International Business Review*, 48(5): 623–42.

Amore, M. D. and Bennedsen, M. 2013. The value of local political connections in a low-corruption environment. *Journal of Financial Economics*, 110(2): 387–402.

Bertrand, M., Kramarz, F., Schoar, A., and Thesmar, D. 2006. Politicians, firms and the political business cycle: Evidence from France. Working paper. University of Chicago.

Bian, Y. and Logan, J. R. 1996. Market transition and the persistence of power: The changing stratification system in urban China. *American Sociological Review*, 61(5): 739–58.

Biggart, N. W. and Guillén, M. F. 1999. Developing difference: Social organization and the rise of the auto industries of South Korea, Taiwan, Spain, and Argentina. *American Sociological Review*, 64(5): 722–47.

Birnbaum, P. H. 1985. Political strategies of regulated organizations as functions of context and fear. *Strategic Management Journal*, 6(2): 135–50.

Bitektine, A. 2011. Toward a theory of social judgments of organizations: The case of legitimacy, reputation, and status. *Academy of Management Review*, 36(1): 151–79.

Boddewyn, J. J. and Brewer, T. L. 1994. International-business political behavior: New theoretical directions. *Academy of Management Review*, 19(1): 119–43.

Boddewyn, J. and Doh, J. 2011. Global strategy and the collaboration of MNEs, NGOs, and governments for the provisioning of collective goods in emerging markets. *Global Strategy Journal*, 1(34): 345–61.

Bonardi, J.-P., Holburn, G. L., and Vanden Bergh, R. G. V. 2006. Non-market strategy performance: Evidence from US electric utilities. *Academy of Management Journal*, 49(6): 1209–28.

Bown, C. P. and Tovar, P. 2011. Trade liberalization, antidumping, and safeguards: Evidence from India's tariff reform. *Journal of Development Economics*, 96(1): 115–25.

Braggion, F. and Moore, L. 2013. The economic benefits of political connections in late Victorian Britain. *Journal of Economic History*, 73(01): 142–76.

Bunkanwanicha, P. and Wiwattanakantang, Y. 2009. Big business owners in politics. *Review of Financial Studies*, 22(6): 2133–68.

Chaney, P. K., Faccio, M., and Parsley, D. 2011. The quality of accounting information in politically connected firms. *Journal of Accounting and Economics*, 51(1): 58–76.

Chen, C. J., Ding, Y., and Kim, C. F. 2010. High-level politically connected firms, corruption, and analyst forecast accuracy around the world. *Journal of International Business Studies*, 41(9): 1505–24.

Claessens, S., Feijen, E., and Laeven, L. 2008. Political connections and preferential access to finance: The role of campaign contributions. *Journal of Financial Economics*, 88(3): 554–80.

Cohen, L., Frazzini, A., and Malloy, C. 2010. Sell-side school ties. *Journal of Finance*, 65(4): 1409–37.

Cooper, M. J., Gulen, H., and Ovtchinnikov, A. V. 2010. Corporate political contributions and stock returns. *Journal of Finance*, 65(2): 687–724.

Cuervo-Cazurra, A. 2006. Who cares about corruption? *Journal of International Business Studies*, 37(6): 807–22.

Cuervo-Cazurra, A. and Genc, M. 2008. Transforming disadvantages into advantages: Developing-country MNEs in the least developed countries. *Journal of International Business Studies*, 39(6): 957–79.

Dacin, M. T., Oliver, C., and Roy, J. P. 2007. The legitimacy of strategic alliances: An institutional perspective. *Strategic Management Journal*, 28(2): 169–87.

Dahan, N., Doh, J., and Guay, T. 2006. The role of multinational corporations in transnational institution building: A policy network perspective. *Human Relations*, 59(11): 1571–600.

Darendeli, I. S. and Hill, T. L. 2013. Delicate diplomacy: Lessons from Libya about balancing political and social legitimacy. Working paper.

Delmas, M. A. and Montes-Sancho, M. J. 2010. Voluntary agreements to improve environmental quality: Symbolic and substantive cooperation. *Strategic Management Journal*, 31(6): 575–601.

Demirguc-Kunt, A. and Maksimovic, V. 1996. Stock market development and financing choices of firms. *World Bank Economic Review*, 10(2): 341–69.

Djelic, M.-L., Nooteboom, B., and Whitley, R. 2005. Introduction: Dynamics of interaction between institutions, markets and organizations. *Organization Studies*, 26(12): 1733–41.

Doh, J. P., Lawton, T. C., and Rajwani, T. 2012. Advancing non-market strategy research: Institutional perspectives in a changing world. *Academy of Management Perspectives*, 26(3): 22–39.

Eden, L. and Lenway, S. 2001. Introduction to the symposium multinationals: The Janus face of globalization. *Journal of International Business Studies*, 32(3): 383–400.

Faccio, M. 2006. Politically connected firms. *American Economic Review*, 96(1): 369–86.

— 2010. Differences between politically connected and nonconnected firms: A cross-country analysis. *Financial Management*, 39(3): 905–28.

Faccio, M., Masulis, R. W., and McConnell, J. 2006. Political connections and corporate bailouts. *Journal of Finance*, 61(6): 2597–635.

Faccio, M. and Parsley, D. C. 2009. Sudden deaths: Taking stock of geographic ties. *Journal of Financial and Quantitative Analysis*, 44(3): 683–718.

Farashahi, M. and Hafsi, T. 2009. Strategy of firms in unstable institutional environments. *Asia Pacific Journal of Management*, 26(4): 643–66.

Feinberg, S. E., Magelssen, C., and Smith, M. G. 2014. Timing is everything: Political action and the value of experience over the policy life cycle. Working paper.

Fisman, R. 2001. Estimating the value of political connections. *American Economic Review*, 91(4): 1095–1102.

Frynas, J. G., Mellahi, K., and Pigman, G. A. 2006. First mover advantages in international business and firm-specific political resources. *Strategic Management Journal*, 27(4): 321–45.

Gelos, R. G. and Werner, A. M. 2002. Financial liberalization, credit constraints, and collateral: Investment in the Mexican manufacturing sector. *Journal of Development Economics*, 67(1): 1–27.

Getz, K. A. and Oetzel, J. 2009. MNE strategic intervention in violent conflict: Variations based on conflict characteristics. *Journal of Business Ethics*, 89(4): 375–86.

Goldman, E., Rocholl, J., and So, J. 2009. Do politically connected boards affect firm value? *Review of Financial Studies*, 22(6): 2331–60.

— 2013. Politically connected boards of directors and the allocation of procurement contracts. *Review of Finance*, 17(5): 1617–48.

Greenwood, R. and Suddaby, R. 2006. Institutional entrepreneurship in mature fields: The big five accounting firms. *Academy of Management Journal*, 49(1): 27–48.

Guthrie, D. 1998. The declining significance of guanxi in China's economic transition. *China Quarterly*, 154: 254–82.

Henisz, W. J. and Delios, A. 2004. Information or influence? The benefits of experience for managing political uncertainty. *Strategic Organization*, 2(4): 389–421.

Hillman, A. J. and Hitt, M. A. 1999. Corporate political strategy formulation: A model of approach, participation, and strategy decisions. *Academy of Management Review*, 24(4): 825–42.

Hillman, A. and Keim, G. 1995. International variation in the business–government interface: Institutional and organizational considerations. *Academy of Management Review*, 21(1): 193–214.

Hillman, A. J., Zardkoohi, A., and Bierman, L. 1999. Corporate political strategies and firm performance: Indications of firm-specific benefits from personal service in the US government. *Strategic Management Journal*, 20(1): 67–81.

Hirsch, P. M. and Lounsbury, M. 1997. Ending the family quarrel toward a reconciliation of "old" and "new" institutionalisms. *American Behavioral Scientist*, 40(4): 406–18.

Holburn, G. L. F. and Zelner, B. A. 2010. Political capabilities, policy risk, and international investment strategy: Evidence from the global electric power generation industry. *Strategic Management Journal*, 31(12): 1290–315.

Jäger, K. 2013. Sources of Franco-German corporate support for the euro: The effects of business network centrality and political connections. *European Union Politics*, 14(1): 115–39.

Jallat, F. and Shultz, C. J. 2011. Lebanon: From cataclysm to opportunity – crisis management lessons for MNCs in the tourism sector of the Middle East. *Journal of World Business*, 46(4): 476–86.

Johnson, S. and Mitton, T. 2003. Cronyism and capital controls: Evidence from Malaysia. *Journal of Financial Economics*, 67(2): 351–82.

Khanna, T. and Palepu, K. 2000. The future of business groups in emerging markets: Long-run evidence from Chile. *Academy of Management journal*, 43(3): 268–85.

Khanna, T., Palepu, K. G., and Sinha, J. 2005. Strategies that fit emerging markets. *Harvard Business Review*, 83(6): 63–7.

Khatri, N., Tsang, E. W. K., and Begley, T. M. 2006. Cronyism: A cross-cultural analysis. *Journal of International Business Studies*, 37(1): 61–75.

Khwaja, A. I. and Mian, A. 2005. Do lenders favor politically connected firms? Rent provision in an emerging financial market. *The Quarterly Journal of Economics*, 120(4): 1371–411.

Kivleniece, I. and Quelin, B. V. 2012. Creating and capturing value in public–private ties: A private actor's perspective. *Academy of Management Review*, 37(2): 272–99.

Knight, B. 2006. Are policy platforms capitalized into equity prices? Evidence from the Bush/Gore 2000 presidential election. *Journal of Public Economics*, 90(4): 751–73.

Kogut, B., Walker, G., and Anand, J. 2002. Agency and institutions: National divergences in diversification behavior. *Organization Science*, 13(2): 162–78.

Kostova, T., Roth, K., and Dacin, M. T. 2008. Institutional theory in the study of multinational corporations: A critique and new directions. *Academy of Management Review*, 33(4): 994–1006.

Lawton, T. and Rajwani, T. 2011. Designing lobbying capabilities: managerial choices in unpredictable environments. *European Business Review*, 23(2): 167–89.

Lester, R. H., Hillman, A., Zardkoohi, A., and Cannella, A. A. 2008. Former government officials as outside directors: The role of human and social capital. *Academy of Management Journal*, 51(5): 999–1013.

Leuz, C. and Oberholzer-Gee, F. 2006. Political relationships, global financing, and corporate transparency: Evidence from Indonesia. *Journal of Financial Economics*, 81(2): 411–39.

Levine, R. 1997. Financial development and economic growth: Views and agenda. *Journal of Economic Literature*, 35(2): 688–726.

Li, H., Meng, L., Wang, Q., and Zhou, L.-A. 2008. Political connections, financing and firm performance: Evidence from Chinese private firms. *Journal of Development Economics*, 87(2): 283–99.

London, T. and Hart, S. L. 2004. Reinventing strategies for emerging markets: Beyond the transnational model. *Journal of International Business Studies*, 35(5): 350–70.

Lounsbury, M. 2001. Institutional sources of practice variation: Staffing college and university recycling programs. *Administrative Science Quarterly*, 46(1): 29–56.

— 2007. A tale of two cities: Competing logics and practice variation in the professionalizing of mutual funds. *Academy of Management Journal*, 50(2): 289–307.

Luo, X. and Chung, C.-N. 2005. Keeping it all in the family: The role of particularistic relationships in business group performance during institutional transition. *Administrative Science Quarterly*, 50(3): 404–39.

Mahon, J. F., Heugens, P. P., and Lamertz, K. 2004. Social networks and non-market strategy. *Journal of Public Affairs*, 4(2): 170–89.

Makino, S., Isobe, T., and Chan, C. M. 2004. Does country matter? *Strategic Management Journal*, 25(10): 1027–43.

Margolis, J. D. and Walsh, J. P. 2003. Misery loves companies: Rethinking social initiatives by business. *Administrative Science Quarterly*, 48(2): 268–305.

Mauro, P. 1995. Corruption and growth. *Quarterly Journal of Economics*, 110(3): 681–712.

Morck, R. K., Stangeland, D. A., and Yeung, B. 1998. Inherited wealth, corporate control and economic growth: The Canadian disease. National Bureau of Economic Research, No. w10692.

Morck, R., Wolfenzon, D., and Yeung, B. 2005. Corporate governance, economic entrenchment and growth. *Journal of Economic Literature*, 43(3): 655–720.

Nee, V. 1989. A theory of market transition: From redistribution to markets in state socialism. *American Sociological Review*, 31(4): 663–81.

North, D. C. 1990. *Institutions, Institutional Change and Economic Performance*. Cambridge: Cambridge University Press.

Oliver, C. and Holzinger, I. 2008. The effectiveness of strategic political management: A dynamic capabilities framework. *Academy of Management Review*, 33(2): 496–520.

Park, S. H. and Luo, Y. 2001. Guanxi and organizational dynamics: Organizational networking in Chinese firms. *Strategic Management Journal*, 22(5): 455–77.

Patriotta, G., Gond, J. P., and Schultz, F. 2011. Maintaining legitimacy: Controversies, orders of worth, and public justifications. *Journal of Management Studies*, 48(8): 1804–36.

Peng, M. W. 1997. Firm growth in transitional economies: Three longitudinal cases from China, 1989–96. *Organization Studies*, 18(3): 385–413.

— 2003. Institutional transitions and strategic choices. *Academy of Management Review*, 28(2): 275–96.

Peng, M. W. and Heath, P. S. 1996. The growth of the firm in planned economies in transition: Institutions, organizations, and strategic choice. *Academy of Management Review*, 21(2): 492–528.

Peng, M. W. and Luo, Y. 2000. Managerial ties and firm performance in a transition economy: The nature of a micro-macro link. *Academy of Management Journal*, 43(3): 486–501.

Peng, M. W. and Zhou, J. Q. 2005. How network strategies and institutional transitions evolve in Asia. *Asia Pacific Journal of Management*, 22(4): 321–36.

Peng, M. W., Wang, D. Y., and Jiang, Y. 2008. An institution-based view of international business strategy: A focus on emerging economies. *Journal of International Business Studies*, 39(5): 920–36.

Powell, W. W., White, D. R., Koput, K. W., and Owen-Smith, J. 2005. Network dynamics and field evolution: The growth of interorganizational collaboration in the life sciences. *American Journal of Sociology*, 110(4): 1132–205.

Rajan, R. G. and Zingales, L. 1998. Which capitalism? Lessons from the East Asian crisis. *Journal of Applied Corporate Finance*, 11(3): 40–8.

Ramamurti, R. and Doh, J. P. 2004. Rethinking foreign infrastructure investment in developing countries. *Journal of World Business*, 39(2): 151–67.

Schuler, D. A., Rehbein, K., and Cramer, R. D. 2002. Pursuing strategic advantage through political means: A multivariate approach. *Academy of Management Journal*, 45(4): 659–72.

Scott, W. R. 2008. Lords of the dance: Professionals as institutional agents. *Organization Studies*, 29(2): 219–38.

Siegel, J. 2005. Can foreign firms bond themselves effectively by renting US securities laws? *Journal of Financial Economics*, 75(2): 319–59.

— 2007. Contingent political capital and international alliances: Evidence from South Korea. *Administrative Science Quarterly*, 52(4): 621–66.

— 2009. Is there a better commitment mechanism than cross–listings for emerging–economy firms & quest: Evidence from Mexico. *Journal of International Business Studies*, 40(7): 1171–91.

Stratmann, T. 1991. What do campaign contributions buy? Deciphering causal effects of money and votes. *Southern Economic Journal*, 57(3): 606–20.

Sun, P., Mellahi, K., and Thun, E. 2010. The dynamic value of MNE political embeddedness: The case of the Chinese automobile industry. *Journal of International Business Studies*, 41(7): 1161–82.

Sun, P., Mellahi, K., and Wright, M. 2012. The contingent value of corporate political ties. *Academy of Management Perspectives*, 26(3): 68–82.

Tashman, P. and Marano, V. 2009. Dynamic capabilities and base of the pyramid business strategies. *Journal of Business Ethics*, 89(4): 495–514.

Thornton, P. H. 2004. *Markets from Culture: Institutional Logics and Organizational Decisions in Higher Education Publishing*. Stanford, CA: Stanford University Press.

Thornton, P. H. and Ocasio, W. 2008. Institutional logics. In R. Greenwood, C. Oliver, R. Suddaby, and K. Sahlin (eds.), *The Sage Handbook of Organizational Institutionalism*: 840. Los Angeles, CA: Sage.

Thornton, P. H., Ocasio, W., and Lounsbury, M. 2012. *The Institutional Logics Perspective: A New Approach to Culture, Structure, and Process*. Oxford: Oxford University Press.

Topalova, P. 2008. India: Is the rising tide lifting all boats? IMF Working Paper 08/54. Washington, DC: International Monetary Fund.

Vachani, S., Doh, J. P., and Teegen, H. 2009. NGOs' influence on MNEs' social development strategies in varying institutional contexts: A transaction cost perspective. *International Business Review*, 18(5): 446–56.

Vasudeva, G., Zaheer, A., and Hernandez, E. 2013. The embeddedness of networks: Institutions, structural holes, and innovativeness in the fuel cell industry. *Organization Science*, 24(3): 645–63.

Wood, G. and Frynas, J. G. 2006. The institutional basis of economic failure: Anatomy of the segmented business system. *Socio-Economic Review*, 4(2): 239–77.

Zhang, J. and Luo, X. R. 2013. Dared to care: Organizational vulnerability, institutional logics, and MNCs' social responsiveness in emerging markets. *Organization Science*, 24(6): 1742–64.

4

How regulatory uncertainty drives integrated market and non-market strategy[1]

Allison F. Kingsley and Richard G. Vanden Bergh

Regulatory policy affects the profitability of regulated firms. So why do some regulated entities invest significant resources to influence regulation while others invest relatively little? This is the fundamental research question we address in this chapter. To analyze this question we draw from and build upon the regulatory economics, positive political theory, political markets, and non-market strategy literatures.

Beginning with Buchanan and Tullock (1962), economists modeled the public policy process by assuming political actors' behavior reflects their self-interest. Using these assumptions, Stigler (1971) and Peltzman (1976) showed that regulators make policy choices, under certain conditions, that help regulated firms. Positive political theorists (e.g., McCubbins et al., 1987; Gilligan et al., 1989) criticized the Stiglerian approach for treating regulatory decisions as taking place within a vacuum. The positive political theorists developed models where regulators are constrained by other policy-makers and gained new insights into drivers of regulatory policy. Throughout all of these models, however, the regulated firms are passive, and do not act strategically to influence policy outcomes. Snyder (1990) complemented these insights by showing that firms' resource allocation decisions are consistent with investment in the policy-making process. With evidence of active firm influence in the policy-making process, economists began developing models of the non-market strategies employed by firms (e.g., Baron, 1995). Building from this foundational stream of research, the more current literature shows that regulated firms develop non-market strategies in a systematic way (e.g., Bonardi et al., 2006; de Figueiredo and Edwards, 2007; Holburn and Vanden Bergh, 2008; Kingsley et al., 2012). However, the literature says little on how or why regulated firms employ different non-market strategies, particularly when non-market rivals elevate regulatory uncertainty.

By way of example, take the recent case of Entergy, an integrated utility and the second-largest nuclear power company in the United States. Entergy operates nuclear units in several states, including Arkansas[2] and Vermont.[3] Although the firm's market strategy is consistent – to pursue cash flow stability by balancing stable regulated utility operations with merchant generation exposure – Entergy's non-market strategies in Arkansas and Vermont have been decidedly different over the past few years. In Arkansas, Entergy pursued a generic, modest non-market strategy, using inexpensive but fast-paced and upbeat advertisements about the firm's efficiency and reliability. In Vermont, Entergy executed a costly low- and high-profile strategy focused broadly on multiple political actors. Advocating for its Vermont Yankee plant, Entergy's advertising campaign with its partners was somber, dramatic, and defensive.

What explains the divergence in Entergy's non-market strategies in Vermont and Arkansas? Why did Entergy choose to allocate resources so differently in these two states? We argue – and will show – that Entergy's exposure to higher regulatory uncertainty in Vermont drove the firm to choose a more expensive and extensive non-market strategy. The different political environments in which Entergy operated required two different strategies. In other words, the higher the regulatory uncertainty faced by firms, the more expensive and expansive their non-market strategy must become.

Indeed, regulatory uncertainty is costly to firms. In the World Bank's 2012 survey of global investors from diverse industries and countries, respondents viewed "adverse regulatory changes" (i.e., regulatory uncertainty) as the single most important type of political risk their firms face, of greater concern than breach of contract, expropriation, or terrorism, for instance (World Bank, 2012). In the twelve months prior to the survey, nearly 30 percent of firms withdrew existing investments or canceled new investments on account of adverse regulatory changes, and over the three years prior more than one-third suffered losses owing to adverse regulatory changes.

The regulatory environment also affects firms' growth and profitability. For instance, PricewaterhouseCoopers conducted a CEO survey between September and December 2012 (PwC, 2013). In 1,330 interviews with CEOs in 68 countries across a range of industries, 85 percent of CEOs believed governments and regulators have some or a significant influence on their business profitability, and over two-thirds saw overregulation as a significant threat to business growth. Clearly, regulatory uncertainty matters to firms.

In this chapter, we build from the growing literature addressing political markets (e.g., Buchanan and Tullock, 1962; Bonardi et al., 2005; Kingsley et al., 2012) and multinational political risk (e.g., Henisz, 2000, 2004; Holburn and Zelner, 2010; Graham, Johnston, and Kingsley, 2013) to explain the drivers of regulatory uncertainty, and the implications for firms' non-market strategies. We analyze both the demand and supply sides of the political market. On the demand side of the political market, we first introduce how the ideology and policy preference alignment of rival demanders affects regulatory uncertainty. On the supply side of the political market, we focus on how the concept of political constraints, from the multinational political risk literature, also affects regulatory uncertainty. We then bring these two sides of the political market together, arguing that the specific regulatory context (ideology of rival, policy preference alignment, and degree of political constraints) allows a focal firm to predict the level of regulatory uncertainty it will face if it makes (or already has made) an investment.

We then discuss how firms design efficient non-market strategies to match the level of regulatory uncertainty. We characterize three primary dimensions of firms' non-market strategies: profile level, coalition breadth, and pivotal target. Finally, we investigate how this theoretical framework applies to the case of Entergy in Vermont and Arkansas between 2010 and 2012.

Theorizing about regulatory uncertainty and integrated strategy

Firms investing in new markets, whether expanding product or geographic scope, need well-designed market strategies to enhance economic market performance. Investments face risk due not only to market forces but also to uncertainties emanating from the political market. The level of political uncertainty varies across firms and political boundaries. Firms that face some positive level of political uncertainty need well-designed non-market strategies to enhance performance in a political market. Furthermore, scholars have argued that the strategies for success in the economic market may differ from the strategies for success in the political market (e.g., Boddewyn and Brewer, 1994; Hillman and Keim, 1995; Bonardi et al., 2005). While the empirical evidence is limited, recent research suggests that when firms face political risk, their success requires integration of their market and non-market strategies (de Figueiredo, 2009; Bach and Allen, 2010; Holburn and Vanden Bergh, 2014). In this section of the paper, we address these two main issues. First, we analyze how characteristics of the political market lead to different levels of regulatory uncertainty for firms. Second, given a level of regulatory uncertainty, we discuss the implications for firms designing integrated market and non-market strategies.

Political market characteristics and regulatory uncertainty

To characterize the level of regulatory uncertainty, we rely on the growing literature on political markets (e.g., Buchanan and Tullock, 1962; Bonardi et al., 2005; Kingsley et al., 2012). In a political market there are demanders of regulation – firms, interest groups, unions, consumers, activists, and so on – and suppliers of regulation – elected politicians, regulatory agencies, and courts (Bonardi et al., 2006). Demanders and suppliers exchange regulatory policies for resources such as votes, finances, and information (Hillman and Hitt, 1999; de Figueiredo and Edwards, 2007). We argue that characteristics of the demanders and suppliers in the political markets determine the level of regulatory uncertainty. Furthermore, we address, in turn, three primary questions related to the level of regulatory uncertainty the focal firm faces. Figure 4.1 depicts these three questions.

Question 1: Are demand side rivals ideological?

In the political market, firms and other interest groups are the demanders of public policy. Demanders have preferences over the policy choices of the suppliers. Consistent with the political economy literature, we assume that firms seek regulation that increases economic profits (e.g., Baron, 2010). We also assume that other interest groups affected by a regulation have preferences over the set of regulatory policy choices. However, while other interest groups also have preferences over the regulatory outcome, we argue that their objectives may or may not be motivated by efficiency concerns (i.e., exploring gains from trade).

In political markets where the preferences of interest groups are aligned with the preferences of the firm, the firm has allies. In these types of political markets, where the entire set of active demanders of regulation have homogeneous preferences, we tend to see regulators captured by the firm (Stigler, 1971) and the design of political strategy is focused entirely on influencing suppliers (Baron, 1999; Holburn and Vanden Bergh, 2004).

The focus of our analysis, however, is on political markets where the policy preferences of the other demanders are different from those of the firm. Following Wilson (1980) and others, we describe these political markets as involving intense political rivalry (see also Baron, 2010), and the non-market strategies of the firm must account for attempts by its demand side rivals to reduce the firm's political market performance.

We assume that an interest group has some ideal policy, defined herein as IG, and that as regulatory policy moves away from that ideal policy IG the value associated with the policy declines.[4]

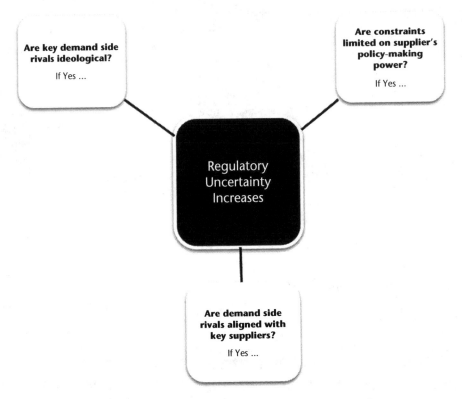

Figure 4.1 Three political market questions related to regulatory uncertainty

We illustrate this with a simple function $V^{IG}(x)$, where x is the policy and V^{IG} is the value for the interest group with ideal policy IG. So the function $V^{IG}(x)$ is the value for the interest group associated with policy x. Now consider how interest groups can be characterized as different types.

Baron (2010) argues that when a firm faces a demand side rival one tactic is for the firm to find substitutes for the rival that reduce the negative effects associated with a policy. The substitute, in essence, compensates the rival interest group for losses associated with a final regulatory policy (y) relative to the value of the most likely alternative policy (x). Baron's argument can be captured in the following equation:

$$\alpha V^{IG}(y) + (1 - \alpha)S^{IG}(y) > V^{IG}(x) \tag{1}$$

In Equation (1) α is the weight the rival interest group places on the value of the policy and $1 - \alpha$ is the weight on the substitute. One can think of α representing the saliency of the policy to the rival interest group. As saliency increases, the rival places a greater weight on the regulatory policy. $S^{IG}(y)$ is the value that the rival interest group places on the substitute policy. The tactical issue arises for the firm only when $V^{IG}(y) < V^{IG}(x)$. In this case the rival interest group prefers x to y and will fight in the political market to implement x. However, if $S^{IG}(y)$ is large enough and receives sufficient weight, then Equation (1) holds and the rival interest group will be less active influencing policy. This improves the probability that the firm's preferred policy y will be implemented by the regulator.

Baron provides an example of a rival interest group accepting a change of policy because it is compensated with a substitute. In his teaching case about the extension of Daylight Savings Time (DST), Baron describes how the National Association of Broadcasters (NAB) preferred the status quo policy (x) to the proposed policy (y) which would extend DST ($V^{NAB}(x) > V^{NAB}(y)$). The NAB opposed extension because they would lose valuable advertising time. The proponents of the extension expended resources to identify a substitute that allowed the NAB to avoid losing valuable advertising time while still implementing the extension to DST (see Baron, 2010: 210).

Implicit in the NAB example is that rival interest groups are motivated by efficiency objectives. That is, these types of interest groups are willing to trade less valuable regulatory policy in exchange for some compensation. We refer to these types of rival interest groups as *efficiency rivals*. However, some interest groups will refuse any form of trade for less valuable regulatory policy. The extreme type of interest group places all weight on the value of the policy ($\alpha = 1$). In this case, Equation (1) never holds for the rival interest group (restricting our attention to only those relevant cases where $V^{IG}(y) < V^{IG}(x)$) and thus the rival will fight any attempts to move regulatory policy away from its ideal policy. The rival interest group will not consider potential gains from trade for moving policy further from x. We refer to these types of rival interest groups as *ideological rivals*.

More generally, ideological rivals place too high a demand on firms to accept any policy further from their ideal. While technically this type of rival may have an α value of less than one,[5] the demands they place on the value of compensation ($S^{IG}(y)$) are so severe that the set of feasible gains from trade is empty. To negotiate with an ideological rival would require the firm to allocate a level of resources that would more than eliminate all marginal profit gains from a more favorable regulatory policy. As a result, ideological rivals will fight hard to prevent any movement in policy closer to the firm's ideal.

This analysis leads to the hypothesis that, relative to efficiency rivals, ideological rivals create greater uncertainty over the outcome of regulatory policy. Ideological rivals tend to use public campaigns such as mailings, boycotts, reports, and/or advocacy advertising to leverage public pressure (Holburn and Vanden Bergh, 2004; Baron, 2010) on issues that are usually highly polarized (Bonardi and Keim, 2005; Bonardi et al., 2006). By contrast, efficiency rivals are more often linked with narrower issues that are not defined along partisan lines but rather reflect bottom-line concerns. This allows for more bargaining over alternatives and lowers transaction costs of negotiation (Coase, 1960).

Question 2: Are constraints limited on supplier's policy-making power?

Drawing from the political economy literature, we assume that the suppliers of public policy, similar to demanders, have well-defined preferences over the set of regulatory policy choices (for examples, see Stigler, 1971; Ferejohn and Shipan, 1990; Holburn and Vanden Bergh, 2004). An important insight from this literature is that regulators are constrained by the preferences of other suppliers, such as the courts or elected officials (McCubbins et al., 1987; Gilligan et al., 1989). These constraints are key drivers of policy uncertainty.

In his influential article Henisz (2000) argues that as the number of constraints on policy-making increases so too does the difficulty in changing policy. Constraints are first and foremost a function of the number of veto players in the political environment. A supplier of public policy is considered a veto player if the supplier has the authority to block a policy change. In totalitarian regimes, for example, there is one veto player. By contrast, in

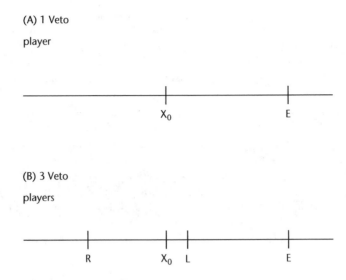

(A) 1 Veto

player

X_0　　　　E

(B) 3 Veto

players

R　　　X_0　L　　　E

Figure 4.2　Veto players

constitutional republics there are typically multiple veto players. A simple diagram of veto players demonstrates Henisz's insight. In Figure 4.2 we present two simple political environments. In environment (A) there is one veto player; in environment (B) there are three veto players (e.g., executive, regulators, and legislature).

As in our discussion of interest groups, we assume that a veto player has an ideal policy point and that it prefers policies as close to its ideal as possible. Furthermore, the value of a policy for veto player i is represented by the function $V_i(x)$. The further the policy is from its ideal, the lower the V_i to the veto player. In policy environment (A) there is one veto player (executive), which has an ideal policy equal to E and for which the value of a policy outcome is maximized at $V_E(x = E)$. So it is straightforward to see that the value of the status quo policy $V_E(X_0) < V_E(E)$. Without any influence from firms or other interest groups, the single veto player will move policy closer to E. We characterize political environment (A) as one with *limited constraints*.

Contrast this to political environment (B), where there are three veto players: the executive, regulator, and legislature. Their ideal policy preferences are represented by E, R, and L, respectively. Consider an attempt by the regulator to move the status quo policy (X_0) closer to R to increase its value associated with the policy. Any movement in policy closer to R increases V_R. However, at the same time this movement toward R reduces V_L and V_E. Similarly, consider an attempt by the legislature to move X_0 closer to L. While V_L and V_E would both increase, V_R would decline.

This simple illustration shows that any attempt to move policy will be vetoed by at least one other supplier of policy. As a result, without influence from firms or other interest groups, policy is more stable. Each veto player represents a constraint on the policy-making power of the other suppliers of policy. As such, we describe political environment (B) as one with *multiple constraints*. We note that in some cases there are more constraints than presented in panel (B). For instance, in some political markets the legislature is composed of two separate veto players – an upper and a lower house. In other political markets, the public can be viewed as a veto player because they have the power to overturn law through a popular

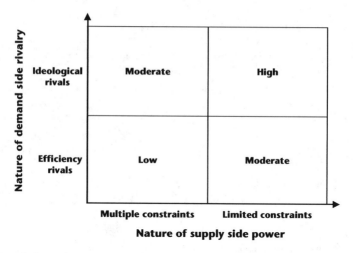

Figure 4.3   Level of regulatory uncertainty for firm

initiative or referendum process. The details of the firm's specific political market therefore need to be built into the analysis.

Henisz (2000, 2004) shows theoretically and empirically that, as the constraints on policy-making power of suppliers increase, the level of policy uncertainty declines. In addition to the number of veto players, other factors constrain the power of policy-makers. The extent of party alignment across the various veto players in the government is positively correlated with uncertainty. For example, in Figure 4.2 (B), if all three veto players were controlled by the same political party, the ideal points of each would be close together, making policy change much easier. Additionally, preference heterogeneity within any multi-member branch of government (e.g., legislature or regulator) adds constraints on the power of policy-makers. Therefore, it is important to look at the details of the political market in which the firm operates. While the political market may appear at first to be characterized as multiple constraints, after factoring in single-party control and homogeneity of preferences within and across branches of government, the political market may be better characterized as limited constraints.

The analysis above leads to the hypothesis that as constraints on the power of policy-makers increases, the level of regulatory uncertainty declines. In Figure 4.3, we combine the effects of the type of rivalry the firm faces and the degree of constraints on the power of policy-makers into a two-by-two framework of regulatory uncertainty.[6] The greatest uncertainty arises for a firm when it faces ideological rivals and limited constraints. By contrast, the lowest uncertainty arises when the firm faces efficiency rivals and multiple constraints. The other two cases create moderate regulatory uncertainty but have different implications for the design of integrated market and non-market strategies, as we discuss in the next section.

Question 3: Are demand side rivals aligned with key suppliers?

Whether rivals are ideological or efficiency oriented, the extent to which they are aligned with the key suppliers of public policy affects the probability of a favorable policy outcome for the firm. Referring to Figure 4.2 (A), where the firm is operating in a political market with limited constraints, a demand side rival is considered aligned with key suppliers (in this case the executive) if its ideal policy is closer to E than X_0 and the firm's ideal policy is closer to X_0 than E. The executive will want to move policy from X_0 to E. Additionally, the executive has the support of the demand side rival for the policy change. By contrast, the firm prefers that the executive maintain the current policy. While the firm can develop a strategy to influence the executive, so too will the firm's demand side rival. This alignment between the rival and the executive increases the cost to the firm of improving regulatory policy and increases the probability of a less favorable regulatory outcome. This analysis also applies to political markets with multiple constraints. Once the key supplier is identified, if the firm's rival is aligned with this key supplier then the probability of a less favorable regulatory outcome increases.

Alignment between demand side rivals and key suppliers poses another threat to the firm. An important component of a regulated firm's non-market strategy is to foster long-term relationships with key suppliers (Hillman and Hitt, 1999). In order to do so the firm must develop and maintain a solid reputation through fair and honest exchange with key suppliers. When the key suppliers' and rival demander's policy preferences are aligned, the rival demander is in a position to frame the policy argument with key suppliers. The risk to the firm is that the rival interest group will use facts in a way that compromises the trustworthiness and/or the integrity of the firm. The firm has to be very careful to limit this potential damage. To do so requires carefully designed strategy.

In the next section we analyze how firms design their integrated market and non-market strategies to mitigate the damage to their reputation as well as the higher degree of regulatory uncertainty that arises with ideological rivals and limited constraints.

Regulatory uncertainty and integrated market and non-market strategy

The nature of demand side rivalry and supply side power can be used to make predictions about market entry and implications for investment. With efficiency rivals and multiple constraints, regulatory uncertainty is low. Therefore, we expect that the regulated firm will expand its product scope or enter into a new geographic market with these characteristics. By contrast, when the firm faces ideological rivals and limited constraints, regulatory uncertainty is high. As a result, the overall uncertainty associated with a market investment may be too great. However, with high regulatory uncertainty, firms have two choices: they can delay investment to avoid an expected negative return, or they can develop and implement an integrated strategy that sufficiently mitigates the negative effects of the regulatory uncertainty and turns the expected returns to positive.

Building from Kingsley et al. (2012), we argue that as the level of regulatory uncertainty increases, so too does the cost of developing a non-market strategy that is well integrated with the firm's market strategy. Specifically, firms leverage specific market assets – financial, human, and network resources – to support their non-market strategy. Firms design non-market strategy along three dimensions: profile level; coalition breadth; and pivotal supplier. To increase the probability of success, we argue that the firm's strategic design along these three dimensions will differ systematically with the nature of demand side rivalry and/or the nature of supply side constraints.

Profile level

Firms' non-market strategies can be divided into low profile and high profile. These two differ in terms of their level of public and political engagement and ultimately the costs of implementation. High-profile strategies are costlier to employ than low-profile strategies because firm tactics either engage the public directly or are likely to receive public scrutiny. The tactics of high-profile strategies include: self-regulation (Maxwell et al., 2000); testifying in front of Congress (Hillman and Hitt, 1999); contributing resources to politicians or political parties (Vanden Bergh and Holburn, 2007); mobilizing a grassroots campaign (Lyon and Maxwell, 2004); and establishing political ties and personal relations with key officials in the government (Faccio, 2006). By contrast, low-profile strategies include such tactics as: commissioning white papers; providing financial resources for speaking engagements; and transmitting technical or political information through lobbying (Hillman and Hitt, 1999; Bonardi and Keim, 2005). By using these low-profile tactics, the firm is more likely to avoid the scrutiny of the media and the public in general.

We posit that firms tailor the profile of their strategy primarily based upon the nature of demand side rivalry. As the nature of demand side rivalry changes, firms adjust the relative resources they direct toward a specific profile. Firms will place greater emphasis on high-profile tactics when they face ideological rivals than when they face efficiency rivals. High-profile tactics, while more costly and risky, may be necessary for the firm to counteract the tactics of ideological rivals. When facing efficiency rivals, by contrast, firms are more likely to negotiate win–win solutions with rivals and the suppliers of policy by working behind the scenes to provide information and identify substitutes.

There are two moderating factors that affect the relative emphasis placed on high-profile tactics. First, if the key supplier of policy is the public, then the firm will naturally need to place greater emphasis on high-profile tactics which reach the public. As mentioned in the previous section, the public or electorate can be considered a key supplier of policy when they have the power to change law through a ballot initiative or referendum. Second, when ideological rivals are aligned with the key suppliers of policy, the firm will be concerned with maintaining its reputational capital. It will also be cognizant of the difficult position that the suppliers of policy face if they move policy away from the desires of their natural ally and the firm's ideological rival. In these political markets, the firm must still use some high-profile tactics to counteract the actions of their rival, but they will also increase the emphasis on low-profile actions to minimize the risk of hurting their reputation and to be sensitive to the needs of the key suppliers of policy.

Coalition breadth

The nature of demand side rivalry has an impact on the types and breadth of coalitions a firm will form to garner support from suppliers of policy. Firms can create a vertical coalition through their factor inputs, value chains, channels of distribution, or customers (Baron, 1995). Alternatively firms can create horizontal coalitions with any interest group ally, outside of their conventional business partner coalition, that seeks similar regulatory policy outcomes. Aligning with interests separate from their established coalition of business-related groups makes horizontal coalitions more costly for regulated firms to implement. To identify allies from outside their vertical chain of production, firms must incur significant search and transaction costs.

We hypothesize that firms are more likely to build horizontal coalitions when they face ideological rivals, and vertical coalitions when they face efficiency rivals. When competing against efficiency rivals, firms need to communicate information about how policy changes affect both firm and stakeholder profits and simultaneously identify substitutes that may compensate efficiency rivals. Direct business partners are better positioned than unrelated coalition groups to provide this type of information to the firm. While vertical coalitions may be valuable in combating ideological rivals, firms are likely to need more grassroots support than that found by just mobilizing their business partners across the entire rent chain. One tactic a firm may employ is to search for and form a horizontal coalition with an ideological ally to help counteract the actions of an ideological rival. Whether developing a vertical or horizontal coalition, when the firm's rivals are aligned with the key suppliers, the cost to form an effective coalition will increase on the margin because the firm will need to expand the scale of its coalition to convince suppliers of policy to move policy closer to the firm's desired outcome.

Pivotal target

Sensible strategies consist of knowing enough about governmental processes to ascertain who are the likely key suppliers of public policy and entail targeting of decision-makers whose support is neither hopeless nor certain but rather is necessary for success and, thus, pivotal (Krehbiel, 1999). With its non-market strategy, the regulated firm will target based on the relative policy preferences and formal structure of the policy-making institutions (Holburn and Vanden Bergh, 2004, 2008; Vanden Bergh and Holburn, 2007). When a firm operates in an extremely limited constraints environment (e.g., a totalitarian regime), the pivotal supplier does not change and is likely to reside in the executive office or with leaders of the political party that controls the executive. By contrast, within multiple constraints environments, the pivotal target varies depending upon the current policy preferences of the various veto players and the current decision-making process (Holburn and Vanden Bergh, 2008). More importantly, with limited constraints, pivotal targets are in a much stronger bargaining position vis-à-vis the firm and will thus extract greater resources from the firm in exchange for its support. This drives up the cost to the firm of designing an effective strategy.

Figure 4.4 summarizes this relationship between the characteristics of the political market that determine regulatory uncertainty and the design of a firm's integrated market and non-market strategy to reduce the overall risk associated with its investments. As uncertainty increases, a firm must change the structure and balance of its non-market strategy, even as the cost of doing so increases. Moreover, when a firm confronts a rival aligned with the key policy suppliers, its non-market strategy must increasingly emphasize low-profile tactics and, more importantly, must expand the scope of its profile, coalition, and targets. Such changes are understandably more costly, but they have an increased probability of success.

Entergy: a case study of regulatory uncertainty and integrated strategy

To apply this theoretical framework, we return to the case of Entergy, the nuclear power company operating in Vermont and Arkansas. State regulation of nuclear power plants like Entergy's creates the potential for regulatory uncertainty. Although nuclear plants do not need operating licenses at the state level (only at the federal level, through the Nuclear Regulatory Commission), they must obtain valid state permits and certificates of public good from state-level regulators. The most common permits are for water usage, air quality control, and wetlands protection. While states do not have the authority to regulate the safety of nuclear power plants in current operation, many have adopted restrictions (e.g., outright bans, demonstrating technology for high-level waste disposal, approval of state legislature, voter approval, findings of economic benefit to ratepayers) on the construction of new

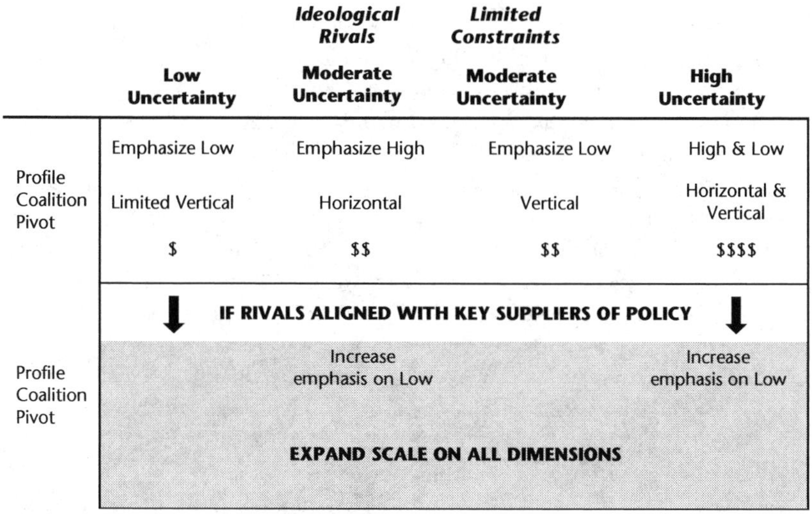

| | Ideological Rivals | | Limited Constraints | |
	Low Uncertainty	**Moderate Uncertainty**	**Moderate Uncertainty**	**High Uncertainty**
Profile Coalition Pivot	Emphasize Low	Emphasize High	Emphasize Low	High & Low
	Limited Vertical	Horizontal	Vertical	Horizontal & Vertical
	$	$$	$$	$$$$

IF RIVALS ALIGNED WITH KEY SUPPLIERS OF POLICY ↓ ↓

| Profile Coalition Pivot | | Increase emphasis on Low | | Increase emphasis on Low |

EXPAND SCALE ON ALL DIMENSIONS

Figure 4.4　Uncertainty and integrated strategy

facilities. In addition, energy rates are regulated and nuclear power plants frequently need state approval to recover additional costs by passing them to consumers through increases in rates. Finally, nuclear power plants must set aside funds for eventual decommissioning, which can run into hundreds of millions of dollars. Some states also require operators of these plants to verify the status of these funds and disclose how the money is invested.[7]

Given the role of states in regulating nuclear power plants, the following section analyzes the political environment for Entergy in the states of Arkansas and Vermont from 2010 to 2012. We first analyze the states' demand side opponents and supply side constraints. Then we discuss Entergy's divergent non-market strategies. We illustrate that while Entergy's market investment and associated regulatory policy issues are nearly identical across the two states, the characteristics of the political markets differ significantly. These differences in the political markets help us understand the differences in Entergy's integrated strategy across the two states.

Political market characteristics and regulatory uncertainty

Question 1: Are Entergy's demand side rivals ideological?

The nature of demand side rivalry for Entergy in Vermont is quite different from that in Arkansas. This difference is due to the presence of extensive ideological rivals in Vermont. Interestingly, Entergy faces competition from efficiency rivals in both Vermont and Arkansas. In both states there is a statutorily created consumer advocate who can participate in regulatory policy-making processes that affect regulated power companies. They represent the interests of consumers but do not have any policy-making authority.[8] A study by Fremeth, Holburn, and Spiller (2014) shows that a consumer advocate is not an ally of the firm. At the same time, this rival interest group is willing to identify gains from trade with the regulated power companies. For example, consumer advocates will often negotiate directly with the regulated power companies to identify reasonable service options. The two groups will then present these options to the regulator for approval. This willingness to negotiate leads to characterizing consumer advocates as efficiency rivals. However, the degree of ideological rivalry Entergy faces is dramatically different in the two states.

Entergy's Vermont Yankee plant faced vocal and vehement opposition from ideological rivals with unequivocal antinuclear preferences. Most of these interest groups were experienced activists sophisticated in leveraging public pressure against non-complying energy companies. Locally, citizens and community stakeholders framed Entergy as unaccountable to Vermonters and Vermont Yankee as dangerously unsafe (Watts, Hines, and Dowds, 2010). Examples include the Safe and Green Campaign, Traprock Center for Peace and Justice, VT Citizen Action Network, VT Yankee Decommissioning Alliance, and Vermont Public Interest Research Group. Regionally, rivals to Entergy were the Sierra Club of the Upper Valley, the Citizens' Awareness Network, the Clamshell Alliance, and the Shut It Down Affinity Group. Opposing nuclear plants was a highly salient issue for these regional groups. Nationally, two antinuclear organizations actively opposed Vermont Yankee: Beyond Nuclear and the Nuclear Information and Resource Service.

In Arkansas, on the other hand, there was no local opposition to Entergy and minimal or perfunctory national opposition (e.g., Beyond Nuclear). Even the regional environmentalist group Sierra Club had only a limited and relatively inactive presence in Arkansas, with a fifth of the membership (on per capita basis) of Vermont.[9] What few rivals Entergy had in Arkansas were efficiency rivals not motivated by ideology but by maintaining low-cost and reliable power (e.g., the consumer advocate).

Question 2: Are constraints limited on supplier's policy-making power in Vermont and Arkansas?

In 2010–12, Vermont's veto players were the governor (E), senate (S), house (H), and regulator (R), and there was strong party alignment across these pivotal players. Peter Shumlin, a Democrat strongly and vocally opposed to Vermont Yankee, won the governorship in 2010.[10] His policy preference is denoted in Figure 4.5 (A). Historically, the issue of nuclear power has been highly partisan in the United States. Republicans typically support nuclear power companies like Entergy based on the logic of jobs, lower retail power prices, and "clean energy." By contrast, Democrats typically oppose nuclear power and have tended to focus on environmental and safety concerns.

Vermont's Democrats also solidly and consistently controlled both legislative houses, with greater than 70 percent control of the state senate (e.g., 21 out of 30 senators) and 63 percent control of the house (e.g., 95 out of 150 representatives). Democratic dominance was unsurprising, given that the public is heavily skewed left, toward the Democratic Party. For instance, in the 2012 presidential election 67 percent of Vermonters voted Democrat.[11] Based upon a detailed ideological measure from 0 (most conservative) to 100 (most liberal), the median ideal point of Vermont's "active electorate" was 86 and the median ideal point of public officials, weighted according to the power they have over public policy decisions, was 81.[12]

Regulators on the Public Service Board, the energy regulator in Vermont, held slightly different policy preferences from those of the governor and the legislative houses. Vermont regulators are appointed – some by former Republican governors, making the Public Service Board more moderate at the time. However, state regulation of nuclear plants in Vermont occurs first in the senate and then at the Public Service Board, meaning that Vermont's regulator was not the pivotal policy supplier to Entergy.

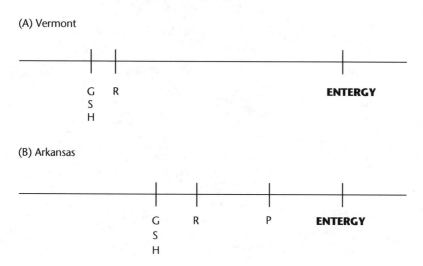

(A) Vermont

G   R   ENTERGY
S
H

(B) Arkansas

G   R   P   ENTERGY
S
H

Figure 4.5   Veto players

Taken together, Vermont's political actors stood in striking opposition to Entergy between 2010 and 2012. The most pivotal veto players – the governor and legislature – held similar policy preferences. This created an environment of limited constraints. The policy suppliers were also uniformly opposed to Entergy, adding to the firm's regulatory uncertainty.

By contrast, in Arkansas, Entergy encountered a political environment of multiple constraints with some diverse preferences. The governor (G) was a Democrat. In addition, the state senate (S) was 57 percent Democrat (e.g., 20 out of 35 Senators) and the house (H) was 54 percent Democrat (e.g., 54 out of 100 Representatives). However, the state's public officials' ideological point was measured at 65, significantly more centrist than Vermont's 81. This moves the G, S, and H veto players closer to Entergy's ideal point (x) than is the case in Vermont.

Two further differences characterize Arkansas's political environment. First, the state's energy regulators (R) are important veto players with slightly more moderate preferences (R) than the governor and legislature, given the appointment and tenure process. Second, the public (P) counts as a veto player due to the state's public ballot initiative process.[13] This is notable because the public (P) was decidedly Republican between 2010 and 2012. Sixty-three percent voted Republican in the 2012 presidential election, and the public's ideological point was measured at 33 (compared to Vermont's 86). Having the public's preferences closer to the firm's provided important opportunities for Entergy to execute its non-market strategy.

Question 3. Are Entergy's demand side rivals aligned with key suppliers in Vermont and Arkansas?

The extent to which Entergy's rivals were aligned with the key suppliers of public policy in Vermont and Arkansas also affected the probability of a favorable policy outcome for Entergy. In Vermont, Entergy's ideological rivals were aligned with the key Democratic policy suppliers that were opposed to Entergy. In Figure 4.5 (A), the ideological rivals' ideal point is closer to the governor (G), senate (S), and house (H) than Entergy, placing Entergy's rivals in an advantageous position to influence the pivotal suppliers. In Arkansas (B), on the

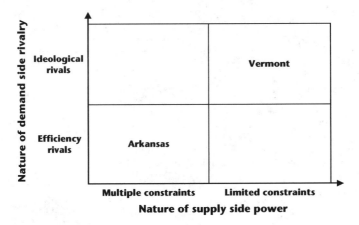

Figure 4.6 Entergy's level of regulatory uncertainty

other hand, Entergy faced very few rivals (e.g., the consumer advocate) who were not closely aligned with key policy suppliers.

Using the answers from these three questions to determine the nature of the demand side and supply side rivalries, we conclude that Entergy was exposed to significantly more regulatory uncertainty in Vermont than in Arkansas (Figure 4.6). Vermont was characterized by relatively limited constraints, meaning that policy suppliers had homogeneous preferences and were able to make policy change easily. Uncertainty was increased because those actors stood in opposition to Entergy. Moreover, Entergy in Vermont was opposed by ideological rivals aligned with those key policy suppliers and fundamentally unwilling to trade on policy outcomes. Arkansas, on the other hand, has multiple constraints on the supply side (e.g., the public) with preferences closer to Entergy's and a political market composed of efficiency rivals.

The conflict around Vermont Yankee's relicensing is a case in point. Experienced antinuclear activist groups leveraged political and public sentiment against Entergy through protests and an advertising campaign focused on Vermont Yankee's problems (e.g., a cooling tower collapse, radioactive triulim leaks, and misleading statements by Entergy executives; Watts, Hines, and Dowds, 2010). In 2010, Vermont senators aligned with these ideological rivals and voted twenty-six–four to cancel Vermont Yankee's state permit or certificate of public good,[14] despite the federal Nuclear Regulatory Commission's twenty-year license extension.[15] While the issue ultimately went to district and appellate courts (which ruled in favor of Entergy), Vermont's governor and legislators actively opposed the firm and, by virtue of the limited political constraints, exposed Entergy to significant and costly regulatory uncertainty.

Entergy's integrated market and non-market strategies

Given these different levels of regulatory uncertainty in Vermont and Arkansas, our theory argues that Entergy's strategy should be distinctive across the two political markets. We predict that the firm would have a more expensive and expansive strategy in Vermont than in Arkansas. As Figure 4.7 details, Entergy's Arkansas strategy would have been inexpensive, emphasizing mainly low-profile tactics and its vertical coalition. In Vermont, on the other

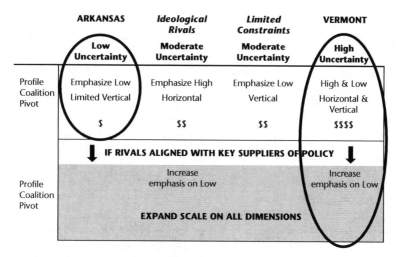

Figure 4.7 Entergy's integrated strategy

hand, Entergy would: use both high- and low-profile strategies but emphasize its low-profile tactics, given ideological rivals' alignment with policy suppliers; build expansive horizontal and vertical coalitions; and allocate significant resources to targeting multiple policy suppliers.

Specifically, Entergy executed a baseline but narrow and inexpensive non-market strategy in Arkansas. The firm's main high-profile tactic was to contribute modestly to political actors (approximately $280,597 – 0.6 percent of all recorded state campaign donations – between 2010 and 2012).[16] For low-profile tactics, Entergy employed twelve state lobbyists on average – a meager one lobbyist per 250,000 state residents. Not bothering even to mobilize a vertical coalition, Entergy undertook non-market action itself. Indeed, to influence the public, the key policy supplier in Arkansas, to maintain its policy preference closer to the firm's, Entergy focused its non-market action on advertising its value to the state's residents. It periodically employed its generic, multi-state "Power to the People" campaign to deliver a fast-paced, upbeat message about Entergy's proactive approach to the environment, energy efficiency, energy conservation, energy reliability, and storm preparation.[17] Lively and diverse problem-solving Entergy employees were portrayed as cutting the public's cost for energy, keeping the state safe with power, and helping the local economy.

Entergy's non-market strategy in Arkansas contrasts starkly with that in Vermont. In terms of profile level, Entergy used both high- and low-profile tactics, emphasizing the latter. For high-profile tactics, the firm donated small amounts to Vermont state campaigns (approximately $9,150 – 0.07 percent of all state campaign donations – between 2010 and 2012). The firm also rolled out a significant publicity campaign: "VT4VY." For low-profile tactics, Entergy spent a staggering $657,303 lobbying behind the scenes in Vermont. On a per capita basis, this was more than four times what the firm spent in other states with nuclear plants.[18] Entergy also employed ten lobbyists in Vermont, on average, an impressive one lobbyist per 62,000 state residents (or four lobbyists per 250,000). Relative to the states' populations, Entergy's lobbying power was four times more concentrated in Vermont than it was in Arkansas. By all accounts, Entergy executed a broad non-market strategy with emphasis on its low-profile tactics.

In terms of coalition breadth, Entergy mobilized a comprehensive coalition of partners. The firm actively recruited vertically from Vermont Yankee employees, plant suppliers and distributors, and Entergy customers. It also built a horizontal coalition that included, among others, the local Vernon community, economic development agencies, the American Nuclear Society, and Yes Vermont Yankee. One of its primary horizontal partners was the Vermont Energy Partnership, a consortium of pro-nuclear businesses and their stakeholders that champions clean, low-cost, reliable electricity solutions. In support of Entergy's Vermont Yankee plant, the Vermont Energy Partnership issued briefs and held public forums.

In terms of pivotal targets, Entergy focused on the governor and legislature but also the regulator. It did so by lobbying the policy suppliers and trying – through "VT4VY" – to diffuse the public anti-nuclear campaign executed by its ideological rivals. The firm widely publicized advertisements in which Vermont Yankee employees, key elements of its vertical chain, advocated the benefits of an active nuclear plant and employer in the state (e.g., economic progress, low-priced electricity, lower greenhouse gas emissions, more jobs). Six small business owners in Vermont also expressed concern over the possible failure of Vermont Yankee to win a state permit. The business owners were somber and the music slow and wistful. Extreme concern about shutting down Vermont Yankee was expressed by the business owner in each commercial: local business Cercosimo Lumber "might not be able to remain here in Vermont"; 200-year-old farm Holyoke might "be forced out of business"; the Vermont Wood Pellet Company "will probably have to close"; and Stowe Flake Mountain Resort said the plant's closure would be the "last straw for a lot of businesses."[19] The message was clear: if Vermont's government did not grant Vermont Yankee a certificate of public good, these businesses would have to close or move.

In sum, Entergy was more active, allocated more resources, and executed a significantly more expansive non-market strategy in Vermont than it did in Arkansas. It did so because it faced more regulatory uncertainty in Vermont, where the political environment had limited constraints, ideological rivals, and alignment amongst those rivals and suppliers in opposition to the firm.

Conclusion

In this chapter, we constructed a theoretical framework to understand the political market, regulatory uncertainty, and firms' non-market strategies. We applied this framework to Entergy's non-market strategies in Vermont and Arkansas between 2010 and 2012. In explaining how regulatory uncertainty drives firms' integrated market and non-market strategies, we aim to contribute to the literatures on regulatory economics, positive political theory, political markets, and non-market strategy. Firms are self-interested (Stigler, 1971), actively constructing integrated strategies (Baron, 1995) in a vibrant political market of demanders (Snyder, 1990) and suppliers (Ferejohn and Shipan, 1990; Henisz, 2004).

On the demand side of the political market, we introduced how ideological rivals, unwilling to negotiate or trade policies like efficiency rivals, increase firms' regulatory uncertainty. This is a novel take on competing demanders. On the supply side of the political market, we argue that political constraints meaningfully mitigate uncertainty. As firms face political markets with limited constraints, they are exposed to more regulatory uncertainty; in markets with multiple constraints, firms find more and less costly opportunities to advance their policy objectives. Further, as firms' rivals become aligned with the key policy-makers, regulatory uncertainty increases, especially if those rivals and suppliers are aligned in opposition to the firm.

To manage the levels of regulatory uncertainty, we theorized that firms must design efficient and custom non-market strategies. We identified three primary dimensions of firms' non-market strategies: profile level, coalition breadth, and pivotal target. When firms face low uncertainty or moderate uncertainty due to limited constraints, they emphasize low-profile strategies, such as lobbying targeted at pivotal policy suppliers. As uncertainty increases due to ideological rivals, firms must emphasize high-profile strategies, such as campaign contributions and public advertising campaigns. In cases of high uncertainty, firms must execute both low- and high-profile strategies. In most cases, firms activate their vertical coalition or rent chain partners to support their policy objectives. In some cases, when uncertainty increases due to ideological rivals, firms must recruit a horizontal coalition of allies pulled from stakeholders or interest groups aligned with their policy objectives. Should the firms' ideological rivals be aligned with key policy suppliers, the firms must layer in additional low-profile strategies to manage their reputations, relationships, and information, and, more importantly, they must expand the scale (and thus the allocated resources) of their non-market strategy in all dimensions.

Notes

1 The authors acknowledge excellent research assistance from Matthew Kehoe and Alexis Reed.
2 Arkansas Nuclear One and Two: 846MW and 930MW (Russellville, AR).
3 Vermont Yankee: 605MW (Vernon, VT).
4 We are assuming that the suppliers and demanders of policy have well-defined ideal policy points and single peaked preferences. This is a standard assumption in models of political decision-making (e.g., Krehbiel, 1999) and in formal models of interest group influence of policy-makers (e.g., Baron, 1999; Holburn and Vanden Bergh, 2004).
5 As Holburn and Vanden Bergh (2004) demonstrate, for relatively high values of α (at least greater than 0.5) it is not in the interest of the firm to bear the cost of advocating for a substitute to compensate a rival for a movement in regulatory policy away from the rival's ideal.
6 We recognize that the two variables – nature of supply side power and nature of demand side rivalry – are continuous in nature rather than the discrete form we present here. For example, a totalitarian regime is the extreme form of limited constraints. By contrast, a political market consisting of the veto players executive, upper house, lower house, independent judiciary, independent regulator, and public and with no single political party control is an extreme form of multiple constraints. There are many examples of political markets that fit between these two extremes. The Entergy case in the discussion provides good examples.
7 Rumelt (2012) discusses the rights of states versus the federal government in the regulation of nuclear power.
8 Holburn and Vanden Bergh (2006) studied the creation of consumer advocates across the fifty US states. They show that approximately two-thirds of the US states have created an independent consumer advocate to represent consumer interests in regulatory policy-making processes affecting regulated power companies.
9 The Sierra Club provided the authors with annual membership data by US state.
10 All election and partisan data on governors and legislators was compiled from *The Book of States*, published annually by the Council of State Governments.
11 Presidential election data was compiled from the National Archives General Election Results. See www.archives.gov/federal-register/electoral-college/2012/popular-vote.html.
12 State ideology data was based on revised calculations using methodology in Berry et al. (1998).
13 Public initiative data gathered from Initiative and Referendum Institute at www.iandrinstitute. org/statewide_i%26r.htm.
14 See Vermont State Legislature, 2006–7 biennium, No. 160, An Act Relating to a Certificate of Public Good for Extending the Operating License of a Nuclear Power Plant, at www.leg.state.vt. us/jfo/VY%20Legislative%20Briefing/ACT160.pdf.
15 VY NRC application is available at www.nrc.gov/reactors/operating/licensing/renewal/applications/ vermont-yankee.html and http://pbadupws.nrc.gov/docs/ML0921/ML092110054.pdf.

16 Campaign contribution and lobbyist data was compiled from the National Institute on Money in State Politics. Lobbyist data averaged over three years: 2010, 2011, and 2012. See www. followthemoney.org.

17 See www.youtube.com/watch?v=DGm4dKiVU9M (Uploaded 04/02/10 – Environment); www. youtube.com/watch?v=jAB0ddAQnI8 (Uploaded 06/04/10 – Storm Preparation); www.youtube. com/watch?v=2QR3VKFryDg (Uploaded 06/07/10 – Energy Conservation); www.youtube.com/ watch?v=zOSqbbG-p5M (Uploaded 09/13/10 – Efficient Energy); and www.youtube.com/ watch?v=-b69QYqsV94 (Uploaded 09/13/10 – Reliability).

18 Data from the Vermont Secretary of State office was compared with data from the Mississippi Secretary of State office. Entergy files lobbying expenditure reports with each of these offices.

19 See www.youtube.com/watch?v=K66wULi08ys (Fabtech Inc); www.youtube.com/watch?v= 4l7K8q59Wag (Cercosimo Lumber); www.youtube.com/watch?v=_fx48PmtfBY (Stowe Flake Mountain Resort); www.youtube.com/watch?v=aZXXkpmabqU (Holyoke Farm); www.youtube. com/watch?v=3P7bZdKaqjQ (Bromley Mountain); and www.youtube.com/watch?v=ziiyQ8tHdkw (VT Wood Pellet Company).

References

Bach, D. and Allen, D. (2010) What every CEO needs to know about non-market strategy, *MIT Sloan Management Review*, Spring, 41–8.

Baron, D. (1995) The non-market strategy system, *MIT Sloan Management Review*, 37, 73–85.

— (1999) Integrated market and non-market strategies in client and interest group politics, *Business and Politics*, 1(1), 7–34.

— (2010) *Business and its Environments* (6th edn), Upper Saddle River, NJ: Prentice Hall.

Berry, W., Ringquist, E., Fording, R., and Hanson, R. (1998) Measuring citizen and government ideology in the American states, 1960–93, *American Journal of Political Science*, 42(1), 327–48.

Boddewyn, J. and Brewer, T. (1994) International business political behavior: New theoretical directions, *Academy of Management Review*, 19, 119–43.

Bonardi, J. P. and Keim, G. (2005) Corporate political strategies for widely salient issues, *Academy of Management Review*, 30(3), 555–76.

Bonardi, J. P., Hillman, A., and Keim, G. (2005) The attractiveness of political markets: Implication for firm strategy, *Academy of Management Review*, 30(2), 397–413.

Bonardi, J. P., Holburn, G., and Vanden Bergh, R. (2006) Non-market performance: Evidence from US electric utilities, *Academy of Management Journal*, 49(6), 1209–28.

Buchanan, J. and Tullock, G. (1962) *The Calculus of Consent: Logical Foundations of Constitutional Democracy*, Ann Arbor: University of Michigan Press.

Coase, R. (1960) The problem of social cost, *Journal of Law and Economics*, 3(1), 1–44.

de Figueiredo, J. M. (2009) Integrated political strategy, *Advances in Strategic Management*, 26, 459–86.

de Figueiredo, J. M. and Edwards, G. (2007) Does private money buy public policy? Campaign contributions and regulatory outcomes in telecommunications, *Journal of Economics and Management Strategy*, 16, 547–76.

Faccio, M. (2006) Politically connected firms, *American Economic Review*, 96(1), 369–86.

Ferejohn, J. and Shipan, C. (1990) Congressional influence on bureaucracy, *Journal of Law, Economics and Organization*, 6, 1–20.

Fremeth, A., Holburn, G., and Spiller, P. (2014) The impact of consumer advocates on regulatory policy in the electric utility sector, *Public Choice*, 161(1–2), 157–81.

Gilligan, T., Marshall, W., and Weingast, B. (1989) Regulation and the theory of legislative choice: The Interstate Commerce Act of 1887, *Journal of Law and Economics*, 32, 35–61.

Graham, B., Johnston, N., and Kingsley, A. (2013) Even constrained governments steal: The domestic politics of transfer and expropriation risks, unpublished manuscript.

Henisz, W. (2000) The institutional environment for multinational investment, *Journal of Law, Economics and Organization*, 16, 334–64.

— (2004) Political institutions and policy volatility, *Economics and Politics*, 16(1), 1–27.

Hillman, A. and Hitt, M. (1999) Corporate political strategy formulation: A model of approach, participation and strategy decisions, *Academy of Management Review*, 20, 193–214.

Hillman, A. and Keim, G. (1995) International variation in the business–government interface: Institutional and organizational considerations, *Academy of Management Review*, 20, 193–214.

Holburn, G. and Vanden Bergh, R. (2004) Influencing agencies through pivotal political institutions, *Journal of Law, Economics and Organization*, 20(2), 458–83.

— (2006) Consumer capture of regulatory institutions: The creation of public utility consumer advocates in the United States, *Public Choice*, 126(1–2), 45–73.

— (2008) Making friends in hostile environments: Political strategy in regulated industries, *Academy of Management Review*, 33(2), 521–40.

— (2014) Integrated market and non-market strategies: Political campaign contributions around merger and acquisition events in the energy sector, *Strategic Management Journal*, 35(3), 450–60.

Holburn, G. L. F. and Zelner, B. A. (2010) Political capabilities, policy risk and international investment strategy: Evidence from the global electric power industry, *Strategic Management Journal*, 31(12), 1290–315.

Kingsley, A., Vanden Bergh, R., and Bonardi, J.-P. (2012) Political markets and regulatory uncertainty: Insights and implications for integrated strategy, *Academy of Management Perspectives*, 26(3), 52–67.

Krehbiel, K. (1999) Pivotal politics: A refinement of non-market analysis for voting institutions, *Business and Politics*, 1(1), 63–81.

Lyon, T. and Maxwell, J. (2004) Astroturf: Interest group lobbying and corporate strategy, *Journal of Economics and Management Strategy*, 13(4), 561–97.

Maxwell, J., Lyon, T., and Hackett, T. (2000) Self-regulation and social welfare: The political economy of corporate environmentalism, *Journal of Law and Economics*, 43(2), 583–618.

McCubbins, M., Noll, R., and Weingast, B. (1987) Administrative procedures as instruments of political control, *Journal of Law, Economics and Organization*, 3, 243–77.

Peltzman, S. (1976) Toward a more general theory of regulation, *Journal of Law and Economics*, 19(2), 211–40.

PwC (2013) *16th Annual Global CEO Survey*, London: The Design Group PwC.

Rumelt, K. J. (2012) Power grab: Preempting states' rights to turn off nuclear power, *Natural Resources and Environment*, 27(1), 24–7.

Snyder, J. M., Jr. (1990), Campaign contributions as investments: The US House of Representatives, 1980–86. *Journal of Political Economy*, 98(6), 1195–227.

Stigler, G. (1971) The theory of economic regulation, *Bell Journal of Economics and Management Science*, 2, 3–21.

Vanden Bergh, R. and Holburn, G. (2007) Targeting corporate political strategy: Theory and evidence from the US accounting industry, *Business and Politics*, 9(2), 1–31.

Watts, R., Hines, P., and Dowds, J. (2010) The debate over re-licensing the Vermont Yankee nuclear power plant, *The Electricity Journal*, 23(4), 59–67.

Wilson, J. (1980) *The Politics of Regulation*, New York: Basic Books.

World Bank (2012) *World Investment and Political Risk*, Washington, DC: Multilateral Investment Guarantee Agency.

5

A politics and public policy approach

David Bach

Through the title of perhaps his most influential book, Harold Lasswell (1936) famously defined politics as "who gets what, when, how." In an increasingly global world in which markets and free enterprise have largely prevailed over their twentieth-century rivals, and where so much wealth, power, and influence is concentrated in private hands, anybody taking Lasswell's elegant definition seriously should immediately recognize that business is inherently political. When Walmart considers where to open its next store, Nestlé chooses a supplier, and Apple weighs an exclusive deal with a telecom provider, these firms' managers take political decisions, whether they are conscious of it or not.

Many managers, no doubt, would think of these as pure business decisions. My experience working with companies and executives across many different sectors and geographies suggests that the view of business as largely apolitical remains prevalent. And how could you blame them? At business schools around the world, the firm is commonly depicted alternatively as a transaction cost minimizer (e.g., Coase 1937), a production function (e.g., Alchian and Demsetz 1972), a set of contracts (e.g., Hart 1988), a bundle of resources (e.g., Barney 1991), or a complex organization driven by the interests and cognitive limitations of the people who comprise it (e.g., Cyert and March 1963). A perspective on the firm as political actor is largely absent.

Non-market strategy is important, first, because its ontology encompasses a depiction of the firm as political actor and, second, because it remains practice-focused and can therefore inform decision-making inside the firm. Too many business-and-society approaches commit what I call the "fallacy of outside-in." Under labels such as corporate citizenship (e.g., Maignan, Ferrell, and Hult 1999; Matten and Crane 2005), business ethics (e.g., Trevino 1986; Donaldson and Dunfee 1999), stakeholder management (e.g., Freeman 1984; Donaldson and Preston 1995; Hillman and Keim 2001), and corporate social responsibility (e.g., Andrews 1987; McWilliams and Siegel 2001; Margolis and Walsh 2003), scholars, policy-makers, and activists have lectured firms on what they ought to do. While this has generated a vibrant and at times insightful academic debate, the impact on management practice has been limited. This should not surprise. How can we expect to change management practice when we have collectively put forth so many different definitions of CSR that one scholar felt compelled to conduct a content analysis of thirty-seven of them just to identify some common themes (Dahlsrud 2008)? In contrast, more than any other approach, non-market strategy offers an inside-out perspective – a view of politics from the perspective of the firm that is both grounded in theory and actionable in practice.

In this contribution, I outline a politics and public policy approach to non-market strategy. I explain how normal business operations in the presence of market failures link the firm's market- and non-market environments and thereby make strategic non-market management a managerial imperative. Once business operations have spilled over into the non-market environment, as they frequently and inevitably do, the firm becomes a political actor along-side a multitude of other interest groups with varying degrees of organization vying for political influence and power (Schattschneider 1960; Dahl 1961; Lipset 1963; Lindblom 1977). As Baron (2006) observed, the non-market environment of business is just as competitive as the market environment, but the rules of the game and resulting dynamics are significantly different. Failure to adjust to and account for these differences is the primary cause of the countless corporate non-market debacles that fill syllabi on the subject.

In the following section, I sketch a simple model of business operations that link the market- and non-market environments and introduce the principal types of actors and institutions. The focus is on the political ramifications of market failures and the interplay between different political actors, including firms, in remedying them. Subsequent sections unpack each of the principal pieces and illustrate underlying dynamics with reference to specific firms and cases. The final section concludes with observations on the state of non-market strategy, both as managerial practice and as a field of study.

Beyond the market

As a moral philosopher, Adam Smith's interest in markets stemmed from his desire to show that egoism was not necessarily reprehensible. "By pursuing his own interest," Smith (2003: 572) explained, "he frequently pursues that of the society more effectually than when he really intends to promote it." After all, he reasoned,

> It is not from the benevolence of the butcher, the brewer, or the baker, that we expect our dinner, but from their regard to their own interest. We address ourselves, not to their humanity but to their self-love, and never talk to them of our own necessities but of their advantages.
>
> *(Smith 2003: 23–4)*

What makes this astonishing feat possible is the "invisible hand" of the market, perpetually sending to economic agents price signals that reflect the prevailing scarcity of goods and services. Without a doubt, the market system has enabled the creation of more wealth and has lifted more people out of poverty than any other human-devised scheme.

But what happens when these price signals are distorted, when they do not reflect true cost or costs cannot be allocated appropriately? In such situations markets inevitably fail to allocate resources efficiently: that is, resources are allocated in a socially suboptimal way. A lack of competition, externalities, information asymmetries, and the non-excludability of certain goods are the most common causes of so-called "market failures" (Samuelson 1948; Coase 1960; Friedman 1962; Olson 1965; Akerlof 1970). Of these, externalities are the most prevalent cause. The classic example is pollution. Driving to work is fun in part because I do not have to inhale the exhausts my car generates. The poor person behind me on her bike, however, is stuck with them even though she did not cause them. Since I get the benefits of driving without some of its costs – costs that are externalized and borne by society at large – I will keep on driving. In contrast, she will soon stop using her bike to protect her health. As a result, there is more driving and less biking than might be socially optimal. The most brutal but undoubtedly most effective method to remedy this unfortunate situation would be to attach a garden hose to my exhaust pipe and to direct the exhausts into my car through the front window. Driving would be a lot less fun and our biker might take up biking again since the air behind my car would be much cleaner. This, quite literally, is what internalizing an externality means: that is, making the originator of a cost bear it in full and thereby ensuring that marginal social cost and marginal private cost are equal.

Externalities and market failures more generally generate political demand for remedies. Clearly, any suboptimal allocation of scarce resources should concern a government committed to maximizing economic welfare. More commonly, however, governments spring into action in response to the grievances of those who claim they are being harmed by the actions of others, particularly if the complainers are politically powerful. Alternatively, a government may take action if it believes prevailing market competition undermines the public interest or to ensure the supply of public goods. Whatever the motivation, public policy in the form of rules, taxes, or other forms of intervention alters market dynamics.

The presence of market failures means that market competition inevitably spills over into the non-market domain. Since transaction costs are not zero, private parties can often not negotiate private remedies for externalities (Coase 1960). Government is consequently called upon to step in and the firm finds itself embroiled in political dynamics that bear little resemblance to the market dynamics we ordinarily consider firms' natural habitat. In this situation, firms can either passively await the implications of public policy or, more sensibly, try to prevent or shape ensuing rules through lobbying and other forms of political engagement. In any case, government intervention, as Coase – and Knight (1924) before him – reminded us, is not costless. Besides transactions costs stemming from policy-making, monitoring, and enforcement, regulation frequently leads to other inefficiencies. Politicians commonly want to maximize votes, even if this means supplying public policies that are economically inefficient or not taking necessary actions (e.g., Dixit 1996). While regulation by arm's-length, technocratic agencies is supposed to buffer from electoral populism, Stigler (1971) and others have shown that regulatory agencies are often "captured" by the industries they are supposed to regulate, leading to policies that favor entrenched interests at the expense of the public at large. All of these are instances of what Coase (1964) first dubbed "government failures" and which Wolf (1979) later aptly referred to as "non-market failures."

In a pluralist system, however, the government is not the only political actor. Myriad non-governmental organizations (NGOs) and interest groups seek to shape policy, particularly when they believe the government is not doing its job. These groups pressure government to adopt certain policies or to repeal others, often with an eye on changing market dynamics. They do this directly, through reports to the government, expert testimonies, and the like, as well as indirectly, by mobilizing voters for or against a particular policy. Frustrated by slow or unresponsive governments, and empowered by technology and 24/7 media coverage, many of these groups increasingly take matters into their own hands and pressurize firms to change directly via campaigns, calls for consumer boycotts, and other forms of activism, a dynamic Baron (2001) calls "private politics." Crucially, citizens play a dual role as (non-market) voters and (market) consumers. Figure 5.1 depicts the various actors, identifies typical interactions between them, and highlights the boundary of market- and non-market environments.

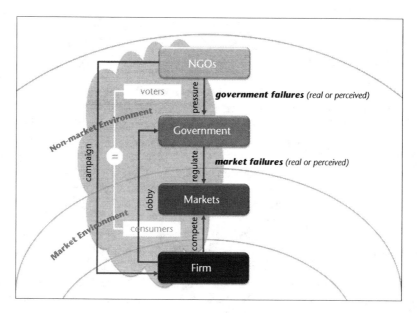

Figure 5.1　A model of politics for non-market strategy

Having sketched a simple model of politics for the purpose of non-market strategy, the following sections unpack the various elements and illustrate them through references to business practice and specific cases.

The politics of market failures

How frequently markets fail is a question of intense debate among economists. While Milton Friedman, for example, accepted the need for government intervention to address market failures, and particularly to promote competition, he thought such occasions to be rare (Friedman 1962).[1] More recent work, especially on information economics and the economics of the environment, has produced a rather different view, one where market failures due to information asymmetries and externalities are pervasive. Growing evidence of the harmful impact of manmade industrial activity in particular has changed the perception of welfare maximizing private competition. The Stern Report (Stern 2006: viii), for example, argued, "Climate change is the greatest market failure the world has ever seen, and it interacts with other market imperfections." This is why, when it comes to the environment, "polluter pays" has become the underlying principle informing public policy in many countries. The idea is to internalize the environmental cost of a product into the price of the product itself, or, alternatively, to hold the original producer accountable for eventual disposal, recycling, or clean up.

As central as the economic concept of market failures is for non-market strategy, for politics the mere *perception* of a market failure, the extent of the resulting disequilibrium, and the necessary remedy are what matter. A simple example will illustrate. Many critics contend that violence on TV fosters violence in society, particularly among adolescents and young adults. There is ample evidence that violence "sells" – that TV content that includes violence attracts greater audiences. Higher ratings, in turn, enable networks to charge more for their advertising slots. In other words, by broadcasting more violence, the networks can earn more money. If more violence on TV means more violence in society, however, the public at large bears the cost in the form of more crime and/or higher law enforcement costs. Since social cost exceeds private cost, a negative externality causes a market failure – the networks supply more violence on TV than is socially optimal. Following the logic above, government action is called for, such as regulating how much violence can be shown on TV, when, and to whom, or maybe even a "TV-per-murder-tax" that supports law enforcement expenses.

While some might support such drastic government intervention, others are understandably skeptical – if not outright hostile – to such proposals. The problem is that the links alleged above are contested – or at the very least *contestable* – in the political arena. Lots of studies show that exposing test subjects to prolonged screen violence will make them more aggressive in subsequent interactions. There are also macro studies that demonstrate a close correlation between the number of violent acts on TV and aggregate national crime statistics. Yet none of this establishes a direct cause-and-effect relationship linking TV violence to violence in society. There are counter-examples of countries – such as Japan – with lots of TV violence yet very low levels of crime. This is why Hollywood and TV networks can contest charges of their alleged culpability and blame other factors, such as absent parents, failing schools, and lax law enforcement. Even if there were consensus that TV violence has adverse effects on society, quantifying the costs and figuring out how to distribute them among originators would be a daunting undertaking. In short, as compelling as the economics of market failures might be in theory, the actual politics of managing alleged market failures in the non-market arena are considerably more complex. The debate about TV violence and what, if anything, to do about it has been going on for more than two decades, but the underlying politics make any definitive resolution highly unlikely.

PepsiCo has been mired in a similar complexity for the past several years. As studies show alarming levels of obesity, particularly among children, with devastating individual- and staggering public-health consequences, critics have taken aim at the fast-food and processed-food industries (e.g., Schlosser 2001; Brownell and Horgen 2004; Weber 2009). Indeed, the amounts of fat, sugar, and salt contained in many industrial food products far exceed levels recommended by doctors and public health experts. Yet the instinct of most food and beverage company executives has been to blame others. "If all consumers exercised . . . obesity wouldn't exist," argued PepsiCo CEO Indra Nooyi in 2010 (Mangalindan 2010). Despite this rhetoric, PepsiCo, in contrast to many of its rivals, has decided to take on the obesity challenge. While continuing to deny responsibility for causing the problem, the company believes it can be part of the solution. To this end, Nooyi brought in a new innovations team, redesigned existing products to make them less unhealthy, and invested in healthy products the company had either acquired or developed in-house (Seabrook 2011).

Using the market failure lens, under Nooyi's leadership PepsiCo is trying to reduce the negative externalities that many critics and a growing number of policy-makers attribute to its product portfolio. Arguably motivating such efforts is the experience of the tobacco industry, a keen reminder of the potential consequences of prolonged inaction in the face of growing public determination to hold business accountable for costs imposed on society. As early as 1994, Yale obesity expert Kelly Brownell made the comparison explicit: "While the government has imposed so-called sin taxes on cigarettes and alcohol in order to reduce consumption," he argued in the *New York Times*, "it has yet to consider taxing low-nutrition foods or banning commercials for fatty snacks targeted at children" (Brownell 1994).

Responding to calls for action from constituents and experts alike, governments around the world have taken action or are contemplating steps to change the industry's opportunity set. In 2011, Denmark became the first country to impose a "fat tax," which "added 16 kroner [$2.70; £1.68] per kilogram of saturated fats in a product, and was levied on everything containing saturated fats, including raw ingredients like butter and milk to prepared foods like pizzas" (Khazan 2012). The tax was short-lived, however. Its scrapping barely a year later highlights the above-mentioned costs of regulation, including unintended consequences as "the measure . . . only increased companies' administrative costs and caused Danes to venture across the border to purchase their unhealthy snacks" in neighboring Germany and Sweden (Khazan 2012).

The challenge is how to price externalities, both negative and positive, and how to deal with second-order effects, including substitutes. As the *Washington Post* reports,

> A May [2012] *British Medical Journal* study found that "fat taxes" would have to increase the price of unhealthy food by as much as 20 percent in order to cut consumption by enough to reduce obesity, and they should be paired with subsidies on fruits and vegetables so consumers don't swap out one unhealthy habit for another.
>
> *(Khazan 2012)*

Denmark's public policy U-turn and the inherent difficulties of changing the incentives of consumers and producers notwithstanding, countries as diverse as Hungary, France, Japan, Ireland, Israel, and the UK have introduced or are planning to introduce similar measures.

While the public policy debate in the US has focused on labeling – essentially an effort to overcome information asymmetries – and regulating food at (public) school cafeterias, New York City, led by then-mayor Michael Bloomberg, went further and tried to ban the sale of sugary drinks larger than sixteen fluid ounces (about 475ml) in restaurants, delis, soda machines, and cinemas (Grynbaum 2012a). This triggered ferocious lobbying activities by the carbonated-beverage industry. Lobbying is another key piece of the model sketched above. The industry did not have to ramp up its activities from scratch. Organized nationally by the American Beverage Association (ABA), an organization that represents "producers and bottlers of soft drinks, bottled water, and other non-alcoholic beverages," the industry (led by heavyweights Coca-Cola and PepsiCo) has been particularly active in recent years.[2] With the election of Barack Obama, a Democratic majority in Congress, and the First Lady's personal interest in fitness and healthy nutrition for children, the association's direct lobbying expenses in Washington, DC increased tenfold between 2008 and 2009, to almost $20 million.[3] In 2010, ABA successfully defeated legislation at the New York state level that would have imposed a one-cent-an-ounce tax on sodas (Grynbaum 2012b). Politically, the New York City initiative by Mayor Bloomberg was considerably more challenging to the industry than the proposed state tax or similar initiatives. It lends itself well to an explication of the politics of non-market strategy and therefore warrants closer examination.

Whereas a soda tax merely increases the cost to consumers of buying a can of Coke or Pepsi, Bloomberg's proposed sales ban of large soda containers outside of supermarkets would have significantly restricted the industry's competitive space. Widespread availability of its products in all kinds of shapes, flavors, and sizes has been a hallmark of the way Coca-Cola and PepsiCo compete. Bloomberg's policy would conceivably have reduced the whole industry's sales. After all, that was the goal. However, weighing even more heavily in the leading soda firms' decision to fight back vigorously was the precedent of a de facto regulation of their industry, particularly at the point of sale. Again, the experience of the tobacco industry loomed large in the background.

In order to defeat the measure, the industry adopted a multi-pronged approach spanning distinct political arenas. First, it sued New York City on the grounds that the Board of Health had overstepped its authority by unilaterally issuing the restrictions. Second, it launched a public relations campaign to turn public opinion against the measure. Finally, it continued to tout its own proactive measures to tackle the obesity challenge. Deployed simultaneously, these three prongs reinforced one another and highlighted the power of effective non-market management.

Suing to ban the implementation of perceived unfavorable rules is a standard weapon in the arsenal of non-market strategy. As is frequently the case, business focused its legal offensive on procedure rather than substance. The industry deliberately sidestepped the question of whether the ban might be in the public interest and instead charged that the Board of Health lacked the authority to enact by "executive fiat" sweeping changes to the way a set of consumer products is regulated (Grynbaum 2012c). As the industry argued in its filing,

> This case is not about obesity in New York City or the motives of the Board of Health in adopting the rule being challenged. This case is about the Board of Health, appointed by the Mayor, bypassing proper legislative process of governing the City.[4]

Sweeping changes of this nature, the industry contended, required the City Council to enact new legislation after a proper public consultation. Crucially, and already anticipating the next round of the struggle, the ABA signed up several allies for its lawsuit, including the National Restaurant Association, the American Grocers Association, the Statewide Coalition of Hispanic Chambers of Commerce, the New York Korean-American Grocers Association, the National Association of Theater Owners, and various labor unions representing workers in the beverage and hospitality industries. It even managed to win the support of the National Association for the Advancement of Colored People (NAACP) – the leading organization of African Americans. In an amicus brief supporting the ABA, lawyers for the NAACP argued that, even though "obesity was a significant problem among blacks and Hispanics," the proposed policy "would disproportionately hurt minority-owned small businesses" (Grynbaum 2013a). By challenging the rule on procedural grounds, the industry sought a forum switch, away from the executive branch and into the arenas of the legislature and more broadly the public sphere, where it felt it would be in a better position to prevail.

In parallel to challenging the proposed rules in a court of law, the ABA and its allies began a campaign in the court of public opinion. To this end, the industry formed an ad hoc advocacy platform called New Yorkers for Beverage Choices. As the name suggests, this massive campaign was not aimed at negating the link between sugary beverages and obesity. Rather, the industry and its allies deliberately reframed the issue around "choice" and more specifically the freedom to choose. Framing is a powerful tool for non-market strategy, just as it is in politics more broadly (Lakoff 2004). By trying to impose a specific frame on an issue, a political actor shapes the way other actors view that issue and what positions they are likely to take. Even those highly concerned about obesity, for example, might agree that consumers' freedom to choose is something that should not be sacrificed. Particularly when a frame evokes existing and underlying emotions, it is likely to be highly effective.

Led by the ABA, New Yorkers for Beverage Choices capitalized on this frame with television advertisements blasting the mayor for his alleged assault on freedom. "This is New York

City; no one tells us what neighborhood to live in or what team to root for," an off-camera voice proclaimed in one commercial (Grynbaum 2012b). "So are we going to let our mayor tell us what size beverage to buy?" In keeping with the frame, the campaign's symbol became the Statue of Liberty holding an oversized soda (Grynbaum and Connelly 2012).

The campaign was highly effective, with almost two-thirds of New Yorkers opposing the proposed ban (Weigner 2012). In fact, many reproduced verbatim the arguments put forth by the industry. "The ban is at the point where it is an infringement of civil liberties," said one woman. An older man went even further and proclaimed: "This is like the nanny state going off the wall" (Grynbaum and Connelly 2012). With the support of a broad coalition and clever framing, the industry had persuaded voters to fight on its behalf, creating a public policy environment that was increasingly hostile to the proposed measure.

Of course, it is no coincidence that the tenor of the industry's non-market campaign – the freedom to choose – was perfectly aligned with the leading players' evolving market strategy, forming what Baron (1995) calls an "integrated strategy." PepsiCo again serves as a powerful illustration. After shareholders raised concerns the company might be neglecting its core business in its quest to internalize obesity-related externalities proactively, Indra Nooyi led a course correction stressing the need for a "balanced portfolio" (Colvin 2012). In fact, the company's strategy has been "investing more in what Nooyi called 'fun-for-you' brands such as Pepsi and Doritos as well as PepsiCo's 'good-for-you' brands that include Quaker and the new Muller Yogurt venture" (Buss 2013).

The industry's approach has been remarkably successful. New York state courts twice ruled in favor of the ABA and prevented the city from implementing its proposed rules on the basis of the Board of Health overstepping its authority (Grynbaum 2013b). Even though the city has decided to appeal (Grynbaum 2013c), most observers believe the industry will again prevail in a court of law. And because of its effective, broad-based campaign, the industry has been similarly effective in the court of public opinion. With hostility to the plans running high among voters, it is not surprising that the city's legislature has failed to champion the measure.

The case of New York's proposed tax on outsized sodas serves as a perfect illustration of several core features of the model sketched above. Does market competition among firms selling sugary beverages cause a negative externality when it comes to public health? Many would say "yes." This alone, however, does not mean that the extent of the externality can be easily quantified, pinned on to the originator, and/or internalized through a viable and effective remedy. For sure, firms such as PepsiCo know that the non-market environment for their business will remain challenging, and they have therefore made changes to their market strategy to internalize some externalities proactively. This, in turn, has given rise to a differential positioning in the market. Yet this does not prevent the firm from fighting vigorously against a proposed public policy it deems harmful to its business interests, taking the fight directly to the government in the form of a lawsuit, and mobilizing voters against the policy by building a coalition, reframing the issue, and advocating unapologetically for an alternative vision more closely aligned with its market strategy.

Proponents of the measure will view its defeat as only a temporary setback. Using the language of the model, they will no doubt hold the failure of the legislature to establish clear rules as an instance of government failure by politicians beholden to special interests. They will therefore continue their own efforts to change the status quo, pressuring the government to renew the effort, seeking to change public opinion, and pressuring firms directly to address the problem.

Politics goes private

The principal actors in the fight over New York's proposed regulation of soda sizes are business and government. In many other instances, however, all of the pivotal actors are private. Politics does not require the government. The rise of what Baron (2001, 2006) calls "private politics" is a hallmark of our time (Keck and Sikkink 1998).

In the 1990s, two powerful episodes jolted the global business community and brought home the notion that NGOs, and the advocacy networks they frequently form, were forces to be reckoned with in a globalizing world economy. The first was the campaign by a group of labor activists against Nike's sweatshops in Asia (Sage 1999; Ballinger 2001) and the second was Greenpeace's campaign against Shell over the Brent Spar oil platform (Vorfelder 1995; Jordan 2001; Zyglidopoulos 2002). These two were noteworthy because the companies, in both cases, had fully complied with their legal responsibilities. In the former case, none of the affected workers actually worked for Nike, so responsibility to ensure proper factory conditions arguably fell to local firms and governments. In the latter case, Shell had obtained all the necessary permits for its proposed deep-water disposal of Brent Spar, an approach that both the firm's scientists and the UK government deemed the safest disposal option. Yet, in both cases, unelected private actors forced mighty multinationals into humiliating U-turns through sustained campaigns that led to widespread consumer boycotts and ultimately tarnished reputations. Completely sidestepping legal technicalities, private activists convinced the public that the companies had a moral responsibility to, respectively, treat the workers who made their products fairly and protect the environment.

The lesson from both cases is a central pillar of non-market strategy, one that many CEOs continue to ignore at their peril: whether a company agrees with its critics that it has a moral responsibility to address an issue is irrelevant. When a sufficiently large number of stakeholders believe the company does have a moral responsibility, it should act as if it does, for at this point addressing the issue most likely has become a matter of *fiduciary* responsibility, since a company's reputation is increasingly one of its most precious assets (Roberts and Dowling 2002; Diermeier 2011).

Many of the activist groups that target multinationals are smart, sophisticated, flexible, and quick. Their understanding of the power of simple messages and compelling images dwarfs that of many corporate marketing departments. Consider Greenpeace's campaign against the deforestation of the Indonesian rainforest. Having identified palm-oil and paper-pulp production as the principal industrial culprits (Cornell 2013), the organization's strategists carefully dissected the leading producers' value chains to find their weakest links. In the case of palm oil, Greenpeace identified Golden Agri Resources (GAR), a subsidiary of the powerful and politically well-connected Sinar Mas Group, which was the country's leading producer and the third-largest worldwide. However, since neither GAR nor Sinar Mas is a household name in the West, where Greenpeace is strongest, the group targeted GAR's better-known customers to exert upward pressure in the value chain. It first approached Unilever, and that company, in keeping with its strong record in sustainability, quickly dropped GAR as a supplier. Next, Greenpeace targeted Nestlé. Indonesian palm-oil constituted a tiny fraction of the company's total resource use, but that did not stop Greenpeace from launching a blistering boycott campaign against Kit-Kat, one of Nestlé's best-known products. In a graphic and somewhat grotesque video that (partly for this reason) quickly went viral, the environmental group twisted Kit-Kat's slogan and asked Nestlé to "give the orangutan a break," drawing an alleged causal chain from Kit-Kat consumption to Nestlé's palm-oil procurement to GAR's plantations to rainforest destruction to a vanishing habitat for universally beloved primates. Nestlé initially badly mishandled the ensuing social media frenzy (Steel 2010) and then quickly caved in, following Unilever's lead in dropping GAR as a supplier and pledging to purchase only verifiably sustainable palm oil (Fortson 2010). Perhaps surprising even Greenpeace, GAR then reached out to the environmental group, involved it in the elaboration of an action plan, and made substantial changes to its operations that led one observer to remark that the "palm oil giant battles to save the world and itself" (Fortson 2011).

In the case of Indonesian pulp production, Greenpeace's point of departure was another Sinar Mas subsidiary, pulp market leader Asian Pulp and Paper (APP). As in the case of GAR, the target of the environmental group became not the originator of the alleged externality but rather one of its prominent customers down the value chain, in this case Mattel, the US-based global toy manufacturer. Accusing Mattel of using APP products in its packaging, especially for Barbie dolls, the NGO launched a campaign consisting of viral videos, social media, and store protests that accused "Chainsaw Barbie" of "killing the rainforest" and culminated with boyfriend Ken declaring: "Barbie, it's over, I don't date girls who are into deforestation" (De Souza 2011a; Jackson 2011).

Having won praise in 2007 for protecting its reputation by swiftly acting on allegations that Chinese-made toys were lead contaminated (Curtin 2010), Mattel once again wasted no time and pledged a thorough investigation within two days of Greenpeace's charge. On its Facebook account the company posted: "Today Mattel launched an investigation into deforestation allegations. While Mattel does not contract directly with Sinar Mas/APP, we have directed our packaging suppliers to stop sourcing pulp from them as we investigate the allegations" (*Environmental Leader* 2011). Four months later, the company announced new policies for its paper and pulp purchasing and quickly earned Greenpeace's praise: "We're very happy that Barbie has retired her pink chainsaw," a Greenpeace official said. "It has taken [Mattel officials] a while, but they have a very complicated supply chain that they needed to figure out and we think the policy and the principles that they put in place and raised today are strong. Of course, we'll be watching the implementation."[5]

Notice that Greenpeace quite unapologetically assumes the roles of legislature, executive, and judiciary in these cases. GAR and APP may have been fully compliant with applicable Indonesian law, but according to Greenpeace they ran afoul of the rules to which, at the very least, Greenpeace and its members believe business should be held accountable. Rather than working to change Indonesian law and thereby relying on the government to change the terms of market competition, as in the obesity case discussed above, Greenpeace simply took on the role of executive and sought to enforce its own rules on the companies involved (and countless others that annually draw the ire of its activists). Put differently, instead of appealing to citizens-as-*voters* who might work to change public policy, Greenpeace mobilized citizens-as-*consumers* by calling for boycotts of companies and products it deemed responsible for – or at least complicit in – the generation of substantial negative externalities. And when these companies relented and changed their policies, pledging to reduce or fully internalize the externality, Greenpeace vowed to remain vigilant and monitor their compliance.

Greenpeace and other activist groups like to set de facto public policy. However, of course, these actors lack a proper political mandate, they are accountable only to their members, and usually they do not engage in deliberative political processes that (should) prevail in pluralist democratic environments. This is precisely what Baron means by "private politics," and the challenge these groups and their frequently disjointed campaigns pose to business – especially to globally operating multinationals – is considerable. The power of non-market strategy – as a managerial prescription rather than merely an academic field of study – is that it provides companies and their leaders with a single lens and a comprehensive toolbox to respond to all kinds of public policy challenges, regardless of whether they emanate in the public sector and impact the firm through formal regulation or whether they involve private politics and direct pressure.

Building on the model of politics sketched at the outset, and the case-based illustrations of both the public and private pathways through which non-market pressure shapes the environment in which firms compete, the following section sketches a simple tool firms can use to map this space and lay the foundation for proactive and strategic non-market management.

Mapping the non-market environment

Michael Porter's seminal contribution to management theory and practice is the demonstration that, first, industry characteristics systematically shape firm performance and that, second, carefully designed strategy can change these characteristics in a way that benefits the firm (Porter 1980, 1998). Non-market environments are, in many respects, more complex than markets and do not lend themselves as easily to a set of generic strategic prescriptions. Nevertheless, research is beginning to yield systematic insights firms can use to manage these parts of their environments more effectively.

To analyze a firm's non-market environment, Baron (1993) first proposed the "4i" framework – issues, interests, institutions, and information. Bach and Allen (2010) expanded on this work and proposed the $(ia)^3$ framework as an analytical tool organized around six sequential questions:

1 What is the *issue*?
2 Who are the *actors* with a stake in this issue?
3 What are these actors' *interests*?
4 In what *arenas* does this issue play out?
5 What *information* moves the issue in these arenas?
6 What *assets* do the actors need to prevail in these arenas?

The appeal of this framework is that it allows managers to obtain a snapshot of the non-market environment, regardless of whether an issue impacts the firm's competitive landscape through the formal public policy pathway, the private politics pathway, or a mix of the two. Notice that in both cases discussed above, non-market actors quite removed from the ultimately affected companies defined the issues. In the PepsiCo case it was the link between sugary beverages and growing obesity rates, especially in children, and New York City's proposed remedy in the form of a sales ban of oversized soda containers. In the Nestlé and Mattel case it was deforestation of the Indonesian rainforest as a result of environmentally harmful palm-oil and paper-pulp production.

In the case of soda, two coalitions quickly formed. Public health advocates shared Mayor Bloomberg's interest in taking decisive action. The firms most affected, PepsiCo, Coca-Cola, and other producers of sugary sodas, had interests that were diametrically opposed and wanted to prevent any new regulations at all cost. However, the industry was smart to enlist a broad set of allies and to assemble a potent coalition. By bringing in associations of restaurant- and convenience-store-owners, as well as the trade unions representing workers in those sectors, the industry considerably increased the potential lobby pressure it could bring to bear. Bloomberg had chosen the arena carefully, electing to proceed with an executive order through the Board of Health rather than the legislature. With this established as the chosen arena, the only relevant information was about the adverse health effects of soda and the anticipated benefits of banning large containers. In this setting, the key asset was votes in the Board of Health, something the measure's opponents thoroughly lacked. This was why they worked so hard to move the issue out of the Board of Health and accomplish a "forum switch" into a more favorable arena. The lawsuits challenged the Health Department's jurisdiction in this matter and once the issue moved to court the key asset became legal muscle, something well-funded multinationals and the trade associations that represent them usually have in abundance. But simultaneously the issue spilled over into a third arena – the public sphere. It became a de facto battle for the hearts of voters between the mayor and his allies, on the one hand, and the industry's coalition, on the other. Using their financial resources and PR prowess – two key assets in this arena – the measure's opponents effectively reframed the issue. Rather than it being an issue of "public health," it became a matter of "choice" and, more specifically, protecting the "freedom to choose." Appealing to New Yorkers' deeply rooted values of independence, freedom, choice, and individual responsibility, the campaign completely sidestepped the question of what to do about obesity and instead mobilized the public against governmental intrusion in people's personal lives. As is so often the case, the most powerful type of information in the public sphere was an appeal to emotions, not objective facts. Members of the City Council saw the writing on the wall and refused to take up the issue, preventing it from reaching yet another arena and effectively burying Bloomberg's initiative. Table 5.1 one summarizes the findings and illustrates the framework.

In the case of Greenpeace's rainforest campaign, the key to understanding the dynamics is the interest divergence among the corporate actors along the value chain. Whereas GAR and APP had a strong interest in running their businesses without outside interference, Unilever, Nestlé, and Mattel all cared most about protecting their reputations. Greenpeace effectively framed the issue in the public sphere and developed informational materials – humorous videos, gripping visuals, and simplistic causal claims – that were ideally suited for social media. In this arena, credibility, the ability to mobilize many people quickly, and understanding how to condense complex issues into simple and actionable prescriptions ("if you want to save orangutans, boycott Kit-Kat and Barbie") are key assets, and Greenpeace possessed them all. With looming reputational damage, neither Nestlé nor Mattel had any interest in publicly defending its suppliers. Rather, their goal was to quickly dissociate themselves from GAR and APP, particularly because neither was a strategic supplier and in both cases alternatives were available. In other words, instead of responding to Greenpeace's non-market challenge in the non-market arena, the two firms decided to tackle the issue in the market by simply dropping their suppliers. In contrast, losing such prominent customers hurt the two Indonesian companies, forcing them into strategic U-turns that set them on to paths of greater sustainability.

Just as the application of Porter's five forces does not yield market strategy, the $(ia)^3$ framework alone does not produce strategic options for firms engaged in challenging non-market situations. Rather, it maps the firm's political environment in a way that is at once accommodating of the diversity of political actors firms face and sufficiently flexible to shed light on political dynamics in very distinct policy arenas. Formulating countervailing strategies without such a comprehensive assessment is likely to be ineffective.

Table 5.1 The (ia)^3 framework applied to the soda case

Issue

Proposed ban on certain soda containers in New York City

Actors	Interests	Arenas
Bloomberg administration	combat negative externalities of soda, reduce consumption, view issue solely as public health challenge	• NYC Board of Health • NY state courts • public sphere/media • NYC City Council
Customers (= voters)	free product choice, opposed to "nanny state," but growing concerns about obesity as public health challenge	
Small merchants, deli and cinema owners/ operators	avoid any product regulations, continue to sell as before, keep up consumption	**Information**
Unions for workers in beverage and hospitality industries	support their employers, as regulations and reduced consumption could endanger jobs, benefits	• statistics on obesity pandemic • evidence of link between large soda containers, consumption, and obesity • opinion polls on voter attitudes regarding proposed policy • effectiveness of precedents, alternative policy tools • beverage company portfolios and sales data
City Council members	get reelected, sensitive to constituents, prepare for post-Bloomberg era	
		...
PepsiCo	avoid any product regulations, keep up consumption, but also seem responsive to growing public health concerns, reposition firm around "balanced portfolio" that enables choice	**Assets** • legal team to fight issue in court • PR team to shape public opinion • credibility in the public's eye • satisfied customers • broad coalition of allies
PepsiCo's competitors	avoid any product regulations, keep up consumption	
American Beverage Association	advocate on behalf of its members, defeat new regulations	

Conclusion

Non-market strategy is one of those rare fields where simultaneously there is growing managerial necessity and a dynamic academic area of study. Irrespective of whether they are aware of the "non-market" label, almost two-thirds of senior executives across a broad range of industries believe that the impact of government and regulation on their businesses will increase over the next three to five years (McKinsey & Company 2011). Similarly, changing government regulation and damage to the firm's reputation – two quintessential non-market risks – occupied spots two and four, respectively, in the 2013 Aon global survey of leading business risks (Aon Risk Solutions 2013). As the demands on companies and their leaders to navigate complex non-market environments increase, there is both an opportunity and a necessity for scholars to engage in research that generates actionable insights.

What is particularly appealing about non-market strategy to practitioners and scholars alike is that it rejects the compartmentalization of firm activities in different arenas that has historically separated lobbying and political strategy from community engagement and CSR. Effective non-market strategy moves seamlessly from formal public policy arenas to the domain of private politics and back. It appreciates the dual role of citizens as both voters and customers. And it never loses sight of the inherently political character of business – everywhere and all the time.

No matter how hard business may try, it cannot escape its political role. Market competition frequently and inevitably spills over into the non-market domain when externalities, information asymmetries, and/or a lack of competition cause market failures. Similarly, as a prime beneficiary of many public goods, business is frequently expected to contribute to their provision. In light of this, firms can remain passive as others shape the environment in which market competition unfolds, or become proactive and manage the non-market environment with the same analytical rigor and strategic purpose that guide leading firms' efforts in the market. The latter requires leaders who understand, accept, and even embrace the inherently political character of business. It also requires scholars to stop lecturing firms on what they ought to do without consideration of competitive realities and to embrace instead the inside-out perspective that integrates non-market considerations into the set of incentives, opportunities, and constraints that firms face.

In many respects, non-market strategy is still in its infancy. Too little is known about whether and when it makes sense to internalize externalities proactively, what factors make a given firm a particularly attractive target to activists, and under what circumstances efforts to reframe an issue or move it into a more favorable political arena will succeed. As more firms confront non-market challenges in a more complex and increasingly global business environment, scholars will have ample opportunity to collect data and conduct systematic analyses. At the same time, firms and their leaders should pay close attention to this line of work, because effective non-market management is sure to be a key success factor across many industries in the future.

Notes

1 Moreover, Chicago School economists, such as Friedman, warned that even if there is evidence of a market failure, there should be no presumption that the government can address the issues in a way that generates net benefits over inaction or private remedies.
2 See "American Beverage Association" at http://en.wikipedia.org/wiki/American_Beverage_Association (accessed January 1, 2014).
3 Center for Responsive Politics at www.opensecrets.org/lobby/firmsum.php?id=D000000491&year=2009 (accessed January 1, 2014).
4 The case is New York Statewide Coalition of Hispanic Chambers of Commerce et al. v. The New York City Department of Health and Mental Hygiene et al., 653584/2012, New York State Supreme Court, New York County.
5 Richard Brooks, as quoted in De Souza 2011b.

References

Akerlof, George A. 1970. "The Market for 'Lemons': Quality Uncertainty and the Market Mechanism." *Quarterly Journal of Economics* 84 (3): 488–500.
Alchian, Armen, and Harold Demsetz. 1972. "Production, Information Costs and Economic Organization." *American Economic Review* 62 (5): 775–95.
Andrews, Kenneth R. 1987. *The Concept of Corporate Strategy.* 3rd edn. Homewood, IL: Irwin.

Aon Risk Solutions. 2013. *Global Risk Management Survey*. Dublin: The AON Centre for Innovation and Analytics.

Bach, David, and David Bruce Allen. 2010. "What Every CEO Needs to Know about Non-market Strategy." *Sloan Management Review* 51 (3): 41–8.

Ballinger, Jeff. 2001. "Nike's Voice Looms Large." *Social Policy* 32 (1): 34–7.

Barney, Jay. 1991. "Firm resources and sustained competitive advantage." *Journal of Management* 17 (1): 99–120.

Baron, David P. 1993. *Business and Its Environment*. 1st edn. Englewood Cliffs, NJ: Prentice-Hall.

—. 1995. "Integrated Strategy: Market and Non-market Components." *California Management Review* 37: 47–65.

—. 2001. "Private Politics, Corporate Social Responsibility, and Integrated Strategy." *Journal of Economics and Management Strategy* 10: 7–45.

—. 2006. *Business and Its Environment*. 5th edn. Upper Saddle River, NJ: Pearson.

Brownell, Kelly D. 1994. "Get Slim with Higher Taxes." *New York Times*, December 15. www.yaleruddcenter.org/resources/upload/docs/press/ruddnews/OpEdNYTimesTaxes1994.pdf. (accessed September 3, 2014).

Brownell, Kelly D., and Katherine Battle Horgen. 2004. *Food Fight: The Inside Story of the Food Industry, America's Obesity Crisis, and What We Can Do about It*. Chicago: Contemporary Books.

Buss, Dale. 2013. "Indra Nooyi Scores as PepsiCo Quarterly Results Show Turnaround." www.brandchannel.com/home/post/2013/02/14/PepsiCo-Earnings-021413.aspx (accessed November 6, 2014).

Coase, Ronald. 1937. "The Nature of the Firm." *Economica*, 4 (16): 386–405.

— 1960. "The Problem of Social Cost." *Journal of Law and Economics* 3: 1–44.

— 1964. "The Regulated Industries: Discussion." *American Economic Review* 54 (3): 194–7.

Colvin, Geoff. 2012. "Indra Nooyi's Pepsi Challenge." *Fortune Magazine*. http://management.fortune.cnn.com/2012/05/29/pepsi-indra-nooyi-2/ (accessed September 3, 2014).

Cornell, Andrew. 2013. "Greenpeace Raises Its Sails." *Australian Financial Review*, May 4.

Curtin, Patricia A. 2010. "Negotiating Global Citizenship: Mattel's 2007 Recall Crisis." In W. Timothy Coombs and Shelley J. Holladay (eds.), *The Handbook of Crisis Communication*: 467. New York: John Wiley & Sons. http://books.google.com/books?hl=en&lr=&id=KMvtvG4zWaYC&oi=fnd&pg=PA467&dq=mattel+reputation&ots=nN1Hwvcaj1&sig=d6fbxLxMDxeaoby_9KbE7eogDgo (accessed September 3, 2014).

Cyert, Richard Michael, and James G. March. 1963. *A Behavioral Theory of the Firm*. Prentice-Hall International Series in Management. Englewood Cliffs, NJ: Prentice-Hall.

Dahl, Robert Alan. 1961. *Who Governs? Democracy and Power in an American City*. Yale Studies in Political Science 4. New Haven, CT: Yale University Press.

Dahlsrud, Alexander. 2008. "How Corporate Social Responsibility Is Defined: An Analysis of 37 Definitions." *Corporate Social Responsibility and Environmental Management* 15 (1): 1–13.

De Souza, Mike. 2011a. "Greenpeace Targets Mattel; Deforestation; Campaign Features 'Chainsaw Barbie' Cutting Rainforest." *The Gazette*, June 8.

—. 2011b. "'Barbie Has Retired Her Pink Chainsaw'; Goes Green; Mattel No Longer Uses Rainforest Packaging Paper." *The Gazette*, October 6.

Diermeier, Daniel. 2011. *Reputation Rules: Strategies for Building Your Company's Most Valuable Asset*. New York: McGraw-Hill.

Dixit, Avinash K. 1996. *The Making of Economic Policy: A Transaction-Cost Politics Perspective*. Cambridge, MA: The MIT Press.

Donaldson, Thomas, and Thomas W. Dunfee. 1999. *Ties that Bind: A Social Contracts Approach to Business Ethics*. Cambridge, MA: Harvard Business School Press.

Donaldson, Thomas, and Lee E. Preston. 1995. "The Stakeholder Theory of the Corporation: Concepts, Evidence, and Implications." *Academy of Management Review* 20: 65–91.

Environmental Leader. 2011. "Mattel Bows to Greenpeace Pressure on APP Packaging." www.environmentalleader.com/2011/06/13/mattel-bows-to-greenpeace-pressure-on-app-packaging/ (accessed September 3, 2014).

Fortson, Danny. 2010. "Palm Oil Giant Hits back at Greenpeace Campaign." *Sunday Times*, July 25.

— 2011. "Palm Oil Giant Battles to Save the World and Itself." *Sunday Times*, August 21.

Freeman, R. Edward. 1984. *Strategic Management: A Stakeholder Approach*. Cambridge: Cambridge University Press. http://books.google.com/books?hl=en&lr=&id=NpmA_qEiOpkC&oi=fnd&

pg=PR5&dq=Strategic+management:+A+stakeholder+approach.+&ots=6_jnD8M6MQ&sig=
TwFL_UbSk_bpfTHsJ-jx3nBu-xo (accessed September 3, 2014).

Friedman, Milton. 1962. *Capitalism and Freedom*. Chicago: University of Chicago Press.

Grynbaum, Michael M. 2012a. "New York Plans to Ban Sale of Big Sizes of Sugary Drinks." *New York Times*, May 30. www.nytimes.com/2012/05/31/nyregion/bloomberg-plans-a-ban-on-large-sugared-drinks.html?pagewanted=all (accessed September 3, 2014).

—. 2012b. "Soda Makers Begin Their Push against New York Ban." *New York Times*, July 1. www.nytimes.com/2012/07/02/nyregion/in-fight-against-nyc-soda-ban-industry-focuses-on-personal-choice.html?pagewanted=all (accessed September 3, 2014).

—. 2012c. "Soda Industry Sues to Stop Bloomberg's Sales Limits." *New York Times*, October 12. www.nytimes.com/2012/10/13/nyregion/soda-industry-sues-to-stop-bloombergs-sales-limits.html (accessed September 3, 2014).

—. 2013a. "In Court, NAACP Adds Voice against Bloomberg's Soda Ban." *New York Times*, January 23. www.nytimes.com/2013/01/24/nyregion/fight-over-bloombergs-soda-ban-reaches-courtroom.html (accessed September 3, 2014).

—. 2013b. "Judge Invalidates Bloomberg's Ban on Sugary Drinks." *New York Times*, March 11. www.nytimes.com/2013/03/12/nyregion/judge-invalidates-bloombergs-soda-ban.html (accessed September 3, 2014).

—. 2013c. "New York Soda Ban to Go before State's Top Court." *New York Times*, October 17. www.nytimes.com/2013/10/18/nyregion/new-york-soda-ban-to-go-before-states-top-court.html (accessed September 3, 2014).

Grynbaum, Michael M., and Marjorie Connelly. 2012. "Most New Yorkers Oppose Bloomberg's Soda Ban." *New York Times*, August 22. www.nytimes.com/2012/08/23/nyregion/most-new-yorkers-oppose-bloombergs-soda-ban.html (accessed September 3, 2014).

Hart, Oliver D. 1988. "Incomplete Contracts and the Theory of the Firm." *Journal of Law, Economics, and Organization* 4 (1): 119–39.

Hillman, Amy J., and Gerald D. Keim. 2001. "Shareholder Value, Stakeholder Management, and Social Issues: What's the Bottom Line?" *Strategic Management Journal* 22 (2): 125–39.

Jackson, Ben. 2011. "Barbie Is Killing the Rainforest." *Sun*, June 8.

Jordan, A. Grant. 2001. *Shell, Greenpeace and Brent Spar*. London: Palgrave Macmillan.

Keck, Margaret E., and Kathryn Sikkink. 1998. *Activists beyond Borders*. Ithaca, NY: Cornell University Press.

Khazan, Olga. 2012. "What the World Can Learn from Denmark's Failed Fat Tax." *Washington Post*, November 11. www.washingtonpost.com/blogs/worldviews/wp/2012/11/11/what-the-world-can-learn-from-denmarks-failed-fat-tax/ (accessed September 3, 2014).

Knight, Frank H. 1924. "Some Fallacies in the Interpretation of Social Cost." *Quarterly Journal of Economics* 38 (4): 582–606.

Lakoff, George. 2004. *Don't Think of an Elephant! Know Your Values and Frame the Debate: The Essential Guide for Progressives*. White River Junction, VT: Chelsea Green.

Lasswell, Harold D. 1936. *Politics: Who Gets What, When, How*. New York: P. Smith.

Lindblom, Charles E. 1977. *Politics and Markets: The World's Political Economic Systems*. New York: Basic Books.

Lipset, Seymour Martin. 1963. *Political Man: The Social Bases of Politics*. Garden City, NY: Anchor Books.

Maignan, Isabelle, Odies Collins Ferrell, and G. Tomas M. Hult. 1999. "Corporate Citizenship: Cultural Antecedents and Business Benefits." *Journal of the Academy of Marketing Science* 27 (4): 455–69.

Mangalindan, JP. 2010. "PepsiCo CEO: 'If All Consumers Exercised . . . Obesity Wouldn't Exist.'" *Fortune/CNN Money*, April 27. http://money.cnn.com/2010/04/27/news/companies/indra_nooyi_pepsico.fortune/index.htm (accessed September 3, 2014).

Margolis, Joshua D., and James P. Walsh. 2003. "Misery Loves Companies: Rethinking Social Initiatives by Business." *Administrative Science Quarterly* 48 (2): 268–305.

Matten, Dirk, and Andrew Crane. 2005. "Corporate Citizenship: Toward an Extended Theoretical Conceptualization." *Academy of Management Review* 30 (1): 166–79.

McKinsey & Company. 2011. "Managing Government Relations for the Future." www.mckinsey.com/insights/public_sector/managing_government_relations_for_the_future_mckinsey_global_survey_results (accessed September 3, 2014).

McWilliams, Abagail, and Donald Siegel. 2001. "Corporate Social Responsibility: A Theory of the Firm Perspective." *Academy of Management Review* 26 (1): 117–27.

Olson, Mancur. 1965. *The Logic of Collective Action: Public Goods and the Theory of Groups*. Cambridge, MA: Harvard University Press.

Porter, Michael E. 1980. *Competitive Strategy: Techniques for Analyzing Industries and Competitors*. New York: Free Press.

—. 1998. *Competitive Advantage: Creating and Sustaining Superior Performance*. New York: Free Press. www.loc.gov/catdir/description/simon032/98009581.html (accessed September 3, 2014).

Roberts, Peter W., and Grahame R. Dowling. 2002. "Corporate Reputation and Sustained Superior Financial Performance." *Strategic Management Journal* 23 (12): 1077–93.

Sage, George H. 1999. "Justice Do It! The Nike Transnational Advocacy Network: Organization, Collective Actions, and Outcomes." *Sociology of Sport Journal* 16 (3): 206–35.

Samuelson, Paul A. 1948. *Economics*. New York: McGraw-Hill.

Schattschneider, E. E. 1960. *The Semisovereign People: A Realist's View of Democracy in America*. New York: Holt, Rinehart and Winston.

Schlosser, Eric. 2001. *Fast Food Nation: The Dark Side of the All-American Meal*. Boston, MA: Houghton Mifflin.

Seabrook, John. 2011. "Snacks for a Fat Planet." *New Yorker*, May 16. www.newyorker.com/reporting/2011/05/16/110516fa_fact_seabrook (accessed September 3, 2014).

Smith, Adam. 2003. *The Wealth of Nations*. New York: Bantam Classic.

Steel, Emily. 2010. "Nestlé Takes a Beating on Social-Media Sites." *Wall Street Journal*, March 29.

Stern, Nicholas. 2006. *Stern Review on the Economics of Climate Change: Summary of Conclusions*. London: UK Government Economic Service.

Stigler, George. 1971. "The Theory of Economic Regulation." *Bell Journal of Economics and Management Science* 2: 3–21.

Trevino, Linda Klebe. 1986. "Ethical Decision Making in Organizations: A Person-Situation Interactionist Model." *Academy of Management Review* 11 (3): 601–17.

Vorfelder, Jochen. 1995. *Brent Spar Oder Die Zukunft Der Meere*. Munich: Beck.

Weber, Karl. 2009. *Food, Inc.: How Industrial Food Is Making Us Sicker, Fatter and Poorer – and What You Can Do about It*. New York: Public Affairs.

Weigner, Mackenzie. 2012. "NYC Soda Ban Opposed by a Majority, Poll Says." *POLITICO*, June 8. www.politico.com/news/stories/0612/77212.html (accessed September 3, 2014).

Wolf, Charles. 1979. "A Theory of Non-market Failure: Framework for Implementation Analysis." *Journal of Law and Economics* 22 (1): 107–39.

Zyglidopoulos, Stelios C. 2002. "The Social and Environmental Responsibilities of Multinationals: Evidence from the Brent Spar Case." *Journal of Business Ethics* 36 (1–2): 141–51.

6

The uneasy interplay between non-market strategy and international relations

Steven McGuire

Management studies and political science are both social sciences and they share certain common characteristics. Both are interested in the allocation of resources given conflicting demands. Both share an interest in organizational design: in the case of management studies, the variable of interest has traditionally been the for-profit corporation; in political science, the legislative system has taken pride of place. More recently both disciplines have sought to accommodate new actors and influences and in both cases the increasing pluralism and heterogeneity of modern societies and economies has prompted this.

Yet, for all their similarities, political science and management studies have, if not divergent, at least clearly distinctive conceptualizations of the firm as a political organization. The sub-field of political science of interest in this chapter – international relations – has until recently said very little about the firm as a political actor. This is in spite of a widespread belief that firms were and are political actors in the sense that they have preferences in respect of policy-makers and act to advance those preferences. Nonetheless, international relations scholarship, whilst accepting firms are actors, has not done much to conceptualize this "actorness" until recently. More precisely, international relations has left the question of firms' political activity and influence to other sub-fields of political science, notably comparative politics (Brooks, 2013).

This has rendered political science scholarship remote from increasing interest in non-market strategy. Non-market strategy has developed a strong and vibrant presence within strategic management literature over the past twenty years. It is worth noting that one of Baron's (1997) earliest papers on non-market strategy involved an international trade dispute – Kodak–Fuji – and this is illustrative of the essential complementarity of political science and management studies.

Non-market strategy research arguably faces two significant opportunities. The first is to extend its analysis more completely beyond its traditional home regions of the United States and Europe and develop non-market strategy work on the wide range of institutional settings seen in emerging markets (Lawton, McGuire, and Rajwani, 2013; Yuan, Peng, and Macaulay, 2012). Second, in the context of increasing competition for economic resources, non-market strategy must elaborate its current focus on national economic actors as key targets to encompass the increasingly important multilateral fora that help govern the international economy.

The modern international system exhibits the characteristics of a pluralistic and interdependent social system. A range of actors – states, non-governmental organizations of all sorts, as well as intergovernmental organizations – compete and collaborate with each other across myriad issues. However, it is not clear that all these units satisfy what, for international relations scholars, are the key requirements of an actor: resources that can be mobilized in support of a preferred course of action and an ability to influence, even if episodically, the course of events. The latter reflects the ability to exercise power, the currency of all political relations, whilst the former must exist for any exercise in power to have meaning. Moreover, it seems increasingly accepted that governance issues now require collaboration, as no individual actor can formulate and implement a preferred policy merely through an exercise of power. The issues that confront policy-makers – from non-proliferation to economic protectionism to environmental and technological threats – exhibit a deep complexity and interconnectedness sometimes termed "wicked problems."

International relations (IR) has gone some way toward theorizing the firm as a political actor – the field has in general become more eclectic and interested in identifiable problems rather than grand debates – but its roots remain state-centric and this has an effect on way that firms are conceptualized (Lake, 2013). During the past century, international relations scholarship has sought to develop an autonomous theory of international politics. IR theory was autonomous in the sense that the theory was not simply an extension of domestic politics but rather reflected unique aspects of the international system (Gilpin, 2001). Foremost among these system-level characteristics was the lack of an overarching governmental authority able to enforce rules. In the absence of a world government, international relations scholarship necessarily sees political relations in more pessimistic terms than other political science sub-disciplines. This interest in a self-contained conceptualization of international politics leads to a comparative disinterest in how firms come to have policy preferences. As Lake terms it, IR's emphasis on grand theory means that it ignores the micro-foundations of theory: namely, the preferences and resources of all actors involved in the political contest (Lake, 2013: 573). Firms are "black boxes" which generate policy preferences, but the internal political process by which a firm comes to have this preference is not seen as the domain of international relations. In one sense, this is entirely understandable; the boundaries of academic sub-disciplines have be drawn somewhere. But it has led to accusations that international relations scholarship engages in "academic" debate in the worst sense of that word: detached from reality and self-indulgent.

However, the intellectual indifference to firms exerts a more subtle influence on international relations scholarship. In a world of increasing interdependence, IR scholars have been somewhat reluctant to acknowledge that "actorness" in international relations increasingly depends on what an actor does, rather than on what an actor is. In their study of the political influence of cities, Bulkeley and Schroeder (2012) note that until recently the idea that any body other than the nation state could have influence in international affairs would have been regarded as absurd. IR scholarship has been even more distinterested in private actors (at least cities or other regions are public). International relations work has posited a zero-sum conceptualization of the public/private divide in politics, where any privatization of the political process is seen as coming at the expense of the state (Bulkeley and Schroeder, 2012).[1] There is also a strong sense in the discipline that privatization is always a retrograde step, and should be countenanced only when all public options have failed. The dominance of state-centrism also leads to a normative perspective on firms as actors. States are legitimate actors in the sense that they are acceptable actors in the policy process. Firms are not. This leads to an implicit assumption, for instance, that private sector governance arrangements – a popular way to govern supply relationships – are by definition inferior to state-sponsored regulations (Hofferberth, 2011).

This chapter seeks to accomplish two things. First, it offers a *tour d'horizon* of mainstream theories of international relations and more specifically the place of the firm in those theories. I will suggest that international relations has a lot to offer management studies in that it provides a significantly richer account of the international business environment than that provided by international business theory. This, I will suggest, is important for two reasons. First, in the context of increasing resource scarcity and its resultant competition among nation states, assumptions about the durability of the comparatively open and interdependent international economy may be misplaced. As a discipline, management studies existed in a remarkably benign period of international economic growth; more historically informed disciplines might help management scholars understand the prospects for continued openness more clearly.

Second, much of the management studies literature vastly exaggerates the extent to which the state is in decline. Much of the recent corporate social responsibility (CSR) literature moves on the assumption that the state cannot fulfill important social functions (Scherer and Palazzo, 2011).[2] In some cases this is true, yet the success of emerging markets draws our attention to the extraordinary power of the state to direct and encourage economic and social activity. Many of the largest emerging-market firms – some of them leaders in the their sectors – are state-owned enterprises (McGuire, 2013; Yuan, Peng, and Macaulay, 2013). South Korea, Singapore, China, and Brazil all make effective use of a range of government interventions in support of national firms. In developed economies the state accounts for a significant fraction of economic activity, and government procurement is a major source of business for industries from defense to office supplies. There is also a technological story overlooked by management studies: namely, states' use of modern communications technologies. The same technologies that allow firms to use online auctions to source suppliers or sell goods to customers can also be used by governments to operate surveillance systems across the entirety of the population. States remain able to engender loyalty and command obedience among populations that no firm can match. Popular attachment to the state as the principal mechanism for addressing collective action problems over a defined territory remains strong. As Micklethwait and Wooldridge (2014: 10) note, "Even allowing for its recent setbacks, the modern Western state is mightier than any state in history and mightier, by far, than any company. Walmart may have the world's most efficient supply chain, but it does not have the power to imprison or tax people – or to listen to their phone calls."

From kingdoms to states: the realist perspective in international relations

If an academic discipline can be said to have a founding event, for international relations it was the Peace of Westphalia of 1649. The resulting treaties were signed between the rulers of what were then the fragmentary remains of the Holy Roman Empire. These treaties gave birth to the modern notion of territorial sovereignty, the principle that geographical boundaries demarked different states and that within those units the political entity governing that territory could be regarded as having the freedom to govern as it saw fit. The Peace of Westphalia remains a central pillar of international relations, political science, and, for that matter, international law. Flowing from this historical signing was the concept of the state, a territorial and political construct that would form the basic unit of analysis. However, although international relations theory regards the state as the key unit of analysis, the various schools disagree over whether it is the only meaningful actor or whether, notwithstanding its primacy, it can be understood as influenced and constrained by other actors. These actors can be interest groups or international organizations.

For international relations theorists of the Realist School, the state constitutes the basic building block of the international system and all other actors and institutions are merely channels through which it transmits its policy preferences. Domestic interest groups do contest for power within states, and this contestation does have implications and consequences for the external relations among states, but there is no international equivalent of this domestic process. Rather, the discipline of international relations is understood as the interaction of states; it is states that aggregate domestic interests and deploy these as foreign policies. Though realism accepts that economic power and wealth matter to politics, it is rooted in an anthropological and not economic approach to human behavior (Kirshner, 2012). For realists, the human desire for security, not the desire for material goods, is the basis for political action. They argue that a person – or a state – can engage in economic activity only after the basic requirements for security are met.

Two distinct schools of realism feature in the literature. Traditional realism – much of it framed by the global conflicts of the twentieth century – emphasizes the anarchic nature of the international system and the "self-help" doctrine, wherein the only guarantor of a state's security is the state itself. Structural realism, developed during the Cold War and most closely associated with Kenneth Waltz (1979), makes an important addition to realist theory. As the term suggests, structural realists suggest that the international system itself has an important effect on state relations. States (or, more precisely, policy-makers) pay attention to relative changes in their fortunes in the international system. This sense of change in relative capabilities and power explains why states make alliances and engage in other forms of bandwagoning: there are attempts to balance against other states with relatively greater power. Whilst structural realism represents an important development in realist theory, both schools share a disregard for firms and other non-state actors in the conduct of international relations.

The focus of realism is "hard" security – that is, a state's ability to protect itself from other states that could, and would, use violence as a means of advancing the national interest. While actual loss of territory to invasion has receded as a genuine threat, it may still be the case that cyber-warfare, embargoes, or other forms of pressure can be brought to bear (Brooks, 2013). The emphasis on survival flows directly from another central characteristic of realism: anarchy. As the prominent realist John Mearsheimer (2009) points out, anarchy in this context does not refer to constant violence and warfare, but rather to the lack of a supranational mechanism for constructing and restraining state behavior. There is no body remotely similar to domestic political institutions – legislatures, police forces, and regulators – that can enforce rules at the international level. Realists do not argue that nothing else aside from national security matters. Rather, they argue that, in the absence of any substantial supranational actor able to enforce compliance and standards of behavior, cooperation in international affairs will always be contingent on the willingness of states to act cooperatively, and that willingness is a function of the anxiety states feel about their security.

Realism and the international business environment

Though states have primacy, realists admit that other actors can behave politically. They accept, for example, that actors can be influential at the national level and that economic and social concerns do have political salience. They argue, however: first, that many of those concerns will always be filtered and influenced by security relations at the international level; and, second, that in times of crisis, hard security will always trump other concerns. The collapse of the international economy in the 1930s is cited as evidence of the power of realism. In spite of economic interdependence, which was argued by Norman Angell to make war futile, states did, in fact, come to rate national security as more important than maintaining economic ties. And in the 1990s President Clinton found that it was more effective to frame international trade agreements in terms of security – prosperity makes for less violent societies and so less external threat to the United States – than in economic terms. The African Growth and Opportunity Act (AGOA), resisted by domestic manufacturing firms, was passed when Clinton shifted the emphasis to the security gains from economic engagement with Africa (Milner and Tingley, 2011). From a realist perspective, evidence of widespread industrial espionage by countries like China is confirmation that nations are always and ultimately more concerned about security than economic development. In many otherwise capitalist states, there are concerns about selling some domestic firms to the firms of states that are potential rivals. The Chinese telecommunications firm Huawei, for instance, regularly encounters resistance when attempting to buy Western firms. Governments of target firms typically cite national security concerns as justification for caution. In 2005 the Chinese National Offshore Oil Company (CNOOC, a state-controlled Chinese multinational) sought to buy the US petroleum producer Unocal. On the face of it, the acquisition was unproblematic: Unocal was a largely California-based integrated oil company with few assets internationally. However, what international assets it did have began to attract congressional attention, with US politicians eyeing the company's significant holdings in Asia. Chevron ended up acquiring Unocal, after CNOOC withdrew its bid, conceding that, "This political environment has made it very difficult for us to accurately assess our chance of success, creating a level of uncertainty that presents an unacceptable risk to our ability to secure this transaction" (Barboza, 2005).

Patterns of foreign direct investment in recent years can be understood through a realist lens. China's investments in Africa, for instance, can be seen as an effort to secure supplies of valuable raw materials, such as oil and manganese, which underpin its staggering economic growth. China has been seen by some as having an advantage in dealing with African economies and their political masters because the Chinese, viewing these investments through realist lenses, do not make an issue of the host countries' human rights records or make other demands in respect of adherence to international codes of conduct. China, in other words, respects the sovereign power of African states and in so doing extends its influence and power whilst securing resources. In many developed states – not least the United States – foreign state-owned companies often receive a frosty reception when they seek to invest. This is because of fears that these ostensibly corporate deals motivated by profit are, in fact, part of a broader foreign policy in which the firm plays an important, but ultimately subordinate, role. In Canada, foreign ownership of natural resources has long been controversial, but as long as that ownership was largely American or European, there were few objections beyond the questioning of why Canada was so reliant on foreign investment. US and European firms were generally privately owned and came from countries that shared Canada's world view, were allies, and thus could be trusted.

In recent years, though, Canada has adopted a decidedly skeptical view of inward investment, particularly in selected commodities sectors, such as potash and petroleum. In 2012 CNOOC was able to purchase Nexen, a mid-sized Canadian company, but only after the Chinese company engaged in an aggressive non-market strategy to reassure Canadian government officials that the acquisition did not present any national security issues. This was not merely an effort aimed at *Canadian* policy-makers; Nexen also had extensive holdings in the Gulf of Mexico, so US officials had to be mollified, too. The US approval process resulted in the company ceding operational control over the Gulf of Mexico fields (Penty and Forden, 2013).

This Canadian example is a particularly apt demonstration of realism's explanatory power. Canada is a small and relatively open economy that relies on inward investment to create wealth. Its geographic position – particularly since the end of the Cold War – makes it exceptionally secure: it faces no realistic threat of invasion and has a secure alliance with the United States. Yet, even a state that faced little security threat and needed foreign direct investment – and was governed by a right-of-center political party at the time – felt that certain forms of foreign direct investment (FDI) in relation to commodities posed a security threat and demanded careful review.

Realism's interest in state-based power has led to a view that it is a form of nationalism (Gilpin, 2001). This is not the case. Nationalist politicians are generally fixated on their state's relative standing in the world and how changes in power and resources affect it. However, the point about realism is that it is the system that produces this anxiety about relative state power. This might force a state into seeking an alliance with other states. Realism effectively treats the state as a form of "economic man," seeing it as a unitary rational actor in the international system (Watson, 2014). It is an ahistorical (though it accepts a role for contingency in shaping policy; see Lake, 2013) and amoral theory of political action. Nationalism romanticizes the state, and sees culture and history as acting as profound influences on a state's activities. Though it shares realism's view of the international system as anarchic, its historically informed view of the state is a world away from realism's.

Realism's central tenet is that political outcomes are always the result of state–state bargaining. Other actors can be influential in developing policy preferences within states but once the issue escalates to the international level, there is no outcome that requires independent action by non-state actors. International organizations are influential to the extent that powerful states within those organizations allow; firms are influential in generating technical and other standards but their influence is effectively constrained by the willingness of major states to sanction the outcome. As such, realist perspectives on politics have not developed a theory of the firm because there is no point in doing so (Coen, Grant, and Wilson, 2010). Realists might argue that any political theory of the firm represents a different domain: namely, management studies.

Pluralist theories: liberalism and constructivism[3]

Realism has arguably been the most influential theory of international politics of the twentieth and twenty-first centuries, but it has been challenged by competing theories that use as their point of departure the extraordinary linkages – commercial, social, and environmental – that exist among states. Economic interdependence is not new – earlier periods of history had high levels of international economic integration – but the current level of institutionalization of international commerce is comparatively new (Aggarwal and Dupont, 2014). The contemporary international system has multiple sources of authority that act across a range of policy areas. In contrast with realism, pluralist accounts of the international system accept that non-state actors can be important, and influential, and that considerations other than a narrow conception of security can be important in shaping actors' behavior.

As a more pluralistic theory of international relations, liberalism has a place for a range of non-state actors, including firms, but like realism it has tended to view firms as second-order actors whose importance lies in their input into domestic policies through non-market strategy. Nonetheless, liberalism has helped to shape subsequent interest in governance, including economic governance, which has a clearer and more substantial conceptualization of the political role of firms.

Constructivism is often positioned as an alternative or opposing theory of international relations, but it is another pluralistic theory, just like liberalism. Where constructivists part company with liberals is in the much greater weight they assign to the political influence of ideas in shaping and constraining political action. Liberalism, like realism, is still mainly concerned with actors and how and why units interact. Constructivism draws attention to the influences of the rules of the game, and how ideas exert a subtle but important influence in political life. The international system is not a given. It is not an objective reality, but rather a socially constructed space where ideas matter.

Rules of the road: regime theory in international relations

One of the most prominent and controversial liberal theories is regime theory, which arose in the international relations literature in the 1980s. Regimes are bundles of norms and rules that serve as a focus for state preferences in an issue area. The persistence of a regime over time shapes the way that a state approaches policy issues because the actor interactions within the regime generate a series of expectations about acceptable behavior (Krasner, 1982). A regime can be understood as exhibiting a form of path dependence, where an accumulation of activities and decisions sets the path along which the organization continues – and finds it hard to break out of if needed. A regime can be understood as an iterated game, where actors have a good probability of meeting again – and this suggests that the shadow of the future makes states more inclined to cooperate, realizing that reciprocity might be a good basis on which to work. Regimes thus serve to regulate states' behavior by presenting them with a set of agreed "rules of the road" for coordinated policy-making.

For scholars of the constructivist perspective on international relations these rules of the road represent the independent power of ideas to shape political outcomes. Whereas realists would suggest that powerful states use ideas instrumentally, constructivists would argue that certain powerful ideas or world views, even if they begin as instruments of powerful states, can exert pressures of their own over time. Elites across countries come to adopt remarkably similar views – a consensus of sorts – about appropriate policy stances. Siles-Brügge (2014: 537–8), for instance, suggests that:

> Trade policy-makers and a group of leading economists have contributed to constructing an ideational imperative for continued openness (and for concluding the Doha Round, albeit less successfully in this latter case given its continued stagnation) by drawing on a questionable reading of economic history (what I refer to as the Smoot–Hawley myth); by continually stressing protectionism's role as one of the causes of the Great Depression non-liberal responses to the current crisis have been all but ruled out by all except those willing to question the received wisdom.

Though regime theory enjoyed considerable prominence among IR scholars in the 1980s and 1990s, its origins are contested. For some, it was developed as an explanation for the development and seeming durability of international agreements across policy areas that became apparent from the 1970s onward. Previously, many international relations scholars had accepted the notion that a hegemon – a preponderant power like the British Empire or the

United States of the twentieth century – was required, essentially, to force international cooperation. In this sense, proponents of the theory were reacting to the relative decline of the United States in world affairs (Gilpin, 2001). As this hegemon diminished in power, it became more important for nations to cooperate in the coordination of the global economy. Regime theory thus sought to explain economic interdependence. For others, it represented an effort to, if not justify, at least rationalize American hegemonic power by dressing up US dominance of the international economy as a cooperative process where other states had a meaningful say (Strange, 1982).

Regime theory starts from a different premise than realism: that states actually rely on each other for a great many things; that this interdependence is more significant than is appreciated by realists; and that this has implications for the propensity of states to cooperate rather than compete. Whether rationalization or not, regime theory helped to shape international political economy work in profound ways, not least by drawing attention to the range of collective action problems that require international cooperation that extends over time and space. Intergovernmental organizations and the wide range of international agreements – such as voluntary codes of conduct – are manifestations of the need for states to cooperate. As Susan Strange noted, early regime theory tended to replicate the same problems faced by realism – an overarching interest in grand theory and state-centrism – but by accepting a more pluralistic conceptualization of politics, it lent itself to new avenues of analysis where firms and civil society could play roles (Strange, 1982).

Regimes are not new: one of the oldest, the International Telecommunication Union (ITU), was founded in 1865 to facilitate international growth in telegraph traffic. In the case of telecommunications, the nature of the technology requires cooperation among various parties, since communications by definition always involve more than one party. Though few people ever reflect on it, everyday life is made possible via a bewildering array of international regimes whose rules of the road allow for interoperability, standardization, and consistency of services for consumers and firms. Nor are the organizations overseeing the operation of these regimes merely ciphers; they exert an independent effect on international relations and the international economy. This is something realists would not recognize; for them, intergovernmental organizations exist only because states want them to and operate only because states find them useful. By implication, if an international organization did seek to exert influence beyond what states – particularly powerful ones – would allow, it would be prevented from doing so. Yet, as Koppell (2010) notes, across an amazing array of issue areas – from international trade to product standards – international organizations *do* implement work that does not conform to the preferences of powerful states (or, for that matter, powerful firms).

Though management studies literature has tended to ignore them completely, and international relations literature has framed its study of regime theory as entirely one of state–state cooperation, firms are indeed deeply affected by regimes and their attendant international organizations. This is because, to the extent that regimes set the rules of the road, they present non-market opportunities for firms. Strange (1982) was among the few international relations scholars to draw attention to the importance of regimes to firms – and of firms to regimes. From her perspective, regimes were evidence of the domestic political influence of US multinationals, as regimes, for Strange, represented an extension of US power into the international system. Building on work on domestic US politics, Strange developed a stream of literature on state–firm bargaining that would be recognizable to many international business scholars (Strange, 1982, 1987; Strange, Stopford, with Henley, 1991). The obsolescing bargain theory of international business scholarship speaks to this private–public relationship, where the state seeks investment and the firm seeks competitive advantage through cost or location advantages. What Strange added, however, was a deeper conception of political power that suffused this relationship. Whereas international business scholars looked at a state–firm bargaining as largely transactional, Strange understood it as a power relationship. For her, it mattered that the deep legal and political structure of the international political economy was decisively influenced by the United States. It mattered that understandings of expropriation, trade instruments, and international finance were based on US domestic laws (Lawton and McGuire, 2003). US firms did well in the international economy because the regimes that structured and facilitated its development were based on the US experience.

Strange's (1982, 1987) identification of firms as key influences on the international economy was a major development in IR theory, but arguably understated the more nuanced and historical role that firms – and not just US multinational enterprises (MNEs) – played in the institutionalization of the international economy. As goods and services became more complex, the nature of regulating and facilitating trade also changed. Regimes deal not merely with high-level macro issues of coordination among states but also technical standards that have profound effects on firms' operations and strategy. The membership of the International Telecommunication Union included firms as well as states. This reflected the fact that the organization existed to facilitate telecommunications and so required firms – with their knowledge of the actual operation of telecoms – to be members. Similarly, the development of the internet as an effective and profitable route to market for firms required not just state–state agreements on a range of policies, but also deep firm involvement to map out technical aspects, including dispute settlement (Lawton and McGuire, 2003). Technical expertise places firms in positions of political power.

Firms need a well-functioning and regulated market to thrive. Though this is so obvious as to be a truism, work that integrates the development and evolution of markets with an account of international relations remains sparse, and to the extent that this has developed in management studies, it has done so through the prism of institutional theory. Debora Spar's (2001) work, for instance, has shown how international relations were central to the evolution of markets in, among other things, piracy, the internet, and radio. In the case of the first, it was rivalry between Great Britain and Spain that shaped British attitudes to piracy in the Caribbean Sea. Faced with a desire to check Spanish power, Britain decided to allow – indeed license – private ships to intercept and confiscate Spanish galleons carrying gold and other goods from the American colonies. Only when this activity became so lucrative that it threatened to become ungovernable did the British desist. Markets are created and shaped by governments – and government rivalry and competition can be a characteristic of this interaction.

Work on the role of public diplomacy highlights the importance of governments to the export success of firms. Ciuriak (2014), for instance, argues that two characteristics of modern economic diplomacy are important for firms' export success. The presence of an embassy is important: lower-level diplomatic representation – including dedicated trade officials – has less impact than having the highest form of country representation – an embassy headed by an ambassador. This is because of an embassy's signaling effect to prospective trade partners. Rather akin to FDI from a firm, embassies signal the intent to develop long-term diplomatic relations. The effect of this on the propensity of firms then to export remains under-studied. Second, Ciuriak finds that the presence of a formal trade agreement leads to enhanced trade. This demonstrates the importance of political structures shaping and supporting commercial relationships.

Work on the links between diplomacy and business in the case of China show remarkably similar results. Chinese outward foreign direct investment often attracts interest because of the link between investment and China's security concerns, particularly when investments are made for resource-seeking rather than knowledge- or market-seeking reasons (Zhang et al., 2014). When the broad spread of Chinese FDI is considered, however, a somewhat different picture emerges. Levels of Chinese FDI are most closely associated with the quality of diplomatic relations with the host country. Zhang and colleagues (2014) find that the longevity of diplomatic links and the seniority of diplomatic representation are both positively correlated with greater flows of Chinese outward investment. The management studies literature too often sees the state as a potential expropriator and thus conceptualizes relations with the state in terms of political risk. A much more nuanced view emerges from international relations: the state can also be a catalyst and guarantor for commercial activity.

Global governance and the rise of private regulatory regimes

Regime theory essentially set the stage for the next major development in international relations theory: the move toward what might be called global governance studies. Global governance is not a theory of international politics in the sense that realism, liberalism, and constructivism are, but its growth as an area of study has antecedents in regime theory and reflects the gradual movement to admit non-state actors to the group of recognized objects of study in international relations.

International relations places states at the center of analysis, but a significant field of work has acknowledged that private actors – both firms and civil society – have begun to play roles in economic and social governance across a range of issue areas. In fact, work on private governance in international relations is deeply concerned with the firm activities that have long been the focus of studies in supply chain and operations management literatures. In this literature, firms are not merely lobbyists, pursuing strategic advantage through non-market strategy. They are, rather, actors that take on the role of policy-maker and regulator and so act in a way that IR scholarship has typically considered the preserve of the state (or a delegated public authority). International relations work has contributed to management studies accounts of supply chains' better appreciation of the role of power relationships in the development of both supply chain governance and corporate social responsibility initiatives.

As Büthe (2010) notes, scholarly interest in private politics arose more or less simultaneously in both management studies and international relations. For the former, David Baron's (2003) work on private politics sought to examine instances where firms would use power – in the sense of inducing an actor to do something they would not have done without that influence – to gain competitive advantage. Baron's work is well known to strategic management scholars, but as interesting as his development of non-market strategy has been, his other significant contribution was to make the firm "political." Management studies literature has a limited sense of firms acting politically (McGuire, 2012). Whilst management studies accepts that firms interact with public authority, this interaction is conceptualized as apolitical or non-political in the sense that management academics do not place the exercise of power at the center of their analyses. International relations' interest in private governance began with work that built on regime theory but went much further in exploring how and why private actors, in place of the state, seemed to succeed in creating and operating systems of rules and norms. International relations work in this area blends liberalism's focus on material and structural aspects of power with constructivism's concern with the importance of ideas and norms. Thus, for example, in the context of CSR initiatives, firms are influential in the development and operation of the global compact both because of the norms embodied in the compact and because of the resources that firms can bring to bear to operationalize the compact (Berliner and Prakash, 2012; Vormedal, 2010). The early work of scholars such as Claire Cutler laid out a research program that generated an entirely new research stream in international political economy that looked at both the operation of private political actors and the issues of legitimacy and justice that accompanied their operation. As Cutler, Haufler and Porter (1998) noted, in spite of the clear evidence that international commercial law and dispute settlement had a significant role for private actors, international relations theory – their specific example was liberalism – had no conceptualization of private politics. Cutler, both individually and with collaborators such as Virginia Haufler and Tony Porter (1998) articulated a research program that emphasized the heretofore little understood role of private actors in international law and international relations. Private authority, as the concept became known, related to the ability of private actors – essentially firms – to make authoritative decisions in relation to the use of resources – just like state actors – and to have those decisions viewed as legitimate by third parties. The view that these decisions are legitimate is crucial: without acceptance by third parties, such as governments or consumers, there is no genuine authority.

In the ensuing twenty years, a vast amount of international relations scholarship has devoted attention to the growth of regulatory regimes where private actors to varying degrees appropriated the traditional role of the state. Like the management studies work on the topic, there is interest in situations where private governance arrangements essentially substitute for weak or absent government (Prakash and Potoski, 2014). But there is also interest in situations where private governance arrangements do not obviously compensate for state weakness but are instead developed as viable and legitimate modes of governance. This literature does not fall neatly into the main theoretical perspectives outlined above but rather lies in the sub-field of international political economy and is informed by cognate areas such as regulation and environmental studies. It is this significant breadth that gives rise to the increasing use of the term *governance* studies to describe the complete range of work that examines and tries to understand the complex interactions of public and private actors across diverse policy areas – from rainforest protection to electrical product standards to coffee production.

International relations scholarship has taken a particular interest in two, related, forms of private political activity. The first relates to the governance of business functions, notably investment and supply chains, but also to financial regulation, where private governance appears to have supplanted or pre-empted state-based regulation. Interest in the political implications of the globalization of production centered initially on the impact this spatial relocation of production would have on national economic policies, including international policies, such as trade policy. As production (services were not considered as tradable in the same way) globalized, the expectation was that firms would increasingly become indifferent to their home countries' trade policies. Instead, they would be more interested in globalized rules and regimes. In areas like pharmaceuticals, for instance, coalitions of European and American firms sought to extend intellectual property protections enjoyed at home upward to the international system (Auld et al., 2010; Fuchs and Lederer, 2007; Sell, 2003; McGuire, 2013). This work, however, still conceived of the firm as acting politically through domestic (mainly European or US) policy processes (Woll, 2008). In the area of supply relationships, for instance, international relations work focused on whether and how firms sought to transfer their domestic standards and practices internationally, and the extent to which this was institutionalized in codes of practice. The diffusion of ISO 14001 can be seen this way, as multinationals use the standard as an "entry fee" for supplier firms. In respect of financial services, one of the most successful efforts at private politics was the generation and diffusion of the International Accounting Standards Board (IASB) as a rival to the US Generally Accepted Accounting Principles (USGAAP). The generation of a new set of accounting standards shows how private regulation does not need to replace or substitute for state inaction (Porter, 2005). In the case of IASB, the European Commission, if anything, encouraged the creation of a new standard, seeing it as an opportunity to create an alternative to the US standard. Moreover, the IASB was created in Europe, a region not obviously in need of private sector alternatives to public regulation.

The second strand relates broadly to the politics of certification standards, often but not exclusively in relation to corporate social responsibility objectives vis-à-vis consumers. The generation of the global compact can be viewed in this way, though the agreement itself if not a standard, per se. It is, however, an articulation of principles that firms are meant to internalize as part of their broader societal obligations (Berliner and Prakash, 2012). Certification standards in areas such as agriculture and forestry are examples of privately generated standards becoming widely adopted. International relations work on forestry, for example, seeks to understand how standards come to be adopted and, as part of that, why firms might adopt one standard in preference to another. Here interactions with public authority are important. Firms with extensive trade in the European Union, for example, look to work with standards broadly compliant with EU directives on sustainable forestry. Prakash and Potoski (2014) find that issues relating to their design also affect private standards, like public regulations: how the standard works and what behaviors it incentivizes.

Conclusion

In a powerful critique of the limited ability of contemporary strategic management research to contribute to debates surrounding the post-financial crisis landscape, Richard Whittington (2012) argued that the management studies community needed to place more emphasis on the impact of firms on society and rather less emphasis on operational problems that were somewhat simpler to study. Whittington was essentially arguing that without a richer account of how firms are perceived by local and national communities and policy-makers, strategic management scholarship misses an important variable explaining the strategic decisions of firms and their consequences.

IR theory has not, and does not, have firms at the center of its analysis of power. The focal point for all theoretical perspectives within the discipline is the state. That said, IR has developed space for the consideration of firms as political actors. In one of the more important developments in the field in recent years, IR has again drawn on work originally done in the domestic policy realm. More recent scholarship, drawing on pluralist or constructivist perspectives, began to acknowledge how firm policy preferences influenced and constrained state-level policy action in the international system. The role of ideas in generating widespread and durable policy preferences among policy-makers has gained considerable prominence over the past two decades.

Moreover, if, as David Lake argues, IR scholarship is developing a welcome interest in studying and understanding issues in international relations and moving away from grand theorizing, then the value of this work to management studies will increase. Quite apart from its increasing appreciation of firms, IR work – and political science more broadly – alerts management scholars to the importance of understanding non-market activity as an exercise in power. Whittington's critique notes that strategic management's focus on performance leaves management scholars unable to comprehend, let alone explain, public anger at business. Some integration of IR scholarship would help rectify that.

What does this mean for the specific sub-field of non-market strategy? It suggests that non-market work will be enriched and given more explanatory power within the broader field of strategic management.

Notes

1 Management studies scholarship makes a different "zero-sum" error by conceptualizing firms' political actions as a function of the inability of the state to perform its traditional public goods functions (see, e.g., Scherer and Palazzo, 2011).
2 For an exception, see Yuan, Peng, and Macauley, 2013.
3 A note on terminology. "Liberalism" is a somewhat convenient catch-all term for a range of pluralistic theories that draw their inspiration from liberal political theory. It shares assumptions with, but is not co-terminus with, neoliberalism, which refers to the political–economic program of rolling back the state.

Bibliography

Aggarwal, Vinod and Cedric Dupont (2014) "The International Economic System," in John Ravenhill (ed.), *Global Political Economy*, 4th edn, Oxford: Oxford University Press, pp. 50–73.

Auld, Graeme, Benjamin Cashore, Cristina Balboa, Laura Bozzi, and Stefan Renckens (2010) "Can Technological Innovations Improve Private Regulation in the Global Economy?," *Business and Politics*, 12(3), DOI: 10.2202/1469–3569.1323.

Axelrod, Robert (1984) *The Evolution of Cooperation*, New York: Basic Books.

Barboza, David (2005) "China Backs away from Unocal Bid," *New York Times*, August 3, www.nytimes.com/2005/08/02/business/worldbusiness/02iht-unocal.html?_r=0 (accessed June 21, 2014).

Baron, David (1997) "Integrated Strategy in International Trade Disputes: The Kodak–Fujifilm Case," *Journal of Economics and Management Strategy*, 6: 291–346.

— (2003) "Private Politics," *Journal of Economics and Management Strategy*, 12: 31–66.

Berliner, Daniel and Aseem Prakash (2012) "From Norms to Programs: The United Nations Global Compact and Global Governance," *Regulation and Governance*, 6(2): 149–66.

Brooks, Stephen (2013) "Economic Actors' Lobbying Influence on the Prospects for War and Peace," *International Organization*, 67: 863–88.

Bulkeley, Harriett and Heike Schroeder (2012) "Beyond State/Non-state Divides: Global Cities and the Governing of Climate Change," *European Journal of International Relations*, 18(4): 743–66.

Büthe, Tim (2010) "Global Private Politics: A Research Agenda," *Business and Politics*, 12(3), DOI: 10.2202/1469–3569.1345.

Ciuriak, Daniel (2014) "The Impact of Domestic Representation Abroad on Canada's Exports," e-brief, C.D. Howe Institute, April.

Coen, David, Wyn Grant, and Graham Wilson (2010) "Political Science: Perspectives on Business and Government," in David Coen, Wyn Grant, and Graham Wilson (eds), *The Oxford Handbook of Business and Government*, Oxford: Oxford University Press, pp. 9–34.

Cutler, Claire, Virginia Haufler, and Tony Porter (eds) (1998) *Private Authority and International Affairs*, Albany: State University of New York Press.

Fuchs, Doris and Markus Lederer (2007) "The Power of Business," *Business and Politics*, 9(3), DOI: 10.2202/1469–3569.1214.

Hofferberth, Matthias (2011) "The Binding Dynamics of Private Governance Arrangements: The Voluntary Principles of Security and Human Rights and the Cases of BP and Chevron," *Business and Politics*, 3(4), www.bepress.com/bap/vol13/iss4/art5 (accessed November 10, 2014).

Gilpin, Robert (2001) *Global Political Economy: Understanding the International Economic Order*, Princeton, NJ: Princeton University Press.

Kirshner, Jonathan (2012) "The Tragedy of Offensive Realism: Classical Realism and the Rise of China," *European Journal of International Relations*, 18(1): 53–75.

Koppell, Jonathan G.S. (2010) *World Rule: Accountability, Legitimacy and the Design of Global Governance*, Chicago: University of Chicago Press.

Krasner, Stephen (1982) "Regimes and the Limits of Realism: Regimes as Autonomous Variables," *International Organization*, 36(2): 185–205.

Lake, David (2013) "Theory is Dead, Long Live Theory: The End of Great Debates and the Rise of Eclecticism in International Relations," *European Journal of International Relations*, 19(3): 567–87.

Lawton, Thomas and Steven McGuire (2003) "Governing the Electronic Market Space: A Critical Evaluation of the Global Consensus on e-Commerce Self-Regulation," *Management International Review*, Special Issue 1: 51–71.

Lawton, Thomas, Steven McGuire, and Tazeeb Rajwani (2013) "Corporate Political Activity: A Literature Review and Research Agenda," *International Journal of Management Reviews*, 15(1): 86–105.

Mazzucato, Maria (2013) *The Entrepreneurial State: Debunking Public vs Private Sector Myths*, London: Anthem Press.

McGuire, Steven (2012) "What Happened to the Influence of Business? Corporations and Organized Labour in the WTO," in Amrita Narlikar, Martin Daunton, and Robert Stern (eds), *Oxford Handbook of the World Trade Organization*, Oxford: Oxford University Press, pp. 320–39.

— (2013) "Multinationals and NGOs amid a Changing Balance of Power," *International Affairs*, 89(3): 695–710.

Mearsheimer, John (2009) "Reckless States and Realism," *International Relations*, 23(2): 241–56.

Micklethwait, John and Adrian Wooldridge (2014) *The Fourth Revolution: The Global Race to Re-invent the State*, London: Allen Lane.

Milner, Helen, and Dustin Tingley (2011) "Who Supports Global Economic Engagement? The Sources of Preferences in American Foreign Economic Policy," *International Organization*, 65(1): 37–68.

Penty, Rebecca and Sara Forden (2013) "CNOOC Said to Cede Control of Nexen's US Gulf Assets," Bloomberg.com, March 1, www.bloomberg.com/news/2013-03-01/cnooc-said-to-cede-control-of-nexen-s-u-s-gulf-assets.html (accessed December 10, 2014).

Porter, Tony (2005) "Private Authority, Technical Authority and the Globalization of Accounting Standards," *Business and Politics*, 7(3), DOI: 10.2202/1469–3569.1138.

Prakash, Aseem and Matthew Potoski (2014) "Global Private Regimes and Domestic Law: ISO 14001 and Pollution Reduction," *Comparative Political Studies*, 47(3): 369–94.

Ravenhill, John (2014) "The Study of Global Political Economy," in John Ravenhill (ed.), *Global Political Economy*, 4th edn, Oxford: Oxford University Press, pp. 3–24.

Scherer, Andreas Georg and Guido Palazzo (2011) "The New Political Role of Business in a Globalized World: A Review of a New Perspective on CSR and Its Implications for the Firm, Governance and Democracy," *Journal of Management Studies*, 48(4): 899–931.

Sell, Susan (2003) *Private Power, Public Law: The Globalization of Intellectual Property Rights*, Cambridge: Cambridge University Press.

Siles-Brügge, Gabriel (2014) "Explaining the Resilience of Free Trade: The Smoot–Hawley Myth and the Crisis," *Review of International Political Economy*, 21(3): 535–74.

Spar, Debora (2001) *Pirates, Prophets and Pioneers: Business and Politics along the Technological Frontier*, New York: Random House.

Strange, Susan (1982) "*Cave! Hic Dragones*: A Critique of Regime Analysis," *International Organization*, 36(2): 479–96.

— (1987) "The Persistent Myth of Lost Hegemony," *International Organization*, 41(4): 551–74.

— (1988) *States and Markets*, London: Pinter.

Strange, Susan and John Stopford, with John Henley (1991), *Rival States, Rival Firms: Competition for World Market Shares*, Cambridge: Cambridge University Press.

Vormedal, Irja (2010) "States and Markets in Global Environmental Governance: The Role of Tipping Points in International Regime Formation," *European Journal of International Relations*, 18(2): 251–75.

Waltz, Kenneth (1979) *Theory of International Politics*, Reading, MA: Addison-Wesley.

Watson, Matthew (2014) "The Historical Roots of Theoretical Traditions in Global Political Economy," in John Ravenhill (ed.), *Global Political Economy*, 4th edn, Oxford: Oxford University Press, pp. 25–49.

Whittington, Richard (2012) "Big Strategy/Small Strategy," *Strategic Organization*, 10(3): 263–68.

Woll, Cornelia (2008) *Firm Interests: How Governments Shape Business Lobbying on Global Trade*, Ithaca, NY: Cornell University Press.

Yuan, Li, Mike Peng, and Craig Macaulay (2013) "Market–Political Ambidexterity during Institutional Transitions," *Strategic Organization*, 11(2): 2015–213.

Zhang, Jianhong, Jiangang Jiang, and Chaohong Zhou (2014) "Diplomacy and Investment – the Case of China," *International Journal of Emerging Markets*, 9(2): 216–35.

Section B
Non-market foundations and structure

7

Corporate social responsibility

Jonathan P. Doh and Benjamin Littell

Corporate social responsibility (CSR) has emerged as an important business response to pressure emanating from citizens and activists, as an alternative to government action to address pressing social issues, and as a form of non-market strategy. Companies are increasingly viewing their CSR actions and initiatives as part of their overall business strategy and operations. CSR is practiced in one form or another by nearly all publicly traded companies and many private and state-owned firms as well. Initially motivated by government and activist stakeholder pressure, CSR has become a more integral, routine part of a company's portfolio of activities. Some companies have taken an especially proactive approach to CSR, applying the same strategic focus to these social initiatives as they do to more commercially driven projects and ventures.

At the same time, scholars are increasingly observing – and advocating for – "strategic" CSR that explicitly acknowledges the potential benefits of engaging with communities, non-governmental organizations (NGOs), and other non-governmental stakeholders (Doh, Lawton, and Rajwani, 2012; McWilliams, Siegel, and Wright, 2006). Further, as noted in other contributions to this volume, the line between corporate political activity (CPA) and CSR is blurring, reflecting the potential influence of social and environmental stakeholders and issues on government policy, the influence of public policy on these stakeholders and their concerns, and the emergence of "private" approaches to policy challenges, notably the emergence of codes, standards, and private regulation as an alternative response to collective goods failures and negative externalities.

In this chapter, we trace the growth and development of CSR as a concept in practice and scholarship, noting differing perspectives on the antecedents (motivations) and objectives of CSR in corporations. We focus especially on "strategic" views of CSR and their connection to non-market strategy. We describe company-specific and collective approaches to CSR and their relationship to non-market strategic objectives. We profile one company, Odebrecht SA, as an example of CSR as a form of non-market strategy in practice. We conclude with suggestions for future research.

The history and origins of modern CSR

Proto-CSR: business practitioners, 1880–1950

In practice, the modern-day CSR movement traces its roots to the 1880s. Initially, the movement concentrated on the treatment of employees and employee welfare during and after the Industrial Revolution. During the 1880s, companies began to improve working conditions, compensate employees for on-the-job accidents, and donate to employee activities (Heald, 1957, as cited in Kristoffersen, Gerrans, and Clark-Murphy, 2005: 6). Much of this initial CSR push was likely a result of external pressures, including unionization and efforts to preempt more stringent government action (Heald, 1957). Andrew Carnegie and his paternalistic approach to employee relations was a classic example of this proto-CSR.

Two decades later, World War I again brought social issues to the forefront of public discourse. Many large companies, including General Electric and Ford, instituted assistance programs for their employees. These programs remained in place at many corporations postwar and became a foundation of general corporate policies toward employees (Heald, 1957). The Great Depression of the 1930s also called attention to social issues and employee welfare, adding awareness of and support for employee-related CSR actions (Heald, 1957). In the 1940s, Johnson and Johnson instituted its now widely known credo that specified the prioritization of its key stakeholder, preferencing healthcare professionals, employees, and customers over shareholder (Katsoulakos, Koutsodimou, Matraga, and Williams, 2004).

The emergence of CSR scholarship

The 1950s witnessed some of the earliest CSR research, primarily with a focus on CSR as philanthropy – not necessarily as business strategy (Moura-Leite and Padgett, 2011). Frederick (2006) summarized the 1950s CSR movement into three categories: "corporate managers as public trusties," "balancing competing claims to corporate resources," and "acceptance of philanthropy as a manifestation of business's support of good causes" (as cited in Moura-Leite and Padgett, 2011: 530).

In 1953, researcher Howard Bowen published *Social Responsibilities of the Businessman*. In his book, Bowen acknowledged that businesses create secondary impacts on populations, and he encouraged businesspeople to consider the outcomes of their actions from an ethical standpoint (Bowen, 1953; Carroll, 1999). Likewise, Peter Drucker included "public responsibility" in his book *The Practice of Management*, published in 1954. Like Bowen, he stated that it is the responsibility of the businessperson to consider the impact of their actions on the greater good of the population (Drucker, 1954). For both Bowen and Drucker, philanthropy was referenced as the driver for CSR, not big-picture business strategy.

Stockholder interests were not absent from 1950s research. Levitt (1958), an early critic of CSR as philanthropy, stated that business managers need to be transparent about their CSR initiatives. He formed the argument that CSR is acceptable only when profitable, and that businessmen who perform CSR for any reason other than maximizing profit are doing so in a selfish way (Levitt, 1958). Levitt argued that it is not the duty of the private business to be in the business of the public good, and that giving managers the ability to make judgments in regard to what to support through CSR only increases managerial power (Levitt, 1958).

In the 1960s, researchers shifted their focus from CSR as philanthropy to CSR's "importance to business and society" (Moura-Leite and Padgett, 2011: 530). In the early half of the decade, multiple researchers examined the larger economic implications of CSR, reaching conflicting conclusions. Economist Milton Friedman (1962) applied CSR to capitalism and profit creation, stating that CSR should and does occur only when it makes economic sense and increases the bottom line. Frederick (1960) proposed an alternative view, stating that CSR represents a crumbling of the laissez-faire ideology and a rebuke of Adam Smith.

In 1967, Davis wrote that business and society are interdependent and derive their success from each other. According to Davis (1967), a strong business can survive only in a strong society. Therefore, it is mutually beneficial when businesses conduct CSR; by improving the health of a society through socially responsible actions, corporations can improve their businesses (Davis, 1967). At the same time, progressive government legislation continued with the Fair Packaging and Labeling Act of 1960, the Equal Pay Act of 1963, the National Traffic and Motor Safety Act of 1966, the National Environmental Policy Act of 1969, and the Truth in Lending Act of 1969. The passage of this landmark legislation underscores the delicate interplay between voluntary CSR in private markets and codification of practices through law and regulation.

Stakeholder activism, 1970s–1980s

In the 1970s and 1980s, the business environment faced new challenges emanating from social and environmental causes and issues, such as the emergence of the environmental movement. This movement culminated in the establishment of the Environmental Protection Agency in the United States and the passage of the Clean Air Act in 1970.

Researchers also began to extend and revise theoretical and conceptual perspectives on CSR. Friedman (1970) expanded and clarified his earlier writings, reasserting that "the social responsibility of business is to increase profits" but acknowledging that it may be reasonable, and therefore profitable, for companies to engage in CSR actions that do not have immediate stockholder benefits as long as there is a long-term benefit. Likewise, Davis (1973) expanded on his previous research, stating that businesses can survive only by maintaining a social contract with the public. According to Davis, as society changes and evolves, businesses must do the same in order to reflect current public opinion. The evolving public opinion held by a society ultimately dictates a firm's CSR policy (Davis, 1973). Companies must answer to the greater public, as the actions of the company affect all stakeholders.

In 1979, Carroll categorized CSR as the "economic, legal, ethical, and discretionary expectations" that the general public holds companies responsible for achieving (Carroll, 1979: 500). These categories imply that the public society expects companies to follow the law, make a profit, behave in an ethical manner toward society, and provide other discretionary actions that benefit society and employees. Multiple researchers evaluated the organization of companies and how structure relates to CSR implementation (Ackerman, 1973; Fitch, 1976; Sethi, 1975).

In the early 1980s, Post and Preston (1981) defined the scope of a business's social responsibilities. They stated that companies should work to resolve problems that occur from their primary actions, as well as those that occur from the secondary effects of those actions, but that companies do not have an obligation to solve all problems that occur in society (Post and Preston, 1981). In this regard, Post and Preston (1981) advocated for companies to approach CSR governance proactively, including involving themselves in the creation of and advocating for public policies. Jones (1980) concluded that, ideally, all stakeholders should have a voice in terms of a company's actions. Donaldson (1982) expanded on Davis's previous social contract theory of CSR, stating that there is a natural relationship between society at large and business.

In 1984, Freeman's *Strategic Management: A Stakeholder Approach* changed the dialogue regarding the relationships of business strategy to CSR and normative theory around stakeholders. Freeman explicitly linked CSR to the management of stakeholders, and stated that companies should base their success on the benefit to their stakeholders (as opposed to stockholders; Freeman, 1984). That same year, evidence of financial gains from CSR actions were shown through research by both Drucker (1984) and Cochran and Wood (1984). In separate articles, they explored the profitability of companies that participated in CSR. Both found that CSR was not only a business opportunity but that financial profit and socially responsible practices were linked (Moura-Leite and Padgett, 2011).

CSR as a global phenomenon

In the 1980s and 1990s, modern CSR became more widespread in the US, Europe, and, increasingly, other regions of the world, including emerging markets. Companies in Japan – and even India, China, Russia, and Brazil – began to embrace it. By 1990, a study by *Fortune* magazine found that 90 percent of all Fortune 500 companies included CSR as a key element in their annual reports (Lee, 2008). Moreover, beginning in the 1990s, international bodies such as the United Nations, World Bank, OECD, and International Labor Organization accepted and advocated for CSR (Moura-Leite and Padgett, 2011).

On the research front, Wood's (1991) research links CSR to other socially oriented theories, such as stakeholder management and social issues management, illustrating the overlap between and among these theories and concepts. While "corporate citizenship" emerged as a potential rival to CSR as an umbrella term in the mid-1990s (Waddock and Graves, 1997), CSR persisted as the preferred term to encapsulate the range of activities related to a company's social and environmental actions. A bit later, the notion of sustainability as an umbrella concept that incorporates economic, social, and environmental dimensions also gained traction. Holt and Barkemeyer (2012) report a significant spike in worldwide coverage of the terms "sustainability" and "sustainable development," most notably since 2002.

Consistent with the blurring of terms and concepts was a renewed interest in institutional theory as a scholarly lens through which to view a range of firm–society interactions, including CSR. Consistent with this view, DiMaggio and Powell (1983: 148) famously argued, "There is such startling homogeneity in organizational forms and practices." This perspective also lends itself to identifying the particular stakeholders that are exerting those social pressures and obligations and predicting the strategies that emanate from those pressures (Boddewyn and Doh, 2011; Husted and Allen, 2010; Yaziji and Doh, 2009).

Using an institutional framework, Matten and Moon (2008) proposed that there were differences in how CSR manifested in different regions of the world with differing institutional and cultural characteristics. They suggested that differences in "national business systems" in the US and Europe, which are results of long-standing, historically embedded institutions, influenced the level and form of CSR in these two regions. The nature of the US business environment and overall institutional conditions provides more incentive and opportunity for companies to take actions tackling their responsibilities toward society, what Matten and Moon (2008) called "explicit" CSR. They defined this form of CSR as "voluntary programs and strategies by corporations that combine social and business value and address issues perceived as being a part of the social responsibility of the company" (Matten and Moon, 2008: 409). In Europe, by contrast, firms practice "implicit" CSR, which consists of "values, norms, and rules that result in (mandatory and customary) requirements for corporations to address stakeholder issues and that define proper obligations of corporate actors in collective rather that individual terms" (Matten and Moon, 2008: 409). Matten and Moon (2008) helped scholars and practitioners to think about the normative implications of CSR and how it can manifest in different forms depending on the institutional setting.

As scholars and business practitioners began to think more about the connection of CSR to core business strategy, they began to view CSR as a potential strategic lever to advance a firm's overall commercial interests. Hence, this period saw the emergence of strategic theories of CSR that offered a normative endorsement of companies' social practices being integrated into their business and corporate-level strategies (McWilliams, Siegel, and Wright, 2006). David Baron, a proponent of non-market strategy, also coined the term "strategic CSR" to recognize that companies compete for socially responsible customers by explicitly linking their social contribution to product sales (Baron, 2001). Concurrent with this strategic view of CSR was a proliferation of analyses seeking to determine whether and how CSR (sometimes referred to as CSP – corporate social performance – to emphasize these performance implications) contributed to corporate financial performance (CFP). This research stream yielded a series of studies (well over a hundred) that sought to link various aspects of the CSR and CSP of firms to their financial performance (CFP). (See, for example, Griffin and Mahon, 1997; Margolis and Walsh, 2003; McWilliams and Siegel, 2000; Preston and O'Bannon, 1997; Ruf, Muralidhar, Brown, and Paul, 2001; Stanwick and Stanwick, 1998.) During this period there were also a number of meta-analyses (e.g., Margolis, Elfenbein, and Walsh, 2007) that found that the overall effect of CSP on CFP was positive but small, and that there was as much evidence for reverse causality (i.e., CFP leading to CSP).

In the next section, we will explore the antecedents, processes, and outcomes of strategic CSR in more depth. Table 7.1 provides a selective summary of some of the major works in CSR and their principal perspective on CSR as a concept and phenomenon.

CSR as non-market strategy

What is non-market strategy?

According to Doh, Lawton, and Rajwani (2012: 23), market strategy consists of the "suppliers, customers, and competitors" while non-market strategy consists of "social, political, legal, and cultural arrangements that constrain or facilitate firm activity." Both strategies include the ultimate goal of increasing profits. Though it does not directly address business operations, non-market strategy can impact on the economic, political, and social outcomes for a company (Baron, 1995, 1997, as cited in Doh, Lawton, and Rajwani, 2012).

Rooted in the Enlightenment and the Industrial Revolution, non-market strategy has existed in practice for over two hundred years. Owners of large private companies, often guided by moral or religious convictions, aligned their philanthropic giving with their market strategies and goals (Lawton, Doh, and Rajwani, 2014). Contemporary examples of non-market strategy include activities such as donating to political campaigns, lobbying, and building partnerships, all with the purpose of increasing profits (Baron, 1995; Baron and Diermeier, 2007; Doh and Lucea, 2013). As non-market strategy addresses governmental and political stakeholders, it is important to note that non-market strategy can invite corruption and unethical behavior, often in the form of bribery and exploitation (Doh, Lawton, and Rajwani, 2012).

The non-market environment of a corporation includes both its internal and its external stakeholders. External stakeholders are stakeholders who are not directly involved in the

Table 7.1 Evolution of CSR scholarly research

Bowen, 1953	*Social Responsibilities of the Businessman* – businesses create secondary impacts and business actions should be evaluated from an ethical standpoint.
Drucker, 1954	*The Practice of Management* – responsibility of the businessman to consider consequences of actions.
Heald, 1957	Origins of CSR in the improvements of working conditions as early as the 1880s. First World War assistance programs, instituted by corporations, became a foundation for corporate policies towards employees.
Levitt, 1958	CSR should be strategic and not purely philanthropic. Business does not have a duty to provide public goods unless it leads to greater profits.
Frederick, 1960	Growing CSR movement a clear rebuke to Adam Smith and laissez-faire economics.
Friedman, 1962	CSR should and only does occur when those actions increase the bottom line.
Davis, 1967	CSR has mutually beneficial effects: society improves from CSR actions and businesses thrive in healthy societies.
Friedman, 1970	Profits still should drive CSR actions, but some CSR results in longer-term profits as opposed to immediate profitability.
Davis, 1973	Businesses can only survive with public support; the evolving public opinion ultimately shapes a company's CSR.
Carroll, 1979	The public expects companies to follow the law and make a profit while also performing ethical actions to benefit society.
Post and Preston, 1981	Businesses have a duty to correct problems that occur as a result of their actions, but they do not have a duty to resolve all societal problems.
Freeman, 1984	*Strategic Management: A Stakeholder Approach* – links CSR to the successful management of stakeholders.
Drucker, 1984; Cochran and Wood, 1984	Profitability shown to be linked to CSR actions.
Wood, 1991	CSR linked to social issues management and stakeholder management.
Baron, 2001	Coins "strategic CSR." Companies shown to compete for socially responsible customers by linking their CSR actions to sales.
Matten and Moon, 2008	CSR manifests itself in different ways in different regions of the world.

operations of the corporation. Examples that are commonly addressed through non-market strategy include governments, NGOs, the natural environment, and the media. Internal stakeholders are stakeholders who are directly involved in corporate actions and operations. Employees and union organizations are examples (Donaldson and Preston, 1995; Mitchell, Agle, and Wood, 1997, as cited in Doh and Lucea, 2013).

CSR as a part of non-market strategy

Social responsibility is increasingly considered an important element of non-market strategy (Doh, Lawton, and Rajwani, 2012) and was described by Lawton, Doh, and Rajwani (2014: 12) as a "strategic or instrumental tool of the corporation." The term "strategic CSR," originally coined by Baron, means that "a company's social practices can be integrated into its business- and corporate-level strategies" (Baron, 2001, as cited in Lawton, Doh, and Rajwani, 2014: 12). The impact of strategic CSR on a corporation's success is not lost on executives: in a

2007 survey, over 56 percent of executives rated CSR as a "high" or "very high" priority (Erhemjamts, Li, and Venkateswaran, 2013). According to Doh, Lawton, and Rajwani (2012: 29), "Strategic theories of CSR (McWilliams, Siegel, and Wright, 2006), which assert that a company's social practices are integrated into its business and corporate-level strategies, are integral to NMS [non-market strategy]."

When examining the non-market environment, Lawton, Doh, and Rajwani (2014) categorize non-market strategies based on a company's level of "political orientation" and "social responsiveness." Social responsiveness relates directly to the way that a company oversees and handles strategic CSR issues. As part of their non-market strategy, companies with high social responsiveness will be likely to engage in CSR actions and appoint senior officials to oversee their CSR initiatives (Lawton, Doh, and Rajwani, 2014). Both low and high political orientation, coupled with high social responsiveness, lead to a non-market strategy that utilizes CSR. Low political orientation/high social responsiveness companies view CSR as an integral part of their market differentiation strategy for their business, while high political orientation/high social responsiveness companies view CSR as a complementary tool to political engagement (Lawton, Doh, and Rajwani, 2014). A study by Hillenbrand, Money, and Ghobadian (2013) – and built upon in Chapter 13 of this book – highlights the impact that strategic CSR can have on the trust that employees, customers, and other stakeholders have in a corporation. According to their research, attitudes toward and trust in a corporation are linked to the positive intent of the corporation's CSR actions (Hillenbrand, Money, and Ghobadian, 2013). A prevailing theory is that, as a strategic differentiator and an element of their non-market strategy, companies compete for socially conscientious customers by strategically highlighting their CSR initiatives (Baron, 2001). Being perceived as "a good citizen" can increase product sales by appealing to those customers (Doh, Lawton, and Rajwani, 2012: 29). McWilliams and Siegel (2001) also highlight the ways in which strategic CSR, as a non-market strategy, can be used to differentiate and create a competitive advantage. They argue that, as various stakeholders make demands for environmentally friendly products, better working conditions, and more socially responsible practices, companies react by making investments in CSR initiatives (McWilliams and Siegel, 2001). By meeting the non-monetary stakeholder demands through their investments in CSR, companies can increase their overall profits. By comparing the cost of the investments to the financial benefit gained through increased profits, companies can identify the level of CSR that provides the highest profit for their shareholders (McWilliams and Siegel, 2001).

CSR, non-market strategy, and firm growth and profitability

As a part of non-market strategy, successful strategic CSR should translate into increased financial success. As of 2013, over a hundred studies had been conducted to try to determine the links between CSR and the financial performance of companies (Lawton, Doh, and Rajwani, 2014). These studies were inconclusive as to whether CSR leads to greater firm performance, or if greater financial performance leads to higher levels of CSR (Margolis, Elfenbein, and Walsh, 2007). More successful companies, with stronger financial resources, are more likely to embrace CSR, making it unclear if CSR is truly the driver for financial success.

Individual researchers have concluded that there are some connections between CSR and financial performance. Waddock and Graves (1997) concluded from their research that strategic CSR initiatives do bring financial success to companies, and, in return, these companies with increased financial success then have more resources to engage in more strategic

CSR actions (as cited in Erhemjamts, Li, and Venkateswaran, 2013). A separate study by Margolis and Walsh (2003) found that, of 109 studied firms, 54 showed a positive relationship between firm performance and CSR actions, while only 7 showed a negative relationship. More recently, an analysis by Brammer and Millington (2008) found that firms with unusually high social performance had higher long-term profits, and a 2013 study by Erhemjamts, Li, and Venkateswaran (2013) also found that firm performance was positively related to CSR activity.

Porter and Kramer (2002, 2006) make the case that potential areas for CSR actions along the value chain can, in return, create new profit-enhancing opportunities (Doh, Lawton, and Rajwani, 2012). CSR activity has also been shown to provide positive benefits to organizational strategy, indicated by increased advertising spend (Erhemjamts, Li, and Venkateswaran, 2013). Similarly, Lawton, Doh, and Rajwani (2014) conclude that these non-market strategies should be tailored to use capital efficiently on those projects that align with and advance their business goals. There are a multitude of voices in the non-market sector – only those that relate to a company's business strategy should be addressed (Lawton, Doh, and Rajwani, 2014). An example of this targeted strategic CSR as a part of non-market strategy can be seen through the profile of Odebrecht at the end of this chapter.

CSR, non-market strategy, and business strategy: firm and industry actions

The interaction of CSR and non-market strategy has generated a number of firm-level responses to challenges and opportunities emanating from the non-market business environment. These responses include the emergence of private regulation, internal and collective codes of conduct, and collaboration with non-governmental stakeholders. Each of these phenomena may be viewed as a form of non-market strategy designed to buffer companies from threats in the business environment and/or advance their commercial interests to further their growth and profitability.

CSR directed at filling institutional voids

For some firms, a foundational objective of CSR in underdeveloped institutional settings is to fill "institutional voids" (Khanna and Palepu, 1999) resulting from the inability or unwillingness of a government to meet its responsibilities through the provision of basic public services (Boddewyn and Doh, 2011). Boddewyn and Doh (2011) specify how MNEs have invested in the national infrastructure of roads, railroads, ports, airports, electrical-power grids, and communication networks in emerging markets (Boddewyn and Doh, 2011), and have expanded these investments to include basic collective goods (safety, water, electricity, worker health and training, roads, etc.) which MNEs need for their *local* operations.

These collective goods are less readily available in countries in transition to a market economy because of *institutional voids* (also called deficits, discrepancies, gaps, and failures), such as ineffective or unreliable legal systems. These institutional voids affect both indigenous and foreign organizations so that our analyses apply to both types, although multinational enterprises (MNEs) face particular problems due to their crossing of borders and therefore have a strong stake in pursuing this form of CSR non-market strategy. The provision of basic social services is sometimes provided alone or with government or NGO partners, as described below and in our case example.

Private regulation as collective non-market strategy

Private regulation – also called self regulatory codes – are sets of codes and standards, established collectively by some combination of firms, governments, and NGOs or other independent groups, that are designed to self-regulate business operations. Unlike formal law, which applies to actions that occur within a nation's borders, private regulation is usually voluntary and adopted across a corporation's global operations. According to Vogel (2010), the origins of private CSR regulation lie in the large-scale targeted attacks against specific companies for certain business practices that they have conducted (Bartley and Child, 2007; Klein, 2001; O'Rourke, 2005, as cited in Vogel, 2010). Examples include campaigns against certain large MNEs for issues such as harsh working conditions, child labor, and environmentally damaging practices (Vogel, 2010).

Researchers agree that private regulation is becoming increasingly important for CSR business strategy due to the globalization of business practices. Traditional government regulation does not apply across all borders (Scott, Cafaggi, and Senden, 2011), meaning illegal practice in one country may be legal in another. As a result, voluntary codes and regulations have been established to supplement public codes (Lawton, Doh, and Rajwani, 2014).

Corporations strategically use private regulation of CSR for multiple reasons. For some companies, private socially responsible regulations are a method of strategic risk management. As a preemptive measure, companies respond to negative criticisms and attack campaigns by signing up to voluntary private regulations that promote CSR. By proactively signing up to private regulations, companies strategically aim to avoid future negative press and public outrage. Past research has shown that negative campaigns against companies and their business practices do not impact profits and success, but companies still find value in improving their public image and stopping negative press through private CSR regulation. This ultimately improves customer relations and employee satisfaction (Vogel, 2010).

Companies also strategically use private regulation to raise industry standards, thereby creating a more even market competition. By strong-arming all competitors into adopting the same private regulations, companies no longer can gain advantages through unfair labor practices or harmful environmental practices. This enables companies to act in a socially responsible way while still being able to compete in the market place. Furthermore, raising industry standards avoids the creation of industry-wide negative press that can occur when just one company acts unethically (Vogel, 2010). Relatedly, companies tend to imitate the actions of their competitors. When one company agrees to private regulations, that company's competitors are likely to follow suit, resulting in industry-wide acceptance of private CSR regulations. The more companies that are accepting of private regulation, the more likely others will as well (Lieberman and Asaba, 2006; Maitland, 2005).

Some firms attempt to shape or influence industry and governmental regulations by agreeing to certain private regulations. For example, by accepting and encouraging private CSR regulations, MNEs can potentially avoid tougher governmental regulations (Vogel, 2010). This, however, has not been the prevailing reason for companies to embrace private regulations (Vogel, 2010).

Codes of conduct

Codes of conduct are a specific form of private regulation that ensure a company acts in accordance with a particular set of socially responsible practices or rules (Lawton, Doh, and Rajwani, 2014). Codes of conduct may be individual or collective and may include disclosure policies in regards to political, social and trade association payments, and the monitoring of other "social spending" (Lawton, Doh, and Rajwani, 2014: 182).

Researchers state that one way CSR codes of conduct are strategically used is by reassuring stakeholders that the company will act in a socially responsible way (Aaronson and Reeves, 2002). Formal, written codes of conduct show a dedication and enforcement of CSR policy. By adopting these codes and strategically promising to act in a manner consistent with socially responsible practices and stakeholder interests, companies ultimately look for reward from stakeholders in exchange (Lenox and Nash, 2003).

Maintaining a strong reputation within the industry and public domain is another key reason for companies to adopt CSR codes of conduct (Diller, 1999). By achieving a positive reputation, companies improve their public image and bolster their visibility and leadership on important social issues (Brereton, 2002). Ultimately, these benefits and increased trust lead to increased profits (Bondy, Matten, and Moon, 2004).

Similarly, codes have been strategically adopted to mitigate and prevent the negative public opinion of a company's environmental, labor, and other actions widely discussed in the media (Van Tulder and Kolk, 2001). If companies choose not to sign up to codes of conduct, they could be perceived negatively by their non-participation – even if they are acting in a manner that is consistent with the codes (Brereton, 2002).

In the same way as private regulation can be used to attempt to avoid government regulation, CSR codes of conduct are adopted to prevent burdensome regulation from governments (McInnes, 1996; Diller, 1999; Brereton, 2002; Truss, 1998, as cited in Bondy, Matten, and Moon, 2004). Furthermore, government has been shown to fail at regulation, and, as discussed previously in regards to private regulation, government lacks the ability to regulate across borders (McInnes, 1996). Researchers also point to supply chain maintenance, customer relations, and preventing potential backlashes from customers as strategic reasons for CSR codes (Diller, 1999).

Strategic networking with NGOs is another reason why companies voluntarily support private regulation. Many firms choose to embrace private regulations that are written by NGOs, as the latter are perceived to hold significant influence and marketing power and maintain higher levels of trust and legitimacy than their corporate counterparts (Vogel, 2010).

NGO–corporate partnerships

In the same way as corporations are using private regulations to lever social responsibility as a business strategy, they are collaborating with stakeholders, forming NGO–corporate partnerships, and working with nonprofits to advance their business goals through CSR (Dahan, Doh, Oetzel, and Yaziji, 2010, as cited in Lawton, Doh, and Rajwani, 2014). When implementing strategic CSR, NGOs provide corporations with inside information and the unique ability to achieve results that corporate–corporate partnerships cannot provide. Information exchange is a critical component of NGO–corporate partnerships. The corporate partners within the NGO–corporate partnership have the ability to utilize the vast network and the field-tested knowledge of the NGO to address the CSR demands of the stakeholders more effectively and efficiently, easing the financial burden of CSR implementation while quickly adapting to market movements (Rondinelli and London, 2003). In return, the NGO–corporate partnerships provide distinctive benefits to NGOs through access to financial and other resources that large, multinational companies are uniquely positioned to deliver (Chesbrough, Ahern, Finn, and Guerraz, 2006).

A key advantage of NGO–corporate partnerships is the mutually beneficial exchange of resources that such relationships provide – not unlike private partnerships (Eisenhardt and Schoonhoven, 1996). NGO–corporate partnerships are even more distinctive than private same-sector partnerships, as the former often provide both partners with resources that they would not be able to find strictly in their own sectors (Eisenhardt and Schoonhoven, 1996).

With diverse partnerships that include both NGOs and large corporations, however, comes some difficulty in working together. Even though the general goals of the partnership may be common to both partners, NGO–corporate partnerships are known to have trust issues, communication difficulties, and conflict. As the partnership tackles more complicated projects, these difficulties increase. Therefore, a successful strategic CSR program implemented through an NGO–corporate partnership requires continual dedication and maintenance (Parker and Selsky, 2004).

CSR as non-market strategy in action at Odebrecht

Many companies around the world have come to see their CSR activities and initiatives as part of their overall non-market strategy. Odebrecht SA, a privately held Brazilian engineering, construction, and energy conglomerate, is one such organization. The company was founded in 1944 in Salvador da Bahia by Norberto Odebrecht, and is now present in South America, Central America, North America, the Caribbean, Africa, Europe, and the Middle East. Its leading company is Norberto Odebrecht Construtora. Odebrecht controls Braskem, the largest petrochemical company in Latin America and the fifth largest in the world, with exports to sixty countries in all continents. In 2012, Odebrecht SA had revenues of $43 billion ("Annual report," 2013). It is responsible for a number of major projects and investments globally, including several in the Miami area, such as the Miami International Airport, the Miami Mover transit connection, and Florida International University Stadium.

Strategic CSR at Odebrecht has a long history. In 1946, Odebrecht constructed its first social welfare project, the 5000-square-meter mixed-use project "Circulo Operario da Bahia" ("Sustainability policy," 2013). In 1965, the Odebrecht Foundation (discussed below) was formed to support and encourage the resolution of Brazil's social issues, specifically for company members, while also acting as an experimental organization for the for-profit Odebrecht. The foundation was founded with four areas of focus ("Sustainability policy," 2013): Human Capital (education and adolescent development); Social Capital (societal issues); Environmental Capital (environmental sustainability); and Productive Capital (job creation). In the 1990s, it refocused its efforts on sustainable development in regions within northeastern Brazil, where the human development index is far below that of other regions within the country ("Sustainability policy," 2013). In 2007, Odebrecht expanded into bio-energy with its ETH Bioenergia division. Sugarcane ethanol and other sustainable biofuels were established as the focus ("Sustainability policy," 2013). As of 2012, Odebrecht had 162 projects inventoried for greenhouse-gas emissions and achieved 74 percent waste diversion ("Sustainability policy," 2013).

Odebrecht accomplishes its strategic CSR through its code of conduct, the philanthropic Odebrecht Foundation, and its sustainability policy.

Odebrecht: code of conduct

Odebrecht utilizes a strategic CSR code of conduct and cultural philosophy to achieve results. Titled "Odebrecht Entrepreneurial Technology," or "TEO," the code outlines the company's philosophy on business actions and ethics. This document incorporates various sustainable CSR concepts into its principles while also stating that improving shareholder returns is one of its primary goals ("TEO business culture: General criteria," 2013). General criteria for Odebrecht's operations, as outlined in the document, include promoting employee wellbeing and quality of life, ensuring safe operations, and conserving the environment in the regions in which it operates ("TEO business culture: General criteria," 2013).

One of the four sections of the TEO code is dedicated solely to corporate social responsibility. Within this section, Odebrecht outlines the goals of improving quality of life for its customers, conducting business operations that improve socio-economic development within the region, creating local jobs, reinvesting profits to improve local development, and protecting the environment while conducting business ("TEO business culture: General criteria," 2013). These outwardly sustainability-oriented goals all aim to improve the health of the local society in which Odebrecht operates.

Odebrecht Foundation: strategic philanthropy

The Odebrecht Foundation, established in 1965, functions as a separate philanthropic entity sponsored by Odebrecht. In 2012 alone, the foundation invested $18 million across more than 300 communities ("Social programs," 2013). Originally devised as a pension fund for Odebrecht employees, the foundation has since grown into a CSR, sustainability-focused institution. Furthermore, the CSR efforts of the foundation are aimed at preparing the youth of the region to enter the workforce as professionals ("Social programs," 2013). In the 1990s, the primary focus of the Odebrecht Foundation shifted inward to resolving the social issues of the Southern Bahia Lowlands region of northeastern Brazil through employment training and job creation. Ultimately, the long-term goal of the foundation is to bring sustainable revenue through ecotourism to that developing region of Brazil ("Social programs," 2013). To create additional awareness and promote Odebrecht's CSR initiatives in all areas where the company operates, the foundation strategically encourages sustainability in engineering through the "Odebrecht Awards for Sustainable Development," which are awarded to students in various countries for their solutions to environmental issues ("Social programs," 2013).

Odebrecht: sustainability policy

Odebrecht's sustainable corporate initiatives, outlined in its "sustainability policy," strategically divide the company's CSR–sustainable goals into five categories: economic, social, cultural, environmental, and political ("Sustainability policy," 2013).

Economic development includes achieving financial sustainability for clients, shareholders, and the regions where Odebrecht conducts business. Odebrecht has the goal of bringing new technology to the forefront and reinvesting in its areas of operations ("Sustainability policy," 2013). By economically acting in a socially responsible manner, Odebrecht can work towards achieving a sustainable customer base within those regions.

Socially, Odebrecht outlines three CSR-related development pillars: develop jobs and bring income to areas where it conducts business; educate and formulate children into professional adults; and encourage citizenship and governance. The sustainability policy also values culture and encourages diversity amongst employees and respect for all. To help achieve this, local art and culture are encouraged through sponsorship when Odebrecht conducts business in a new region. This sponsorship results in books, CDs, and art that reflect and preserve local culture and customs ("Sustainability policy," 2013).

Environmental responsibility includes waste reduction, energy use, resource renewal, and carbon-dioxide emissions reduction. Odebrecht uses emission reduction as its primary method of measuring environmental CSR impact, starting with the first greenhouse-gas emission inventory to track carbon dioxide at plants. Odebrecht has seen significant success environmentally, with Braskem reducing emissions by 13.6 percent in two years ("Sustainability policy," 2013).

Political participation includes the promotion of political policies in the countries in which Odebrecht operates, with the goal of encouraging sustainability initiatives. Recent examples of Odebrecht's participation include its contribution to the UN Climate Change Conference Carbon Forum, partnering with Angola and UNICEF to distribute polio vaccines, partnering with the government of Peru to train leaders and conserve resources, and joining Brazil's Ministry of Social Development to develop the "Believe" program ("Sustainability policy," 2013). The company's ETH Bioenergia division has worked to end child labor, participated in the sustainability-focused "New Earth Leaders" organization, and successfully campaigned to create the first National Industrial Learning Service unit at the Araguaia Center ("Sustainability policy," 2013).

Conclusions

CSR is a core element of non-market strategy. As the business environment becomes more global, more complex, and more volatile, new actors and issues emerge that challenge and engage business. These non-market actors and issues transcend government officials, agencies, and policies and increasingly include civil society generally, and non-governmental organizations in particular. With growing awareness of the challenges of sustainability, human rights, employment safety and working conditions, and other social issues, companies must actively participate in responses to these vexing problems.

As firms consider CSR as an integral part of their non-market strategies they can create new avenues for growth and development that incorporate social and environmental concerns, and, in some instances, leverage these global trends to advance their commercial success. Countless companies such as Odebrecht have already demonstrated the potential of viewing CSR as an opportunity to advance business interests while also addressing important social issues.

Bibliography

Aaronson, S. and Reeves, J. (2002). *Corporate Responsibility in the Global Village: The Role of Public Policy.* Washington, DC: National Policy Association.

Ackerman, R. W. (1973). How companies respond to social demands. *Harvard Business Review*, 51(4): 88–98.

"Annual report" (2013). Odebrecht. Accessed March 2, 2014. www.odebrecht.com/en/publications/annual-reports.

Baron, D. P. (1995). The non-market strategy system. *Sloan Management Review*, 37(1): 73–85.

— (1997). Integrated strategy and international trade disputes: The Kodak–Fujifilm case. *Journal of Economics and Management Strategy*, 6(1): 291–346.

Baron, D. (2001). Private politics, corporate social responsibility and integrated strategy. *Journal of Economics and Management Strategy*, 10: 7–45.

Baron, D. P. and Diermeier, D. (2007). Strategic activism and non-market strategy. *Journal of Economics and Management Strategy*, 16(3): 599–634.

Bartley, T. and Child, C. (2007). Shaming the corporation: Reputation, globalization, and the dynamics of anti-corporate movements. Working paper, Department of Sociology, Indiana University.

Boddewyn, J. and Doh, J. (2011). Global strategy and the collaboration of MNEs, NGOs, and governments for the provisioning of collective goods in emerging markets. *Global Strategy Journal*, 1(34): 345–61.

Bondy, K., Matten, D., and Moon, J. (2004). The adoption of voluntary codes of conduct in MNCs: A three-country comparative study. *Business and Society Review*, 109(4): 449–77.

Bowen, H. (1953). *Social Responsibilities of the Businessman*. New York: Harper.

Brammer, S. and Millington, A. (2008). Does it pay to be different? An analysis of the relationship between corporate social and financial performance. *Strategic Management Journal*, 29(12): 1325–43.

Brereton, D. (2002). The role of self-regulation in improving corporate social performance: The case of the mining industry. Paper given at the Australian Institute of Criminology Conference on Current Issues in Regulation: Enforcement and Compliance, Melbourne, September.

Carroll, A. B. (1979). A three-dimensional conceptual model of corporate performance. *Academy of Management Review*, 4(4): 497–505.

— (1999). Corporate social responsibility: Evolution of a definitional construct. *Business and Society*, 38(3): 268–95.

Chesbrough, H., Ahern, S., Finn, M., and Guerraz, S. (2006). Business models for technology in the developing world: The role of non-governmental organizations. *California Management Review*, 48(3): 48–76.

Cochran, P. L., and Wood, R. A. (1984). Corporate social responsibility and financial performance. *Academy of Management Journal*, 27(1): 42–56.

Dahan, N. M., Doh, J. P., Oetzel, J., and Yaziji, M. (2010). Corporate–NGO collaboration: Co-creating new business models for developing markets. *Long Range Planning*, 43(2): 326–42.

Davis, K. (1967). Understanding the social responsibility puzzle. *Business Horizons*, 10(4): 45–50.

— (1973). The case for and against business assumption of social responsibilities. *Academy of Management Journal*, 16(2): 312–22.

Diller, J. (1999). A social conscience in the global marketplace? Labour dimensions of codes of conduct, social labelling and investor initiatives. *International Labour Review*, 138(2): 99–129.

DiMaggio, P. and Powell, W. W. (1983). The iron cage revisited: Institutional isomorphism and collective rationality in organizational fields. *American Sociological Review*, 48(2): 147–60.

Doh, J. P. and Lucea, R. (2013). So close yet so far: Integrating global and non-market strategy. *Global Strategy Journal*, 3(2): 171–94.

Doh, J. P., Lawton, T. C., and Rajwani, T. (2012). Advancing non-market strategy research: Institutional perspectives in a changing world. *Academy of Management Perspectives*, 26(3): 22–39.

Doh, J. P., Lawton, T., Rajwani, T., and Paroutis, S. (2013). Why your company may need a chief external officer. *Organizational Dynamics*, 43(2): 96–104.

Donaldson, T. (1982). *Corporations and Morality*. Englewood Cliffs, NJ: Prentice-Hall.

Donaldson, T. and Preston, L. E. (1995). The stakeholder theory of the corporation: Concepts, evidence, and implications. *Academy of Management Review*, 20(1): 65–91.

Drucker, P. F. (1954). *The Practice of Management*. New York: Collins.

— (1984). Converting social problems into business opportunities: The new meaning of corporate social responsibility. *California Management Review*, 26(2): 53–63.

Eisenhardt, K. M. and Schoonhoven, C. B. (1996). Resource-based view of strategic alliance formation: Strategic and social effects in entrepreneurial firms. *Organization Science*, 7(2): 136–50.

Erhemjamts, O., Li, Q., and Venkateswaran, A. (2013). Corporate social responsibility and its impact on firms' investment policy, organizational structure, and performance. *Journal of Business Ethics*, 118: 395–412.

Fitch, H. G. (1976). Achieving corporate social responsibility. *Academy of Management Review*, 1(1): 38–46.

Frederick, W. C. (1960). The growing concern over business responsibility. *California Management Review*, 2(4): 54–61.

— (2006). *Corporation, Be Good! The Story of Corporate Social Responsibility*. Indianapolis, IN: Dogear.

Freeman, E. R. (1984). *Strategic Management: A Stakeholder Approach*. Boston, MA: Pitman.

Friedman, M. (1962). *Capitalism and Freedom*. Chicago: University of Chicago Press.

— (1970). "The social responsibility of a business is to increase its profits." *New York Times Magazine*, September 13.

Griffin, J. J. and Mahon, J. F. (1997). The corporate social performance and corporate financial performance debate: Twenty-five years of incomparable research. *Business and Society*, 36: 5–31.

Heald, M. (1957). Management's responsibility to society: The growth of an idea. *Business History Review*, 31(4): 375–84.

Hillenbrand, C., Money, K., and Ghobadian, A. (2013). Unpacking the mechanism by which corporate responsibility impacts stakeholder relationships. *British Journal of Management*, 24(1): 127–46.

Holt, D. and Barkemeyer, R. (2012). Media coverage of sustainable development issues: Attention cycles or punctuated equilibrium? *Sustainable Development*, 20(1): 1–17.

Husted, B. W. and Allen, D. B. (2010). *Corporate Social Strategy: Stakeholder Engagement and Competitive Advantage*. Cambridge: Cambridge University Press.

Jones, T. M. (1980). Corporate social responsibility revisited, redefined. *California Management Review*, 22(3): 59–67.

Katsoulakos, P., Koutsodimou, M., Matraga, A., and Williams, L. (2004). *A Historic Perspective on the CSR Movement*. CSRQuest Sustainability Framework. Accessed December 8, 2014. www.csrquest. net/uploadfiles/1D.pdf.

Khanna, T. and Palepu, K. (1999). The right way to restructure conglomerates in emerging markets. *Harvard Business Review*, July–August: 125–33.

Klein, N. (2001). *No Logo: Taking Aim at the Brand Bullies*. New York: Picador.

Kristoffersen, I., Gerrans, P., and Clark-Murphy, M. (2005). The corporate social responsibility and the theory of the firm. Finance and Economics and FIMARC Working Paper Series, Edith Cowan University.

Lawton, T. C., Doh, J. P., and Rajwani, T. (2014). *Aligning for Advantage: Competitive Strategies for the Political and Social Arenas*. Oxford: Oxford University Press.

Lee, M. D. P. (2008). A review of the theories of corporate social responsibility: Its evolutionary path and the road ahead. *International Journal of Management Reviews*, 10(1): 53–73.

Lenox, M. J. and Nash, J. (2003). Industry self-regulation and adverse selection: A comparison across four trade association programs. *Business Strategy and the Environment*, 12(6): 343–56.

Levitt, T. (1958). The dangers of social responsibility. *Harvard Business Review*, 36(5): 41–50.

Lieberman, M. and Asaba, S. (2006). Why do firms imitate each other? *Academy of Management Review*, 31: 366–85.

Maitland, A. (2005). Industries seek safety in numbers. *FT Responsible Business*, Special Report, November 18.

Margolis, J. D. and Walsh, J. P. (2003). Misery loves companies: Rethinking social initiatives by business. *Administrative Science Quarterly*, 48(2): 268–305.

Margolis, J. D., Elfenbein, H. A., and Walsh, J. P. (2007). Does it pay to be good? A meta-analysis and redirection of research on the relationship between corporate social and financial performance. Working paper, Harvard Business School.

Matten, D. and Moon, J. (2008). "Implicit" and "explicit" CSR: A conceptual framework for a comparative understanding of corporate social responsibility. *Academy of Management Review*, 33(2): 404–24.

McInnes, D. (1996). Can self-regulation succeed? *Canadian Banker*, 103(2): 30–6.

McWilliams, A. and Siegel, D. (2000). Corporate social responsibility and financial performance: Correlation or misspecification? *Strategic Management Journal*, 21: 603–9.

— (2001). Corporate social responsibility: A theory of the firm perspective. *Academy of Management Review*, 26(1): 7–127.

McWilliams, A., Siegel, D. S., and Wright, P. M. (2006). Guest editors' introduction: Corporate social responsibility: Strategic implications. *Journal of Management Studies*, 43: 1–18.

Mitchell, R. K., Agle, B. R., and Wood, D. J. (1997). Toward a theory of stakeholder identification and salience: Defining the principle of who and what really counts. *Academy of Management Review*, 22(4): 853–86.

Moura-Leite, R. C. and Padgett, R. C. (2011). Historical background of corporate social responsibility. *Social Responsibility Journal*, 7(4): 528–39.

O'Rourke, D. (2005). Market movements: Nongovernmental organization strategies to influence global production and consumption. *Journal of Industrial Ecology*, 9: 115–28.

Parker, B. and Selsky, J. W. (2004). Interface dynamics in cause-based partnerships: An exploration of emergent culture. *Nonprofit and Voluntary Sector Quarterly*, 33(3): 458–88.

Porter, M. E. and Kramer, M. R. (2002). The competitive advantage of corporate philanthropy. *Harvard Business Review*, 80(12): 56–68.

— (2006). Strategy and society: The link between competitive advantage and corporate social responsibility. *Harvard Business Review*, 84: 78–92.

Post, J. and Preston, L. (1981). *Private Management and Public Policy: The Principle of Public Responsibility*. Stanford, CA: Stanford University Press.

Preston, L. E. and O'Bannon, D. P. (1997). The corporate social–financial performance relationship: A typology and analysis. *Business and Society*, 36: 419–29.

Ramamurti, R. and Doh, J. (2004). Rethinking foreign infrastructure investment in developing countries. *Journal of World Business*, 39(2): 151–67.

Rondinelli, D. A. and London, T. (2003). How corporations and environmental groups cooperate: Assessing cross-sector alliances and collaborations. *Academy of Management Executive*, 17(1): 61–76.

Ruf, B. M. K., Muralidhar, R. M., Brown, J. J., and Paul, K. (2001). An empirical investigation of the relationship between change in corporate social performance and financial performance: A stakeholder theory perspective. *Journal of Business Ethics*, 32(2): 143–57.

Scott, C., Cafaggi, F., and Senden, L. (2011). The conceptual and constitutional challenge of transnational private regulation. *Journal of Law and Society*, 38(1): 1–19.

Sethi, S. P. (1975). Dimensions of corporate social performance: An analytical framework. *California Management Review*, 17(3): 58–64.

"Social programs" (2013). Odebrecht. Accessed February 22, 2014. www.odebrecht.com/relatorio2012/en/acao-social/.

Stanwick, P. A. and Stanwick, D. (1998). The relationship between corporate social performance and organizational size, financial performance, and environmental performance: An empirical examination. *Journal of Business Ethics*, 17: 195–204.

"Sustainability policy" (2013). Odebrecht. Accessed February 22, 2014. www.odebrecht-usa.com/en/sustainability/sustainability-policy.

"TEO business culture: General criteria" (2013). Odebrecht. Accessed February 22, 2014. www.odebrecht.com/en/odebrecht-organization/teo-business-culture#general_criteria.

Truss, W. M. P. (1998). Codes of conduct policy framework. Competitive Australia, Industry Science Tourism Consumer Affairs, Government of Australia. Accessed November 7, 2003. www.selfregulation.gov.au/publications/CodesOfConduct-PolicyFramework/Conduct_Policy Framework.pdf.

Van Tulder, R. and Kolk, A. (2001). Multinationality and corporate ethics: Codes of conduct in the sporting goods industry. *Journal of International Business Studies*, 32(2): 267–83.

Vogel, D. (2010). The private regulation of global corporate conduct achievements and limitations. *Business and Society*, 49(1): 68–87.

Waddock, S. A. and Graves, S. B. (1997). The corporate social performance. *Strategic Management Journal*, 8(4): 303–19.

Wood, D. J. (1991). Corporate social performance revisited. *Academy of Management Review*, 16(4): 691–718.

Yaziji, M. and Doh, J. (2009). *NGOs and Corporations: Conflict and Collaboration*. Cambridge: Cambridge University Press.

8

Corporate political activity

Anna John, Tazeeb S. Rajwani and Thomas C. Lawton

The creation and preservation of competitive advantage remains the central concern of strategic managers (Lawton et al., 2013). Throughout this book, the contributors argue that in the modern world economy, the competitive advantage of a company is determined as much by its non-market strategy as it is by its market engagement. Following on Chapter 7's discussion of corporate social responsibility (CSR), in this chapter we focus on the second pillar of non-market strategy, usually referred to in the literature as "corporate political activity" (CPA). This ranges from lobbying government through the use of political campaign contributions, to sharing information with political or regulatory actors, to attending political action committee meetings on policy formulation. Therefore, the key objectives of this chapter are to reflect on the various perspectives in the field, shed light on the dominant theoretical constructs in CPA, and set out a future research agenda. Our discussion underpins numerous subsequent chapters of this book.

In this chapter we present a CPA framework and discuss it from the perspective of value creation. A particular emphasis is placed on how value is viewed by different research domains and how it is shaped by corporate political options and choices. Even though there is a broad range of theoretical constructs and approaches in CPA research (Getz, 2001), we focus on the two main approaches in the field: institutional theory; and the resources and capabilities perspective (Hillman, 2003).

CPA and the non-market

Non-market strategy is often conceived of as a bi-dimensional activity. In addition to CSR, it comprises CPA – corporate attempts to influence government policy for the firm's benefits (Lawton et al., 2013). Figure 8.1 shows the CPA aspect of non-market strategy used by firms. It is worth noting that it should not be considered in isolation from CSR. Instead, the two forms of non-market activity may interact and mutually reinforce each other, resulting in "responsible CPA." Furthermore, this relationship may shape the overall non-market strategy and influence its effectiveness.

Non-market strategy scholars focusing on CPA are often organized into three research threads, focusing on value, options, and choices and structure of firm-level political action

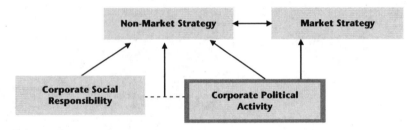

Figure 8.1 CPA as an element of non-market strategy

Source: Adapted from Lawton et al. (2014).

Figure 8.2 A conceptual framework of a CPA system

Source: Based on Lawton et al. (2013).

(Getz, 2001; Mitnick, 2001; Lawton et al., 2013: 9). A conceptual framework in Figure 8.2 shows the structure of CPA systems as a composite of these three issues. While considering the issue of value, we will discuss why firms engage in political activity. The issues of options and choices aim to explain how firms generate value from CPA. Specifically, the issue of options comes across the question of how firms organize their political efforts in response to environmental pressures by adopting different approaches, strategies, and tactics. In the discussion of choices of CPA we look into factors underlying firms' selection of certain political options.

An issue of value

Is CPA beneficial to firms?

CPA is believed to be a useful complement to market activities because of its favorable implications for firms and their value (Shaffer, 1995). Traditionally, with very few exceptions (Shepsle and Weingast, 1984), the research assumed positive effects of CPA on business (Baysinger et al., 1985; Keim and Zeithaml, 1986; Hillman et al., 1999; Puck et al., 2013). By and large, the empirical substantiation of this assumption was very scarce (Shaffer, 1995; Hillman et al., 2004). According to Hillman et al. (1999, 2004), the inability of earlier studies to supply empirical evidence about the political behavior–firm benefits link might be explained by measuring difficulties. The major challenge was in linking political activities to measurable firm-level performance outcomes. For example, it was hard to establish political impact on intangible performance variables such as legitimacy, influence, and access to resources (Hillman et al., 1999). Moreover, some studies stressed that the benefits from CPA do not always accrue solely to that firm. Instead, there are always some "free-riding" firms, suggesting a collective impact from individual political efforts (Keim and Baysinger, 1988; Hillman et al., 1999).

Despite these challenges, recent studies have become increasingly concerned with empirical validation of this assumption. Yet, the results are inconclusive. On the one hand, some authors have found that CPA can have a positive impact on the market performance of firms

(Bonardi et al., 2006; de Figueiredo and Silverman, 2006; Niessen and Ruenzi, 2010). For example, using data from the international air transport sector, Shaffer et al. (2000) showed that firms with a greater level of political activity attained a positive change in their market position, relative to competitors. Also, some research concluded that CPA improves the financial performance of firms. For instance, Hill et al. (2013) suggested that prior investments in lobbying helped to accrue greater excess returns and shareholder wealth. In a similar manner, Cooper et al. (2010) suggested that contributions to political campaigns might help firms to increase their future returns. Moreover, Wei (2006) showed that a firm's ability to engage and associate with government significantly improved its financial performance.

Furthermore, political activity may entail favorable decisions by government officials. For instance, Wei (2006) found that different political strategy elements, such as involvement in government affairs and direct association with governmental agents, increased access to government resources. Bonardi et al. (2006) found that US utility firms capable of initiating reviews of public utilities commissions and having experience in working with rate regulators were more likely to be granted higher rates of return, which are the major source of profit. In a similar manner, de Figueiredo and Silverman (2006: 598) discovered that an increase in expenditures on lobbying of legislators by a university resulted in an increase in its earmarks, or "non-competitive grants written into appropriations bills by legislators."

On the other hand, some authors found that political activities did not always predetermine favorable outcomes for firms (Hadani and Schuler, 2013; Puck et al., 2013). Specifically, political engagement might pose a risk to the security of assets. For example, Li and Qian (2013) suggested that, as they are often incompatible with the interests of controlling shareholders, the political ties of CEOs increased firms' risks of corporate takeover. In a similar vein, political activity did not always improve the market performance of firms. For instance, Sheng et al. (2011) found that political connections did not necessarily contribute to growth in sales and market share.

Likewise, it has been suggested that political activity might have an undesired impact on the financial performance of firms. For instance, Hadani and Schuler (2013) demonstrated that larger cumulative political investments reduced market value and return on sales of firms. Furthermore, market value dropped in firms whose boards of directors comprised more members with political ties (Hadani and Schuler, 2013). Similarly, Sheng et al. (2011) found that political ties, or *guanxi*, in the Chinese context did not always help firms to improve their financial performance (e.g., return on investment and profit growth). This is consistent with the argument of Sun, Mellahi, and Wright (2012) that different types of political activity (e.g., political ties) do not always benefit a firm; instead, they may occasionally transform into liabilities.

The inconsistencies in results may be explained by the interference of temporal, contextual, and firm factors. The temporal moderators are those that consider the role of timing in political activity effectiveness. For instance, the coincidence of a political action with an unforeseen political or business event, process, or change, and their duration, may occasionally enhance or distort the intended effects of political efforts. However, scholars have generally overlooked this group of moderators. An exception is a study by Frynas et al. (2006) that discussed the role of political business environment changes in the effects of political resources on the first-mover advantage of firms. The authors suggested that political resources will be less conducive to first-mover advantage in a new market in times of changes in political business environment. Overall, the temporal moderators should be explored in greater detail in future research.

As for the contextual moderators, these may include factors in the external environment, such as institutions, government activity, and market ambience. For example, Sheng et al.

(2011) suggested that the effectiveness of political ties may have two major groups of moderators: institutional environment and market environment. The institutional environment was a composite of enforcement inefficiency and government support moderators, whereas technological turbulence and demand uncertainty constituted the market environment. It was found that political ties helped to improve the financial and market performance of firms where government support and technological turbulence are lower. By contrast, political ties worsened performance under conditions with greater law enforcement efficiency and higher technological turbulence.

Some authors discussed the role of governmental and competition moderators. Specifically, Frynas et al. (2006) postulated that political resources are more likely to lead to first-mover advantage in contexts with greater host government interference in the industry, greater assistance from the home and host governments, and greater cooperation between the home and host governments. Regarding the competition moderations, the study posited that political resources will be more conducive to first-mover advantages when second movers have less political and non-political resources (Frynas et al., 2006).

In addition, some authors emphasized the importance of firm-related moderators. For instance, Puck et al. (2013) concluded that the effects of political strategies depend upon firm visibility. Specifically, political strategies tended to increase risk exposure for firms with high visibility. In a similar vein, Frynas et al. (2006) proposed that political resources are more likely to help to achieve first-mover advantages for firms with greater richness of non-political resources and a higher degree of integration between political and non-political resources. Furthermore, Oliver and Holzinger (2008) emphasized the role of political and non-political firm dynamic capabilities in the effectiveness of their political strategies.

Even though it does not always entail positive outcomes, CPA remains on the agendas of many managers. Some authors argue that firms do not necessarily engage in political activity because of its value. Instead, engagement in political activity may be driven by personal managerial imperatives and biases (Hadani and Schuler, 2013). However, despite their personal motives, most managers aspire to increase the legitimacy of their CPA by enhancing its benefits to the firm.

Meanwhile, it is possible that inconsistencies in the effects of CPA on firm value may be explained by differences in theoretical views underlying studies. Aiming to address this problem, Lawton et al. (2013) revisited the issue of CPA value by integrating existing studies into distinctive domains that have implications for performance. Having examined different theoretical approaches and conceptual views across papers, Lawton et al. (2013) proposed three domains: resources and capabilities; institutions; and political environment.

Resources and capabilities focus on CPA value

The resources and capabilities domain incorporates studies extending the resource-based view from the market environment to an element of the non-market environment – CPA. Specifically, this domain assumes that each firm is a unique bundle of political resources and capabilities that are deployed to improve competitiveness both in the political environment and in the market. Aiming to surpass its competitors, a firm may refer to organizational resources (e.g., an in-house office or a permanent regulatory person), relational resources (e.g., relationships with policy-makers), public image (e.g., perception of stakeholders), reputation (e.g., firm responsibility), or finances (e.g., direct contributions to political campaigns and indirect contributions to events and conferences) (Lawton et al., 2013).

A closer look at this domain suggests that some of its studies discussed political resources in relatively predictable, or endogenous, contexts where firms can anticipate political events, such as market deregulation and the adoption of new legislation, and prepare responses to them (Kim and Prescott, 2005; Frynas et al., 2006; Capron and Chatain, 2008). However, drawing on an extension of the resource-based view – the dynamic capabilities perspective – Teece et al. (1997) suggested conceptualizing political capabilities as a form of higher-order dynamic capabilities allowing for sustainable competitive advantage or maintaining existing competitive parity in highly unpredictable, or exogenous, environments (Oliver and Holzinger, 2008).

The major contribution of the resources and capabilities domain is that, while taking a firm as a unit of analysis, it helps to develop a better understanding of CPA micro-foundations and how they create firm benefits, such as the ability to reduce risk exposure, the ability to generate and sustain competitive advantage, and the ability to improve performance (Lawton et al., 2013). Another contribution of this domain is that it considers not only the reactive nature of CPA where firms respond to threats in the political environment but also the possibility of using resources and capabilities in a proactive manner in order to take advantage of political opportunities.

Yet, Lawton et al. (2013) argue that, despite its contributions to research on the value of CPA, the resources and capabilities domain has some weaknesses that should be addressed. First and foremost, it considers the benefits of political action only at the firm level, without consideration of the collective efforts of firms in the political field. Meanwhile, for firms with scarce resources (e.g., new entrants to the market and SMEs), individual actions may be too costly and, when this is the case, the collective measures allowing pulling resources and capabilities from several co-negotiators may be an alternative way of gaining greater political weight and attaining the desired political outcomes. Another weakness is that this domain does not clarify if and how some political resources and capabilities may occasionally transform from assets into liabilities for firms (Sun et al., 2011).

Meanwhile, the resources and capabilities domain has a number of avenues for researchers to explore in the future. Lawton et al. (2013) call for studies that will look at political-resources configurations within different countries that are directly involved in market and non-market strategy simultaneously. They suggest that such configurations might include: the combinations of political resources and capabilities with financial systems and their regulation; the labor market institutions and their regulations (e.g., trade unions, dispute settlement mechanisms, training and education); the corporate sector (e.g., ownership types, trade associations, value/supply chain relationships); and the culture of the country (attitudes toward business).

Institutions focus on CPA value

This domain draws upon an institutional perspective (Lawton et al., 2013). Drawing on the important work of Hotho and Pedersen (2012), we find that a better understanding of the value of CPA can benefit from three distinctive approaches: new institutional economics (North, 1990), new institutional perspectives (DiMaggio and Powell, 1983), and national business systems (Jackson and Deeg, 2008a). The new institutional economics perspective (North, 1990) contributes to the research into political activity benefits by focusing on how political and regulatory uncertainty shapes firms' decisions. By and large, studies in this stream are concerned with deterring the effects of institutional voids, instability in regulatory institutions, and risks of changes in institutional environment on firms and their decisions, competitiveness, and performance. Many studies agree that uncertainty due to opaque regulatory environments, underdeveloped judicial and financial systems, corruption, and engagement in inter-state political conflicts increase costs and, therefore, impede operations, strategic moves, and performance of firms (Delios and Henisz, 2000; Wei, 2000; Henisz and Delios, 2001; Grosse and Trevino, 2005; Li and Vashchilko, 2010). The theoretical emphasis on institutional voids and political and regulatory uncertainty may be particularly helpful in exploring the effectiveness of CPA in the context of developing and emerging economies (Lawton et al., 2013).

Another stream in this domain approaches the issue of CPA effectiveness from the new institutional perspective (DiMaggio and Powell, 1983), often referred to as institutional or organizational sociology (Doh, Lawton, and Rajwani, 2012). Studies in this literature strand place a particular emphasis on social structures and relationships within societies and on how their pressures influence CPA.

A distinctive feature of the new institutional research is its assumption that firms' political actions are socially embedded into softer aspects (e.g., cultures and history) and harder aspects (e.g., formal rules and enforcement systems) of institutions (Granovetter, 1985; Jackson and Deeg, 2008a, 2008b; Lawton et al., 2013). This assumption predetermines the conceptualization of political actions and their value. Specifically, political actions are conceived of as responses to institutional pressures. As in other areas (Barreto and Baden-Fuller, 2006), the value of such responses is a trade-off between a defensive objective – survival – and an offensive objective – performance. The survival objective is reactive as it aims to eliminate threats rather than search for opportunities. For example, it may be associated with the need to prevent undesired actions of policy-makers to be able to improve the competitive position and use it to remain in the market and make normal profits. By contrast, the performance objective is proactive as it presumes shaping rather than responding to the institutional environment and, most importantly, availing of its opportunities not exploited by rivals. For example, this objective may be related to gaining access to key policy-makers in order to accrue privileges needed to generate and sustain advantage over competitors and make super-normal profits.

The new institutional studies explain the survival-performance trade-off in the value of CPA. Initially, firms make political responses to the institutional pressures in order to ensure survival in both non-market and market environments. Nonetheless, triggered by similar institutional pressures, such survival-driven responses become increasingly similar and lead to homogeneity, or isomorphism, among firms. This, in turn, jeopardizes performance levels in the organizational field.

CPA may weaken performance through mimetic, normative, and coercive mechanisms of isomorphism. For example, in the case of mimetic isomorphism, politically successful firms in the market, or leaders, become a point of reference for the remaining firms, or followers, in the conditions of uncertainty (DiMaggio and Powell, 1983). The followers mimic best political practices (e.g., lobbying and corruption) of the leaders in order to survive in both non-market and market environments (Venard and Hanafi, 2008; Venard, 2009; Lawton et al., 2013). If the best practices work well for the followers too, such emulation reduces the competitive disparity between the leaders and the followers. By accumulating political benefits similar to those of the leaders, the followers may strengthen their market positions and even financial performance. Whereas the followers gradually improve their competitive position, the leaders steadily lose their competitive advantage in both non-market and market environments. In sum, mimetic isomorphism may worsen the performance of politically successful forms in the market (Barreto and Baden-Fuller, 2006). Yet, another scenario is also possible. Having emerged as economically rational choices emphasizing value maximization (Paauwe and Boselie, 2003), the best practices may be successful for the leaders (Oliver, 1997). However, following normative rationality principles and being an outcome of mere susceptibility to social influence (Paauwe and Boselie, 2003), imitation of these practices may not necessarily fit well into the followers' strategies and, if this is the case, may lead to a sub-optimal choice that damages performance (Oliver, 1997).

Likewise, the normative isomorphism in political responses to institutional pressures may also distort performance over time. The normative pressures originate in the professionalization of political activity in firms. Formal education (e.g., universities), professional networks (e.g., trade associations), and employment of professionals (e.g., former politicians) are major sources of professionalization. They inform the management of norms of behavior and make them more confident actors in the realm of business–state relations. However, by acquiring similar political skills, firms adopt homogeneous political strategies and tactics. The converging political approaches have little capacity to generate competitive advantage (Paauwe and Boselie, 2003). First, they may be sub-optimal choices imposing limits on considering alternative and, perhaps, more effective approaches. Second, professionalization-driven approaches may be more effective when adopted by a small number of firms, but they may be of little value when adopted by the majority of firms.

Also, isomorphism in CPA may weaken performance of firms through the coercive mechanism. This is typical for situations when, aiming at defending their legitimacy, firms comply with international-, national-, and industry-level legislations and regulations. Such compliance means that firms have little or no choice as to whether and which corporate political measures to undertake. This also implies that the value of corporate political decisions is constrained by the obligation to conform to a set of coercive instruments (e.g., laws, rules, directives, and regulatory body approaches) and sub-optimal choices may originate from little or no control over corporate political decisions (Oliver, 1997). For example, some coercive instruments may undermine organizations' ability and motivation to influence governmental policies to their benefit. According to Hansen and Mitchell (2000), some pro-government regulations on business–state bargaining procedures reduce firms' power and increase their costs and put them at a disadvantage vis-à-vis governments. Similarly, government regulations on, and approaches to, funding negotiations may reduce the value of – and therefore discourage – political activity among nonprofit organizations (Chavesc et al., 2004).

Studies centering on national business systems, or comparative capitalisms, comprise the third stream in the institutions domain (Hotho and Pedersen, 2012). This literature strand aims to explain the persistence of differences in CPA among national economic systems (Doh et al., 2012). Its particular emphasis is on the issue of why, despite globalization pressures to converge, firms' political approaches remain divergent across nations. Similar to other streams, this literature cluster acknowledges that firms from different jurisdictions refer to different political means to attain their goals and that a deep understanding of national peculiarities of political institutions is paramount to developing competitive advantage (Jackson and Deeg, 2008a, 2008b). However, there is a scarcity of studies providing empirical evidence as to how cross-national differences in institutional systems influence effectiveness of corporate political activities. For example, drawing upon qualitative longitudinal data from the Chinese automotive sector, Sun et al. (2010) explored the role of political embeddedness strategies in developing long-term competitive advantages by firms in host-country markets. Nonetheless, to the best of our knowledge, no studies have attempted to test the suggested hypotheses in cross-sectional research or other contexts. In addition, it remains unclear how differences across national economic systems influence firms' ability to affect policy change and their performance (e.g., market share, sales, and profitability). In sum, further research is needed to explain how the value of firms' political actions forms across jurisdictions.

Therefore, compared to other streams in this domain, the national business systems strand seems to be under-researched. Lawton et al. (2013) suggest that future work is needed to develop a better understanding of business–state relations in emerging economies. First, it is important to move beyond the institutional voids perspective of Khanna and Palepu (2005). Indeed, as the developing economies grow, it is possible to assume that their institutions become more established, too.

Political environment focus on CPA value

Lawton et al. (2013) propose this domain to describe studies having political uncertainty environment focus. This research cluster may be conceived of as an extension of the previous domain, where institutions shape corporate political activities and their effectiveness. Nonetheless, its major distinction from the institutional studies is that it shifts attention from soft aspects (e.g., national culture, uncertainty, and historical development) and toward the hard elements (e.g., norms, formal rules, enforcement systems, and uncertainty) of institutions.

An important contribution of this domain is that it takes into account political environment as a setting for CPA effects on firm performance. Political environment may either enhance or hinder the effectiveness of firms' political efforts (Lawton et al., 2013). For instance, intended corporate political measures may occasionally lead to adverse effects in politically risky contexts (Henisz and Delios, 2004; Young, 2010). According to Henisz and Delios (2004), it may be hard for firms to guarantee corporate political effectiveness in highly uncertain political contexts allowing little or no control over governmental policies. Specifically, firms' difficulty in controlling governmental policies may increase in jurisdictions where, due to the lack of veto players and the subsequent insufficiency of checks and balances in the formal policy-making apparatus, government officials feel unconstrained in their choice of policies (Henisz and Delios, 2004). Alternatively, firms may be unable to control government policies in contexts with political regime changes (Henisz and Delios, 2004). On a similar note, Young (2010) found that, contrary to their expectations, firms in Central and Eastern Europe failed to capture institutional changes and benefit from them.

Taking different standpoints to analyses of the value of CPA, the three domains have ontological boundaries. In a way, the institutions and political environment domains do not substantially differ. In fact, the political environment perspective may be conceived of as an extension of the institutions stream, with greater focus on institutions, hard elements and an additional moderator – political environment. Yet, these two domains are standing aside from the resources and capabilities cluster. For example, using a firm as a central unit of analysis, the resources and capabilities perspective centers on the micro-foundations of how the value of CPA forms. By contrast, looking at the organization fields, the institutions and political environment domains offer a macro-view as to how firms may be affected by institutional pressures.

Another distinction is related to the environmental focus. The external environment is the center of attention in the institutions and political environment domains, whereas the internal ambience is the starting point of analyses in the resources and capabilities domain. Because external environment is important to the institutions and political environment studies, they accommodate a possibility of collective political actions. By contrast, with their focus on the internal environment, the resources and capabilities studies look into the internal capacity of firms to manage their CPA and, because of this, place greater emphasis on the role of individual political efforts.

Furthermore, the domains differ in their conceptualization of the value of political efforts as well as their approaches to, and the way they see the role of a firm in, managing the effectiveness of CPA. By and large, studies in the institutions and political environment perspectives assume a passive role of the firm in the political environment. Firms do not influence environments; instead, they respond to institutional pressures. Their overall approach to corporate political activities is reactive. The value of political efforts in this case is a function of institutional pressures and is often reduced to survival objectives. Overall, the institutional pressures are assumed to have a negative impact on the effectiveness of CPA. For example, a firm may opt to leave a foreign market after an abrupt, unfavorable change in political regime. Nonetheless, the resources and capabilities domain assumes that firms are proactive players in the environment. Using unique bundles of resources and capabilities, they relentlessly search for, and take advantage of, new opportunities in order to improve their positions in the political environment and market. The proactive political behavior of firms is motivated by the desire to outperform competitors and generate super-normal profits. For instance, building upon dynamic capabilities, a firm may adjust to sudden regime changes in a country and remain in its market.

Despite their ontological boundaries, the three domains have the potential for convergence. For example, the institutions and political environment domains may benefit from ideas in the resources and capabilities domain. Some authors bring in a resource-based view to reconceptualize firms from actors which passively respond to institutional pressures into proactive players which adopt influence strategies (Frynas and Mellahi, 2003; Henisz and Delios, 2004). For instance, Frynas and Mellahi (2003) suggest that firms may use their political capabilities to avail themselves of opportunities and design highly effective political strategies even in jurisdictions with under-developed institutions (e.g., Nigeria); hence, there is a possibility to counteract the negative implications of institutions. The authors further conclude that institutions do not always constrain firm performance. Instead, companies may take advantage of fluid and risky political environments. In a similar vein, Henisz and Delios (2004) contend that the discouraging impact of institutional weaknesses and associated risks may be counterbalanced by a resource such as experience in unstable environments. In fact, by systematically entering into hazardous environments, firms are able to accumulate the capabilities they need to reduce their future risk exposure to potentially adverse effects and expand their influence on policy-makers (Henisz and Delios, 2004).

Likewise, the resources and capabilities domain may benefit from the institutions and political environment perspectives. As mentioned earlier, these place particular emphasis on the external environment. By shifting their focus from the internal ambience to the external environment, studies in the resources and capabilities domain may address their lack of focus on collective political efforts and their value. Specifically, they may examine if and how different firms in an organizational field may unite their unique resources and capabilities in order to gain a greater political weight and attain their individual goals (Oliver, 1997).

Notwithstanding, integration between the three domains is a potential avenue for future research. Lawton et al. (2013) suggest that rather than treating these research areas as largely discrete, it might be beneficial to move toward a more integrated approach that links different levels of analysis. Combining advances from three perspectives may better inform research into CPA and its value. Drawing on Oliver (1997), we argue that the resources of firms and

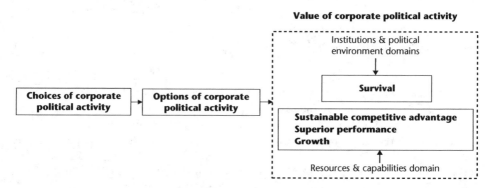

Figure 8.3 Corporate political activity with an extended version of the value component

institutions where they are embedded are complementary sources of the CPA value and, for this reason, should not be considered in isolation. This implies that firms enhance their political value by using both resources and institutions capital. In this view, political resource capital is a set of assets and competencies (e.g., the ability to build ties with key government officials in politically stable countries and the ability to adapt to new political regimes in unstable areas), which help to enhance the value in the political context and translate it into competitive advantages on the market. By contrast, the institutional capital refers to the decision context (e.g., political information systems and inter-firm alliances to share political resources) surrounding the resource capital. Figure 8.3 shows the CPA system with an extended version of the value component.

The value of CPA depends upon its options (e.g., types of corporate political tactics and strategy). According to Hill et al. (2013), the effectiveness of political tactics depends on the choice of the right channel. For example, in the case of a lobbying activity, this implies a choice between direct contributions to political campaigns from the corporate treasury and contributions via political action committees (PACs). We revisit the issue of options in the next section.

An issue of options

Firms have different options as to how they generate value from CPA. These options are related to approaches, strategies, and (associated with them) tactics of political action.

Many scholars acknowledge that political options are outcomes of firm–environment interaction. They also agree that the environment exerts pressure and poses threats to firms. According to Baysinger (1984), firms are expected to deal with three broad categories of threats to their economic activity: a threat of competition; a threat to the legitimacy of organizational goals and purposes; and a threat to methods underlying their organizational goals and purposes.

Even though researchers agree that, to a lesser or greater extent, all firms are exposed to threats and pressures in the political and institutional environments, there seems to be a divergence between studies with the institutions focus and those with the resources and capabilities focus as to how firms respond to these threats and pressures. Having different assumptions about the firm–environment interaction, the two literature streams adopt two different approaches to political activity. Specifically, the institutions studies offer a better explanation for – and, therefore, are biased to – reactive or bridging (Meznar and Nigh, 1995; Blumentritt,

2003) approaches, whereas the resources and capabilities research allows for the analysis of proactive or buffering approaches (Meznar and Nigh, 1995; Blumentritt, 2003).

The institutions focus on corporate political options

The institutional scholarship makes an assumption that firms are reactive political players who passively respond to threats and pressures of other political actors, such as competitors (Hersch and McDougall, 2000; Venard and Hanafi, 2008; Venard, 2009; Lawton et al., 2013), professionals (Greenwood et al., 2002), and government bodies (Boddewyn and Brewer, 1994; Hansen and Mitchell, 2000). These are conceptualized as constraints beyond managerial control. For instance, followers of the new institutional economics suggest that firms are repelled by political threats and, for this reason, are more likely either never to enter or to leave a potentially threatening market (Boddewyn and Brewer, 1994). In a similar manner, the new institutional studies argue that firms do not influence, but passively respond to, political actors. For example, they mimic the best practices of leading competitors in the market (Hersch and McDougall, 2000; Venard and Hanafi, 2008; Venard, 2009; Lawton et al., 2013), follow norms established by professionals (Greenwood et al., 2002), and comply with governments' coercive measures, such as new legislation and regulations (Boddewyn and Brewer, 1994).

Overall, the institutional research seems to be biased to reactive approaches at the expense of proactive options. This is because it is theoretically equipped to offer a better explanation to reactive rather than proactive political actions. Firms opt for reactive approaches to political action because they have no control over the external environment. Interestingly, the institutional research does not deny the possibility that imitating other politically active firms or following professional norms might – occasionally – result in influence strategies. Nonetheless, looking at the political activity as a macro-phenomenon without consideration of its micro-foundations fails to demonstrate if and how these influence strategies become effective at the firm level. As a result of this weakness, the institutional research into proactive options has been rather scant.

The reactive approaches underpin reactive strategies and tactics in political activity (Hillman and Hitt, 1999). For example, according to Boddewyn and Brewer (1994), reactive approaches form the basis for non-bargaining strategies – avoidance, circumvention, and compliance – which enable the avoidance of engagement into public policy. In the avoidance strategy, firms make decisions to "leave it" or opt for "no-go" (Boddewyn and Brewer, 1994). By choosing a compliance strategy, a firm passively accepts and adjusts to public policy changes without any resistance (Boddewyn and Brewer, 1994). The circumvention strategy involves illegal actions (e.g., smuggling of products and tax evasion) that firms use to reinstate their independence from governmental constraints and incentives (Stephens et al., 1991; Boddewyn and Brewer, 1994). The non-bargaining strategies are akin to Weidenbaum's (1980) passive reaction and positive anticipation. In passive reaction, a firm reacts to changes on an ad hoc basis; by contrast, it anticipates changes and incorporates them into its strategy in the case of positive anticipation. With those elements in mind, Figure 8.3, above, shows reactive approaches and strategies in the CPA system.

The resources and capabilities focus on corporate political options

The resources and capabilities studies usually neglect the assumption of the submissive role of firms in relation to their political and institutional environments. For example, scholars drawing on a resource dependence theory (Pfeffer and Salancik, 1978) stress that, despite being embedded into, and constrained by, their context, firms can undertake active political measures to reduce their environmental uncertainty and dependence upon major institutions such as governments and other organizations (Hillman et al., 2009).

In a similar manner, followers of the resource-based view claim that firms can actively manage their environments by using political resources and capabilities. By managing their environments, firms reduce their threats. For instance, with political ties and lobbying resources, they can reduce a threat of undesired actions of some competitors by getting preferential treatment terms from the government. Likewise, by means of political action committees (PACs) and in-kind contributions during elections, firms can eliminate the risk of future government initiatives against those organizational goals that conflict with societal safety and values (e.g., alcohol and tobacco production and advertising). Similarly, using grassroots campaigns, firms may influence regulations affecting methods whereby they attain their organizational goals (e.g., waste disposal, hiring, and job design).

Unlike the institutions research, the resources and capabilities studies allow for the development of a better understanding of proactive approaches to political activity. For example, bridging a macro-perspective of organizational ecology theories with a micro-view of firms, the resource dependence research directly focuses on a means to generate successful performance within a given political environment (Hillman et al., 2009). Also, looking into micro-foundations of political actions, the resource-based view studies illustrate how firms manage their performance by influencing public policy (Lawton and Rajwani, 2011).

Having more rigorous theoretical explanations, to date, scholars agree on three major stages of a decision-making process within proactive CPA. The first decision comes across as a choice between transactional and relational proactive approaches (Hillman and Hitt, 1999). The former implies that a firm postpones its political strategy development until a particular public policy issue arises. The interaction between firms and policy-makers in this case is not continuous; rather, it takes the form of a series of ad hoc transactions where the parties engage in short-term exchange relations on an issue-by-issue basis.

By contrast, the latter approach to CPA implies that businesses develop long-term relationships with policy-makers across a broad range of issues (Hillman and Hitt, 1999). Firms that follow this approach are fully equipped in advance with the necessary resources, such as political connections and experience, before a public policy issue arises (Hillman and Hitt, 1999). The relational approach has two major features. First, it usually begins with internalization of political activity as a function within a firm. Indeed, as the amount of government regulation in Europe and the USA had increased dramatically by the 1990s, many firms opted for relational approaches by creating government relations offices in Washington and Brussels and by hiring full-time representatives for government affairs (Walker, 1991; Grant, 1993). Second, the relational approach implies a deeper and more frequent involvement with governments, which has some advantages. For example, in contexts where the risk of political regime change are not very high, relational behavior allows for the control of policy-making processes and outcomes. Also, having political resources to hand helps to reduce transaction costs. According to Hillman and Keim (1995), as trust develops between the two parties, the marginal transaction costs of their relationship decline. Nonetheless, some authors sound cautious about the relational approach effectiveness in highly volatile contexts where an abrupt political regime change can transform relational political assets into liabilities (Sun et al., 2010).

The second decision of proactive political activity in the resources and capabilities research refers to the choice of participation levels (Olson, 1965; Hillman and Hitt, 1999). Firms can pursue their competitive advantage through either individual or collective participation. Individual participation refers to solitary efforts by firms to affect public policy, whereas collective participation is about the collaboration and cooperation of two or more firms in the public policy process (Hillman and Hitt, 1999). For example, firms may lobby either individually or collectively, as members of trade associations.

The third decision in a proactive political process is related to the choice of strategies. By and large, political strategies proposed in earlier studies were not justified theoretically (Sethi, 1982; Baysinger et al., 1985; Keim and Zeithaml, 1986; Getz, 1993; Oberman, 1993; Lord, 1995). In reply to those classifications, Hillman and Hitt (1999) developed a taxonomy based on an exchange theory. Conceptualizing a public policy process as a market with a mutual interdependence between those supplying and demanding policy, Hillman and Hitt (1999) introduced three generic strategies based on major political resources exchanged: information; financial incentive; and constituency-building. The information strategy targets policy-makers by providing information. The financial incentive strategy aims at influencing policy-makers by providing financial incentives. The constituency-building strategy helps to affect policy-makers indirectly through the support of constituents (e.g., voters and grassroots). Figure 8.4 presents the CPA system with an extended version of the options element.

Corporate political options and value

As mentioned earlier, firms have different options as to how they generate value from CPA. Yet, the link between corporate political options and value has not been fully explored. Meanwhile, it seems that following either the institutions approach or the resources and capabilities approach may impede future advances in this under-researched area. As shown earlier, reactive options remain the domain of the institutions research. This offers a macro-view as to how firms respond to institutional pressures in order to survive (de Villa et al., 2014). However, as micro-level analyses are beyond its scope, this research does not go further by looking at what happens to firm performance after such responses have been made. As a result, the value of reactive political options remains unclear. Future studies may need to explore the assumption that reactive political strategies are of value to firms by helping them to survive and minimize the negative effects of institutional pressures. To develop a better understanding of the link between reactive political options and their value to firms, scholars may need to enrich the institutions macro-view with firm-level analyses of the resources and capabilities approach. This would also help to examine another under-researched issue – the role of resources and capabilities of firms in generating value out of reactive political activities. For example, it would enable exploring which reactive political strategies and their outcomes draw on which resources and capabilities. It is possible that non-political resources and capabilities may be sufficient for the successful implementation of passive reaction, or ad hoc action strategies. Therefore, firms may need to be more resourceful and develop not only non-political resources but also political resources (e.g., political intelligence) to pursue anticipation strategies (e.g., de Villa et al., 2014).

By contrast, the research into proactive political options has benefited mainly from the resources and capabilities approach. This refers to the internal capacity of firms to generate value out of proactive political activity. Yet, despite its explicit focus on the political activity–value link, the research into proactive options has not fully explored the role of institutional environment. With very few exceptions (Frynas et al., 2006; Sheng et al., 2011), it makes an assumption that firms can manage institutional environment by using resources and

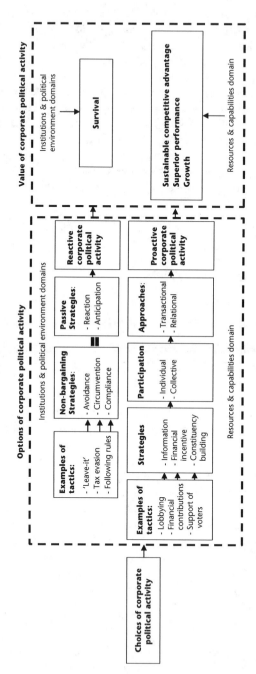

Figure 8.4 Corporate political activity system with extended versions of the value and options components

capabilities, but does not explain if and how institutional pressures impede or enhance the efforts of firms. To address this gap, future studies may need to refer to the institutions perspective by bringing an institutional context moderator into their analysis.

In sum, the future research into the link between corporate political options and value will benefit from integrating the institutions and resources and capabilities approaches. Blending the institutions approach to reactive political options with the resources and capabilities approach will help to explain how firms generate value by responding to institutional pressures. In a similar manner, bringing together the resources and capabilities and institutions approaches will facilitate a more holistic view of performance outcomes of proactive political options as a function of not only firms' efforts but also institutional forces enabling or weakening those efforts.

An issue of choice

The choice of corporate political options depends upon a range of factors (Lawton et al., 2013). These have been considered within various theoretical frameworks. However, the largest proportion of factors originates from two literature streams: the research on institutions and the research on resources and capabilities.

The institutions focus on corporate political choices

The studies looking at institutions agree that corporate political choices are a function of the institutional environment. For instance, new institutional economics research (North, 1990) centers on how institutional voids, instability in regulatory institutions, and risks of changes in the institutional environment influence corporate political choices. Interestingly, the environmental uncertainty is a predictor of both reactive and proactive political approaches (Meznar and Nigh, 1995). This implies that, in the face of political instability, firms do not refer to a single method, but rather combine avoidance and adaptation measures with influence initiatives.

The new institutional perspective (DiMaggio and Powell, 1983) explores how corporate political choices are affected by institutional pressures. Some authors have shown that decisions about political approaches, strategies, and tactics are the result of mimetic isomorphism among industry competitors. For example, Schuler et al. (2002) found that the political practices of firms were related to overall industry-level political activity. Likewise, competitors imitated each other's contributions in Hersch and McDougall's (2000) study of PAC donations.

Studies that center on national business systems (Jackson and Deeg, 2008a) examine different corporate political choices across national economic systems. According to Hansen and Mitchell (2001), firm preferences for certain political practices vary across countries: significant differences were found between political activities in the USA and UK; likewise, political initiatives in the USA differed substantially from those in Canada and Japan.

The resources and capabilities focus on corporate political choices

Studies in this stream assume that decisions about corporate political options depend upon the amount of resources and capabilities a firm owns and the dependence on other political stakeholders (e.g., government) in its access to these resources and capabilities (Meznar and Nigh, 1995). Resource-based view advocates posit that endowment in resources defines a firm's ability to engage in political activity (Schuler and Rehbein, 1997). Specifically, the more resources and capabilities a firm has, the greater its power in the political arena and the more active it is in influencing public policy. Yet, in line with the resource-dependence perspective (Pfeffer and Salancik, 1978), political activity will be greater among those firms whose access to resources depends upon other actors in the political environment (e.g., government). By and large, the research into resource-related factors – firm size, firm slack, firm diversification level, firm ownership, firm age, firm structures, firm culture, and firm dependency upon other political actors (e.g., government) – confirms these hypotheses. The next section will look at each of these factors in detail.

Resource-based view

Firm size

The resource-based view scholars agree that firm size predetermines the approach to, and the level of participation in, political activity. Firm size is measured by sales, assets (Meznar and Nigh, 1995), market share (Schuler, 1996), public visibility (Hansen and Mitchell, 2000), and number of employees (Meznar and Nigh, 1995). Larger firms – those with greater sales, assets, market share, greater visibility, and number of employees (Meznar and Nigh, 1995) – have more resources and are more likely to follow proactive approaches to political activity and to act individually. The opposite holds for smaller firms.

Looking at the firm-size factor, Drope and Hansen (2008) suggest that smaller firms are more likely to opt for "do-nothing" free-riding strategies in order to benefit from the political efforts of larger firms pursuing influence strategies. Also, Schuler (1996) suggests that firms with larger shares in an industry are more likely to oppose unfair trade policies by testifying at court hearings and filing petitions. Moreover, firms with larger workforces and assets were more politically active in Meznar and Nigh's (1995) study. In a similar vein, Hart (2001) concluded that PAC contributions were higher among larger firms.

Furthermore, smaller firms are more likely to act collectively to attain their political goals. According to Hillman and Hitt (1999), firms with greater financial and intangible resources have greater capacity to engage in political activity on an individual basis whereas collective actions are more typical for firms with fewer resources. In Cook and Fox (2000), smaller firms were more likely to join forces to influence public policy. As they have fewer resources, smaller firms choose political options which allow them to attain political goals with minimum inputs. Therefore, free-riding behaviors are adopted where collective participation takes place, and resources are pooled together from several members. These are more common choices among smaller firms, as they allow them to keep their costs low.

Firm resource slack

Having more resources at their disposal, firms with greater resource slack (e.g., higher free cash flow, debt-to-equity ratio, and current assets:current liabilities ratio) can afford to be, and are therefore more likely to be, politically active (Hillman et al., 2004).

Firm diversification level

Similar to other products of resource endowment, diversification predicts the involvement in and strategy type of political activity. For example, Hillman (2003) suggested that firms with greater international diversification levels are more likely to adopt relational approaches to political strategies. Furthermore, as they have more financial resources, they are more likely to adopt a financial incentive strategy to influence public policies (Hillman, 2003).

Firm ownership

Firm ownership may be considered as a resource in CPA (Getz, 1996). Compared to firms with foreign ownership, domestic firms are more likely to have such resources as experience, skills, and confidence when dealing with major political actors in the home country and, for this reason, they are more likely to undertake influence strategies to turn government policies to their advantage (Hillman et al., 2004). According to Hansen and Mitchell (2000), domestic firms in the USA tended to use PACs and testify at congressional hearings more often than their foreign counterparts.

Firm age

Measured by such constructs as firm experience, reputation, and credibility, firm age predicts corporate political options (Hillman, 2003). Some studies argue that older firms are expected to be more politically active. They suggest that firm performance is a function of their experience and legitimacy (Hillman and Hitt, 1999; Hillman, 2003). Firms learn from their past experiences and, over time, become more adept at building and sustaining competitive advantage by actively managing their political environment (March and Simon, 1958; Schuler and Rehbein, 1997). As a consequence, firms choose corporate political options which require greater managerial attention, political capabilities, and commitment to political activity. For example, more experienced firms tend to adopt relational approaches to corporate political strategy implementation (Hillman, 2003).

Also, over time, firms become more concerned with another source of profits – legitimacy, a composite of reputation and credibility indicating congruence with the values dominant in non-market environments (Boddewyn and Brewer, 1994). To preserve this important asset, firms engage in relations with one of the most powerful groups of non-market stakeholders – policy-makers (Boddewyn and Brewer, 1994). Looking at the empirical data from China, Luo (2001) showed that firms with greater legitimacy tended to foster relationships between their managers and government officials.

Formalized firm structures

Formal structures, such as government or public affairs units, may be conceived of as a resource of firms that engage in political activity. These structures bring together professionals and create conditions for more active implementation of political practices on an ongoing basis (Lawton et al., 2013). For instance, Martin (1995) found that firms with government affairs offices in Washington, DC, were more likely to support national reforms in the healthcare sector.

Firm culture

Blumentritt (2003) argues that the political beliefs and influence of top managers are often more important political resources than the amount of bargaining power resources a firm owns. Hillman (2003) explains that firm culture is important because it forms a system of subjective and cognitive elements that shapes influence processes. Nonetheless, the empirical research into the political culture of firms has been scarce. Future studies might concentrate on how managers' political orientation (e.g., affiliation and ethics) defines their choice of political options, such as approaches, strategies, and tactics.

Resource-dependence theory

Firm dependency on other political actors

Firms deal with and depend upon multiple constituents in the political environment (Brenner and Cochran, 1991; Hosseini and Brenner, 1992). Yet, as it is the major determinant of policies, government has been recognized as one of the most important political actors (Schuler and Rehbein, 1997). Resource-dependence theory proponents (Pfeffer and Salancik, 1978) suggest that firms whose access to resources needed to generate revenues (e.g., contracts and sales channels) and reduce costs (e.g., tax relief and subsidies) depends upon the government are more motivated to manage this dependency via CPA (Meznar and Nigh, 1995; Mitchell et al., 1997; Hillman and Hitt, 1999; Schuler, 1999; Hansen and Mitchell, 2000; Hart, 2001; Magee, 2002; Schuler et al., 2002; Hillman et al., 2004). It is worth noting that "resource dependence" is often used as a synonym for "issue salience." Some authors explain that a firm's dependence on the government in regard to a specific political issue makes that issue more salient and creates the need for the firm's interaction with the government (Brenner, 1980; Schuler and Rehbein, 1997): that is, a firm is more likely to gauge a political initiative against that policy whose impact on the firm's competitive position and performance is more significant (Schuler and Rehbein, 1997).

By and large, the empirical research supports the resource-dependence hypothesis. For example, Magee (2002) confirmed that, as their sales depend upon decisions about national defense bills, defense firms make financial contributions to congressional members voting on those bills. According to Hart (2001), sales of defense contractors to government were positively related to PAC formation and size. Furthermore, Meznar and Nigh (1995) confirmed empirically that firms whose access to critical resources depends upon government were eager to regain their power on both political and real markets by influencing public policy. Finally, Schuler (1996) found that, as imports grow, domestic firms experience greater dependence upon national policies in regard to foreign products and, for this reason, attempt to persuade governments to introduce protectionist measures.

Figure 8.5 shows the CPA system with an extended version of the choices element.

Corporate political choices and value

Both the institutions and the resources and capabilities approaches agree that the institutional environment and firm-related factors influence the value of CPA (Hillman and Hitt, 1999; Lawton et al., 2013). However, the opposite causality of the corporate political choices–value relationship has not received the same attention in the two domains. On the one hand, it has been addressed in studies of the resources and capabilities research. They acknowledge the reverse directionality, suggesting that CPA may be driven by firm performance. Indeed, it follows from the resource-based view studies that firms with better performance generate more resources needed to engage and succeed in political initiatives (Meznar and Nigh, 1995; Schuler, 1996). Also, from the resource-dependence theory standpoint, firms whose

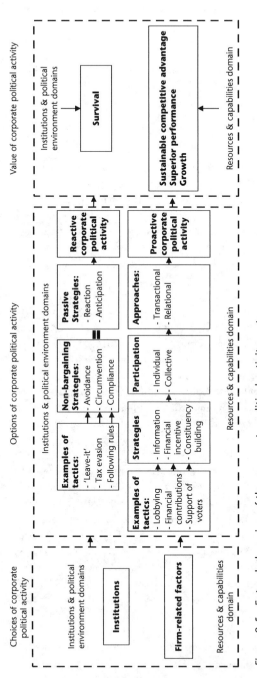

Figure 8.5 Extended version of the corporate political activity system

performance depends upon access to resources controlled by the government are more motivated to build ongoing relations with government officials (Hart, 2001; Magee, 2002).

On the other hand, the opposite directionality of the corporate political choices–value relationship has received little attention in the institutions domain. This is because, implicitly following the idea of environmental determinism (Hannan and Freeman, 1984), this domain assumes that firms and their performance are outcomes, but not factors, of environmental forces. As a result, it is unclear if and how firms with better performance shape institutions in the political field. This will help when exploring the link between firm performance, a construct inherent in the resources and capabilities domain, and institutions, a unit of analysis in the institutions domain.

CPA in action

A closer look at the political behavior of firms suggests that their approaches to influence practices in the political arena vary substantially across contexts. In advanced economies, CPA is formally accepted and viewed as a legitimate voice of firms in the non-market sphere. Most political activities of firms are institutionalized and have legislation guiding their implementation. For instance, lobbying in the USA is recognized as an official paid activity whereby well-connected advocates, or lobbyists, represent a company in order to dispute legislation in various decision-making bodies, such as the Congress. In line with the Lobbying Disclosure Act of 1995, each individual rendering lobbying services to another individual or firm in the USA is expected to register with the Secretary of the Senate and the Clerk of the House of Representatives (Senate, 2014). In addition, lobbyists are expected to register their clients and file reports detailing their lobbying activities and contributions for each of those clients (Senate, 2014). This system guarantees transparency in business–government lobbying relations. In the UK, the Transparency of Lobbying, Non-party Campaigning and Trade Union Administration Act 2014 provides for a Statutory Register of Consultant Lobbyists. Following consultations, the UK government is committed to introducing a Statutory Register for Lobbyists from 2015 onwards, which should have a similar effect to the US Congressional registration process.

By contrast, CPA in emerging economies is not formally accepted and its practitioners operate under weak or no legislation. Such a system creates additional pressures for companies entering these economies. On the one hand, multiple legislative loopholes induce unethical political behaviors, such as bribery and corruption. Whereas some foreign companies mimic unethical local practices in order to survive, other firms refrain from them at the expense of losing lucrative investment opportunities and market positions as well as bearing greater transactional costs due to slow negotiations. For example, because of its commitment to a no-bribery approach to business–government relations, John Deere, an American company specializing in the manufacture of agricultural, forestry, and construction equipment, had to cope with delays in its investments in India (John Deere, 2014).

On the other hand, companies from advanced economies may have to deal not only with host-country practices but also with home-country legislation and regulations, and with host-government initiatives that impose curbs on some forms of political activity. For instance, US companies operating in countries where corruption is the norm are bound by federal law not to engage in bribery activities. Also, companies operating in emerging economies may become targets of host-country initiatives against unethical political behaviors. For example, the Chinese Ministry of Public Security has recently accused GlaxoSmithKline, a British healthcare corporation, of bribing doctors and hospital officials to prescribe its products, generating several billion yuan in illegal revenue (PMLive, 2014).

Conclusions and directions for future research

In this chapter, we examined CPA as an element of non-market strategy generating value to firms. Even though research into CPA has advanced substantially over the past several decades, several issues have received little attention and may become an agenda for future studies. For example, those centering on the value of CPA may need to consider the following research directions. First, in the research on institutions, future work is needed to understand business–state relations and their value in emerging economies. Scholars will need to move beyond the institutional voids perspective (Khanna and Palepu, 2005) to consider if and how the formation of institutions in emerging economies leads to convergence between their political practices and those of advanced economies. Second, several issues deserve greater attention from advocates of the resources and capabilities approach. For instance, future research is needed to develop a better understanding not only of the benefits of CPA at the firm level but also of the value of firms' collective efforts in the political field. Also, it is important to explore if and how some political resources (such as political ties) may occasionally become liabilities rather than assets for firms. Furthermore, Lawton et al. (2013) call for studies looking at political resource configurations within different countries that are directly involved in market and non-market activities simultaneously. These configurations might include the combinations of political resources and capabilities with financial systems and their regulation, labor market institutions and their regulations, the corporate sector, and the culture of the country. Third, scholars may need to integrate the institutions and the resources and capabilities approaches in order to develop a more holistic view of CPA value as a function of both resource capital and institution capital (Oliver, 1997).

Likewise, several issues have received little attention in the research into corporate political options. Reactive political options have been the primary concern in the institutions domain. However, as micro-level analyses are beyond its scope, institutions studies have de-emphasized the link between reactive political options and value. As a result, it is not known if and how reactive political strategies help firms to generate value by responding to institutional pressures. To fill this gap, scholars will need to enrich the institutions macroview with firm-level analyses of the resources and capabilities domain.

By contrast, proactive political options have been considered mainly within the resources and capabilities perspective. This makes the assumption that firms can manage the institutional environment by using resources and capabilities but does not explain if and how institutional pressures impede or enhance firms' efforts. To address this issue, future studies may need to refer to the institutional research. This will help to create a more holistic view of performance outcomes of proactive political options as a function not only of firms' efforts but also of institutional forces enabling or weakening those efforts.

Finally, future work is needed to develop a better understanding of corporate political choices and, most importantly, the corporate political choices–value link. Prior research has confirmed that, as they affect decisions about corporate political options, institutional environment and firm-related factors influence the value of CPA. Furthermore, resources and capabilities research has shown that corporate political choices may also be driven by firm performance. However, the possibility of opposite causality of the corporate political choices–value relationship has not been explored in the institutions domain. As a consequence, it is unclear if and how firms with better performance shape different institutions in the political field. To examine this issue, future studies looking at multi-level institutions will need to incorporate the construct of firm performance into their analyses by integrating the resources and capabilities approach.

Bibliography

Andres, G. J. (1985). Business involvement in campaign finance: Factors influencing the decision to form a corporate PAC. *PS: Political Science and Politics*, 18(02), 213–20.

Baron, R. M., and Kenny, D. A. (1986). The moderator–mediator variable distinction in social psychological research: Conceptual, strategic, and statistical considerations. *Journal of Personality and Social Psychology*, 51(6), 1173.

Barreto, I., and Baden-Fuller, C. (2006). To conform or to perform? Mimetic behaviour, legitimacy-based groups and performance consequences. *Journal of Management Studies*, 43(7), 1559–81.

Baysinger, B. D. (1984). Domain maintenance as an objective of business political activity: An expanded typology. *Academy of Management Review*, 9(2), 248–58.

Baysinger, B. D., Keim, G. D., and Zeithaml, C. P. (1985). An empirical evaluation of the potential for including shareholders in corporate constituency programs. *Academy of Management Journal*, 28(1), 180–200.

Beblawi, H. (1987). The rentier state in the Arab world. *Arab Studies Quarterly*, 9(4), 383–98.

Blumentritt, T. P. (2003). Foreign subsidiaries' government affairs activities: The influence of managers and resources. *Business and Society*, 42(2), 202–33.

Boddewyn, J. J., and Brewer, T. L. (1994). International-business political behavior: New theoretical directions. *Academy of Management Review*, 19(1), 119–43.

Bonardi, J. P. (2004). Global and political strategies in deregulated industries: The asymmetric behaviors of former monopolies. *Strategic Management Journal*, 25(2), 101–20.

Bonardi, J. P., Holburn, G. L., and Vanden Bergh, R. G. (2006). Nonmarket strategy performance: Evidence from US electric utilities. *Academy of Management Journal*, 49(6), 1209–28.

Brenner, S. N. (1980). CPA: An exploratory study in a developing industry. In Lee Preston (ed.), *Research in Corporate Social Performance and Policy*, Vol. 2. Greenwich, CT: JAI, 197–236.

Brenner, S. N., and Cochran, P. (1991). A stakeholder theory of the firm: Implications for business and society theory and research. *Proceedings of International Association for Business and Society,* UT: Sundance, 449, 457.

Capron, L. C., and Chatain, O. (2008). Competitors' resource-oriented strategies: Acting on competitors' resources through interventions in factor markets and political markets. *Academy of Management Review*, 33(1), 97–121.

Carretta, A., Farina, V., Gon, A., and Parisi, A. (2012). Politicians "on board": Do political connections affect banking activities in Italy? *European Management Review*, 9(2), 75–83.

Chavesc, M., Stephens, L., and Galaskiewicz, J. (2004). Does government funding suppress nonprofits' political activity? *American Sociological Review*, 69(2), 292–316.

Chen, Y., and Touve, D. (2011). Conformity, political participation, and economic rewards: The case of Chinese private entrepreneurs. *Asia Pacific Journal of Management*, 28(3), 529–53.

Claessens, S., Feijen, E., and Laeven, L. (2008). Political connections and preferential access to finance: The role of campaign contributions. *Journal of Financial Economics*, 88(3), 554–80.

Cook, R. G., and Fox, D. R. (2000). Resources, frequency, and methods: An analysis of small and medium-sized firms' public policy activities. *Business and Society*, 39(1), 94–113.

Cooper, M. J., Gulen, H., and Ovtchinnikov, A. V. (2010). Corporate political contributions and stock returns. *Journal of Finance*, 65(2), 687–724.

De Figueiredo, J. M., and Silverman, B. S. (2006). Academic earmarks and the returns to lobbying. *Journal of Law and Economics*, 49(2), 597–625.

De Villa, M. A., Rajwani, T., Lawton, T. and Mellahi, T. (2014). A taxonomy of adaptive political strategies: Managing host political contexts in emerging economies. *Academy of International Business Ireland–UK Chapter Proceedings*, April 10–12, University of York, 56.

Delios, A., and Henisz, W. (2000). Japanese firms' investment strategies in emerging economies. *Academy of Management Journal*, 43(3), 305–23.

DiMaggio, P., and Powell, W. (1983). The iron cage revisited: Institutional isomorphism and collective rationality in organizational fields. *American Sociological Review*, 48(2), 147–60.

Doh, J. P., Lawton, T. C., and Rajwani, T. (2012). Advancing nonmarket strategy research: Institutional perspectives in a changing world. *Academy of Management Perspectives*, 26(3), 22–39.

Drope, J., and Hansen, W. (2008). Futility and free riding: Corporate political participation and taxation rates in the United States. *Business and Politics*, 10(3), 1–25.

Frynas, J. G., and Mellahi, K. (2003). Political risks as firm-specific (dis)advantages: Evidence on transnational oil firms in Nigeria. *Thunderbird International Business Review*, 45(5), 541–65.

Frynas, J. G., Mellahi, K., and Pigman, G. A. (2006). First mover advantages in international business and firm-specific political resources. *Strategic Management Journal*, 27(4), 321–45.

Getz, K. (1993). Selecting corporate political tactics. In B. M. Mitnick (ed.), *Corporate Political Agency: The Construction of Competition in Public Affairs*, Newbury Park, CA: Sage Publications, 242–73.

— (1996). Politically active foreign-owned firms in the US: Elephants or chickens? In D. Woodward and D. Nigh (eds.), *Beyond Us and Them: Foreign Ownership and US Competitiveness*. Columbia: University of South Carolina Press, 231–53.

— (1997). Research in corporate political action integration and assessment. *Business and Society*, 36(1), 32–72.

— (2001). Public affairs and political strategy: Theoretical foundations. *Journal of Public Affairs*, 1(4), 305–29.

Giddens, A. (2000). *The Third Way and Its Critics*. London: Polity.

Granovetter, M. (1985). Economic action and social structure: The problem of embeddedness. *American Journal of Sociology*, 91(3), 481–510.

Grant, W. (1993). Pressure groups and the European Community: An overview. In J. R. Lynton and B. Jones (eds.), *Half a Century of British Politics*. Manchester: Manchester University Press, 27–46.

Greenwood, R., Suddaby, R., and Hinings, C. R. (2002). Theorizing change: The role of professional associations in the transformation of institutionalized fields. *Academy of Management Journal*, 45(1), 58–80.

Grosse, R., and Trevino, L. J. (2005). New institutional economics and FDI location in Central and Eastern Europe. *MIR: Management International Review*, 45(2), 123–45.

Hadani, M., and Schuler, D. A. (2013). In search of El Dorado: The elusive financial returns on corporate political investments. *Strategic Management Journal*, 34(2), 165–81.

Hannan, M. T., and Freeman, J. (1984). *Organizational Ecology*. Cambridge, MA: Harvard University Press.

Hansen, W. L., and Mitchell, N. J. (2000). Disaggregating and explaining CPA: Domestic and foreign corporations in national politics. *American Political Science Review*, 94(4), 891–903.

— (2001). Globalization or national capitalism: Large firms, national strategies, and political activities. *Business and Politics*, 3(1), 5–19.

Hart, D. M. (2001). Why do some firms give? Why do some give a lot? High-tech PACs, 1977–96. *Journal of Politics*, 63(4), 1230–49.

Henderson, A. (1999). Firm strategy and age dependence: A contingent view of the liabilities of newness, adolescence and obsolescence. *Administrative Science Quarterly*, 44, 281–314.

Henisz, W., and Delios, A. (2001). Uncertainty, imitation, and plant location: Japanese multinational corporations, 1990–1996. *Administrative Science Quarterly*, 46(3), 443–75.

— (2004). Information or influence? The benefits of experience for managing political uncertainty. *Strategic Organization*, 2(4), 389–421.

Hersch, P. L., and McDougall, G. S. (2000). Determinants of automobile PAC contributions to house incumbents: Own versus rival effects. *Public Choice*, 104(3–4), 329–43.

Hill, M. D., Kelly, G. W., Lockhart, G. B., and Ness, R. A. (2013). Determinants and effects of corporate lobbying. *Financial Management*, 42(4), 931–57.

Hillman, A. J. (2003). Determinants of political strategies in US multinationals. *Business and Society*, 42(4), 455–84.

Hillman, A. J., and Hitt, M. A. (1999). Corporate political strategy formulation: A model of approach, participation, and strategy decisions. *Academy of Management Review*, 24(4), 825–42.

Hillman, A., and Keim, G. (1995). International variation in the business–government interface: Institutional and organizational considerations. *Academy of Management Review*, 20(1), 193–214.

Hillman, A. J., Keim, G. D., and Schuler, D. (2004). CPA: A review and research agenda. *Journal of Management*, 30(6), 837–57.

Hillman, A. J., Withers, M. C., and Collins, B. J. (2009). Resource dependence theory: A review. *Journal of Management*, 35(6), 1404–27.

Hillman, A. J., Zardkoohi, A., and Bierman, L. (1999). Corporate political strategies and firm performance: Indications of firm-specific benefits from personal service in the US government. *Strategic Management Journal*, 20(1), 67–81.

Hirschman, A. O. (1970). *Exit, Voice, and Loyalty: Responses to Decline in Firms, Organizations, and States*, Vol. 25. Cambridge, MA: Harvard University Press.

Holburn, G. L., and Zelner, B. A. (2010). Political capabilities, policy risk, and international investment strategy: Evidence from the global electric power generation industry. *Strategic Management Journal*, 31, 1290–315.

Hosseini, J. C., and Brenner, S. (1992). The stakeholder theory of the firm: A methodology to generate value matrix weights. *Business Ethics Quarterly*, 2, 99–119.

Hotho, J. J., and Pedersen, T. (2012). Beyond the "rules of the game": Three institutional approaches and how they matter for international business. In M. Demirbag and G. Wood (eds.), *Handbook of Institutional Approaches to International Business*. Cheltenham: Edward Elgar, 236–73.

Jackson, G., and Deeg, R. (2008a). Comparing capitalisms: Understanding institutional diversity and its implications for international business. *Journal of International Business Studies*, 39(4), 540–61.

— (2008b). From comparing capitalisms to the politics of institutional change. *Review of International Political Economy*, 15(4), 680–709.

John Deere (2014). Code of ethics. Accessed July 9, 2014. Available at: www.deere.com/wps/dcom/en_US/corporate/our_company/investor_relations/corporate_governance/code_of_ethics/code_of_ethics.page.

Keim, G., and Baysinger, B. (1988). The efficacy of business political activity: Competitive considerations in a principal–agent context. *Journal of Management*, 14(2), 163–80.

Keim, G. D., and Zeithaml, C. P. (1986). Corporate political strategy and legislative decision making: A review and contingency approach. *Academy of Management Review*, 11(4), 828–43.

Khanna, T., and Palepu, K. (2005). Spotting institutional voids in emerging markets. Harvard Business School Background Note 106014.

Kim, B., and Prescott, J. E. (2005). Deregulatory forms, variations in the speed of governance adaptation, and firm performance. *Academy of Management Review*, 30(2), 414–25.

Lane, D. (2008). From chaotic to state-led capitalism. *New Political Economy*, 13(2), 177–84.

Lawton, T., and Rajwani, T. (2011). Designing lobbying capabilities: Managerial choices in unpredictable environments. *European Business Review*, 23(2), 167–89.

Lawton, T., McGuire, S., and Rajwani, T. (2013). CPA: A literature review and research agenda. *International Journal of Management Reviews*, 15(1), 86–105.

Lawton, T. C., Doh, J. P., and Rajwani, T. (2014). *Aligning for Advantage: Competitive Strategies for the Political and Social Arenas*. Oxford: Oxford University Press.

Lenway, S. A., and Rehbein, K. (1991). Leaders, followers, and free riders: An empirical test of variation in corporate political involvement. *Academy of Management Journal*, 34(4), 893–905.

Li, J., and Qian, C. (2013). Principal–principal conflicts under weak institutions: A study of corporate takeovers in China. *Strategic Management Journal*, 34(4), 498–508.

Li, Q., and Vashchilko, T. (2010). Dyadic military conflict, security alliances, and bilateral FDI flows. *Journal of International Business Studies*, 41, 765–82.

Liu, N., Wang, L., and Zhang, M. (2013). Corporate ownership, political connections and M&A: Empirical evidence from China. *Asian Economic Papers*, 12(3), 41–57.

Lord, M. D. (1995). An agency theory assessment of the influence of corporate grassroots political activism. *Academy of Management Proceedings*, August (1), 396–400.

Luciani, G. (2008). Rentierism and repression. *Arabia*, 4, 5.

Luo, Y. (2001). Toward a cooperative view of MNC–host government relations: Building blocks and performance implications. *Journal of International Business Studies*, 32, 401–19.

Magee, C. (2002). Do political action committees give money to candidates for electoral or influence motives? *Public Choice*, 112, 373–99.

Mahdavy, H. (1970). The patterns and problems of economic development in rentier states: The case of Iran. *Life*, 1000, 1.

Mahon, J. F. (1983). Corporate political strategies: An empirical study of chemical firm responses to superfund legislation. *Research in Corporate Social Performance and Policy*, 5, 143–82.

Mahon, J. F., Bigelow, B., and Fahey, L. (1989). Toward a theory of corporate political strategy. Paper presented at the Annual Meeting of the Academy of Management, Washington, DC, August.

March, J. G., and Simon, H. (1958). *Organizations*. New York: John Wiley.

Martin, C. J. (1995). *Nature or nurture? Sources of firm preference for national health reform. American Political Science Review*, 89(4), 898–913.

Masters, M. F., and Baysinger, B. D. (1985). The determinants of funds raised by corporate political action committees: An empirical examination. *Academy of Management Journal*, 28(3), 654–64.

Meznar, M. B., and Nigh, D. (1995). Buffer or bridge? Environmental and organizational determinants of public affairs activities in American firms. *Academy of Management Journal*, 38(4), 975–96.

Mitchell, N., Hansen, W., and Jepsen, E. (1997). The determinants of domestic and foreign CPA. *Journal of Politics*, 59, 1096–113.

Mitnick, B. M. (2001). The uses of political markets. Paper presented at the National Meetings of the Academy of Management, Washington, DC, August.

Moore, P. W. (2002). Rentier fiscal crisis and regime stability: Business–state relations in the Gulf. *Studies in Comparative International Development*, 37(1), 34–56.

Niessen, A., and Ruenzi, S. (2010). Political connectedness and firm performance: Evidence from Germany. *German Economic Review*, 11(4), 441–64.

North, D. (1990). *Institutions, Institutional Change and Economic Performance*. Cambridge: Cambridge University Press.

Oberman, W. (1993). Strategy and tactic choice in institutional resource context. In B. M. Mitnick (ed.), *Corporate Political Agency*. Newbury Park, CA: Sage, 301–24.

Oliver, C. (1997). Sustainable competitive advantage: Combining institutional and resource-based views. *Strategic Management Journal*, 18(9), 697–713.

Oliver, C., and Holzinger, I. (2008). The effectiveness of strategic political management: A dynamic capabilities framework. *Academy of Management Review*, 33(2), 496–520.

Olson, M. (1965). *The Logic of Collective Action*. Cambridge: Cambridge University Press.

Paauwe, J., and Boselie, P. (2003). Challenging "strategic HRM" and the relevance of the institutional setting. *Human Resource Management Journal*, 13(3), 56–70.

Pfeffer, J. S., and Salancik, G. (1978). *The External Control of Organizations: A Resource Dependence Perspective*. New York: Harper and Row.

PMLive (2014). China targets UK executive in GSK corruption probe. Accessed July 9, 2014. Available at: www.pmlive.com/pharma_news/china_targets_uk_exec_in_ gsk_corruption_probe_568499.

Puck, J. F., Rogers, H., and Mohr, A. T. (2013). Flying under the radar: Foreign firm visibility and the efficacy of political strategies in emerging economies. *International Business Review*, 22(6), 1021–33.

Ring, P. S., Lenway, S. A., and Govekar, M. (1990). Management of the political imperative in international business. *Strategic Management Journal*, 11(2), 141–51.

Schuler, D. (1996). Corporate political strategy and foreign competition: The case of the steel industry. *Academy of Management Journal*, 39(3), 720–37.

— (1999). Corporate political action: Rethinking the economic and organizational influences. *Business and Politics*, 1(1), 83–97.

Schuler, D. A., and Rehbein, K. (1997). The filtering role of the firm in corporate political involvement. *Business and Society*, 36(2), 116–39.

Schuler, D. A., Rehbein, K., and Cramer, R. D. (2002). Pursuing strategic advantage through political means: A multivariate approach. *Academy of Management Journal*, 45(4), 659–72.

Senate. (2014). Lobbying Disclosure Act of 1995. Accessed July 9, 2014. Available at: www.senate.gov/legislative/Lobbying/Lobby_Disclosure_Act/4_Registration_of_Lobbyists.htm.

Sethi, S. P. (1982). Corporate political activism. *California Management Review*, 24(3), 32–42.

Shaffer, B. (1995). Firm-level responses to government regulation: Theoretical and research approaches. *Journal of Management*, 21(3), 495–514.

Shaffer, B., and Hillman, A. J. (2000). The development of business-government strategies by diversified firms. *Strategic Management Journal*, 21(2), 175–90.

Shaffer, B., Quasney, T. J., and Grimm, C. M. (2000). Firm level performance implications of nonmarket actions. *Business and Society*, 39(2), 126–43.

Sheng, S., Zhou, K. Z., and Li, J. J. (2011). The effects of business and political ties on firm performance: Evidence from China. *Journal of Marketing*, 75(1), 1–15.

Shepsle, K. A., and Weingast, B. R. (1984). Political solutions to market problems. *American Political Science Review*, 78(2), 417–34.

Stephens, R. A., Boddewyn, J. J., and Sproul, S. R. (1991). International smuggling: Environmental factors and corporate implications. *International Journal of Commerce and Management*, 1(1/2), 4–25.

Sun, P., Mellahi, K., and Liu, G. S. (2011). Corporate governance failure and contingent political resources in transition economies: A longitudinal case study. *Asia Pacific Journal of Management*, 28(4), 853–79.

Sun, P., Mellahi, K., and Thun, E. (2010). The dynamic value of MNE political embeddedness: The case of the Chinese automobile industry. *Journal of International Business Studies*, 41(7), 1161–82.

Sun, P., Mellahi, K., and Wright, M. (2012). The contingent value of corporate political ties. *Academy of Management Perspectives*, 26(3), 68–82.

Teece, D. J., Pisano, G., and Shuen, A. (1997). Dynamic capabilities and strategic management. *Strategic Management Journal*, 18(7), 509–33.

Venard, B. (2009). Organizational isomorphism and corruption: An empirical research in Russia. *Journal of Business Ethics*, 89(1), 59–76.

Venard, B., and Hanafi, M. (2008). Organizational isomorphism and corruption in financial institutions: Empirical research in emerging countries. *Journal of Business Ethics*, 81(2), 481–98.

Vogel, D. (1996). *Kindred Strangers: The Uneasy Relationship between Politics and Business in America.* Princeton, NJ: Princeton University Press.

Walker, J. L. (1991). *Mobilizing Interest Groups in America: Patrons, Professions, and Social Movements.* Ann Arbor: University of Michigan Press.

Wang, H., and Qian, C. (2011). Corporate philanthropy and corporate financial performance: The roles of stakeholder response and political access. *Academy of Management Journal*, 54(6), 1159–81.

Wei, S.-J. (2000). How taxing is corruption on international investors? *Review of Economics and Statistics*, 82(1), 1–11.

Wei, W. (2006). The relationship among corporate political resources, political strategies and political benefits of firms in China based on resource dependency theory. *Singapore Management Review*, 2(2), 85–14.

Weidenbaum, M. L. (1980). Public policy: No longer a spectator sport for business. *Journal of Business Strategy*, 1(1), 46–53.

WITRG. (2014). Oil price history and analysis. Accessed July 9, 2014. Available at: http://wtrg.com/prices.htm.

Yakovlev, A. (2006). The evolution of business–state interaction in Russia: From state capture to business capture? *Europe–Asia Studies*, 58(7), 1033–56.

Yoffie, D. B. (1987). Corporate strategies for political action: A rational model. In A. Marcus, A. Kaufman, and D. Beam (eds.), *Business Strategy and Public Policy*. New York: Quorum, 43–60.

Yoffie, D. B., and Bergenstein, S. (1985). Creating political advantage: The rise of the corporate political entrepreneur. *California Management Review*, 28(1), 124–9.

Young, P. (2010). Captured by business? Romanian market governance and the new economic elite. *Business and Politics*, 12(1), 1–38.

Yu, F., and Yu, X. (2011). Corporate lobbying and fraud detection. *Journal of Financial and Quantitative Analysis*, 46(6), 1865–91.

9

Non-market strategies in legal arenas

Ariel A. Casarin

Firms create and capture value through competitive interactions in legal domains. Apple has been plaintiff or defendant in legal actions against other parties in its value chain all over the globe. The firm has litigated claims with consumers, competitors, suppliers, and regulators. Apple's litigation generally involves intellectual property disputes, but the firm has also been a party in lawsuits that involve antitrust claims, consumer actions, commercial unfair trade practices, defamation demands, and corporate espionage. Some of these actions have determined significant case law for the information technology industry, and many have captured the attention of the public and media.[1] Apple's actions in legal domains have, however, allowed it to sustain and enhance unique product features. To some extent, Apple's competitive advantage, like its capabilities to develop media switch technology, largely rests on its strategic conduct in legal arenas.[2]

Like Apple, other firms can use the legal process strategically to preserve their rights, to protect valuable assets, and to create and sustain competitive advantages.[3] They can purposefully use courts to resolve contractual and administrative issues that arise when they believe another actor has unlawfully caused damage or changed the rules of the game (North, 1990).[4] Strategic behavior in legal arenas can then complement and substitute for market and other non-market action. Firms can opt to rely on courts to settle, legally, market and non-market issues when reputation, bargaining, or alternative private dispute resolution mechanisms – like arbitration – fail,[5] or when their specific resources in legal arenas are superior relative to others (Peteraf and Barney, 2003). Similarly, firms can rely on courts to complement and substitute for lobbying, financial, and coalition-building strategies so as to shape regulations and challenge policies in favorable ways (Hillman, Keim, and Schuler, 2004). All in all, legal arenas offer firms unique opportunities to integrate market and non-market strategies (Baron, 2003).

Legal arenas permit firms' strategic non-market behavior. Like bureaucrats and politicians, judges are ordinary people driven by well-defined preferences behaving in a purposive, forward-looking way and responding rationally to ordinary incentives – power, popularity, reputation, and the value of choosing (Posner, 1993; Spiller and Gely, 2007); they also decide on the basis of personal rewards, which may include bribes, and under conditions of threats and intimidation (Dal Bó, Dal Bó, and Di Tella, 2006). As bureaucrats and politicians, judges are appointed by other political actors under close public scrutiny, or elected by popular vote.[6] Courts are thus, to a degree, formed by political actors subject to generic political non-market strategies (Hillman and Hitt, 1999). Unlike other arenas in corporate public politics, the passive role of courts offers firms more control over their agendas, as courts cannot "table" an issue but must rule on the disputes brought to them (Cross, 2003). Non-market legal action is thus strategic because it involves long-lasting sequential choices: the option to file for suit, the level playing field, ensuing competitive interactions among parties – that involve preemption, threats, and commitments – and hence a change on rivals' incentives and courses of action (Priest and Klein, 1984).[7]

Firms can accommodate in legal arenas a variety of strategic choices and opt for various degrees of organizational activeness. For example, some firms choose to dispute proactively in court the validity or accuracy of all potential contractual infringements or policy changes originating from government action, while others seek to avoid legal arenas at all costs and anticipate actions to avoid future legal disputes. Many firms comply with environmental, safety, or product regulations, but some do not comply and defensively opt to pay fines and change practices on a case-by-case basis. Alternative strategies imply different internal and external capabilities and therefore demand for varying organizational responses (Oliver and Holzinger, 2008). In all cases, the decisions to comply and to sue – which need not be substitutes – offer room to maintain, create, or redistribute value with consequential direct economic and reputational impacts on firms.

Non-market strategies in legal arenas should thus depend on firms' legal resources and capabilities, be integrated into the overall strategy of the firm, and therefore should be conditional on market and other non-market strategies, the nature of competition, and the features of the institutional environment. Then, non-market strategies in legal arenas are not a lawyer's redoubt. Laws regulate and constrain activities, but they also offer an opportunity set that managers can use as part of their market and non-market strategies. Every legal dispute is a business problem affecting the risk:reward ratio of a given venture (Bagley, 2008). Apple's extensive multinational litigation over technology patents against competitors and suppliers, for example, is part of the mobile-device "smartphone patent wars" and a central component of the fierce competition in the global market for consumer mobile communications.

In this chapter I discuss and elaborate how legal arenas offer firms strategic options to sustain and create realizable value in relation to other players in the value chain. While politics plays a large role in judicial domains, I narrow the focus to firms' non-market strategic behavior in legal arenas and pay no attention to strategic behavior on the part of judges and policy-makers. My goal is to examine how generic non-market political strategies can be taken to legal arenas, so I pay little attention to the law and economics of litigation.[8] Also, my assessment and empirical review mostly focus on the direct effects of firms' actions in legal environments, so I only occasionally emphasize the indirect or secondary reputational, relational, or financial impacts firms might experience when disputing issues in legal domains.[9]

The chapter is organized as follows. The first section reviews how legal strategies can change the business game. I rely on the approach of value-based business strategies to illustrate how firms can use legal arenas to develop favorable asymmetries vis-à-vis other players in the value chain. The next section examines the theory of firms' strategic behavior in legal arenas. I look at some theoretical models of firms' strategic decisions to enter legal domains, firms' options for strategic behavior once in legal arenas, and the strategic use of judicial process as a complement of and substitute for market actions – such as bargaining – and non-market activities in administrative and legislative arenas. The third section reviews empirical studies that use firm-level data to illustrate the strategic behavior and performance of firms in the legal environment. The fourth section takes a macro-institutional perspective and revisits features of countries' legal environments and the consequent implications for firms' non-market strategies. The final section summarizes and suggests implications for academics, students, and practitioners.

How strategies in legal arenas can change the game

Laws and judicial processes establish the rules of the game for firms striving to create and capture value in their market environment; they also offer firms and other interest groups room to affect competitive positioning by means of individual or collective actions executed beyond markets (Whitford, 2003).[10] Non-market strategies in legal arenas consist of the concerted pattern of activities firms take before laws and judicial processes that are aimed at developing and protecting favorable asymmetries in the value chain, with the ultimate goal of creating or redistributing value to the firms' benefit (Baron, 2003; Sokol, 2012). Firms can then strategically use legal arenas to complement relational governance with formal contracting so as to define and strengthen relationships and reduce transaction costs. Legal arenas also allow firms to protect and leverage the value of their resources, to create options that complement market and non-market bargaining against private and public parties, and to go beyond compliance with the letter of the law and translate regulatory constraints into opportunities for value creation and capture (Bagley, 2008).

Laws play an important role in creating value, reinforcing price positioning and reducing costs (Brandenburger and Stuart, 1996). Figure 9.1 illustrates how legal arenas contribute to the development of value-based integrated strategies. Essentially, firms may construct one of four different non-market strategies in the public politics environment. They may choose to direct non-market action exclusively at bureaucratic or political arenas – which can influence or overturn administrative decisions – to litigate only or to develop some sequential or simultaneous combination of actions, as courts can determine the legal statutes of norms and new policy outcomes, while legislatures and executives, which I refer to as "political arenas," have the potential to reverse or, in practice, ignore a judicial decision (Spiller and Gely, 2007).

Strategic behavior in legal environments can enable firms to offer prices and products that provide unique benefits to consumers. Firms can then use the legal process to raise and

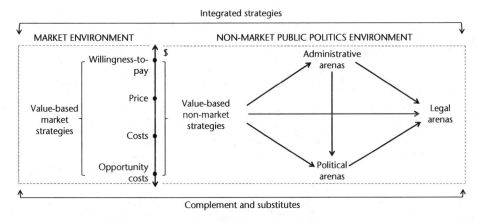

Figure 9.1 Value-based integrated strategies

protect the willingness-to-pay of buyers for the firm's product, or to lower the willingness-to-pay of buyers for other firms' products. For example, a firm can sue a competitor for false advertising or product counterfeiting to introduce asymmetries in product attributes and thereby advance classic differentiation strategies. Legal arenas can also help firms to develop cost advantage strategies by shifting the relative costs or quality of rivals' inputs, or by making it more difficult to procure them (Capron and Chatain, 2008). Backus & Johnston, once a local brewer in Peru, proactively used legal strategies to restrict the exchange of returnable glass bottles between brewers, thereby raising consumers' switching costs and increasing InBev's entry and post-entry operation costs.

In addition to using legal arenas to protect and dispute attributes and costs, firms can actively participate in legal domains to affect pricing policies. They can strategically use judicial processes to help disorganize tacit collusion schemes or to press rivals to forgo discounts, rebates, and selective price cuts. For example, predatory pricing complaints may afford plaintiffs strategic advantages whether or not they ultimately prevail. Then, less efficient firms may use the threat of a predation lawsuit to overcome efficiency deficits (Marsh, 1998; Crane, 2005).[11] Firms can also rely on legal arenas to challenge competitors' tying (Asker and Bar-Isaac, 2010) and product-bundling practices and thus unmask price discrimination and market power practices. For example, the US government's case against Microsoft rested on allegations that the latter compelled computer manufacturers to license and install the Internet Explorer web browser, entered into contracts that tended to exclude rivals, and engaged in various forms of predatory conduct (Gilbert and Katz, 2001).

Much of a firm's value for actively participating in legal arenas comes from the ability to attach legal protections and privileges to knowledge assets such as patents, capabilities, and business processes. Firms can therefore use laws and legal processes to copyright works, to patent inventions and processes, and to protect proprietary information. For example, a patent can differentiate a product and make it more likely that a buyer will pay a premium price; it can both reduce costs and create a barrier to entry. Patents can also be licensed to others to generate revenues. Brand-association trademarks such as slogans, packaging, colors, scents, and shapes increase consumers' willingness-to-pay, make products less price elastic, and therefore reduce cash flow variability. Intellectual property rights can be used defensively, as a bargaining tool, and proactively to shut down a competing line of business (Bagley, 2010). Similarly, strategic compliance of environmental regulations can increase the demand for a firm's product or decrease its costs (Karpoff, Lott, and Wehrly, 2005).

Legal arenas create options firms can use to complement and substitute for other market and non-market strategies. Firms can strategically use or threaten to use judicial process to change the arena where the game is played, away from market or administrative arenas, toward the court (Spiller and Liao, 2006). Customers, competitors, and suppliers may then sue each other so as to dispute (legally) market and non-market issues. Corporate lawsuits can then involve a wide spectrum of issues, from antitrust, breach of contract, corporate governance, and environmental issues to patent infringement, product liability and securities exchange, and free-trade-type of suits.[12] All these issues can potentially create or redistribute value among players in the value chain. For example, a firm might legally challenge the awarding of a contract to a rival in order to attempt to win the contract for itself. If successful, this strategy would shift output between the firms and might also affect both firms' marginal costs.

Firms can also rely on courts to litigate rulings or policy outcomes emanating from regulators, administrative offices, or legislatures. For instance, firms can strategically choose not to comply with regulations when enforcers – say, bureaucrats – are not subject to influence, and to litigate policy outcomes strategically when issuers – say policy-makers – are subject to lobbying. The legal challenge of regulations, administrative decisions, and laws, generally a long-lasting process (see, for instance, Marsh, 1998), potentially creates asymmetries in costs or product attributes between compliant and non-compliant firms that might result in temporary competitive advantages. In some cases, non-compliance with waste disposal environmental standards most frequently gives non-compliant firms a cost advantage over compliant ones. Government lawsuits can, however, debar firms from public contracts and attract large amounts of publicity, which could bring large reputational losses (Karpoff and Lott, 1993).

Governments sue firms for regulatory misconduct, but also bring antitrust cases to offset competitive distortions in markets. Evidence suggests, however, that corporations file ten antitrust cases for every case filed by the government (Bizjak and Coles, 1995).[13] The expensive nature of antitrust lawsuits and the fact that it is typically cheaper to bring a lawsuit than to defend against one makes antitrust disputes a strategic instrument to raise rivals' costs. A firm may strategically bring its own case (which is costly) and/or have the government bring a case on its behalf (which is less expensive) against another firm (Sokol, 2012). Firms can defensively use antitrust disputes to impose restrictions on business decisions, but also as an aggressive strategic weapon, for instance to obtain a ban for a certain merger which might threaten their own market position (Yao, 1988). Antitrust lawsuits against competitors can also be an effective way to send market signals or to voice displeasure with, for example, a competitive price cut.

Legal arenas can, however, be misused. Firms can (ab)use antitrust law to extract funds from successful rivals, punish non-cooperative behavior, respond to an existing (non-antitrust) lawsuit, prevent a hostile takeover, or prevent successful firms from competing vigorously (McAfee and Vakkur, 2004). Firms can also use anti-dumping laws to discourage the entry of foreign rivals (Marsh, 1998). Non-price predatory litigation, which seeks to raise rivals' costs (Salop, 1979; Salop and Scheffman, 1983) or to prevent, delay, or raise the costs of competitors' entry (Milgrom and Roberts, 1982), may have similar effects.[14] In industries with some entry regulation, for example, an incumbent firm may repeatedly file lawsuits of little merit against an entrant to impose costs of defense, delay financing or other contractual arrangements, and ultimately discourage other potential entrants from entering.[15]

Firms can also use other tactical choices, like preliminary court orders, to cause an immediate impact on competitive advantage. Preliminary injunctions, a strategic instrument firms can use once in legal domains, prevent "irreparable harm" and therefore are a remedy to protect the value of assets, patents, and other rights.[16] These court orders, which are issued before a full hearing or final decision on a case's merits, can delay mergers, mandate compulsory licenses, block strikes, prohibit product launches, or retire products already in the market. Twentieth Century Fox, for example, has relied on preliminary injunctions in several countries to prevent local producers from selling Duff beer.[17] Firms' requests for preliminary injunctions may avoid "irreparable harm," but also drive up a rival's cost, as an injunction proceeding itself raises the legal expenditure required to pursue a case in the courts. If a plaintiff can also shut down a fraction of a defendant's operations for months while the issue is being resolved, as Twentieth Century Fox did with Duff Sudamerica in Colombia, the defendant is likely to experience a reduction in operating cash flow and risk bankruptcy.[18]

In short, firms can manage risks and dispute value in legal arenas against other firms, non-firm private actors, and governmental bodies, such as regulators and legislatures. The above examples illustrate that non-market action in the legal environment can encompass several stages of the business life cycle, from the development of the business concept, the assembling of the management team, and the raising of capital to the development, production, and marketing of the product or service and the harvesting of the endeavor. Legal arenas are not a niche for only a few firms. Large and established firms like Apple and small and nascent firms like Aylus Networks can all strategically use legal arenas to secure property, avoid liability from illegal acts, enforce rights, challenge regulations and policies, and therefore create and sustain a competitive advantage.[19]

Strategic behavior in legal arenas

The study of firm behavior in legal arenas can be traced back to Becker's (1968) treatment of the criminal justice system. Becker's work was soon followed by Landes (1971) and Posner (1973), who began to consider the determinants of settlement and the effect on court outcomes of the actions and reactions of several participants in the system. These works applied economic principles of optimization to participants in the legal system in order to generate predictions consistent with casual observation of the courts and, later, to generate hypotheses which could be tested empirically. The study of strategic behavior in legal arenas eventually grew out of the study of the determinants of pre-trial settlements (Gould, 1973). Cooter and Rubinfeld (1989), Daughety (2000), and Spier (2007) provide comprehensive surveys.

The basic premise of this literature is that the decision to bring a suit – that is, formally to enter a legal arena – is an investment decision.[20] A plaintiff will then rationally choose to bring a suit when the expected return from litigation x_p outweighs the trial costs c_{tp}. As was discussed in the previous section, suits and countersuits may be brought on their own merit or to force a collateral outcome favorable to the plaintiff. The return x_p can then capture issues that are somewhat beyond the scope of the dispute, such as a transitory rise in the other party's costs, the impact that a court decision will have on future cases, or the plaintiff's concern for its reputation. Similarly, the costs of the plaintiff and defendant, c_{tp} and c_{td}, respectively, include out-of-pocket and opportunity costs, such as time and effort. The plaintiff will choose to pursue litigation when the strategy has positive expected net present value, $x_p > c_{tp}$.[21]

Several models predict that in a world of symmetric information, all else being equal, the higher the stakes in a case, the more likely it is to be litigated, as the potential gains from litigating tend to dominate litigation costs. Given the costs of litigation and no information asymmetries – that is, the parties have full information about each other's expectations on the litigation outcome – litigation occurs only as a result of a genuine disagreement between parties on the case outcome. Such difference in expectations can be due to uncertainty over the facts or the law, or differences of opinion as to the applicable facts or law. Settlement may then occur during litigation as new information causes the expectations of plaintiffs and defendants to converge.[22]

More interesting situations develop when the parties have asymmetric information. For example, when the parties do not know each other's expectations, litigation may ensue due to strategic behavior, even when the parties actually agree on the merits of the case. Limited information opens the way for each party to try to affect the other's expectation of the value of litigation to its own advantage. Then, the plaintiff's expected benefits are not only determined by the merits of the case, but also by the efforts the two parties devote to winning. In other words, the plaintiff's litigation costs are endogenous. The expected payoff to the plaintiff is thus given by the function $x_p (c_{tp}, c_{td})$, which includes the defendant's effort. The plaintiff's expected gain from bringing the suit, prior to trial and net of trial costs, is thus given by

$$x_p (c_{tp}, c_{td}) - c_{tp} \tag{1}$$

The defendant's expected loss x_d is

$$x_d\,(c_{tp},\,c_{td}) + c_{td} \tag{2}$$

The derivative $\partial x_p / \partial c_{tp}$ can be thought of as the marginal productivity of the plaintiff's effort at trial. If effort is productive, then $\partial x_p / \partial c_{tp} > 0$ and $\partial x_p / \partial c_{td} < 0$. The same applies for the defendant. The variables c_{tp} and c_{td} are chosen by the parties as part of their strategy at trial. The plaintiff chooses c_{tp} to maximize her expected gain, and so does the defendant with c_{td} to minimize expected loss. The first order condition for the plaintiff is:

$$\left(\frac{\partial x_p}{\partial c_{tp}}\right) + \left(\frac{\partial x_p}{\partial c_{td}}\right) i_p = 1 \tag{3}$$

where $i_p = \partial c_{td} / \partial c_{tp}$ measures how the defendant's cost will change in response to a change in the plaintiff's costs. Equation (3) indicates that the plaintiff will expend money at trial so that the marginal benefit from more effort is equal to the marginal cost. This shows that effort at trial can serve as an important signaling function. The decision about how much to expend at trial thus depends on strategic considerations related to i_p.

The equilibrium litigation investments can be viewed as the outcome of a non-cooperative game (which could be simultaneous or sequential) where the plaintiff maximizes x_p. The structure of this game is similar to those of other types of non-market contests (see Baron, 2001, for example). The dynamic strategies employed by the participants in these games hinge on the anticipated reaction of rivals i_p – each player would like their opponent to "back off" and invest less in the contest. To this end, the plaintiff might derive a strategic benefit from aggressive spending, for example, when the defendant's best response function is decreasing in the plaintiff's investment. Conversely, the plaintiff would benefit from a commitment to lower spending levels if the defendant's best response curve slopes upward. Then, a credible commitment by the defendant to build a defensive strategy could lower the plaintiff's expected litigation return and make them drop the suit altogether. Legal and political science scholars have shown that court outcomes are a function of the resources firms bring to bear in legal arenas (Songer and Sheehan, 1992).

Private litigants have incentives to settle a dispute when doing so would be mutually beneficial. However, government litigants may not have the same incentives as private parties to reach cost-effective and efficient outcomes when litigating a dispute. Government authorities may choose not to settle even if the settlement might be more efficient and cost effective for both the agency and the other party. For example, an agency may be more concerned with obtaining a legal ruling on a new statute, and the associated legal precedent, rather than settling the case and reaching a private agreement with a particular firm even if a settlement would be more cost effective. In addition, the source of funding for many government litigants is legislative appropriation, not the market. If government agencies are less constrained in terms of financial and legal resources, they will have an advantage in pursuing a lawsuit or defending against one.

Firms can use litigation to complement and substitute for other non-market strategies in public policy arenas. A firm that wishes to change a law, for example, has the option of lobbying the legislature for a new law or suing in court for a precedent that changes the law. Bouwen and McCown (2007) weigh these options in the context of the European Union's decision process. Rubin, Curran, and Curran (2001) model such tradeoff in a one-stage game where net payoffs result from relative marginal cost of effort and benefits in using legislative and judicial arenas and from the disputants' relative technological advantage in those two competing domains. Somewhat predictably, they show that a firm will choose litigation over lobbying weighing payoffs according to the competitive edge the firm and the rival both have in the competing domains. Rubin, Curran, and Curran (2001), however, do not provide for an equilibrium outcome. The model therefore does not consider that the counterparty could respond by seeking change in a more advantageous arena.

The dependence of judicial outcomes, at least in part, on the resources used in courts implies that firms must choose between resources used up in administrative and legislative arenas and resources spent on litigation when disputing non-market issues. De Figueiredo and de Figueiredo (2002) go beyond Rubin, Curran, and Curran (2001) and theoretically examine in a two-stage game how competing interest groups with differential resources configure their non-market spending between lobbying and litigation to maximize the chance of a favorable policy outcome. In the lobbying game, two differently endowed firms compete over a policy outcome issued by a regulator or policy-maker. This first stage of the game predicts vote-buying biases policy outcomes toward more endowed players, although the size of the offer of the smaller player puts a limit on how far the larger player can go in requesting policy. Firms can then challenge the policy outcome in courts, which decide based on their own preferences and on groups' (remaining) resources.[23]

The model shows that the existence of litigation alters the nature of the first-stage lobbying game. It also points out that the availability of litigation means that, in many cases, firms should forgo lobbying altogether in order to ensure that first-stage gains can be upheld and defended in the courts. The analysis also illustrates how the non-market environment conditions firms' best integrated lobbying–litigation strategy. In particular, de Figueiredo and de Figueiredo (2002) suggest that as, (1), the court's reversion point becomes more extreme, the transfer made in the lobbying stage will be smaller; as, (2), the endowed firm's resources increase, the transfers are higher and the outcome of the lobbying stage is closer to the ideal point; as, (3), the underlying probability that the court might overturn the decision increases, the transfers to the regulator decrease and therefore lobbying outcomes are driven toward non-results, and this effect may eliminate lobbying altogether; and as, (4), the responsiveness of the court to resources changes, the effect it has on lobbying will depend upon the ideology of the court.

Once in legal arenas, firms can use information, financial, and coalition strategies (Hillman and Hitt, 1999) to affect litigation outcomes. Firms cannot lobby the courts in the same way as they may lobby agencies or legislatures, but that does not mean that the application of the law may not be considered a part of politics. Firms can then use alternative mechanisms to channel out-of-court information to judicial decision-makers. One mechanism is to provide evidence in regulatory and legislative processes that can add value to the litigation that may follow. Letters and testimony seemingly aimed at persuading bureaucrats signal interest groups' political preferences. Taken alone, presentations would appear designed to persuade the agency, but evidence added to the rule-making record also builds anticipated legal cases from existing structures of statutory obligations and judicial precedent (Schmidt, 2002). Courts' difficulties in interpreting complex scientific or technical evidence add to the uncertainty of legal judgment, so regulatory evidence and factual propositions reduce uncertainty and may also constrain judges' ideological preferences (Hillman and Hitt, 1999).

The news media plays an essential role in society by providing information to the public that somehow conditions individual and collective decision-makers. Firms can then embrace demand-side media bias strategies (Mullainathan and Shleifer, 2005; Baron, 2006) and fuel reputational cascades to voice information publicly so as to influence judicial decision-making

(Bonardi and Keim, 2005). Evidence shows that media bias affects voter preferences (DellaVigna and Kaplan, 2007), which then influences political behavior. Lim, Snyder, and Stromberg (2010) find that active media coverage does not influence court decisions independent of voter preferences, but it substantially magnifies the influence of voter preferences on court decisions. They also find that media influence on court decisions depends very much on judicial selection mechanisms.

Private money can also have an impact on judicial politics. As in administrative (de Figueiredo and Edwards, 2007) and legislative domains (Baron, 1994; Ansolabehere, de Figueiredo, and Snyder, 2003), money can affect judicial decision-making directly, by changing the bias and competence of the judges who sit in court, and indirectly, by inducing a strategic response to the other judges' votes. Bonneau and Cann (2009) find that campaign contributions drive rulings of popular-vote-elected judges. Iaryczower and Shum (2012) model courts' decisions based on judges' information, preferences, and strategic behavior and predict empirically individual voting based on both judges' and case features. They then use predicted outcomes to examine, in a second stage, how campaign contributions affect individual and courts' conditional voting probabilities. They show that a judge's voting strategy leans more heavily toward an interest group the larger its campaign contributions are to that judge and the smaller its contributions are to other court members. They also find that contributions have a larger effect on the behavior of individual judges than on aggregated court decisions.

Judicial strategies are high-cost efforts. Coalitions are then a low-cost means for assembling aligned interests into more powerful blocs, though the possibility to form them depends on a group's purpose, its means of maintenance, and the benefits of collective action.[24] Whitford (2003) reviews a variety of coalition micro-structures in US environmental groups' participation as amici curiae before the Supreme Court. He observes that, for any one event, the micro-structure of a coalition varies, but that coalitions take on general forms across events. The events of firms bringing joined legal cases to court are studied very little. It is possible to argue, however, that in order to use strategies of one-off or repeated joint litigation effectively, firms must be organizationally structured so that they can maintain focus and consistent preferences over complex policy issues during long time periods. Specialized sectoral associations are therefore more likely to engage in group litigation.

Evidence of firms' behavior and performance in legal arenas

Case studies dominate early research on firms' strategic behavior in legal domains and on the impact of legal disputes upon firms. These small-sample studies provide evidence of the features of particular disputes and often explore the institutional setting in rich detail (see, for instance, Cutler and Summers, 1988; Fields, 1990; and Hertzel and Smith, 1993, for alternative analyses of a single inter-firm dispute). Empirical work then moved to the use of larger data samples to identify and measure the implications of inter-firm lawsuits statistically. In practice, however, the vast majority of disputes that are filed ultimately settle before trial and countless others are settled before a case is even filed. Empirical studies on firms' behavior and performance in legal arenas must therefore deal with sample selection bias. One type of selection bias is that cases going to litigation are not a random sample but rather cases that could not be settled (Priest and Klein, 1984).[25] The other sample selection problem is that lawsuits are instances when plaintiffs believe that their benefits from suing outweigh their costs.

The evidence provided in empirical studies contributes to our understanding of the hazards and the nature of the costs and benefits firms face in legal arenas.[26] Bhagat, Bizjak, and Coles (1998) were probably the first to provide large-sample empirical evidence on the risks and overall costs for firms' actions in legal environments.[27] They collected data on filings and settlements announced in the *Wall Street Journal* between 1981 and 1983 involving firms' disputes with other firms, a government entity, and individuals on a wide spectrum of legal issues: antitrust, breach of contract, corporate governance, environmental, patent infringement, product liability, and SEC-(Securities and Exchange Commission) and FTC-(Federal Trade Commission) type suits. They then used event study methods to estimate the abnormal stock market reaction to filing and settlement announcements. The authors recognize that their sample is not bias free: most of the cases reported in the newspaper probably involve large firms or what the *Journal* perceives as important legal issues; and the sample includes only firms for which stock market returns data are available.

Despite these limitations, the results of the study are relevant for firms' strategies in legal domains. The findings indicate that, no matter who brings a lawsuit against a firm – be it another firm, individuals, or the government – defendants suffer economically meaningful and statistically significant wealth losses of close to 1 percent of the equity market value upon the filing of a suit. Plaintiffs, however, experience no significant wealth effects around filings. The authors also find that the wealth effects upon filing vary with the identity of the plaintiff. Defendant firms involved in government suits suffer larger declines in shareholder wealth (−1.73 percent) than defendants in inter-firm (−0.75 percent) or private parties' (−0.81 percent) lawsuits. This suggests that the type of suit most frequently disputed against the government is typically more serious, or that government agencies have more leverage and resources to use in legal battles. The study also finds that certain types of suit are more costly for defendant firms. Environmental (−3.08 percent), product-liability (−1.46 percent), and security-law violations suits (−2.71 percent) result in significantly greater wealth losses than antitrust (−0.81 percent) or breach-of-contract (−0.16 percent) disputes. Interestingly, the authors find that defendant firms benefit from a significant wealth increase when they settle a suit with another firm, but that such an increase does not occur when they settle with governments or non-corporate parties. For plaintiff firms, again, the wealth implications of settlements appear to be trivial.

Bhagat et al.'s (1998) results suggest that environmental suits are the most costly for firms. Karpoff et al. (2005) also use *Wall Street Journal* data and the stock price reaction as a measure of the present value of the net costs to a firm accused of violating an environmental regulation, and then partition such costs into components that reflect legal and reputational penalties. Their sample consists of a wide variety of actions involving different types of harms and initiated by different regulators or private parties. Karpoff et al. (2005) find that allegations or charges that a firm violated environmental regulations correspond to economically meaningful and statistically significant losses in the firm's share value. Initial press announcements containing allegations of a violation are associated with an average abnormal stock return of −1.69 percent. When the initial announcement indicates that the firm formally has been charged with a violation, the average abnormal stock return is −1.58 percent.[28] Interestingly, they find that the market value losses are similar in size to firms' legal penalties. Karpoff et al. (2005) therefore conclude that legal penalties, not reputational penalties, are the primary deterrents to environmental violations.[29]

Firms' environmental suits appear to be the most costly, but private antitrust suits the most frequent. Bizjak and Coles (1995) analyze a large sample of inter-firm antitrust disputes. Their study finds that defendants experience economically and statistically significant wealth losses at the announcement of a filing of a private antitrust suit, while plaintiffs experience a significant wealth gain. Plaintiffs can and do damage defendants by initiating a lawsuit. The analysis also reveals that the wealth effects depend on the nature of the allegation and the statute invoked, as those alleging horizontal violations do somewhat better than those seeking damages from vertical allegations. Jarrell (1985) finds that target firms that litigate the takeovers and then settle are often successful at increasing the purchase price of their stock. In this case, the strategic use of litigation increases stockholders' returns. Yoffie and Kwak (2001) show the relevance of so-called antitrust compliance programs as an integral part of a firm's business strategy and illustrate how Intel avoids antitrust litigation while Microsoft has to cope with multiple suits.

In a methodologically leading study, Perloff, Rubinfeld, and Ruud (1996) also use data for inter-firm antitrust cases in five US federal district courts; the claims that appeared more often were refusals to deal, tying, price fixing, price discrimination, and vertical restraint. They estimate how much an increase in the probability that the plaintiff wins at trial and how much an increase in the variance of the trial outcome affect the probability of a pre-trial settlement. These estimates allow them to determine the extent to which parties are risk averse, which encourages settlement. Perloff et al. (1996) innovate because they jointly estimate the trial and settlement equations. Results show that the likelihood of plaintiffs' success in antitrust trials varies substantially by jurisdiction, which permits forum shopping by antitrust allegation, size of firm, industry, and whether or not a jury trial occurs. Interestingly, they also find that defendants do not worry about reputation effects, which implies that their attitudes toward risk are no different from those of plaintiffs when explaining settlement. They also find that risk aversion plays a role in settlement: for every 1 percent increase in the probability that the plaintiff wins, the probability of settlement rises by nearly 0.13 percent.

Many settlements occur between the request for a preliminary injunction and the hearing on the motion or after the plaintiff has threatened to file such a request. Lanjouw and Lerner (2001) explore empirically the relationship between the financial status of disputants and the use of preliminary injunctions in a sample of patent lawsuits. The results suggest that injunctions may be available only to financially stronger plaintiffs. In univariate comparisons, disputes in which preliminary injunctions are requested have plaintiffs almost twice as large in terms of sales, employment, and cash as those in disputes where preliminary injunctions are not requested. Regression analyses confirm that the strength of the plaintiff has a substantial and statistically significant effect on the probability that an injunction will be requested. Results also indicate that strong defendants are targeted along with those that are weak.

Other studies have obtained similar findings. Marsh (1998) finds that firms filing for anti-dumping protection experience an increase in market value – magnitudes are similar to those of Bhagat et al. (1998). She also finds, however, that firms experience a market value loss if petitions receive a negative determination at the final stage of the process. As the author acknowledges, this result is probably biased since cases going to final determination are not a random sample but cases that could not be settled (Priest and Klein, 1984). Somaya (2003) investigates systematic reasons for non-settlement in patent lawsuits and finds that non-settlement is increased by strategic stakes. Somewhat relatedly, Hall and Ziedonis (2007) find little evidence that semiconductor firms have adopted a more aggressive stance toward patent enforcement since the 1970s, despite the effective strengthening of US patent rights in the 1980s and widespread entry by small firms. They find those firms' litigation rates as enforcers of patents remained relatively stable, though they also find an escalation in their baseline risk as targets of litigation brought by outside patent owners.

All of the studies discussed above pay little attention to judges' decision-making. Judges, however, may have some set of preferences over case outcomes because of ideological or political preferences (Spiller and Gely, 1992). If ideological behavior exists, litigants would be aware of this behavior and act strategically in choosing the cases they bring to trial.

De Figueiredo (2005) methodologically follows Perloff et al. (1996) and conducts a joint estimation of the probability of bringing a case before the US Federal Communications Commission and of winning it, given that cases have been brought to trial. De Figueiredo (2005) contributes by applying the analysis to regulatory cases where the government is always a defendant and also because he explicitly incorporates judicial ideology into the joint estimation procedures. His paper shows that judges do vote in ideologically predictable ways in regulatory cases.[30] It also shows that firms, anticipating judges' ideological votes, select regulatory cases for litigation strategically, and that this selection effect is much larger than the effect on litigated case outcomes.

The world is not legally flat

Firms can sometimes choose non-market playing fields within and across countries based on their competitive edge and institutional conditions. For example, in April 2011 Apple sued its component supplier Samsung in the US District Court for the Northern District of California, alleging that several of Samsung's Android phones and tablets infringed Apple's intellectual property.[31] The following week, Samsung counter-sued Apple, filing federal complaints in courts in Seoul, Tokyo, and Mannheim, alleging that Apple infringed Samsung's patents for mobile-communications technologies. In June 2011, Samsung also filed suits against Apple in the British High Court of Justice, in the US District Court for the District of Delaware, and with the US International Trade Commission in Washington, DC. By July 2012, Apple and Samsung were embroiled in more than fifty lawsuits in several countries, all alike in their institutional features.[32]

Non-market strategies are all context specific. The institutional conditions and underlying philosophy of a country may determine firms' preferred approach to market and non-market strategy formulation and execution (Henisz and Zelner, 2001).[33] Firms' non-market strategies in legal arenas are therefore conditional on the features of the institutional environment, both political and legal. Variations across countries in the rule of law, procedural formalism, and courts' discretion are then relevant for the formulation of non-market strategies in legal domains. Such differences should be apparent in different strategic approaches. Some firms, then, will legally contend with a competitor in one country but seek an extrajudicial resolution with the same rival in another nation. For example, Twentieth Century Fox adopted different strategies in Australia, Colombia, and Germany against local producers of Duff beer. Even within a single country, firms might choose to comply with laws or legally compete with an actor but choose to dispute some rules, or settle out of court with others because of the intertwined roles played by firm features, the nature of disputes, and the legal and political environment.

Legal systems around the world regulate dispute resolution: they rely on lawyers and professional judges, order the steps that disputants must follow, regulate the collection and presentation of evidence, insist on legal justification of claims and judges' decisions, give predominance to written submissions, and so on (Hadfield, 2005). Predictably, courts' effectiveness in resolving disputes varies across countries. For instance, the World Economic Forum has for years conducted a survey that inquires into legal arenas' effectiveness in both settling disputes and challenging regulation. Figure 9.2 illustrates that widespread differences exist between countries. On average, surveyed managers perceive that countries' legal arenas are more efficient at settling firms' disputes against regulations and policy outcomes than they are at settling disputes between firms.

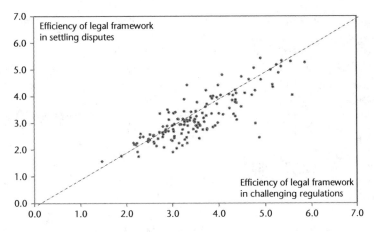

Figure 9.2   The effectiveness of courts in settling disputes

Source: Schwab (2013).

Note: The data is generated by a survey of firm executives operating in a given country. The responses to the following two questions are reported: "How efficient is the legal framework in your country for private businesses to settle disputes?" and "How efficient is the legal framework in your country for private businesses to challenge the legality of government actions and/or regulations?" 1 = extremely inefficient; 7 = highly efficient.

Djankov, La Porta, Lopez-de-Silanes, and Shleifer (2003) empirically examine the factors that make courts function more or less effectively. Using original data from questionnaires answered by attorneys in 109 countries, they combine records on substantive and procedural statutory intervention in two specific disputes – the eviction of a non-paying tenant and the collection of a bounced check – to develop a formalism index that measures the duration of disputes once they are in the legal process and gauges judicial quality. The study finds that some countries regulate dispute resolution more heavily than others.[34] Legal procedures systematically differ across legal families, as common law countries have less formalized and French civil law countries have more formalized dispute resolution mechanisms.[35] Djankov et al. (2003) also find that richer countries exhibit lower levels of procedural formalism than poorer ones.

Djankov et al. (2003) also find huge variation among countries in the speed and quality of courts. Their results indicate that, in most countries, courts resolve (these simple) disputes extremely slowly, taking an average of over 200 days. There is, however, remarkable variation in the estimated duration of each procedure among countries. Eviction is estimated to take 49 days in the United States, but 547 days in Austria and 660 in Bulgaria. Check collection is estimated to take 60 days in New Zealand, but 527 days in Colombia and 645 in Italy. Predictably, expected duration is highly correlated with procedural formalism. Results also indicate that higher formalism is associated with inferior justice, holding other things constant. All in all, these results suggest that legal structure, rather than level of development, shapes the efficiency and efficacy of courts.[36]

Greater formalism can be efficient in some countries: it can reduce error and protect the judicial process from subversion by powerful interests. The various steps of the process, such as reliance on professional judges and collection of written evidence, are there to secure a fair judicial process. Still, the existence of laws has no practical effect if judges are incapable of deciding according to their interpretation of laws and freed from eventual external pressures (North and Weingast, 1989). Judges and courts do not count as political actors when they are subjected to incapacitating interferences such as threats, bribes, and physical violence, which can effectively annul their will (Dal Bó et al., 2006).[37] A judge who changes a ruling after receiving a threat or rules according to the preference he or she imputes to a legislative majority is behaving strategically (Spiller and Gely, 2007).[38] The notion of judicial autonomy, however, distinguishes between the two cases; it simply requires that judges are not subject to incapacitating interferences when they decide upon cases.

The extent of independent courts has captured the attention of both academics and practitioners. The literature distinguishes between de jure and de facto concepts of judicial independence (Feld and Voigt, 2003). The notion of de jure judicial independence relates to the formal rules aimed at insulating judges from undue pressure, from either outside or within the judiciary. The concept of de facto judicial independence is behavioral and looks at the autonomy and enforcement of judicial measures. Both measures involve saying something about behaviors that are not directly observable. Ríos-Figueroa and Staton (2012) evaluate and compare thirteen cross-national indicators of judicial independence covering several countries over long periods.[39] They find that de jure and de facto measures do not covary among them, and that different de jure indicators are not correlated with each other. In practice, these findings suggest that management should thus be creative in their efforts to identify how independent judicial behavior is likely to manifest (Bagley, 2008).

Weak institutional quality implies lax enforcement, because of incompetence, political interference, or bribery and corruption. Variations in the quality of legal arenas should, then, result in dissimilar firm conducts. Chong and Gradstein (2011) examine how the rule of law translates into legal compliance by business firms using data from the World Business Environment Survey, which contains firm-level survey responses on features of firms' environment and modus operandi in regard to law compliance. They examine how the strength of legal monitoring and enforcement impacts illegal activities, as measured by the percentage of sales off the books. Results show that firm-level features, such as the nature of firm ownership, its size and age, do matter for illegal practices. Still, most of the variation in illegality across firms comes from countrywide measures of institutional quality. These results appear to be robust for the measures of illegal activity and countries' institutional quality.

Berkowitz, Moenius, and Pistor (2006) argue that differences in the quality of legal arenas also affect international trade. Their position is that, in complex products' industries, importers bear most of the risks of transactions, as exporters can hedge commercial risks before importers verify the quality of goods. A potential breach of contract between the exporter and importer about product quality can be taken to the importer's court, the exporter's court, or a third country's arbitrator. However, if the exporter does not comply with a foreign ruling when it loses, the importer's last resort for enforcing a resolution is the court system in the exporter's country.[40] The importer's ability to make and enforce a ruling then depends upon the overall quality of institutions of the exporter's country, and the importer's competitive edge in that country. Berkowitz et al. (2006) find strong evidence that the quality of exporter- and importer-country institutions exhibits a strong positive association with trade flows in complex markets, but has no significant association with trade flows in simple markets.

It can be argued that judiciaries may favor local firms. Bhattacharya, Galpin, and Haslem (2007) rely on a comprehensive sample of public US and foreign corporate defendants in US federal courts and use event studies methods to examine whether firms have an advantage in their own country's courts. They examine antitrust, breach-of-contract, employment-related, patent-infringement, and product-liability cases, whose outcomes can be further classified into four general groups: cases dismissed by a judge; cases resolved with a summary judgment by a judge; cases resolved in formal trial; and settlement. The study's results show that the market reaction upon the announcement of a federal lawsuit is less negative for US corporate defendants. They also indicate that the dismissal rates for US defendants are similar to the dismissal rates for foreign defendant firms, but if the case goes to trial, US firms are less likely to lose. Similar to Moore (2003), who relies on patent-infringement cases, Bhattacharya et al.'s (2007) results provide evidence that local firms have a home-court advantage in US federal courts. Interestingly, they further show that there is a prejudice against foreign firms in US courts, and that such prejudice rests on the judges.[41]

Conclusion

In recent years there has been a rapidly developing path of research on corporate public politics. This research has, however, focused overwhelmingly on the legislative and executive branches while too often ignoring the judiciary.

Legal arenas play an important part in non-market strategy. Judicial action may be pursued against a participant in the value chain, but also against a particular policy or its implementation. The purpose of suing is to shift the game away from the market or the legislative or bureaucratic arena and towards the courts, where the interest group expects to get via litigation what it was unable to obtain with other strategies. The goal of firms' conduct in legal domains may be direct – such as reversing an adverse bureaucratic outcome – or indirect – such as putting the regulatory agency on notice that pursuing this particular policy line would be extremely expensive.

The main purpose of the court system is to facilitate value-creating activities and deter value-destroying activities through the enforcement of contracts and laws. For many, the courts and the application of law may not be considered a part of politics. Revisiting theoretical approaches and empirical evidence, however, shows that legal arenas offer room for strategic non-market behavior with a consequent effect on firms' integrated competitive positioning. Issues brought to legal domains are resolved at various stages of a sequential decision-making process in which parties have limited information and act in their own self-interest. Whether to use the legal system and what actions to take once a suit is filed are decisions to be solved recursively by computing the expected values of subsequent stages of the dispute. Ultimately, trial outcomes are determined by the interaction between the effort that the parties make at trial, their relative costs and resources, the underlying facts and law of the case, and differences in judges and juries across jurisdictions.

Firms' non-market strategies in legal arenas therefore comprise whether and when to take an issue into legal domains, how to use legal arenas as substitutes for or complements of market and other non-market strategies, and how to behave strategically once in the legal process. Disputes in legal domains are not rare. Government entities tend to file a large number of environmental and product liability suits; firms file many antitrust, breach-of-contract, and patent-infringement actions; and non-firm private parties dispute issues involving corporate governance and securities law violations. Because litigation is expensive, complex, and time consuming, interest groups may also use litigation as a threat to obtain policies advocated through their lobbying process. The extent to which litigation threats can alter bureaucratic and political behavior depends on the probability that the interest group is likely to win. Thus, the compositions of the legislature and the courts impact the credibility of litigation threats. One way in which lobbying and litigation strategies are related is that interest groups must choose how to allocate resources to the first-stage lobbying effort and then – should they or their opponents choose to litigate – to the litigation that might ensue.

Empirical evidence suggests that lawsuits are not zero-sum games. It indicates that the strategic use of litigation increases stockholders' returns, and that litigation is generally bad news for defendants. In an ideal world, every court system would be accurate, unbiased, and free. The world is far from ideal, however, which makes non-market strategies context specific. The empirical evidence indicates that the likelihood of a plaintiff's success varies substantially by jurisdiction, as judges and juries may bring their personal or political biases into the courtroom. The tradeoff between campaign contributions, lobbying, and litigation is also affected by the nature of the institutional environment. Litigation loses its power in unified systems, limiting successful interest group activities to direct lobbying and buying.

For courts to play an important enforcement role, they must be at least somewhat independent from interference. Again, the evidence shows huge variation between countries in the efficacy and quality of their courts. Then, countries with good contract enforcement specialize in the production of goods for which relationship-specific investments are more important, while weak investor protection limits the scale of multinational firms' activities and alter the decision to deploy technology through foreign direct investment rather than licensing. Yet, the evidence points to extremely long expected duration of dispute resolution, suggesting that courts are not an attractive venue for resolving disputes. The evidence also suggests that the systems of dispute resolution in many countries are inefficient, which may explain why alternative strategies of securing property and contract, including private dispute resolution, are so widespread in developing countries.

All in all, the growing appreciation of the significance of legal arenas in non-market strategy offers many additional important avenues for future research.

Acknowledgment

I am very grateful to Monica Bedoya Denegri for valuable discussions on legal views and for passionately sharing with professional rigor her experience as a corporate counsel. The usual disclaimer applies.

Notes

1 Source: http://en.wikipedia.org/wiki/Apple_Inc._litigation; accessed December 2013.
2 Throughout this paper by "legal arenas" I mean the formal entities – judges and courts – that enforce rules and regulations and resolve disputes based on private and public law.
3 Firms are even created to arbitrate stakes in legal arenas and to capture value from marketable assets and rights. See, for example, "Second-hand suits", *The Economist*, April 6, 2013.
4 Moral and ethical considerations impinge upon most legal questions and, unquestionably, determine how the law is applied. Throughout the chapter I take the (unconvincing) position that managers, office-holders, and judges embrace the rule of law and recognize the moral aspects of strategic choice.
5 Private litigants have incentives to settle a dispute when doing so becomes mutually beneficial. With no transaction costs and income effects, private settlement would yield efficient outcomes (Coase, 1960).
6 As Posner (1993) also notes, politics, personal friendships, ideology, and pure serendipity play too large a role in the appointment of judges to warrant treating the judiciary as a collection of genius–saints miraculously immune to the tug of self-interest.
7 For example, firms can settle cases that are assigned unsympathetic judges or have "bad facts," while pressing forward with likely winners not only because of the merits of those cases but to set favorable precedents for future market and non-market disputes.
8 See, for example, Spiller and Gely (2007) for theoretical approaches and empirical reviews on judges' strategic decision-making, and Spier (2007) for a law and economics review of litigation.
9 Secondary effects can take several forms. For example, firms that defraud customers lose sales, and those that cheat suppliers face higher input costs or lost trade credit.

10 I use the term "law" to include national and sub-national constitutions, statutes enacted by legislatures, regulations and rules established by regulators and their enforcement agencies, and the common laws established by courts in the course of deciding specific cases.

11 Predatory pricing law is perhaps the antitrust theory most susceptible to strategic use because it involves an effort to punish the lowering of prices, a behavior that ordinarily counts as a virtue. Refer again to note 4.

12 Fraudulent actions are a potential source of competitive advantage and improved financial performance. However, I reemphasize the focus on the moral and legal conducts that firms can take in legal environments to secure a competitive advantage, and therefore discuss very little the strategic decision to engage in dubious behavior (Becker, 1968). Rather than strategic, fraud appears to be path dependent (Baucus and Near, 1991). Karpoff and Lott (1993) provide evidence that firms accused or convicted of corporate fraud experience a large reputational cost, which largely surpasses the costs of penalties and fines. Firms may also make fraudulent use of legal processes. Fraudulent litigation between firms may be due to rent-seeking, the search for favorable settlements through nuisance suits, or anticompetitive effects.

13 This is probably due to the fact that private firms may have better information than governments about potential antitrust violations (McAfee, Mialon, and Mialon, 2008).

14 It is generally argued that non-price predation will be a profitable strategy more frequently than will price predation. While the benefits of the two strategies to the predator are usually similar, the costs of non-price predation to the predator may be much lower.

15 See Hemphill (2004) for an analysis of ethical dilemmas in antitrust.

16 A preliminary injunction is typically issued shortly after the filing of a lawsuit on the basis of an abbreviated pre-trial hearing. Preliminary injunctions consider whether the petitioner has no adequate remedy at law or faces the threat of irreparable harm if the injunction is denied, the balance between irreparable harm and the injury that granting the injunction would inflict on the defendant, the probability that the plaintiff will win the case on its merits, and the public interest.

17 See Arrow (2010) for a thorough analysis of this case.

18 See www.larepublica.co/asuntos-legales/la-superindustria-protegi%C3%B3-los-derechos-de-la-marca-duff-de-fox_103806; accessed January 2014.

19 See www.patentlyapple.com/patently-apple/2013/10/apples-airplay-and-apple-tv-are-targeted-in-new-patent-lawsuit.html for an account of a legal dispute between Apple and Aylus Networks; accessed December 2013.

20 This discussion of the law and economics of litigation follows Spier (2007).

21 Note that plaintiffs motivated by an external or collateral gain may decide to sue even if the costs of litigating cannot be offset by the expected benefits of winning on the merits. Here, the costs of litigating can be justified solely by the collateral gain.

22 While x represents a transfer from the defendant to the plaintiff, the total cost of litigation is $c_{tp} + c_{td}$. The parties can avoid these costs through a private agreement to end the dispute before litigation costs are incurred. Several games with symmetric information use backward induction to resolve out-of-court settlement or case dropouts. The probability of settlement, however, depends on various factors, such as the timing of offers and counter-offers, the information and beliefs of the two litigants, and the way that the particular dispute fits into the broader economic, legal, and strategic environment.

23 For example, more money translates into better expert witnesses and better lawyers.

24 See again Spier (2007) for a law and economics analysis of multiparty litigations, such as class action lawsuits.

25 Priest and Klein (1984) first argued that cases in which the outcome is clear – the defendant has a strong case or the defendant has a weak case – are likely to be settled, whereas the cases that go to trial have outcomes that are unclear. This means that each litigant is likely to win about 50 percent of the time. This paper spawned a large amount of literature. Waldfogel (1995) tested some other predictions for different case types, while Siegelman and Waldfogel (1999) find that the Priest and Klein (1984) model fits the data when one more parameter is introduced: plaintiffs face greater uncertainty than defendants.

26 I mostly concentrate on inter-firm disputes. There is, however, a large body of empirical literature examining suits and settlement in product liability and medical malpractice, where plaintiffs are individuals. See, for instance, Polinsky and Shavell (2007).

27 This study largely follows from Bhagat, Brickley, and Coles (1994).

28 Note these costs are similar to those of Bhagat et al. (1998).

29 Firms that violate environmental regulations typically do not impose direct harm on their customers, employees or suppliers. Karpoff et al. (2005) argue that reputational penalties are then negligible because there are no repeat market transactions through which firms internalize violations costs. Koh, Qian, and Wang (2013) find that corporate social performance provides reputational insurance to litigation risk.

30 Bhattacharya et al. (2007) address judicial bias against foreign firms.

31 Apple's complaint included specific federal claims for patent infringement, false designation of origin, unfair competition, and trademark infringement, as well as state-level claims for unfair competition, common law trademark infringement, and unjust enrichment.

32 Source: http://en.wikipedia.org/wiki/Apple_Inc._v._Samsung_Electronics_Co.,_Ltd.; accessed December 2013.

33 Khoury, Junkunc, and Mingo (2012) find that differences in the legal environment of countries affect venture capital's investment strategies.

34 The correlation of the formalism index between the eviction of a non-paying tenant and the collection of a bounced check is 0.83.

35 See Shleifer, Lopez-de-Silanes, and La Porta (2008) for a thorough discussion of the consequences of countries' legal origins on economics- and business-related issues.

36 Results in Djankov et al. (2003) are highly correlated with those of Djankov, Hart, McLiesh, and Shleifer (2006), who study the efficiency of debt enforcement incorporating estimates of time, cost, and resolution of a standardized insolvency case. LaPorta, Lopez-de-Silanes, Pop-Eleches, and Shleifer (2004) take a different approach, as they collect information from national constitutions on judicial independence (as measured by judicial tenure) and the acceptance of appellate court rulings as a source of law. They ask whether judicial independence contributes to the quality of contract enforcement and the security of property rights.

37 This strategy also applies to lobbying in legislative arenas.

38 These situations are the same and have different moral and normative consequences.

39 For example, academic measures of de jure and de facto judicial independence are those of LaPorta et al. (2004) and Henisz (2000), respectively. The Global Competitiveness Reports offer more practical-oriented measures of judicial independence.

40 The exporter is also more likely to keep the bulk of its assets in its home jurisdiction.

41 Moore (2003), however, finds the prejudice in the jury.

References

Ansolabehere, S. D., de Figueiredo, J. M., and Snyder, J. M. (2003). Why is there so little money in US politics? *Journal of Economic Perspectives*, 17(1), 105–30.

Arrow, B. M. (2010). Real-life protection for fictional trademarks. *Fordham Intellectual Property, Media, and Entertainment Law Journal*, 21, 111.

Asker, J., and Bar-Isaac, H. (2010). *Exclusionary Minimum Resale Price Maintenance*. No. w16564. Cambridge, MA: National Bureau of Economic Research.

Bagley, C. E. (2008). Winning legally: The value of legal astuteness. *Academy of Management Review*, 33(2), 378–90.

— (2010). What's law got to do with it? Integrating law and strategy. *American Business Law Journal*, 47(4), 587–639.

Baron, David P. (1994). Electoral competition with informed and uninformed voters. *American Political Science Review*, 88(1), 33–47.

— (2001). Theories of strategic non-market participation: Majority-rule and executive institutions. *Journal of Economics and Management Strategy*, 10(1), 47–89.

— (2003). *Business and its Environment*. Englewood Cliffs, NJ: Prentice-Hall.

— (2006). Persistent media bias. *Journal of Public Economics*, 90(1), 1–36.

Baucus, M. S., and Near, J. P. (1991). Can illegal corporate behavior be predicted? An event history analysis. *Academy of Management Journal*, 34(1), 9–36.

Becker, G. S. (1968). Crime and punishment: An economic approach. *Journal of Political Economy*, 76(2), 169–217.

Berkowitz, D., Moenius, J., and Pistor, K. (2006). Trade, law, and product complexity. *Review of Economics and Statistics*, 88(2), 363–73.

Bhagat, S., Bizjak, J., and Coles, J. L. (1998). The shareholder wealth implications of corporate law-suits. *Financial Management*, 50(4), 5–27.

Bhagat, S., Brickley, J. A., and Coles, J. L. (1994). The costs of inefficient bargaining and financial distress: Evidence from corporate lawsuits. *Journal of Financial Economics*, 35(2), 221–47.

Bhattacharya, U., Galpin, N., and Haslem, B. (2007). The home court advantage in international corporate litigation. *Journal of Law and Economics*, 50(4), 625–60.

Bizjak, J. M., and Coles, J. L. (1995). The effect of private antitrust litigation on the stock-market valuation of the firm. *American Economic Review*, 85(3), 436–61.

Bonardi, J.-P., and Keim, G. D. (2005). Corporate political strategies for widely salient issues. *Academy of Management Review*, 30(3), 555–76.

Bonneau, C., and Cann, D. (2009). The effect of campaign contributions on judicial decision-making. Unpublished manuscript.

Bouwen, P., and McCown, M. (2007). Lobbying versus litigation: Political and legal strategies of interest representation in the European Union. *Journal of European Public Policy*, 14(3), 422–43.

Brandenburger, A. M., and Stuart, H. W. (1996). Value-based business strategy. *Journal of Economics and Management Strategy*, 5(1), 5–24.

Capron, L., and Chatain, O. (2008). Competitors' resource-oriented strategies: Acting on competitors' resources through interventions in factor markets and political markets. *Academy of Management Review*, 33(1), 97–121.

Chong, A., and Gradstein, M. (2011). Is the world flat? Country-and firm-level determinants of law compliance. *Journal of Law, Economics, and Organization*, 27(2), 272–300.

Coase, R. H. (1960). Problem of social cost. *Journal of Law and Economics*, 4(1), 1–44.

Cooter, R. D., and Rubinfeld, D. L. (1989). Economic analysis of legal disputes and their resolution. *Journal of Economic Literature*, 27, 1067–97.

Crane, D. A. (2005). The paradox of predatory pricing. *Cornell Law Review*, 91, 1.

Cross, F. B. (2003). Business and judicial politics. *Business and Politics*, 5(1), 3–5.

Cutler, D., and Summers, L. (1988). The costs of conflict resolution and financial distress: Evidence from the Texaco–Pennzoil litigation. *Rand Journal of Economics*, Summer, 157–72.

Dal Bó, E., Dal Bó, P., and Di Tella, R. (2006). Plata o Plomo? Bribe and punishment in a theory of political influence. *American Political Science Review*, 100(1), 41–53.

Daughety, A. F. (2000). Settlement. In B. Bouckaert and G. De Geest (eds.), *Encyclopedia of Law and Economics*, Vol. 5. Cheltenham: Edward Elgar, 95–158.

De Figueiredo, J. M. (2005). Strategic plaintiffs and ideological judges in telecommunications litigation. *Journal of Law, Economics, and Organization*, 21(2), 501–23.

De Figueiredo, J. M., and de Figueiredo Jr, R. J. (2002). The allocation of resources by interest groups: Lobbying, litigation and administrative regulation. *Business and Politics*, 4(2), 161–81.

De Figueiredo, R. J. P., and Edwards, G. (2007). Does private money buy public policy? Campaign contributions and regulatory outcomes in telecommunications. *Journal of Economics and Management Strategy*, 16(3), 547–76.

DellaVigna, S., and Kaplan, E. (2007). The Fox News effect: Media bias and voting. *Quarterly Journal of Economics*, 122(3), 1187–234.

Djankov, S., Hart, O., McLiesh, C., and Shleifer, A. (2006). *Debt Enforcement around the World*. No. w12807. Cambridge, MA: National Bureau of Economic Research.

Djankov, S., La Porta, R., Lopez-de-Silanes, F., and Shleifer, A. (2003). Courts. *Quarterly Journal of Economics*, 118(2), 453–517.

Feld, L. P., and Voigt, S. (2003). Economic growth and judicial independence: Cross-country evidence using a new set of indicators. *European Journal of Political Economy*, 19, 497–527.

Fields, M. A. (1990). The wealth effects of corporate lawsuits: Pennzoil v. Texaco. *Journal of Business Research*, 21(2), 143–58.

Gilbert, R. J., and Katz, M. L. (2001). An economist's guide to US v. Microsoft. *Journal of Economic Perspectives*, 15(2), 25–44.

Gould, J. P. (1973). The economics of legal conflicts. *Journal of Legal Studies*, 2(2), 279–300.

Hadfield, G. K. (2005). The many legal institutions that support contractual commitment. In M. M. Shirley and C. Ménard (eds.), *Handbook of New Institutional Economics*. Netherlands: Kluwer Academic Publishers, 175–203.

Hall, B. H., and Ziedonis, R. H. (2007). An empirical analysis of patent litigation in the semiconductor industry. University of California at Berkeley Working Paper, 217–42.

Hemphill, T. A. (2004). Antitrust, dynamic competition, and business ethics. *Journal of Business Ethics*, 50(2), 127–35.

Henisz, W. J. (2000). The institutional environment for multinational investment. *Journal of Law, Economics, and Organization*, 16(2), 334–64.

Henisz, W. J., and Zelner, B. A. (2001). The institutional environment for telecommunications investment. *Journal of Economics and Management Strategy*, 10(1), 123–47.

Hertzel, M. G., and Smith, J. K. (1993). Industry effects of interfirm lawsuits: Evidence from Pennzoil v. Texaco. *Journal of Law, Economics, and Organization*, 9, 425.

Hillman, A. J., and Hitt, M. A. (1999). Corporate political strategy formulation: A model of approach, participation, and strategy decisions. *Academy of Management Review*, 24(4), 825–42.

Hillman, A. J., Keim, G. D., and Schuler, D. (2004). Corporate political activity: A review and research agenda. *Journal of Management*, 30(6), 837–57.

Iaryczower, M., and Shum, M. (2012). The value of information in the court: Get it right, keep it tight. *American Economic Review*, 102(1), 202–37.

Jarrell, G. A. (1985). The wealth effects of litigation by targets: Do interests diverge in a merge? *Journal of Law and Economics*, 28, 151–77.

Karpoff, J. M., and Lott Jr, J. R. (1993). Reputational penalty firms bear from committing criminal fraud. *Journal of Law and Economics*, 36, 757.

Karpoff, J. M., Lott Jr, J. R., and Wehrly, E. W. (2005). The reputational penalties for environmental violations: Empirical evidence. *Journal of Law and Economics*, 48(2), 653–75.

Khoury, T. A., Junkunc, M., and Mingo, S. (2012). Navigating political hazard risks and legal system quality venture capital investments in Latin America. *Journal of Management*.

Koh, P.-S., Qian, C., and Wang, H. (2013). Firm litigation risk and the insurance value of corporate social performance. *Strategic Management Journal*, 35(10), 1464–82.

Landes, W. M. (1971). An economic analysis of the courts. *Journal of Law and Economics*, 14(1), 61–107.

Lanjouw, J. O., and Lerner, J. (2001). Tilting the table? The use of preliminary injunctions. *Journal of Law and Economics*, 44(2), 573–603.

LaPorta, R., Lopez-de-Silanes, F., Pop-Eleches, C., and Shleifer, A. 2004. Judicial checks and balances. *Journal of Political Economy*, 112(2), 445–70.

Lim, C. S. H., Snyder Jr, J. M., and Stromberg, D. (2010). Measuring media influence on US state courts. Unpublished manuscript.

Marsh, S. J. (1998). Creating barriers for foreign competitors: A study of the impact of anti-dumping actions on the performance of US firms. *Strategic Management Journal*, 19(1), 25–37.

McAfee, R. P., and Vakkur, N. V. (2004). The strategic abuse of antitrust laws. *Journal of Strategic Management Education*, 1(3), 1–18.

McAfee, R. P., Mialon, H. M., and Mialon, S. H. (2008). Private v. public antitrust enforcement: A strategic analysis. *Journal of Public Economics*, 92(10), 1863–75.

Milgrom, P., and Roberts, J. (1982). Predation, reputation, and entry deterrence. *Journal of Economic Theory*, 27(2), 280–312.

Moore, K. (2003). Xenophobia in American courts. *Northwestern University Law Review*, 97, 1497–550.

Mullainathan, S., and Shleifer, A. (2005). The market for news. *American Economic Review*, 95(4), 1031–53.

North, D. C. (1990). *Institutions, Institutional Change and Economic Performance*. Cambridge: Cambridge University Press.

North, D. C., and Weingast, B. R. (1989). Constitutions and commitment: The evolution of institutions governing public choice in seventeenth-century England. *Journal of Economic History*, 49(4), 803–32.

Oliver, C., and Holzinger, I. (2008). The effectiveness of strategic political management: A dynamic capabilities framework. *Academy of Management Review*, 33(2), 496–520.

Perloff, J. M., Rubinfeld, D. L., and Ruud, P. (1996). Antitrust settlements and trial outcomes. *Review of Economics and Statistics*, 789(3), 401–9.

Peteraf, M. A., and Barney, J. B. (2003). Unraveling the resource-based tangle. *Managerial and Decision Economics*, 24(4), 309–23.

Polinsky, A. M., and Shavell, S. (eds.). (2007). *Handbook of Law and Economics*, Vol. 2. Netherlands: Elsevier.

Posner, R. A. (1973). An economic approach to legal procedure and judicial administration. *Journal of Legal Studies*, 2(2), 399–458.

— (1993). What do judges and justices maximize? (The same thing everybody else does.) *Supreme Court Economic Review*, 30, 1–41.

Priest, G. L., and Klein, B. (1984). The selection of disputes for litigation. *Journal of Legal Studies*, 13(1), 1–55.

Ríos-Figueroa, J., and Staton, J. K. (2012). An evaluation of cross-national measures of judicial independence. *Journal of Law, Economics, and Organization*, 24(3), 104–37.

Rubin, P. H., Curran, C., and Curran, J. F. (2001). Litigation versus legislation: Forum shopping by rent seekers. *Public Choice*, 107(3–4), 295–310.

Salop, S. C. (1979). Strategic entry deterrence. *American Economic Review*, 69(2), 335–8.

Salop, S. C., and Scheffman, D. T. (1983). Raising rivals' costs. *American Economic Review*, 73(2), 267–71.

Schmidt, P. (2002). Pursuing regulatory relief: Strategic participation and litigation in US OSHA rulemaking. *Business and Politics*, 4(1), 71–89.

Schwab, K. (2013). *The Global Competitiveness Report 2013–2014*. Switzerland: World Economic Forum.

Shleifer, A., Lopez-de-Silanes, F., and La Porta, R. (2008). The economic consequences of legal origins. *Journal of Economic Literature*, 46(2), 285–332.

Siegelman, P., and Waldfogel, J. (1999). Toward a taxonomy of disputes: New evidence through the prism of the Priest/Klein model. *Journal of Legal Studies*, 28, 101.

Sokol, D. (2012). The strategic use of public and private litigation in antitrust as business strategy. *Southern California Law Review*, 85, 689–95.

Somaya, D. (2003). Strategic determinants of decisions not to settle patent litigation. *Strategic Management Journal*, 24(1), 17–38.

Songer, D. R., and Sheehan, R. S. (1992). Who wins on appeal? Upperdogs and underdogs in the United States courts of appeals. *American Journal of Political Science*, 36(1), 235–58.

Spier, K. E. (2007). Litigation. In A. M. Polinsky and S. Shavell (eds.), *Handbook of Law and Economics*, Vol. 1, Netherlands: Elsevier, 259–342.

Spiller, P., and Gely, R. (1992). Congressional control or judicial independence: The determinants of US Supreme Court labor-relations decisions, 1949–88. *RAND Journal of Economics*, 23(4), 463–92.

— (2007). *Strategic Judicial Decision Making*. No. w13321. Cambridge, MA: National Bureau of Economic Research.

Spiller, P. T., and Liao, S. (2006). *Buy, Lobby or Sue: Interest Groups' Participation in Policy Making: A Selective Survey*. No. w12209. Cambridge, MA: National Bureau of Economic Research.

Waldfogel, J. (1995). The selection hypothesis and the relationship between trial and plaintiff victory. *Journal of Political Economy*, 103, 229–60.

Whitford, A. B. (2003). The structures of interest coalitions: Evidence from environmental litigation. *Business and Politics*, 5(1), 45–64.

Yao, D. (1988). Beyond the reach of the invisible hand: Impediments to economic activity, market failures, and profitability. *Strategic Management Journal*, 9, 59–70.

Yoffie, D. B., and Kwak, M. (2001). Playing by the rules. How Intel avoids antitrust litigation. *Harvard Business Review*, 79(6), 119.

10
Culture and international investment

Rodrigo Bandeira-de-Mello

Non-market factors have long been on the agenda of international business literature as an important explanatory and managerial variable (Rodriguez, Siegel, Hillman, and Eden, 2006). A central task for multinational corporation (MNC) managers is learning how to cope with non-market differences between their home market and foreign markets. These differences have an impact on decisions such as entry and establishment modes, location, and governance, and reflect on the performance and survival of international operations (Kirkman, Lowe, and Gibson, 2006; Ambos and Hakanson, 2014). This chapter relates two important non-market components, namely culture and politics, to the international investment decisions of developing country multinational corporations (DMNCs).

Existing theory suggests there are two factors linking cultural aspects to the international investments of DMNCs (Cuervo-Cazurra, 2012). First, DMNC managers are accustomed to hostile and volatile environments in their home countries and, as a result, are less risk-averse than their colleagues from advanced country multinational corporations (AMNCs). Second, DMNCs are more likely to move to culturally dissimilar countries, rather than learning incrementally from their international operations in culturally similar countries. This is because the former present more market opportunities than the latter. This tradeoff is not faced by AMNCs, since similar countries are also rich and developed.

In this chapter I show that politics at home has an effect on how DMNC managers cope with cultural differences when deciding about foreign direct investment (FDI) locations. I draw hypotheses from international business and political economy perspectives to show that a firm's political connections at home make DMNCs more likely to move to culturally distant places when making FDI investments. The mechanism producing the hypothesized effects undergoes changes in managerial perception toward risk and opportunity assessments that happen when firms benefit from three major rents that are the result of policy-induced market imperfections: subsidies, favorable competition policy, and reduced red tape. The politically connected DMNC manager tends to assess risks and opportunities in the foreign market favorably and is, therefore, more likely to jump cultural distances.

I test my argument by using large, traditional Brazilian DMNCs as a sample. The sample choice is important for several reasons. First, Brazil is a good laboratory for testing the effect of political connections, since firms and governments operate in a close mutual relationship when putting forward development policies (Lazzarini, Musacchio, Bandeira-de-Mello, and Marcon, 2012). Second, Brazil is a variety of hierarchical democratic capitalism, which induces strong individual political behavior from firms, making it possible to observe the private benefits obtained from political strategies (Schneider, 2013). Third, the electoral system in Brazil makes corporate financial contributions to political candidates a good investment for both firms and candidates, who exchange favors for money (Samuels, 2001, 2002; Boas, Hidalgo, and Richardson, 2014). Official data that match donor firms and individual candidate recipients allow the election effect between winning and losing candidates to be measured and isolated. This is important for reducing endogeneity problems (Claessens, Feijen, and Laeven, 2008). Finally, the Brazilian MNCs in the sample are among the largest and most traditional in the country.

I address an empirical gap in the culture-based explanation for the internationalization of DMNCs. In particular, I specify the political nature of the phenomena that affect the location of FDI in culturally distant places. Not all DMNCs in a given country are equally capable of jumping cultural distance, but those that are more closely connected to the home government are more likely to cope with cultural distance. This argument also contributes to specifying the value of the political connections with the home government in democratic governments.

Theoretical background

Cultural distance and FDI

Cross-national distance is a key concept in international business and in management in general (Berry, Guillén, and Zhou, 2010). It has been used as a variable to explain virtually every phenomenon related to international investment (Kirkman, Lowe, and Gibson, 2006). Cross-national distances have been operationalized in many ways, using several- or single-dimension measures, but maybe the most popular has been the dimensions of psychic distance and its even more popular offspring, cultural distance (Kirkman, Lowe, and Gibson, 2006; Ambos and Hakanson, 2014).

The Uppsala incremental internationalization theory gives the concept of psychic distance a central role in predicting the internationalization process of MNCs. According to this theory, psychic distance is correlated with the presence of non-market attributes in the foreign market, such as language, culture, and regulations, which prevent knowledge about markets and operations from flowing to the home market. More precisely, this concept is defined as "factors preventing or disturbing the flows of information between firm and market. Examples of such factors are differences in language, culture, political systems, level of education, level of industrial development, etc." (Johanson and Wiedersheim-Paul, 1975: 307). International investment for Uppsala scholars is a gradual process by which the firm copes with greater psychic distances, and acquires knowledge and experience, in order to engage in committing resources to distant markets. At the initial stages, the firm targets places that are familiar to its home country, that is, places with low psychic distances. As the firm learns how to acquire information from and communicate with the market it becomes more inclined to commit resources (from sales agents to fully owned subsidiaries) to more psychically distant places (Johanson and Vahlne, 1977).

Cultural distance is a common proxy for psychic distance (Kogut and Singh, 1988; Ambos and Hakanson, 2014). Culture is defined as the "collective programing of the mind which distinguishes the members of one human group from another" (Hofstede, 1980: 25) and it is manifested through symbols such as language and codes of conduct that reflect shared values and taken-for-granted assumptions. Cultural differences play a great role in explaining international business decisions as one of the main tasks of international managers is to cope with different cultures. For researchers, the great challenge is how to grasp the complexity of cultural differences in research design. Usual measures of cultural distance include indices such as Hofstede's dimensions and the GLOBE Project (Kirkman, Lowe, and Gibson, 2006). These indices assign scores to countries for specific cultural dimensions that refer to the attitude of people towards values, such as individuality, family, work, authority, etc. Kogut and Singh (1988) proposed a measure for cultural distance using Hofstede's dimensions that became widely used in the field. They constructed a final average score based on the Euclidean distances between foreign and host countries for each dimension.

In spite of its popularity, the cultural distance concept has faced criticism. The main problems refer to hidden properties of symmetry (the difference between country A and country B is the same as between country B and country A), the stability of the differences over time, the linearity of the causal effect on international business decisions, the causality of a single dimension of distance (culture), and that differences generate discordance and lack of fit among individuals (Shenkar, 2001). Also, the use of score-based indices raises the issue of aggregating individual scores to build country-level scores, which is called "ecological fallacy" (Berry, Guillén, and Zhou, 2010).

These conceptual and operationalization problems might explain why empirical research has produced mixed findings. In a review paper, Kirkman, Lowe, and Gibson (2006) report that cultural distance has been found to affect outward foreign direct investment (OFDI) from the US negatively (Li and Guisinger, 1992; Loree and Guisinger, 1995), but also to have no impact on initial or subsequent FDI decisions (Benito and Gripsrud, 1992), and to have a positive impact on increasing FDI in Mexico (Thomas and Grosse, 2001). Despite the controversy, cultural distance still remains a popular explanatory variable to explain FDI (Ambos and Hakanson, 2014).

Government-induced OFDI

Government-induced OFDI may be a result of restrictive policies or institutional misalignment between the MNC and the home country institutional environment (Witt and Lewin, 2007). But, as emerging economies occupied a prominent position in the world flow of FDI (Rasiah, Gammeltoft, and Jiang, 2010), researchers and practitioners turned their attention to home country government policies that promoted OFDI and nurtured global companies (Hong, Wang, and Kafouros, 2014).

From a political economy perspective, MNCs and government are in a mutually dependent relationship. Emerging economy governments, like any other government, want to improve macroeconomic and social conditions, achieve sustainable economic growth, and, of course, maximize the likelihood of remaining in power. To this end, such governments implement development policies that usually include the integration of the country in the world economy through the investment of domestic firms (Luo, Xue, and Han, 2010). Nurturing OFDI produces positive externalities, as DMNCs bring home new technologies and help increase the country's productivity.

Literature has tried extensively to model the effect of government policies on OFDI theoretically. Brewer (1993) highlights the importance of government policies that make FDI an attractive option for MNCs. The author builds on the core idea that government policies produce market imperfections that are responsible for making FDI a rational economic alternative over trade and licenses (Boddewyn, 1988). Major market imperfections come from two sources: Hymer's market power and its origin in industry structure; and Williamson's transaction costs. According to Brewer (1993), Dunning's Eclectic paradigm takes both sources into account in predicting FDI: oligopolistic competition at home gives MNCs superiority to compete with local firms abroad (ownership); the internalization of operations through FDI is preferred because of high transaction costs in governing trade or licensing in the foreign country (internalization); and firms will seek locations where such superiority has a higher value when compared with alternative places (location). Since major sources of transaction costs are the consequence of erratic, weak governments that are incapable of enforcing laws and contracts, for instance, both home and host government policies matter in FDI decisions. In another model, Murtha and Lenway (1994) explain how and why governments can deliberately influence the strategic choices of MNCs. Governments can issue and implement industrial strategies that reallocate resources to achieve national objectives that have an impact on an MNC's strategic choices. The major policy components, according to Murtha and Lenway (1994), are: to what extent the government imposes credible commitments on firms; the scope of the policy target (industry or firm); the extent to which property rights are assigned to private or state-owned corporations; and the extent to which transactional government happens by way of the market or government authority.

In the context of emerging economies, the burgeoning empirical research on home government-induced OFDI has documented the major features of promoting policies: tax relief; privileged information and investment coordination; financial aid; and bilateral and regional agreements to reduce red tape (Rasiah, Gammeltoft, and Jiang, 2010). Brewer (1993) suggests the following home government policies that may have a positive impact on OFDI: monetary policies with regard to money supply, interest and exchange rates; subsidies; and export and price controls. Brewer (1993) also mentions that lax antitrust policies that allow for the over-concentration of firms in the domestic market generate market imperfections that promote OFDI.

China has largely been used as a context for measuring the effect of government policies on OFDI. Results show that favorable government policies are more important for driving a firm's level of OFDI than technological and advertising resources (Wang, Hong, Kafouros, and Wright, 2012). Luo, Xue, and Han (2010) extensively documented the evolution of Chinese policies that culminated with the recent provision of strong support for Chinese MNCs. They identify the following promotional policies: a financial and taxation policy through tax relief; credit and loan support; a favorable foreign exchange policy; risk-safeguard mechanisms, such as an insurance subsidiary for expatriates and a mutual protection agreement; information service network to inform managers about the rules on investment in different countries; bank information; and OFDI direction guidance, which provides information about firms and foreign countries.

In democratic countries like Brazil, where the promotion policy is less formal and more diffuse than in China, Bazuchi et al. (2013) identified the following mechanisms that have an influence on OFDI: subsidized loans from the National Development Bank (BNDES) at half the market rate; minority government ownership of government-controlled, state-owned pension funds and the BNDES Holding Company; privileged treatment in conflict resolution when the home government deploys diplomatic resources to solve conflicts with host governments in order to facilitate investments; and favorable regulation. The government issues a wide range of regulations, such as all-encompassing industrial policy for specific sectors, approval to gain above-normal market power, and preferential treatment for issuing licenses.

In sum, Luo, Xue, and Han (2010) summarize the following institutional mechanisms that positively affect OFDI: fiscal incentives; insurance against political risk; assistance in international expansion through government agencies (chamber or ministry of commerce, etc.); double taxation avoidance agreements; bilateral and regional treatment to protect investments abroad; a bilateral or multilateral framework to liberalize investment conditions in host countries; and help for firms in dealing with a host country's government institutions.

Development of hypotheses

Governments affect OFDI flows. Favorable policies can influence international investments that otherwise would not have been made (Murtha and Lenway, 1994). However, the rents generated by government policies are not equally appropriated by local DMNCs. The theory underpinning the different effects of government policies on MNC activity was set out in a seminal paper by Boddewyn (1988). He draws attention to the fact that the government and market imperfections generated are not exogenous, or a "given," as considered by the dominant internationalization models. Drawing from several theoretical traditions, including political economy and political science, Boddewyn (1988) models the political behavior of MNCs as a strategic interplay between firms and governments: instead of passively responding to government policies, MNCs can actively shape them in their favor, thus generating asymmetric benefits. By way of strategic political behavior, politically competent MNCs can induce market imperfections from government actions and then appropriate ownership advantages (Boddewyn, 1988; Brewer, 1993).

Empirical research into the heterogeneous distribution of political capabilities in the home country and their effect on the internalization of firms has flourished (see Hong, Wang, Kafouros, 2014 for a review). As an example, Wang, Hong, Kafouros, and Wright (2012) show how company idiosyncrasies cause different effects on foreign investment by Chinese multinationals. They build their argument upon institutional and resource-based theories to show that the degree of government ownership and level of government affiliation (state, provincial, city, county, etc.) affect both the type (market- or resource-seeking) and location (developing and developed country) of OFDI. Bandeira-de-Mello, Arreola, and Marcon (2012) found that the greater the political connection of Brazilian multinationals through campaign contributions, the greater the speed at which they commit assets abroad.

I have discussed why home governments may induce OFDI from local multinationals as well as how government policies affect MNC decisions. Considering that MNCs will seek out rents, two issues become important for deriving my hypotheses about the effect of home country political connections on jumping cultural distances: first, the underlying mechanism by which rents deriving from policy-generated market imperfections affect the decision to internationalize to a culturally distant location; and, second, how those rents are asymmetrically distributed for selected DMNCs.

I address these questions by focusing my argument on three types of rent that are most typical for supporting OFDI policies: subsidies; a favorable competition policy; and reduced red tape. Subsidies usually come as soft budget constraints. Kornai (1986) proposed the concept of soft budget constraint to explain the inefficiencies of socialist regimes and later transition economies. It implies a particular and paternalistic role of the state in providing special treatment for some economic agents, for example in the form of cheap loans or in choosing not to enforce loan contracts. The soft budget constraint has been used to explain the outward FDI of Chinese companies. Using state ownership as a proxy for soft budget constraint, Shi (2013) shows that soft budget constraint is the main reason why Chinese state-owned enterprises (SOEs) invest in riskier locations than their private counterparts.

Favorable competition policies allow for the breeding of national champions. "National champions may be created or protected in a number of ways, such as by the granting of state aid, the encouragement of domestic mergers, or opposition to the takeover of a domestic company by a foreign company" (OECD, 2009: 11). The selection of these firms tends to respond to the attainment of industrial and economic objectives (Stal and Cuervo-Cazurra, 2011). Governments allow for above-normal industry concentration through mergers and acquisitions. Being strong in the domestic market also allows the consolidator to become a worldwide industry champion. Governments are also likely to pick national champion candidates from among firms that are influential in the national arena and for which owning a controlling stake can help protect what may be seen as an issue of national pride or sovereignty (Bagwell and Staiger, 1999).

Reduced red tape may come as the speeding up of bureaucratic processes, reduced paperwork, and/or privileged access to the diplomatic agenda and agencies. The home government may directly negotiate with host governments in order to mitigate political risk or reduce requirements for issuing licenses, reduce sanitary requirements, or even help in reducing legitimacy problems (Luo, Xue, and Han, 2010). Chinese companies, for instance, cope with considerable risk in their international investments by going to risky locations, largely thanks to home–host government relationships (Wang, Hong, Kafouros, and Wright, 2012).

I argue that subsidies, favorable competition policies, and reduced red tape affect managerial perception and the assessment of the risks and opportunities associated with investing in the host country. According to culture-based models of internationalization, bounded-rational and risk-averse managers will frame risk and opportunities in order to decide how to commit their resources (Johanson and Vahlne, 1977). The difference is that managerial assessment is contingent upon experience, and I argue that it is contingent upon the appropriation of policy rents.

Since one tenet of the soft budget constraint concept is that the entrepreneur should perceive and act upon their perception, a high probability of being bailed out by the government (Kornai, 1986) and the donor's expectation of receiving something in exchange are very important for understanding how the soft budget mechanism will lead to a downward bias in risk evaluation and an upward bias in opportunity assessment. The same reasoning applies to a favorable competition policy and reduced red tape. Institutional pressures to create and develop global champions at home urge firms to pursue foreign opportunities (Wang, Hong, Kafouros, and Wright, 2012). Through its agencies, the government may help reduce any market information bias and provide to the politically connected firm privileged information about possible subsidies and bureaucratic requirements from the host government. Foreign market information is usually channeled via contacts with partners and fairs.

I argue that home government support at home reduces uncertainty and favors risk and opportunity assessment by managers, making them more prone to commit resources in culturally distant places. But how are these selected DMNCs chosen in the first place? Boddewyn (1988) suggests the existence of a political market where government decision-makers (supply) and firms (demand) meet. In fact, the political market metaphor has been further developed and has helped in predicting what kind of political strategy firms should use to cope with specific political market structures (Bonardi, Hillman, and Keim, 2005). Hillman and Hitt (1999) propose three types of political strategy: financial (corporate campaign contribution); informational (lobbying); and constituency-building (advocacy).

These existing political strategy typologies, however, are designed for the pluralist institutional setting, which is typical of the United States. Faccio (2006) measured a more direct type of influence based on personal connections between politicians and businesspeople. She found that connections are pervasive around the world, but more prominent in institutionally weak countries. The value of such connections has been measured in many ways and the results are usually positive for the firm (Faccio, 2006).

I focus on a specific type of connection that is formed when the firm directly finances the electoral campaign of the elected candidate. Unlike the US, where firms usually donate via political action committees, or provide parties with soft money, I model the direct financing of the political candidate. Firms donate to receive early favors from the candidate in office. Candidates need money to get elected and reelected. This is akin to a relational contract type of transaction that is assigned to a mutual hostage exchange type of governance: both parties sink non-salvageable assets into the relationship in the form of money and in the need to refinance the campaign continuously and obtain rents from the government. Connected MNCs signal to the government that they are more likely to participate in government plans. Elected politicians will pay back the contribution by facilitating access to subsidized loans and government contracts.

Based on my previous arguments, politically connected firms at home will assess risks and opportunities in a way that will make them more inclined to make resource commitments by jumping cultural distances. Hence, my first hypothesis is:

H1: Political connections at home positively affect a DMNC's direct investment in culturally distant countries.

The underlying mechanism producing the effect of jumping cultural distances is the bounded-rational and risk-averse manager's favorable perception of the risks and opportunities in the foreign market. However, might one argue that other mechanisms are also in play and produce the same effects? It is important to address alternative explanations in order to make my arguments stronger.

I propose two alternative mechanisms that are substitutes for political connections at home. First, while Hypothesis H1 proposes that political connections at home have this effect on managerial perception, one might argue that having a foreign partner might produce an equivalent effect. Foreign ownership in DMNCs is a common phenomenon. Foreign investors possess international networks that make the flow of information more fluid. Experienced foreign investors, like DMNC partners, may endow the firm with superior knowledge and expertise about foreign markets as well as about managing subsidiaries abroad.

Political connections at home and foreign ownership are expected to be equally beneficial to the DMNC. However, I argue that these two "jumping mechanisms" are substitutes for each other. Foreign ownership, even if it is minority ownership, requires governance compliance that is not usually compatible with establishing close relationships with the powerful. Chaney, Faccio, and Parsley (2008) find that, because politically connected firms are not prone to revealing their actual financial status to politicians and are, thus, less accountable to market pressures, they produce significantly poorer earnings reports than do their non-connected counterparts. Since most DMNCs are business groups, Khanna and Yafeh (2007) note that foreign ownership of business groups affects the relationship between groups and government. Political connections enable affiliates to access valuable country resources for repeated market entry (Guillén, 2000; Wan, 2005), which conflicts with the refocusing requirements demanded by foreign associates (Hoskisson, Johnson, Tihanyi, and White 2005). Therefore, I propose a second hypothesis.

H2: Foreign ownership negatively moderates the effect of political connections at home on direct DMNC investment in culturally distant countries.

The second alternative "jumping mechanism" is a firm's capabilities. A capable firm has stable routines and heuristics that make it more efficient than its competitors. For a DMNC, superior capabilities may include searching, assessing, and transferring assets in order to leverage and upgrade knowledge abroad (Luo and Tung, 2007). It is expected that a DMNC that possesses superior FDI capabilities is also more likely to engage in resource commitments in culturally distant places (Cuervo-Cazurra, 2008). On the other hand, DMNCs with weak capabilities are more likely to connect politically in order to compensate for their weak firm-specific advantages (Hong, Wang, and Kafouros, 2014). Therefore, DMNCs possessing superior FDI capabilities will be more likely to exploit these capabilities rather than explore political ones (Luo and Rui, 2009).

Experiential knowledge acquired over time is the underlying substrate of company capabilities (Kogut and Zander, 1992). Therefore, I expect that older DMNCs will be less likely to profit from the effect of political connections at home than younger firms. Hence, the third hypothesis:

H3: Experiential knowledge negatively moderates the effect of political connections at home on a DMNC's direct investment in culturally distant countries.

Methods

Research setting

Brazil is a good natural laboratory to test my hypotheses about the role of political connections in the relationship between culture and international investments. The country is a typical representation of hierarchical capitalism (Schneider, 2013): business groups are the preferred organizational form for large firms and MNCs; there is a lot of informality; and job tenure is low. Historically, business associations have weakened since the 1930s. There is no all-encompassing and peak business association. Emerging markets, particularly in Latin America, are typical hierarchical economies and thus favor individual, corporate political activity. In Brazil, particularly, financing the right candidates gives superior access to government contracts (Boas, Hidalgo, and Richardson, 2014) and cheap credit (Claessens, Feijen, and Laeven, 2008; Lazzarini, Musacchio, Bandeira-de-Mello, and Marcon, 2012). That is why corporate campaign finance is by far the major source of election funding for candidates. Firms donate to candidates of both the left and the right, seeking a hedge for their vulnerable position.

Legislation allows direct, corporate financial contributions to political candidates of up to 2 percent of their gross revenue (although this law is poorly enforced, so the actual contribution is usually higher). Considering that competing in an election under an open-list proportional representation system in electoral districts as big as England is very costly, successful candidates usually trade pork for money to pay their campaign expenses (Samuels, 2001, 2002).

Brazil has also adopted an overt policy of favoring OFDI. It has used the BNDES to orchestrate industry concentration and nurture national champions. Lazzarini, Musacchio, Bandeira-de-Mello, and Marcon (2012) found that BNDES allocations are both technical and political. The bank seems not to select bad performers, but political connections through the financing of elected candidates increase the likelihood of receiving debt and equity from the bank. This policy has produced important global firms, such as world leaders JBS (food) and Fibria (pulp and paper).

Table 10.1 Sampled industries and firms

Industry	Number of observations	Firms
Food and Beverage	15	Ambev, JBS and Marfrig
Retail	7	Natura
Mining	7	Vale
Machinery	7	Weg
Pulp and Paper	18	Klabin, Suzano and Fibria
Oil and Gas	7	Petrobras
Chemicals	13	Braskem and Ultrapar
Steel	18	Gerdau, Lupatech and Usiminas
Textiles	7	Coteminas-Springs Global
Transportation	7	ALL Logistica
Vehicles and Parts	42	DHB, Embraer, Iochp-Maxion, Marcopolo, Randon and Tupy
Total	148	

Finally, legislation requires candidates to report information about their donors. This publicly available information makes it possible to connect donor firms to politicians. This is a unique data source that makes it possible to make better estimates.

Sample

I used a sample of large privately owned Brazilian multinationals listed on the São Paulo Stock Exchange. I used only secondary sources to collect data. Financial figures were available from the stock exchange, cultural distance measures were taken from the Hofstede Center website, and information about foreign investment was obtained primarily from the transnationality indices series, provided by *Valor Econômico*, a major business newspaper in Brazil. It was also cross-checked with several sources, such as the companies' own websites, specialist publications, and other public data sources.

Nevertheless, some considerations about sampling and sample size need to be taken into account. First, listed firms are the only source of reliable company data in Brazil, even though this considerably limits sample size and imposes self-selection problems. Second, not all the information about internationalization activity is publicly available, which made me proceed with skepticism and use the triangulation of different sources. Third, and most importantly, the final sample size was severely reduced due to a lack of available information. I was able to assemble panel data for 23 large multinationals, from 2003 to 2010, totaling 148 firm–year observations in an unbalanced panel. Table 10.1 shows the representativeness of the industries in the sample.

A small sample size makes it more difficult to reject the null hypothesis, but the effects may be produced by outlier firms. I ran robustness tests that removed outlier firms and the results were stable. I also tested the results using different models.

Variables and measures

Dependent variable

I used the cultural distance variables, as provided by the Hofstede Center website. Today the center measures six Hofstede dimensions. Exhibit 10.1 describes each of these in turn.

I followed Kogut and Singh (1988) to average out the dimensions to calculate a single measure also. However, I could not use the variance of each indicator to weight the average. For each firm-year, I averaged the distance between Brazil and the countries where the firm had fully or partially owned subsidiaries for each dimension. Then I computed the average of the six dimensions to represent the FDI location as an aggregate measure of the dyadic cultural distance.

Exhibit 10.1 Description of Hofstede dimensions

Hofstede dimension	Description
Hosftede 1 (power distance)	This dimension expresses the degree to which the less powerful members of a society accept and expect that power is distributed unequally. The fundamental issue here is how a society handles inequalities between people. People in societies that have a large degree of power distance accept a hierarchical order in which everybody has a place and which needs no further justification. In societies with a low power distance, people strive to equalize the distribution of power and demand justification for power inequalities.
Hosftede 2 (individualism versus collectivism)	The up side of this dimension, called individualism, can be defined as a preference for a loosely knit social framework in which individuals are expected to take care only of themselves and their immediate families. Its opposite, collectivism, represents a preference for a tightly knit framework in society in which individuals can expect their relatives or members of a particular in-group to look after them in exchange for unquestioning loyalty. A society's position in this dimension is reflected in whether people's self-image is defined in terms of "I" or "we."
Hosftede 3 (masculinity versus femininity)	The masculinity side of this dimension represents a preference in society for achievement, heroism, assertiveness, and material rewards for success. Society at large is more competitive. Its opposite, femininity, stands for a preference for cooperation, modesty, caring for the weak, and quality of life. In this instance, society at large is more consensus-oriented.
Hosftede 4 (uncertainty avoidance)	The uncertainty avoidance dimension expresses the degree to which the members of a society feel uncomfortable with uncertainty and ambiguity. The fundamental issue here is how a society deals with the fact that the future can never be known: should we try to control the future or just let it happen? Countries having a high uncertainty avoidance index (UAI) maintain rigid codes of belief and behavior and are intolerant of unorthodox behavior and ideas. Weak UAI societies have a more relaxed attitude in which practice counts more than principles.

(Continued)

Exhibit 10.1 (Continued)

Hofstede dimension	Description
Hosftede 5 (pragmatic versus normative)	This dimension describes how people in the past, as well as today, relate to the fact that so much that happens around us cannot be explained. In societies with a normative orientation most people have a strong desire to explain as much as possible. People in such societies have a strong concern with establishing the absolute truth; they are normative in their thinking. They exhibit great respect for traditions, a relatively small propensity to save for the future, and a focus on achieving quick results. In societies with a pragmatic orientation, most people don't have a need to explain everything, as they believe that it is impossible fully to understand the complexity of life. The challenge is not to know the truth but to live a virtuous life. In societies with a pragmatic orientation, people believe that truth depends very much on situation, context, and time. They show an ability to adapt traditions easily to changing conditions, a strong propensity to save and invest, thriftiness, and perseverance in achieving results.
Hosftede 6 (indulgence versus restraint)	Indulgence stands for a society that allows relatively free gratification of basic and natural human drives related to enjoying life and having fun. Restraint stands for a society that suppresses gratification of needs and regulates it by means of strict social norms.

Source: Hofstede Center (http://geert-hofstede.com/dimensions.html), accessed February 2014.

Independent variables

Three independent variables were used to test my three hypotheses. The first variable captures the degree of the company's political connectedness at home. I used a measure taken from corporate campaign contributions. This measure is constructed so as to mitigate endogeneity problems. It takes into account the election as an exogenous event. I assume that Brazilian elections are competitive so that a single firm has little effect on the outcome. The degree of political connection of a firm in a given election is the number of winning candidates from those who received financial support. I also expect an opposite effect for losing candidates. In some models I built a composite measure, by subtracting the number of winning candidates from the number of losing candidates, considering the total number of recipient candidates who received financial support from the firm.

The second independent variable is foreign ownership. I measured this variable as the ratio of voting shares in the hands of non–Brazilian investors to total voting shares. I had to take the natural logarithm to fit a normal distribution.

Finally, I use the year the company was founded as a proxy for experiential knowledge.

Observed control variables

I used the following observed variables to control for possible factors affecting the decision to commit resources abroad: the firm's size, as the natural logarithm of the firm's total assets; capital expenditure, as the ratio of Capital Expenditure (CAPEX) to total assets; operational performance, as the ratio of Earns Before Interest and Taxes (EBIT) to total assets; group affiliation, if the firm belongs to a business group or not; industry stable effects, industry transient effects, and year dummies. Control of time effects was important since I wanted to rule out, among other things, the effect of gradual learning over time while committing resources to more culturally distant places.

Models

I estimated random effect models using panel data that cover two major elections and their subsequent terms: 2002 election (2003–6) and the 2006 election (2007–9). I opted for random effects over fixed effects because the independent variables of interest are either time invariant (the firm's age) or show very little within variability (political connection at home and foreign ownership). However, I am aware of possible unobservable variables that are not controlled (even though the main variable – political connection at home – has few endogeneity problems).

The general model equation is represented in Equation 1. The dependent variable (Y_{it}) is the aggregate cultural dyadic distance for all FDI locations of firm i in year t. To test hypothesis H1, I used only the main effect model with only political connections at home. If the coefficient of political connection ($\beta1$) is positive and significant, H1 is accepted. When I introduce foreign ownership ($X2_{it}$) and the interaction term, I expect the interaction coefficient ($\beta3$) to be negative and significant, representing the substitution effect proposed in H2. The same reasoning applies for H3, when I introduce company age ($X2_{it}$), but since the higher the variable, the younger the firm, I expect the interaction coefficient ($\beta3$) to be positive and significant for H3 to be accepted.

$$Y_{it} = \alpha_{it} + \beta1.X1_{it} + \beta2_{it}X2 + \beta3(X1_{it} * X2_{it}) + \sigma\beta.controls_{it} + \sigma_{it} \tag{1}$$

One may argue that the Brazilian MNCs in the sample are already outstanding firms, that they would have made these investments anyway, and that it was the politicians who sought them out to offer rents, reversing the causality. I believe that the way I measure political connections (which is almost a random distribution of numbers among the firms) and the separation between winning and losing candidates reduce this endogeneity issue (Claessens, Feijen, and Laeven, 2008).

Results

The final sample of 23 Brazilian multinationals comprised an eight-year unbalanced panel of 148 firm-year observations. These sampled firms are listed companies, representing the most important Brazilian multinationals. Table 10.2 presents descriptive statistics for the sampled firms. On average, they were founded in 1956, with the oldest founded in 1899 and the youngest in 2002. The average capital expenditure is 9 percent and operational profitability is 12 percent. As expected, 92 percent of the sample are affiliates of some of the 200 largest business groups in Brazil. On average, these Brazilian MNCs seem to have good political

Table 10.2 Descriptive statistics

Variable	Mean	sd	1	2	3	4	5	6	7	8	9
1 Cultural distance	21.10	7.33									
2 Firm size (ln)	14.84	1.72	.26								
3 Capital expenditure	.09	.07	−.13	.18							
4 Operational profitability	.12	.08	.03	−.06	−.02						
6 Group affiliation	.92	.26	.17	.47	−.20	.14					
5 Foreign ownership	.07	.17	.25	.22	−.07	−.04	.15				
7 Founding year	1956	28.47	−.14	.03	−.06	−.08	−.16	.29			
8 Political connections (winning candidates)	12.97	21.83	−.04	.21	.06	−.18	.16	−.16	−.57		
9 Losing candidates	9.74	17.76	−.09	.16	.05	−.11	.15	−.17	−.56	.94	
10 Winning minus losing candidates	3.22	7.81	.09	.23	.08	−.25	.10	−.06	−.31	.65	.35

Note: n = 148 firm-year observations. Correlations are simple bivariate correlations. Statistics in italics are significant at 5 percent.

Table 10.3 Descriptive comparison between elections

	2002 Election			2006 Election		
	Mean	Min.	Max.	Mean	Min.	Max.
Political distance*	20.90	6.25	54.66	21.32	13.5	44.91
Hofstede 1	20.73	7.34	42.50	20.56	8.71	42.50
Hofstede 2	28.17	7.20	64.00	28.60	8.14	53.00
Hofstede 3	16.23	4.39	50.00	16.50	8.00	43.50
Hofstede 4	18.22	3.33	60.00	20.09	7.29	55.50
Hofstede 5	27.51	7.00	67.00	28.00	7.00	41.50
Hofstede 6	14.57	3.00	56.00	14.17	3.00	33.50
Political connections (winning candidates)*	11.16	0	82	15.04	0	89
Losing candidates*	9.40	0	76	10.13	0	82
Winning minus losing candidates	1.75	−3	11	4.91	−4	38

Notes: n = 79 firm-year observations for 2002 election; n = 69 firm-year observations for 2006 election.
*Differences between the four-year periods after each election are non-significant.

capability as the number of winning candidates is statistically greater than the number of losing candidates.

Table 10.3 shows data comparing the periods after the 2002 election (2003–6) and the 2006 election (2007–9). There is no statistical improvement in the value of the political connection, for either winning or losing candidates. But when the difference between winning and losing candidates is considered for each firm, they seem to have learned from experience, as there is a significant difference ($p < .01$) between the political connection proxies of the two elections: 1.75 in 2002 and 4.91 in 2006. Interestingly, the maximum number of winning candidates, which may be as many as 82 in the 2006 election, is an expressive figure. The firm which financially supports the largest number of candidates in an election contributed to 158 candidates in 2002 and to 171 candidates in 2006.

The Brazilian MNCs in the sample have also not increased the average cultural distance of their foreign FDI locations. There is statistically no change in the average cultural distance, but only an increase in minimum values and a decrease in maximum values. Analyzing each dimension individually, greater differences are found for the individualism versus collectivism dimension and pragmatic versus normative dimension. Brazil is located close to the collectivism extreme and scores in an intermediate position for the pragmatic–normative dimension. These numbers make sense if one considers that major market opportunities for FDI are in developed Western economies, which are usually individualistic and pragmatic countries.

Table 10.4 shows the random-effect parameter estimates for Model 1 to Model 5. Firm size is positive and significant in all models. All other controls are non-significant, except for Model 5, where Group Affiliation (Model 5: $\beta = 6.28$, p < .05) and Foreign Ownership

Table 10.4 Random-effect estimates for cultural distance

Variables	(1)	(2)	(3)	(4)	(5)
Firm size (ln)	1.65**	1.49*	1.49*	1.45*	1.28+
	(.64)	(.64)	(.62)	(.61)	(.79)
Capital expenditure	−1.98	−1.64	−1.79	−1.89	−11.67+
	(3.27)	(3.29)	(3.13)	(3.09)	(7.08)
Operational profitability	−3.17	−2.38	−2.41	−3.6	10.60
	(4.46)	(4.46)	(4.28)	(4.27)	(8.20)
Group affiliation	7.82	8.66	8.68	8.78	6.28*
	(8.40)	(5.82)	(8.43)	(9.06)	(3.20)
Foreign ownership (ln)	.56	.12	.08	.34	1.01**
	(.24)	(.24)	(.22)	(.27)	(.40)
Founding year	.05	.06	.06	.07	−.02
	(.08)	(.06)	(.09)	(.09)	(.03)
Political connections (winning candidates)		.12**			.28**
		(.04)			(.09)
Losing candidates		−.13**			−.50***
		(.01)			(0.13)
Winning minus losing candidates			.13***	.16***	
			(.04)	(.04)	
Winning minus losing candidates* Foreign ownership (ln)				−.05+	
				(0.3)	
Political connections (winning candidates)* Founding year					.01**
					(0.00)
Losing candidates* Founding year					−.01**
					(0.04)
Stable industry effects	Yes	Yes	Yes	Yes	Yes
Transient industry effects	Yes	Yes	Yes	Yes	Yes
Year dummies	Yes	Yes	Yes	Yes	Yes
N	148	148	148	148	148
R-squared (overall)	46.9%	50.1%	48.15%	50.2%	4%

Notes: Standard errors are in parentheses; the constant term is included in all models; parameters are General Least Squares (GLS) estimates; the dependent variable in all models is cultural distance.
***p <.001; **p <.01; *p <.05; +p <.10

(Model 5: β = 1.01, p < .01) are, as expected, positively associated with cultural distance. I introduce the Political Connection variable in Model 2 as well as the Losing Candidate variable. As predicted by H1, the coefficient for Political Connection is positive and significant (Model 2: β = .12, p < .01) and the coefficient for Losing Candidate is negative and significant (Model 2: β = −.13, p < .01). These two opposite effects have about the same magnitude; their marginal effects are non-negligible, considering the number of winning and losing candidates assigned to each firm. This result provides support for H1.

Looking at Models 3 and 4, I use another proxy for political connections that captures both effects together: the difference between winning and losing candidates. The same pattern for political connection is repeated in Model 3, and the interaction term in Model 4 is negative and significant (Model 4: β = −.05, p < .10). This implies that political connection and foreign ownership are substitutes for each other. As foreign ownership increases, it tends to diminish the effect of political connection on cultural distance. Indeed, the main effect of political connection in Model 4 (β = .16, p < .001), for MNCs without foreign ownership, is greater than the same unconditional effect in Model 3 (β = .13, p < .001). However, this result needs to be considered with caution. First, the significance of the interaction term is weak (p < .10), and, second, the use of the two variables separately, as used in the other models (number of winning and losing candidates), did not prove to be significant for the interaction terms. Therefore, H2 is partially supported.

Finally, Model 5 shows the estimates for the interaction between political connections and the firm's capabilities proxy by the founding year of the firm. The main effects for Political Connection (Model 5: β = .28, p < .01) and Losing Candidate (Model 5: β = −.50, p < .01) show the expected sign and significance. They capture the respective effect of political connections on cultural distance for a firm founded in the average of the sample (the variable is centered). The interaction terms also show the expected signs and significance. The younger the firm is, the greater the effect of political connections on cultural distance (Model 5: β = .01, p < .01), and the worse the effect of losing candidates on cultural distance (Model 5: β = −.01, p < .01). As predicted by H3, younger firms with weak developed capabilities will be more likely to allocate resources in order to seek government support. The marginal effects of the interaction terms are quite small, but sufficient to give support to H3.

I ran a series of robustness tests to account for the stability of the results. First, I fit fixed-effect models in the sample. Fixed-effects estimations take into account non-observable variables, such as managerial intentions and international capability. The results showed support for Hypotheses H1 and H2. Hypothesis H3 did not hold good, mostly because the founding year is time invariant and the interaction term was only capturing the variation in political connections.

Second, I left one firm at a time out of the sample from a set of outlier firms. I defined outlier firms as being those MNCs that are SOEs, or previous SOEs. In the sample they are Embraer (airplane manufacturer), Vale (mining company), Petrobras (state oil company), and Usiminas (steel company that has the largest values for cultural distance). The results were stable and in most cases even more significant for all hypotheses.

Discussion

I derive hypotheses that are drawn from international business and political economy perspectives to show that political connections at home positively affect the decision regarding investing in culturally distant countries. I fit random-effect models in a sample of 23 large Brazilian multinationals, forming a panel ranging from 2003 to 2009.

The results show strong support for the hypothesis that the degree of political connection has a positive effect on the allocation of FDI to culturally distant places. The magnitude of the effect suggests that, on average, a firm that has financially supported forty elected candidates is more likely to jump five points on the cultural distance scale to an FDI location. Two other alternative mechanisms were tested against political connections. They all showed good results. First, foreign ownership negatively moderates the effect of political connections on jumping cultural distances. Both mechanisms may produce the same effect but conflict one with another, by helping information flow from foreign markets and changing managerial perception towards risk and opportunity assessment. Second, results suggest that younger firms, which in general are less experienced than older firms, are more influenced by home government political connections than older firms when deciding on locating FDI in culturally distant markets.

The implications for theory are threefold. First, this study extends our understanding of the internationalization of DMNCs. Existing internationalization theories need further specification in order to explain the phenomenon of DMNCs. Cuervo-Cazurra (2012) suggests extending the Uppsala incremental theory by showing that DMNCs face a tradeoff in which most FDI opportunities are located in psychically (or culturally) distant countries. This tradeoff makes DMNCs more inclined to jump cultural distances to locate FDI in attractive places. I extend his argument further by showing that politically well-connected firms at home are more likely to jump cultural distances when compared to less connected DMNCs. Politically connected firms are more prepared to face obligating non-market pressures in "strange" countries than non-connected DMNCs (Cuervo-Cazurra and Genc, 2011).

Second, the interaction between these two non-market components – culture and politics – increases knowledge about the value of political connections found in international business literature. General knowledge in the field is that DMNCs deploy political strategies to seek government protection in order to compensate for their weakness vis-à-vis AMNCs (Hong, Wang, Kafouros, 2014). However, I add to this debate the contingent effect of political connections at home on the relationship between culture distance and the FDI location.

While the literature recognizes that both home and host governments are important factors in generating market imperfections and promoting the internalization of ownership advantages through FDI, most of the empirical research has historically addressed the detrimental effect of host country governments (Boddewyn, 1988; Brewer, 1993). More recently, a series of studies in the Chinese context has addressed the role of home governments in promoting and affecting the location of FDI. They point, in particular, to the importance of party affiliation and state ownership for achieving local legitimacy and gaining institutional support (see Hong, Wang, Kafouros, 2014 for a review). However, the type of political connection I test here is more direct, because it operationalizes a relational contract between local politicians and the firm. It also allows for splitting the effect between the winning and losing candidates in a political campaign, which makes it possible to build a reasonable counterfactual to test the effect of connections through elected officials.

Third, the research setting of Brazil provides interesting implications. Unlike China, Brazil is a vibrant democracy. The effect of home country governments and the differential effect of a company's political behavior on the FDI location have not been investigated in depth for a democratic and capitalist country (Bandeira-de-Mello, Arreola, and Marcon, 2012). The Chinese context empirically represents an interesting setting but, at the same time, it is an outlier context that does not represent most features of the democratic representation of developing countries. In order to generalize the Brazilian case, I propose to use the framework of varieties of capitalism (Hall and Soskice, 2001). Countries where the institutional environment favors pluralistic competition for rent-seeking, like the US, are more likely to have firms individually pursuing political strategies, such as lobbying, campaign financing, personal service, board participation (revolving door), and personal contacts. On the other hand, corporatist negotiation between top business associations, unions, and governments favors more collective action by firms seeking political rents, such as in the coordinated market economies of Germany and Scandinavia.

Brazilian DMNCs, and most emerging MNCs from Latin America, originate in hierarchical capitalist countries, characterized by atomistic labor relations, small and weak unions, low-skill workers, and highly integrated and diversified business groups. In such a context, hierarchical relations and power asymmetries that favor the firm promote individual political behavior over actions through associations or negotiations with unions (Schneider, 2013). The difference between hierarchical and pluralistic countries with regard to a company's political behavior is that in the former firms and governments are strong forms of authority and hierarchies, and hence they develop close ties with each other. In the latter, firms and governments also develop close ties, but there is more competition with other organizations, such as business associations, labor associations, and non-governmental organizations in the political market place. The consequence is that rents can go to zero due to competition among interest groups in pluralistic forms of capitalism, while they may be directed towards closely connected firms in hierarchical societies.

The results also inform the practice. Consider the following examples that illustrate the location of FDI in culturally distant places. Braskem, an Odebrecht Group company, which is highly innovative and a leader in Latin America in the petrochemical sector, was founded in 1972 and consolidated its position in the sector through acquisitions in 2002. Its FDI investments began in 2006 in Argentina, Chile, Uruguay, and the Netherlands, then, in 2008, in the UK, and in 2010 in the US. This increase in FDI was accompanied by a fourfold increase in the degree of its political connections. JBS, the leading food company in the world, was founded in 1958 as a small meat-packing firm. In 2005 the company made its first cross-border acquisition when it bought Swift Armour in Argentina. In 2007, it entered the American market, when it acquired Swift Food and later Smithfield Beef. It then entered Australia through the acquisition of Tasman, and it also now has a presence in Belgium. JBS is one of the most connected companies and achieved twenty-seven successful candidates (winners minus losers) in the 2006 election (the largest number was thirty-eight). Klabin is an important multinational in the pulp and paper sector. It was founded in 1899 and expanded domestically in the 1970s. Its first FDI investment was in Argentina; it entered the UK in 2004. Klabin expanded its political connections (winners minus losers) from six in the 2002 election to twenty-six candidates in the 2006 election.

Finally, the industrial electrical engine manufacturer WEG was founded in 1961. It opened its first office in the US thirty years later and the following year acquired a firm in Belgium to serve the European market. In 1994 it entered Japan through acquisition, and the following year entered Australia. Throughout the 1990s it extended its presence in Europe by establishing offices in Germany, the UK, France, Spain, and Sweden. In 2000, it acquired manufacturing plants in Mexico and Argentina and later set up offices in Venezuela, Italy, the Netherlands, Chile, and Colombia. In 2002, it acquired a manufacturing plant in Portugal, in 2004 a plant in China, and in 2007 it established distribution offices in India, Singapore, and Dubai. It began manufacturing in India in 2008 and in South Africa in 2010. In spite of all these movements, in the sampled period, from 2003 to 2009, WEG did not increase but rather decreased its average cultural distance. As expected, the degree of political connection also decreased as the company supported more losing than winning candidates.

These examples corroborate the traditional DMNC internationalization path of entering both developed and developing countries at the same time (Guillén and Garcia-Canal, 2009). During this process, managers should consider playing the political game in order to profit from policy rents. However, there are two notes of caution. First, government offers aim to achieve national objectives, which will not necessarily correlate with a company's objectives. Therefore, it is important to assess whether available rents are beneficial or detrimental to a firm's performance. This is a difficult task, particularly if the DMNC belongs to a business group in which calculating the compound performance of several firms is cumbersome and sometimes based on political rather than economic reasoning (Costa, Bandeira-de-Mello, and Marcon, 2013). While government-induced FDI may, at one and the same time, favor risk and the opportunity for managerial assessment, managers may feel constrained to accept some offers in order to please the government with regard to future favors.

Second, the playing field of politics, particularly in countries with weak law enforcement, blurs the frontier between legality and illegality. Corruption, in all its forms, is sometimes hard to distinguish. That is why political advice firms offer tutorials to CEOs about how to talk with politicians, what to accept, and what to offer. In recent Brazilian corruption scandals, judged by the Supreme Court, businesspeople were punished more severely than politicians.

These results have limitations. The model did not take into account the purpose of the FDI, or the political distance. Even though the type of resource commitment measured includes any investment in the value chain activity, there is no variable that takes into account whether the FDI is market-, efficiency-, or resource-seeking. One may also argue that firms seek locations that are not politically distant and that political distance is negatively correlated with cultural distance. Although this might be true, it is unlikely, since these two dimensions are virtually uncorrelated (Berry, Guillén, and Zhou, 2010). In fact, DMNCs tend to choose valuable locations where their political capabilities are also valuable, and this is highly linked to the cultural environment. I also did not control for the size of the FDI investments. Firms might choose to invest less in culturally distant places.

Conclusion

Culture and international investments are closely interrelated. Culture-based explanations for international investment consider that managers will commit resources abroad based on incremental adjustments. Considering risk-averse managers and relatively closed organizational boundaries, few factors may interfere in the managerial evaluation of possible foreign opportunities. Existing theoretical extensions suggest that DMNC managers are less risk averse and jump cultural distances to seek market opportunities in "strange" foreign countries. However, this home-country, context-specific effect is not homogeneously distributed among DMNCs. In the case of hierarchical economies, where non-market strategies are pervasive and mutual dependency on the government is high, political connections at home have a positive impact on jumping cultural distances. Furthermore, political connections at home are a substitute for foreign ownership in providing incoming flows of knowledge about foreign markets and also a substitute for the weak capabilities of less experienced, young firms.

Bibliography

Ambos, B.; Hakanson, L. The concept of distance in international management research. *Journal of International Management*, 20, pp. 1–7, 2014.

Bagwell, K.; Staiger, R. W. Domestic policies, national sovereignty and international economic institutions. *Quarterly Journal of Economics*, 116(2), pp. 519–62, 1999.

Bandeira-de-Mello, R.; Arreola, F.; Marcon, R. The importance of nurturing political connections for emerging multinationals. In: Hadjikhani, A.; Elg, U.; Ghauri, P. (eds.), *Business, Society, and Politics: Multinationals in Emerging Markets*. Bingley: Emerald, 2012.

Bazuchi, K.; Zacharias, S.; Broering, L.; Arreola, M.; Bandeira-de-Mello, R. The role of home country political resources for Brazilian multinational companies. *Brazilian Administration Review*, 10(4), pp. 415–38, 2013.

Benito, G. R. G.; Gripsrud, G. The expansion of foreign direct investments: Discrete rational location choices or a cultural learning process? *Journal of International Business Studies*, 23(3), pp. 461–76, 1992.

Berry, H.; Guillén, M.; Zhou, N. An institutional approach to cross-national distance. *Journal of International Business Studies*, 41, pp. 1–21, 2010.

Boas, T.; Hidalgo, D.; Richardson, N. The spoils of victory: campaign donations and government contracts in Brazil. *Journal of Politics*, 76(2), pp. 415–29, 2014.

Boddewyn, J. Political aspects of MNE. *Journal of International Business Studies*, 19(3), pp. 341–63, 1988.

Boddewyn, J.; Brewer, T. International-business political behavior: new theoretical directions. *Academy of Management Review*, 19(1), pp. 119–143, 1994.

Bonardi, J.; Hillman, A.; Keim, G. The attractiveness of political markets: implications for firm strategy. *Academy of Management Review*, 30(2), pp. 397–413, 2005.

Brewer, T. Government policies, market imperfections, and foreign direct investment. *Journal of International Business Studies*, 24(1), pp. 101–20, 1993.

Chaney, P.; Faccio, M.; Parsley, D. The quality of accounting information in politically connected firms. Unpublished working paper, Vanderbilt University, Nashville, TN, 2008.

Claessens, S.; Feijen, E.; Laeven, L. Political connections and preferential access to finance: the role of campaign contributions. *Journal of Financial Economics*, 88, pp. 554–80, 2008.

Costa, M.; Bandeira-de-Mello, R.; Marcon, R. A influência da conexão política na diversificação dos grupos empresariais brasileiros. *Revista de Administração de Empresas*, 53, pp. 376–87, 2013.

Cuervo-Cazurra, A. The multinationalization of developing country MNE: the case of multilatinas. *Journal of International Management*, 14, pp. 138–54, 2008.

— Extending theory by analyzing developing country multinational companies: solving the Goldilocks debate. *Global Strategy Journal*, 2, pp. 153–67, 2012.

Cuervo-Cazurra, A.; Genc, H. Obligating, pressuring, and supporting dimensions of the environment and the non-market advantages of developing-country multinational companies. *Journal of Management Studies*, 48(2), pp. 441–55, 2011.

Cui, L.; Jiang, F. State ownership effect on firms' FDI ownership decisions under institutional pressure: a study of Chinese outward-investing firms. *Journal of International Business Studies*, 43, pp. 264–84, 2012.

Faccio, M. Politically connected firms. *American Economic Review*, 96, pp. 369–86, 2006.

Guillén, M. Business groups in emerging economies: a resource-based view. *Academy of Management Journal*, 43(3), pp. 362–80, 2000.

Guillén, M.; Garcia-Canal, E. The American model of the multinational firm and the "new" multinationals from emerging economies. *Academy of Management Perspectives*, 43(3), pp. 23–35, 2009.

Hall, P.; Soskice, D. (eds.) *Varieties of Capitalism: The Institutional Foundations of Comparative Advantage*. New York: Oxford University Press, 2001.

Hillman, A.; Hitt, M. Corporate political strategy formulation: a model of approach, participation, and strategy decisions. *Academy of Management Review*, 24(4), pp. 825–42, 1999.

Hofstede, G. *Culture's Consequences: International Differences in Work Related Values*. Beverly Hills, CA: Sage, 1980.

Hong, J.; Wang, C.; Kafouros, M. The role of the state in explaining the internationalization of emerging market enterprises. *British Journal of Management*, 2014.

Hoskisson, R. E.; Johnson, R. A.; Tihanyi, L.; White, R. Diversified business groups and corporate refocusing in emerging economies. *Journal of Management*, 31(6), pp. 941–65, 2005.

Johanson, J.; Vahlne, J. The internationalization process of the firm: a model of knowledge development and increasing foreign market commitments. *Journal of International Business Studies*, 8(1), pp. 23–32, 1977.

Johanson, J.; Wiedersheim-Paul, F. The internationalization of the firm: four Swedish cases. *Journal of Management Studies*, 12(3), pp. 305–22, 1975.

Khanna, T.; Yafeh, Y. Business groups in emerging markets: paragons or parasites? *Journal of Economic Literature*, 45(2), pp. 331–72, 2007.

Kirkman, B.; Lowe, K.; Gibson, C. A quarter century of Culture's consequences: a review of empirical research incorporating Hofstede's cultural values framework. *Journal of International Business Studies*, 37, pp. 285–320, 2006.

Kogut, B.; Singh, H. The effect of national culture on the choice of entry mode. *Journal of International Business Studies*, Fall, pp. 411–32, 1988.

Kogut, B.; Zander, U. Knowledge of the firm, combinative capabilities, and the replication of technology. *Organization Science*, 3(3), pp. 383–97, 1992.

Kornai, J. The soft budget constraint. *Kyklos*, 39(1), pp. 3–30, 1986.

Lawton, T.; McGuire, S.; Rajwani, T. Corporate political activity: a literature review and research agenda. *International Journal of Management Reviews*, 15, pp. 86–105, 2013.

Lazzarini, S.; Musacchio, A.; Bandeira-de-Mello, R.; Marcon, R. What do development banks do? Evidence from Brazil, 2002–2009. Working paper, 2012. Available at: http://papers.ssrn.com/sol3/papers.cfm?abstract_id=1969843 (accessed September 3, 2014).

Lecraw, D. Direct investment by firms from less developed countries. *Oxford Economic Papers*, 29(3), pp. 442–57, 1977.

Li, J.; Guisinger, S. The globalization of service multinationals in the 'triad' regions: Japan, Western Europe, and North America. *Journal of International Business Studies*, 23(4), pp. 675–96, 1992.

Loree, D. W.; Guisinger, S. E. Policy and non-policy determinants of US equity foreign direct investment. *Journal of International Business Studies*, 26(2), pp. 281–99, 1995.

Luo, Y.; Rui, H. An ambidexterity perspective toward multinational enterprises from emerging economies. *Academy of Management Perspectives*, 23(4), pp. 49–70, 2009.

Luo, Y.; Tung, R. International expansion of emerging market enterprises: a springboard perspective. *Journal of International Business Studies*, 38, pp. 481–98, 2007.

Luo, Y.; Xue, Q.; Han, B. How emerging market governments promote outward FDI: experience from China. *Journal of World Business*, 45, pp. 68–79, 2010.

Murtha, T.; Lenway, S. Country capabilities and the strategic state: how national political institutions affect multinational corporations' strategies. *Strategic Management Journal*, 15, pp. 113–29, 1994.

OECD. *Competition Policy, Industrial Policy and National Champions*. 2009. Available at: www.oecd.org/daf/competition/44548025.pdf (accessed December 8, 2014).

Rasiah, R.; Gammeltoft, R.; Jiang, Y. Home government policies for outward FDI from emerging economies: lessons from Asia. *International Journal of Emerging Markets*, 5(¾), pp. 333–57, 2010.

Rodriguez, P.; Siegel, D.; Hillman, A.; Eden, E. Three lenses on the multinational enterprise: politics, corruption, and corporate social responsibility. *Journal of International Business Studies*, 37, pp. 733–46, 2006.

Samuels, D. Money, elections, and democracy in Brazil. *Latin American Politics and Society*, 43(2), pp. 27–48, 2001.

— Pork barreling is not credit claiming or advertising: campaign finance and sources of the personal vote in Brazil. *Journal of Politics*, 64, pp. 845–63, 2002.

Schneider, B. *Hierarchical Capitalism in Latin America: Business, Labor, and the Challenges of Equitable Development*. New York: Cambridge University Press, 2013.

Shenkar, O. Cultural distance revisited: towards a more rigorous conceptualization and measurement of cultural differences. *Journal of International Business Studies*, 32, pp. 519–35, 2001.

Shi, W. Risky business? A firm-level analysis of Chinese outward direct investments. Working paper, 2013. Available at: https://ncgg.princeton.edu/IPES/2013/papers/S115_rm3.pdf (accessed September 3, 2014).

Stal, E.; Cuervo-Cazurra, A. The investment development path and FDI from developing countries: the role of pro-market reforms and institutional voids. *Latin American Business Review*, 12(3), pp. 209–31, 2011.

Thomas, D. E.; Grosse, R. Country-of-origin determinants of foreign direct investment in an emerging market: The case of Mexico. *Journal of International Management*, 7(1), pp. 59–79, 2001.

Wan, W. Country resource environments, firm capabilities, and corporate diversification strategies. *Journal of Management Studies*, 42, pp. 161–82, 2005.

Wang, C.; Hong, J.; Kafouros, M.; Wright, M. Exploring the role of government involvement in outward FDI from emerging economies. *Journal of International Business Studies*, 43, pp. 655–76, 2012.

Witt, M.; Lewin, A. Outward foreign direct investment as escape response to home country institutional constraints. *Journal of International Business Studies*, 38, pp. 579–94, 2007.

11

Managing business–government relationships through organizational advocacy

Howard Viney and Paul R. Baines

Few areas of organizational life have come under such intense public scrutiny as the firm's attempt to engage in building and sustaining relationships with government or regulatory oversight bodies. Despite this increased scrutiny, and concerns regarding the legitimacy of any form of corporate political activity, non-market strategies demand increasing attention. The necessity to align all aspects of organizational strategy to create the possibility of competitive advantage has become increasingly recognized and important (Lawton et al., 2014). Engaging with government continues to prove challenging but the importance for organizations of doing so as part of a comprehensive aligned strategic approach should not be underestimated, especially in industries where government is an active stakeholder. A key challenge for senior managers involves understanding the options available and how and why they may be deployed. This chapter therefore focuses on the process of managing non-market strategic engagement with government.

In this chapter, we discuss and exemplify a typology of different levels of relationship engagement (or LRE) (Baines and Viney, 2010; Viney and Baines, 2012) based upon the non-market strategic options available to an organization. We discuss how managers with responsibility for government relations can use this typology to tailor an appropriate and contingent non-market strategy which complements and aligns with the overall strategic direction of their organization. The typology is not intended to be seen as sequential; rather, we believe that organizations can develop a nuanced strategic approach which may involve the enacting of several options simultaneously or a systematic plan for engagement as events occur. In similar fashion, we believe that the typology provides the potential for organizations to plan their long-term engagement with oversight bodies as well as to respond to urgent opportunities or threats emerging from decisions taken by government or regulators.

The focus of this chapter is upon corporate political activity, rather than corporate social responsibility. We are concerned with non-market options that depend upon the "advocacy" of organizational interests rather than other corporate political activity that involves establishing or maintaining direct ties to political actors. In that sense, we are interested in what Bouwen and McCown (2007) describe as "voice" strategies rather than "access" strategies that are commonly and extensively addressed elsewhere. Some forms of the voice strategies we discuss are closely aligned to the information strategy variant of corporate political activity identified by Hillman and Hitt (1999). However, the intent of different forms of relationship engagement would enable us to distinguish between different types of business political behavior characterized as "bargaining" by Boddewyn and Brewer (1994: 121). As we will discuss, some engagements are intended primarily to build partnerships between business and government while some options also acknowledge the potential for conflict between business and government actors.

There exist strong arguments that non-market strategies are of highly questionable legitimacy; yet these exist alongside other perspectives which argue that all organizations possess a legitimate right to have their voice heard in situations where their interests are affected. Before expanding upon the relationship engagement typology, we briefly need to reflect upon arguments for and against organizational engagement with oversight bodies. This review is not focused directly upon the corporate political activity literature, which is discussed extensively elsewhere in this volume. Rather, we broaden the discussion by considering perspectives on this theme emerging from related but tangential literatures, principally the business ethics and public affairs literatures.

Engaging with government or regulatory bodies

Whether organizations should pursue non-market strategies to support their market strategies (Baron, 1995; Bonardi, 1999; Ring et al., 2005; Bonardi et al., 2006; Pearce et al., 2008) and what the impact of this decision will have upon organizational performance are areas of increasing attention (McWilliams et al., 2002; Dahan, 2005; Capron and Chatain, 2008; Keim and Hillman, 2008; Pearce et al., 2008). These conversations have contributed to the development of literatures around corporate political activity (CPA) (Baysinger, 1994; Shaffer, 1995; Hillman and Hitt, 1999; Hillman et al., 2004, among many) and strategic political management (SPM) (Oliver and Holzinger, 2008) and focused upon the critical question of how organizations can pursue non-market strategies allied to their more traditional market strategies. There are several authoritative reviews of these literatures, and we will not seek to replicate them here (Hillman et al., 2004; Lawton et al., 2013).

There exists a need, however, to reflect upon work which has focused upon the legitimacy of an organization seeking to engage with oversight bodies, from both a positive and a negative perspective, in order to establish a common understanding of some of the dominant economic and political arguments for and against organizations' lobbying of government. Such a review is necessary to set the context prior to presenting our framework and exploring arguments as to why it would be helpful to managers to understand the options available to them as they approach engagement with government or regulatory bodies.

To begin the process, let us refine our understanding of the concept of relationship engagement. Most discussion of engagement has traditionally focused upon organizations' attempts to align government interests with their own or even to seek to shape government interests (Delmas and Montes-Sancho, 2010). Often pejoratively defined as lobbying, this practice has been defined broadly as the process by which organizations seek to gain influence in government decision-making (Nownes, 2001), typically by targeting influential public officials (Green et al., 1972). The defining characteristics of relationship engagement with public organizations and officials therefore would be that it appears motivated by self-interest and focused upon forwarding an organization's agenda (Milbrath, 1963). However, as we will discuss below, organizational self-interest should not automatically be viewed with distrust and there are strong arguments in favor of the legitimacy of such behavior.

Nevertheless, arguments in the literature portray behavior of this sort, where organizations seek to influence government actions, negatively as they fail to consider wider social interests and are potentially damaging to the good conduct of business in an economy. This has led lobbying to be described as a "grabbing-hand" (Shleifer and Vishny, 1998) which has the effect of enforcing unfair competition or leading to a small number of well-resourced or -connected organizations exercising unjustified levels of market power. Other economic arguments have suggested that lobbying has the effect of enforcing, not rectifying, market failure (Henderson, 2001), implying a serious cost to the general public (Keffer and Hill, 1997), which has led to strong arguments that lobbying results in morally reprehensible outcomes (Gowthorpe and Amat, 2005) or affronts to fairness (Charki et al., 2011).

Furthermore, organizations' lobbying has been described as a rent-seeking activity (Barker, 2008; Boatright, 2009) aimed at exploiting an organization's existing competitive advantage, held in contrast to the more acceptable market-making activity. Rent-seeking is identified as "wasteful" from a societal perspective as it represents an inefficient use and allocation of resources "intended to gain a monopoly position" (Boatright, 2009: 541). Rent-seeking is contrasted with other, legitimate, rents which arise naturally from business activities. Implicitly, resources spent on lobbying to raise rents could be spent more efficiently upon market-making that would increase the general sum of wellbeing (Posner, 1975). Rent-seeking has also been seen by some critics, such as Mantere et al. (2009), as socially wasteful and possibly immoral. Adding to this negative interpretation of lobbying, there is a widely held view that *only* well-resourced organizations can afford to lobby (e.g., see Bouwen and McCown, 2007: 427; Delmas and Montes-Sancho, 2010: 583), while other research has found specifically that reputation, position, and track record in markets are necessary for the achievement of political access (Moss et al., 2012). In extending this argument a link has been identified between politically well-connected organizations and positive government intervention in difficult times (see Faccio, 2006; Faccio et al., 2006; Galang, 2012), while Galang (2012) has gone so far as to identify political connections as an explanation for some government action after the 2008 economic crisis. Other evidence that lobbying activity works, and that organizations that engage in it benefit from government decisions (e.g., see Grossman and Helpman, 1994; Nelson, 2006), makes these criticisms even more damning.

However, despite the abundance of negative interpretations, positive interpretations do exist. For instance, it has been argued that any entity (any individual, interest group, or corporation) has a legitimate right to petition an oversight body for the consideration of their interests when laws, regulations, and rules are being developed or applied. This concept is termed "interest representation" by Coen (2007). Based on this view, lobbying/relationship engagement is a legal, and even a necessary, aspect of representative democracy. If that is so, however, we are left with the question as to why the practice is so widely mistrusted and often identified as being of questionable economic, social, and ethical validity? Does the fact that organizations that have engaged in lobbying have benefited from government decisions imply that those decisions were wrong? Is it not possible that the effect of lobbying may lead to improved government decision-making that has a net beneficial effect for society as a whole? Some critics, such as Stigler (1971), have argued that regulation is biased towards protecting powerful incumbent firms that would imply that lobbying simply protects existing interests rather than creates the possibility of identifying a more equitable outcome.

Various authors have highlighted the positive aspects of lobbying, providing information or advice that is potentially socially valuable and takes the place of expenditure that would otherwise have had to be funded from the public purse. This is the notion of a "legislative subsidy" suggested by Hall and Deardorff (2006) and based upon giving government access to experts who are able to provide "an invaluable source of information" to government (Keffer and Hill, 1997: 1371). Examples of the positive impact of lobbying exist in the literature, such as reported by Charki et al.'s (2011) example of the improved regulation of online reverse auctions in France. This is an interesting case as it reveals the ways in which organizations have far greater awareness of the implications of disruptive technological change and can alert government or regulatory authorities to the need to act (and achieve a broadly positive social and economic outcome). This perspective is argued strongly by Fairbrass (2003, 2006), who emphasizes the positive relationship between government and firms that are essentially trading "legitimacy, support, information, and expertise . . . [for] . . . the economic and political environment they find favorable" (Fairbrass and Zueva-Owens, 2012: 331) or appropriate. Fairbrass and Zueva-Owens (2012) further emphasize the reality that in many instances there are partnerships between governmental, business, and civil society actors. Sawant (2012) highlights the exchange relationship between firms and political actors, where both parties will seek to gain from the interaction (although this can be negatively or positively interpreted).

The challenge for organizations wishing to engage in relationship engagement with oversight bodies is to undertake approaches that are seen as legitimate (in order to overcome suspicions of illegitimacy) and that do not affect the socially positive operation of markets. In a recent paper, Sawant (2012: 204) noted the tendency of research to suggest that legitimacy (on the part of the firm) is a necessity to influence public policy positively (in their favor). This would therefore seem to increase the premium or incentive for firms to be seen to be engaging in open and transparent lobbying practice. In the remainder of this chapter, we discuss the options that are available to firms to be seen to be engaged in legitimate relationship engagement.

The different levels of relationship engagement

CPA by organizations is designed based upon what they perceive to be the intended outcomes of their engagement with government or regulatory bodies. We have previously designed a series of different "levels of relationship engagement" that correspond with such strategic intentions (see Baines and Viney, 2010; Viney and Baines, 2012). These levels of relationship engagement can be characterized by the corporate behaviors organizations pursue to achieve the intended CPA outcomes. This framework allows organizations the opportunity to assess how they should engage with government and regulatory authorities, and what resources to commit.

Figure 11.1 illustrates the five-level relationship engagement classification system, where each level corresponds to a type of CPA (see Viney and Baines, 2012). In addition, Figures 11.2 and 11.3 describe the correlating levels of decreasing engagement with government actors at each level, which we describe as the "nature of the CPA" undertaken at each level. Readers will note that we divide the model into two to reflect a distinct hierarchy within our conceptualization of CPA. The top three levels of CPA (Levels 5, 4 and 3, as shown in Figure 11.2) are strategic, and the last two levels (Levels 2 and 1, as shown in Figure 11.3) are tactical. For the purposes of clarification, we do not consider our relationship engagement taxonomy to be sequential. Organizations can adopt a level of relationship engagement appropriate to their needs. Some firms will undertake relationship engagement at different levels as their operational contexts dictate. Others may pursue relationship engagement simultaneously at different levels. Yet others might consistently effect their relationship engagement at a particular level over time (Viney and Baines, 2012).

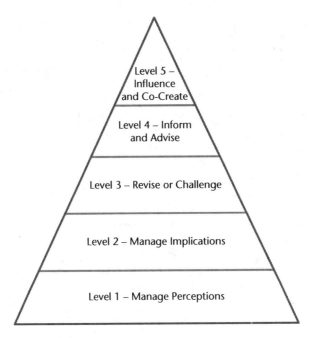

Figure 11.1 A five-level relationship engagement classification system

Source: Viney and Baines (2012) (Reproduced with kind permission of *European Business Review*).

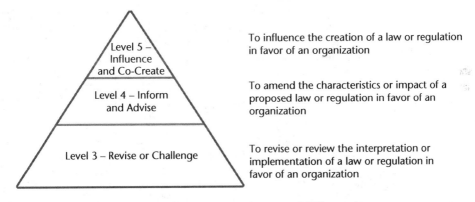

Figure 11.2 Strategic relationship engagement – nature of CPA

Source: Viney and Baines (2012) (Reproduced with kind permission of *European Business Review*).

We suggest that there are distinct strategic rationales for CPA at each level. At Level 5, organizations partner with governmental or regulatory agencies to engage in a process by which laws or regulations are co-created. This is a very high-level interaction with law-makers and represents very high levels of influence. This is likely to be an infrequently witnessed option available to very few organizations within each political system. At Level 4, organizations are closely involved with the definition of laws or regulations through partic-ipation in consultations, providing information or guidance that shapes the detail of laws and regulations. This also represents high-level interaction with law-makers, and considerable

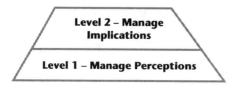

To understand how change as a product of a law or regulation affects an organization

To manage perceptions of change to create a favorable impression of an organization

Figure 11.3 Tactical relationship engagement – nature of CPA

Source: Viney and Baines (2012) (Reproduced with kind permission of *European Business Review*).

influence within the process through information provision and advice, but where the intention is to encourage the legislator to find favor with one's own firm's interests. In Level 3 engagement, organizations are not involved in framing laws or regulations but, instead, seek to influence the interpretation of law, regulation, or policy in their favor through some form of challenge, or by minimizing its implications. At this level, engagement is used to attempt to exercise external power and influence, with a focus on revision or challenge.

In contrast, for tactical CPA, there is a tacit recognition that the firm is unable to affect the content of legal or regulatory activity. Thus, Level 2 engagement suggests that organizations will seek dialogue with law-makers or regulatory authorities to determine the nature of impending legal or regulatory change. This will not necessarily involve privileged access, but rather working "channels of communication" to permit effective responses to change that the organization has not been involved in creating. This level of engagement assumes management of these channels rather than an attempt to exert influence. This strategy constitutes managed reactivity through political environmental scanning. Finally, in Level 1 engagement, organizations respond to changes produced by laws or regulations, and attempts to manage perceptions in their wider stakeholder community. This reflects a desire to create a favorable impression of the organization and its response to political environmental change. Again, this approach is essentially managed reactivity through political environmental scanning, but activity is aimed at image control rather than effective management of processes.

In summary, not all firms undertake CPA at the same level of relationship engagement. This is partially a response to a lack of information, experience, or opportunity (i.e., the access required to pursue CPA at Levels 5 or 4 is typically strictly limited in any political system), but also a lack of need. Obtaining access at Levels 5, 4, or 3 requires a high level of resource deployment, which may or may not be justified. All organizations will want government and regulatory agencies to develop legislation or regulations that are beneficial to their organizational objectives. However, for some, this process becomes critical, justifying the extra investment needed to operate potentially at Levels 4 or 5. For many, such an investment is less critical, so they focus upon lower levels.

Influencing relationship engagement through rhetoric

In any CPA situation, it is important to determine not just which governmental stakeholders need to be influenced but also how that influence should be achieved. This process is fraught with difficulties, typically legal, ethical, and philosophical. However, it is clear that firms are extremely active in attempting to influence governments, and US lobbying practices and techniques now pervade the EU (Coen, 1999). A key element of the CPA process at the strategic levels of relationship engagement is to determine how to persuade legislative actors of the legitimacy of a firm's perspective. Whilst legislators have a remit to engage stakeholders in the legislative process (as part of the wider representative democratic process), they must

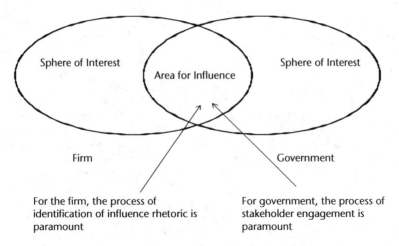

Figure 11.4 CPA and the identification of influence rhetoric

first take into account the needs of other stakeholders and society in general. This makes the process of identifying the influence rhetoric required for the firm to persuade the legislative actors a cornerstone of the CPA process; yet there is only anecdotal consideration of this persuasion process. The process of identifying the rhetoric necessary to influence a relation-ship with government arises from a consideration of the overlapping spheres of interest of the firm and the government actors. However, a key principle of the process of the identification of influence rhetoric is that the firm's rhetoric is framed from the perspective of the benefits to government for the proposed legislative amendment/change since government actually controls legislation and has veto power (see Figure 11.4).

The identification of influence rhetoric is therefore the fundamental building block of the CPA process. In Table 11.1, we outline some examples of companies that have successfully influenced governments at different strategic levels of relationship engagement and the rhet-oric they pursued to obtain that legislative advantage.

Exploring and illustrating the different levels

In this section, we explore what we understand about the different levels of engagement and their principal characteristics. This is achieved through exemplification, exploring how organ-izations have attempted to operationalize their CPA strategy. LRE should not be viewed as a continuum of activity options but as a portfolio available to organizations to be deployed when required. We provide a range of examples of the different types of relationship engagement used by organizations at each "level" as they pursue CPA in support of their corporate agendas.

Level 5 engagement – influence and co-create

Few firms are permitted access at the very highest levels of government or regulatory deci-sion-making to co-create laws, or are able to exploit close relationships with oversight bodies to achieve favorable decisions. Access to this level of engagement is necessarily limited; few citizens in democracies would be comfortable with the notion of policy being created by firms that are, in theory, governed by that policy. However, there is evidence of its existence in a number of industries where the specialized nature or strategic importance of the sector

189

Table 11.1 Relationship engagement and the identification of influence rhetoric: strategic examples

Relationship engagement level	Detail	Example	Rhetoric identified to influence relationship engagement
5	To influence the creation of a law or regulation in favor of an organization	Formula 1 and the 2004 EU directive banning tobacco sponsorship	There should be a two-year stay on tobacco sponsorship because implementation of the directive at the suggested time would mean Formula 1 would need to move to the Far East, with the loss of thousands of jobs and considerable tax revenue to the UK government
4	To amend the characteristics of a proposed law or regulation in favor of an organization	The introduction of the Carbon Reduction Commitment (CRC) cap and trade program	UK supermarkets, hotels and manufacturers, asked to comment as part of a consultation process on a new draft regulation, pointed to the potential impact of the regulation upon their profitability and were able to extract concessions from the UK's Department of Energy and Climate Change when the scheme was introduced in October 2009
3	To revise or review the interpretation or amendment of a law or regulation in favor of an organization	The merger of Price Waterhouse and Coopers and Lybrand in 1999 to form PwC	The two companies successfully persuaded EU merger control authorities that the combined entity would be more capable of auditing large state and private companies newly entering the EU after the 2004 enlargement program meant that a further twelve countries joined, and that failure to approve the merger would mean that there would be limited capacity in the market to audit these organizations

is reflected in very close relationships with government. For instance, the policy decisions favoring the banking and automotive industries in the 2008 global economic crisis suggest Level 5 influence over government actors. The question is: what is the nature of this influence and is it legitimate?

Level 5 sees engagement at the highest level, requiring considerable resource application. The key characteristic of Level 5 engagement is that organizations act to achieve very strong influence by shaping the proposed or potential legislation, regulation, or policy. Relationship engagement practice can take two main forms, as follows:

- Formal co-creation: the organization partners legislative, regulatory, or policy-making bodies.
- Policy inspiration: the organization creates awareness of and/or desire for legislation, regulation, or policy.

Inspirational Level 5 behavior is more typical than co-creation, although the latter is possible. This is explained as a consequence of the characteristics of representative democracy and the concerns which exist when sectional interests like those of a company or pressure group establish any kind of influence over the legislative or oversight process (creating an extreme form of the concept of regulatory capture) (Dal Bó, 2006). Level 5 engagement can be particularly controversial, whether it is co-created or inspired by sectional interests (see Exhibit 11.1).

Exhibit 11.1 Level 5 relationship engagement – the KC-X airborne refueling contract

The potentially controversial nature of high-level relationship engagement is well illustrated in the protracted bidding process for the US Air Force's (USAF) new generation of airborne refueling aircraft.

The requirement for new-generation airborne refueling aircraft was identified at the turn of the century and the USAF set about establishing a set of capabilities that the new aircraft should be able to perform. This resulted in the selection of the Boeing 767 airframe in 2002 and the award of a contract in 2003 to lease 100 B767s from Boeing in a deal worth around $20 billion. However, a subsequent congressional investigation into the selection process suggested that the USAF had unfairly favored the Boeing bid, permitting the firm to amend the capabilities the new tanker was expected to fulfill. According to documents retrieved by the Senate Commerce Commission investigation, Boeing eliminated nineteen of the twenty-six capabilities contained in the original specification to make its product more competitive. Furthermore, Airbus was permitted only twelve days to prepare its counter-bid (after Boeing had amended the specification in its favor), clearly indicating and reflecting the USAF's preference to award the contract to the American company. This, the Senate Commerce Commission suggested, did not represent a competitive bidding process and could not guarantee value for money. The deal was abandoned in December 2003 and a number of Boeing executives were forced from their posts following allegations of corruption. As a consequence of the failure of the initial process, a formal bidding competition was initiated but that too resulted in controversy. The original decision in February 2008 to award the contract (now valued at around $100 billion) to a Northrup Grumman/EADS consortium was challenged by Boeing in a protest to the US Government Accountability Office (GAO), which upheld the challenge and insisted the USAF must restart the contract competition. A final decision, which once again went in favor of Boeing, was taken in February 2011.

This example provides evidence of two levels of relationship engagement being used by Boeing at different times and reflecting the company's changing fortunes. The USAF's relationship with Boeing in the initial contract award appears to indicate Level 5 influence or co-creation, with the USAF's preference for working with Boeing reflected in favorable access to the design of the product specification. However, following the cancelation of the original contract and the apparent ending of the potential for Level 5 influence or co-creation, Boeing had to resort to Level 3 revision or challenge to reassert its interests after the award of the contract to a rival in 2008. Some commentators have suggested that the embarrassing revelation of the closeness of the USAF and Boeing, ending the potential for Level 5 engagement, resulted in a bias *against* Boeing and in favor of EADS, necessitating Boeing's resort to a Level 3 challenge.

It is interesting that the "failed" Level 5 approach was portrayed as potentially corrupt after it emerged that a Boeing procurement manager working on the deal had previously worked with the Pentagon team that initiated the project. However, the exchange of personnel between buyers and suppliers is a relatively common occurrence in many industry sectors and an aspect of effective Level 5 relationship engagement.

One clear-cut example of Level 5 engagement is the relationship between aerospace companies, such as EADS/Airbus Industries, and their various European host governments. When Airbus was seeking launch aid for its proposed A350 project, French, German, and UK governments were all ready to provide it on favorable terms. This speaks not only to the closeness of the relationship between EADS and European governments, but also to the importance in political and economic terms of maintaining Airbus Industries' position in the global airline industry. A further example, this time involving direct co-creation of regulations, can be seen in the UK government's policy to decommission nuclear industry facilities. The wording of the Energy Act of 2004 makes it clear that industry participants must work within a regulatory framework to plan and undertake the activities necessary to achieve the policy's overall objective. The nuclear industry is a partner of government rather than a supplicant, demonstrating co-creative Level 5 engagement because of its specialist capabilities and its importance to the overall success of the policy.

A key motivation for Level 5 engagement is that emerging legislation, regulation, or policy might either not appear (when its introduction would be otherwise favored by the organization) or might appear in a substantially different format from that desired. The government's motivations are worth consideration here, and will vary depending upon the type of Level 5 engagement attempted. Co-creation is more likely to be considered when the industry in question is large and strategic or new and innovative, where expertise is specialized, rare, and expensive to develop (and scarce or non-existent in government). Organizations in the high-technology industries, for example, have expertise and industry understanding that are significantly ahead of government or regulatory understanding. Eising (2007) has noted a far more pragmatic explanation, at the European level at least. He notes that the EU looks to work with organizations as a means of overcoming the inertia of the EU policy processes (described as "Eurosclerosis"). Level 5 LRE therefore helps make policy possible in an environment where, without engagement activity, it would be impossible.

The key characteristic of engagement at this level is that it resembles a close partnership. There is a mutual interest in government working very closely with organizations affected by the outcome of the process. In that sense, the company could be seen to be implementing government policy. To summarize, influence at Level 5 is extremely rare in representative democracies. The characteristic of Level 5 engagement which makes it unlike Level 4 or 3 is that it instigates or exists at the inception or pre-inception of policy.

Level 4 – inform and advise

Many firms, individually or collectively, attempt to impact the characteristics of legislation, regulation, or policy by participating in Level 4 engagement. The principal characteristic of Level 4 is that it involves participation in a formal legislative process through the provision of advice or information rather than recommendation or argument. Therefore, organizations act when the concept, if not the content, of policy already exists. Level 4 engagement has the following two forms:

- Solicited, as part of a formal consultative process.
- Unsolicited, within the boundaries of a consultative system.

Here, the general principles of the legislation, regulation, or policy are already established. However, in order to establish legitimacy, acquire a mandate, or enhance the efficiency or effectiveness of the legislative process, the regulatory body requests input from influential stakeholders. Hence, the content of legislation requires confirmation. The oversight body recognizes its own limited information access and therefore invites contributions to satisfy the information gap. Large legislative, regulatory, or policy-making bodies engage in consultation to varying degrees, depending upon political expediency, actual concern for opinion, or as a signifier of real uncertainty as to their understanding of the subject. For example, in the European Parliament hearings are held by committees to ascertain expert opinion on aspects of their work. Commercial organizations and trade bodies frequently send representatives to engage with such bodies in order to influence legislation and policy. Examples of solicited and unsolicited SPM activities are presented in Exhibit 11.2.

Exhibit 11.2 Level 4 relationship engagement – informing government

Consultation provides all sides in an argument with opportunities to propose alternative perspectives. For example, in August 2009, the UK government concluded a formal consultation process on the adoption of the Agency Workers Directive, which is "a piece of EU legislation designed to provide more protection for . . . temporary workers employed by British companies by giving them almost the same status as full-time employees" (Gribben, 2009: 8). Contrasting opinions were provided by the Trades Union Congress, arguing for early adoption, and a variety of business groups such as the British Chambers of Commerce and the Recruitment and Employment Confederation, which argued for late adoption (with the potential for rejection by any future Conservative government).

Information is important in the legislative process, but its collection can be expensive and governments are often wary of the cost of obtaining all of the information needed to inform a legislative process. Organizations with an argument to make are aware of this dilemma, and offer information to government with the hope and expectation that in doing so they will shape government thinking. For example, the CBI (Confederation of British Industry) commissioned a report by McKinsey, the international consulting house, to provide an overview of the UK electricity industry to highlight the need for infrastructure investments to ensure generation capacity was maintained in the long term (Mason, 2009). The CBI's members all have an interest in ensuring the integrity and low price of energy and hence have an interest in provoking a debate on future infrastructure investment; this explains the decision to commission a report highlighting this need.

The discussion of fracking, a technique designed to recover gas and oil deposits from shale rock, illustrates the importance of Level 4 relationship engagement for a range of organizations motivated by interest in a major contentious issue. For example, at a 2013 UK House of Lords

Selection Committee on Economic Affairs session to discuss the economic impact on UK energy policy of shale gas and oil (HOL, 2013), written evidence was received from thirty different witnesses, including trade associations, such as the United Kingdom Onshore Operators Group and the Chemical Industries Association, companies actively engaged in the energy industry, such as E.ON, EDF and Cuadrilla, and organizations opposed to the use of the technique, along with academic experts.

Consultation of this type is intended to ensure that all voices are heard in a legislative process. Inevitably, however, the stakes are higher for some than for others. For example, it was suggested that as a consequence of the open consultation process during the creation of the European Union's emissions trading scheme that the large steel companies were able to shape the scheme in a manner which favored them and led to them obtaining options worth tens of millions of dollars through their engagement with the consultation process and the strength of their arguments (Macalister, 2009).

Overall, Level 4 engagement sees organizations recognizing an opportunity to exert influence through a variety of channels. This is a well-known and understood option for an organization, and a relatively low-cost way of ensuring that its opinion is heard among regulatory or legislative bodies, although without certainty of success. Organizations with specialist knowledge will seek to provide government bodies with the benefit of their expertise in the hope of achieving a positive outcome. There is, nevertheless, the potential for governments to use the consultation opportunity as a fig leaf to legitimize a policy that would otherwise be implemented in a hostile environment. From the organization's perspective, however, this approach offers some positive benefits, including:

- An invitation or an audience does provide some exposure to the organization's opinions and any such opportunity is valuable.
- There remains the option for an organization to pursue Level 3 engagement if Level 4 engagement is unsuccessful because of, for example, general public concerns, perhaps generated by adverse media commentary.
- Through participation in discussions with oversight bodies, and any subsequent publicity, momentum may be created or allies identified for future relationship engagement.
- The cost of involvement may be relatively low, but the value of the information to the oversight body may be considerable, making the oversight body more likely to be receptive, even if it ultimately fails to act on that information.

Key characteristics at this level include the provision of assistance to the legislative process in the hope of accessing decision-makers so that an organization's case may be heard and evaluated in the decision-making process. In summary, Level 4 engagement implies proximity to the process, and in some fashion the possibility to achieve mutual interests by participation. However, there is the scope for disappointment as an organization's opinions can be ignored. The characteristic of Level 4 engagement that makes it unlike other levels is that it is undertaken through formal channels. This level is characterized by the provision of information, rather than inspiration or argument.

Level 3 – revise or challenge

Level 3 engagement shifts from the provision of information and persuasion to confrontation and argument. Arguably, this marks the difference between bargaining behavior aimed at establishing "partnership" to that which represents "conflict" in the terms outlined by Boddewyn and Brewer (1994). Of the strategic levels, Level 3 is perhaps the most commonly used. Whereas the preceding levels attempt to access the policy process early, Level 3 comes later, once decisions on legislation, regulation, or policy have been taken but the legislation, regulation, or policy is still open to challenge. At Level 3, the focus is on seeking to "stress-test" legislation, regulation, or policy by probing its boundaries or flexibility. As with previous levels, Level 3 engagement has two forms. It is either:

- rhetorical – by challenging the implementation of new legislation, regulation, or policy publicly; or
- legal – by challenging the implementation of new legislation, regulation, or policy through formal legal avenues.

The execution of either type of Level 3 engagement and the key political nature of many of the decisions that are challenged mean that while it is often portrayed as a less legitimate approach, it is nonetheless a valid and potentially effective form of engagement.

Level 3 engagement is likely to be attuned to the national legislative program. For example, Delmas and Montes-Sancho (2010) noted the development of the "Climate Challenge program" by the US energy industry appeared to be an attempt to preempt legislation relating to climate change emerging from the White House during the Clinton era. An example in the European context is outlined in Exhibit 11.3.

Exhibit 11.3 Level 3 relationship engagement – testing the polluter pays principle

In April 2007, the European Union introduced a directive intended to ensure that "those who cause environmental damage should bear the costs of avoiding it or compensating for it." This was the culmination of a lengthy process, begun when the European Community was first created but taken up seriously in the late 1980s, resulting in a green paper in 1993 and a white paper in 2000. The polluter pays principle was intended to ensure that public financing of environmental policy be minimized, with problem creators bearing the responsibility for financing its solution. The green and white papers initiated lengthy consultations, during which many stakeholders (described as "operators of risky or potentially risky activities") made representations taking advantage of Level 4 inform and advise engagement.

However, having established the principle, the EU recognized that there needed to be some scope for "allowable exceptions." These were permitted under the founding treaty of the European Community, which sought to recognize the diversity of the union and the right of member states to interpret certain directives in their own contexts. One key aspect of the principle concerned the extent to which national governments can require polluters to assume responsibility for pollution created prior to the introduction of the directive (i.e., before 2008, when the directive came into force) or for which there was no direct evidence that pollution was created by the operator of risky activities.

This aspect of the directive was tested by a court case brought before the Administrative Court of Sicily which culminated in a 2010 ruling by the European Court of Justice. Several Italian utility companies (ERG, ENI, and Syndial) challenged the Italian government's interpretation of the directive that found them responsible for pollution in the Priolo–Augusta–Melilli area of Sicily and required them to clean up the affected areas. The companies argued that no formal investigation into the cause of the pollution had been undertaken. No direct correlation had been established between their activities and the pollution, and hence no responsibility could be established for the liability to clean up the area. The EU Court of Justice ruled that appropriate national bodies can presume liability on account of the fact that "the operator's installations are located close to the polluted areas." This was a strict interpretation of the directive and imposed a severe limit on the scope for exceptions.

The action taken by ERG, ENI, and Syndial can be seen as evidence of Level 3 revision or challenge relationship engagement motivated by a desire to test the extent of a directive with potentially significant scope to impose liabilities upon them. This action was necessitated by the failure of Level 4 inform and advise engagement to reach a settlement that was deemed acceptable for companies of this type. Furthermore, their actions can be seen to have been undertaken, unofficially at least, on behalf of other "operators of risky or potentially risky activities" to test the extent of the directive and the European Court of Justice's interpretation of its application of the directive. There will have been a free-rider effect here, even though the outcome was ultimately unsatisfactory for the energy companies.

Legal challenges are far less common in the EU than in the USA. The less litigious nature of Europeans may be a reason for this; the effectiveness of rhetorical positioning may be another, although Coen (2007) notes that cost may be the main reason why legal Level 3 LRE has been used only sparingly. An organization considering Level 3 engagement recognizes that previous opportunities to shape legislation by itself or other organizations have either failed or been missed, but that opportunities to shape how that legislation is interpreted remain.

Level 3 engagement is the most frequently recognized form of lobbying – where organizations exploit opportunities to question, challenge, and (re-)shape legislation, regulation, or policy. Methods include seeking judicial review and the formation of common interest group alliances. In earlier assessments we have seen evidence of large coalitions banding together to engage at Level 4 (such as when the UK's hedge-fund industry responded to the threat of EU regulatory action), but this option of collaborative action remains during Level 3 engagement.

Level 2 – manage implications

Organizations might choose to undertake different levels of engagement at the same time. For example, energy companies tend to be active in the pursuit of strategic relationship engagement. However, there are also examples of tactical relationship engagement in this industry. For example, the UK government's decision to pursue clean coal technology was applauded by a variety of interested parties, including E.ON UK (the UK subsidiary of the

German power company), which declared that it was "committed to fit capture technology to Kingsnorth [its coal-powered power station] in accordance with the government's proposed conditions, as long as it is properly funded" (Vidal and Jowit, 2009: 6). In relationship engagement terms, E.ON UK acknowledged that it had to accept the government's decision, but to make that decision more palatable it attempted to move the debate in its favor. This action suggests E.ON has appropriated the aim of the decision (to improve its green credentials) by pointing out the necessity of government subsidy in order to achieve its objectives.

Level 2 engagement is often focused upon making objections to a policy clear as part of a longer-term policy of relationship engagement. For example, when the UK's Freight Transport Association criticized the government's decision to impose a two-pence rise in fuel duty, it was both an attempt to demonstrate its opposition and an attempt to ensure the issue remained in the public eye with the hope of building support for a long-term policy change (Booth, 2009). Level 2 engagement therefore aims to develop an awareness of the implications of unopposable change and to project a positive interpretation of that change. A recent paper by Du and Vieira (2012) offers a variety of examples of Level 2 (and Level 1) engagement and makes it clear that the corporate website is now a very important vehicle for such engagement.

Level 1 – manage perceptions

Organizations that fundamentally disagree with government policy might use corporate communications to illustrate their opposition. Gallaher ran a campaign by M&C Saatchi prior to the tobacco poster advertising ban in 2003 featuring an advert with an overweight opera-singer wearing a purple dress, implying that "It isn't over 'til the fat lady sings." Around the same time, British American Tobacco, Japan Tobacco, and Philip Morris ran anti-smoking adverts aimed at young people, perhaps in an attempt to head off the ban (Viney and Baines, 2012).

The key characteristic in Level 1 is the management of perceptions of the implications of change. This is undertaken either when change is or seems inevitable or there is a need to build a grassroots following. It therefore bears some similarity to the constituency-building options identified in work by authors such as Baysinger et al. (1985) and Keim and Baysinger (1982). Their notion of constituency-building develops a "bottom-up" approach to achieving influence, where the emphasis is placed upon mobilizing citizens (in their capacities as voters and party members) to lobby oversight bodies on behalf of an organizational interest.

Conclusion

The aim of this chapter is to offer guidance to managers on the options available to them as they seek to manage their relationship engagement with government. The emphasis has been placed upon non-market "voice" strategies intended to achieve and enhance organizational advocacy which we argue sit alongside more traditional market strategies to create a truly aligned strategy for an organization. Underlying this work is the belief that, despite continued skepticism regarding CPA, organizations possess a legitimate right to develop and build relationships with oversight bodies. We believe that, in line with many contributions to this volume, these legitimate non-market strategies help to create the potential for organizational competitive advantage. The relationship engagement classification system (Baines and Viney, 2010; Viney and Baines, 2012) and the examples we have presented here are intended to show how organizations can craft a relationship engagement strategy which is appropriate, contingent, and flexible in the face of an increasingly dynamic competitive environment.

Many observers have noted that the industry in which a firm operates matters, and in those industries where government is an active participant the need for relationship engagement will be particularly evident. In such cases, organizations will have to engage; the only choice will be in *how* they engage. In determining an answer to this question, the resources an organization possesses will be particularly relevant. The institutional environment is also important, as the type of "voice" options we discuss here are dependent upon a policy process that is open to advice, scrutiny, or challenge. It is possible to conceive of country contexts experiencing institutional voids (North, 1990), or where institutions are emergent rather than established (Henisz and Zelner, 2005), where these options are currently unavailable or offer limited potential, reflecting the very limited role firms play in the policy process. Discussion of non-market strategies in countries engaged in filling institutional voids, or where institutions are emerging, remains an item of importance for future research in this field (Puck et al., 2013).

There are costs associated with relationship engagement, so deciding which level to pursue, for how long, in what way, and with whom is critical. (As we have discussed, there is real potential to cooperate with other organizations to achieve mutual benefits.) Of considerable importance also will be the sophistication of the engagement strategy adopted. We note that organizations are unlikely to limit their relationship engagement to one level all of the time, and anticipate that they will change their engagement as need dictates, or as resources permit. Organizations may develop a core relationship engagement strategy but it may include elements drawn from across the range of options identified. They may move between levels as the success or failure of earlier efforts becomes clear. They may, in addition, pursue different non-market strategies simultaneously to influence a plurality of stakeholders, such as different levels of government actors, other industry players, non-governmental organizations (NGOs), or the general public. The aim of strategic alignment should sit at the heart of choices regarding non-market "voice" strategies of the type discussed here.

Throughout this chapter, we have posited that CPA and relationship engagement provide a new set of strategic insights to organizations seeking to pursue their legitimate right to establish relationships with government or regulatory oversight bodies. The approach we have advocated relies upon organizations committing to pursue legitimate, ethical, and legal means to advance their causes, as only through such commitment will the skepticism felt towards corporate political activity be reduced.

Our underlying argument, therefore, is a belief that a more open and frank discussion of the motivations of organizational non-market strategy is consistent with the achievement of organizational objectives. Observers expect for-profit organizations to seek to make profits, and the health of market economies depends upon them doing so consistently over time. Legitimate non-market strategies assist in this search for competitive advantage. In closing this chapter, we argue that there is a strong need for more research focused upon testing the positive benefits of pursuing open and transparent non-market strategies. The potential of "voice" options of the type discussed above will be enhanced, we argue, if they are pursued in a context of openness. Only when such openness exists might the wider community be persuaded to accept that relationship engagement between government and industry is not suspicious per se. Indeed, this might lead to widespread appreciation that it has an important role to play in a democratic society more generally. Perhaps in the (probably distant) future, we might even see organizations voting formally on legislation that affects them directly – a veritable corporate political market place.

References

Baines, P. and Viney, H. (2010). An unloved relationship? Dynamic capabilities and political-market strategy: A research agenda. *Journal of Public Affairs*, 10, 1, 258–64.

Barker, D. (2008). Ethics and lobbying: The case of real estate brokerage. *Journal of Business Ethics*, 80, 23–35.

Baron, D. P. (1995). Integrated strategies: Market and non-market components. *California Management Review*, 37, 47–65.

Baysinger, B. D. (1994). Domain maintenance as an objective of business political activity: An expanded typology. *Academy of Management Review*, 9, 248–58.

Baysinger, B. D., Keim, G. D., and Zeithaml, C. P. (1985). An empirical evaluation of the potential for including shareholders in corporate constituency programs. *Academy of Management Journal*, 28, 180–200.

Boatright, J. (2009). Rent seeking in a market with morality: Solving a puzzle about corporate social responsibility. *Journal of Business Ethics*, 88, 541–52.

Boddewyn, J. J. and Brewer, T. L. (1994). International business political behavior: New theoretical directions. *Academy of Management Review*, 19, 119–43.

Bonardi, J.-P. (1999). Market and nonmarket strategies during deregulation: The case of British Telecom. *Business and Politics*, 1/2, 203–31.

Bonardi, J.-P., Holburn, G.L. F., and Vanden Bergh, R. G. (2006). Nonmarket strategy performance: Evidence from US electric utilities. *Academy of Management Journal*, 49, 1209–28.

Booth, R. (2009). Fuel duty rise is end of road for many drivers, says freight lobby. *Guardian*, September 1, 7.

Bouwen, P. and McCown, M. (2007). Lobbying versus litigation: Political and legal strategies of inter-est representation in the European Union. *Journal of European Public Policy*, 14(3), 422–43.

Capron, L. and Chatain, O. (2008). Competitors' resource-oriented strategies: Acting on competitors' resources through interventions in factor markets and political markets. *Academy of Management Review*, 33, 97–121.

Charki, M. H., Josserand, E., and Charki, N. B. (2011). Toward an ethical understanding of the controversial technology of online reverse auctions. *Journal of Business Ethics*, 98, 17–37.

Coen, D. (1999). The impact of US lobbying practice on the European business–government relation-ship. *California Management Review*, 41(4), 27–44.

— (2007). Empirical and theoretical studies in EU lobbying. *Journal of European Public Policy*, 14, 333–45.

Dahan, N. (2005). Can there be a resource-based view of politics? *International Studies of Management and Organizations*, 35, 8–27.

Dal Bó, E. (2006). Regulatory capture: A review. *Oxford Review of Economic Policy*, 22, 203–24.

Delmas, M. A. and Montes-Sancho, M. J. (2010). Voluntary agreements to improve environmental quality: Symbolic and substantive cooperation. *Strategic Management Journal*, 31, 575–604.

Du, S. and Vieira, E. T. (2012). Striving for legitimacy through corporate social responsibility: Insights from oil companies. *Journal of Business Ethics*, 110, 413–27.

Eising, R. (2007). The access of business interests to EU institutions: Towards elite pluralism. *Journal of European Public Policy*, 14, 384–403.

Faccio, M. (2006). Politically connected firms. *American Economic Review*, 96, 369–86.

Faccio, M., Masulis, R., and McConnell, J. (2006). Political connections and corporate bailouts. *Journal of Finance*, 6, 2597–635.

Fairbrass, J. (2003). The Europeanisation of business interest representation: UK and French firms compared. *Comparative European Politics*, 1, 313–34.

— (2006). Organised Interests. In Bache, I. and Jordan, A. (eds.), *The Europeanisation of British Politics*, London: Palgrave Macmillan.

Fairbrass, J. and Zueva-Owens, A. (2012). Conceptualising corporate social responsibility: "Relational governance" assessed, augmented and adapted. *Journal of Business Ethics*, 105, 321–35.

Galang, R. M. (2012). Victim or victimizer: Firm responses to government corruption. *Journal of Management Studies*, 49, 429–62.

Gowthorpe, C. and Amat, O. (2005). Creative accounting: Some ethical issues of macro- and micro-manipulation. *Journal of Business Ethics*, 57, 55–64.

Green, M. J., Fallows, J. M., and Zwick, D. R. (1972). *Who Runs Congress?* New York: Bantam/Grossman.

Gribben, R. (2009). Employees and unions at odds over EU plan for agency workers: Conflict surrounds legislation to give temporary workers more protection. *Sunday Telegraph*, August 2, 8.

Grossman, G. and Helpman, E. (1994). Protection for sale. *American Economic Review*, 84, 833–50.

Hall, R. and Deardorff, A. (2006). Lobbying as legislative subsidy. *American Political Science Review*, 100, 69–84.

Henderson, D. (2001). *Misguided Virtue: False Notions of Corporate Social Responsibility*. London: Institute of Economic Affairs.

Henisz, W. and Zelner, B. (2005). Legitimacy, interest group pressures, and change in emergent institutions: The case of foreign investors and host country governments. *Academy of Management Review*, 30, 361–82.

Hillman, A. J. and Hitt, M. A. (1999). Corporate political strategy formulation: A model of approach, participation and strategy decisions. *Academy of Management Review*, 24, 825–42.

Hillman, A. J., Keim, G. D., and Schuler, D. (2004). Corporate political activity: A review and research agenda. *Journal of Management*, 30, 837–57.

House of Lords (HoL) (2013). *The Economic Impact on UK Energy Policy of Shale Gas and Oil: Oral and Written Evidence*. Select Committee on Economic Affairs, October 14. Retrieved from: www.parliament.uk/documents/lords-committees/economic-affairs/EnergyPolicy/Evidence%20Volume/OnlineEvVol3.pdf (accessed 4 March 2015).

Keffer, J. M. and Hill, R. P. (1997). An ethical approach to lobbying activities of business in the United States. *Journal of Business Ethics*, 16, 1371–9.

Keim, G. and Baysinger, B. D. (1982). Corporate political strategies examined: Constituency building may be the best of all. *Public Affairs Review*, 3, 77–87.

Keim, G. and Hillman, A. (2008). Political environments and business strategy: Implications for managers. *Business Horizons*, 54, 47–53.

Lawton, T. C., Doh, J. P., and Rajwani, T. (2014). *Aligning for Advantage: Competitive Strategies for the Political and Social Arenas*. Oxford: Oxford University Press.

Lawton, T., McGuire, S., and Rajwani, T. (2013). Corporate political activity: A literature review and research agenda. *International Journal of Management Reviews*, 15, 86–105.

Macalister, T. (2009). Steel firms make millions from EU carbon trading scheme. *Guardian*, September 10, 28.

Mantere, S., Pajunen, K., and Lamberg, J.-A. (2009). Vices and virtues of corporate political activity: The challenges of international business. *Business and Society*, 48, 105–32.

Mason, R. (2009). CBI calls for rise in Britain's nuclear spend. *Daily Telegraph*, July 13, 3.

McWilliams, A., van Fleet, D. D., and Cory, K. D. (2002). Raising rivals' costs through political strategy: An extension of resource-based theory. *Journal of Management Studies*, 39, 707–23.

Milbrath, L. W. (1963). *The Washington Lobbyists*. Chicago: Rand McNally.

Moss, D., McGrath, C., Tonge, J., and Harris, P. (2012). Exploring the management of the corporate public affairs function in a dynamic public environment. *Journal of Public Affairs*, 12, 47–60.

Nelson, D. (2006). The political economy of anti-dumping: A survey. *European Journal of Political Economy*, 22, 554–90.

North, D. C. (1990). *Institutions, Institutional Change, and Economic Performance*. New York: Cambridge University Press.

Nownes, A. J. (2001). *Pressure and Power: Organized Interests in American Politics*. Boston, MA: Houghton-Mifflin.

Oliver, C. and Holzinger, I. (2008). The effectiveness of strategic political management: A dynamic capabilities framework. *Academy of Management Review*, 33, 496–520.

Pearce, J. L., De Castro, J. O., and Guillen, M. F. (2008). Influencing politics and political systems: Political strategies and corporate strategies. *Academy of Management Review*, 33, 493–95.

Posner, R. (1975). The social costs of monopoly and regulation. *Journal of Political Economy*, 83, 807–27.

Puck, J., Rogers, H., and Mohr, A. (2013). Flying under the radar: Foreign firm visibility and the efficacy of political strategies in emerging economies. *International Business Review*, 22, 1021–33.

Section C

Non-market impact and performance

Environmental performance and non-market strategy

The impact of inter-organizational ties

Thomas Graf and Carl Joachim Kock

Environmental issues such as global warming or the harm caused to people and nature through the release of chemicals are critical concerns for society and politics today. OECD data, for instance, make clear that the goal set in 2010 of stabilizing the climate at a two-degree Celsius global average temperature increase cannot be reached without serious policy change (OECD, n.d.). According to the US Environmental Protection Agency, 4.09 billion pounds of toxic chemicals were disposed of or released into the environment (i.e., air, water or land) in 2011 (EPA, 2011). As a result of this, firms are increasingly under pressure from non-market actors to improve their environmental impact.

An increasingly important part of any modern firm's non-market strategy is therefore its response to institutional pressures for more sustainable production processes and toxic emissions management. These pressures are brought to bear on the firm from a wide variety of market and non-market constituencies, including governments (Reid and Toffel, 2009), non-governmental organizations (NGOs) (Boli and Thomas, 1997), the media (Bansal and Clelland, 2004; Hamilton, 1995), suppliers (Vachon and Klassen, 2007), employees (Turban and Greening, 1997), consumers, and even socially minded investors (Delmas and Toffel, 2008).

Interestingly, firms seem to respond to these pressures in very different ways, leading to rather heterogeneous efforts in terms of reducing or avoiding waste or developing environmentally friendly or even enhancing products or service ideas. While the extant literature has examined various factors that may cause firms to become environmental champions or laggards, we propose that these efforts also differ depending on the interaction with a firm's heterogeneous stakeholders. In the first part of this chapter, we will therefore provide a newly arranged overview of the key issues uncovered by the environmental management literature, particularly emphasizing the impact of market versus non-market stakeholders. Furthermore, we will highlight one particular area that has not received much attention so far: the potential impact of inter-organizational linkages, such as alliances or director interlocks, on a firm's environmental management. The second half of the chapter, accordingly, proposes an organizing framework for thinking about these potentially important effects.

Environmental management and non-market strategy

On a broad level, the extant literature suggests two generic environmental strategies of how firms respond to institutional expectations toward more sustainable management (Hart, 1995). Firms following a reactive strategy, on the one hand, do only what appears to be necessary to build or maintain environmental legitimacy in the eyes of their stakeholders. They improve their environmental performance no further than the minimum level required – for instance, through end-of-pipe technologies that control waste at the end of the production process – or manage stakeholder expectations through rather symbolic gestures when not even reaching such required minimum levels. The overall goal of this strategy is to avoid reputational penalties and regulatory sanctions at the lowest possible cost (Klassen and Whybark, 1999).

By contrast, environmentally proactive firms go beyond regulatory rules and aim to perform better in terms of their environmental efforts than what they are legally required or even socially expected to do (Russo and Fouts, 1997; Sharma and Vredenburg, 1998). Instead of implementing waste control technologies at the end of a production process, for instance, they aim at preventing the generation of new waste from the early production stages on and throughout the whole production process (Klassen and Whybark, 1999).

We suggest that these two distinct approaches to environmental management have rather different implications for management, depending on whether the targets of these strategies (or, alternatively, the impetus behind these strategies) are market or non-market stakeholders (Table 12.1). In fact, stakeholder theory has been used in many contexts as a lens to differentiate between entities that are important for a firm and strategic moves toward them (Freeman, 1984; Laplume, Sonpar, and Litz, 2008). In the environmental management literature, however, stakeholder approaches have been applied mostly in the context of proactive strategies. Stakeholder integration, following this view, is perceived as a necessary condition for environmental leadership and affiliated competitive advantages (e.g., Buysse and Verbeke, 2003; Sharma and Vredenburg, 1998). By contrast, we consider a stakeholder perspective as an effective tool to analyze environmental management tactics and strategies in general and not only limited to one specific strategy. Rearranging the extant literature (Bansal and Roth, 2000; King and Lenox, 2002; Reid and Toffel, 2009) according to these two dimensions allows us to provide an organizing framework for thinking about environmental strategies in the context of market versus non-market stakeholders.

Table 12.1 Environmental management and stakeholder engagement

	Reactive environmental strategies	*Proactive environmental strategies*
Market stakeholders Customers, investors, employees, or suppliers	E.g. environmental certification to impress customers or corporate governance gestures to impress investors (symbolic management)	E.g. competitive advantages based on cost advantage, environmental innovation, and competitor preemption
Non-market stakeholders Government, NGOs, or communities	E.g. self-auditing to express commitment to environmental norms vis-à-vis regulatory organizations (symbolic management)	E.g. competitive advantages based on the shaping of political processes or "strategic bridging" with NGOs

Reactive environmental strategies and non-market stakeholders

At the core of reactive environmental strategies is the "not doing more than necessary" logic. Firms that follow such a logic will tend to respond to pressures for better environmental performance from non-market stakeholders such as regulatory institutions (Majumdar and Marcus, 2001), the media (Bansal and Clelland, 2004), or NGOs (Jasanoff, 1997) with activities that may help to reassure these stakeholders but without actually following up with substantive changes to their environmental performance. Such "window-dressing" activities to express conformity with environmental norms publicly without a real follow-up are essentially a form of symbolic management, as described by Westphal and Zajac (1994) and other authors (e.g., Berrone and Gomez-Mejia, 2009; Boiral, 2007).

Firms pursuing such a strategy might pretend to reduce the emission of chemicals, for instance by adding end-of-pipe technologies that "control" waste rather than reduce it (Klassen and Whybark, 1999). Likewise, they may adopt self-regulatory commitments without actually implementing them, particularly in the absence of strong regulatory surveillance (Short and Toffel, 2010), or they may participate in voluntary agreements within collective corporate political strategies without actually generating much improvement in their environmental performance (King and Lenox, 2000). Particularly when the respective voluntary agreement program is already well established and when many firms have adapted to it, the potential for such free-riding would seem to be high. Late adopters, specifically, may experience similar reputational benefits, such as lower scrutiny from governmental institutions, without the substantial investments in environmental management of early adopters (Delmas and Montes-Sancho, 2010). In this way they may comply with formal requirements of governmental institutions and mitigate potential pressures and at the same time forgo the costs for the actual environmental performance improvements.

Environmentally weak firms may also use the simple publication of environmental data as an expression of environmental commitment (Philippe and Durand, 2011). Furthermore, they may apply typical political strategy means such as constituency-building or financial-incentive tactics to prevent regulatory sanctions due to weak environmental performance (Clark and Crawford, 2012).

Overall, reactive strategies are characterized by symbolic management techniques to express environmental commitment without actually improving a firm's environmental performance. These allow firms with weaker environmental performance to avoid the scrutiny of non-market stakeholders. At the same time, however, they also incur costs – for instance, for installing end-of-pipe technologies or the remediation of waste – and leave aside potential competitive opportunities from actively shaping their non-market environment. Surprisingly, the literature has so far not considered the cost of firms practicing symbolic management in sensitive areas such as environmental issues. One might imagine a rather strong backlash if consumers or non-market stakeholders feel betrayed in a matter that may be considered ethical.

Reactive environmental strategies and market stakeholders

Environmentally reactive firms are also likely to attempt to create or maintain environmental legitimacy with respect to market stakeholders. The implementation of waste control technologies, for instance, has been found to be one means to avoid negative signals to customers (Vachon and Klassen, 2007). In addition, firms may try to portray themselves as reliable and sustainable organizations by adopting internationally recognized management standards, such as the ISO 14001 certification (Delmas, 2002). As long as such standards bind adopters only to particular environmental process regulations and not to concrete environmental performance levels, they could again be (mis)used for window-dressing purposes (Boiral, 2007; King, Lenox, and Terlaak, 2005; Melnyk, Sroufe, and Calantone, 2003).

Moreover, corporate governance mechanisms, such as the establishment of environmental committees or an explicit environmental compensation policy, have been found to act in some instances as rather symbolic tools that may avoid potential pressures from investors or other stakeholders while having no or only a weak impact on a firm's actual environmental performance (Berrone and Gomez-Mejia, 2009). Bansal and Clelland (2004), furthermore, identified the voluntary disclosures of environmental liabilities as another means for environmentally weak firms to mitigate negative reactions from investors.

Reactive firms, in sum, engage in several efforts to avoid negative reputational consequences from market stakeholders. Waste control activities, thereby, aid them in avoiding negative signals to customers or investors, while symbolic management – for example, through corporate governance initiatives – allows them to build up a positive image.

Proactive environmental strategies and market stakeholders

In contrast to environmentally reactive firms, proactive firms aim to achieve a strong environmental performance by investing in substantive waste reduction throughout the production process. This strategy may allow proactive firms to differentiate themselves from competitors (as one type of market stakeholders) and cater to the desires of another set of market stakeholders in terms of customers who increasingly value greener products and services. In particular, proactive firms learn to generate cost advantages through a better utilization of raw materials, more efficient production cycles, and/or the avoidance of liability costs (Hart, 1995). Moreover, through life-cycle thinking, the integration of stakeholder views into the product design process, and the resulting product differentiation (product stewardship), as well as through environmental innovation, they may preempt competitors and eventually develop unique products that environmentally conscious customers will buy (Berrone, Fosfuri, Gelabert, and Gomez-Mejia, 2013).

Building on the resource-based view of the firm (Barney, 1991), the extant literature argues that the aforementioned processes generate and are the result of environmental capabilities and best practices (Berchicci, Dowell, and King, 2012; Christmann, 2000; Sharma and Vredenburg, 1998), which can be exploited with respect to a firm's market stakeholders. In fact, since these capabilities generate positive financial outcomes for the firm while being path-dependent, often embedded in organizational routines, and hence, at the same time, also quite tacit, they provide a source of competitive advantage (Boiral, 2002; King and Lenox, 2002; Shrivastava, 1995).

In addition to the generation of valuable organizational capabilities, proactive firms are considered more successful at developing a "green" reputation that may create intangible advantages, such as employee retention (Turban and Greening, 1997), or a lower unsystematic stock market risk (Bansal and Clelland, 2004). Finally, waste prevention has been found to aid in integrating and strengthening partner relationships across supply chains by the transfer of practices and the alignment of logistics and technologies, thereby creating another source of competitive advantage (Vachon and Klassen, 2007). Proactive firms, overall, tend to develop advantages by integrating market stakeholders more strongly than other firms, whereas reactive firms tend to use symbolic management tactics to mislead the same.

Proactive environmental strategies and non-market stakeholders

Environmentally proactive firms also differ from reactive firms in the way they interact with non-market stakeholders. Specifically, through their superior levels of waste prevention, proactive firms present themselves as entities that are credible and committed to sustainability, which may be positively perceived by regulatory institutions (Majumdar and Marcus, 2001), the media (Bansal and Clelland, 2004), and NGOs (Jasanoff, 1997). Instead of merely reacting to new regulations, for instance, they aim to shape public policies and influence regulatory institutions for their benefit (Hillman, Keim, and Schuler, 2004). As, for instance, Russo and Fouts (1997: 540) have pointed out, proactive firms may develop "political acumen [as an] ability to influence public policies in ways that confer a competitive advantage," and foster the regulation of specific chemicals where the firm performs better than its competitors or to initiate independent audits that hurt the firm's competitors more than itself (Leone, 1986).

Instead of just engaging in purely symbolic environmental commitments, proactive firms try to integrate important non-market stakeholders, such as NGOs or local communities, in the development of new products or to use them as door-openers to other important stakeholders – something that has been described as "strategic bridging" (Stafford, Polonsky, and Hartman, 2000; Westley and Vredenburg, 1991). Their environmental reputation may be enhanced further by serious and engaged participation in collective voluntary agreements, such as the US Climate Challenge program, even at the cost of tolerating free-riding by late joiners, as discussed above (Delmas and Montes-Sancho, 2010).

Taken together, proactive firms do not only improve their environmental performance through internal process changes, they also express their environmental ambition publicly to gain environmental legitimacy and the support of non-market stakeholders and use this support as knowledge sources for their environmental management.

Environmental management and non-market strategies

Altogether, environmental management must clearly be considered as a key part of firms' non-market challenges. For example, environmental management involves several dimensions that are central to non-market competition, such as the potential influence of firms on public policies that may hurt their competitors while benefiting themselves, the cooperation with NGOs that may aid them in producing superior environmental products, or the cooperation with a local community that may endow them with political influence in that region. Yet, when compared with other non-market contexts, such as social welfare programs and philanthropy, environmental issues – particularly in more proactive firms – seem to pertain more specifically to the organization of the production process per se.

Inter-organizational ties and environmental management

One of the underexplored areas in the emerging literature on environmental management is the potential influence that a firm's partner network has on a focal firm's environmental performance. In fact, a large literature has explored the effect of inter-firm linkages, such as strategic alliances or director interlocks, on a variety of other strategic issues, including innovation, diversification, and organizational structure. For these areas, prior research (reviewed briefly below) has found significant effects resulting from at least two distinct processes: learning; and reputational spillovers. Yet, while it is a very reasonable assumption that similar effects also exist in the area of environmental management, extant research has been comparatively muted on this topic, thus offering promising avenues for future research.

Alliances and interlocks: knowledge and reputation transfers

The extant literature on inter-firm ties has particularly focused on strategic alliances and director interlocks. The resource-based view (Barney and Arikan, 2001) and the related knowledge-based view of the firm (Grant, 1996) have often been used to explain the formation of learning alliances where knowledge transfers and mutual learning are the primary purpose of cooperation (see, for instance, a comprehensive review provided by Eunni, Kasuganti, and Kos, 2006).

Alliances can enable a firm to access the knowledge of the other firms in the alliance and pursue strategic goals with the combined resource base (Grant and Baden-Fuller, 2004) or even allow for the actual transfer or co-production of knowledge (Kale and Singh, 2007). In addition, the literature on interlocking directorships (instances where directors sit on the boards of multiple firms) often applies vicarious learning or institutional theory perspectives to explain the transfer of knowledge across boards of directors (Mizruchi, 1996; Shipilov, Greve, and Rowley, 2010; Shropshire, 2010).

Besides such knowledge transfers, the alliance and interlock literature has explored reputational spillovers among linked firms. Firms may form alliances or interlocks with highly legitimate institutions to increase their own legitimacy in the eyes of stakeholders (Baum and Oliver, 1991; Mizruchi, 1996). Based on signaling theory (Spence, 1973), the extant literature explains such spillovers by suggesting that stakeholders use inter-firm linkages as alternative signals of quality in the presence of uncertainty. Similar to an employer who cannot assess the full and actual quality of a job applicant and who needs to rely on alternative signals, such as CVs or assessment centers, stakeholders may not always see the actual quality of a firm and rely instead on its ties to other firms as proxies of quality (Stuart, Ha, and Hybels, 1999).

Inter-firm ties and the environment

We next explore the potential impact of inter-firm linkages on the environmental strategies of firms, with a particular focus on gaps in the extant literature and promising avenues for future inquiry. While there is a general paucity of work in this area, some researchers have looked at a number of related issues.

One literature stream, for instance, has discussed the importance of inter-firm knowledge transfers in the context of environmental management by exploring supply chain integration and the use of environmental technologies (for a literature review, see Srivastava, 2007). The key notion developed and tested in this literature is that important suppliers need to become technologically integrated in order to make waste prevention investments effective (Vachon and Klassen, 2007). A second literature stream has explored collaborations between businesses and environmental NGOs such as Greenpeace as an alternative way of self-regulation vis-à-vis governmental regulators (e.g., Arts, 2002; Glasbergen and Groenenberg, 2001). Ortiz-de-Mandojana and her colleagues (2011) also provided support for the importance of inter-firm knowledge transfers in the context of environmental management. Specifically, they showed that firms engage more in environmentally proactive strategies when directors from knowledge-intensive service firms sit on their boards and provide them with consulting service.

Yet, only a few studies have tackled the specific contribution that other firms' green capabilities or strategies could have for a somehow linked focal firm's environmental strategy. Albino, Dangelico and Pontrandolfo (2012), for example, explored several types of inter-organizational collaborations but could not find an impact of such collaborations on a firm's position in *Newsweek*'s US 500 Green Ranking, 2010. Lin (2012), by contrast, found that non-equity exploration alliances with diverse partners have a positive impact on a focal firm's proactive environmental performance.

In terms of reputational spillovers, the literature has likewise addressed a number of relevant issues. Specifically, a theoretical paper by Dacin, Oliver, and Roy (2007) suggested that firms may form strategic alliances in order to gain social legitimacy through linkage with partners, while other studies demonstrated that firms experience negative reputational spillovers just by being in the same industry (Barnett and King, 2008) or merely by using chemicals that were similar to those used by a firm that committed an error or suffered an accident (Diestre and Rajagopalan, 2013). Delmas and Montes-Sancho (2010), moreover, looked at the effect of linkages between firms and non-market actors – specifically, governmental institutions – and suggested that firms profit from established environmental voluntary agreements even if they join only symbolically and without improving their environmental performance substantially. Lin (2012), finally, suggests a "legitimacy-oriented type of alliance" whereby focal firms build equity-based exploitation ties with homogeneous partners to influence stakeholder perceptions beneficial for the firm.

Yet, here too a comprehensive model of reputational effects between firms and their potential consequences on environmental strategies remains to be defined.

Taking together the abundance of the inter-firm linkage literature on knowledge and reputation transfers in general and the few examples in the wider realm of social issues, further research on the impact of inter-firm linkages specifically on environmental management seems very promising.

One reason why the impact of inter-firm linkages on environmental management has been largely ignored may be that the focus of academic research interests is usually on the primary motivation of inter-firm cooperation per se. The alliance literature explores, for instance, the conditions under which firms can create value (Rothaermel and Deeds, 2004) or appropriate value in an alliance (Diestre and Rajagopalan, 2012). More specifically, research questions analyzed in the literature include how alliances can strengthen a firm's innovation capabilities (Sampson, 2007), when alliances are superior to acquisitions (Wang and Zajac, 2007), and how trust can increase inter-firm learning (Muthusamy and White, 2005).

Environmental management as part of a firm's non-market strategy might be seen as more of a side-issue that is of less – or no – concern for the purposeful creation of an alliance or an interlocking directorship between firms. Accordingly, learning about environmental knowledge from partners or reputational spillovers may simply be side-effects of such co-operations and, hence, overlooked by researchers. Research on interlock directorships, by contrast, often includes a perspective on potential unintended effects of inter-firm ties: for example, when interlocks foster the diffusion of various organizational practices such as the accounting of stock option grants (Kang and Tan, 2008) or corporate governance practices (Shipilov et al., 2010). In these cases, it seems rather unlikely that learning about such practices was the primary purpose for setting up the interlock in the first place. Similarly, it seems unlikely that negative reputational spillovers – for example, the damage that linked firms suffered by having interlocks with firms that committed financial fraud as documented by Kang (2008) – were intended when firms created an interlock. Given these unintended effects of inter-firm

Table 12.2 The inter-firm linkage and environmental management interplay

	Inter-firm knowledge transfers	Inter-firm reputational spillovers
Intention of inter-firm linkage formation	E.g. linkages to "green" firms built for the purpose of acquiring environmental capabilities	E.g. linkages to "green" firms built for the purpose of enhancing environmental legitimacy
Side-effects of inter-firm linkages	E.g. learning from other firms' capabilities due to long-term cooperation, even if these learning effects were not the purpose for starting the cooperation	E.g. experiencing environmental reputation increases from partners without being aware of or intending to generate them

linkages, the dearth of studies on environmental knowledge and reputation spillovers even for the area of director interlock is even more surprising.

Based on these considerations, we suggest a new framework (Table 12.2) for the relationship between inter-firm linkages and environmental management. In particular, we propose to distinguish between intended and unintended effects of ties, on one hand, and the type of potential "transfer" – environmental knowledge or reputation – on the other.

Intended environmental knowledge transfers

As empirical studies have shown, firms, even in the same industry, differ greatly with respect to their environmental performance. A likely reason for this is that it is difficult in most industrial contexts to reduce the generation and emission of waste efficiently, and firms accordingly differ in their ability or dedication to tackle these issues (King and Lenox, 2002). One important but so far unanswered question, in this context, is the degree to which inter-firm relationships can be attractive sources of knowledge on how to engage effectively and efficiently in proactive environmental strategies.

Some studies have started to examine this research question and have provided initial evidence that firms attempt to absorb environmental capabilities from external organizations, for instance by acquiring the relevant facilities (Berchicci et al., 2012). It seems plausible to assume, however, that firms also perceive alliances and interlocking directorships as valuable sources of environmental knowledge and created these linkages specifically for the purpose of acquiring environmental capabilities.

Alliances, for example, have been found to create learning opportunities for rather complex and tacit knowledge that may be embedded in the partner's routines, as such alliances allow for close interaction, immediate feedback communication, and face-to-face imitation (Lyles and Salk, 2007). Such knowledge transfers seem to be particularly strong when partners build trustful relationships (Muthusamy and White, 2005), have alliance management capabilities (Kale and Singh, 2007), and are technologically related (Mowery, Oxley, and Silverman, 1996; Sampson, 2007). Alliances with environmentally strong partners, thus, may be formed based on the intention to acquire or co-develop complex environmental capabilities that are necessary for proactive strategies (Lin, 2012).

Furthermore, interlock directors have been found to be conducive for one firm imitating the strategies of another (Haunschild, 1993), and knowledge flows through internet ties appear to push firms into more proactive environmental strategies (Ortiz-de-Mandojana et al., 2011).

Accordingly, a reasonable assumption is that firms may indeed, in some situations, build an interlock with a "green" firm specifically to gain insights into how successful the other firm's proactive strategy is or what the key pitfalls are that the focal firm needs to understand if they intend to roll out a similar strategy. Hence, further research is needed on the conditions and modes of such intended environmental knowledge transfers through inter-firm linkages.

Unintended environmental knowledge transfers

We also find it likely – perhaps even more likely – that inter-firm linkages are formed initially due to organizational considerations that have scarcely anything to do with environmental management issues. Yet, the process of linking with other firms may induce unintended as well as intended consequences.

The director-interlock literature, for example, has shown that organizational practices such as the poison pill takeover defense mechanism (Davis, 1991) are adopted between interlocked firms. It appears unlikely, however, that such imitation was intended ex ante or even the purpose of creating the interlock tie. Similarly, interlocked firms have been found to imitate corporate governance practices (Shipilov et al., 2010). Yet, it seems reasonable to assume that such imitation was a side-effect rather than a key – or even *any* – consideration at the beginning of the interlock relationship. Furthermore, even though resource-dependence theory (Pfeffer and Salancik, 1978) and theoretical studies on interlocks (Mizruchi, 1996) suggest that interlocks are set up to gain insights into other firms' practices, it seems reasonable to assume that the object of these insights remains a priori rather unspecified. The insights a director gains during his or her tenure and board attendances, may, instead, be the result of a rather unintended learning or imitation process and subject to chance, suggesting that the actual outcomes of an interlock linkage – that is, the actual knowledge that is being transferred – are not the originally intended purpose of the link formation. Overall, it seems fair to state that the extant literature on interlock directorships remains rather silent on the classification of inter-firm knowledge transfers as being intended or unintended.

By contrast, the strategic alliance literature has concentrated primarily on the academic exploration of predefined performance outcomes (for a literature review, see Christoffersen, 2013). Partners are assumed to be selected on the basis of predefined goals (Diestre and Rajagopalan, 2012) and resource complementarities (Mitsuhashi and Greve, 2009), and the vast majority of studies explore the conditions under which such predefined and intended goals of alliance partners are achieved (Muthusamy and White, 2005). However, as De Rond and Bouchikhi (2004) emphasized in their alliance literature review, alliances often do not behave as linearly, goal-oriented, or recurrently as tends to be suggested by life-cycle, teleological, or evolutionary approaches. Instead, they may be conceptualized as the coexistence of multiple competing forces and dialectic tensions that allow for the possibility of unexpected consequences.

Taken together, both literature streams on inter-firm linkages appear to suggest that interlocked and allied firms may learn from each other even if this learning occurs as a side-effect and was not the primary reason for why the tie had been created in the first place. Moreover, such unintended learning processes may likely be fostered by certain contingencies, such as the specific knowledge characteristics transferred across firms, the duration of an alliance or interlock, or the respective purpose of an alliance.

Clearly, the longer two firms are allied or interlocked, the more interaction they have with each other. Accordingly, the higher should be the exposure to a firm's partners' knowledge bases and the more unintended learning effects should occur. Similarly, research and development alliances may provide firms with a deeper insight into the actual environmental processes of their partners than marketing or supplier alliances that in turn might be more helpful in discovering environmentally relevant product or supplier knowledge. Finally, unintended learning effects across firms are more likely to occur when the respective knowledge is rather simple, codifiable, and – due to such characteristics – easy to transfer across firms (Davis, 1991; Westphal and Zajac, 2001). A firm's experience with the ISO 14001 certification, for instance, or specific waste control technologies may easily spill over to affiliated firms and instigate isomorphic imitation effects (Delmas, 2002). Complex, tacit, and embedded knowledge, by contrast, may be less likely to spill over by accident, and thus rather require an actual intention to learn from partners and the development of appropriate structures for the same.

Research on such unintended knowledge spillover effects is widely absent, however, and may provide a promising research direction for understanding knowledge spillovers and inter-firm imitation of environmental strategies.

Intended environmental reputation spillovers

Inter-firm linkages have been identified by both the interlock and the alliance literature as potential sources of reputation and legitimacy spillovers (Deephouse and Carter, 2005). Pfeffer and Salancik (1978: 145), for instance, suggested that firms build interlocks to "provide confirmation to the rest of the world of the value and worth of the organization." Mizruchi (1996: 276), likewise, suggested that the "quest for legitimacy" is a reason for firms to form an interlock tie with another firm: "By appointing individuals with ties to other important organizations, the firm signals to potential investors that it is a legitimate enterprise worthy of support." Similarly, the alliance literature demonstrated that young firms receive higher IPO (initial public offering) evaluations when they are endorsed by prestigious partners (Stuart et al., 1999) or that suppliers of prestigious buyers can acquire new clients more easily (Kang, Mahoney, and Tan, 2009).

In all these cases, firms actively take advantage of other organizations' reputations by linking with them and exploiting the information asymmetry between themselves and their stakeholders, who may not be able to assess the actual quality of a firm. This phenomenon is similar to a job market situation when a potential employer is unable to assess the quality of a job applicant directly and relies on proxies, such as assessment centers, instead, as signaling theory suggests (Spence, 1973). It is also like the adverse selection problem in agency theory, where firm owners (principals) do not have direct means to assess the quality of a CEO (agent) and need to rely on proxies instead, as the corporate governance literature has discussed (Akerlof, 1970; Eisenhardt, 1989).

In the context of environmental strategies, it therefore seems reasonable to assume that firms deliberately build linkages with particularly "green" organizations in order positively to affect stakeholders' perception of their own environmental ethics (Lin, 2012). Given that the environmental performance of firms has become an important issue over the last few decades and that environmentally illegitimate firms may experience regulatory penalties, media and pressure group surveillance, or negative customer or stock market reactions, environmental legitimacy transferred from partner firms may indeed be a valuable resource. By allowing firms to establish or maintain a green image or at least to avoid external scrutiny (Bansal, 2005), such environmental reputation spillovers may provide a powerful and cost-efficient opportunity for firms to shape their stakeholders' view of the firm in a positive way (Bansal and Roth, 2000).

Unintended environmental reputation spillovers

While the extant literature has explored "intended" reputation spillovers and suggested that firms actively form inter-firm linkages in order to profit from their partners' reputations, there is also evidence for "unintended" spillovers, primarily in the context of unethical acts and reputational damages. According to Barnett and King (2008), for example, a firm's reputation suffers if another firm within the same industry suffers a major accident. Kang (2008), furthermore, suggested that firms experience reputational damages if they are interlocked with other firms that have committed financial fraud, and Sullivan, Haunschild, and Page (2007) found evidence that firms cut their interlock ties with other firms engaged in unethical behaviors, such as tax evasion or workers' safety violations.

In all these cases, firms experience reputational damages not because they have committed errors themselves but because of their links with other organizations. As the categorization literature has shown, stakeholders seem to classify firms as belonging to the same category because they are perceived as similar (e.g., Hsu, Hannan, and Koçak, 2009). For instance, if one firm suffers a major environmental accident, stakeholders may expect similar risks to exist for other firms in the same industry, independent of these latter firms' actual safety and risk management activities (Diestre and Rajagopalan, 2013). Similarly, if one firm commits financial fraud, stakeholders may perceive its outside directors as having violated their monitoring role and find it likely that these directors behave in a similarly lax fashion in their other firms. The firms interlocked with such a financially fraudulent firm may then suffer from reputational damages (Kang, 2008). Clearly, none of these negative reputation spillovers was intended when the original inter-organizational links were formed.

Despite the aforementioned studies on such negative unintended reputation spillovers, the extant literature remains silent when it comes to the exploration of *positive* unintended reputation spillovers. In the context of environmental management, we find it very likely that such spillovers from "green" firms to affiliated firms with a weaker environmental performance exist – and that they happen independently of whether the respective linkage was built for the purpose of environmental reputation spillovers or for other purposes altogether.

Building on the extant literature, we therefore propose that firms may engage in alliances or interlocks with "green" firms for other – perhaps more market-oriented – reasons, such as research and development or marketing purposes, and still experience environmental reputation increases. As a consequence, such firms may experience less stakeholder pressure to become "greener" than firms without "green" ties and, accordingly, invest less in environmental management than they would have done without the ties. If the positive reputation spillover has not been intended, the firm may even be unaware of the reputation spillovers and how their environmental strategy became influenced by them. Hence, studies on unintended positive reputation spillovers in the field of environmental management may be an interesting research avenue and should aid our understanding of firm behaviors in both the market and the non-market spheres.

Conclusion

This chapter has reviewed a key challenge for firms' non-market strategies – how they deal with environmental pressures – and has provided an organizing framework for thinking about environmental strategies from the perspective of market versus non-market stakeholders. Specifically, we have analyzed the implications of firms' taking either a reactive stance (e.g., through waste control and symbolic stakeholder management tactics) or a proactive stance (e.g., through waste prevention and stakeholder integration) toward environmental management and performance for their interactions with market and non-market stakeholders.

In addition, we have identified a major gap in the extant literature that pertains to the impact of inter-organizational ties on environmental issues. Again, we have proposed a novel organizing framework by distinguishing between environmental knowledge and reputation spillovers, on one hand, and intended versus unintended effects, on the other. Based on this framework, we suggest that inter-organizational ties, such as alliances and interlocks, should have an important impact on a firm's environmental stance and the attractiveness of either a reactive or a proactive strategy. Our organizing framework should guide further research into these important issues.

For the academic world, such research could enrich our theoretical understanding of how knowledge and reputation spill over across firms and what impact this can have on the receiving firms' strategies. Practitioners, likewise, should be interested in the intended or unintended repercussions that linkages with other firms can have on their own ability to achieve environmental goals and to deal with the wide variety of pressure groups that are increasingly forcing environmental issues on to the central stage of corporate decision-making.

References

Akerlof, G. A. 1970. The market for "lemons": quality uncertainty and the market mechanism. *Quarterly Journal of Economics*, 84(3): 488–500.

Albino, V., Dangelico, R. M., and Pontrandolfo, P. 2012. Do inter-organizational collaborations enhance a firm's environmental performance? A study of the largest US companies. *Journal of Cleaner Production*, 37: 304–15.

Arts, B. 2002. "Green alliances" of business and NGOs: new styles of self-regulation or "dead-end roads"? *Corporate Social Responsibility and Environmental Management*, 9(1): 26–36.

Bansal, P. 2005. Evolving sustainably: a longitudinal study of corporate sustainable development. *Strategic Management Journal*, 26(3): 197–218.

Bansal, P., and Clelland, I. 2004. Talking trash: legitimacy, impression management, and unsystematic risk in the context of the natural environment. *Academy of Management Journal*, 47(1): 93–103.

Bansal, P., and Roth, K. 2000. Why companies go green: a model of ecological responsiveness. *Academy of Management Journal*, 43(4): 717–36.

Barnett, M. L., and King, A. A. 2008. Good fences make good neighbors: a longitudinal analysis of an industry self-regulatory institution. *Academy of Management Journal*, 51(6): 1150–70.

Barney, J. 1991. Firm resources and sustained competitive advantage. *Journal of Management*, 17(1): 99–120.

Barney, J., and Arikan, A. M. 2001. The resource-based view: origins and implications. In M. A. Hitt, R. E. Freeman, and J. S. Harrison (eds.), *Blackwell Handbook of Strategic Management*. Oxford: Blackwell.

Baum, J. A. C., and Oliver, C. 1991. Institutional linkages and organizational mortality. *Administrative Science Quarterly*, 36(2): 187–218.

Berchicci, L., Dowell, G., and King, A. A. 2012. Environmental capabilities and corporate strategy: exploring acquisitions among US manufacturing firms. *Strategic Management Journal*, 33(9): 1053–71.

Berrone, P., and Gomez-Mejia, L. R. 2009. Environmental performance and executive compensation: an integrated agency–institutional perspective. *Academy of Management Journal*, 52(1): 103–26.

Berrone, P., Fosfuri, A., Gelabert, L., and Gomez-Mejia, L. R. 2013. Necessity as the mother of "green" inventions: institutional pressures and environmental innovations. *Strategic Management Journal*, 34(8): 891–909.

Boiral, O. 2002. Tacit knowledge and environmental management. *Long Range Planning*, 35(3): 291–317.

— 2007. Corporate greening through ISO 14001: a rational myth? *Organization Science*, 18(1): 127–46.

Boli, J., and Thomas, G. M. 1997. World culture in the world polity: a century of international non-governmental organization. *American Sociological Review*, 62(2): 171–90.

Buysse, K., and Verbeke, A. 2003. Proactive environmental strategies: a stakeholder management perspective. *Strategic Management Journal*, 24(5): 453–70.

Christmann, P. 2000. Effects of "best practices" of environmental management on cost advantage: the role of complementary assets. *Academy of Management Journal*, 43(4): 663–80.

Christoffersen, J. 2013. A review of antecedents of international strategic alliance performance: synthesized evidence and new directions for core constructs. *International Journal of Management Reviews*, 15(1): 66–85.

Clark, C. E., and Crawford, E. P. 2012. Influencing climate change policy: the effect of shareholder pressure and firm environmental performance. *Business and Society*, 51(1): 148–75.

Dacin, M. T., Oliver, C., and Roy, J. P. 2007. The legitimacy of strategic alliances: an institutional perspective. *Strategic Management Journal*, 28(2): 169–87.

Davis, G. F. 1991. Agents without principles – the spread of the poison pill through the intercorporate network. *Administrative Science Quarterly*, 36(4): 583–613.

De Rond, M., and Bouchikhi, H. 2004. On the dialectics of strategic alliances. *Organization Science*, 15(1): 56–69.

Deephouse, D. L., and Carter, S. M. 2005. An examination of differences between organizational legitimacy and organizational reputation. *Journal of Management Studies*, 42(2): 329–60.

Delmas, M. A. 2002. The diffusion of environmental management standards in Europe and in the United States: an institutional perspective. *Policy Sciences*, 35(1): 91.

Delmas, M. A., and Montes-Sancho, M. J. 2010. Voluntary agreements to improve environmental quality: symbolic and substantive cooperation. *Strategic Management Journal*, 31(6): 575–601.

Delmas, M. A., and Toffel, M. W. 2008. Organizational responses to environmental demands: opening the black box. *Strategic Management Journal*, 29(10): 1027–55.

Diestre, L., and Rajagopalan, N. 2012. Are all "sharks" dangerous? New biotechnology ventures and partner selection in R&D alliances. *Strategic Management Journal*, 33(10): 1115–34.

— 2013. Toward an input-based perspective on categorization: investor reactions to chemical accidents. *Academy of Management Journal*, 57(4): 1130–53.

Eisenhardt, K. M. 1989. Agency theory – an assessment and review. *Academy of Management Review*, 14(1): 57–74.

EPA. 2011. *2011 Toxic Release Inventory National Analysis Overview*. www2.epa.gov/sites/production/files/documents/complete_2011_tri_na_overview_document.pdf (accessed September 3, 2014).

Eunni, R. V., Kasuganti, R. R., and Kos, A. J. 2006. Knowledge management processes in international business alliances: a review of empirical research, 1990–2003. *International Journal of Management*, 23(1): 34–42.

Freeman, R. E. 1984. *Strategic Management: A Stakeholder Approach*. Boston, MA: Pitman.

Glasbergen, P., and Groenenberg, R. 2001. Environmental partnerships in sustainable energy. *European Environment*, 11(1): 1–13.

Grant, R. M. 1996. Toward a knowledge-based theory of the firm. *Strategic Management Journal*, 17: 109–22.

Grant, R. M., and Baden-Fuller, C. 2004. A knowledge accessing theory of strategic alliances. *Journal of Management Studies*, 41(1): 61–84.

Hamilton, J. T. 1995. Pollution as news: media and stock market reactions to the toxics release inventory data. *Journal of Environmental Economics and Management*, 28(1): 98–113.

Hart, S. L. 1995. A natural-resource-based view of the firm. *Academy of Management Review*, 20(4): 986–1014.

Haunschild, P. R. 1993. Interorganizational imitation – the impact of interlocks on corporate acquisition activity. *Administrative Science Quarterly*, 38(4): 564–92.

Hillman, A. J., Keim, G. D., and Schuler, D. 2004. Corporate political activity: a review and research agenda. *Journal of Management*, 30(6): 837–57.

Hsu, G., Hannan, M. T., and Koçak, Ö. 2009. Multiple category memberships in markets: an integrative theory and two empirical tests. *American Sociological Review*, 74(1): 150–69.

Jasanoff, S. 1997. NGOs and the environment: from knowledge to action. *Third World Quarterly*, 18(3): 579–94.

Kale, P., and Singh, H. 2007. Building firm capabilities through learning: the role of the alliance learning process in alliance capability and firm-level alliance success. *Strategic Management Journal*, 28(10): 981–1000.

Kang, E. 2008. Director interlocks and spillover effects of reputational penalties from financial reporting fraud. *Academy of Management Journal*, 51(3): 537–55.

Kang, E., and Tan, B. R. 2008. Accounting choices and director interlocks: a social network approach to the voluntary expensing of stock option grants. *Journal of Business Finance and Accounting*, 35(9–10): 1079–102.

Kang, M.-P., Mahoney, J. T., and Tan, D. 2009. Why firms make unilateral investments specific to other firms: the case of OEM suppliers. *Strategic Management Journal*, 30(2): 117–35.

King, A., and Lenox, M. 2002. Exploring the locus of profitable pollution reduction. *Management Science*, 48(2): 289–99.

King, A. A., and Lenox, M. J. 2000. Industry self-regulation without sanctions: the chemical industry's Responsible Care Program. *Academy of Management Journal*, 43(4): 698–716.

King, A. A., Lenox, M. J., and Terlaak, A. N. N. 2005. The strategic use of decentralized institutions: exploring certification with the ISO 14001 management standard. *Academy of Management Journal*, 48(6): 1091–106.

Klassen, R. D., and Whybark, D. C. 1999. The impact of environmental technologies on manufacturing performance. *Academy of Management Journal*, 42(6): 599–615.

Laplume, A. O., Sonpar, K., and Litz, R. A. 2008. Stakeholder theory: reviewing a theory that moves us. *Journal of Management*, 34(6): 1152–89.

Leone, R. A. 1986. *Who Profits? Winners, Losers, and Government Regulation*. New York: Basic Books.

Lin, H. 2012. Strategic alliances for environmental improvements. *Business and Society*, 51(2): 335–48.

Lyles, M. A., and Salk, J. E. 2007. Knowledge acquisition from foreign parents in international joint ventures: an empirical examination in the Hungarian context. *Journal of International Business Studies*, 38(1): 3–18.

Majumdar, S. K., and Marcus, A. A. 2001. Rules versus discretion: the productivity consequences of flexible regulation. *Academy of Management Journal*, 44(1): 170–9.

Melnyk, S. A., Sroufe, R. P., and Calantone, R. 2003. Assessing the impact of environmental management systems on corporate and environmental performance. *Journal of Operations Management*, 21(3): 329–51.

Mitsuhashi, H., and Greve, H. R. 2009. A matching theory of alliance formation and organizational success: complementarity and compatibility. *Academy of Management Journal*, 52(5): 975–95.

Mizruchi, M. S. 1996. What do interlocks do? An analysis, critique, and assessment of research on interlocking directorates. *Annual Review of Sociology*, 22: 271–98.

Mowery, D. C., Oxley, J. E., and Silverman, B. S. 1996. Strategic alliances and interfirm knowledge transfer. *Strategic Management Journal*, 17: 77–91.

Muthusamy, S. K., and White, M. A. 2005. Learning and knowledge transfer in strategic alliances: a social exchange view. *Organization Studies*, 26(3): 415–41.

OECD. n.d. *Environmental Outlook to 2050: The Consequences of Inaction*. www.oecd.org/environment/indicators-modelling-outlooks/oecdenvironmentaloutlookto2050theconsequencesofinaction.htm (accessed September 3, 2014).

Ortiz-de-Mandojana, N., Aragón-Correa, J. A., Delgado-Ceballos, J., and Ferrón-Vílchez, V. 2011. The effect of director interlocks on firms' adoption of proactive environmental strategies. *Corporate Governance: An International Review*, 20(2): 164–78.

Pfeffer, J., and Salancik, G. R. 1978. *The External Control of Organizations: A Resource Dependence Perspective*. New York: Harper and Row.

Philippe, D., and Durand, R. 2011. The impact of norm-conforming behaviors on firm reputation. *Strategic Management Journal*, 32(9): 969–93.

Reid, E. M., and Toffel, M. W. 2009. Responding to public and private politics: corporate disclosure of climate change strategies. *Strategic Management Journal*, 30(11): 1157–78.

Rothaermel, F. T., and Deeds, D. L. 2004. Exploration and exploitation alliances in biotechnology: a system of new product development. *Strategic Management Journal*, 25(3): 201–21.

Russo, M. V., and Fouts, P. A. 1997. A resource-based perspective on corporate environmental performance and profitability. *Academy of Management Journal*, 40(3): 534–59.

Sampson, R. C. 2007. R&D alliances and firm performance: the impact of technological diversity and alliance organization on innovation. *Academy of Management Journal*, 50(2): 364–86.

Sharma, S., and Vredenburg, H. 1998. Proactive corporate environmental strategy and the development of competitively valuable organizational capabilities. *Strategic Management Journal*, 19(8): 729–53.

Shipilov, A. V., Greve, H. R., and Rowley, T. J. 2010. When do interlocks matter? Institutional logics and the diffusion of multiple corporate governance practices. *Academy of Management Journal*, 53(4): 846–64.

Short, J. L., and Toffel, M. W. 2010. Making self-regulation more than merely symbolic: the critical role of the legal environment. *Administrative Science Quarterly*, 55(3): 361–96.

Shrivastava, P. 1995. Environmental technologies and competitive advantage. *Strategic Management Journal*, 16(S1): 183–200.

Shropshire, C. 2010. The role of the interlocking director and board receptivity in the diffusion of practices. *Academy of Management Review*, 35(2): 246–64.

Spence, M. 1973. Job market signaling. *Quarterly Journal of Economics*, 87(3): 355–74.

Srivastava, S. K. 2007. Green supply-chain management: a state-of-the-art literature review. *International Journal of Management Reviews*, 9(1): 53–80.

Stafford, E. R., Polonsky, M. J., and Hartman, C. L. 2000. Environmental NGO–business collaboration and strategic bridging: a case analysis of the Greenpeace–Foron alliance. *Business Strategy and the Environment*, 9(2): 122–35.

Stuart, T. E., Ha, H., and Hybels, R. C. 1999. Interorganizational endorsements and the performance of entrepreneurial ventures. *Administrative Science Quarterly*, 44(2): 315–49.

Sullivan, B. N., Haunschild, P., and Page, K. 2007. Organizations non gratae? The impact of unethical corporate acts on interorganizational networks. *Organization Science*, 18(1): 55–70.

Turban, D. B., and Greening, D. W. 1997. Corporate social performance and organizational attractiveness to prospective employees. *Academy of Management Journal*, 40(3): 658–72.

Vachon, S., and Klassen, R. D. 2007. Supply chain management and environmental technologies: the role of integration. *International Journal of Production Research*, 45(2): 401–23.

Wang, L., and Zajac, E. J. 2007. Alliance or acquisition? A dyadic perspective on interfirm resource combinations. *Strategic Management Journal*, 28(13): 1291–317.

Westley, F., and Vredenburg, H. 1991. Strategic bridging: the collaboration between environmentalists and business in the marketing of green products. *Journal of Applied Behavioral Science*, 27(1): 65–90.

Westphal, J. D., and Zajac, E. J. 1994. Substance and symbolism in CEOs' long-term incentive plans. *Administrative Science Quarterly*, 39(3): 367–90.

— 2001. Decoupling policy from practice: the case of stock repurchase programs. *Administrative Science Quarterly*, 46(2): 202–28.

13

Corporate responsibility and stakeholder relationship impact

Carola Hillenbrand, Kevin Money and Abby Ghobadian

Scholars have advocated the integration of stakeholder theory within non-market strategy literature as a means to test claims that corporate responsibility (CR) increases trust in, and support of, organizations (e.g. Galbreath 2010; Barnett 2007; Doh and Guay 2006). However, despite the volume of recent work (for a review, see Peloza and Shang 2011; Laplume et al. 2008), stakeholder studies continue to be challenged in two ways. First, stakeholder theory currently presents a set of pragmatic approaches rather than offering testable theories about the nature or development of relationships with stakeholders (Carvalho et al. 2010; Bhattacharya et al. 2009; Basu and Palazzo 2008; Friedman and Miles 2002; Jones 1995). Second, research often focuses on the perspective of the organization and lacks the involvement of actual stakeholders in the conceptual development and empirical measurement of theory (Fisher et al. 2009; Vaaland et al. 2008; Friedman and Miles 2002). Lack of involvement of real-world stakeholders prevents scholars from acting with confidence when advising practitioners on non-market strategies of CR (Carvalho et al. 2010; Basu and Palazzo 2008; Starkey and Madan 2001).

This chapter addresses these two challenges. First, it develops a theoretical model of how CR impacts customer and employee relationships. It does so by building on literature from social psychology and drawing on the tradition of theory of reasoned action (TRA) research (Fishbein and Ajzen 2010; Armitage and Christian 2003). Second, to foster empirical research with actual stakeholders, the model is empirically tested with customers and employees of a service organization in the UK that had implemented a range of CR-related activities into its business operations. Our chapter differs notably from existing CR frameworks in that it operationalizes the impact of CR activities of firms at the level of customer and employee experiences of such activities. CR-related experiences are differentiated into experiences that impact individuals themselves ("self-related" CR experiences) and those that impact other stakeholders ("others-related" CR experiences). A theoretical model is developed that places both sets of CR-related experiences as exogenous (independent) variables in the model.

In testing the theoretical linkages, our chapter provides some novel insights. Customer and employee self-related CR experiences are found to impact their beliefs about, and trust towards, the organization significantly. More interestingly, we find evidence that others-related CR experiences drive the development of beliefs and trust both independently and in the presence of self-related CR experiences. The impact of CR initiatives within wider society can thus be conceptualized and measured in terms of the radial impact that these activities have on groups such as customers and employees. Perhaps most interestingly, we find evidence that beliefs partially mediate how experiences of CR, both self-related and others-related, impact the development of trust. This finding implies that customers and employees assimilate CR-related experiences cognitively, at least in part, and may provide organizations with a resource that will help buffer the effects of negative experiences as well as magnify the effects of positive experiences. Together, these findings have important implications for the management of CR and non-market strategies of firms, which we explore at the end of this chapter.

Theoretical foundation

Corporate responsibility

The term corporate responsibility is used in this chapter to convey a scholarly shift from corporate social responsibility (CSR), focusing on social obligations of business, to analyzing business responsibilities comprehensively (Vaaland et al. 2008; Berger et al. 2007; Pirsch et al. 2007), encompassing day-to-day operating practices and processes as well as long-term strategy and decision-making of organizations (Maon et al. 2010; Lee 2008; Ahmad et al. 2003). This chapter thus investigates CR in terms of customer and employee experiences of wide-ranging manifestations of CR in organizational practice towards themselves and other stakeholders, building on Waddock (2004: 10), who defines CR as "the degree of (ir)responsibility manifested in a company's strategies and operating practices as they impact stakeholders and the natural environment day-to-day" and in line with Basu and Palazzo (2008: 130), who define the depth of a company's CR commitment as "the extent to which it manifests itself across various types of activities." Matten and Moon (2008) depict a conceptualization of CR as embedded in a wide range of organizational actions and functions as "implicit" CR, which they suggest European stakeholders, such as customers and employees, often implicitly expect. Similarly, CR as embraced in policies and practices throughout the organization and in relation to all stakeholder interactions is described by Pirsch et al. (2007) as "institutionalized" CR, which they argue is most effective in enhancing stakeholder attitude towards the company and decreasing skepticism.

Firm motives for engaging in CR have been classified as instrumental (self-interest driven), relational (concerned with relationships among group members) and normative/moral motives (concerned with ethical standards and moral principles) (Aguilera et al. 2007). Most empirical studies examine the instrumental line and find a modest positive association between CR-related concepts and corporate financial performance (CFP) (Vaaland et al. 2008; Luo and Bhattacharya 2006; Husted and Salazar 2006; Orlitzky et al. 2003; Margolis and Walsh 2001). A number of theories have been put forward to explain the positive correlation between these two measures (Carroll and Shabana 2010; Peloza 2009). Instrumental theorists argue that CR creates positive relationships with key stakeholders (Waddock and Graves 1997), which in turn enable the organization to use its resources more effectively (Orlitzky and Benjamin 2001). CR is therefore seen as an intangible asset (in this case reputation) with a positive impact on CFP (Gardberg and Fombrun 2006). The protagonists of slack resources theory offer a different explanation and direction of causality. They argue that firms with a strong CFP enjoy an abundance of resources and therefore are in a position to address social issues (McGuire et al. 1988). Surroca et al. (2010) combine these two points of view and argue CR is both a predictor and consequence of CFP and the relationship between the two is mediated by a firm's intangible resources, such as reputation, culture and human capital. The focal point for much of this research is the organization but at the heart of instrumental theory and the combined instrumental/slack resources theory is the positive stakeholder attitude towards the organization (Surroca et al. 2010).

Despite the central assumption of the importance of stakeholders in this circuit, however, there is a paucity of theoretical and empirical research focusing on the actual development of stakeholder attitude and behavior (Neville et al. 2005). Vlachos (2010: 356) specifically urges scholars to investigate predictors of stakeholder CR perceptions as well as the process by which individual stakeholder perceptions translate into supportive behavior towards organizations. It is the aim of this study to go some way towards addressing this long-standing lacuna by providing a coherent framework for investigating the role of CR in the development of trust and positive intent towards organizations.

The stakeholder relationship impact of CR

In the non-market literature, CR is often seen as a useful means to engage with stakeholders. Within the stakeholder landscape, customers and employees are the focus in this chapter as they are described as the most immediate stakeholders of any organization (Peterson 2004a, 2004b) and they are said to have the greatest impact on the way firms manage CR expectations in the future (Carvalho et al. 2010; Walsh et al. 2009; Aguilera et al. 2007). Literature relating to customer and employee relationships is now reviewed in turn.

It is widely suggested that CR can provide a useful approach for enhancing the quality of customer relationships. The types of benefits include differentiation of products, brands and firms (e.g. McWilliams et al. 2006; McWilliams and Siegel 2001; Russo and Fouts 1997; Creyer and Ross 1997), easier introduction of new products (e.g. Brown and Dacin 1997), possibility of asking for premium prices (Creyer and Ross 1997), development of positive customer attitudes towards products and firms (Scholder Ellen et al. 2000; Folkes and Kamins 1999; Brown and Dacin 1997), increased customer loyalty, word-of-mouth and retention (e.g. Maignan et al. 1999; Handelman and Arnold 1999), increased customer purchase intent (Mohr and Webb 2005; Mohr et al. 2001) and a lower inclination to punish companies (Creyer and Ross 1997).

A number of relationship studies explore moderating effects at both an individual and a contextual level. Customer awareness of issues relating to responsibility (Mohr et al. 2001) and heterogeneity, in terms of importance that customers place upon such issues (Sen and Bhattacharya 2001), are the two most influential moderating factors. These range from customers who are solely driven by traditional purchase criteria, such as price, quality and convenience, to highly active and committed customers who hold strong beliefs about CR, actively search for related information and make their purchase decisions on social and environmental issues (Mohr et al. 2001). While customers seem to differ in how receptive they are to CR, empirical findings suggest that all customers react negatively to irresponsible business behavior (Sen and Bhattacharya 2001). The irresponsible business behaviors studied include ethical breach by a firm (Folkes and Kamins 1999) and exploitation of a non-profit organization (Mohr et al. 2001). Negative reactions on the part of customers include boycotts and switch of providers, speaking out against companies and refusal to invest in stocks (e.g. Brammer and Pavelin 2005; DaSilva 2004; Brown and Dacin 1997). However, existing studies in the customer domain have been accused of two main limitations. First, the concept of responsibility is often defined as a narrow social and voluntary function of business. Maignan and Ferrell (2004) conclude in an extensive review that scholars have generally focused on very limited social marketing dimensions. Typical research areas include cause-related marketing (e.g. Webb and Mohr 1998), support of charities (e.g. Barone et al. 2000), support of local communities (e.g. McWilliams and Siegel 2001; Brown and Dacin 1997), protection of the environment (Menon and Menon 1997; Drumwright 1994) and support of social initiatives (e.g. Sen and Bhattacharya 2001; Brown and Dacin 1997). Second, studies are often based on experimental designs, such as fictitious information about pro-social company behavior (e.g. Mohr and Webb 2005; Handelman and Arnold 1999; Folkes and Kamins 1999; Murray and Vogel 1997), hypothetical company donations (Strahilevitz and Myers 1998) and hypothetical cause-related marketing scenarios (Becker-Olsen et al. 2006; Scholder Ellen et al. 2000; Barone et al. 2000). Such experimental research designs have been described as problematic in terms of external validity and limited in their usefulness to real-life situations (Mohr and Webb 2005), especially due to low levels of customer awareness in real life of the issues studied.

At the same time, it has been suggested that CR can impact employee relationships in three ways: by positively influencing employees' work attitudes and behaviors (Collier and Esteban 2007; Greening and Turban 2000); through other competitive advantages, such as related to prospective employees, wider skill-sets of employees and spill-over effects on customers (Siegel 1999; Ahmad et al. 2003); and by avoiding negative consequences from a lack of responsibility, such as labour disputes, strikes and other subversive behaviors (e.g. Dane 2004; Hopkins and John 2002). More specifically, benefits related to the development of positive attitudes and behaviors of employees include enhanced levels of commitment (Collier and Esteban 2007; Brammer et al. 2006; Peterson 2004b; Maignan et al. 1999), feelings of pride (Maignan et al. 1999), staff motivation and higher levels of morale (Dane 2004; Greening and Turban 2000) and a willingness to go beyond the call of duty (Maignan et al. 1999). Benefits related to other competitive advantages include easier recruitment and higher application pursuit (Brown 2003; Greening and Turban 2000; Siegel 1999), enhancement of job-related skills and the development of new skills (Peterson 2004a), spill-over effects on customers' satisfaction and retention (Ahmad et al. 2003) and links to innovation and successful introduction of new products (Ahmad et al. 2003). Benefits related to a lack of negative consequences include lower turnover intentions of staff (Peterson 2003; Luce et al. 2001; Sims and Keon 2000), fewer feelings of discomfort and role conflict among the workforce (Sims and Keon 2000), lower levels of staff self-doubt (Dane 2004) and lower likelihood of labor disputes and strikes (Hopkins 2005; Foulkes 1980). It has also been shown that employees like to be associated with organizations that stand for honesty, transparency and accountability (e.g. Lozano 2002; Luce et al. 2001).

Compared to customer studies, employee studies operationalize responsibility with much less focus on social dimensions but include broader elements, such as training and development (Brammer et al. 2006), adoption of codes of conduct (Peterson 2004b; Maignan et al. 1999), fairness and employee empowerment (Brammer et al. 2006; Peterson 2004b; Ahmad et al. 2003), implementation of diversity programs (Peterson 2004b), flexibility in procedures (Peterson 2004b), monitoring of potential harmful effects of corporate operations (Maignan et al. 1999) and embedding of responsible procedures in day-to-day routines (Brown 2003). While some employee studies rely on experimental designs (e.g. Greening and Turban 2000), overall they do so to a lesser extent than customer studies. A number of employee studies control for variables such as gender, job satisfaction and length of employment (Brammer et al. 2006). Existing studies in the employee domain, however, show two main limitations. First, there is a lack of theory in many studies as to how benefits in employee relationships develop based on responsibility. While social identity theory is sometimes used as an explanation (Brammer et al. 2006), many studies fail to outline underlying processes or provide a rationale without empirical testing (Maignan and Ferrell 2004). Second, while responsibility is operationalized in a number of ways in employee studies, existing studies fail to establish whether these issues are indicative of CR in the eyes of employees. This is particularly noticeable as responsibility is often operationalized in ways other than the social activities of business, the predominant way of operationalization in customer studies. As such, it is unclear whether examined relationship variables express CR in the eyes of employees, whether they are self-related – that is, towards themselves in their role as staff – or others-related – that is, towards customers and external stakeholders. In this chapter, we differentiate between these two important aspects of stakeholder experiences of business behavior, as reviewed in the following section.

Self-related and others-related CR experiences

Interestingly, the need to understand stakeholder experiences of CR was described more than a decade ago by Wood and Jones (1995), who defined stakeholders as the "recipients" of corporate actions and outputs, who therefore experience the effects of corporate behavior. We label such experiences *self-related CR experiences* (e.g. customers' experiences while receiving goods and services and employees' experiences of working terms and conditions). Wood and Jones (1995) furthermore described stakeholders as "evaluators" of how organizational behaviors have affected the groups and organizations in their environment. Through their observations, stakeholders will thus have what we call *others-related CR experiences* (e.g. whether an organization gives something back to local communities, how fairly it treats suppliers or competitors, and how positively – or negatively – it impacts the natural and physical environment in which it operates).

A self-related versus others-related conceptualization of CR experiences reflects recent advances proposing a differentiated view of target recipient and audience of firm CR (Peloza and Shang 2011; Aguilera et al. 2007). The former is manifested in experiences of how the organization relates to an individual stakeholder directly, often in routine interactions and regular processes. Customers and employees, in their natural roles, will typically hold implicit expectations (Matten and Moon 2008) as to what constitutes (ir)responsible business conduct (Pirsch et al. 2007) and, according to Bhattacharya et al. (2009), will judge CR activities first and foremost along returns to themselves. Empirical research investigating self-related value from CR activities of firms is, however, largely missing (Peloza and Shang 2011), despite claims that CR is most immediately expressed and experienced in such direct interactions (Waddock 2004). This is even more surprising given that self-related experiences may be linked most closely to stakeholder attitudes and behaviors (Peloza and Shang 2011; Mohr and Webb 2005; Peterson 2004b).

Others-related CR experiences, on the other hand, are manifested in observations of how the organization relates to stakeholders other than oneself, both in routine interactions and in extramural activities. While most non-market strategy scholars would probably agree that CR is inherently a multi-stakeholder concept (Freeman 1984), an others-related dimension of how stakeholders experience CR activities of firms has been suggested only recently (Peloza and Shang 2011; Turker 2009b; Holbrook 2006). In particular, organizational justice and trust literatures are advancing a more deontic approach, considering not only individuals' own experiences but how individual stakeholders react to the (ir)responsible treatment of others (Gillespie and Dietz 2009; Aguilera et al. 2007; Colquitt et al. 2001). Gillespie and

Dietz (2009) argue that the way an organization relates to various stakeholders sends out cues that together build a collective experience of that organization. Employees, for example, look for cues of how the organization is experienced by external stakeholders (Gillespie and Dietz 2009), while customers also take cues of how employees and other stakeholders are treated (Turker 2009b; Pirsch et al. 2007). While individuals may lack detailed exposure to how an organization relates to all of its stakeholders (Pomering and Dolnicar 2009), they nevertheless form impressions from anything they see and hear (Gardberg and Fombrun 2006), based, for example, on observations of ongoing firm interactions with communities or suppliers as well as experiences of contributions to society and corporate philanthropy (Podnar and Golob 2007). In fact, it has been suggested that individuals actively look for cues from other sources to form judgments about CR (Pomering and Dolnicar 2009; Brammer et al. 2007).

Beliefs about the CR of the organization

The application of TRA suggests that beliefs about the CR of the organization result from prior experience (Fishbein and Ajzen 2010). Beliefs are understood as cognitive judgments about experiences of CR practices, which are suggested as a missing element in much empirical research (Walker et al. 2010; Vlachos 2010). In fact, some argue that any attempt by organizations to leverage CR activities to their advantage will be ineffective unless based on a firm understanding of how individuals make sense of such activities and whether they judge experiences positively (Hanke and Stark 2009). CR activities may backfire if stakeholders do not infer genuine motives or if they do not perceive alignment between an organization and its CR activities (Carvalho et al. 2010; Becker-Olsen et al. 2006; Godfrey 2005). The study of CR can build on insights from reputation literature, where it is widely understood that emotional appeal and trust of stakeholders depend on subjective interpretations of past experiences with organizations (Gardberg and Fombrun 2006; Bansal and Clelland 2004). In particular, Davis et al. (2003) explore customer and employee beliefs (such as how competent, innovative or ruthless an organization is) based on prior experience and linked to subsequent behavior. The impact of beliefs on outcome behaviors is likely to work both ways: positive beliefs about CR of the organization can act as a buffer, protect the organization from negative consequences and provide an opportunity platform to create stakeholder support (Gardberg and Fombrun 2006; Klein and Dawar 2004); negative beliefs can lead to overconstrued and negative inferences and hamper trust-building efforts (Gillespie and Dietz 2009; Pomering and Dolnicar 2009). Interestingly, scholars suggest that individuals may be more susceptible to negative beliefs if CR activities are implemented narrowly rather than in a comprehensive, institutionalized manner (Carvalho et al. 2010; Pirsch et al. 2007; Rupp et al. 2006).

Conceptual model and hypotheses

Drawing inspiration from theorists who apply advances in psychology to management literature (e.g. Brammer et al. 2007), this study draws on insights from TRA research to place the concepts discussed in the previous section in a causal framework (Fishbein and Ajzen 2010; Ortiz de Guinea and Markus 2009). In its original form, the TRA proposes a sequentially related process linking experiences, beliefs, attitudes and intentions that ultimately result in an actual behavior. Positioning key stages of human experience and behavior in an order of their development allows for systematic and rigorous investigation: it helps to position qualities of successful relationships (trust and positive intent) into a framework that

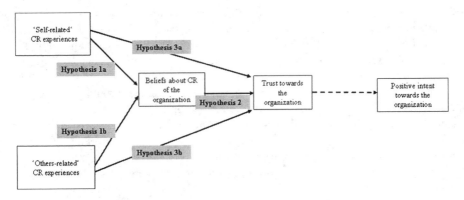

Figure 13.1   Theoretical research model

Source: Building on the theory of reasoned action (Fishbein and Ajzen 2010).

Note: All non-dashed paths are hypothesized relationships. The dashed path has been studied extensively in past research and is therefore not hypothesized, but it is included in the full model for empirical testing.

allows for understanding the development of these concepts in terms of experiences and beliefs that relate to CR.

The theoretical research model utilized in this study is illustrated with accompanying hypotheses in Figure 13.1.

Positive intent is the outcome of the proposed research model and is preceded by trust towards the organization.[1] Trust, in turn, is influenced by beliefs about the CR of an organization. Beliefs are anteceded by self-related and others-related experiences of CR. In addition, CR experiences are hypothesized to impact directly on the development of trust towards the organization, following recent advances in literature that cognitive and emotional pathways may work simultaneously and independently (Ortiz de Guinea and Markus 2009). Emerging evidence from the field of neuroscience suggests that both pathways should be considered for issues of personal salience (Tobler et al. 2008), while scholars such as Aguilera et al. (2007) and Lerner (2003) believe CR is of personal salience to customers and employees. The model in Figure 13.1 is associated with five research hypotheses, outlined below.

Research Hypothesis 1a: Increases in self-related CR experiences lead to increases in positive beliefs about the CR of the organization.

TRA theorists propose that direct experiences with a given object result in the formation of beliefs about that object (Fishbein and Ajzen 2010). They also suggest that since the validity of one's own senses is rarely questioned, beliefs based on direct experiences are often held with maximal certainty, particularly if experiences result in consequences for the self (e.g. Manstead 1997). In a seminal work, Bem (1970) goes as far as to suggest that, ultimately, any belief can be doubted unless it is based on the credibility of one's own sensory experiences. Some business and society scholars have explored stakeholder perceptions in relation to CR (Carvalho et al. 2010; Turker 2009a, 2009b; Brammer et al. 2007; Becker-Olsen et al. 2006; Scholder Ellen et al. 2006), but studies that link CR-related experiences explicitly to the development of beliefs remain elusive (Vlachos 2010; Lee 2008). It has been suggested that

CR and experiences thereof need to be identified and interpreted based on unique organizational activities (e.g. Vlachos 2010; Lee 2008; Morsing and Schultz 2006). Recently, scholars have claimed that stakeholders need to experience CR in all corporate processes and procedures in an institutionalized and routine way (Matten and Moon 2008; Basu and Palazzo 2008; Pirsch et al. 2007) and have suggested such categories as experiences of open, fair and rewarding behaviors as useful indicators of CR (Du et al. 2010; Kim et al. 2010; Turker 2009b).

Research Hypothesis 1b: Increases in others-related CR experiences lead to increases in positive beliefs about the CR of the organization.

Theorists furthermore propose that, alongside experiences that have direct impact on the self, experiences retrieved from observing others contribute towards shaping human beliefs. This is a well-researched area of psychology (Campbell-Meiklejohn et al. 2010; Dumontheil et al. 2010; Van Lange 2000), based on Bandura's (1986) seminal work on social learning theory, which suggests that people often learn through observing the actions and experiences of reference groups. Experiences of how organizations treat other stakeholders provide qualitatively different information from own experiences, which are of particular interest in the context of CR (Turker 2009a; Pirsch et al. 2007), for example if different stakeholder groups possess different levels of power over the organization (Mitchell et al. 1997). A stakeholder with high power will be unable to know how the organization treats stakeholders with low power, unless they observe organizational interactions with low-power stakeholders. Business and society scholars have suggested for some time that individuals are concerned with issues of fairness and responsibility even if there is no apparent benefit to the person or if the recipient of the organizational act is a stranger (Aguilera et al. 2007; Godfrey 2005; Turillo et al. 2002; Barbian 2001). Turker (2009a), for example, suggests that employees perceive experiences of CR activities directed towards society, non-governmental organizations (NGOs), the natural environment and future generations as important as benefits for themselves. Once again, though, while business and society scholars make these claims, there is a dearth of empirical evidence to support them (Laplume et al. 2008).

Research Hypothesis 2: Increases in positive beliefs about the CR of the organization lead to increases in trust towards the organization.

TRA theorists propose that as a person forms beliefs about an object, she/he automatically and simultaneously acquires a positive or negative attitude towards that object (Fishbein and Ajzen 2010). At the most basic level, psychological theory assumes that individuals learn to like and trust objects associated with positive connotations and learn to dislike and distrust objects with negative connotations. While the term "beliefs" refers to attributes of an object without implying any personal inclination towards it (Harvey 1997), the concept of "trust" is often defined as including an emotional bond, a willingness to engage and a confident expectation towards an exchange partner (McEvily and Tortoriello 2011). By assuming that CR is generally seen as a "good thing," it can be assumed that positive beliefs about the CR of an organization lead to trust, whereas negative beliefs lead to a lack of trust towards the organization (Pivato et al. 2008; Brammer and Pavelin 2004; Waddock 2004). A number of CR scholars suggest that stakeholder perceptions of the CR of an organization impact feelings of trust, which in turn result in support directed towards the organization (e.g. Vlachos 2010; Morsing 2006; Gueterbock 2004; Riordan et al. 1997; Murray and Vogel 1997). Aguilera et al. (2007) review the justice literature to suggest that CR activities provide employees with critical information to guide fairness perceptions, which then, through a reciprocal mechanism, impact trust, commitment and performance (see also Gillespie and Dietz 2009). Scholars such as Marin et al. (2009) and Pirsch et al. (2007) suggest that customers judge CR activities in terms of how embedded they are in company processes and procedures, and only positive evaluations lead to increases in customer feelings of loyalty.

Research Hypothesis 3a: Increases in self-related CR experiences lead to increases in trust towards the organization.

Scholars from the fields of psychology and management suggest that day-to-day experiences of stakeholders with organizations may also impact directly on the development of trust (McEvily and Tortoriello 2011; Deery et al. 2006; Gakovic and Tetrick 2003; Susskind et al. 2003). It is not surprising that many studies have examined the impact of product- and service-related experiences upon customer trust towards organizations (e.g. Gruen et al. 2000), while studies of employees have focused upon investigating the remuneration- and culture-based experiences that drive employee trust and engagement (e.g. Gellatly et al. 2009). As discussed under Hypothesis 1a, this study follows conceptual advancements that suggest CR experiences should be operationalized as relating to customer and employee experiences of day-to-day interactions with organizations and experiences of CR in institutionalized company processes (Matten and Moon 2008; Pirsch et al. 2007; Waddock 2004).

Research Hypothesis 3b: Increases in others-related CR experiences lead to increases in trust towards the organization.

In line with Hypothesis 1b (which discussed the influence of outside sources on the development of beliefs), Hypothesis 3b captures the influence of others-related CR experience on the development of trust. It has been suggested that people take into account the interest of other parties when emotionally judging behaviors of organizations and trusting or distrusting firms (McEvily and Tortoriello 2011; Gillespie and Dietz 2009; Zsolnai 2002; Turillo et al. 2002). Maignan and Ferrell (2004), for example, suggest that consumers not only show emotional concern for their own welfare (for example, calling for improved product safety) but also care about issues that do not affect them directly (for example, child labor). Kitchin (2003) suggests that trust is conditional not only on how a business is seen to act towards others but also on how one imagines a business *might be acting* towards others in situations that one cannot see.

In this context it is useful to consider how scholars building on TRA have elaborated on the notion of subjective norm, which refers to our views of what is socially acceptable or unacceptable behavior (Fishbein and Ajzen 2010; Manstead and Van der Pligt 1998). An organization that violates norms in relation to how it treats stakeholders other than ourselves (e.g. misleading customers, underpaying employees or taking advantage of suppliers) may not impact us directly, but might violate our understanding of social norms and leave us feeling suspicious about how trustworthy the organization is (Pomering and Dolnicar 2009; Morsing et al. 2008). The measurement of subjective norms, however, has been criticized for relying too heavily on subjects' interpretation of perceived influence (Manstead and Van der Pligt 1998). This study thus measures the impact of others-related CR experiences in terms of subjects' own perceptions.

Mediating role of beliefs

In addition to testing individual hypotheses, it is important to consider the implications of the complex system that the whole model represents. Viewed in its entirety, the theory in the proposed model suggests that beliefs about the CR of the organization partially mediate the relationship between experiences related to CR and the development of trust. This partial mediation is important because it suggests that beliefs may act as a buffer between stakeholder experiences and their subsequent trust (Ortiz de Guinea and Markus 2009; Manstead 1997; Petty 1995).

Research methodology

The financial services sector was purposely chosen for this study because institutions in that sector typically have ongoing and high-involvement relationships with both customers and employees (Pomering and Dolnicar 2009). The participating research organization was chosen as it exhibits a keen interest in CR and is a long-established financial services institution in the UK with a policy to value relationships with stakeholders and view these as crucial to its long-term success. The organization, in the year prior to the study, had designed and implemented a range of CR-related activities with a view to enhancing stakeholder experiences and improving levels of customer and employee commitment and support. These CR-related activities were implemented to improve customers' and staff's direct experiences of the organization (self-related CR experiences) as well as their wider perceptions of the organization in society (others-related CR experiences). Activities addressing the former included significant efforts to ensure fair and transparent practices in all customer interactions, extensive training and development programs for staff, a procedure of openness about policies and services, and an explicit effort to listen to, and act upon, concerns expressed by any member of staff or customer. With regard to the latter (others-related CR experiences), the decision was taken to retain branches/outlets in small communities, with the stated aim to achieve a positive impact on society. The organization also engaged in initiatives to help worthy causes to market themselves effectively, encouraged business partners to make contributions to the local community and honored such engagements with community awards.

Separate questionnaires for customers and employees were developed following the works of Churchill (1979) and Rossiter (2002). The constructs trust, beliefs about CR of the organization and positive intent are operationalized through the use of reflective indicators (Fornell and Cha 1994; Bollen 1989). Items belonging to self-related CR experiences and others-related CR experiences are operationalized formatively (e.g. Goldberg and Hartwick 1990).

Operationalization of CR-related concepts

Scholars have suggested that measures of CR must be tailored to the context of the researched organization (Orlitzky and Benjamin 2001). Methodologically, if CR is to be understood in the context of a focal organization, integrating customers and employees in the development of measures ensures construct and content validity (Rossiter 2002). In line with scholars such as Peloza and Shang (2011) and Turker (2009a), the study employed a qualitative phase that was conducted, in separate settings, with customers and employees of the participating organization to shape meaningful and relevant measures of CR experiences. Customers and employees were asked to describe what they understand by CR and how they can tell from their experiences whether the organization is responsible or not. Interestingly, it emerged from this exploratory phase of the research that customers and employees describe self-related CR experiences as wide ranging, in line with scholarly claims for a holistic, complex and broad conceptualization (Peloza and Shang 2011; Matten and Moon 2008; Brammer et al. 2007, Vuontisjaervi 2006): both groups highlight issues such as fair processes and procedures, the importance of keeping promises and open and honest communication, while customers also mention issues related to products and services, and employees mention such issues as training and compensation. Self-related CR experiences were therefore operationalized through differentiated measures relevant to the specific customer and employee context. Others-related CR experiences were operationalized as experiences of care that organizations demonstrate towards other stakeholder groups that were mentioned by customers and employees, such as (other) customers, (other) employees, local communities, society at large and the organization itself. Beliefs about the CR of the organization are operationalized as beliefs about the transparency, integrity, consideration of business impacts, non-financial purpose, competence and continuity of the organization (Waddock 2004).

Operationalization of trust and positive intent

Trust towards the organization is operationalized based on Rempel et al. (1985). Positive intent towards the organization is operationalized with regard to commitment and loyalty of customers and employees. For customers, measures of commitment and loyalty are expressed in terms of repurchasing intentions, positive word of mouth and effort invested in the relationship (Walsh et al. 2009; Morgan and Hunt 1994). For employees, measures of commitment and loyalty are expressed in terms of intentions to maintain the relationship, positive world of mouth and efforts to make an impact with their work (Gellatly et al. 2009; Meyer et al. 1990).

Piloting and sampling

Measures were piloted with eight customers and six employees following the process suggested by Summers (2001), which resulted in minor changes. A seven-point Likert-type scale was applied to the questionnaire. A randomized sample of 5000 customers representing different geographical areas of the UK were invited by letter to participate; 708 usable responses were received (a response rate of 14 percent). The service organization employed 700 members of staff, all of whom were invited by letter to participate, resulting in 359 usable employee responses (a response rate of 51 percent). These response rates are in line with guidelines for academic research (Baruch 1999).

Statistical techniques

Data from the two questionnaires were analysed separately, starting with checks for missing data, outliers and assessment of normality (Hair et al. 2006). A two-stage approach was applied for assessing reliability and validity of measures (Hair et al. 2006). Stage one involved the use of exploratory factor analysis to explore the empirical data structure; stage two involved the application of confirmatory factor analysis with the items of the reflective scales to assess the robustness of the scales and their interrelationships. Based on a satisfactory assessment, data were analysed using structural equation modeling. As the research model consisted of formative and reflective indicators, the component-based approach of partial least squares (PLS) was utilized (Chin 2001; Fornell and Cha 1994). The PLS outcome was analyzed by starting with the outer model (measurement model) and then moving to the inner model (structural model), following Hulland (1999) and Gerbing and Anderson (1988).

For reflective measures of the outer model, individual item reliability was assessed by examining the significance of item loadings (Hulland 1999), while internal scale reliability was assessed through composite scale reliability (Werts et al. 1974) and average variance extracted (AVE) (Fornell and Larcker 1981). For formative measures of the outer model, the significance of item weights was analyzed utilizing one-tailed t-tests (Chin 1998). For the inner model, path coefficients were assessed as well as the model's explanatory power R^2 and predictive relevance Q^2 (Chin 1998). In line with Podsakoff et al. (2003), design controls and statistical controls were used to assess the impact of common method bias (see Podsakoff et al. 2003: 898). A post-hoc analysis, Harman's single factor test reveals the presence of ten distinct factors for both customer and employee data in the unrotated factor solution (Podsakoff et al. 2003).

Results

Customer model

For reflective measures, all but one outer model loadings are in the region of .6 or greater and composite reliability scores of all constructs are above the recommended level of .7 (Nunnally 1978). AVE scores of all constructs are above the recommended level of .5 (Fornell and Larcker 1981), confirming satisfactory convergent validity. For formative measures, an examination of the weights illustrates the relevance of the items to the research model (Wixom and Watson 2001), and the application of the variance inflation factor (VIF) as a measure of multicollinearity shows the VIF of all items below the suggested cut-off of 10 (Hair et al. 2006). The customer estimated path model with path coefficients and R^2 values is shown in Figure 13.2. Several bootstrapping exercises yielded robust estimates (Chin 1998). The results reported in Figure 13.2 are based on 200 samples of 500 cases (Mathieson et al. 2001). The R^2 values provide evidence of the explanatory power of the model: positive intent, trust and beliefs about CR have R^2 values of .48, .46 and .35, respectively, indicating large effect sizes (Clark-Carter 1997).

Table 13.1 shows the path coefficient estimates for each of the six hypothesized path linkages of the customer inner model and includes respective t-values with their significance level. All hypothesized relationships are significant at the $p = .01$ level.

Table 13.2 presents means and standard deviations of the latent constructs and the latent variable correlation matrix. The square root of AVE for the measures can be found in the diagonal of the matrix. Discriminant validity is deemed satisfactory as the diagonal elements are larger than off-diagonal elements (Hair et al. 2006).

Explanatory power of the customer model is demonstrated by assessing changes in R^2 via the partial F-test (Chin 1998) and through the pseudo F-test (Mathieson et al. 2001): all predictor latent variables have small to medium effect sizes (Chin 1998) and the results of all pseudo F-tests are significant at the .01 level. Predictive relevance of the customer model is

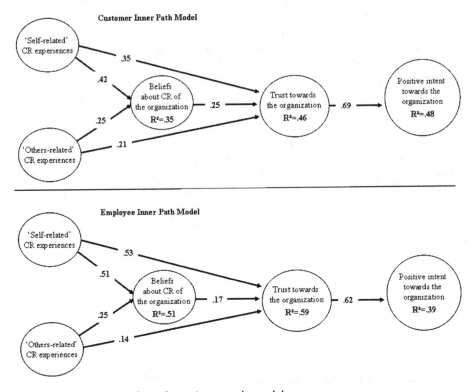

Figure 13.2 Customer and employee inner path model

demonstrated as all $Q^2 > 0$ (Chin 1998; Geisser 1975; Stone 1974). Changes in the omission distance from 25 to 100 to 200 showed consistent results.

Employee model

For reflective measures, one outer model loading that was not in the region of or greater than .6 was excluded from the analysis, which resulted in composite reliability scores of all constructs above the recommended level of .7 (Nunnally 1978). AVE scores of all constructs were above .5 (Fornell and Larcker 1981), confirming satisfactory convergent validity. For formative measures, an examination of the weights again illustrates the relevance of the items to the research model (Wixom and Watson 2001), and the VIF of all items was below 10 (Hair et al. 2006). The estimated path model with path coefficients and R^2 values is shown in Figure 13.2. Bootstrapping procedures yielded stable results (Chin 1998). The results reported in Figure 13.2 are based on 200 samples of 300 cases (Mathieson et al. 2001). The R^2 values provide evidence for the explanatory power of the employee model (positive intent, trust and beliefs about CR have R^2 values of .39, .59 and .51, respectively). These R^2 values can be interpreted as large in effect size (Clark–Carter 1997: 353).

Table 13.1 presents the path coefficient estimates and t-values. All hypothesized relationships are significant at the .01 level, with the exception of one that is significant at the .05 level. Table 13.2 suggests discriminant validity to be satisfactory. Assessment of R^2 and Q^2 values suggests good explanatory power and good predictive relevance of the employee model.

Table 13.1 PLS estimation output for customer and employee model

Path linkages	Path coefficient (original sample estimate)	Path coefficient (mean of sub-samples)	T-value	Level of significance	Support for hypotheses
CUSTOMER					
H1a: Self-related CR experiences – Beliefs about CR of the organization	.42	.44	9.17	**	supported
H1b: Others-related CR experiences – Beliefs about CR of the organization	.25	.25	5.32	**	supported
H2: Beliefs about CR of the organization – Trust towards the organization	.25	.25	4.23	**	supported
H3a: Self-related CR experiences – Trust towards the organization	.35	.36	5.34	**	supported
H3b: Others-related CR experiences – Trust towards the organization	.21	.20	4.08	**	supported
Trust towards the organization – Positive intent	.69	.70	24.22	**	not hypothesized
EMPLOYEE					
H1a: Self-related CR experiences – Beliefs about CR of the organization	.51	.51	7.66	**	supported
H1b: Others-related CR experiences – Beliefs about CR of the organization	.25	.27	3.47	**	supported
H2: Beliefs about CR of the organization – Trust towards the organization	.17	.17	3.22	**	supported
H3a: Self-related CR experiences – Trust towards the organization	.53	.52	8.35	**	supported
H3b: Others-related CR experiences – Trust towards the organization	.14	.15	2.11	*	supported
Trust towards the organization – Positive intent	.62	.62	16.00	**	not hypothesized

Notes:
*Significance at the .05 level;
**Significance at the .01 level.

Table 13.2 Latent variable correlation matrix for customer and employee data

Latent variable correlation matrix	Self-related experiences of CR	Others-related experiences of CR	Beliefs about CR of the organization	Trust towards the organization	Positive intent	M	Std
CUSTOMER							
Self-related CR experiences	formative					5.56	.87
Others-related CR experiences	.53	formative				5.17	.89
Beliefs about CR of the organization	.55	.47	**.72**			5.24	.87
Trust towards the organization	.61	.52	.55	**.94**		5.31	.99
Positive intent	.66	.53	.54	.68	**.74**	4.96	1.07
EMPLOYEE							
Self-related CR experiences	formative					4.65	1.40
Others-related CR experiences	.73	formative				5.22	.79
Beliefs about CR of the organization	.69	.62	**.74**			5.76	.81
Trust towards the organization	.71	.63	.63	**.83**		4.91	1.14
Positive intent	.53	.50	.55	.62	**.73**	5.16	1.00

Partial mediation

Mediation was tested based on Baron and Kenny (1986) through regressing the mediator on independent variables (Hypotheses 1a and 1b); regressing the dependent variable on independent variables (Hypotheses 3a and 3b); and regressing the dependent variable on both independent variables and mediator (Hypotheses 2, 1a and 1b). As all hypotheses are supported, the results suggest that beliefs about CR of the organization partially mediate the relationship between self-related experience of CR and the development of trust as well as between others–related experiences of CR and trust, in both customer and employee models.

Discussion, implications and future research

Discussion

Application of TRA in this study allows for bridging of the gap between constructs related to CR (customer and employee experiences of, and beliefs about, the CR of the organization) and beneficial organizational outcomes (trust and positive intent towards the organization), thereby helping to unpack the underlying psychological process that drives responses to CR activities (Peloza and Shang 2011; Bhattacharya et al. 2009; Margolis and Walsh 2001; Wood and Jones 1995). The strong path coefficients between CR-related concepts and important organizational outcomes, such as intended commitment and loyalty, suggest that psychological theory is applicable and useful in the context of CR. CR-related experiences and beliefs are shown as critical building blocks of how CR impacts customer and employee relationships. In terms of theory-building, this suggests conceptual frameworks ought to incorporate experiental as well as cognitive elements, and at the same time focus on individuals' own experiences as well as how individuals experience others to be impacted by the organization. In practical terms the findings suggest that organizations need to balance a variety of issues and that CR activities can have radial impacts on a wide stakeholder constituency.

The impact of self-related CR experiences

The results suggest that increases in self-related CR experiences – that is, experiences related to fairness in interactions, direct communication and perceived individual benefits – lead to increases in positive beliefs about the CR of an organization (Hypothesis 1a) as well as trust in the organization (Hypothesis 3a). While these links have been suggested, they have not yet been proven from a stakeholder perspective. The finding that large amounts of variance are explained in beliefs about the CR of the organization suggests that customers and employees base their judgments of whether they perceive an organization as honest, responsible or transparent to a large extent on the CR-related experiences that are measured in this study. This supports the view of theorists such as Matten and Moon (2008), Pirsch et al. (2007) and Waddock (2004) that CR is expressed (by the organization) and experienced (by stakeholders) in a wide range of day-to-day operating practices of business.

Interestingly, the findings reveal higher R^2 values for beliefs and trust in the employee compared with the customer model. The findings also reveal stronger path links from self-related CR experiences to beliefs and trust in the employee compared to the customer model, while the impact of others-related CR experiences is more similar in both models. This may indicate that customers base their perceptions of CR on a comparatively wider variety of issues than employees and/or than is measured in this study. It could also mean that self-related CR experiences are even more important to employees than to customers in building their beliefs about, and trust in, the organization, possibly due to the closeness and intensity of a typical employee–organization relationship.

Importantly, however, the findings in this study provide empirical evidence that both customers and employees base their perceptions of the CR of the organization to a large extent on how the organization relates to them directly in a number of institutionalized processes and day-to-day interactions. This might come as a surprise to managers who see CR as more peripheral rather than central to organizational behavior and performance, and demonstrates that there is a significant impact from CR-related experiences and beliefs on customer and employee trust and positive intent.

The impact of others-related CR experiences

Our findings suggest that increases in others-related CR experiences also lead to increases in positive beliefs about the CR of the organization (Hypothesis 1b) and trust in the organization (Hypothesis 3b) and thereby provide the first empirical evidence that customers and employees conceptualize CR in a way in which they take account of how both they themselves and other stakeholders are treated when making judgments.

It is well established in the business and society literature that CR incorporates the way organizations relate to various stakeholder groups (Laplume et al. 2008; Wood et al. 2006;

Freeman 1984). So far, however, it has been less well established whether the way an organization relates to others impacts individuals in their own relationships with the organization (Holbrook 2006). Conceptually, this finding provides a fresh take on CR as a multi-stakeholder concept, in that it demonstrates that customers and employees, in their own understandings of CR, care significantly about how organizations relate to their wider stakeholder constituency, including local communities and society as a whole. In practical terms this implies that managers need to think beyond stakeholder groupings when implementing CR activities. It also suggests that managers wanting to measure and demonstrate impact from CR activities need to measure the radial impact of corporate behaviors across stakeholder groups.

It is interesting to note that the link from others-related CR experiences to beliefs about the CR of the organization is stronger than the link from others-related CR experiences to trust, in both the customer and the employee models. This suggests that observations of how others are treated may have a stronger direct impact at a cognitive level than at an emotional level. The exact influence of self-related versus others-related CR experiences may differ from one situation to another, however.

The mediating role of beliefs about the CR of the organization

The finding that positive beliefs about CR lead to increases in trust (Hypothesis 2) is in line with theorists such as Morgan and Hunt (1994), who argue that trust results from beliefs about honesty, integrity, consistency, benevolence and responsibility of organizations. The finding also supports claims that evaluative thoughts may help or hinder the development of benefits derived from CR (e.g. Scholder Ellen et al. 2006; Riordan et al. 1997). While scholars have used cognitive theories to explain negative consequences from a lack of responsible business behaviors (e.g. Folkes and Kamins 1999; Creyer and Ross 1997), the results of this study provide support for the impact that positive beliefs about CR can have on the development of trust.

Importantly, the results suggest that the model is partially mediated. This has important implications for theory development in the context of CR as well as in the wider context of relationship theories. It suggests that beliefs about the CR of the organization can act as a buffer in relationships between individuals and organizations. For example, stakeholders holding positive beliefs about an organization who experience a negative event may not react negatively towards the organization immediately, especially if an experience is not in line with the beliefs people have about the organization more generally. Like a positive reputation, beliefs about CR can act as a form of goodwill protecting the organization from negative events that will occur from time to time (Godfrey 2005). It is important to note that negative beliefs may act in a similar way by preventing positive experiences from impacting trust immediately. This suggests it may take time to develop positive relationships with stakeholders who hold negative connotations of an organization.

Managerial implications

The study has a number of managerial implications. In simple terms it demonstrates that corporate responsibility matters to stakeholders in a material way: experiences and observations of high levels of corporate responsibility increase positive intentions of stakeholders towards the firm while low levels of responsibility decrease positive intentions. Organizations would be well advised to invest in non-market strategies that supported activities related to corporate responsibility, so this chapter goes some way to answering the "So what?" question related to CR that practitioners often have to answer.

While this may make intuitive sense, what is novel about the study reported in this chapter is that it sheds light on the mechanism by which responsibility impacts stakeholder attitudes and behavior. Most importantly, it demonstrates that stakeholders are influenced not just by their own direct experiences of an organization but by how that organization treats other stakeholders. The results suggest that customers are influenced by the ways organizations treat employees, suppliers and other customers. At the same time, employees are influenced by the way in which organizations treat customers, suppliers and other employees. As such, organizations would be well advised to let a broad stakeholder base act (and speak) on their behalf when wishing to convey a positive message about CR (Morsing et al. 2008). Such recommendations are in line with suggestions by other scholars such as Pirsch et al. (2007: 137), who elaborate on spill-over effects of CR activities to other stakeholder constituencies, claiming that consumers "do not always have their 'consumer hat' on, they are also employees, investors, advocates and community members."

Furthermore, managers and leaders can use the evidence reported in this study to justify expenditure and effort devoted towards a wide range of non-market strategy stakeholders, as such efforts are likely to have a material impact on direct as well as indirect stakeholders (through experiences and observations of self-related and others-related corporate activities) and as such will pay off in the long-term.

The stakeholder dynamics explored in this chapter are particularly interesting to consider in the context of non-market strategy, as they demonstrate that stakeholders pay attention to how organizations treat others and not only how organizations behave in terms of their direct relationship with a stakeholder. If an organization were to treat a focal stakeholder well but at the same time others badly this would probably be counter-productive. Stakeholders may be suspicious of an organization's real intent. They may be committed, but only superficially, never really committing or giving their full trust to the organization. The following messages are thus emerging from this chapter for leaders and managers:

1 Stakeholders are looking at all organizational actions, not just actions directed towards them.
2 Stakeholders care about not only themselves but others in different parts of the world, which is particularly relevant in today's globalized and connected world.
3 Authenticity matters – it is advisable for managers and leaders to aim for consistent behavior in all organizational relations rather than trying to please one stakeholder group at the expense of another.

Limitations and implications for future research

As with any empirical investigation, this study has a number of limitations that lend themselves to future exploration. Most importantly, the results from this study should not be generalized without further exploration as they present findings from customers and employees of just one organization in one sector. This study is useful in building up theory incrementally (Hitt et al. 1994), but it would be useful to conduct similar research with other organizations in other industries and with more stakeholder groups to increase current knowledge and practice of non-market strategy more widely. It would also be useful to expand the theoretical model to include moderating impacts of demographic and attitudinal variables that have been studied in the non-market strategy literature, to explore the notion of heterogeneity among stakeholder groups, to explore the impact of irresponsible corporate behaviors and to incorporate measures of actual behaviors of stakeholders.

Conclusions

It was the aim of this study to unpack the mechanism by which CR impacts stakeholder relationships in a non-market environment. In pursuing this objective, previous work is extended to examine the psychological process that drives individual stakeholder responses to CR experiences (Bhattacharya et al. 2009; Aguilera et al. 2007). Our results suggest that CR impacts customers and employees through three distinct but interrelated processes: first, in terms of self-related CR experiences that customers and employees have through their own interactions with the organization; second, in terms of others-related CR experiences that customers and employees have of how organizations relate to a wider stakeholder constituency; and, third, in terms of beliefs that stakeholders form about the CR of the organization, which result from these two types of experiences. The partial mediation found in this study furthermore highlights the importance that cognitive assessments play in this circuit.

We hope that this study will lay the theoretical and empirical foundation to further unpack the nuances and contingencies of how non-market strategies impact on a wider range of stakeholder relationships.

Notes

1 The dashed path has been studied extensively in past research (see, for example, Lewin and Johnston 1997; Pearson et al. 1997). It is therefore not hypothesized, but it is included in the full model for empirical testing.

Bibliography

Aguilera, R. V., Rupp, D. E., Williams, C. A. and Ganapathi, J. (2007). Putting the S back in corporate social responsibility: a multilevel theory of social change in organizations. *Academy of Management Review*, 32(3), 836–63.

Ahmad, S. J., O'Regan, N. and Ghobadian, A. (2003). Managing for performance: corporate responsibility and internal stakeholders. *International Journal of Business Performance Management*, 5, 141–53.

Ajzen, I. and Heilbroner, R. L. (1980). *Understanding Attitudes and Predicting Social Behaviour*. Englewood Cliffs, NJ: Prentice-Hall.

Armitage, C. J. and Christian, J. (2003). From attitudes to behaviour: basic and applied research on the theory of planned behaviour. *Current Psychology: Developmental, Learning, Personality, Social*, 22, 187–95.

Bandura, A. (1986). *Social Foundations of Thought and Action: A Social Cognitive Theory*. Englewood Cliffs, NJ: Prentice-Hall.

Bansal, P. and Clelland, I. (2004). Talking trash: legitimacy, impression management, and unsystematic risk in the context of the natural environment. *Academy of Management Journal*, 47, 93–103.

Barbian, J. (2001). The charitable worker. *Training*, 38, 50–5.

Barnett, M. (2007). Stakeholder influence capacity and the variability of financial returns to corporate social responsibility. *Academy of Management Review*, 32(3), 794–816.

Baron, R. M. and Kenny, D. A. (1986). The moderator–mediator variable distinction in social psychological research: conceptual, strategic, and statistical considerations. *Journal of Personality and Social Psychology*, 51, 1173–82.

Barone, M. J., Mjyazaki, A. D. and Taylor, K. A. (2000). The influence of cause-related marketing on consumer choice: does one good turn deserve another? *Journal of the Academy of Marketing Science*, 28, 248–62.

Baruch, Y. (1999). Response rate in academic studies – a comparative analysis. *Human Relations*, 52, 421–38.

Basu, K. and Palazzo, G. (2008). Corporate social responsibility: a process model of sensemaking. *Academy of Management Review*, 33(1), 122–36.

Becker-Olsen, K. L., Cudmore, A. B. and Hill, R. P. (2006). The impact of perceived corporate social responsibility on consumer behavior. *Journal of Business Research*, 59, 46–53.

Beckmann, S. C. (2007). Consumers and corporate social responsibility: matching the unmatchable. *Australasian Marketing Journal*, 15(1), 27–36.

Bem, D. J. (1970). *Beliefs, Attitudes, and Human Affairs*. Belmont, CA: Brooks/Cole.

Berger, I. E., Cunningham, P. and Drumwright, M. E. (2007). Mainstreaming corporate social responsibility: developing markets for virtues. *California Management Review*, 49, 132–57.

Bhattacharya, C. B., Korschun, D. and Sen, S. (2009). Strengthening stakeholder–company relationships through mutually beneficial corporate social responsibility initiatives. *Journal of Business Ethics*, 85, 257–72.

Bird, R., Hall, A. D., Momente, F. and Reggiani, F. (2007). What corporate social responsibility activities are valued by the market? *Journal of Business Ethics*, 76, 189–206.

Bollen, K. (1989). *Structural Equations with Latent Variable*. New York: John Wiley & Sons.

Brammer, S. and Pavelin, S. (2004). Voluntary social disclosures by large UK companies. *Business Ethics: A European Review*, 13, 86–99.

— (2005). Corporate reputation and an insurance motivation for corporate social investment. *Journal of Corporate Citizenship*, 20, 39–51.

— (2006). Corporate reputation and social performance: the importance of fit. *Journal of Management Studies*, 43, 435–55.

Brammer, S., Millington, A. and Rayton, B. (2006). Do CSR policies affect employees' commitment to their organisations? *People Management*, 12, 52.

— (2007). The contribution of corporate social responsibility to organizational commitment. *International Journal of Human Resource Management*, 18(10), 1701–19.

Brown, D. (2003). From Cinderella to CSR. *People Management*, August, 21.

Brown, T. J. and Dacin, P. A. (1997). The company and the product: corporate associations and consumer product responses. *Journal of Marketing*, 61, 68–84.

Campbell-Meiklejohn, D., Bach, D. R., Roepstorff, A., Dolan, R. J. and Frith, C. D. (2010). How the opinion of others affect our valuation of objects. *Current Biology*, 20, 1165–70.

Carroll, A. B. and Shabana, K. M. (2010). The business case for corporate social responsibility: a review of concepts, research and practice. *International Journal of Management Reviews*, 12(1), 85–105.

Carvalho, S. W., Sen, S., de Oliveira Mota, M. and de Lima, R. C. (2010). Consumer reactions to CSR: a Brazilian perspective. *Journal of Business Ethics*, 91, 291–310.

Chin, W. W. (1998). Issues and opinions on structural equation modelling. *MIS Quarterly*, 22, 7–16.

— (2001). *PLS Graph User's Guide*. Version 3.0. http://carma.wayne.edu/documents/oct1405/plsgraph3.0manual.hubona.pdf (accessed December 13, 2014).

Churchill, G. A. J. (1979). A paradigm for developing better measures of marketing constructs. *Journal of Marketing Research*, 16, 64–73.

Clark-Carter, D. (1997). *Doing Quantitative Psychological Research: From Design to Report*. East Sussex: Psychological Press.

Collier, J. and Esteban, R. (2007). Corporate social responsibility and employee commitment. *Business Ethics: A European Review*, 16, 19–33.

Colquitt, J. A., Conlon, D. E., Wesson, M. J., Porter, C. O. L. H. and Ng, K. Y. (2001). Justice at the millennium: a meta-analytic review of 25 years of organizational justice research. *Journal of Applied Psychology*, 86, 425–45.

Conner, M. and Norman, P. (1996). *Predicting Health Behaviour: Research and Practice with Social Cognition Models*. Milton Keynes: Open University Press.

Creyer, E. H. and Ross, W. T. J. (1997). The influence of firm behavior on purchase intention: do consumers really care about business ethics? *Journal of Consumer Marketing*, 14, 421–32.

Curras-Perez, R., Bigne-Alcaniz, E. and Alvarado-Herrera, A. (2009). The role of self-definitional principles in consumer identification with a socially responsible company. *Journal of Business Ethics*, 89, 547–64.

Dane, K. (2004). The relationship between perceptions of corporate citizenship and organizational commitment. *Business and Society*, 43, 296–319.

DaSilva, A. (2004). *Cone Citizenship Study*. Boston, MA: Cone Strategic Marketing.

Davis, G., Chun, R., da Silva, R. V. and Roper, S. (2003). *Corporate Reputation and Competitiveness*. London: Routledge.

Deery, S. J., Iverson, R. D. and Walsh, J. T. (2006). Toward a better understanding of psychological contract breach: a study of customer service employees. *Journal of Applied Psychology*, 91(1), 166–75.

Doh, J. P. and Guay, T. R. (2006). Corporate social responsibility, public policy, and NGO activism in Europe and the United States: an institutional-stakeholder perspective. *Journal of Management Studies*, 43, 47–73.

Drumwright, M. E. (1994). Socially responsible organizational buying: environmental concern as a noneconomic buying criterion. *Journal of Marketing*, 58, 1–19.

Du, S., Bhattacharya, C. B. and Sen, S. (2010). Maximizing business returns to corporate social responsibility (CSR): the role of CSR communication. *International Journal of Management Reviews*, 12(1), 8–19.

Dumontheil, I., Kuester, O., Apperly, I. A. and Blakemore, S.-J. (2010). Taking perspective into account in a communicative task. *NeuroImage*, 52, 1574–83.

Edelman, L. F., Bresnen, M., Newell, S., Scarbrough, H. and Swan, J. (2004). The benefits and pitfalls of social capital: empirical evidence from two organizations in the United Kingdom. *British Journal of Management*, 15, 559–69.

Fishbein, M. (1997). Predicting, understanding and changing socially relevant behaviours: lessons learned. In MacGarty, C. and Haslam, S. A. (eds.), *The Message of Social Psychology*. Oxford: Blackwell.

Fishbein, M. and Ajzen, I. (2010). *Reasoned Action: Predicting and Changing Behaviour*. Reading, MA: Addison-Wesley.

Fisher, K., Geenen, J., Jurcevic, M., McClintock, K. and Davis, G. (2009). Applying asset-based community development as a strategy for CSR: a Canadian perspective on a win–win for stakeholders and SMEs. *Business Ethics: A European Review*, 18(1), 66–82.

Folkes, V. S. and Kamins, M. A. (1999). Effects of information about firms' ethical and unethical actions on consumers' attitudes. *Journal of Consumer Psychology*, 8, 243–59.

Fornell, C. and Cha, J. (1994). Partial least squares. In Bagozzi, R. P. (ed.), *Advanced Methods of Marketing Research*. Cambridge: Blackwell.

Fornell, C. and Larcker, D. F. (1981). Evaluating structural equation models with unobservable variables and measurement error. *Journal of Marketing Research*, 18, 39–50.

Foulkes, F. K. (1980). *Personnel Policies in Large Non-union Companies*. Englewood Cliffs, NJ: Prentice-Hall.

Freeman, E. (1984). *Strategic Management: A Stakeholder Approach*. New York: Basic Books.

Friedman, A. L. and Miles, S. (2002). Developing stakeholder theory. *Journal of Management Studies*, 39, 1–21.

Gakovic, A. and Tetrick, L. E. (2003). Psychological contract breach as a source of strain for employees. *Journal of Business and Psychology*, 18, 235–46.

Galbreath, J. (2010). Drivers of corporate social responsibility: the role of formal strategic planning and firm culture. *British Journal of Management*, 21, 511–25.

Gardberg, N. A. and Fombrun, C. J. (2006). Corporate citizenship: creating intangible assets across institutional environments. *Academy of Management Review*, 31(2), 329–46.

Geisser, S. (1975). The predictive sample reuse method with applications. *Journal of the American Statistical Association*, 70, 320–8.

Gellatly, I. R., Hunter, K. H., Currie, L. G. and Irving, P. G. (2009). HRM practices and organizational commitment profiles. *International Journal of Human Resource Management*, 20(4), 869–84.

Gerbing, D. W. and Anderson, J. C. (1988). Structural equation modelling in practice: a review and recommended two-step approach. *Psychological Bulletin*, 103, 411–23.

Gillespie, N. and Dietz, G. (2009). Trust repair after an organization-level failure. *Academy of Management Review*, 34(1), 127–45.

Godfrey, P. C. (2005). The relationships between corporate philanthropy and shareholder wealth: a risk management perspective. *Academy of Management Review*, 30, 777–98.

Goldberg, M. E. and Hartwick, J. (1990). The effects of advertiser reputation and extremity of advertising claim on advertising effectiveness. *Journal of Consumer Research*, 17, 172–9.

Greening, D. W. and Turban, D. B. (2000). Corporate social performance as a competitive advantage in attracting a quality workforce. *Business and Society*, 39, 254–80.

Gruen, T. W., Summers, J. O. and Acito, F. (2000). Relationship marketing activities, commitment, and membership behaviors in professional associations. *Journal of Marketing*, 64, 34–49.

Gueterbock, R. (2004). Greenpeace campaign case study – Stop Esso. *Journal of Consumer Behaviour*, 3, 265–71.

Hair, J. F., Black, W. C., Babin, B. J., Anderson, R. E. and Tatham, R. L. (2006). *Multivariate Data Analysis*. Upper Saddle River, NJ: Pearson Prentice-Hall.

Handelman, J. M. and Arnold, S. J. (1999). The role of marketing actions with a social dimension: appeals to the institutional environment. *Journal of Marketing*, 63, 33–48.

Hanke, T. and Stark, W. (2009). Strategy development: conceptual framework on corporate social responsibility. *Journal of Business Ethics*, 85, 507–16.

Harvey, O. J. (1997). Beliefs, knowledge, and meaning from the perspective of the perceiver: need for structure-order. In McGarty, C. and Haslam, S. A. (eds.), *The Message of Social Psychology*. Oxford: Blackwell.

Hitt, M. A., Hoskisson, R. E. and Ireland, R. D. (1994). A mid-range theory of the interactive effects of international and product diversification on innovation and performance. *Journal of Management*, 20, 297–326.

Holbrook, M. B. (2006). Rosepekiceciveci versus CCV. In Lusch, R. F. and Vargo, S. L. (eds.), *The Service-Dominant Logic of Marketing: Dialog, Debate and Directions*. Armonk, NY: Sharpe.

Hopkins, M. (2005). Measurement of corporate social responsibility. *International Journal of Management and Decision Making*, 6, 213–31.

Hopkins, M. and John, D. (2002). Sustainability in the internal operations of companies. *Corporate Environmental Strategy*, 9(2), 1–11.

Houghton, S. M., Gabel, J. T. A. and Williams, D. W. (2009). Connecting the two faces of CSR: does employee volunteerism improve compliance? *Journal of Business Ethics*, 87, 477–94.

Hulland, J. (1999). Use of partial least squares in strategic management research: a review of four recent studies. *Strategic Management Journal*, 20, 195–204.

Husted, B. W. and Salazar, J. (2006). Taking Friedman seriously: maximising profits and social performance. *Journal of Management Studies*, 43(1), 75–91.

Jones, T. M. (1995). Instrumental stakeholder theory: a synthesis of ethics and economics. *Academy of Management Review*, 20, 404–37.

King, W. R. and He, J. (2006). A meta-analysis of the technology acceptance model. *Information and Management*, 30, 1–16.

Kim, H.-R., Lee, M., Lee, H.-T. and Kim, N.-M. (2010). Corporate social responsibility and employee–company identification. *Journal of Business Ethics*, 95, 557–69.

Kitchin, T. (2003). Corporate social responsibility: a brand explanation. *Journal of Brand Management*, 10, 312–26.

Klein, J. and Dawar, N. (2004). Corporate social responsibility and consumers' attributions and brand evaluations in a product–harm crisis. *International Journal of Research in Marketing*, 21, 203–17.

Komiak, S. Y. X. and Benbasat, I. (2006). The effects of personalization and familiarity on trust and adoption of recommendation agents. *MIS Quarterly*, 30, 941–60.

Kozinets, R. V. and Handelman, J. M. (2004). Adversaries of consumption: consumer movements, activism, and ideology. *Journal of Consumer Research*, 31, 691–704.

Laplume, A. O., Sonpar, K. and Litz, R. A. (2008). Stakeholder theory: reviewing a theory that moves us. *Journal of Management*, 34, 1152–89.

Lee, M.-D. P. (2008). A review of the theories of corporate social responsibility: its evolutionary path and the road ahead. *International Journal of Management Reviews*, 10(1), 53–73.

Lerner, M. J. (2003). The justice motive: where social psychologists found it, how they lost it, and why they might not find it again. *Personality and Social Psychology Review*, 7, 388–99.

Lewin, J. E. and Johnston, W. J. (1997). Relationship marketing theory in practice: a case study. *Journal of Business Research*, 39, 23–31.

Lozano, J. (2002). Organizational ethics. In L. Zsolnai (ed.), *Ethics in the Economy*. Bern: Peter Lang.

Luce, R. A., Barber, A. E. and Hillman, A. J. (2001). Good deeds and misdeeds: a mediated model of the effect of corporate social performance on organizational attractiveness. *Business and Society*, 40, 397–416.

Luo, X. and Bhattacharya, C. B. (2006). Corporate social responsibility, customer satisfaction, and market value. *Journal of Marketing*, 70(4), 1–18.

Maignan, I. and Ferrell, O. C. (2004). Corporate social responsibility and marketing: an integrative framework. *Journal of the Academy of Marketing Science*, 32, 3–19.

Maignan, I., Ferrell, O. C. and Hult, G. T. (1999). Corporate citizenship: cultural antecedents and business benefits. *Journal of the Academy of Marketing Science*, 27, 455–69.

Manstead, A. S. R. (1997). Situations, belongingness, attitudes, and culture: four lessons learned from social psychology. In McGarty, C. and Haslam, A. S. (eds.), *The Message of Social Psychology: Perspectives on Mind in Society*. Oxford: Blackwell.

Manstead, A. S. R. and Van der Pligt, J. (1998). Should we expect more from expectancy-value models of attitude and behavior? *Journal of Applied Social Psychology*, 28, 1313–16.

Maon, F., Lindgreen, A. and Swaen, V. (2010). Organizational stages and cultural phases: a critical review and a consolidative model of corporate social responsibility development. *International Journal of Management Reviews*, 12(3), 20–38.

Margolis, J. D. and Walsh, J. P. (2001). *People and Profits? The Search for a Link between a Company's Social and Financial Performance*. Mahwah, NJ: Lawrence Erlbaum Associates.

Marin, L., Ruiz, S. and Rubio, A. (2009). The role of identity salience in the effects of corporate social responsibility on consumer behavior. *Journal of Business Ethics*, 84, 65–78.

Mathieson, K., Peacock, E. and Chin, W. W. (2001). Extending the technology acceptance model: the influence of perceived user resources. *Database for Advances in Information Systems*, 32, 86–112.

Matten, D. and Moon, J. (2008). Implicit and explicit CSR: a conceptual framework for a comparative understanding of corporate social responsibility. *Academy of Management Review*, 33(2), 404–24.

McEvily, B. and Tortoriello, M. (2011). Measuring trust in organizational research: review and recommendations. *Journal of Trust Research*, 1(1), 22–62.

McGuire, J. B., Sundgren, A. and Schneeweis, T. (1988). Corporate social responsibility and firm financial performance. *Academy of Management Journal*, 31(4), 854–72.

McWilliams, A. and Siegel, D. (2001). Corporate social responsibility: a theory of the firm perspective. *Academy of Management Review*, 26, 117–27.

McWilliams, A., Siegel, D. S. and Wright, P. M. (2006). Corporate social responsibility: strategic implications. *Journal of Management Studies*, 43, 1–18.

Menon, A. and Menon, A. (1997). Enviropreneurial marketing strategy: the emergence of corporate environmentalism as marketing strategy. *Journal of Marketing*, 61, 51–67.

Meyer, J. P., Allen, N. J. and Gellatly, I. R. (1990). Affective and continuance commitment to the organization: evaluation of measures and analysis of concurrent and time-lagged relations. *Journal of Applied Psychology*, 75(6), 710–20.

Mitchell, R. K., Agle, B. R. and Wood, D. J. (1997). Toward a theory of stakeholder identification and salience: defining the principle of who and what really counts. *Academy of Management Review*, 22, 853–86.

Mohr, L. A. and Webb, D. J. (2005). The effects of corporate social responsibility and price on consumer responses. *Journal of Consumer Affairs*, 39, 121–47.

Mohr, L. A., Webb, D. J. and Harris, K. E. (2001). Do consumers expect companies to be socially responsible? The impact of corporate social responsibility on buying behavior. *Journal of Consumer Affairs*, 35, 45–72.

Morgan, R. M. and Hunt, S. D. (1994). The commitment–trust theory of relationship marketing. *Journal of Marketing*, 58, 20–38.

Morsing, M. (2006). Corporate social responsibility as strategic auto-communication: on the role of external stakeholders for member identification. *Business Ethics: A European Review*, 15, 171–82.

Morsing, M. and Schultz, M. (2006). Corporate social responsibility communication: stakeholder information, response and involvement strategies. *Business Ethics: A European Review*, 15, 323–38.

Morsing, M., Schultz, M. and Nielsen, K. U. (2008). The "Catch 22" of communicating CSR: findings from a Danish study. *Journal of Marketing Communications*, 14(2), 97–111.

Murray, K. B. and Vogel, C. M. (1997). Using a hierarchy-of-effects approach to gauge the effectiveness of corporate social responsibility to generate goodwill toward the firm: financial versus nonfinancial impacts. *Journal of Business Research*, 38, 141–59.

Muthuri, J. N., Matten, D. and Moon, J. (2009). Employee volunteering and social capital: contributions to corporate social responsibility. *British Journal of Management*, 20, 75–89.

Neville, B. A., Bell, S. J. and Menguec, B. (2005). Corporate reputation, stakeholders and the social performance–financial performance relationship. *European Journal of Marketing*, 39, 1184–220.

Nunnally, J. C. (1978). *Psychometric Theory*, New York: McGraw-Hill.

Orlitzky, M. and Benjamin, J. D. (2001). Corporate social performance and firm risk: a meta-analytic review. *Business and Society*, 40(4), 369–97.

Orlitzky, M., Schmidt, F. L. and Rynes, S. L. (2003). Corporate social and financial performance: a meta-analysis. *Organization Studies*, 24, 403–41.

Ortiz de Guinea, A. and Markus, M. L. (2009). Why break the habit of a lifetime? Rethinking the roles of intention, habit, and emotion in continuing information technology use. *MIS Quarterly*, 33(3), 433–44.

Pearson, C. M., Misra, S. K., Clair, J. A. and Mitroff, I. I. (1997). Managing the unthinkable. *Organizational Dynamics*, 26, 51–64.

Peloza, J. (2009). The challenge of measuring financial impacts from investments in corporate social performance. *Journal of Management*, 35(6), 1518–41.

Peloza, J. and Shang, J. (2011). How can corporate social responsibility activities create value for stakeholders? A systematic review. *Journal of the Academy of Marketing Science*, 39, 117–35.

Peterson, D. K. (2003). The relationship between ethical pressure, relativistic moral beliefs and organizational commitment. *Journal of Managerial Psychology*, 18, 557–73.

— (2004a). Benefits of participation in corporate volunteer programs: employees' perceptions. *Personnel Review*, 33, 615–27.

— (2004b). The relationship between perceptions of corporate citizenship and organizational commitment. *Business and Society*, 43, 296–319.

Petty, R. E. (1995). Attitude change. In Tessser, A. (ed.), *Advanced Social Psychology*. New York: McGraw-Hill.

Pickett, M. C. (2007). 'Theory of reasoned action: reassessing the relationships of moral and ethical climates in organizations. *Journal of the American Society of Business and Behavioural Sciences*, 3(1), 1–10.

Pirsch, J., Gupta, S. and Grau, S. L. (2007). A framework for understanding corporate social responsibility programs as a continuum: an exploratory study. *Journal of Business Ethics*, 70, 125–40.

Pivato, S., Misani, N. and Tencati, A. (2008). The impact of corporate social responsibility on consumer trust: the case of organic food. *Business Ethics: A European Review*, 17, 3–12.

Podnar, K. and Golob, U. (2007). CSR expectations: the focus of corporate marketing. *Corporate Communications: An International Journal*, 12(4), 326–40.

Podsakoff, P. M., MacKenzie, S. B., Lee, J.-Y. and Podsakoff, N. P. (2003). Common method biases in behavioral research: a critical review of the literature and recommended remedies. *Journal of Applied Psychology*, 88, 879–903.

Pomering, A. and Dolnicar, S. (2009). Assessing the prerequisite of successful CSR implementation: are consumers aware of CSR initiatives? *Journal of Business Ethics*, 85, 285–301.

Rempel, J. K., Holmes, J. G. and Zanna, M. P. (1985). Trust in close relationships. *Journal of Personality and Social Psychology*, 49(1), 95–112.

Riordan, C. M., Gatewood, R. D. and Bill, J. B. (1997). Corporate image: employee reactions and implications for managing corporate social performance. *Journal of Business Ethics*, 16, 401–12.

Rodrigo, P. and Arenas, D. (2008). Do employees care about CSR programs? A typology of employees according to their attitudes. *Journal of Business Ethics*, 83, 265–83.

Rossiter, J. R. (2002). The C-OAR-SE procedure for scale development in marketing. *International Journal of Research in Marketing*, 19, 305–35.

Rupp, D. E., Ganapathi, J., Aguilera, R. V. and Williams, C. A. (2006). Employee reactions to corporate social responsibility: an organizational justice framework. *Journal of Organizational Behaviour*, 27, 537–43.

Russo, M. V. and Fouts, P. A. (1997). A resource-based perspective on corporate environmental performance and profitability. *Academy of Management Journal*, 40, 534–59.

Scholder Ellen, P., Mohr, L. A. and Webb, D. J. (2000). Charitable programs and the retailer: do they mix? *Journal of Retailing*, 76, 393–406.

Scholder Ellen, P., Webb, D. J. and Mohr, L. A. (2006). Building corporate associations: consumer attributions for corporate socially responsible programs. *Journal of the Academy of Marketing Science*, 34, 147–57.

Sen, S. and Bhattacharya, C. B. (2001). Does doing good always lead to doing better? Consumer reactions to corporate social responsibility. *Journal of Marketing Research*, 48, 225–43.

Siegel, D. (1999). *Skill-biased Technological Change: Evidence from a Firm-level Survey*. Kalamazoo, MI: Upjohn Institute Press.

Sims, R. L. and Keon, T. L. (2000). The influence of organizational expectations on ethical decision-making conflict. *Journal of Business Ethics*, 23, 219–28.

Starkey, K. and Madan, P. (2001). Bridging the relevance gap: aligning stakeholders in the future of management research. *British Journal of Management*, 12, S3–S26.

Stone, M. (1974). Cross-validatory choice and assessment of statistical predictions. *Journal of the Royal Statistical Society*, 36, 111–47.

Strahilevitz, M. and Myers, J. G. (1998). Donations to charity as purchase incentives: how well they work may depend on what you are trying. *Journal of Consumer Research*, 24, 434–47.

Summers, J. O. (2001). Guidelines for conducting research and publishing in marketing: from conceptualization through the review process. *Journal of the Academy of Marketing Science*, 29, 405–15.

Surroca, J., Tribo, J. A. and Waddock, S. (2010). Corporate responsibility and financial performance: the role of intangible resources. *Strategic Management Journal*, 31(5), 463–90.

Susskind, A. M., Kacmar, K. M. and Borchgrevink, C. P. (2003). Customer service providers' attitudes relating to customer service and customer satisfaction in the customer–server exchange. *Journal of Applied Psychology*, 88, 179–87.

Tobler, P. N., Kalis, A. and Kalenscher, T. (2008). The role of moral utility in decision making: an interdisciplinary framework. *Cognitive, Affective and Behavioral Neuroscience*, 8(4), 390–401.

Turillo, C. J., Foler, R., Lavelle, J. J., Umphress, E. E. and Gee, J. O. (2002). Is virtue its own reward? Self-sacrificial decisions for the sake of fairness. *Organizaional Behavior and Human Decision Processes*, 89, 839–65.

Turker, D. (2009a). Measuring corporate social responsibility: a scale development. *Journal of Business Ethics*, 85, 411–27.

— (2009b). How corporate social responsibility influences organizational commitment. *Journal of Business Ethics*, 89, 189–204.

Trudel, R. and Cotte, J. (2009). Does it pay to be good? *MIT Sloan Management Review*, 50(2), 60–8.

Vaaland, T. I., Heide, M. and Gronhaug, K. (2008). Corporate social responsibility: investigating theory and research in the marketing context. *European Journal of Marketing*, 42(9/10), 927–53.

Van Breukelen, W., Van Der Vlist, R. and Steensma, H. (2004). Voluntary employee turnover: combining variables from the "traditional" turnover literature with the theory of planned behavior. *Journal of Organizational Behavior*, 25, 893–914.

Van Lange, P. A. M. (2000). Beyond self-interest: a set of propositions relevant to interpersonal orientations. *European Review of Social Psychology*, 11, 297–331.

Vlachos, P. A. (2010). Predictors and outcomes of corporate social responsibility: a research framework. *International Journal of Business Governance and Ethics*, 5(4), 343–59.

Vuontisjaervi, T. (2006). The European context for corporate social responsibility and human resource management: an analysis of the largest Finnish companies. *Business Ethics: A European Review*, 15(3), 271–91.

Waddock, S. (2004). Parallel universes: companies, academics, and the progress of corporate citizenship. *Business and Society Review*, 109, 5–42.

Waddock, S. and Graves, S. B. (1997). The corporate social performance–financial performance link. *Strategic Management Journal*, 18(4), 303–19.

Walker, M., Heere, B., Parent, M. M. and Drane, D. (2010). Social responsibility and the Olympic Games: the mediating role of consumer attributions. *Journal of Business Ethics*, 95, 659–80.

Walsh, G., Mitchell, V.-W., Jackson, P. R. and Beatty, S. E. (2009). Examining the antecedents and consequences of corporate reputation: a customer perspective. *British Journal of Management*, 20, 187–203.

Webb, D. J. and Mohr, L. A. (1998). A typology of consumer responses to cause-related marketing: from sceptics to socially concerned. *Journal of Public Policy and Marketing*, 17, 226–38.

Werts, C. E., Linn, R. L. and Joereskog, K. G. (1974). Intraclass reliability estimates: testing structural assumptions. *Educational and Psychological Measurement*, 34, 25–33.

Whittington, R., Jarzabkowski, P., Mayer, M., Mounoud, E., Nahapiet, J. and Rouleau, L. (2003). Taking strategy seriously: responsibility and reform for an important social practice. *Journal of Management Inquiry*, 12(4), 396–409.

Wixom, B. H. and Watson, H. J. (2001). An empirical investigation of the factors affecting data warehousing success. *MIS Quarterly*, 25, 17–41.

Wood, D. J. and Jones, R. E. (1995). Stakeholder mismatching: a theoretical problem in empirical research on corporate social performance. *International Journal of Organizational Analysis*, 3, 229–67.

Wood, D. J., Logsdon, J. M., Lewellyn, P. G. and Davenport, K. (2006). *Global Business Citizenship. A Transformative Framework for Ethics and Sustainable Capitalism*. New York: M. E. Sharpe.

Zsolnai, L. (2002). The moral economic man. In Zsolnai, L. (ed.), *Ethics in the Economy (Handbook of Business Ethics)*. Bern: Peter Lang.

14

Strategic CSR, value creation and competitive advantage

Jedrzej George Frynas

Since the early 1970s, there has been a long-standing research interest in the potential of corporate social responsibility (CSR) for creating value (Bragdon and Marlin 1972; Moskowitz 1972), as evidenced by hundreds of studies that investigated the correlation between CSR and financial performance (for reviews, see Margolis and Walsh 2003; Molina-Azorín et al. 2009). Since the late 1990s, CSR has been increasingly linked to strategic management and strategic CSR research has emphasized CSR as a mechanism for enhancing differentiation and achieving a competitive advantage (e.g. Russo and Fouts 1997; Sharma and Vredenburg 1998; Porter and Kramer 2006).

Therefore, CSR is no longer simply viewed as public relations or as a tool towards enhancing employee motivation but as an integral part of a firm's strategy and value capture. Leading scholars such as Michael Porter, Rosabeth Moss Kanter and Philip Kotler have embraced CSR as an important concern in strategic management (Kanter 1999, 2008; Kotler and Lee 2005; Porter and Kramer 2006). Porter and Kramer (2006: 84) argued that "a company must integrate a social perspective into the core frameworks it already uses to understand competition and guide its business strategy."

The interface between strategic CSR, value creation and competitive advantage deserves our attention as it is linked to important practical concerns. Most large global companies view CSR as important to the success of their business, but many find it difficult to link CSR to value creation and competitive advantage. In a survey of 1000 global CEOs from 107 countries by the consulting firm Accenture in 2013, 93 percent of CEOs believed that sustainability will be important to the future success of their business. However, the lack of a clear link between social and environmental concerns and business value drivers has been rising in importance as a critical barrier to integrating social and environmental concerns in business strategy. In 2013, 37 percent of CEOs regarded the lack of a clear link to business value as a critical barrier, an increase from 18 percent in a similar survey in 2007 and 30 percent in a 2010 survey (Accenture 2013).

This chapter investigates the links between strategic CSR, value creation and competitive advantage, by summarizing key ideas and theoretical frameworks. The chapter starts with a definition of strategic CSR. Then the key theoretical perspectives on CSR and the key papers on the organizational benefits of strategic CSR are summarized. A section is specifically devoted to innovation, which is regarded as a key potential benefit of strategic CSR. Two case vignettes are then used to illustrate the application of the VRIO (Value, Rarity, Imitability and Organization) framework and to explore the link between strategic CSR, value creation and sustainable competitive advantages. The chapter ends with a brief discussion and directions for future research.

Defining strategic CSR

As Doh and Littell implied in Chapter 7, there is no agreement on what exactly CSR stands for or where the boundaries of CSR lie (Lockett et al. 2006; Blowfield and Murray 2008). The responsibilities of companies are often defined differently, depending on the social – especially national – context (Baskin 2006; Waldman et al. 2006), the industry context (Frynas 2009; Runhaar and Lafferty 2009) or ownership structure (Johnson and Greening 1999; Berrone et al. 2010). Furthermore, CSR is a dynamic concept and its meaning can change over time (Carroll 1999; Matten and Moon 2008). Therefore, it is most appropriate to define CSR as an umbrella term for a variety of theories and practices, all of which recognize that companies have a responsibility for their impact on society and the natural environment, often beyond legal compliance and the liability of individuals (Blowfield and Frynas 2005: 503; see also Matten and Crane 2005).

Similarly, there is no agreement on what exactly strategic CSR stands for. Key papers on CSR and strategy by authors such as by Burke and Logsdon (1996), Baron (2001), McWilliams and Siegel (2001; 2011) and Siegel and Vitaliano (2007) have not provided a universal working definition of strategic CSR. According to Burke and Logsdon (1996: 496), CSR is strategic when "it yields substantial business related benefits to the firm, in particular by supporting core business activities and thus contributing to the firm's effectiveness in accomplishing its mission." According to Baron (2001: 9), "strategic CSR is simply a profit-maximization strategy motivated by self-interest and not by a conception of corporate social responsibility." McWilliams and Siegel (2011: 1481) define "strategic CSR as any 'responsible' activity that allows a firm to achieve SCA [sustainable competitive advantage], regardless of motive." These authors do not elaborate on these statements much further and do not provide clear examples to distinguish between CSR and strategic CSR.

Going beyond the work by these strategy authors and building on the above definition by Blowfield and Frynas (2005: 503), this paper defines strategic CSR as following "an organizational strategy that addresses the organization's responsibility for its impact on society and the natural environment." Following a process or organic view of strategy, we define it as "the planned or actual coordination of the firm's major goals and actions, in time and space, that continuously co-align the firm with its environment" (Farjoun 2002: 570). In line with prior studies on CSR and strategy that pointed to the contribution of strategic CSR to profit-maximization and attaining competitive advantages for the firm (e.g. Baron 2001; McWilliams and Siegel 2001; Porter and Kramer 2006), strategic CSR involves "key organizational decisions" related to social and environmental matters that are coordinated and integrated in order to achieve important objectives for and on behalf of the entire organization. By CSR strategy, we therefore do not mean individual social or philanthropic activities decided by subsidiaries of multinational firms, or ad hoc initiatives by the firm's headquarters to address public relations. We do not equate strategy with social and environmental effectiveness – an organization may pursue a coherent and integrated strategy based on its own cost–benefit analyses and may achieve organizational performance outcomes that ultimately may prove ineffective in social and environmental terms.

Following the above strategy definition and in line with applied strategic CSR contributions (e.g. Kanter 1999; Porter and Kramer 2006; Rangan et al. 2012), examples of strategic CSR may include, inter alia:

- Strategic philanthropy (e.g. bottom-of-the-pyramid strategies targeting low-income customers by companies such as Unilever; or IBM's philanthropic support for US-based schools which helped the company to develop new internet tools).
- Strategic reengineering of the value chain (e.g. use of fair trade goods by companies such as Starbucks; or the reengineering of the value chain to source more sustainable products by retailers such as Marks and Spencer).
- Strategic transformation of the organization's skills or overall business strategy (e.g. the use of closed-loop manufacturing by companies such as Interface; or General Electric's transportation solutions for reducing carbon-dioxide emissions, such as electric vehicle charging stations and electrical grid improvements).

Theoretical perspectives on strategic CSR

CSR scholarship has been dominated by the stakeholder theory (see Laplume et al. 2008) and the institutional theory (see Brammer et al. 2012). Stakeholder theory spawned different variants and interpretations (e.g. Donaldson and Preston 1995; Gray et al. 1996; Egels-Zandén and Sandberg 2009), but generally predicts CSR strategies as a direct result of relative pressures from different actors (e.g. Brammer and Millington 2004; Bremmers et al. 2007; Zietsma and Winn 2008). Institutional theory predicts that CSR strategies and practices will become similar within a defined business environment, as similar firms face similar social expectations – a process known as "institutional isomorphism" (e.g. Jennings and Zandbergen 1995; Doh and Guay 2006; Husted and Allen 2006). Hence both of these perspectives focus predominantly on explaining organizational adaptation to external social and environmental pressures. However, this focus on external stimuli fails to explain satisfactorily why specific firms use CSR strategically to gain a competitive advantage. Indeed, Porter and Kramer (2006) argued that only "proaction" strategies are genuinely "strategic" in the sense that they can help the firm to gain a competitive advantage from CSR. A proactive strategy allows the firm to align social and environmental goals with its core business strategy. While a few applications of stakeholder theory and institutional perspectives suggested that companies can occasionally manipulate stakeholder and institutional pressures (e.g. Child and Tsai 2005; Lamberti and Lettieri 2009), stakeholder and institutional perspectives largely lack the methodological tools to explain proactive strategic CSR.

Different economic and managerial theories have been proposed as an explanation of strategic CSR. For example, work linking the theory of the firm to CSR has previously suggested that CSR strategies can be conceived as a function of supply of/demand for social and environmental activities in the market place and that strategic CSR is an outcome of cost–benefit analyses by the organization (McWilliams and Siegel 2001; Husted and de Jesus Salazar 2006), while work linking game theory to CSR has suggested that CSR strategies can be conceived as the result of interdependent decision-making between rational actors with expected payoffs of different strategies (Baron 2001; Fairchild 2008). Most notably, a dynamically growing body of scholarship has applied the resource-based view (RBV) to explain proactive strategic choices of firms with regards to CSR, and the RBV has become the dominant instrumental theory within the CSR literature (e.g. Hart 1995; Russo and

Fouts 1997; Branco and Rodrigues 2006; Marcus and Anderson 2006; McWilliams and Siegel 2011).

The RBV emphasizes the importance of valuable resources for successful firm strategies (see Priem and Butler 2001), including specifically non-market strategies (see Oliver and Holzinger 2008), and points to the heterogeneity of firms in terms of valuable resources as a source of competitive advantage. Barney (1997: ch. 5) devised a practical tool for identifying valuable resources called the VRIO framework (sometimes referred to as the VRIN framework, in which the "N" stands for Non-substitutability), which asks four related questions: whether a firm's resources and capabilities are valuable, rare, costly to imitate, and exploited by the organization. In the words of one key review of the RBV field, Barney's framework "has supplied the footing for many RBV studies, with subsequent work based on either his framework or an extension" (Priem and Butler 2001: 23). Empirical applications of the VRIO framework have found that companies with valuable and rare resources achieve higher levels of organizational performance and sustainable competitive advantage (Newbert 2008; Talaja 2012).

Unsurprisingly, a significant part of RBV empirical applications to CSR has tested the statistical relationship between social/environmental performance and economic returns (Russo and Fouts 1997; Menguc and Ozanne 2005; Menguc et al. 2010) or has applied the VRIO framework (Falkenberg and Brunsael 2011; Peters et al. 2011) in order to provide evidence that social and environmental capabilities can lead to competitive advantages. Other CSR studies have found, for example, that capabilities related to research and development positively affect CSR (Padgett and Galan 2010) and that the difficulty of acquiring and duplicating social/environmental capabilities can reduce isomorphism within an industry (Escobar and Vredenburg 2011).

Linking the RBV to CSR implies that specialized skills or capabilities related to investment in CSR can lead to firm-specific competitive advantages. In the context of CSR, a strategic capability could be a firm's reputation for socially responsible behavior, a firm's ability to innovate green products or a firm's relational skills for dealing with non-governmental organizations. Hart (1995) developed propositions on the conditions under which companies may develop firm-specific social and environmental competences two decades ago. Strategic CSR could then be justified as an investment in capabilities that will allow the firm to differentiate itself from its competitors and will help the firm to gain a competitive advantage.

In summary, the RBV lens implies that companies can be strategically proactive in terms of searching for CSR-related business opportunities, in marked contrast to the reactive view presented by stakeholder theory and institutional theory. Table 14.1 contrasts these three perspectives.

Table 14.1 Comparison of theoretical perspectives on CSR strategy

	Institutional theory	Stakeholder theory	Resource-based view
Main focus	Adherence to rules and norms	Relationships with external actors	Firm resources and capabilities
Determinants of CSR strategy	Conformity to different institutional contexts	Relative dependence of a firm on stakeholders	Social and environmental capabilities of a firm
Main unit of analysis	Institutional context	Organization	Organization
Scope for independent managerial action	Non-choice behavior	Limited choice behavior	Substantial choice behavior

Organizational benefits from strategic CSR

There has been a long tradition of researching the correlation between social responsibility and financial performance, with hundreds of research papers devoted to this topic (the earliest studies include Bragdon and Marlin (1972) and Moskowitz (1972)). While some research findings on the CSR–performance correlation have been contradictory and fundamental questions about methodology design remain (for reviews, see Margolis and Walsh 2003; Carroll and Shabana 2010), overall these studies have pointed to a positive correlation between CSR and financial performance, but they have not, by and large, treated CSR as a strategic firm activity.

Over the last decade and a half, research has shown that strategic CSR can yield many organizational benefits for a company. Studies suggest that it can enhance product differentiation and erect barriers to entry (McWilliams and Siegel 2001), enhance recruitment as part of the organization's human resource management (HRM) (Brekke and Nyborg 2008), enhance global brands as part of reputational management (Polonsky and Jevons 2009), preempt government regulation (Baron 2001) or lead to first-mover advantages (Sirsly and Lamertz 2008). Table 14.2 provides a summary of selected key papers.

Table 14.2 Organizational benefits from strategic CSR – selected key papers (alphabetical, by author)

Author/Year	Summary	Theory applied
Baron 2001	Strategic CSR as a mechanism for protecting the organization from activist group campaigns	Game theory
Baron and Diermeier 2007	Strategic CSR as a mechanism for protecting the organization from activist group campaigns	Game theory
Brekke and Nyborg 2008	Strategic CSR as a mechanism for developing human resource capabilities	–
Buysse and Verbeke 2003	Strategic CSR as a mechanism for improving stakeholder relations	Stakeholder theory
McWilliams and Siegel 2001	Strategic CSR as a mechanism for enhancing product differentiation and erecting barriers to entry	Theory of the firm
Polonsky and Jevons 2009	Strategic CSR as a mechanism for enhancing global branding	–
Porter and Kramer 2006	Strategic CSR as a source of competitive advantage and innovation	–
Russo and Fouts 1997	Strategic CSR as a mechanism for developing environmental resources and capabilities	RBV
Sharma and Vredenburg 1998	Strategic CSR as a mechanism for developing organizational capabilities	RBV
Turban and Greening 1997	Strategic CSR as a mechanism for enhancing the organization's attractiveness to prospective employees	Signaling theory
Zhao 2012	Strategic CSR as a mechanism for obtaining government support in emerging markets	–

In line with the fundamental tenet of strategic management that firms obtain sustainable competitive advantages through differentiation strategies, strategic CSR research has likewise emphasized CSR as a mechanism for enhancing differentiation and achieving a competitive advantage (e.g. Russo and Fouts 1997; Sharma and Vredenburg 1998; Porter and Kramer 2006). According to Porter and Kramer (2006: 91), CSR strategies should be seen as "a long-term investment in a company's future competitiveness," that is, a mechanism for discovering future business opportunities and resulting in a competitive advantage for selected firms. The popular VRIO model can then be used to identify the firm-specific capabilities that can lead to a sustainable competitive advantage by identifying CSR-related capabilities that are valuable, rare, difficult to imitate and appropriately exploited by the organization. Given that sustainable competitive advantage can be expected to result in value creation, a fundamental question is to consider the link between strategic CSR activities and value creation.

Almost two decades ago, Burke and Logsdon (1996: 496) outlined five key strategic criteria or dimensions in order – in their words – to "capture the full range of strategic behaviour and opportunities for business to benefit from CSR." These five strategic dimensions can be useful for assessing the contribution of strategic CSR to value creation:

- *Centrality* refers to a measure of closeness of fit between between a CSR strategy or initiative and the organization's mission and goals. CSR strategies or initiatives with a high level of centrality are likely to receive high priority within the organization's management, to align with the organization's core competencies and to yield future benefits.
- *Specificity* refers to the organization's ability to internalize the benefits of a CSR strategy or initiative, instead of creating a collective good which can be shared by others within the industry, the community or wider society. CSR strategies or initiatives with a high level of specificity (e.g. related to cost savings or patentable products) are likely to result in value creation.
- *Proactivity* refers to the degree to which behavior is planned in anticipation of trends in the external business environment and in the absence of crisis conditions. An organization that recognizes business opportunities related to new social and environmental trends early is likely to be in a better position to create value.
- *Voluntarism* refers to the scope of discretionary decision-making within the organization and the absence of externally imposed compliance requirements, which is closely related to proactivity. A high level of voluntarism (e.g. exceeding the existing anti-pollution regulatory standards or providing higher levels of employee care, compared with industry standards) is more likely to result in value creation.
- *Visibility* refers to the degree of observability of a CSR activity and the organization's ability to gain recognition from stakeholders. Value creation can result from both a high level of visibility to external stakeholders (e.g. related to customer loyalty or enhanced public perception of product reliability) and a high level of visibility to internal stakeholders (e.g. related to improved productivity or better employee motivation).

Strategic management of these five dimensions in search of a competitive advantage can consequently translate into value creation, which – in the words of Burke and Logsdon (1996: 499) – constitutes "the ultimate measure of strategic benefits from CSR activities." Several more recent studies explicitly apply the Burke and Logsdon framework for considering value creation from strategic CSR (Husted and Allen 2007; Sirsly and Lamertz 2008; Bruyaka et al. 2013).

CSR and innovation

Value creation occurs when an organization's resources are combined in new ways to increase the value of these resources. Thus, Husted and Allen (2007: 597) have argued, with reference to CSR, "value creation is necessarily about innovation" and the main benefit of strategic CSR is in helping firms to find new ways to grow and develop. According to Blowfield and Murray (2008: 152), the authors of a leading CSR textbook, CSR strategies should be treated as a "critical link in innovation and learning."

Several studies show that CSR strategies can lead to business innovations (Bhatnagar and Cohen 1997; Kanter 1999; Wagner 2010; Bocquet et al. 2013). CSR-related innovations are particularly concentrated in two areas: environmental improvements and local community development. According to a study of 129 CSR-related innovations (Louche et al. 2010), the key areas of innovation were related to environmental sustainability (34 percent), poverty and hunger (18 percent) and partnerships for development (17 percent). (The last two areas are directly related to corporate activities in local communities.)

The biggest opportunities for innovation arguably arise with regards to environmental improvements, such as reduction in the use of materials and emissions, recycling and other eco-friendly practices, because they potentially generate considerable win–win outcomes (SustainAbility 2001, 2002). For instance, a study by Sharma and Vredenburg (1998) compared seven Canadian oil companies and found that the two that were most proactive on environmental improvements greatly benefited from related innovations, such as technology patents in the areas of process improvement, sulfur-dioxide recovery, waste reduction and disposal, soil restoration, and less polluting fuels. In turn, innovations helped the development of new revenue streams for those companies, such as sales of less polluting fuels. As another example, a more recent study by Davis (2010) assessed strategic CSR among Japanese companies. While the study found that most Japanese companies lack proactive CSR strategies, it showed that Ito-Yokado, a large Japanese supermarket chain, was handsomely rewarded from introducing an innovative branded system for product traceability within its food supply chain as part of an attempt to reassure consumers of the safety of its products, which resulted in improvements in product quality, access to new sources of knowledge and innovations in farming, improved customer feedback and enhanced customer satisfaction.

Another important area of innovation is the development of new products and services targeted at low-income customers in emerging economies, known as "bottom-of-the-pyramid" strategies (Prahalad and Hammond 2002; Prahalad 2005; Wilson and Wilson 2006). The underlying assumption here is that global products of multinational firms are often too expensive or unsuited for the low-end market of four billion consumers who live on less than $2000 a year. New business models for targeting poor consumers suggest that private firms can help reduce poverty and make profits at the same time. Most notably, Prahalad (2005, 2012) has demonstrated that multinational firms have tapped into new sources of innovation when developing products specifically targeted at poor consumers in emerging markets, such as Unilever's micronutrients and other health products or a GE Healthcare battery-operated electrocardiogram machine developed for use in rural India. These products potentially allow poor people to improve their health or simply access new consumer goods, while helping multinational firms to broaden their markets in often poor neighborhoods in countries such as India and Brazil.

These examples imply that innovation depends on the area of activity and the industry sector. Studies on strategic CSR and innovation suggest that a company should align its social and environmental strategies with its core competencies in order to maximize innovation (Kanter 1999; Porter and Kramer 2006). Indeed, successful innovating companies such as the above-mentioned Ito-Yokado and Unilever focus on social and environmental issues that allow them to leverage their core competencies. One could generalize, for example, that chemicals and petroleum companies that are focused on engineering solutions are in an advantageous position to develop eco-engineering innovations; large retail chains are in an advantageous position to develop supply chain innovations; and consumer product manufacturers are in an advantageous position to develop new consumer products aimed at poor people. Strategic CSR requires specialist skills and capabilities already within the company; in turn, these skills and capabilities are upgraded as a result of being used in a new, different context.

CSR and competitive advantage – case-study illustrations

The achievement of sustainable competitive advantage through CSR may be difficult to achieve in practice for many companies because many types of socially responsible activity may not be costly to imitate for competitors. For example, in the coffee shop sector, the adoption of fair trade has become a key high-profile indicator of a responsible firm, and leading coffee shop chains, such as Starbucks and Costa, have widely adopted fair trade coffee in their outlets. However, the competitive advantages resulting from this adoption by first movers proved to be temporary as other companies were able to imitate the approach (Falkenberg and Brunsael 2011). As another example, BP's initiatives on climate change in the late 1990s and early 2000s helped the company to differentiate itself from its competitors, save significant costs through decreased gas flaring and stimulate innovation. However, the competitive advantages ultimately proved to be temporary as other oil companies, such as Shell, Exxon and Chevron, soon supported policies such as greenhouse-gas emission reductions (Frynas 2009).

These two examples raise the question of how a company can genuinely gain and maintain a sustainable competitive advantage through strategic CSR. I will use the examples of fair trade in global coffee shop chains and climate change initiatives in the oil and gas sector as brief illustrations of the applicability of the VRIO framework. For each case, I have selected three companies for illustrative purposes.

Fair trade in coffee shop chains in the UK

Background

Fair trade is a concept intended to improve the welfare of small-scale producers in developing economies by providing "fair" prices (often guaranteed minimum prices) for producers and by abiding by certain social and environmental rules, albeit there are different fair trade models with varying rules (Tallontire 2000; Macdonald 2007). Coffee is now the most popular fair trade product, although the coffee shop chain conversion to fair trade was gradual and initially reluctant. In the late 1990s, Starbucks came under pressure from activists to introduce fair trade coffee. In the company's home market the US Organic Consumers Association (OCA) called for a boycott of the chain until it agreed to stock fair trade coffee in all of its outlets. Starbucks duly introduced its own CAFÉ Practices fair trade pilot program in 2001, which was launched throughout the company in 2002. However, UK activist groups continued to criticize Starbucks, and the OCA boycott call remained in place until 2006.

Since then, fair trade has become a widely adopted and visible CSR initiative among coffee shop chains in the UK. Since 2009, all Starbucks coffee sold in the UK has been fairly traded and Starbucks has become the largest buyer of fair trade coffee in the world. Similarly, the largest coffee shop chain in the UK – Costa – has introduced fair trade coffee. Since 2010, all of its coffee has been Rainforest Alliance certified.

However, the fair trade initiatives of all of the large coffee chains have been criticized for their lack of comprehensiveness. For instance, Costa's Rainforest Alliance certification label only guarantees that 30 percent of the coffee beans in a particular product have been certified. Meanwhile, Starbucks' coffee is not independently certified at all, and, more importantly, the company has been accused of double standards as it has performed poorly on other CSR dimensions (e.g. its anti-trade union stance and low wages for staff).

AMT Coffee was an early adopter of fair trade coffee in the UK when it decided to become 100 percent fair trade in 2004, and the company has gone much further than either Costa or Starbucks by also stocking 100 percent fair trade tea and organic milk (not just 100 percent fair trade coffee) and introducing a range of other fair trade and sustainable products, including juices and snacks. In a 2011 ranking of eight UK coffee shop chains by Ethical Consumer, AMT Coffee was ranked top in terms of its overall ethical and environmental performance, while Starbucks was ranked bottom. Yet AMT Coffee remains a niche player: it has about 60 outlets in the UK, compared with approximately 1600 Costas and 700-plus Starbucks (2013 figures).

VRIO framework

IS A FAIR TRADE LABEL VALUABLE FOR COFFEE SHOP CHAINS?

Fair trade is valuable in terms of promoting a positive customer image and deflecting the key past ethical criticism of coffee shop chains. It might also help to increase sales. Consumer behaviour studies have specifically shown that consumers have a strong preference for fair trade coffee over conventional coffee and are willing to pay a premium for certified fair trade coffee (Rotaris and Danielis 2011; Stratton and Werner 2013). This is supported by the continued commitment to fair trade among the two biggest UK coffee shop chains – Starbucks and Costa – for whom fair trade is a core part of their strategic CSR. Competitors such as Caffè Nero and Coffee Republic that do not have any fair trade certification promote themselves as paying a "fair" price for their coffee, and thereby try to benefit from the positive association with fair trade.

IS A FAIR TRADE LABEL RARE AMONG COFFEE SHOP CHAINS?

Fair trade coffee is not rare. While Caffè Nero and Coffee Republic do not offer fair trade coffee, the two main UK chains and a few smaller players, such as Pret A Manger, AMT Coffee and Soho Coffee, do. However, AMT Coffee's approach of offering a wide range of fair trade and organic products, in addition to coffee, is relatively rare. In other words, a fair trade label does not offer significant scope for differentiation, although specificity is higher for the broader approach adopted by AMT Coffee.

IS A FAIR TRADE LABEL DIFFICULT TO IMITATE AMONG COFFEE SHOP CHAINS?

Fair trade adoption is easy to imitate, as it does not involve substantial firm-specific capabilities. There are multiple providers of fair trade certifications, each with varying rules, including Fairtrade International, 4C Association, UTZ Certified and Rainforest Alliance. An imitator company may choose the certification scheme with which it finds easiest to comply. However,

AMT Coffee's approach is more difficult to imitate as it relies on a full range of fair trade and organic products, and reinforces its ethical appeal through a number of other unusual and publicized initiatives, such as withdrawing Nestlé's KitKat from its outlets as an unethical choice and using only free-range eggs in its sandwiches.

IS A FAIR TRADE LABEL EXPLOITED BY THE ORGANIZATION?

The fair trade label is widely exploited by Starbucks, Costa and AMT Coffee. All three companies promote fair trade very prominently on their websites – each website has a section devoted specifically to "ethics" or "responsible coffee," where fair trade is the key highlighted issue. Fair trade is also present in other publicity materials. In 2012, Starbucks notably launched an integrated advertising campaign that prominently featured fair trade. This comprised TV adverts and a promotional offer of a free fair trade brownie with every purchase of Starbucks fair trade coffee. (AMT Coffee had run a similar promotional campaign three years earlier.)

DOES A FAIR TRADE LABEL OFFER A SUSTAINABLE COMPETITIVE ADVANTAGE?

Coffee is a key input for all coffee shop chains and any product improvements may be seen as aligned with the companies' goals and capabilities, while a fair trade label is seen as a key indicator of social responsibility among coffee shop chains and can create value. However, application of the VRIO dimensions suggests that a fair trade label does not currently offer significant differentiation for large chains. In contrast, AMT Coffee's approach is more differentiated and more difficult to imitate than those of the other companies. It is also able to exploit the opportunities of fair trade with its distinctive ethical stance and close alignment with the company's mission and customer appeal. Therefore, fair trade may constitute the basis for AMT Coffee's sustainable competitive advantage as a niche player. However, its approach might ultimately be imitated by competitors, as the company's small size and relatively little-known brand offer little protection against larger competitors.

Climate change initiatives in global oil companies

Background

Climate change is the key environmental sustainability issue globally, and reductions in greenhouse-gas emissions are regarded as a key indicator of sustainability among companies. However, historically, there has been a varying degree of responsiveness among oil companies to addressing climate change concerns (Rowlands 2000; Levy and Kolk 2002; Skjaerseth and Skodvin 2003). For instance, Exxon denied the validity of scientific evidence on climate change and opposed any mandatory reductions in greenhouse-gas emissions for a long time. In stark contrast, in 1997 BP set itself the target of reducing greenhouse-gas emissions from its own facilities by 10 percent from 1990 levels by 2010. Three years later, it introduced an internal emissions trading system to achieve emissions reductions, whereby each of the company's 150 business units was assigned a target for the emission of greenhouse gases and a number of "permits," which the business units were able to trade between themselves. Thanks to the trading system, which introduced incentives for pursuing the most cost-effective methods for emission reductions, BP was able to attain its reduction objective nine years early, at the end of 2001. Thereafter, the company made further progress on emission reductions.

Its greenhouse-gas emissions declined by a further 22 percent between 2002 and 2006, while the company's oil production increased in the same period.

Since then, climate change initiatives have become a widely adopted and visible CSR priority among all the major global oil companies. Exxon has finally accepted the importance of climate change and reduced its greenhouse-gas emissions by 6.5 percent between 2009 and 2012. At the same time, BP lost its climate change leadership in the industry, which had depended largely on the enthusiasm of the company's CEO John Browne (in that post between 1995 and 2007). Its proactive strategy quickly dissipated when Browne was replaced by a new CEO who placed less emphasis on leadership in climate change. Today, neither Exxon nor BP could claim to use climate change initiatives for competitive differentiation.

In contrast, the Norwegian state-owned Statoil explicitly uses strategic CSR to pursue competitive advantages and aims to be a CSR best-practice company in the global oil and gas sector. Firm-specific capabilities have helped the company to obtain competitive advantages. For example, robust health, safety and environment (HSE) training provision previously helped Statoil to obtain a commercial foothold in Iraq's oil sector, while its forging of responsible local community relations in Norway and Canada helped it to operate successfully in Alaska. Statoil's mission statement starts with a commitment "to accommodate the world's energy needs in a responsible manner" and the company's vision is very simple: "crossing energy frontiers." Statoil has set itself a strategic objective of being an industry leader in carbon efficiency. While its oil and gas production (and hence total greenhouse-gas emissions) has been rising, it has one of the lowest rates of carbon-dioxide emissions per unit of production in the global oil and gas sector (46 tonnes per 1000 tonnes of hydrocarbon production in 2010, compared with a European average of 74 tonnes, a global average of 133 tonnes and a North American average of 166 tonnes).

The VRIO framework

ARE CLIMATE CHANGE INITIATIVES VALUABLE FOR GLOBAL OIL COMPANIES?

Climate change initiatives are valuable in terms of promoting a positive image of the company and significant savings related to energy efficiency. Studies tend to show a positive and significant relationship between environmental performance and financial performance (e.g. King and Lenox 2002; Molina-Azorín et al. 2009) and specifically postulate firm-specific advantages from proactive climate change initiatives (e.g. Boiral 2006; Frynas 2009). Following the twelve-month operation of the carbon emission trading scheme in 2000–1, BP estimated that the company was able to save US$650 million through decreased natural gas venting and flaring, either by selling the natural gas or by increased energy efficiency (Victor and House 2006) and one can expect other oil companies to benefit similarly from climate change initiatives.

ARE CLIMATE CHANGE INITIATIVES RARE AMONG GLOBAL OIL COMPANIES?

Climate change initiatives are common among the large global oil companies, and key competitors such as Shell and Chevron have invested in this area. However, beyond energy efficiency and gas flaring measures, there have been some distinctive features of climate change initiatives. BP (like its key rival Shell) invested in renewable energy from the late 1990s and used the marketing slogan "Beyond Petroleum," although renewable energy was never close to BP's core competencies and it is not a global leader in biofuels or wind energy.

Neither BP nor Exxon can claim leadership on climate change today, while Statoil has a strategic objective of being an industry leader in carbon efficiency and regards "carbon capture and storage" (a process of safely capturing and storing carbon dioxide underground in order to prevent it from entering the atmosphere) as a major potential business opportunity. There is no existing market for carbon storage and it is not yet certain that the technology will be widely used in future, hence Statoil's long-standing significant investment in this technology is relatively unusual and pioneering.

ARE CLIMATE CHANGE INITIATIVES DIFFICULT TO IMITATE AMONG GLOBAL OIL COMPANIES?

Most energy efficiency measures related to greenhouse-gas reductions, such as measures related to the reduction of methane venting or improvements to plant and equipment, are relatively easy to imitate. In contrast, Statoil's carbon capture and storage (CCS) technology is leading edge in this field globally and is more difficult to imitate. Statoil's investment in CCS dates back to the 1990s and Statoil participated in key innovative partnerships related to CCS, owns CCS facilities in Norway and Algeria, and built the world's first liquefied natural gas (LNG) plant with a CCS facility in Norway. It would be costly to match Statoil's investment and capabilities in CCS. However, other global oil companies have huge financial resources at their disposal and are already investing in this area; notably, Chevron is working on a gas project in Australia which will become the world's largest saline reservoir carbon-dioxide injection facility when completed.

ARE CLIMATE CHANGE INITIATIVES EXPLOITED BY THE ORGANIZATION?

Exxon, BP and Statoil all exploit climate change initiatives widely. The three companies promote their climate change initiatives very prominently on their websites and in their annual sustainability reports. They are also taking advantage of opportunities for energy efficiency savings. Statoil's long-standing investment in CCS is probably the most significant distinctive capability, but all three companies are working on research and development related to climate change (e.g. Exxon opened a new research facility on algae-based biofuels in 2010).

DO CLIMATE CHANGE INITIATIVES OFFER A SUSTAINABLE COMPETITIVE ADVANTAGE?

Just as climate change initiatives are seen as a key indicator of social responsibility among oil companies and can create value, application of the VRIO dimensions suggests that climate change initiatives do not offer considerable opportunities for differentiation for most oil companies. For all oil companies, including Exxon and BP, climate change initiatives are arguably fundamentally misaligned with their main function of producing hydrocarbon resources, which emit greenhouse gases and contribute to global warming. Statoil's commitment to climate change initiatives is somewhat more aligned with its wider obligations to society, given that it is a 63 percent state-owned national oil company, and is aligned with the company's vision of being the CSR best-practice company in its sector. Its CCS investment is more differentiated and more difficult to imitate than the climate change initiatives of other oil companies. However, CCS might ultimately be imitated by competitors with considerable financial resources. They have the capacity to commit billions of dollars to any new technology and are already starting to experiment with CCS themselves.

Discussion

It is evident that CSR is not merely a reaction to external pressures; companies also use it proactively for strategic purposes. The RBV can help towards conceptualizing CSR in the same way as it conceptualizes companies' resources and capabilities related to technology or marketing. Today's global companies face strong competitive pressures and they may use any available methods to create value and gain a competitive advantage over their rivals, including the use of strategic CSR.

The literature review in this chapter and the two case vignettes demonstrate that strategic CSR can contribute to value creation. The literature demonstrates that there are many organizational benefits of strategic CSR, including innovation, and empirical studies tend to show a positive correlation between CSR and financial performance. In the case vignettes, the CSR initiatives of all six companies have contributed to value creation.

At the same time, the case vignettes demonstrate that obtaining a sustainable competitive advantage through strategic CSR is much more difficult to achieve. AMT Coffee and Statoil have developed distinctive strategic CSR capabilities. However, these capabilities might ultimately be imitated by wealthier competitors in the future. Starbucks is already attempting to gravitate towards AMT Coffee's approach (e.g. by introducing a wider range of fair trade products and investing in marketing itself as an ethical consumer choice), while Chevron and other global oil companies are gravitating towards Statoil's approach (notably by investing in CCS research and experimenting with new CCS facilities). The example of BP after the departure of John Browne, or the well-known example of The Bodyshop after the departure of Anita Roddick, illustrates that a sustainable competitive advantage through strategic CSR can dissipate rapidly once the key architect of the firm's strategic CSR leaves the company.

Conclusion and future research directions

Linkages between strategic CSR, value creation and competitive advantage require much more careful conceptualization and much more in-depth research. One can identify at least three key directions for future research.

Managerial process

Given the demonstrated importance of entrepreneurship (e.g. Spear 2006; Baron 2007; Dixon and Clifford 2007) and the role of innovation (e.g. Lanjouw and Mody 1996; Kanter 1999; Porter and Kramer 2006) for firm-level CSR strategies, future research needs to go further in unpacking the managerial process that is behind strategic CSR. While many studies explore a positive correlation between CSR and different organizational outcomes or the relevance of CSR-related capabilities or the importance of leadership for CSR, there is very little research on how CSR-related firm-specific capabilities are conceptualized, acquired and developed by top managers. This may be partly related to the limitations of the RBV (the main instrumental perspective on CSR), which has been criticized in general for treating processes by which resources and capabilities are deployed as a "black box" (Kraaijenbrink et al. 2010: 356) and largely confining the role of managers to sorting "among the firm's resources to see if any conform to the criteria" that resources must meet in order to yield rents in equilibrium, rather than "*creating* strategic resources" (Foss 2012: n.p.; original emphasis). Future studies may either apply the RBV in new ways or apply other theoretical perspectives in order to unpack the managerial process behind strategic CSR.

Individual level of analysis

Closely related to the previous argument, most applications of CSR have focused on the macro and meso levels of analysis but have failed to explain strategic CSR adequately at the individual level of analysis. In a recent survey of 181 papers on CSR, Aguinis and Glavas (2012) found that only 4 percent focused on the individual level of analysis, while 57 percent focused on the organizational level and 33 percent focused on the institutional level. The literature linking the RBV and CSR ignores the significance of individuals, as argued by one of its earliest proponents: "Socially complex resources depend upon large numbers of people or teams engaged in coordinated action such that few individuals, if any, have sufficient breadth of knowledge to grasp the overall phenomenon" (Hart 1995: 989). In general, the RBV has been criticized for failing to recognize "the role of the individual judgments or mental models of entrepreneurs and managers" (Kraaijenbrink et al. 2010: 356) sufficiently. Future studies may potentially apply the RBV with regards to the individual level (for instance, exploring how social and environmental capabilities are conceptualized by individual managers within an organization).

Multi-level and multi-theory studies

The literature review and the case vignettes in this chapter demonstrate that a company's CSR approach is a mixture of reactive and proactive elements. Firms partly adopt CSR in response to isomorphic or stakeholder pressures and partly adopt proactive CSR strategies in order to exploit opportunities for value creation. Strategic CSR may be an outcome of factors at different levels of analysis: the macro level (e.g. government tax incentives), the meso level (e.g. specific business opportunities) and the individual level (e.g. cognition of individual CEOs). Therefore, future studies may benefit from multi-theory and multi-level approaches. Indeed, multi-theory studies that apply a combination of institutional theory and the RBV have recently been on the rise (Branco and Rodrigues 2008; Menguc et al. 2010; Escobar and Vredenburg 2011; Aguilera-Caracuel et al. 2012; Lin 2012; Lourenço et al. 2012; Perego and Kolk 2012; Arevalo et al. 2013), although none of these has addressed the individual level of analysis.

In conclusion, future research on strategic CSR should usefully provide more systematic assessments of the managerial process and the importance of the individual level of analysis behind strategic CSR and of the interactions between different CSR predictors, mediators and moderators at different levels of analysis, applying multi-theory approaches.

References

Accenture. 2013. *The UN Global Compact – Accenture CEO Study on Sustainability 2013 – Architects of a Better World*. Available at: www.accenture.com/SiteCollectionDocuments/PDF/Accenture-UN-Global-Compact-Acn-CEO-Study-Sustainability-2013.PDF (accessed December 8, 2014).

Aguilera-Caracuel, J., Aragón-Correa, J., Hurtado-Torres, N. and Rugman, A. 2012. The effects of institutional distance and headquarters' financial performance on the generation of environmental standards in multinational companies. *Journal of Business Ethics* 105(4): 461–74.

Aguinis, H. and Glavas, A. 2012. What we know and don't know about corporate social responsibility: a review and research agenda. *Journal of Management* 38(4): 932–68.

Arevalo, J. A., Aravind, D., Ayuso, S. and Roca, M. 2013. The Global Compact: an analysis of the motivations of adoption in the Spanish context. *Business Ethics: A European Review* 22(1): 1–15.

Barney, J. B. 1997. *Gaining and Sustaining Competitive Advantage*. Reading, MA: Addison-Wesley.

Baron, D. 2001. Private politics, corporate social responsibility and integrated strategy. *Journal of Economics and Management Strategy* 10: 7–45.

— 2007. Corporate social responsibility and social entrepreneurship. *Journal of Economics and Management Strategy* 16(3): 683–717.

Baron, D. and Diermeier, D. 2007. Strategic activism and nonmarket strategy. *Journal of Economics and Management Strategy* 16(3): 599–634.

Baskin, J. 2006. Corporate responsibility in emerging markets. *Journal of Corporate Citizenship* 24: 29–47.

Berrone, P., Cruz, C., Gomez-Mejia, L. R. and Larraza-Kintana, M. 2010. Socioemotional wealth and corporate responses to institutional pressures: do family-controlled firms pollute less? *Administrative Science Quarterly* 55: 82–113.

Bhatnagar, S. and Cohen, M. A. 1997. *The Impact of Environmental Regulation on Innovation: A Panel Data Study*. Nashville, TN: Owen Graduate School of Management, Vanderbilt University.

Blowfield, M. and Frynas, J. G. 2005. Setting new agendas: critical perspectives on corporate social responsibility in the developing world. *International Affairs* 81(3): 499–513.

Blowfield, M. and Murray, A. 2008. *Corporate Responsibility – A Critical Introduction*. Oxford: Oxford University Press.

Bocquet, R., Le Bas, C., Mothe, C. and Poussing, N. 2013. Are firms with different CSR profiles equally innovative? Empirical analysis with survey data. *European Management Journal* 31(6): 642–54.

Boiral, O. 2006. Global warming: should companies adopt a proactive strategy? *Long Range Planning* 39(3): 315–30.

Bragdon, J. H., Jr. and Marlin, J. A. T. 1972. Is pollution profitable? *Risk Management* 19(4): 9–18.

Brammer, S. and Millington, A. 2004. The development of corporate charitable contributions in the UK: a stakeholder analysis. *Journal of Management Studies* 41(8): 1411–34.

Brammer, S., Jackson, G. and Matten, D. 2012. Corporate social responsibility and institutional theory: new perspectives on private governance. *Socio-Economic Review* 10: 3–28.

Branco, M. C. and Rodrigues, L. L. 2006. Corporate social responsibility and resource-based perspectives. *Journal of Business Ethics* 69(2): 111–32.

— 2008. Factors influencing social responsibility disclosure by Portuguese companies. *Journal of Business Ethics* 83(4): 685–701.

Brekke, K. A. and Nyborg, K. 2008. Attracting responsible employees: green production as labor market screening. *Resource and Energy Economics* 30(4): 509–26.

Bremmers, H., Omta, O., Kemp, R. and Haverkamp, D.-J. 2007. Do stakeholder groups influence environmental management system development in the Dutch agri-food sector? *Business Strategy and the Environment* 16: 214–31.

Bruyaka, O., Zeitzmann, H., Chalamon, I., Wokutch, R. and Pooja, T. 2013. Strategic corporate social responsibility and orphan drug development: insights from the US and the EU biopharmaceutical industry. *Journal of Business Ethics* 117(1): 45–65.

Burke, L. and Logsdon, J. M. 1996. How corporate social responsibility pays off. *Long Range Planning* 29(4): 495–502.

Buysse, K. and Verbeke, A. 2003. Proactive environmental strategies: a stakeholder management perspective. *Strategic Management Journal* 24(5): 453–70.

Carroll, A. B. 1999. Corporate social responsibility: evolution of a definitional construct. *Business and Society* 38: 268–95.

Carroll, A. B. and Shabana, K. M. 2010. The business case for corporate social responsibility: a review of concepts, research and practice. *International Journal of Management Reviews* 12(1): 85–105.

Child, J. and Tsai, T. 2005. The dynamic between firms' environmental strategies and institutional constraints in emerging economies: evidence from China and Taiwan. *Journal of Management Studies* 42(1): 95–125.

Davis, S. 2010. Strategic CSR in the Japanese context: from business risk to market creation. In C. Louche, S. O. Idowu and W. L. Filho (eds.), *Innovative CSR: From Risk Management to Value Creation*. Sheffield: Greenleaf: 374–97.

Dixon, S. E. A. and Clifford, A. 2007. Ecopreneurship: a new approach to managing the triple bottom line. *Journal of Organizational Change Management* 20(3): 326–45.

Doh, J. P. and Guay, T. R. 2006. Corporate social responsibility, public policy, and NGO activism in Europe and the United States: an institutional-stakeholder perspective. *Journal of Management Studies* 43(1): 47–73.

Donaldson, T. and Preston, L. E. 1995. The stakeholder theory of the corporation: concepts, evidence, and implications. *Academy of Management Review* 20(1): 65–91.

Egels-Zandén, N. and Sandberg, J. 2009. Distinctions in descriptive and instrumental stakeholder theory: a challenge for empirical research. *Business Ethics: A European Review* 19(1): 35–49.

Escobar, L. F. and Vredenburg, H. 2011. Multinational oil companies and the adoption of sustainable development: a resource-based and institutional theory interpretation of adoption heterogeneity. *Journal of Business Ethics* 98(1): 39–65.

Ethical Consumer. 2011. Free shopping guide to coffee shops. Manchester: Ethical Consumer.

Fairchild, R. 2008. The manufacturing sector's environmental motives: a game-theoretic analysis. *Journal of Business Ethics* 79(3): 333–44.

Falkenberg, J. and Brunsael, P. 2011. Corporate social responsibility: a strategic advantage or a strategic necessity? *Journal of Business Ethics* 99(Supp. 1): 9–16.

Farjoun, M. 2002. Towards an organic perspective on strategy. *Strategic Management Journal* 23(7): 561–94.

Foss, N. J. 2012. Entrepreneurship in the context of the resource-based view of the firm. In K. Mole and M. Ram (eds.), *Perspectives in Entrepreneurship: A Critical Approach*. New York: Palgrave Macmillan: 120–33.

Frynas, J. G. 2009. *Beyond Corporate Social Responsibility: Oil Multinationals and Social Challenges*. Cambridge: Cambridge University Press.

Gray, R., Owen, D. and Adams, C. 1996. *Accounting and Accountability*. London, New York: Prentice-Hall.

Hart, S. L. 1995. A natural resource-based view of the firm. *Academy of Management Review* 20: 986–1014.

Husted, B. W. and Allen, D. B. 2006. Corporate social responsibility in the multinational enterprise: strategic and institutional approaches. *Journal of International Business Studies* 37(6): 838–49.

— 2007. Strategic corporate social responsibility and value creation among large firms. *Long Range Planning* 40: 594–610.

Husted, B. W. and de Jesus Salazar, J. 2006. Taking Friedman seriously: maximizing profits and social performance. *Journal of Management Studies* 43(1): 75–91.

Jennings, P. and Zandbergen, P. 1995. Ecologically sustainable organizations: an institutional approach. *Academy of Management Review* 20: 1015–52.

Johnson, R. A. and Greening, D. W. 1999. The effects of corporate governance and institutional ownership types on corporate social performance. *Academy of Management Journal* 42: 564–76.

Kanter, R. M. 1999. From spare change to real change: the social sector as beta site for business innovation. *Harvard Business Review* 77(3): 122–32.

— 2008. Transforming giants. *Harvard Business Review* 86(1): 43–52.

King, A. and Lenox, M. 2002. Exploring the locus of profitable pollution reduction. *Management Science* 48: 289–99.

Kotler, P. and Lee, N. 2005. *Corporate Social Responsibility: Doing the Most Good for Your Company and Your Cause*. Hoboken, NJ: John Wiley and Sons.

Kraaijenbrink, J., Spender, J.-C. and Groen, A. J. 2010. The resource-based view: a review and assessment of its critiques. *Journal of Management* 36(1): 349–72.

Lamberti, L. and Lettieri, E. 2009. CSR practices and corporate strategy: evidence from a longitudinal case study. *Journal of Business Ethics* 87: 153–68.

Lanjouw, J. O. and Mody, A. 1996. Innovation and the international diffusion of environmentally responsive technology. *Research Policy* 25: 549–71.

Laplume, A. O., Sonpar, K. and Litz, R. A. 2008. Stakeholder theory: reviewing a theory that moves us. *Journal of Management* 34(6): 1152–89.

Levy, D. L. and Kolk, A. 2002. Strategic responses to global climate change: conflicting pressures on multinationals in the oil industry. *Business and Politics* 4(3): 275–300.

Lin, H. 2012. Strategic alliances for environmental improvements. *Business and Society* 51(2): 335–48.

Lockett, A., Moon, J. and Visser, W. 2006. Corporate social responsibility in management research: focus, nature, salience and sources of influence. *Journal of Management Studies* 43(1): 115–36.

Louche, C., Idowu, S. O. and Filho, W. L. 2010. Innovation in corporate social responsibility: how innovative is it? An exploratory study of 129 global innovative CSR solutions. In C. Louche, S. O. Idowu and W. L. Filho (eds.), *Innovative CSR: From Risk Management to Value Creation*. Sheffield: Greenleaf: 284–304.

Lourenço, I., Branco, M., Curto, J. and Eugenio, T. 2012. How does the market value corporate sustainability performance? *Journal of Business Ethics* 109(1): 417–28.

Macdonald, K. 2007. Globalising justice within coffee supply chains? Fair trade, Starbucks and the transformation of supply chain governance. *Third World Quarterly* 28(4): 793–812.

Marcus, A. A. and Anderson, M. H. 2006. A general dynamic capability: does it propagate business and social competencies in the retail food industry? *Journal of Management Studies* 43(1): 19–46.

Margolis, J. D. and Walsh, J. P. 2003. Misery loves companies: rethinking social initiatives by business. *Administrative Science Quarterly* 48(2): 268–305.

Matten, D. and Crane, A. 2005. Corporate citizenship: towards an extended theoretical conceptualization. *Academy of Management Review* 30(1): 166–79.

Matten, D. and Moon, J. 2008. "Implicit" and "explicit" CSR: a conceptual framework for a comparative understanding of corporate social responsibility. *Academy of Management Review* 33(2): 404–24.

McWilliams, A. and Siegel, D. S. 2001. Corporate social responsibility: a theory of the firm perspective. *Academy of Management Review* 26: 117–27.

— 2011. Creating and capturing value: strategic corporate social responsibility, resource-based theory, and sustainable competitive advantage. *Journal of Management* 37(5): 1480–95.

Menguc, B. and Ozanne, L. 2005. Challenges of the "green imperative": a natural resource-based approach to the environmental orientation–business performance relationship. *Journal of Business Research* 58(4): 430–8.

Menguc, B., Auh, S. and Ozanne, L. 2010. The interactive effect of internal and external factors on a proactive environmental strategy and its influence on a firm's performance. *Journal of Business Ethics* 94(2): 279–98.

Molina-Azorín, J. F., Tarí, J. J., Claver-Cortés, E. and López-Gamero, M. D. 2009. Quality management, environmental management and firm performance: a review of empirical studies and issues of integration. *International Journal of Management Reviews* 11(2): 197–222.

Moskowitz, M. 1972. Choosing socially responsible stocks. *Business and Society Review* 1: 71–5.

Newbert, S. L. 2008. Value, rareness, competitive advantage, and performance: a conceptual-level empirical investigation of the resource-based view of the firm. *Strategic Management Journal* 29(7): 745–68.

Oliver, C. and Holzinger, I. 2008. The effectiveness of strategic political management: a dynamic capabilities framework. *Academy of Management Review* 33(2): 496–520.

Padgett, R. C. and Galan, J. I. 2010. The effect of R&D intensity on corporate social responsibility. *Journal of Business Ethics* 93(3): 407–18.

Perego, P. and Kolk, A. 2012. Multinationals' accountability on sustainability: the evolution of third-party assurance of sustainability reports. *Journal of Business Ethics* 110(2): 173–90.

Peters, M., Siller, L. and Matzler, K. 2011. The resource-based and the market-based approaches to cultural tourism in Alpine destinations. *Journal of Sustainable Tourism* 19(7): 877–93.

Polonsky, M. and Jevons, C. 2009. Global branding and strategic CSR: an overview of three types of complexity. *International Marketing Review* 26(3): 327–47.

Porter, M. E. and Kramer, M. R. 2006. Strategy and society: the link between competitive advantage and corporate social responsibility. *Harvard Business Review* 84(12): 78–92.

Prahalad, C. K. 2005. *The Fortune at the Bottom of the Pyramid: Eradicating Poverty through Profits*. Upper Saddle River, NJ: Wharton School Publishing.

— 2012. Bottom of the pyramid as a source of breakthrough innovations. *Journal of Product Innovation Management* 29(1): 6–12.

Prahalad, C. K. and Hammond, A. 2002. Serving the world's poor, profitably. *Harvard Business Review* 80(9): 48–57.

Priem, R. L. and Butler, J. E. 2001. Is the resource-based "view" a useful perspective for strategic management research? *Academy of Management Review* 26(1): 22–40.

Rangan, K., Chase, L. A. and Karim, S. 2012. *Why Every Company Needs a CSR Strategy and How to Build It*. Harvard Business School Working Paper 12–088, April 5.

Rotaris, L. and Danielis, R. 2011. Willingness to pay for fair trade coffee: a conjoint analysis experiment with Italian consumers. *Journal of Agricultural and Food Industrial Organization* 9(1): 1–22.

Rowlands, I. H. 2000. Beauty and the beast? BP's and Exxon's positions on global climate change. *Environment and Planning C* 18: 339–54.

Runhaar, H. and Lafferty, H. 2009. Governing corporate social responsibility: an assessment of the contribution of the UN Global Compact to CSR strategies in the telecommunications industry. *Journal of Business Ethics* 84(4): 479–95.

Russo, M. V. and Fouts, P. A. 1997. A resource-based perspective on corporate environmental performance and profitability. *Academy of Management Journal* 40(3): 534–9.

Sharma, S. and Vredenburg, H. 1998. Proactive corporate environmental strategy and the development of competitively valuable organizational capabilities. *Strategic Management Journal* 19: 729–53.

Siegel, D. S. and Vitaliano, D. F. 2007. An empirical analysis of the strategic use of corporate social responsibility. *Journal of Economics and Management Strategy* 16(3): 773–92.

Sirsly, C.-A. T. and Lamertz, K. 2008. When does a corporate social responsibility initiative provide a first-mover advantage? *Business and Society* 47(3): 343–69.

Skjaerseth, J. B. and Skodvin, T. 2003. *Climate Change and the Oil Industry: Common Problem, Varying Strategies.* New York: Manchester University Press.

Spear, R. 2006. Social entrepreneurship: a different model? *International Journal of Social Economics* 33(5/6): 399–410.

Stratton, J. P. and Werner, M. J. 2013. Consumer behavior analysis of fair trade coffee: evidence from field research. *Psychological Record* 63(2): 363–74.

SustainAbility. 2001. *Buried Treasure: Uncovering the Business Case for Corporate Sustainability.* London: SustainAbility and United Nations Environment Programme.

— 2002. *Developing Value: The Business Case for Sustainability in Emerging Markets.* London: SustainAbility, International Finance Corporation and Ethos.

Talaja, A. 2012. Testing VRIN framework: resource value and rareness as sources of competitive advantage and above average performance. *Management: Journal of Contemporary Management Issues* 17(2): 51–64.

Tallontire, A. 2000. Partnerships in fair trade: reflections from a case study of Cafédirect. *Development in Practice* 10(2): 166–77.

Turban, D. B. and Greening, D. W. 1997. Corporate social performance and organizational attractiveness to prospective employees. *Academy of Management Journal* 40: 658–72.

Victor, D. G. and House, J. C. 2006. BP's emissions trading system. *Energy Policy* 34(15): 2100–12.

Wagner, M. 2010. Corporate social performance and innovation with high social benefits: a quantitative analysis. *Journal of Business Ethics* 94: 581–94.

Waldman, D. A. et al. 2006. Cultural and leadership predictors of corporate social responsibility values of top management: a GLOBE study of 15 countries. *Journal of International Business Studies* 37(6): 823–37.

Wilson, C. and Wilson, P. 2006. *Make Poverty Business: Increase Profits and Reduce Risks by Engaging with the Poor.* Sheffield: Greenleaf.

Zhao, M. 2012. CSR-based political legitimacy strategy: managing the state by doing good in China and Russia. *Journal of Business Ethics* 111: 439–60.

Zietsma, C. and Winn, M. I. 2008. Building chains and directing flows: strategies and tactics of mutual influence in stakeholder conflicts. *Business and Society* 47(1): 68–101.

15

Managing non-market risk

Is it possible to manage the seemingly unmanageable?[1]

Jennifer Oetzel and Chang Hoon Oh

A key challenge for scholars interested in non-market strategy is to improve understanding of the complex risks that firms face and to formulate effective strategies for responding to them. Non-market risks, which include social, political, legal, environmental, and techno-logical risks (among others), can create major business disruptions and threaten firm survival. The cause of these risks is generally attributed to factors outside the control of most firms. To gain a comprehensive understanding of these risks, scholars and managers must not only examine the risks themselves, but the broader context in which they occur. The institutional environment can greatly influence the likelihood that a major risk will occur, the severity of the risk, and the appropriate strategic responses available to managers (Doh, Lawton, and Rajwani, 2012; Lawton, McGuire, and Rajwani, 2013).

In this chapter, we aim to contribute to the research on non-market strategy by focusing on non-market discontinuities, their characteristics, the factors that influence the likelihood that these discontinuities will affect businesses, and the range of strategic responses available to managers. In particular, we discuss the innovative strategic responses that some firms have adopted to address non-market discontinuities.

Broadly speaking, non-market risks can be categorized as continuous or discontinuous in nature. Continuous or systematic non-market risks are those that firms face on a regular or semi-regular basis, such as policy uncertainty and corruption (Delios and Henisz, 2003; Doh, Rodriguez, Uhlenbruck, Collins, and Eden, 2003; Henisz and Delios, 2001; Mauro, 1995). Research on continuous risks has tended to focus on the actions or inactions of a particular government or administration as the source of risk. Discontinuous risks are "episodic occurrences that are often difficult to anticipate or predict" (Oetzel and Oh, 2014: 732; see also Lampel, Shamsie, and Shapira, 2009; Ramanujam, 2003; Slovic, Fischhoff, and Lichtenstein, 2000). Examples of these major discontinuities range from terrorist attacks and violent conflicts to technological or natural disasters (Oetzel and Getz, 2012; Oetzel and Oh, 2014; Oh and Oetzel, 2011; Perrow, 2007; Wernick, 2006).

While both types of non-market risks can threaten firm profitability and even survival, discontinuous risks have tended to receive less attention in contemporary research, probably because of their episodic nature and the perception that these discontinuities tend to be "unmanageable." It is often possible for managers to gain a significant amount of information – prior to an investment decision – on the existence of continuous risks in the country that may pose a problem for a firm. For example, the existence and prevalence of corruption in a given country is generally widely known prior to market entry (Doh et al., 2003). So, too, is the structure of the government and the process in which policy decisions are made. In contrast, major disasters and discontinuities are often unexpected, taking unprepared managers by surprise. As a generalization, managers may also perceive risks such as natural disasters, violent conflicts, and the like to be threats outside their area of expertise and training.

Thus, our rationale for focusing our attention on discontinuous risks is that they have received somewhat less attention in the management literature and they are more difficult to prepare for since they tend to occur with relatively little notice. Furthermore, because major discontinuous risks tend to be destabilizing, at least in the geographic vicinity in which they occur, they are more likely to threaten firm survival and create major business discontinuities in a very short period of time. In addition, there is less understanding about these risks (as opposed to continuous risks) in the strategic management research, and existing tools and strategies for managing risk – such as risk avoidance or modifying ownership structure – are not necessarily effective in the face of major discontinuities.

Rather than proposing a comprehensive review of non-market risks more generally, the focus of this chapter is to challenge the traditional emphasis in the risk management literature on risk avoidance, and instead to focus on gaining a better understanding of the characteristics of major risk events and the factors that influence them so that managers and their firms are better equipped to develop effective response strategies. In the case of violent conflict, for example, it may be possible for managers to adopt strategies that enable firms to manage risk in the operating environment, not just avoid it. In fact, managers that focus solely on mitigating risk may find that they are able to achieve only a temporary, short-term reprieve from the impact of a given risk event. For other non-market risks, such as terrorist attacks and natural and technological disasters, understanding the characteristics of these threats and the factors that influence their impact on business can guide managers toward more effective response strategies.

A common thread linking non-market risk, such as terrorist attacks, violent conflicts, and major technological or natural disasters, is the perception that these events are outside the control of the firm and therefore "unmanageable" (March and Shapira, 1987; Slovic, Fischhoff, and Lichtenstein, 2000). As a result, managers may believe that there is little that their firm can do to mitigate the effects of such events (aside from buying insurance where possible and affordable), so they rely on reactive rather than proactive response strategies. While this may be a common perception, an intriguing question is: why do some firms experiencing these risks exit in response while others stay or even plan and carry out new ventures? Can managers develop capacities around managing complex risks that are a valuable source of competitive advantage for the firm? In practice, we regularly find businesses that survive and continue to operate despite highly destructive and destabilizing events, while others go beyond simply operating as usual and plan new entries and expansions despite these disasters.

Understanding how risk events affect firms, why businesses stay and continue to operate versus exit when faced with these events, and how firms respond has important implications for businesses as well as policy-makers seeking to retain foreign investment and support local businesses despite major crises. Policy-makers also have a stake in minimizing the possibility of long-term economic and social setbacks. Enhancing business continuity in the face of crises may improve the social and economic wellbeing of society and increase the possibility of a more rapid recovery post-disaster.

The purpose of the next section is to address the relevance of different types of discontinuous risk to firms. How important are these risks to firms? Are they rare events or do they occur with enough frequency to merit managerial attention and the formulation of an integrated strategy response? Do these events substantially impact firms, employees, localities, and nations, or is the cost in human and economic terms generally low? These and other questions will be explored throughout this chapter.

Understanding seemingly "unmanageable risk"

Frequency and impact of major discontinuous risks

Unfortunately, the major non-market risks[2] described in this chapter are not rare events. In a recent study of terrorist events and natural and technological disasters, researchers found that of the 71 European Fortune Global 500 multinational enterprises (MNEs) whose subsidiaries were located in 101 host countries between 2001 and 2006, 60 percent experienced terrorist activities, 96 percent experienced natural disasters, and 80 percent experienced technological disasters (Oh and Oetzel, 2011). Violent conflicts are not uncommon, either. According to the Heidelberg Institute for International Conflict Research, in 2013 there were 414 political conflicts around the world, of which 221 involved violence (HIIK, 2014: 15).

The loss of life and economic costs of these events can be staggering. For example, the terrorist attacks on September 11, 2001 in the United States resulted in approximately 3000 casualities and an estimated financial cost of $3.3 trillion (Carter and Cox, 2011). With respect to natural disasters, at least 1836 people died in Hurricane Katrina and the economic costs are estimated to be $156 billion (Vigdor, 2008). In comparison, according to the US Geological Survey, 227,898 people died across multiple countries, the vast majority in Indonesia (approximately 167,000), as a result of the earthquake and tsunami in the Indian Ocean in 2004 (USGS, 2004). In terms of economic costs, hardest-hit Aceh Province in Indonesia reportedly had $4 billion in reconstruction costs (BBC News, 2005). Between 2002 and 2011 in Asia more generally, natural disasters caused over 65,000 deaths and affected almost 220 million people each year (CCTV, 2014). This difference in impact between disasters is consistent with research findings that the loss of life associated with major disasters is greater in developing and emerging market countries, but the financial cost of these events is greater in developed countries. Table 15.1 shows the number of incidents and human victims by type of discontinuous risk between 1980 and 2011.

Relevance to business

Although both continuous and discontinuous risks can lead to tremendous economic and monetary damages for firms, the business literature has not paid much attention to how these risks are relevant to business strategy and operations. Outside of academia, however, the media frequently covers the impact of these risks on businesses, and in practice firms widely acknowledge their importance to their operations. For instance, once President Obama declared the Boston Marathon bombings in 2013 to be an act of terrorism, many businesses on Boylston Street, where the bombing occurred, found that since they did not have terrorism insurance they were not covered for either damage to property or disruption of business

Table 15.1 Incidents and damages of major discontinuous risks

Year	Number of events			Number of human victims		
	Natural disasters	Technological disasters	Terrorism activities	Natural disasters	Technological disasters	Terrorism activities
1980	151	44	523	26097	2357	2349
1981	148	40	469	117197	2749	1537
1982	153	41	423	13973	2034	2237
1983	206	48	428	461061	3682	8797
1984	156	63	471	16273	6442	5607
1985	180	76	524	60232	4586	5831
1986	174	102	533	10349	6766	4406
1987	231	165	503	21533	11776	4384
1988	237	165	417	57509	7880	2487
1989	188	223	360	12599	10214	3322
1990	304	190	372	53160	8614	3252
1991	266	233	578	189707	9412	155
1992	231	148	359	16680	7453	190
1993	266	173	552	21811	9486	8339
1994	255	193	375	15590	9299	3507
1995	277	179	310	27166	7343	2310
1996	273	210	219	31595	9403	5565
1997	323	201	189	30124	7992	2266
1998	363	220	95	62673	8589	2410
1999	416	303	295	76906	8703	3122
2000	526	369	167	16646	11383	3263
2001	450	325	52	39505	8546	3365
2002	533	360	130	21761	12451	653
2003	392	334	275	113088	10750	15588
2004	410	359	235	245013	10329	8659
2005	497	371	110	94043	11652	12337
2006	446	302	84	28795	10004	6152
2007	449	277	91	22422	7651	1458
2008	400	260	92	242243	6946	3312
2009	382	230	101	16005	6865	1592
2010	436	235	113	308114	6744	1441
2011	352	244	91	34139	6583	719
Total	8809	5946	9231	2,319,470	235,018	126,860
Average	304	205	318	79,982	8104	4374

Sources: EM-DAT (2014); Mickolus et al. (2012).

(Associated Press, 2013). In areas that are dependent upon tourism, terrorist attacks can affect a country or region for years. The terrorist bombing in Bali in 2002, for example, killed 202 people and devastated the island's economy for several years (Baker and Coulter, 2007). In the months following the bombing, hotel occupancy rates fell from 75 percent to just 14 percent (Baker and Coulter, 2007).

According to the Global Competitiveness Index produced by the World Economic Forum (2013), business costs of terrorism vary between countries. The index is based on a

Table 15.2 Business costs of terrorism: to what extent does the threat of terrorism impose costs on business in your country?

Ranking	Country	Score
1	Slovenia	6.7
2	Finland	6.7
3	Iceland	6.6
4	Austria	6.6
5	Czech Republic	6.5
94	United Kingdom	5.2
110	India	4.8
111	Thailand	4.8
112	Nicaragua	4.8
113	Mexico	4.7
114	Russian Federation	4.7
120	United States	4.4
136	Algeria	3.5
137	Yemen	3.2
138	Egypt	3.1
139	Pakistan	3.1
140	Colombia	2.9

Source: World Economic Forum (2013).

Note: 1 = to a great extent; 7 = not at all.

survey of top corporate executives' assessments of the costs. In 2013, Slovenia, Finland, Iceland, Austria, and the Czech Republic ranked as the top five countries (where the threat of terrorism does not impose significant costs on businesses), while Algeria, Yemen, Egypt, Pakistan, and Colombia are the bottom five countries (where the threat of terrorism imposes huge business costs). The United Kingdom, India, and the United States were rated far below many other countries (94th, 110th, and 120th, respectively). However, over the years there has been a tremendous amount of fluctuation in the rankings. This only accentuates the need to emphasize risk management over risk prediction. In Table 15.2, we show the top five, the bottom five, and selected other countries from the 140 countries listed in the index.

Natural disasters often directly hit plants or industrial complexes. In 2011, floods in Thailand killed more than 800 people and caused huge disruptions to industry, cutting the country's economic growth for that year to 0.1 percent. Toshiba Corp was one of the foreign companies that had to halt its production at ten plants near Bangkok due to the floods. Even though the Thai government and commercial industrial parks had invested in flood mitigation equipment, in 2013 two foreign-owned factories producing electronic parts at Amata Nakorn industrial park, east of Bangkok, had to close their factories due to floods. The floods also indirectly affected other manufacturers by forcing delays in shipments. Infrastructure was also affected, leading to the disruption of supply chains (Lefevre, 2013).

Technological disasters can also have a major impact on business. Some examples include train derailments, chemical leaks, and certain health crises. For example, in 2013 there was a devastating train derailment in Quebec, Canada. A seventy-two-car freight train loaded with crude oil from North Dakota was parked near the town of Lac-Mégantic. During the night approximately sixty tank cars broke away and ultimately derailed. At least five of the cars exploded (CBC News, 2014). Forty-seven people died, and thirty buildings in the town were destroyed (*Atlantic*, 2013; CBC News, 2014). MM&A Railway, the company involved in the accident, is now insolvent (CBC News, 2014).

Numerous companies have reported that such major disasters may adversely affect corporate performance. According to the 2006 annual report of Anheuser-Busch Companies (2006: 13), natural disasters and the threat of terrorist acts may affect business continuity and corporate financial results if these disasters result in shortages of raw materials and commodities, and in heightened security and higher costs for imports and exports. Likewise, VINCI Group, a French construction multinational corporation (MNC), noted:

> [L]ike all companies, VINCI may be affected by natural disasters such as earthquakes, floods, cyclones, lightning or exceptional meteorological conditions which could lead to the collapse or accidental destruction of Group infrastructure assets under construction or in use. Such events can lead locally to a significant reduction in the Group's revenue or to an increase in the costs to maintain or repair its facilities
>
> *(VINCI Group, 2008: 105)*

DaimlerChrysler similarly noted, "[P]roduction and business processes could also be affected by unforeseeable events such as natural disasters or terrorist attacks on our facilities or data centers" (DaimlerChrysler, 2004: 40).

Even though firms are unable to predict discontinuous risks, experience operating during these risks without a disaster plan in place has led some firms to prepare their operations against future risk events.[3] One of these companies, Continental Airlines, developed an emergency plan in 2006 after barely avoiding Hurricane Rita in 2005 (Worthington, Collins, and Hitt, 2009). In 2008, when Hurricane Ike threatened the Houston area, the airline temporarily transferred its business operations from that city (Continental's hub) to an underground bunker in Conroe, Texas (Harrington, 2008). Doing so enabled Continental to continue to conduct its airline operations in any region where airports were operational.

Another example is the safety management plan of AREVA, a French utility firm. Due to the increasing level of government requirements regarding industrial safety, the company reinforced its use of lessons learned to ensure the highest level of safety in its facilities. It has also carried out a number of impact studies on both its home and its foreign operations. Although the company has implemented strategies and procedures to manage terrorism, natural disasters, and technological risks, it admits that it is not always able to control the factors that influence the severity of potential accidents that may affect its operations (AREVA, 2009).

Characteristics of risks

As managers formulate response strategies to different types of risk, it is important to understand how the characteristics of different risk types might affect their overall threat to firms. Non-market risks can differ substantially from one another. For instance, risks vary in terms of their duration, geographic scope, intensity, and underlying causes (Getz and Oetzel, 2010). Furthermore, it is well established that individuals perceive risks very differently, and this too affects managers' responses to discontinuous events. Each of the variable characteristics will now be discussed in turn.

Duration and intensity

All else being equal, the longer the duration of a major discontinuous risk, the more likely a firm is to develop an integrated and sustained response plan. Short-lived events, particularly in countries where the government is well equipped to respond to a disaster and provide relief, are generally seen as isolated events that do not require a fundamental rethinking of corporate strategy (regardless of whether this might be an appropriate response). When a risk event extends over a long period of time, however, such as in the case of a violent conflict, this suggests that the government is incapable of containing the risk. In such situations, it is also unlikely that the government will be able to provide post-disaster assistance and mitigate the impact of the disaster and its human and economic impact on society. Discontinuities that persist for a lengthy period of time are likely to necessitate more extensive response plans as the firm prepares for the continued risk of discontinuity over the foreseeable future.

In addition, different types of risk may interact and generate even more complex risks. For example, the India–Pakistan war in 1970 exacerbated the damages from the Bhola cyclone (Oh and Reuveny, 2010). Another example is the 2011 Fukushima nuclear plant accident in Japan which were initiated by an earthquake and tsunami. Although Japan is considered the most advanced country in managing these natural disasters, the radioactive water spills are now a major global concern. It is expected that the decontamination work will take at least until early 2016 due to frequent earthquakes in the region (Lui, 2013). As a result, many countries have either banned or imposed restrictions on food and fish imports from Japan (Reuters, 2011).

Other key characteristics affecting firm response to risk are the intensity and impact of a given event. Low-intensity events are less likely to affect firm operations, particularly for any substantial period of time. Furthermore, the loss of life and financial and social impacts are minimized when the intensity is lower. Generalizing, then, events that are short in duration and low in intensity will pose less risk to firms and their investments.

Geographic scope

For obvious reasons, risks that are geographically widespread are likely to affect a greater number of individuals and organizations either directly or indirectly than highly concentrated risk events. The direct effects are obvious: damage or destruction to firm facilities and supply chains and the targeting of employees pose serious and immediate threats to firm survival. Firms that are not directly targeted may be indirectly affected when transportation networks, utilities, and infrastructure systems are disrupted.

Although disasters that cover a large geographic area tend to affect a greater number of individuals and firms, there are exceptions to this general principle. For example, there are times when natural disasters may strike large swathes of relatively unpopulated portions of a country. In this case, the loss of life, disruption to infrastructure, and potential discontinuity in business operations are likely to be minimal. The urgency associated with responding to risk events – even those involving large geographic areas – is likely to be lessened when the event happens in an area remote from the business centers and where the impact of a risk event is minimized. Scholars have tried to capture the interplay between the threat of an event, such as a violent conflict, a firm's exposure to that event, and the geographic location of the conflict (Dai, Eden, Beamish, 2013).

Perceptions of risk

Although discontinuous risks can be quantified in a variety of ways – by their duration, intensity, impact, and geographic scope – it is well established that risk perceptions play an important role in how people respond to risk events (Lampel, Shamsie, and Shapira, 2009; Slovic, Fischhoff, and Lichtenstein, 2000). For instance, reactions to a terrorist attack are often disproportionate to the actual impact of the event (Slovic, Fischhoff, and Lichtenstein, 2000). Financial markets and the broader society are likely to respond with greater panic than the actual impact of the event would suggest (Garvey and Mullins, 2008). In contrast, natural disasters are often seen as "acts of God" and therefore outside the control of managers (Slovic, Fischhoff, and Lichtenstein, 2000). Not surprisingly, when we examine the differential effects of major risks on foreign firm investments we find that MNEs may be less likely to exit a country after a natural disaster (e.g., floods, earthquakes, tsunamis, etc.) than they are after a terrorist attack or technological disaster (e.g., breakdowns of technological systems, industrial accidents, train crashes, etc.), regardless of the severity of the event (Oh and Oetzel, 2011). It is not difficult to anticipate that the effects also vary across sub-types of disasters or risks.

These findings can yield potentially valuable insights for managers. A firm may overreact to socially magnified events but underreact to more costly and deadly discontinuities. An overreaction can result in lost business if a firm exits too abruptly. If a firm fails to plan for less dramatic events like natural disasters, however, it risks incurring substantial losses to property and disruption to business. Furthermore, to the extent that perceptions influence reality, public dread relating to terrorist events may cause real damage to the economy, even though the actual loss of time and property does not warrant it.

Causes of risk

Political scientists have devoted a tremendous amount of time and effort to studying the factors that may cause or contribute to events such as terrorist attacks and violent conflicts. While much progress has been made, there is still substantial debate among scholars about the role that economic, religious, and environmental factors play in causing violent conflict or terrorism. Furthermore, other issues, such as access to water and other natural resources or ethnic homogeneity (or fractionalization), can contribute to instability and conflict. Interaction effects between these factors may further complicate researchers' attempts to disentangle the causes of various risk events.

While political scientists work to increase understanding of the causes of political strife, climatologists, biologists, urban planners, and others are studying the factors that may be causing what seems to be an increase in natural disasters – or at least in their severity – in many parts of the world. Risk analysts in the insurance industry are at the forefront of understanding natural disasters and their impact on businesses and communities. Quoted in an article published by the *Smithsonian* magazine, Robert Muir-Wood, the chief scientist of Risk Management Solutions – whose job includes calculating the odds of catastrophic weather-related disasters – indicates that something is changing in the industry. He states that, "In the past, when making these assessments, we looked to history. But in fact, we've now realized that that's no longer a safe assumption – we can see, with certain phenomena in certain parts of the world, that the activity today is not simply the average of history" (Stromberg, 2013). Other analysts and organizations are quoted in the same article essentially calling for a paradigm shift in how risk assessments for natural disasters are conducted (Stromberg, 2013).

In the management literature, relatively little emphasis is placed on understanding the causes of regional, national, or international discontinuities. To the extent that understanding the causal factors behind discontinuities is relevant to the formulation of appropriate response strategies by firms, this is an important gap in the literature. When and whether the factors driving conflict should influence firm strategy remains an open question. We discuss this issue in greater detail in the section on strategic responses to risk, below.

Factors influencing firm response

While it is intuitively appealing to assume that there is a linear relationship between major discontinuities and firm response, studies that solely examine the direct effects of various types of risk on firm/subsidiary response may yield incomplete or misleading results. This is because the direct effects are almost always statistically negative but there are numerous factors that influence the relationship between risk and firm response. For example, country context and firm experience can influence whether a risk will negatively impact a firm, how severe the impact will be, and, possibly, how the firm should respond. With respect to violent conflict, local and international stakeholder pressures appear to play different but important roles in influencing firm response. Figure 15.1 illustrates the variables, strategy choices, and relationships described in this chapter, and we discuss each of these factors in greater detail below.

Country context

A wide variety of factors affects how a particular risk will influence a given company. The quality of country governance, for one, plays a significant moderating role between risk events and subsidiary investment. By "country governance" we are referring to the ability of

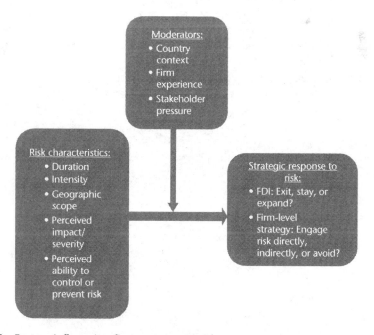

Figure 15.1   Factors influencing firm response to risk

the government to develop and implement sound policies, rule of law, political stability, the quality of public service, freedom of expression, and citizens' voice in selecting their government, among other factors (Kaufmann, Kraay, and Mastruzzi, 2008). For example, high-quality regulations reduce the likelihood that an MNE will divest from a country that is affected by natural disasters. One explanation for this finding is that building code regulations tend to reduce property damage and loss of life during natural disasters. Proper enforcement of these codes and related regulations can minimize the impact of a natural disaster. For technological disasters, "voice and accountability," the ability of citizens to participate in their government, was found to increase the likelihood that MNEs would divest after a technological disaster (Oh and Oetzel, 2011). Managers may consider techno-logical disasters to be more preventable than other types of risk events. It is possible that political protest and attention to disasters can be destabilizing to governments during an emergency and inspire a loss of investor confidence (Oh and Oetzel, 2011: 676). In com-parison, high-quality governance across multiple dimensions was necessary to reduce the likelihood that MNE subsidiaries would disinvest after a terrorist attack.

As the previous discussion demonstrates, the aspects of governance that are important for addressing one type of discontinuity are not necessarily the same for others. More research on the country-level institutional factors that affect firm risk in the face of crisis is needed to improve understanding of how governance can mitigate the impact of risk on firms. It would also help managers to formulate better policies for managing risk.

Experience

Managers can obtain various types of experience managing risk. The experience can be risk specific, country specific, or a combination of the two and may involve managing risks with different levels of severity, duration, and geographic impact, among other characteristics. Central questions in the study of experience managing risk are which types of experience are valuable, can the experience be leveraged across countries, and how does the value of expe-rience vary by type of risk? Research on the relationship between experience with risk and firm investment behavior indicators that experience with some types of risk can be leveraged across borders while other types are country specific. Firms with experience managing during discontinuous risks, such as terrorist events and natural and technological disasters, can leverage this experience in expansions within their existing location but not for initial entry into other countries experiencing similar high-impact problems (Oetzel and Oh, 2014: 2). This finding appears to hold for other types of discontinuous risk, such as violent conflict risk. Scholars have demonstrated that country-specific knowledge is necessary when firms are facing conflicts involving host country governments. While corporate-level experience may be equally valuable when facing what amount to security threats posed by non-state-related conflicts, country-specific knowledge is necessary for state-related violence (Oh and Oetzel, 2014).

These findings underscore the importance of research on discontinuous as opposed to continuous risks since there are notable differences in the value of experience. Studies of firm response to continuous risks, such as policy uncertainty, reveal that firm experience in high-risk environments is positively related to higher entry rates into other high-risk countries (Delios and Henisz, 2003; Holburn and Zelner, 2010). For discontinuous risks, then, there appear to be limits on the ability of firms to leverage experience from one country into another.

Stakeholder pressure

Another factor influencing how firms may respond to different risks is the role of stakeholder pressure. In communities that have experienced major disasters and discontinuities, business associations, nonprofit groups, and government actors may urge the private sector to engage in post-disaster relief efforts and possibly in disaster planning for future events (Muller and Whiteman, 2008; Zhang, Rezaee, and Zhu, 2009). In some communities, private sector firms may be the largest and most politically and economically powerful organizations. Non-profit groups realize this latent power and are increasingly seeking greater firm participation in solving problems that impact the community or region as a whole. These multisectoral efforts are sometimes aimed at mitigating the conditions that create crises in the first place. Since firms have a direct interest in the wellbeing of the countries and communities in which they operate, and because firms experience the negative impact of major discontinuities, managers may be willing to learn new strategies and skills for addressing discontinuous non-market risk.

Rather than relying primarily on risk avoidance or mitigation, it is not surprising that there is growing evidence that managers may be more willing than previously thought to adopt non-traditional strategies for managing risk, strategies that might mitigate conflict risk altogether rather than temporarily reduce it. Local stakeholder pressure, in particular, may motivate firms in ways that international stakeholders do not (Oetzel and Getz, 2012). Such pressure may be more salient than that of international stakeholders because local stakeholders are directly affected by major disasters and may feel a greater sense of urgency to address crises in their communities (Oetzel and Getz, 2012). In the case of natural disasters, local employees may experience a loss of personal property or an inability to get to work because of damage to roads or other infrastructure. When faced with violent conflicts, employees may fear physical attacks and refuse to work, putting greater pressure on firms to resolve the risk (Oetzel and Getz, 2012).

Next, we discuss some of the strategic responses that have been used to address non-market risk, particularly for firms seeking foreign direct investment.

Strategic responses to risk

Managing non-market risk prior to investment

Scholars studying firms' strategic responses to non-market risk have tended to emphasize risk avoidance over risk management. The political risk literature has traditionally focused on how managers and their firms can identify "riskier" markets before an investment is made. To avoid risk, particularly for foreign direct investments that are often planned for multi-year or multi-decade time horizons, decision-makers need to be able to predict risk years in advance. Once an investment has been made and a firm's operations are established, managers must decide whether to continue after a major discontinuity or adopt a more avoidance-oriented approach, such as exiting the country. While market exit may be the most prudent response, automatically disinvesting from a country may result in lost opportunities and future options.

Managing risk prior to making an investment also involves foreign entry and ownership decisions. Assessing the level of political risk in a country prior to an investment may lead a firm to choose one company over another. In many other situations, however, firms may be obliged to enter certain markets regardless of the risk if they need access to specific resources or markets. In addition, it is extremely difficult to forecast what the risk profile of a country will be several years down the road (Oetzel, Bettis, and Zenner, 2001). Analysts certainly did not predict the Arab Spring or the ensuing political turmoil in Tunisia and Egypt two years prior to these events.

A firm's ownership choice offers another opportunity for mitigating risk in new foreign entry decisions. Joint ventures with local partners (as compared to wholly owned subsidiaries as an entry mode) have often been considered valuable for multinationals seeking to reduce their exposure to non-market risk (Delios and Henisz, 2000). Of course, MNC–local partnerships are beneficial only so long as the contractual relationship between the two entities is robust and the local partner has the necessary skills and capabilities (Henisz, 2000). In addition, if a firm can manage risks better than its local competitors, lowering their level of ownership might not be an optimal strategy when the principle of risk and return is considered.

As important as market entry and ownership decisions are prior to investment – decisions that should not be minimized in any way – they cannot fully protect firms from risk. Other mechanisms for managing risk – such as insurance for natural or technological hazards, terrorist attacks, or violent conflict – are also only partially effective. Companies may find that private sector insurance is unavailable for ventures in high-risk markets or for periods longer than three years. Policies are also limited in their coverage. Given the limitations of existing approaches, it may be possible for firms in certain situations to consider alternative approaches to managing non-market risk.

Innovative responses to non-market risk

While not widely taught in business schools, a growing number of firms are exploring and in some cases adopting innovative responses to discontinuous non-market risks (Kolk and Lenfant, 2013; Oetzel and Getz, 2012; Reade and Lee, 2012; Tevault, 2013). The United Nations Global Compact has sponsored case studies on local and multinational firms engaged in positive efforts to promote peace and stability in war-torn environments (UN Global Compact, 2010, 2013). These case studies, along with important scholarly work in the area, show that conflicts occurring in the wider environment can spill over to the workplace, creating complex management challenges (Chua, 2013; Reade and Lee, 2012). If left unaddressed, these challenges can affect firm performance at a variety of levels. Other studies have examined the role that partnerships between MNEs and other organizations can play in mitigating conflict (Kolk and Lenfant, 2013; Tevault, 2013).

There is evidence that managers are open to new ways of addressing major risks. Researchers have found that a substantial portion of United Nations Global Compact survey respondents would be willing to adopt a range of strategies that would directly or indirectly impact a conflict itself. In many cases, managers indicated that they would likely act in collaboration with other firms, non-governmental organizations, business associations, and the like rather than do so alone (Oetzel and Getz, 2012). Direct actions might include such responses as lobbying the government to resolve the conflict, speaking out publicly against violence and/or its causes, mediating interactions between the various parties to the conflict, and organizing negotiations among those parties, among others. Indirect strategies could include adopting human resource policies that avoid aggravating social and ethnic tensions in society, verifying that the participants in the firm's supply chain have not contributed to the conflict, adopting industry codes of conduct for operating in conflict areas, and donating resources to respond to local humanitarian crises (Oetzel and Getz, 2012).

To the extent that managers and their firms engage directly or indirectly in mitigating risk in the countries where they operate, this has the potential to offer a paradigm shift in how we think about risk management. Rather than responding to non-market risks by exiting a country, hiring security firms to protect firm assets, or focusing on post-hoc risk mitigation, managers might be able to address certain types of risk at their source.

Local firms often provide the best examples of innovative non-market risk management approaches. Since they may have fewer alternative investment options when faced with risk (e.g., shifting production to another country), they are pushed to find creative ways to survive. In numerous countries, local businesses are playing a significant role in developing partnerships aimed at overcoming the security and institutional voids created by years of conflict. Two business-led initiatives in Sri Lanka are said to have played important roles in bringing to an end the civil war that hobbled the economy for decades: the Business for Peace Alliance (BPA) and Sri Lanka First. The BPA, which was founded in 2002 by a group of business leaders from the seventeen regional chambers of commerce, represented all of Sri Lanka's provinces and ethnic business communities (Banfield, Gunduz, and Killick, 2006). The conflict is estimated to have cost $12 billion between 1971 and 1996 alone (it finally ended in 2009), and a total of 80,000–100,000 casualties.

Another initiative, the Caucasus Business and Development Network (CBDN) in the South Caucasus, was profiled in *The Economist* (2008). Businesses in the region joined forces in 2005 and formed the CBDN to reopen borders that had inhibited trade, advocate for greater regional economic cooperation, support cross-divide production chains (e.g., production and machinery lending schemes), establish secure economic zones, and create and promote regional brands (Caucasian cheese, tea, wine, etc.). As the CBDN states on its website, a key aim is to alleviate the negative social consequences of protracted conflicts in the region through the development of the private sector in border regions, conflict zones, and among small and medium-sized businesses.

Although the above responses took place in areas of violent conflict risk, they are equally applicable to other discontinuities, such as natural disasters. It is well documented that natural disasters result in a greater loss of life in developing countries than they do in developed nations (Kasperson and Pijawka, 1985; Oh and Oetzel, 2011). In addition, in countries where there is poor enforcement of building codes, damage from earthquakes and other natural disasters is likely to be magnified. Firms may be able to work collectively through business associations, chambers of commerce, and governmental or non-governmental organizations to reduce the impact of future disasters. The value of mitigating risk in this way is obvious, but the motivation to do so when everything is running smoothly is often weak. We argue that firms that focus their risk management efforts on risk mitigation rather than avoidance will gain a competitive advantage over other firms when a disaster occurs. The mindset associated with active community engagement to build more resilient communities will yield economically and socially valuable dividends for firms.

Conclusions

The risks we have highlighted in this chapter are challenging and complex. For this reason, traditional approaches aimed at risk avoidance over risk management are unlikely to be feasible or effective. Thus, managers are beginning to rethink traditional responses to political risks and major disasters, particularly those risks that are often seen as "unmanageable" – those that arise from terrorist attacks, violent conflict, and natural disasters. It is increasingly clear that managers must learn to manage these seemingly unmanageable risks by improving their understanding of the characteristics and natures of various types of risk, of host country governments and their effects on risk, and of how different types of experience enable firms to manage risk effectively in different contexts. Regardless of whether they choose to respond to risk in a proactive manner, stakeholders may push firms to engage.

Notes

1 Financial support was partially provided by the Social Sciences and Humanities Research Council of Canada (435-2013-0394).
2 Terrorist events are defined as the use of violence or threat of violence in order to achieve political or ideological goals (Oh and Oetzel, 2011: 660; Wernick, 2006). Terrorism may be domestic in origin or may result from international groups or networks of individuals. Natural disasters are caused by events such as earthquakes, volcanic eruptions, floods, tsunamis, and the like. Technological disasters arise from industrial accidents, a breakdown of technical systems, such as malfunctions leading to train or plane crashes, and other related incidents (Oh and Oetzel, 2011). Violent conflicts are the organized and sustained use of physical force that results in injury or death to persons and/or damage or destruction to property (Oetzel, Getz and Ladek, 2007).
3 The two examples below (i.e., Continental Airlines and AREVA) were introduced in Oetzel and Oh (2014).

References

Anheuser-Busch. 2006. Annual report.
AREVA. 2009. Annual report.
Associated Press. 2013. Business frets at terrorism tag of Boston Marathon attack. May 13.
Atlantic. 2013. Freight train derails and explodes in Lac-Mégantic, Quebec. www.theatlantic.com/infocus/2013/07/freight-train-derails-and-explodes-in-lac-megantic-quebec/100548/ (accessed May 14, 2014).
Baker, K., Coulter, A. 2007. Terrorism and tourism: The vulnerability of beach vendors' livelihoods in Bali. Journal of Sustainable Tourism 15(3): 249–66.
Banfield, J., Gunduz, C., Killick, N. (eds.). 2006. Local business, local peace: The peacebuilding potential of the domestic private sector. London: International Alert.
BBC News. 2005. Tsunami economic impact. March 22. http://news.bbc.co.uk/2/hi/business/4154277.stm#Indonesia (accessed May 22, 2012).
Carter, S., Cox, A. 2011. One 9/11 tally: $3.3 Trillion. New York Times, September 8.
CBC News. 2014. MM&A Railway faces charges in Lac-Mégantic disaster. May 13. www.cbc.ca/news/canada/montreal/mm-a-railway-faces-charges-in-lac-mégantic-disaster-1.2640654 (accessed May 14, 2014).
CCTV. 2014. Chinese public urged to play bigger role in disaster management. February 28.
Chua, R. Y. J. 2013. The costs of ambient cultural disharmony: Indirect intercultural conflicts in social environment undermine creativity. Academy of Management Journal 56(6): 1545–7.
Dai, L., Eden, L., Beamish, P. W. 2013. Place, space, and geographical exposure: Foreign subsidiary survival in conflict zones. Journal of International Business Studies 44: 554–78.
DaimlerChrysler. 2004. Annual report.
Delios, A., Henisz, W. J. 2000. Japanese firms' investment strategies in emerging markets. Academy of Management Journal 43(3): 305–23.
— 2003. Political hazards, experience, and sequential entry strategies: The international expansion of Japanese firms, 1980–98. Strategic Management Journal 24(11): 1153–64.
Doh, J., Lawton, T., Rajwani, T. 2012. Advancing nonmarket strategy research: Institutional perspectives in a multipolar world. Academy of Management Perspectives 26(3): 22–39.
Doh, J. P., Rodriguez, P., Uhlenbruck, K., Collins, J., Eden, L. 2003. Coping with corruption in foreign markets. Academy of Management Executive 17(3): 114–27.

Economist, The. 2008. A Caucasian cheese circle: The secret diplomacy of cheesemaking. May 22.

EM-DAT. 2014. The OFDA/CRED International Disaster Database (www.em-dat.net). Brussels: Université Catholique de Louvain.

Garvey, J., Mullins, M. 2008. Contemporary terrorism: Risk perception in the London options market. *Risk Analysis* 28(1): 151–60.

Getz, K., Oetzel, J. 2010. MNE strategic intervention in violent conflict: Variations based on conflict characteristics. *Journal of Business Ethics* 89(4): 375–86.

Harrington, G. 2008. Bunker mentality: Business continuity. *Continental Magazine*, December, 64.

Heidelberg Institute for International Conflict Research (HIIK). 2014. *Conflict barometer 2013.* www. hiik.de/en/konfliktbarometer/pdf/ConflictBarometer_2013.pdf (accessed December 9, 2014).

Henisz, W. J. 2000. The institutional environment for multinational investment. *Journal of Law, Economics and Organization* 16(2): 334–64.

Henisz, W. J., Delios, A. 2001. Uncertainty, imitation, and plant location: Japanese multinational corporations, 1990–96. *Administrative Science Quarterly* 46(3): 443–75.

Holburn, G. L. F., Zelner, B. A. 2010. Political capabilities, policy risk, and international investment strategy: Evidence from the global electric power industry. *Strategic Management Journal* 31(12): 1290–315.

Kasperson, R. E., Pijawka, K. D. 1985. Societal response to hazards and major hazard events: Comparing natural and technological hazards. *Public Administration Review* 45: 7–8.

Kaufmann, D., Kraay, A., Mastruzzi, M. 2008. *Governance matters VII: Aggregate and individual governance indicators, 1996–2007.* Working Paper No. 4654. World Bank: Washington, DC.

Kolk, A., Lenfant, F. 2013. Multinationals, CSR and partnerships in Central African conflict countries. *Corporate Social Responsibility and Environmental Management* 20(1): 43–54.

Lampel, J., Shamsie, J., Shapira, Z. 2009. Experiencing the improbable: Rare events and organizational learning. *Organization Science* 20(5): 835–45.

Lawton, T., McGuire, S., Rajwani, T. 2013. Corporate political activity: A literature review and research agenda. *International Journal of Management Reviews* 15(1): 86–105.

Lefevre, A. S. 2013. Thailand flooding closes 2 factories at industrial park. Reuters, October 9.

Lui, M. 2013. Fukushima radiation cleanup may take 3 more years, Kyodo Reports. Bloomberg, December 22.

March, J. G., Shapira, Z. 1987. Managerial perspectives on risk and risk taking. *Management Science* 33(11): 1404–18.

Mauro, P. 1995. Corruption and growth. *Quarterly Journal of Economics* 110(3): 681–712.

Mickolus, E. F., Sandler, T., Murdock, J. M., Flemming, P. A. 2012. *International terrorism: Attributes of terrorist events (ITERATE), 1968–2011.* Dunn Loring, VA: Vinyard Software.

Muller, A., Whiteman, G. 2008. Exploring the geography of corporate philanthropic disaster response: A study of Fortune Global 500 firms. *Journal of Business Ethics* 84: 589–603.

Oetzel, J., Getz, K. 2012. When and how might firms respond to violent conflict? *Journal of International Business Studies* 32(6): 658–81.

Oetzel, J., Oh, C. H. 2014. Learning to carry the cat by the tail: Firm experience, disasters, and multinational subsidiary entry and expansion. *Organization Science* 25(3): 732–56.

Oetzel, J., Getz, K., Ladek, S. 2007. The role of multinational enterprises in responding to violent conflict: A conceptual model and framework for research. *American Business Law Journal* 44(3): 331–58.

Oetzel, J., Bettis, R., Zenner, M. 2001. Country risk measures: How risky are they? *Journal of World Business* 36(2): 128–45.

Oh, C. H., Oetzel, J. 2011. Multinationals' response to major disasters: How does subsidiary investment vary in response to the type of disaster and the quality of country governance? *Strategic Management Journal* 32(6): 658–81.

— 2014. *Once bitten twice shy? Experience managing risk and MNC subsidiary-level investment and expansion.* Working paper.

Oh, C.H., Reuveny, R. 2010. Climatic natural disasters, political risk and international trade. *Global Environmental Change* 20(2): 243–54.

Perrow, C. 2007. *The next catastrophe: Reducing our vulnerabilities to natural, industrial, and terrorist disasters.* Princeton, NJ: Princeton University Press.

Ramanujam, R. 2003. The effects of discontinuous change on latent errors in organizations: The moderating role of risk. *Academy of Management Journal* 46(5): 608–17.

Reade, C., Lee, H.-J. 2012. Organizational commitment in time of war: Assessing the impact of attenuation of employee sensitivity to ethnopolitical conflict. *Journal of International Management* 18(1): 85–101.

Reuters. 2011. Factbox: Restrictions on Japanese food imports. March 23.

Slovic, P., Fischhoff, B., Lichtenstein, S. 2000. Rating the risks. In P. Slovic (ed.), *Perception of risk*. London: Earthscan: 104–20.

Stromberg, J. 2013. How the insurance industry is dealing with climate change. *Smithsonian*. http://blogs.smithsonianmag.com/science/2013/09/how-the-insurance-industry-is-dealing-with-climate-change/ (accessed December 18, 2013).

Tevault, A. 2013. How institutional and business power theory shapes business strategy in fragile states: The case of Sierra Leone. *Business, Peace, and Sustainable Development* 1(1): 43–62.

United Nations Global Compact. 2010. Doing business while advancing peace and development. www.unglobalcompact.org/docs/issues_doc/Peace_and_Business/DBWAPD_2010.pdf (accessed December 19, 2013).

— 2013. Responsible business advancing peace: Examples from companies, investors, & Global Compact local networks. www.unglobalcompact.org/docs/issues_doc/Peace_and_Business/B4P_Resource_Package_company.pdf (accessed December 19, 2013).

United States Geological Survey (USGS). 2004. Earthquake Hazards Program: Magnitude 9.1 – off the west coast of northern Sumatra. http://earthquake.usgs.gov/earthquakes/eqinthenews/2004/us2004slav/#summary (accessed May 22, 2012).

Vigdor, J. 2008. The economic aftermath of Hurricane Katrina. *Journal of Economic Perspectives* 22(4): 135–54.

VINCI Group. 2008. Annual report.

Wernick, D. 2006. Terror incognito: International business in an era of heightened geopolitical risk. In G. S. Suder (ed.), *Corporate strategies under international terrorism and adversity*. Cheltenham: Edward Elgar: 59–82.

World Economic Forum. 2013. The global competitiveness report 2013–14. Geneva: World Economic Forum.

Worthington, W. J., Collins, J. D., Hitt, M. A. 2009. Beyond risk mitigation: Enhancing corporate innovation with scenario planning. *Business Horizons* 52(5): 441–50.

Zhang, R., Rezaee, Z., Zhu, J. 2009. Corporate philanthropic disaster response and ownership type: Evidence from Chinese firms' response to the Sichuan earthquake. *Journal of Business Ethics* 91: 51–63.

16

States, markets, and the undulating governance of the global electric power supply industry

Scholarship meets practice

Sinziana Dorobantu and Bennet A. Zelner

The global electricity supply industry has cycled between state-centered and market-mediated models of governance since its inception in the 1880s. Initially funded and operated by private players with little government oversight, the industry soon experienced a prolonged trend of increasing government intervention that culminated in a series of nationalizations between 1945 and 1978. During the 1980s and 1990s this trend reversed, as dozens of countries implemented "neoliberal" reforms intended to restore the role of the market – and reduce that of the state – in the industry's operation. Though it is too early to be certain, the tide may once again be turning.

What accounts for this undulating pattern? Part of the explanation lies in the realm of realpolitik. Two world wars sensitized national governments in Europe and elsewhere to the strategic significance of the industry, which was deemed too vital to national security to be governed by the vagaries of the market. In many countries, strong economic growth during the following two decades was interpreted as evidence of the success of the state-centered model, which effectively subsidized the provision of a critical input to macroeconomic growth. However, by the late 1970s, decades of politicized operations, together with rising fuel prices following the oil shock of 1973, had so impaired industry performance in many cases that national governments turned back to the market and its promise of economic "discipline." This trend gained momentum during the 1980s and 1990s, as privatization, regulatory restructuring, and other market-oriented reforms diffused throughout the global electricity industry.

Shifting scholarly views about government's ability to manage the economy paralleled these broad waves of change in industry governance. For economists, the key questions to ask in relation to any policy intended to govern the provision of infrastructure services are: when and how should governments intervene in markets in which the economics of existing technologies "naturally" limit competition, reducing social welfare and, ultimately, economic growth? Though the basic formulation of these questions had entered scholarly discourse by the end of the nineteenth century, the answers supplied by the academy have fluctuated over time. Support for state-centered solutions dominated such discourse through the middle of the twentieth century. In the 1960s, however, the libertarian views of the Chicago School became more prominent, and support for market-oriented approaches to infrastructure governance began to supplant the interventionist ideology that had prevailed earlier. By the 1980s, these views had elided with the broader ideological movement known as "neoliberalism," which continued to dominate intellectual and policy discussions through the turn of the twenty-first century.

In what follows, we trace these undulating patterns of industry governance and academic discourse in a historical sketch of the global electricity industry. The correspondence between shifting approaches to industry governance and prevailing economic wisdom suggests that the latter facilitated the former, whether as a source of ex ante influence, a tool of ex post justification, or a more subtle conspiratorial force.[1]

A global industry at its inception (1880s–1942)

The electricity industry owes much of its initial development to multinational companies and international capital originating from such early industrializers as the United Kingdom, Germany, Belgium, France, Switzerland, and the United States. Electrification was a gradual process driven primarily by private investors' drive to generate large returns in highly populated locations abroad, as well as by the needs of privately owned multinationals operating in capital-intensive industries (e.g., natural resources and agricultural commodities). Before the First World War, foreign ownership of electric utilities ranged as high as 90–5 percent in Latvia, Russia, and most of the countries in the Balkans; 75–100 percent in Mexico and much of Latin America; and virtually 100 percent in colonized territories in Africa, Asia, and the Caribbean (Hausman, Hertner, and Wilkins 2011: 31–3).

Though government regulation of the electricity industry was minimal at first, municipalities soon became involved, either directly through the provision of electricity and gas (which were typically supplied together) or indirectly through the issuance of franchises dictating the terms of service provision (Troesken 1997, 2006). Discussions about the right approach to ensure an appropriate level of political control intensified in the early 1900s, by which point most European and North American cities had undergone electrification, the utilities serving them had expanded significantly, and long-distance transmission had grown in importance.

The intellectual debate over the industry's governance revolved around the economic concept of natural monopoly, the roots of which lay in the work of economists going back to Adam Smith (1776), and the rudiments of whose current conceptualization – as an industry in which it is most cost-efficient to have a single firm responsible for all production (Gans 2014) – crystallized during the electricity industry's first decade of operation (Ely 1894; see Mosca 2008: 322–4). Infrastructure industries were viewed as exhibiting strong tendencies toward natural monopoly due to deep economies of scale exposing consumers to monopolistic pricing behavior by sole providers (Knight 1921; Sraffa 1926). The two main solutions proposed to address this hazard were government ownership (Ely 1894) and regulation (Hadley 1886). Additional normative rationales for government intervention in infrastructure industries included the use of "eminent domain" to acquire the contiguous tracts of land necessary for the construction of infrastructure facilities, the large social returns to infrastructure investment, and health and safety considerations (Baldwin, Cave, and Lodge 2013). Political considerations augmented these intellectual arguments, as the provision of universal access to basic services was incorporated into the expanding definition of "statehood."

National governments, for their part, also recognized infrastructure industries' potential to serve as vehicles of mass employment as well as instruments of political patronage.

The demand for resources during the First World War highlighted an additional, strategic rationale reason for government intervention in the electricity industry. The disruption of cross-border flows of capital, fuel, and equipment during the war, as well as initiatives to eliminate financial capital originating from non-allied nations and private investors' fear of creating a post-war capacity glut, led many European governments to invest directly in generating facilities. The stock market crash of 1929 and the ensuing Great Depression bolstered the case for government involvement, providing new evidence to support the view that the electricity industry was too critical to be under the control of fickle profit-seekers. Additional forms of government involvement included the creation of new oversight agencies, the development of comprehensive national grids, initiatives to reduce dependence on imported fuels, and, in some cases, the provision of tax incentives to electric utilities (Hausman et al. 2011: 127–9). Despite the trend of increased state involvement across Europe, only the Russian and Turkish governments nationalized their systems during this period – in 1917 (after the Russian Revolution) and 1938, respectively.

Commanding heights: government ownership and regulation (1942–78)

Beginning in the Second World War, national governments throughout the world assumed a more active role in the electricity industry, on the basis of wartime requirements as well as the diffusing view that the market was ill equipped to govern the provision of basic infrastructure services (Hausman et al. 2011: 227). The timing and the content of different countries' policy choices reflected their experience during the two world wars as well as the political shifts engendered by these conflicts.

In Europe – where the post-war reorganization of national boundaries compounded governments' strategic incentives to control the industry as a way to assert legitimacy over a country's geographic span – and elsewhere, the expropriation of foreign-owned electricity assets that had commenced during the inter-war period culminated in a wave of nationalization programs in the second half of the 1940s, including in France (1946), Austria (1947), Australia (1947), South Africa (1948), Spain (1949), and China (1949). Meanwhile, governments of newly independent states that emerged in the post-war decolonization wave also assumed active roles in the provision of infrastructure services – which were considered to be among an economy's "commanding heights" – as a means of asserting and legitimizing their power.

Such motivations were less salient in the United States, whose geographic separation from Europe had shielded it from the physical destruction wrought by the Second World War. Additionally, the US was culturally "distant" from most other countries in its strong historical preference for private enterprise over public administration. The American electricity industry's history reflected this heritage: strong domestic players such as Thomas Edison and J. P. Morgan had fought each other over the industry's early organization (Granovetter 1992; McGuire, Granovetter, and Schwartz 1993), and private investors in general had always had easy access to financing as well as technical and operational expertise. As a result of these factors, there was little need for the government to step in as provider of either capital or knowledge, or as a direct supplier of electricity services. Instead, the primary motivation for government intervention in the US electricity industry was that of governing an industry prone to natural monopoly, and the governance model that ultimately emerged was one in which private investor-owned utilities (or IOUs) operated under state-level regulation intended to guarantee supply at rates that were remunerative but not exploitative.

Beyond the US and Europe, private electric utilities that had survived the wave of postwar nationalizations experienced greater government pressure to increase production and expand distribution to meet growing demand. At the same time, governments faced pressure from politically powerful industrial consumers and the public at large to keep tariffs low. The result of these discrepant forces was chronic undersupply and, ultimately, another round of nationalization in such countries as Argentina (1958), Cuba (1960), Egypt (1961), Mexico (1962), Chile (1965), and Brazil (1978).

By the 1960s, national or municipal governments helmed infrastructure industries in countries throughout the world (with the notable exception of the United States). Spectacular economic growth rates during the decade appeared to justify governments' earlier decisions to own and operate the electricity industry. Moreover, because electricity represented a basic input to all industrial activities, the use of government debt to finance the industry's expansion was easily justified as a way to promote the policy goal of economic development, which was embraced by virtually all governments.

Within the system of public ownership and operation, however, lay the seeds of its eventual demise. The system did little to resolve the inherent tension between the need to finance expansion, on the one hand, and expectations of universal access and subsidized pricing that had evolved under the state-centered model. Weak incentives for productivity and efficiency at state-owned enterprises, together with frequent interference by politicians seeking to build or maintain support, resulted in capacity shortages, deterioration of existing assets, and, ultimately, poor industry performance on all metrics (Bacon 1995; Bacon and Besant-Jones 2001). Moreover, the prospects for recovery under the existing model were bleak, as politically locked-in prices combined with high government debt in many developing countries choked off access to much-needed funding. Performance was better in developed countries, but high operating expenses, frequent cost overruns in the construction of new facilities, and technological limits on the extent of economies of scale available from new generation technologies created pressures for change (Hirsh 1989; Joskow 1998). Fuel cost spikes following the oil shock of 1973 compounded these pressures by exposing the depth of the industry's problems.

Most scholarship during this period continued to embrace the position that governments should intervene to promote the public interest when markets fail (Pigou 1932), but the seeds of this view's demise were also planted in the 1960s. The Chicago School of economic thought had long rejected the dominant intellectual belief, rooted in Keynesianism, in government's ability to manage the economy. The school's sway grew dramatically in the late 1940s and 1950s, and in 1962 one of its luminaries, George Stigler, published an influential empirical analysis with his associate Clare Friedland that ostensibly demonstrated electricity regulation's inefficacy in the thirty-nine US states that had instituted the practice through 1937. Harvey Averch and Leland Johnson (1962) – who were both economists at the RAND Corporation – mounted another prominent attack in an article published that same year, arguing that the "rate-of-return" form of utility regulation practiced by state-level public utility commissions promoted inefficient investment patterns. Chicago economist Harold Demsetz (1968) went a step further by taking aim at the theory of natural monopoly itself, arguing that ex ante competition among firms bidding to supply a good whose production technology had monopolistic attributes would be sufficient to prevent monopolistic pricing.

In addition to critiques focusing on economic mechanisms, critiques addressing political mechanisms that also appeared during the 1960s contributed to the state-centered model's subsequent demise. New theories depicting public officials as self-interested actors held that producers were better positioned than consumers to "purchase" favorable treatment due to the organizational and financial advantages enjoyed by the former. The roots of this work lay in Stigler's "Theory of economic regulation" (1971; see also Peltzman 1976); Mancur Olson's *Logic of Collective Action* (1965) in the field of political science; and Buchanan and Tullock's *The Calculus of Consent: Logical Foundations of Constitutional Democracy* (1962), which spawned the so-called "Public Choice" School.

All about free markets: privatization and deregulation (1978–2001)

Beginning in 1978, numerous countries embarked on programs to privatize their electricity industries, reform the regulatory apparatus, and implement other market-oriented reforms. The widespread perception that decades of cost-of-service regulation or politically motivated supply, pricing, and employment decisions had led to inefficient operation and poor investment decisions – often culminating in crisis conditions – motivated governments to introduce these programs. Liberalized electricity markets came to exist in Australia, New Zealand, and much of Europe, North America, and South America.

The move to unfettered free markets in the 1980s and 1990s was guided by neoliberal economic principles associated with the "Washington consensus." Proponents of this program – most notably John Williamson, the Washington think-tank economist who coined the term – defined it as "prudent macroeconomic policies, outward orientation, and free-market capitalism" (Williamson 1990: 19).[2] They emphasized the potential of free markets to rectify the effects of failed statist policies, such as import-substitution industrialization (ISI) in Latin America, India, and parts of Africa; and state planning in the socialist economies of Eastern Europe, the former Soviet Union, and China. Critics highlighted that the Washington consensus was pure "market fundamentalism" dictating an undifferentiated set of reform recipes without attention to local economic and institutional conditions in the affected countries prescribed (Stiglitz 2003, 2008, 2010; Rodrik 2006; Serra and Stiglitz 2008).

In the 1980s and 1990s, when most of the developing world was searching for alternatives to development models that favored trade protection and state control, the Washington consensus became a "transnational policy paradigm produced by both intellectual and political forces" (Babb 2013: 269). The model resonated with policy-makers in much of the West, especially in the United States and the United Kingdom, where Ronald Reagan and Margaret Thatcher had also spearheaded the adoption of free-market reforms. Backed by widely accepted ideological principles and well-regarded intellectuals and policy-makers (mostly in Washington), the consensus gained impressive momentum and diffused quickly around the world as international financial institutions – led by the World Bank and the International Monetary Fund – made their loans to developing countries' governments conditional on policy reforms. To obtain a much-needed loan, these governments agreed to remove trade barriers, privatize state-owned enterprises, and reduce the overall level of state intervention in the economy (Williamson 1990, 1994). The combination of normative pressures stemming from the widespread embrace of the "consensus" and the coercive pressures imposed by powerful international organizations translated into widespread adoption of the free-market model embodied by the "Washington consensus" (Henisz, Zelner, and Guillen 2005; Babb 2013).

In addition, political and economic conditions in target countries made them ripe for the adoption of fundamental economic reform. Decades of macroeconomic instability, poor infrastructure development, and insufficient public service provision culminated in the emergence of new government elites supported by publics who demanded change. The so-called "third wave" of democratization (Huntington 1993) refers to the adoption of democratic rule in large parts of the developing world, including Latin America, Eastern Europe and the former Soviet republics, and parts of Africa. The new governments, empowered by the delegitimization of economic models enacted by previous elites and constrained by the poor economic conditions that had resulted (at least in part) from these models, needed to change direction, and the Washington consensus model was either the most powerful alternative or the only option available to those countries that approached international financial institutions for a loan. The confluence of these conditions – delegitimized economic policies, new political leaders, and the conditionality policies imposed by international financial institutions – enabled governments to push against any entrenched economic interests that opposed reform (Przeworski 1991; Haggard and Kaufman 1995; Weyland 1998, 2004).

Infrastructure industries – the most common targets of state ownership and control, and ostensibly the best illustration of the shortcomings of state intervention – underwent dramatic transformations as a result of these market-oriented reforms. The electric power industry was no exception. As discussed above, state ownership and operation had to this point been the norm in most countries. Governments had considerable sway in setting prices, often at levels intended to benefit politically powerful constituencies and interest groups at the expense of other programs funded from the public purse (Henisz and Zelner 2006). Political incentives trumped economic criteria in pricing and investment decisions, and, in many parts of the world, government-run utilities delayed the expansion of generating and distribution capacities needed to meet the rising demand fueled by rapid industrialization. Beginning in the 1970s and continuing throughout the 1980s, rising fuel prices, troubled nuclear programs in developed countries, and inadequate supply in developing economies raised further questions about the economic costs and benefits of the industry's mode of organization.

In contrast to much of the world, the electricity industry in the United States performed relatively well during this period: power was widely and reliably supplied; investment in new capacity matched or exceeded demand growth; and system losses were low, especially when compared with those in other countries (Joskow 1997). Nevertheless, pressure to reform the existing model of private ownership combined with cost-of-service regulation came from large industrial consumers, who perceived opportunities for cost savings from being able to purchase energy directly from wholesale producers. This pressure led to the adoption of the Public Utilities Regulatory Policies Act (PURPA) of 1978. The act required utility firms to buy electricity from "qualifying facilities" and paved the way for the emergence of independent power producers (IPPs) (Russo 2001) and the reform of transmission and distribution functions (Joskow 1997).

The Energy Policy Act of 1992 expanded opportunities for IPPs to sell electricity to utilities for resale. While in the mid-1990s IPPs accounted for only about 8 percent of electricity generating capacity in the US, they accounted for most of the capacity added since 1980 (Joskow 1997). The IPPs themselves soon joined politically powerful industrial consumers to lobby for further reform of the industry. Both groups stood to gain if they were allowed to transact in a deregulated market rather than at prices reflecting the large sunk costs of regulated utilities' prior investments, or from long-term purchase contracts signed in the 1970s and 1980s (White, Joskow, and Hausman 1996).

The rationale for and experience with electricity industry reform in the United States are unique. Pressure for reform in other parts of the world came from consumers dissatisfied with the poor availability and reliability of electricity services resulting from impaired investment incentives and electricity prices driven by political considerations with little regard for economic efficiency. In the same year as PURPA was adopted, Chile established a wholesale market where generators could sell power to retailers, and by 1982 large users were allowed to choose suppliers and negotiate prices directly (Al-Sunaidy and Green 2006). Soon afterwards, it became the first country to implement a sweeping set of market-oriented reforms, including privatization of the state-owned utility, liberalization of market entry, and the reduction of executive influence over the regulatory process (Henisz et al. 2005). Thereafter, market-oriented reform policies were introduced in the United Kingdom (1989), Norway (1990), New Zealand (1992), Australia (1994), and Spain (1994), and they have since diffused to other parts of the world, too (Al-Sunaidy and Green 2006; Williams and Ghanadan 2006; Joskow 2008).

Market-oriented reform policies were intended to foster competition in the generating segment of the industry – whose natural monopoly status has been called into question (Baumol, Panzar, and Willig 1982) – and to reform the regulation of the transmission and distribution functions, which were still viewed as natural monopolies. In developing countries, proponents of market-oriented reform also hoped that institutional changes would increase the industry's efficiency and encourage much-needed private investment (Williams and Ghanadan 2006). Specific reforms included the "unbundling" of generation, transmission, and distribution to allow for market entry liberalization; the privatization of state-owned utilities; the establishment of autonomous regulatory agencies independent of executive control, and the elimination of executive influence over the regulatory process. Market liberalization was first limited to generation but later extended through the creation of wholesale markets and, in some cases, retail markets. England and Wales, Chile, Argentina, New Zealand, Norway, and other countries all adopted variations of consumer choice models that allowed consumers to select their providers.

Scholarship during this period supported the trend of market-oriented reform. During the 1970s, the Chicago School's influence expanded, fueling a broader debate among economists about the relative effectiveness of "demand-side" policies associated with Keynesianism versus the "supply-side" initiatives espoused by neoliberalism (Evans 1997). Though political scientists, sociologists, and historians had previously debated the proper role of the state, economists shifted the locus of discussion from the relative merits of different forms of public administration for governing activities traditionally associated with the state to the choice between governments and markets as alternative modes of governance (Evans 1997: 62–3). The subsequent emergence of the field of "positive political economy" – which embraced the assumptions of self-interested political actors and differential organization costs between producers and consumers (Spulber 1989; Snyder 1991; Baron 1995a, 1995b) – solidified this shift by employing the tools of economics to assess the "credibility" of alternative models for governing utilities in a world of imperfect political and economic "markets" (e.g., Levy and Spiller 1994; see also Perotti 1995).

Empirical analyses of privatization's performance effects reflected shifting conceptual views about the appropriate functions of government and the mechanics of the policy-making process. At the end of the 1980s – relatively early in the global wave of market-oriented infrastructure reform – Boardman and Vining (1989: 1) summarized existing empirical research as providing only "weak support" for the proposition that private sector firms outperform their public sector counterparts. A dozen years later, Megginson and Netter (2001: 389) – surveying the larger body of evidence accumulated in the interim – proclaimed that "research now supports the proposition that privately owned firms are more efficient and more profitable than otherwise-comparable state-owned firms" (see also Megginson, Nash, and Van Randenborgh 1994; Boubakri and Cosset 1998; D'Souza and Megginson 1999; Dewenter and Malatesta 2001).

Letting the state back in: neoliberal retrenchment and state capitalism

By the mid-2000s, liberalized electricity markets had replaced cost-based regulation and government ownership in many countries. However, the experiences of more than two decades of market-oriented reform highlighted the challenges of restructuring the electricity industry. The inability to store large amounts of power renders the electricity industry sector vulnerable to supply manipulations, as exemplified by the California energy crisis of 2000–1 and the resultant rollback of retail deregulation in the state. In the developing world, weak performance in the years following the adoption of market-oriented infrastructure reform has created pressure for governments to intervene with new layers of regulation. Calls for increased state intervention in markets following the 2008–9 global financial crisis (Posner 2011; Piketty 2014) and an agenda to switch to renewable energy sources has created or compounded such pressure in many countries that had previously embraced a more laissez-faire approach. Elsewhere, powerful emerging-market governments in such countries as Brazil, Russia, India, and China are advocating their own vision of economic development in which a powerful state stands strong behind national champions, fledgling industries, and state enterprises expanding abroad.

Recent scholarship has once again reflected these broad trends. First, empirical studies of the relative performances of privately owned firms and their state-owned counterparts have continued to accumulate. Some analyses have echoed the generally rosy assessments published in the 1990s and early 2000s, but many others have reached more nuanced conclusions about privatization experiences during this same period, finding that the performance of privatized firms is contingent on a variety of factors. Some of these factors are technical attributes or other choice variables, such as privatization method (Cabeza-Garcia and Gomez-Anson 2011), owner identity (Frydman et al. 1999; D'Souza, Megginson, and Nash 2005; Omran 2009; Boubakri, Cosset, and Saffar 2013), ownership concentration (Omran 2009; Cabeza-Garcia and Gomez-Anson 2011), the presence and sequencing of other industry-level reforms, such as regulatory restructuring (Bortolotti, Cambini, and Rondi 2013) and the introduction of competition (Li and Xu 2004; Zhang, Parker, and Kirkpatrick 2008), and the choice of industry (Cabeza-Garcia and Gomez-Anson 2011; see also Kwoka 2005). Broader country-level attributes that are less susceptible to the near-term influence of policy-makers – including the availability of market-relevant capabilities (Denisova et al. 2009, 2012), the level of capital market development (D'Souza et al. 2005), the existence of a well-functioning corporate governance regime (Boubakri et al. 2005, 2008; Denisova et al. 2009; Boubakri et al. 2013), the presence of stability-promoting policy-making institutions (Vaaler and Schrage 2009; Bortolotti et al. 2013), and a country's overall level of economic development (Boubakri et al. 2005, 2008; D'Souza et al. 2005; Zhang et al. 2008) – have also been shown to affect post-privatization performance.

A second body of contemporaneous research has examined a less tractable set of influences on the performance of privatized firms – and of market-oriented reform more generally – than the more "technical" factors discussed. Multiple studies have analyzed the diffusion of such reform in the electricity industry (Henisz et al. 2005) and a range of others, distinguishing among coercive, normative, competitive, and knowledge-based influences (Simmons and

Elkins 2004; Henisz et al. 2005; see also Fourcade-Gourinchas and Babb 2002; Bortolotti, Fantini, and Siniscalco 2004; Kogut and Macpherson 2011). By demonstrating the role of belief structures and power dynamics in the global diffusion of market-oriented reform, these analyses called into question the common presumption among proponents of the Washington consensus that the neoliberal prescription's ascent near the end of the twentieth century was the inevitable result of its technical superiority. In so doing, they have also exposed neoliberalism's vulnerability to the same forces that promoted this ascent.

More recent research has directly illuminated this vulnerability. Denisova et al. (2012), using data from a 2006 survey of 28,000 individuals in twenty-eight post-communist countries, found that ideological preferences and concerns about the legitimacy of privatization contributed to popular support for "revising" the process. In the specific context of the electricity industry, Zelner, Henisz, and Holburn (2009) analyzed the influences on governments' renegotiation of the terms of privately owned generation projects in sixty-two countries, finding that less favorable domestic sentiment toward private enterprise and greater domestic political conflict – along with reduced indebtedness to multilateral lenders and renegotiation by peer-country governments – were all positively associated with the incidence of renegotiation.

By highlighting ideational influences on the adoption and performance of market-oriented reform in the electricity industry and others, these studies would seem to accommodate the contention that scholarship has contributed to the economic, political, and social transformations surrounding structural evolution of the global electricity industry. A handful of recent publications further illuminate this argument. In a recent diffusion study, Kogut and Macpherson (2011) demonstrated an association between the spread of privatization and other market-oriented reform policies and the presence of American-trained Ph.D. economists in adopting countries, as well as the level of agreement among economists on a given policy's value. Centeno and Cohen (2012: 328) also considered the role of economists in their historical analysis of neoliberalism's development:

> The market's first great victory was in the academy. The principles underlying neoliberalism first established their monopoly in the field of economics and from there engaged in an imperial conquest (or delegitimation) of other fields (McNamara 2009; Oatley 2011). What is particularly fascinating about the relationship between academic economics and the rise of neoliberalism is that even as the level of abstraction and formalism of the former increased, so did its influence in shaping policy. (Reay 2007)

Nobel laureate and former World Bank chief economist Joseph Stiglitz provided a blunter assessment during the early days of the of the 2008 financial crisis:

> The world has not been kind to neo-liberalism, that grab-bag of ideas based on the fundamentalist notion that markets are self-correcting, allocate resources efficiently, and serve the public interest well. It was this market fundamentalism that underlay Thatcherism, Reaganomics, and the so-called "Washington Consensus" in favor of privatization, liberalization, and independent central banks focusing single-mindedly on inflation.

> For a quarter-century, there has been a contest among developing countries, and the losers are clear: countries that pursued neo-liberal policies not only lost the growth sweepstakes; when they did grow, the benefits accrued disproportionately to those at the top.

> *(Stiglitz 2008)*

Stiglitz subsequently went on to bemoan the "culpability" of "the economics profession" in promoting heroic beliefs about markets, the result of which was that, "Today, not only is our economy in a shambles but so too is the economic paradigm that predominated in the years before the crisis – or at least it should be" (Stiglitz 2010).

If Stiglitz's pronouncement is correct, then the question naturally arises: what next? Scholars who have traced the sociopolitical forces shaping neoliberalism's "arc" concur that there exist no serious contenders to replace the paradigm, due to the sharp real-world political cleavages that any successor would have to surmount (Centeno and Cohen 2012: 332; Babb 2013: 291) as well as the intellectual cleavages around issues of economic development (Babb 2013: 291). Given these circumstances, future structures implemented by national governments to govern the provision of infrastructure services will more likely comprise a "heterogeneous international policy regime that is less uniformly structured by transnational policy paradigms" (Babb 2013: 291).

Whatever the precise makeup of the new regime, relaxation of the neoliberal hegemony seems almost certain to be accompanied by an expanded role for the state. The debate over the advantages and disadvantages of state ownership and involvement in the economy has already regained momentum in the wake of the recent global financial crisis (Bremmer 2010; Wooldridge, Bremmer, and Musacchio 2012; Inoue, Lazzarini, and Musacchio 2013), and research examining the impact of state ownership on such outcomes as foreign investment location choice and entry mode has recently begun to appear (e.g., Cui and Jiang 2012; Wang et al. 2012). In the specific context of the electricity industry, future research should examine the extent to which continued and, in some cases, resurgent government involvement (through either direct ownership or regulation) affects firms' expansion patterns (Doh, Teegen, and Mudambi 2004; Dorobantu and Zelner 2014).

Conclusion

Though intellectual debates over the answers to the questions posed in the introduction – when and how should governments intervene in markets in which existing technologies have natural monopoly properties? – have often been technical in nature, the technical analyses themselves have shifted over time, creating an undulating pattern of state-centered and market-mediated policy prescriptions. In the policy-making arena, security concerns prompted by two world wars and the politics surrounding the provision of critical infrastructure services have also played an explicit role in the design and implementation of structures to govern the electricity industry.

The industry's tendency toward natural monopoly, combined with its economic and strategic importance, pushed governments around the world toward active intervention through the middle of the twentieth century. The United States opted for private ownership combined with strong regulatory oversight decentralized at the state level. In Europe and the rest of the world, government ownership and operation emerged in the middle of the century as the dominant model for the organization of the industry.

State ownership and control, however, did not fare as well as its proponents had hoped, especially after the global energy crises of the 1970s and the economic slowdown that affected most of the developing world in the 1980s. By the turn of the twenty-first century, market-oriented reforms designed to reduce state participation had diffused around the world. Yet this model, too, has failed to live up to its promise in many countries (Denisova et al. 2009, 2012; Zelner et al. 2009).

So the electricity industry appears again poised for change as the global sway of the neo-liberal creed declines. Policy-makers seeking new solutions during this period of ferment would be well advised to favor gradual, incremental changes over another round of dramatic structural overhaul. Scholars, for their part, should also strive to design governance structures that respect the realpolitik of this vital industry by balancing the high-powered incentives of the market with governments' – and societies' – deep-rooted desire for reliability, affordability, and access. They might also step back to assess the extent to which their own beliefs – however "scientific" they might ostensibly be – reflect the peculiar influences of time and place rather than universal truths.

Notes

1 For related analyses focusing on internal domestic politics and corruption, see Henisz and Zelner (2014) and Troesken (2006), respectively. For broader discussions of the role of the academy in the "arc" of neoliberalism, see Centeno and Cohen (2012) and Babb (2013).
2 Williamson intended the term to refer to ten propositions: fiscal discipline; a redirection of public expenditure priorities toward primary healthcare, primary education, and infrastructure; tax reform to lower the marginal rates and broaden the tax base; interest rate liberalization; a competitive exchange rate; trade liberalization; liberalization of inflows of foreign direct investments; privatization; deregulation to remove barriers to entry and exit; and secure property rights (1990: 35).

References

Al-Sunaidy, A., and R. Green. 2006. "Electricity deregulation in OECD (Organization for Economic Cooperation and Development) countries." *Energy, Electricity Market Reform and Deregulation* 31 (6–7): 769–87.

Averch, H., and L. L. Johnson. 1962. "Behavior of the firm under regulatory constraint." *American Economic Review* 52 (5): 1052–69.

Babb, S. 2013. "The Washington consensus as transnational policy paradigm: Its origins, trajectory and likely successor." *Review of International Political Economy* 20 (2, SI): 268–97.

Bacon, R. W. 1995. "Privatization and reform in the global electricity supply industry." *Annual Review of Energy and the Environment* 20 (1): 119–43.

Bacon, R. W., and J. Besant-Jones. 2001. "Global electric power reform, privatization, and liberalization of the electric power industry in developing countries." *Annual Review of Energy and the Environment* 26 (1): 331–59.

Baldwin, R., M. Cave, and M. Lodge. 2013. *Understanding Regulation: Theory, Strategy, and Practice.* 2nd edition. New York: Oxford University Press.

Baron, D. P. 1995a. "Integrated strategy: Market and nonmarket components." *California Management Review* 37 (2): 47–65.

— 1995b. "The nonmarket strategy system." *Sloan Management Review*, Fall: 73–85.

Baumol, W. J., J. C. Panzar, and R. D. Willig. 1982. *Contestable Markets and the Theory of Industry Structure.* New York: Harcourt College Publishing.

Boardman, A. E., and A. R. Vining. 1989. "Ownership and performance in competitive environments: A comparison of the performance of private, mixed, and state-owned enterprises." *Journal of Law and Economics* 32 (1): 1–33.

Bortolotti, B., C. Cambini, and L. Rondi. 2013. "Reluctant regulation." *Journal of Comparative Economics* 41 (3): 804–28.

Bortolotti, B., M. Fantini, and D. Siniscalco. 2004. "Privatisation around the world: Evidence from panel data." *Journal of Public Economics* 88 (1–2): 305–32.

Boubakri, N., and J. C. Cosset. 1998. "The financial and operating performance of newly privatized firms: Evidence from developing countries." *Journal of Finance* 53 (3): 1081–110.

Boubakri, N., J. Cosset, and O. Guedhami. 2005. "Liberalization, corporate governance and the performance of privatized firms in developing countries." *Journal of Corporate Finance* 11 (5): 767–90.

— 2008. "Privatisation in developing countries: Performance and ownership effects." *Development Policy Review* 26 (3): 275–308.

Boubakri, N., J. Cosset, and W. Saffar. 2013. "The role of state and foreign owners in corporate risk-taking: Evidence from privatization." *Journal of Financial Economics* 108 (3): 641–58.

Bremmer, I. 2010. *The End of the Free Market: Who Wins the War between States and Corporations?* New York: Portfolio Hardcover.

Buchanan, J. M., and G. Tullock. 1962. *The Calculus of Consent: Logical Foundations of Constitutional Democracy.* Ann Arbor: University of Michigan Press.

Cabeza-Garcia, L., and S. Gomez-Anson. 2011. "Post-privatisation ownership concentration: Determinants and influence on firm efficiency." *Journal of Comparative Economics* 39 (3): 412–30.

Centeno, M. A., and J. N. Cohen. 2012. "The arc of neoliberalism." *Annual Review of Sociology* 38 (3): 317–40.

Cui, L., and F. Jiang. 2012. "State ownership effect on firms' FDI ownership decisions under institutional pressure: A study of Chinese outward-investing firms." *Journal of International Business Studies* 43 (3): 264–84.

D'Souza, J., and W. L. Megginson. 1999. "The financial and operating performance of privatized firms during the 1990s." *Journal of Finance* 54 (4): 1397–438.

D'Souza, J., W. L. Megginson, and R. Nash. 2005. "Effect of institutional and firm-specific characteristics on post-privatization performance: Evidence from developed countries." *Journal of Corporate Finance* 11 (5): 747–66.

Demsetz, H. 1968. "Why regulate utilities?" *Journal of Law and Economics* 11 (1): 55–65.

Denisova, I., M. Eller, T. Frye, and E. Zhuravskaya. 2009. "Who wants to revise privatization? The complementarity of market skills and institutions." *American Political Science Review* 103 (2): 284–304.

— 2012. "Everyone hates privatization, but why? Survey evidence from 28 post-communist countries." *Journal of Comparative Economics* 40 (1): 44–61.

Dewenter, K. L., and P. H. Malatesta. 2001. "State-owned and privately owned firms: An empirical analysis of profitability, leverage, and labor intensity." *American Economic Review* 91 (1): 320–34.

Doh, J. P., H. Teegen, and R. Mudambi. 2004. "Balancing private and state ownership in emerging markets' telecommunications infrastructure: Country, industry, and firm influences." *Journal of International Business Studies* 35 (3): 233–50.

Dorobantu, S., and B. Zelner. 2014. "State-owned vs. private multinationals: Two motivations of international expansion in the electricity supply industry." Unpublished manuscript.

Ely, R. T. 1894. "Natural monopolies and the workingman: A programme of social reform." *North American Review* 158 (448): 294–303.

Evans, P. 1997. "The eclipse of the state? Reflections on stateness in an era of globalization." *World Politics* 50 (1): 62–87.

Fourcade-Gourinchas, M., and S. L. Babb. 2002. "The rebirth of the liberal creed: Paths to neoliberalism in four countries." *American Journal of Sociology* 108 (3): 533–79.

Frydman, R., C. Gray, M. Hessel, and A. Rapaczynski. 1999. "When does privatization work? The impact of private ownership on corporate performance in the transition economies." *Quarterly Journal of Economics* 114 (4): 1153–91.

Gans, J. S. 2014. "Natural monopoly." In M. Augier and D. Teece (eds.), *The Palgrave Encyclopedia of Strategic Management.* London: Palgrave Macmillan. www.palgraveconnect.com/esm/doifinder/10.1057/9781137294678.0454 (accessed November 15, 2014).

Granovetter, M. 1992. "Economic institutions as social constructions: A framework for analysis." *Acta Sociologica* 35 (1): 3–11.

Hadley, A. T. 1886. "Private monopolies and public rights." *Quarterly Journal of Economics* 1 (1): 28–44.

Haggard, S., and R. R. Kaufman. 1995. *The Political Economy of Democratic Transitions.* Princeton, NJ: Princeton University Press.

Hausman, W. J., P. Hertner, and M. Wilkins. 2011. *Global Electrification: Multinational Enterprise and International Finance in the History of Light and Power, 1878–2007.* New York: Cambridge University Press.

Henisz, W. J., and B. A. Zelner. 2006. "Interest groups, veto points, and electricity infrastructure deployment." *International Organization* 60 (1): 263–86.

— 2014. "The cycling of power between private and public sectors: Electricity generation in Argentina, Brazil, and Chile." In E. Brousseau and J.-M. Glachant (eds.), *The Manufacturing of Markets: Legal, Political and Economic Dynamics.* New York: Cambridge University Press: 253–70.

Henisz, W. J., B. A. Zelner, and M. F. Guillen. 2005. "The worldwide diffusion of market-oriented infrastructure reform, 1977–99." *American Sociological Review* 70 (6): 871–97.

Hirsh, R. F. 1989. *Technology and Transformation in the American Electric Utility Industry.* New York: Cambridge University Press.

Huntington, S. P. 1993. *The Third Wave: Democratization in the Late 20th Century.* Norman: University of Oklahoma Press.

Inoue, C. F. K. V., S. G. Lazzarini, and A. Musacchio. 2013. "Leviathan as a minority shareholder: Firm-level implications of state equity purchases." *Academy of Management Journal* 56 (6): 1775–801.

Joskow, P. L. 1997. "Restructuring, competition and regulatory reform in the US electricity sector." *Journal of Economic Perspectives* 11 (3): 119–38.

— 1998. "Electricity sectors in transition." *Energy Journal* 19 (2): 25–52.

— 2008. "Lessons learned from electricity market liberalization." *Energy Journal* 29 (2): 9–42.

Knight, F. H. 1921. "Cost of production and price over long and short periods." *Journal of Political Economy* 29. http://ideas.repec.org/a/ucp/jpolec/v29y1913p304.html (accessed November 15, 2014).

Kogut, B., and J. M. Macpherson. 2011. "The mobility of economists and the diffusion of policy ideas: The influence of economics on national policies." *Research Policy* 40 (10): 1307–20.

Kwoka, J. E. 2005. "The comparative advantage of public ownership: Evidence from US electric utilities." *Canadian Journal of Economics/Revue canadienne d'economique* 38 (2): 622–40.

Levy, B., and P. T. Spiller. 1994. "The institutional foundations of regulatory commitment: A comparative-analysis of telecommunications regulations." *Journal of Law, Economics, and Organization* 10 (2): 201–46.

Li, W., and L. X. C. Xu. 2004. "The impact of privatization and competition in the telecommunications sector around the world." *Journal of Law and Economics* 47 (2): 395–430.

McGuire, P., M. Granovetter, and M. Schwartz. 1993. "Thomas Edison and the social construction of the early electricity industry in America." In R. Swedberg (ed.), *Explorations in Economic Sociology.* New York: Russell Sage Foundation: 213–48.

McNamara, K. R. 2009. "Of intellectual monocultures and the study of IPE." *Review of International Political Economy* 16: 72–84.

Megginson, W. L., and J. R. Netter. 2001. "From state to market: A survey of empirical studies on privatization." *Journal of Economic Literature* 39 (2): 321–89.

Megginson, W. L., R. C. Nash, and M. Van Randenborgh. 1994. "The financial and operating performance of newly privatized firms: An international empirical analysis." *Journal of Finance* 49 (2): 403–52.

Mosca, M. 2008. "On the origins of the concept of natural monopoly: Economies of scale and competition." *European Journal of the History of Economic Thought* 15 (2): 317–53.

Oatley, T. 2011. "The reductionist gamble: Open economy politics in the global economy." *International Organization* 65: 311–41.

Olson, M. 1965. *The Logic of Collective Action: Public Goods and the Theory of Groups.* Cambridge, MA: Harvard University Press.

Omran, M. 2009. "Post-privatization corporate governance and firm performance: The role of private ownership concentration, identity and board composition." *Journal of Comparative Economics* 37 (4): 658–73.

Peltzman, S. 1976. "Toward a more general theory of regulation." *Journal of Law and Economics* 19 (2): 211–40.

Perotti, E. C. 1995. "Credible privatization." *American Economic Review* 85 (4): 847–59.

Pigou, A. C. 1932. *The Economics of Welfare.* Volume I. New York: Cosimo Classics.

Piketty, T. 2014. *Capital in the Twenty-first Century.* Translated by Arthur Goldhammer. 1st edition. Cambridge, MA: Belknap Press.

Posner, R. A. 2011. *A Failure of Capitalism: The Crisis of '08 and the Descent into Depression.* Cambridge, MA: Harvard University Press.

Przeworski, A. 1991. *Democracy and the Market: Political and Economic Reforms in Eastern Europe and Latin America.* New York: Cambridge University Press.

Reay, M. J. 2007. "Academic knowledge and expert authority in American economics." *Sociological Perspectives* 50: 101–29.

Rodrik, D. 2006. "Goodbye Washington consensus, hello Washington confusion? A review of the World Bank's economic growth in the 1990s: Learning from a decade of reform." *Journal of Economic Literature* 44 (4): 973–87.

Russo, M. V. 2001. "Institutions, exchange relations, and the emergence of new fields: Regulatory policies and independent power production in America, 1978–92." *Administrative Science Quarterly* 46 (1): 57–86.

Serra, N., and J. E. Stiglitz. 2008. *The Washington Consensus Reconsidered: Towards a New Global Governance.* Oxford: Oxford University Press.

Simmons, B. A., and Z. Elkins. 2004. "The globalization of liberalization: Policy diffusion in the international political economy." *American Political Science Review* 98 (1): 171–89.

Smith, A. 1776. *An Inquiry into the Nature and Causes of the Wealth of Nations.* Volume I. London: W. Strahan and T. Cadell.

Snyder, J. M. 1991. "On buying legislatures." *Economics and Politics* 3 (2): 93–109.

Spulber, D. F. 1989. *Regulation and Markets.* Cambridge, MA: MIT Press.

Sraffa, P. 1926. "The laws of returns under competitive conditions." *Economic Journal* 36 (144): 535.

Stigler, G. J. 1971. "Theory of economic regulation." *Bell Journal of Economics and Management Science* 2 (1): 3–21.

Stiglitz, J. E. 2003. *Globalization and Its Discontents.* New York: W. W. Norton & Company.

— 2008. "The end of neo-liberalism?" www.project-syndicate.org/commentary/the-end-of-neo-liberalism- (accessed November 15, 2014).

— 2010. "Needed: A new economic paradigm." *Financial Times*, August 19.

Troesken, Werner. 1997. "The sources of public ownership: Historical evidence from the gas industry." *Journal of Law, Economics, and Organization* 13 (1): 1–25.

— 2006. "Regime change and corruption: A history of public utility regulation." In E. L. Glaeser and C. Goldin (eds.), *Corruption and Reform: Lessons from America's Economic History.* Chicago: University of Chicago Press: 259–82.

Vaaler, P. M., and B. N. Schrage. 2009. "Residual state ownership, policy stability and financial performance following strategic decisions by privatizing telecoms." *Journal of International Business Studies* 40 (4): 621–41.

Wang, C., J. Hong, M. Kafouros, and M. Wright. 2012. "Exploring the role of government involvement in outward FDI from emerging economies." *Journal of International Business Studies* 43 (7): 655–76.

Weyland, K. 1998. "Swallowing the bitter pill sources of popular support for neoliberal reform in Latin America." *Comparative Political Studies* 31 (5): 539–68.

— 2004. *The Politics of Market Reform in Fragile Democracies: Argentina, Brazil, Peru, and Venezuela.* Princeton, NJ: Princeton University Press.

White, M. W., P. L. Joskow, and J. Hausman. 1996. "Power struggles: Explaining deregulatory reforms in electricity markets." *Brookings Papers on Economic Activity, Microeconomics* January: 201–67.

Williams, J. H., and R. Ghanadan. 2006. "Electricity reform in developing and transition countries: A reappraisal." *Energy, Electricity Market Reform and Deregulation* 31 (6–7): 815–44.

Williamson, J. 1990. "What Washington means by policy reform." In J. Williamson (ed.), *Latin American Adjustment: How Much Has Happened?* Washington, DC: Peterson Institute for International Economics: 35–70.

— 1994. *The Political Economy of Policy Reform.* Washington, DC: Peterson Institute for International Economics.

Wooldridge, A., I. Bremmer, and A. Musacchio. 2012. "State capitalism: Statements." *The Economist*, February 2. www.economist.com/debate/days/view/804/print (accessed November 15, 2014).

Zelner, B. A., W. J. Henisz, and G. L. F. Holburn. 2009. "Contentious implementation and retrenchment in neoliberal policy reform: The global electric power industry, 1989–2001." *Administrative Science Quarterly* 54 (3): 379–412.

Zhang, Y. F., D. Parker, and C. Kirkpatrick. 2008. "Electricity sector reform in developing countries: An econometric assessment of the effects of privatization, competition and regulation." *Journal of Regulatory Economics* 33 (2): 159–78.

Section D

Non-market context and challenges

Corporate climate change adaptation

An emerging non-market strategy in an uncertain world

Peter Tashman, Monika Winn, and Jorge E. Rivera

In this chapter, we discuss non-market strategies associated with corporate climate change adaptation (CCCA), or the "changes in behavior of a business organization aimed at coping with the effects of any climate-related event" (Bleda and Shackley, 2008: 517). Most scholarly attention to non-market strategy has explored how firms confront and manage opportunities and threats in their institutional environments, whether political, social, or ethical in nature, with very little attention being paid to forces in the ecological environment of the firm with strategic implications. The situation is changing somewhat as a growing number of studies are exploring the implications of climate change on businesses and their stakeholders through the lens of CCCA (Winn et al., 2011). In particular, a number of scholars have turned their attention to studying explicit climatic impacts on firms, including disruptions to operations, supply and distribution chains, infrastructure, insurable risk, migration patterns of workers, consumer behavior, and the institutions that support markets and economies (Kuhn, Campbell-Lendrum, Haines, and Cox, 2005; Maddison, 2001; Schlenker, Hanemann, and Fischer, 2005). Still, research on CCCA is in a very early stage.

Our goal in this chapter is to draw attention to the importance of non-market strategies for managing climate change-related phenomena, specifically through the area of CCCA. Currently, the area lacks a common organizing framework that scholars can use to structure their approach to identifying, framing, and studying important questions. For this reason, we develop one such framework around the diversity of exposure pathways through which climate change-related pressures may affect the firm, and then propose how this framework might be used as a basis for future research. Firms may be directly biophysically exposed to climate change "perturbations," which are abnormally extreme episodes, or continuous "stressors," which are more subtle changes in weather trends that can disrupt business operations if they persist for long enough (Füssel, 2007). Firms also face a number of indirect exposures to climate variability and change, since they are embedded in "highly variable political, economic, institutional, and biophysical conditions" (Belliveau, Smit, and Bradshaw, 2006: 364) that channel climatic pressures to the firm in unintended and unforeseeable ways. In brief, firms may be subject to a number of climate change-related influences depending on the set of exposures facing them. Thus, we build our framework around categories reflecting the firm's exposure in its biophysical, industrial–economic, and institutional environments, which include political, social, and technological forces related to climate change.

Within each category, we address the constructs of corporate climate change vulnerability (CCCV), corporate climate change adaptive capacity (CCCAC), and CCCA, which have each received consistent attention from scholars of the area (e.g. Belliveau et al., 2006; Berkhout, Hertin, and Gann, 2006; Bleda and Shackley, 2008; Hoffmann et al., 2009; Scott and McBoyle, 2007; Tashman, 2011). CCCV refers to the "possible negative impacts of climate change in real terms" on business (Hoffmann et al., 2009: 257). CCCAC refers to the "ability of business organizations to adjust, moderate potential damages, take advantage of opportunities, or to cope with the consequence of climate related events (both physical and institutional)" (Bleda and Shackley, 2008: 519). As mentioned above, CCCA describes the resultant efforts by firms to cope with threats or seize opportunities related to climate change-related forces. Our framework relies on these constructs because they reflect the external drivers of organizational action on climate change (e.g. CCCV), firms' willingness and capacity to respond to those drivers (e.g. CCCAC), and resultant efforts in this regard (e.g. CCCA). Finally, after reviewing the research on CCCA as it pertains to each climate change exposure pathway, we outline research opportunities for scholars with interests in this area.

The rest of this chapter will be organized as follows. First, we will review the key concepts of CCCV, CCCAC and CCCA. Second, we will organize the extant research on these concepts into categories that reflect how they pertain to the biophysical, industrial–economic, and institutional climate change exposures that are confronting business. We will also outline unanswered research questions and opportunities associated with each type of exposure. Finally, we will discuss the implications of our framework for scholars and practitioners.

Corporate climate change vulnerability

In the broadest sense, CCCV refers to the extent to which businesses can be harmed by climate change-related pressures. Scholars have identified several conditions that determine the presence and extent of a firm's climate change vulnerability, including exposure, sensitivity, and resilience to climate change pressures (e.g. Belliveau et al., 2006; Hoffmann et al., 2009; Linnenluecke, Griffiths, and Winn, 2013; Scott and McBoyle, 2007; Tashman, 2011). Exposure refers to the presence of climate change pressures in the external environment of the firm. Sensitivity refers to the extent to which the firm may be adversely affected by those pressures (Belliveau et al., 2006). Resilience refers to the firm's capacity to recover from adverse climate change-related effects in both substantive (the extent to which affected resources may be restored to their previous state) and temporal (the extent to which the recovery timeframe is feasible for the firm) dimensions (Linnenluecke, Griffiths, and Winn, 2012).

As mentioned above, CCCV can involve "perturbations," which are discrete extreme episodes, or continuous "stressors," which are more subtle changes in weather trends that disrupt business operations if they persist for sufficiently long timeframes (Füssel, 2007). Firms experience CCCV directly through biophysical exposure, or indirectly through industrial–economic and institutional actors and systems that may be sensitive to climate change-related pressures (Belliveau et al., 2006). Finally, direct and indirect forms of CCCV can be highly interactive (Smit, McNabb, and Smithers, 1996), implying that firms can simultaneously experience multiple forms of exposure, sensitivity, and resilience to climate change as well as the effects of these factors in combination.

Corporate climate change adaptive capacity

Like CCCV, CCCAC is an inclusive concept that refers to organizational resources that help firms cope with threats or take advantage of opportunities created by climate change (Berkhout, 2012). Research on this construct has focused on how managerial sensemaking abilities determine recognition of CCCV, as well as the capabilities that are useful in adapting to climate change. Generally, scholars believe that managerial interpretations and responses to climatic stimuli are boundedly rational, where managers face diverse competing demands on their attention that complicate recognizing and responding to CCCV (Berkhout, 2012).

In addition, there is a small but growing amount of research on the capabilities that help firms adapt to climate change by enabling responses to CCCV (e.g. Berkhout et al., 2006; Hertin, Berkhout, Gann, and Barlow 2003; Tashman, 2011; Winn et al., 2011). In particular, Winn and colleagues (2011) suggest that several existing capabilities could be developed and deployed in response to CCCV, including sustainability management, crisis management, and risk management, since CCCV often involves uncertainty- and risk-associated ecological pressures, including massively destructive extreme weather events. These scholars carefully note the discontinuous and non-linear nature of climate change exposure, along with its unknown destructive potential, and suggest that current capabilities will need to become more robust to the future realities of climate change.

Berkhout and colleagues (2006) observed an evolutionary economics approach to building CCCAC in the UK water and housing sectors. They found that firms deployed learning routines and dynamic capabilities to establish a better organizational fit with their changing climatic environment. Less work has examined how industrial–economic and institutional factors shape CCCAC, although organizational theories suggest that they may either enable or constrain such capabilities. Berkhout's (2012: 94) review of the CCCA literature led him to conclude that these contexts "may provide the knowledge, resources, incentives, and legitimacy for (collective) adaptive action, but they may also promote climate vulnerability and constrain adaptive responses."

Corporate climate change adaptation

Management scholars have used a number of definitions for CCCA in their research (Nitkin, Foster, and Medalye, 2009). Bleda and Shackley (2008: 517) view it as "changes in behavior of a business organization aimed at coping with the effects of any climate-related event." Hoffmann and colleagues (2009: 257) define it as "the measures that a company chooses to implement in order to adapt to climate change." Linnenluecke and colleagues (2012: 18) suggest that climate change adaptation involves "longer-term, anticipatory adjustments to observed or expected impacts from weather extremes and greater climate variability." While Belliveau and colleagues (2006), Tashman (2011), and Winn and colleagues (2011) avoid explicit definitions, their papers suggests that adaptation to climate change is consistent with organizational adaptation described in a number of management theories, including the behavioral view of the firm, institutional theory, the resource-based view, and resource dependence theory. We contend that the concept should remain general enough to accommodate a wide range of potential adaptive responses to the various exposure pathways that may confront firms, as well as be inclusive of multiple organizational theories to explain different mechanisms at play with these various exposures.

Current research asserts that CCCA can vary along several dimensions, including type of adaptation, degree of proactivity, and scope of adaptation (Nitkin et al., 2009). Researchers

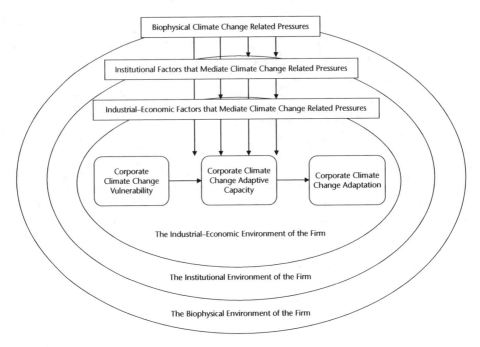

Figure 17.1 Factors and levels of analysis of the corporate climate change adaptation process

focusing on type adaptation have discussed the measures that firms can take to reduce the CCCV of their current business models, or adapt their business models into activities that are less vulnerable (e.g. Hertin et al., 2003; Hoffmann et al., 2009; Tashman, 2011). Degree of proactivity refers to whether firms are engaged in anticipatory (proactive), autonomous, planned, and/or reactive adaptation. Anticipatory adaptation involves measures to reduce CCCV ahead of the firm's climate change exposure. Autonomous adaptation is not consciously planned by managers, but rather is triggered by climate change exposure. Conversely, planned adaptation is deliberately undertaken by management. Reactive adaptation comprises responses to the effects of climate change on firms after the fact (Nitkin et al., 2009). Finally, scope of adaptation refers to whether the adaptation is aimed at providing private benefits for only the firm itself, club benefits for sets of organizations, or public benefits for non-market stakeholders in the firm's institutional environment (Berkhout, 2012). In the next sections, we map the different types of climate change-related exposures that have been discussed in the literature and relate them to CCCV, CCCAC, and CCCA, respectively. Figure 17.1 illustrates these relationships.

Climate change adaptation and biophysical pressures

Biophysical exposure and corporate climate change vulnerability

Biophysical CCCV refers to vulnerability to abnormal weather trends caused by dynamics in the atmospheric environment of the firm (IPCC, 2001). As mentioned above, abnormal weather trends may manifest as perturbations (abnormally extreme weather events) or stressors (prolonged deviations in the statistical norms of climatic variables such as temperature and precipitation amounts) (Füssel, 2007). It is important to note that extreme weather events are not necessarily climate change-related. They are, by definition, rare and expected to happen on an infrequent basis. Extreme weather is a reflection of climate change when events become more frequent, intense, and/or geographically dispersed than historical averages (IPCC, 2001).

Several articles have studied the massive destructive potential of biophysical perturbations that can affect firms (Linnenluecke et al., 2012; Winn et al., 2011). This research has generally focused on extreme weather events and their potential to create spectacular physical impacts on firms. Organizational sensitivity to these events appears to be a function of physical dependence of the assets that are exposed to these events. Firms tend to be resilient to these impacts if their assets are impact-resistant to exposure and they are able to invest in restoring damaged assets (Linnenluecke et al., 2012). Firms might also recover from these impacts if they have insured damaged assets (Mills, 2012).

Some research has examined how biophysical climatic stressors generate incremental and cumulative impacts on organizations' systems over time. Hoffman (2006) briefly described how Arctic-region businesses that depend on ice for transportation routes have been vulnerable to warming winter temperatures that shorten ice-road seasons. Several studies have examined how the ski resort industry is vulnerable to warming winter temperatures because of their effect on ski season length and quality (e.g. Hoffmann et al., 2009; Scott, McBoyle, and Mills, 2003; Tashman, 2011). Schlenker and colleagues (2005) examined how climate change appears to be shifting temperatures and redistributing hydrological resources around the globe, and by extension creating winners and losers in the agricultural industries. In these cases, sensitivity appears to be a function of direct dependence on biophysical resources. For example, ski resorts count reliable snowfall as an essential operating resource, just as agricultural concerns require reliable access to lengthy wet growing seasons (Tashman, 2011). Firms that do not depend on climatic resources, on the other hand, should be insensitive to climatic stressors. With regard to resilience, sensitive firms are unlikely to see the restoration of the climatic resources that are affected by climate change stressors unless the firm's local weather trends revert to previous norms. Again, firms might recover from the impacts of biophysical stressors if they have insured damaged assets against losses (Mills, 2012).

Finally, scholars have also uncovered evidence of positive effects of biophysical exposure on firms. Where temperatures are becoming warmer, tourism firms that rely on hot weather are benefiting from longer seasons (Maddison, 2001). The same positive effects can be seen for some agricultural concerns that are benefiting from longer growing seasons (Schlenker et al., 2005). Similarly, some ski resorts are benefiting from geographic shifts in temperature and precipitation that have resulted in more natural snowfall over the course of the winter season (Scott et al., 2003).

Biophysical exposure and corporate climate change adaptive capacity

Management scholars have given some attention to explaining the firm's capabilities for coping with biophysical climate change exposure, most often when exposure is in the form of extreme weather. Some of this research has focused on managers' ability to make sense of their firms' exposure and identify the resources that could be deployed in efforts to reduce CCCV. Others have examined how firms might engage in organizational learning to improve their response capacities to these pressures (e.g. Berkhout et al., 2006; Hertin et al., 2003). Finally, some research has focused on how firms might deploy existing capabilities to cope with climate change (e.g. Hertin et al., 2003; Hoffmann et al., 2009; Scott et al., 2003; Tashman, 2011).

In general, scholars have found evidence of variability in managers' awareness of their firms' biophysical CCCV, and that many overlook these pressures until they actually experience their effects. Hoffmann and colleagues (2009) found that Swiss ski resort managers were often unaware of their vulnerability to climatic variability, even though the industry has substantial exposure and sensitivity. Haigh and Griffiths (2012) found managers may be unaware of biophysical CCCV until climate "surprises" impacted their physical assets. Scott and McBoyle (2007) concluded that ski resorts were more likely to incorporate climate change-related goals in strategic planning after unusually dry winters. Berkhout and colleagues (2006) found that many managers were aware of their industry's biophysical climate change exposure, but not of their own firm's. They also observed few deliberate efforts to understand the causes or long-term implications of climate change.

Some research has pointed to the importance of organizational learning as a basis for CCCAC to biophysical CCCV. Because of biophysical CCCV's enormous physical destructive potential, and because its prevalence and intensity may intensify substantially in the future, many organizations lack robust capabilities for responding to the potential impacts (Winn et al., 2011). As a result, "learning how to respond to ecological discontinuities will be indispensable to management practice" (Linnenluecke et al., 2012: 18). Berkhout and colleagues (2006) observed that adaptive organizations leveraged "learning cycles" (Zollo and Winter, 2002). These cycles rely on routines that sequence efforts at sensing and interpreting biophysical CCCV, experimenting with new routines, codifying and deploying new routines, and refining them over time. Busch (2011) observed different capabilities in his study of Austrian and Swiss utilities. In particular, he found that adaptive capacity was a function of capabilities that internalize knowledge about biophysical CCCV, respond to its short-term impacts, and enable long-term innovation that could reduce biophysical CCCV in the future.

Finally, a small amount of attention has been paid to examining how firms may leverage existing resources and capabilities to cope with biophysical CCCV. Several scholars have suggested that risk and disaster management capabilities might be a basis for anticipating and responding to destructive extreme weather events (e.g. Berkhout et al., 2006; Mills, 2005; Winn et al., 2011). Hoffmann and colleagues (2009) and Tashman (2011) both observed that some ski resorts are able to draw on biophysical resources when adapting to CCCV associated with biophysical stress. They do so by finding and using alternative hydrological resources when climate variability results in waning natural precipitation. Finally, slack resources and capital can be deployed in efforts to recover from the negative effects of biophysical CCCV, invested in insurance against its potential effects, or used to take advantage of potential opportunities that arise from more favorable weather trends (Winn et al., 2011).

Biophysical exposure and corporate climate change adaptation

To date, little empirical evidence of CCCA to biophysical exposure has been generated by management scholars. Tashman and Rivera (Forthcoming) suggest that one issue associated with studying CCCA is that the phenomenon has barely emerged in practice. This may be the case because relatively few managers have experience perceiving, recognizing, and managing biophysical CCCV (Haigh and Griffiths, 2012). Further, CCCA generally could involve either behavioral or cognitive changes that might be difficult to observe in practice (Berkhout, 2012). Finally, CCCA to biophysical exposure could involve practices that are also responses to non-climatic stimuli (Scott and McBoyle, 2007).

Still, a few studies have generated evidence on the topic. Hertin and colleagues (2003) observed that UK homebuilders engaged in commercial, financial, and technological adaptation to biophysical exposure. Commercial adaptation was done by relocating building sites to areas with less biophysical exposure or building less sensitive buildings. Financial adaptation involved insuring assets and accruing slack resources that could be used in future adaptation efforts. Technological adaptation involved innovating materials and building techniques that are more resilient to climate variability. Berkhout and colleagues (2006) developed a similar scheme to describe adaptation efforts of UK water utilities, noting that firms could also deploy information and monitoring techniques for evaluating CCCV and assessing the effectiveness of adaptation initiatives. They suggested that these additional efforts enabled some firms to shift their CCCA strategies from reactive to proactive. They also observed that adaptation initiatives tended to be more effective when they were based on existing routines for risk-appraisal and decision-making.

Hoffmann and colleagues' (2009) study of Swiss ski resorts observed a complementary scheme in which adaptation involved measures to protect affected businesses, expand into less vulnerable businesses, and/or use financial adaptations to share financial risks. Protecting affected businesses involved technological adaptation that reduced CCCV in either proactive or reactive ways; expanding beyond affected businesses allowed firms to reduce the CCCV of the business with new lines of business with less biophysical CCCV; and financial CCCA included using insurance, building slack resources, and diluting climate risk via horizontal integration or strategic alliances with business partners and competitors. Finally, in a study of US ski resorts, Tashman and Rivera (Forthcoming) found evidence of maladaptation, where CCCA to biophysical exposure led to negative externalities. In this case, ski resorts used snowmaking and terrain expansion to increase their resilience to biophysical exposure; this, however, led to negative environmental impacts in their local ecosystems.

Future research on biophysical exposure and corporate climate change adaptation

We believe that research on biophysical exposure and CCCA still offers a number of opportunities for empirical study and theory development. As noted by Winn and colleagues (2011), there has been little scholarly effort to explain how ecological forces can impact organizations in general. Indeed, the natural environment can be a source of competitive advantage, just as it can generate forces that can destroy organizations. The study of biophysical CCCV represents a significant opportunity to address this lacuna both empirically and theoretically, since it can become manifest as a variety of different perturbations and stressors that impact infrastructure- and natural resource-intensive industries, respectively (Tashman, 2011). Winn and colleagues' (2011) concept of "massive discontinuous change," which describes permanent shifts in ecological and social systems that can result from disequilibria in the natural environment, offers one lens through which to view such research. Tashman and Rivera (Forthcoming) argue that resource dependence theory might be a suitable lens for making sense of biophysical CCCV because it involves organizational interdependence with ecological systems and ecological uncertainty. Other scholars might develop work that integrates ecological theories with organizational theory (e.g. Winn and Pogutz, 2013) to improve understanding of biophysical climate change exposure and the firm's sensitivity and resilience to it.

The study of CCCAC and biophysical climate change exposure also offers interesting opportunities for future research. As noted above, a number of researchers have observed that managers often have difficulty recognizing and interpreting biophysical exposure cues, or understanding the nature and extent of their organizations' biophysical CCCV. Future research might more thoroughly examine the nature of challenges and antecedents of organizational sensemaking of biophysical CCCV, and of ecological pressures on the firm more generally. Whiteman and Cooper (2000, 2011) offer one possible avenue for doing so, through their work on "ecological sensemaking" and "ecological embeddedness." In addition, more research is needed on managers' capacity to build awareness and commitment within their organizations for CCCAC, given that it is not a traditional focus for external analysis in strategy.

With regard to capabilities related to CCCAC, there may be opportunities to extend existing theory on capability development and organizational adaptation. Prior research has examined capabilities for responding to institutional and industry dynamics, including instances of discontinuous change (e.g. Meyer, 1982; Tushman and Anderson, 1986). However, the potentially sudden and massive nature of discontinuities associated with biophysical CCCV suggests that new forms of adaptive capabilities may emerge as firms attempt to build their CCCAC to cope with such pressures. In addition, it suggests new organizational structures that are more resilient to biophysical CCCV may emerge and become interesting areas of study. Finally, the costs associated with CCCA to biophysical exposure may be considerable for many organizations, given that it involves responding to potentially massive discontinuous change. As a result, scholars may have opportunities to observe how organizations convince their external stakeholders to co-create capital and combine and develop the resources necessary for transformative adaptation efforts.

Finally, as mentioned above, research on CCCA to biophysical exposure may have succeeded at classifying its types, but more research is needed to understand the conditions under which adaptation to biophysical CCCV depends on the other objectives of the organization. In particular, future research could examine the conditions under which CCCA to biophysical

Table 17.1 A future research agenda for the area of corporate climate change adaptation to biophysical exposure

Exposure pathway	Climate change vulnerability	Climate change adaptive capacity	Climate change adaptation
Biophysical	How can theories of ecology inform organizational theory to explain biophysical exposure?	What capabilities are needed to respond to massive discontinuities?	Does climate change adaptation complement other competitive or legitimacy-seeking practices?
	What is unique about sensemaking of biophysical exposure?	How do firms develop these capabilities?	How do firms adapt to biophysical exposure autonomously?
	How can biophysical exposure create opportunities as well as threats for organizations?	How do firms promote collective action needed for developing combinative capabilities across stakeholders?	When does climate change adaptation generate positive and negative externalities?

exposure is a response to those stimuli primarily or to many other external pressures or organizational objectives (Berkhout, 2012). Scholars have also observed that planned and proactive adaptation tends to occur after firms have concrete prior experience with CCCA, but the subject of autonomous adaptation has been largely overlooked. In addition, as CCCA to biophysical exposure emerges further in practice, scholars may observe new strategies that reflect the changing nature of the firm's relationship with its biophysical and climatic systems, as well as potentially new organizational forms that are better able to cope with costs of adapting to massive ecological discontinuities (Winn et al., 2011).

Climate change and industrial–economic pressures

Industrial–economic exposure and corporate climate change vulnerability

Management research on indirect CCCV through the industrial–economic environment of the firm is emerging and has thus far been descriptive. In particular, scholars have examined how firms can be affected by climate change through its impacts on stakeholders in their value chains and important industry infrastructure. Some attention has also been paid to how business and industry associations are working to promote climate change awareness and knowledge about adaptation to their members (Thistlethwaite, 2012). With respect to climate change impacts on value chains and infrastructure, the WBCSD (2008) uncovered survey evidence that managers are increasingly concerned with climate change risks to sourcing raw materials, avoiding disruptions in supply chains and logistics, and uncertainty in relationships with employees, distributors, and customers facing climatic or biophysical exposure. Mills (2005, 2012) cited examples of industrial–economic exposure in the insurance industry through firms' customers, claimants, and investors. Here, the primary impacts on the industry occur through policy-holders' claims arising from their own biophysical exposure. Firms in the industry have also been subject to pressures from investors who are concerned about how climate change-related claims affect profitability. Belliveau and colleagues (2006) explained how wineries in British Columbia were indirectly affected by unusually hot and dry weather, which led to increased forest fire activity that discouraged tourism-related demand for local wines.

It appears that sensitivity in these cases is a function of well-studied forms of resource dependence, organizational interdependence, and uncertainty (Pfeffer and Salancik, 1978; Starik and Rands, 1995; Tashman, 2011). The biophysical exposure of the firm's market stakeholders creates uncertainty for the firm because stakeholders' exposure might interfere with their abilities or desire to conduct routine transactions with the firm. Firms may be resilient to CCCV rooted in economic exposure if those stakeholders are themselves resili- ient, or if the firm has alternative sources of the critical resources (Tashman and Rivera, Forthcoming). For example, Belliveau and colleagues (2006) described how larger wine- makers in British Columbia have reduced their dependence on local grape growers who are vulnerable to climate change by purchasing grapes from other growing regions. No research has yet explained how firms manage their climate change exposure through stakeholders that have experienced massive discontinuous change. Such efforts might be warranted because many industries rely on energy, agricultural, and raw natural materials sectors, which could see their business models upended by climate change. In particular, discontinuous impacts on agriculture associated with extreme weather and water scarcity could affect numerous food and beverage production industries that rely on agricultural suppliers (WBCSD, 2008).

Climate change may also create opportunities involving new products, services, technologies, and engineering solutions for organizations and consumers that are attempting to cope with climate change. Mills (2012) reported how the insurance industry has begun developing a new suite of climate-risk management products and services for policy-holders, including climate-risk modeling, consulting, and financing for building adaptive capacity and resilience. Similarly, Smit and Skinner (2002) discuss how agricultural suppliers have developed products and services that improve the resilience of agricultural firms, including new weather-resistant crop varietals, climate information systems, and low-water-intensive irrigation systems.

Industrial–economic exposure and corporate climate change adaptive capacity

Currently, the study of CCCAC to industrial–economic climate change exposure has been largely overlooked by management scholars. One possible reason for this lacuna is that there may be significant overlap between a firm's capacity to adapt to direct biophysical CCCV and indirect CCCV experienced through its industrial–economic environment. The literature on organizational adaptation generally views the role of adaptive capabilities as helping improve the performance of the firm in its business environment (Linnenluecke et al., 2013). Indeed, in the cases of both biophysical and industrial–economic exposure, the role of adaptive capacity is to help the firm reduce sensitivity and improve resilience of resources that may be affected by climate change-related pressures (as well as help the firm take advantage of related opportunities). The primary difference between the two types of exposure is that biophysical exposure involves resources located in the firm's internal value chain, while industrial–economic exposure involves resources in external supply and distribution chains. In other words, the difference is a matter of who controls the resources in question.

Since industrial–economic exposure implies that firms may not control the resources in question, we contend that CCCA might first require establishing cooperative alliances with the firms that have direct exposure, or merger and acquisition (M&A) efforts with those organizations if firms need to find ways to improve their control over the adaptation process. Such behaviors have received extensive attention in the strategic management literature on organizations that wish to acquire and integrate complementary capabilities for the purpose of effective adaptation and/or establish the necessary control over resources needed to implement adaptation (e.g. Das and Teng, 1998; Hamel, 1991). The capabilities that enable effective alliancing and M&A behavior have also been studied extensively (e.g. Dyer and Singh, 1998; Ireland, Hitt, and Vaidyanath, 2002).

Stakeholder dialogue capabilities might also enable CCCA to industrial–economic exposure as a means of incentivizing market stakeholders to reduce their own CCCV (Sussman and Freed, 2008). Where alliancing and M&A activity are unnecessary or infeasible, stakeholder dialogue can be used for knowledge-sharing activities that help stakeholders reduce their sensitivity and build resilience to climate change, and help the firm understand the nature of stakeholders' CCCV. For example, after paying out exorbitant claims to policy-holders after Hurricane Katrina, Swiss Re engaged in "awareness building" and "external outreach" to help its customers build their own adaptive capacity. To support these strategies, the firm now makes available its own research on projected climate scenarios, sponsors conferences, and works with intergovernmental agencies on corporate outreach programs (Hoffman, 2006).

We view such M&A, alliancing, and outreach capabilities as supplemental to resources and capabilities that comprise adaptive capacity to biophysical exposure. Firms that engage in acquisitions, alliances, or cooperative partnerships with organizations that are directly exposed to climate change still need to make sense of their vulnerability and adaptive capacity and implement adaptive measures.

Industrial–economic exposure and corporate climate change adaptation

The research attention devoted to CCCA and industrial–economic exposure is also at an early stage and offers limited insights into how firms address related pressures. Most research on this topic has studied firms' private adaptation efforts involving commercial, technical, or financial adaptation. Belliveau and colleagues (2006) explained how firms may engage in commercial CCCA by establishing alternative supply and distribution chains with less bio-physical CCCV. The WBCSD (2008) discussed opportunities for firms to engage in both commercial and technological CCCA by developing new products and services that help their target markets cope with climate change. With regard to financial adaptation, Scott and McBoyle (2007) explained how horizontal integration can help firms gain control over critical resources that are directly exposed to climate change and diversify their risks from industrial–economic exposure across multiple sub-units. In addition, Sussman and Freed (2008) discussed how some firms have relied on insurance or increased their capital reserves to hedge against the financial risks associated with climate change. A limited amount of research has examined efforts by organizations to establish club benefits for organizations that are jointly affected by climate change. Examples include Mills' (2012) discussion of new insurance industry products that help policy-holders manage their climate-related risks, as well as Smit and Skinner's (2002) description of agricultural supplier products and services that make farming less vulnerable to climate change.

Future research on industrial–economic exposure and corporate climate change adaptation

The paucity of research on this climate change exposure pathway translates into ample research opportunities for management scholars. First, scholars could develop classification schemes of CCCA to industrial–economic exposure. It is possible that the current schemes, including commercial, financial, and technological adaptation, and measures to protect affected businesses, expansion into less vulnerable business, and sharing financial risks, may be applied directly to CCCA to industrial–economic exposure. Still, we contend that such schemes should account for the indirect and inter-organizational nature of CCCA to this pathway.

Second, our understandings of CCCAC and CCCA to industrial–economic exposure require additional theorizing as well as empirical study. As discussed above, building this adaptive capacity to this type of pressure may require integrative research that links sensemaking, learning, and capability development with strategies that enable inter-organizational coordination. However, these processes have yet to become a focus for scholars of CCCA. It is also important to increase understanding of the differences between proactive and reactive adaptation, and to uncover the drivers of both types, particularly those prompting proactive adaptation to this exposure pathway. It is possible that experience with industrial–economic CCCV is crucial to managers' ability to make sense of its potential impacts on the firm, as with biophysical CCCV. Still, the indirect nature of this exposure pathway may further complicate firms' ability to respond proactively. Given the early stage of research on this topic, both description and theory-building are needed. In addition, quantitative studies on the effectiveness of CCCA approaches to this exposure pathway, as well as descriptive research on processes behind building CCCAC, will become increasingly important if the indirect effects of climate change on firms through their industrial–economic systems continue to intensify.

This sub-topic also presents excellent opportunities for scholars interested in extending organizational theories focusing on the boundaries of the firm, and on inter-organizational coordination, learning, and integration. Management scholars have applied a number of perspectives to explain these behaviors in the past, including transaction-cost economics, resource dependence theory, and the resource-based, knowledge-based, and relational views of the firm. However, as Winn and colleagues (2011) noted, climate change exposure may bring about massive discontinuities in the firm's economic environment, which may in turn invoke emergent processes that require extending these theories. For example, the decision to acquire a supplier facing disruptive biophysical CCCV in order to gain control over that supplier's adaptation practices calls for developing practices to assess the value and risks of the acquisition target, as well as subsequent adaptive capacity development. Similarly, cooperative strategies may involve new ways of reconciling sensemaking processes among firms that are directly and indirectly exposed to climate change, as well as new processes for integrating resources, capabilities, and knowledge. Finally, market stakeholders' direct biophysical CCCV could alter power dynamics in inter-organizational fields in heretofore unobserved ways. Each of these possibilities suggests that scholars may have opportunities to observe new organizational structures and forms and interorganizational strategies that are more resilient to the array of industrial–economic climate change pressures that can affect firms.

Climate change adaptation and institutional pressures

Institutional exposure and corporate climate change vulnerability

Existing research into CCCA has generated significant evidence of how the institutional environment of the firm can channel biophysical and/or economic biophysical exposures (Berkhout, 2012). We use the term "institutional environments" to refer to networks of social actors and rules, law, norms, belief systems, and cultural elements that give meaning and structure to their relationships (Scott, 2008). Belliveau and colleagues (2006) explained how small wine producers in British Columbia face institutional exposure through regulations requiring high proportions of sales on site to tourists. When the weather is poor for tourism, the market size for these producers is commensurately affected. Similarly, Thistlethwaite (2012) described how regulations prevented insurance companies from dropping policies that no longer met their perceived risk standards of insurability. In both cases, institutional arrangements appear to make firms more sensitive to climate change, and possibly less responsive. Finally, some research has studied how institutional voids, non-inclusive markets, and poverty all exacerbate stakeholder vulnerability, and, by extension, CCCV rooted in institutional exposure (Adger, 1999; Handmer and Dovers, 1996). For example, the World Bank (2011) linked voids in infrastructure, education, healthcare, and affordable housing in the Philippines with the CCCV of citizens of that country and, by implication, the institutional exposure of its business community.

Table 17.2 A future research agenda for the area of corporate climate change adaptation to industrial–economic exposure

Exposure pathway	Climate change vulnerability	Climate change adaptive capacity	Climate change adaptation
Industrial–economic	How should different forms of industrial–economic exposure be classified?	How can inter-organizational coordination and stakeholder engagement enable sensemaking, learning, and capability to develop for climate change adaptation?	How do proactive and reactive adaptations to industrial–economic exposure differ in form and effectiveness?
	What theoretical lens can explain how industrial–economic systems mediate biophysical pressures to organizations?	How do forces in industrial–economic systems enable and inhibit climate change adaptation?	When should firms engage in private, club, and/or public adaptation to industrial–economic exposure?

Conversely, several scholars have also noted that the strength of public institutions and goods can attenuate CCCV rooted in institutional exposure by reducing the sensitivity or increasing the resilience of citizens and stakeholders. For example, Assadourian (2012) described the Dutch government's efforts to develop a comprehensive climate change adaptation policy that steers investment into societal vulnerability reduction measures, such as building stronger levees, storm surge barriers, and more river volume capacity. He concluded that these investments help industry by protecting their institutional environments from biophysical exposure. In another example, Belliveau and colleagues (2006) explained how government support programs in British Columbia have helped attenuate the impacts of biophysical vulnerability on agricultural firms.

Some research attention has also focused on the roles of tacit institutions and institutional logics in shaping the firm's institutional exposure to CCCV. Mills (2012) and Thistlethwaite (2012) both explained how actuarial practices based on antiquated institutional logics have increased the economic exposure of insurance firms to climate change. Traditionally, these practices followed a taken-for-granted institutional logic that historical risk patterns can adequately value future policy risk, even though the future effects of climate change are predicted to be more severe and variable than past effects. Grothmann and Patt (2005) discussed how Zimbabwean farmers continued to plant maize because of its local cultural importance, even when seasonal forecasts predicted poor weather for that crop.

We are not aware of any research into opportunities associated with institutional exposure to climate change. Still, we expect that corporate institutional entrepreneurs may have opportunities to shape, adapt, and create new institutional arrangements to reduce CCCV rooted in institutional exposure and act as corporate citizens at the same time. As an example, there is evidence from the US ski resort industry of firms playing active roles in the climate change mitigation social movement. Here, some ski resorts appear to be attempting to strengthen social movement pressures to reduce societal greenhouse-gas emissions to mitigate the effects of climate change on their industry (Tashman and Rivera, Forthcoming). Pinkse and Kolk (2011) suggest that firms might also have opportunities to leverage complementary institutional arrangements to reduce institutional exposure to climate change. In particular, they suggest that the global movement for sustainable development overlaps with the emerging movement for societal climate change adaptation. Thus, institutional entrepreneurs concerned with societal CCCA may be more successful by engaging components of the sustainable development movement.

Institutional exposure and corporate climate change adaptive capacity

While scholars have developed significant evidence for how the institutions can channel climate change pressures towards the firm, less effort has been paid to understanding organizational adaptive capacity to this exposure pathway. In theory, CCCAC to institutional exposure could involve the firm's capacity to reduce its exposure or sensitivity or improve its resilience to institutional influences that channeling climate change exposure to the firm (Brooks, Adger, and Kelly, 2005). This might occur in at least two ways. First, firms may have the capacity to buffer themselves from their institutional exposure to climate change (Oliver, 1991). They may also be able to shape their institutional environments in a manner that mitigates the institutional effects of climate change (Pelling, High, Dearing, and Smith, 2008).

Work on the first form of CCCAC to institutional exposure suggested here is currently undeveloped. On the second form, some research has examined the role of informal and formal social networks in shaping institutional arrangements and how they channel climate change pressures to firms. Pelling and colleagues (2008) discussed how informal social networks within and between organizations comprising common institutional fields enabled reflexive learning among individuals and organizations, and, ultimately, action on climate change adaptation within fields. Thistlethwaite (2012) discussed how the ClimateWise cross-sectoral partnership is attempting to shape insurance industry members' and stakeholders' behaviors to reduce the exposure of the institutional environment as a whole to climate change. Pinkse and Kolk (2011) identified several cross-sectoral partnerships in developing countries that help establish collective action among firms, non-governmental organizations (NGOs), and governments for broader societal adaptation efforts. Finally, Tashman and Rivera (Forthcoming) described how the United States' national ski resort industry association was a vehicle for influencing public policy debates about reducing societal greenhouse-gas emissions. In sum, the research suggests that some organizations have developed CCCAC to institutional exposure through informal and formal forms of collective action.

Institutional exposure and corporate climate change adaptation

There has also been very little work on resultant adaptation to institutional pressures associated with climate change. Some research has examined club adaptation efforts undertaken by industries that are attempting to change institutional arrangements so that their members are less susceptible to climate change-related pressures. For example, Mills' (2012) and Thistlethwaite's (2012) research also described insurance industry associations' attempts to redefine the institutional logic guiding actuarial practices so that it better accounts for forward-looking policy risks associated with climate change. Similarly, Pelling and colleagues (2008) observed how Welsh dairy farmers collectively adapted to their warming climate by adopting the New Zealand grazing system, which is based on a logic of lower production outputs and costs.

Other work has examined public adaptation efforts by organizations aimed at reducing the CCCV of non-market stakeholders in the institutional environment of business. This work has also focused on firms' participation in collective action institutions that allow organizations to share the costs associated with engaging in public CCCA. For example, Pinkse and Kolk (2011) described how the Munich Climate Insurance Initiative, a multi-stakeholder initiative involving insurance firms and NGOs, has expanded insurance and knowledge on climate-risk reduction into developing countries. Finally, some research has focused on the role of firms or industries in shaping policy and government responses to regional biophysical climate change pressures. For example, Adger (1999) explained how local tourism operators in Tobago, along with village leaders and government regulators, were able to help enact conservation policies for coral reefs that were invaluable to the local community and economy. The reefs in question were vulnerable to bleaching events from warming ocean temperatures, as well as overuse by local stakeholders. The conservation efforts reduced the vulnerability of the reefs to warming waters by helping prevent local use from negatively impacting resilience.

Future research on institutional exposure and corporate climate change adaptation

While scholars have devoted considerable attention to describing how institutional environments can affect the firm's climate change vulnerability and ability to adapt to it, we believe there are still important opportunities to engage in theoretical development and quantitative study on the topic. Scholars such as Grothmann and Patt (2005), Mills (2012), and Thistlethwaite (2012) have demonstrated anecdotally how existing institutional arrangements can both exacerbate CCCV and inhibit CCCAC. Still, theory development is needed to explain generally and systematically how institutional arrangements impact firms' exposure and abilities to cope with climate change. In addition, more work could be done to explore how public sector institutions might create opportunities associated with exposure to climate change. Such efforts might involve integrative theorizing with institutional theory and a perspective relevant to biophysical CCCV, such as resource dependence theory (e.g. Tashman and Rivera, Forthcoming), ecological sensemaking, or ecological embeddedness (e.g. Whiteman and Cooper, 2000, 2011), as suggested above. Similarly, scholars could study how different institutional arrangements within industries, organizational fields, and regional political environments are set up to cope with climate change-related massive discontinuous change (e.g. Winn et al., 2011).

Future research on CCCAC and institutional exposure could involve opening inquiries into firms' capacities to buffer themselves from institutional influences that may constrain their abilities to adapt to CCCV, or reduce their vulnerability to institutional influences that might channel climate change exposure or constrain the adaptive capacity of firms. Additionally, research in this area could build on the limited attention that has been devoted to institutional entrepreneurship aimed at reshaping firms' institutional exposure to climate change. As mentioned above, existing work in this area has focused on the role of informal and formal networks as collective sensemaking and sensegiving communities for retheorizing institutions that impede CCCA or exacerbate CCCV. Future research might extend these insights by examining how institutional entrepreneurs and their supporting networks might affect public policy outcomes to reduce CCCV or enable CCCA efforts that are affected by public institutions. Scholars could also build on Pinkse and Kolk's (2011)

Table 17.3 A future research agenda for the area of corporate climate change adaptation to institutional exposure

Exposure pathway	Climate change vulnerability	Climate change adaptive capacity	Climate change adaptation
Institutional	What are the theoretical mechanisms through which institutional arrangements impact climate change vulnerability? When do institutions create opportunities related to climate change vulnerability for organizations? How do industry environments shape institutional climate change related pressures on organizations?	What capabilities help firms buffer themselves from institutional climate change related pressures? What are the attributes of institutional entrepreneurs who shape institutions that affect climate change vulnerability? Are there complementary non-climate change related institutional logics that can help enable corporate climate change adaptation?	How can types of adaptation to institutional climate change exposure be classified? How do firms engage in private adaptation to institutional climate change exposure? What forms of adaptation to institutional climate change exposure are most effective?

observation that the sustainable development social movement might contain allies and logics for strengthening institutions related to CCCA, and vice versa.

Finally, the lack of attention paid to institutional exposure and CCCA means that there are a number of research opportunities. First, scholars have yet to develop a typology of corporate adaptive responses to institutional influences related to climate change exposure, even though there is evidence of a number of different types of influence. In addition, while research has started to focus on firms' participation in club and public adaptation efforts, we know of no research into any private CCCA to institutional exposure. Such efforts could involve buffering institutional influences or reducing vulnerability to them, as described above. Finally, research on the effectiveness of these adaptation efforts is also at a very early stage. The practical significance of such research could become extremely important if business communities, civil societies, and governments need to adapt societal institutions to fit better with the ecological realities that may face them.

Conclusions

This chapter has sought to draw attention to the non-market strategy topic of climate change adaption, and organize the extant literature on this subject into a framework that can be used as a basis for future research. The framework is focused on the antecedents, capabilities, and outcomes of CCCA, and how these elements are shaped by climate change exposure from the ecological, industrial–economic, and institutional environments of the firm. Scholars interested in pursuing research in this area may have opportunities to develop critical insights for management practice and theory, because, as Winn and colleagues (2011: 169) note, "climate change presents a new, unprecedentedly disruptive, potentially cascading and profoundly uncertain type of change in organizational environments." Thus, the area may serve as a testing ground for new theory that accounts for the ecological impacts on organizations resulting from climate change and how the industrial–economic and institutional environments of the firm might channel or moderate these impacts.

While research into CCCA is still at an early stage, scholars have discovered some common themes that could form the basis for integrating and extending our understanding of the topic. First, direct ecological pressures associated with climate change are diverse in form and create a wide range of impacts on firms, depending on whether they are discrete perturbations or continuous stressors, and on the nature and extent of the firm's sensitivity and resilience to these pressures. Second, firms are indirectly exposed to climate change through various stakeholders facing biophysical vulnerability. Third, institutions can exacerbate firm and stakeholder vulnerability by magnifying sensitivity, inhibiting resilience, or interfering with the firm's adaptive capacity. Fourth, firms' ability to respond to these influences depends on commonly studied sensemaking, learning, resource orchestration, and inter-organizational economic and institutional processes, as well as necessarily emergent characteristics for responding to potentially massive discontinuous change (Winn et al., 2011). Finally, while research has observed and classified different forms of CCCA, the effectiveness of these efforts has not been studied. We suggest that this is because the attribution of events to climate change has been tenuous, in part because events are in the future and uncertain, and in part because of socio-political and institutional barriers to sensemaking (Hoffman, 2011).

We believe that further research in this area of non-market strategy could be critical for practice in a world where ecological change might disrupt organizations, industries, and institutional systems (Winn and Kirchgeorg, 2005). If the effects predicted by the scientific community of the Intergovernmental Panel on Climate Change continue to intensify on each of these types of systems, research on CCCA could help uncover how firms might cope more effectively with the threats of climate change or even capitalize on the opportunities that it creates. In addition, it could help uncover how industry systems might adapt or even transform themselves to fit with new ecological, industrial–economic, or institutional realities. Finally, our knowledge of societal climate change adaptation, involving new policy approaches, tacit institutional arrangements, and nascent social movements, would undoubtedly be informed by organizational climate change adaptation research, since organizations have critical knowledge, resources, social power, and incentives to participate in public adaptation efforts. For these reasons, we emphasize the need for research that identifies and examines early adopters of CCCA.

Some of this research has already commenced. For example, numerous scholars have studied CCCA in the ski and agricultural industries because of their histories of vulnerability and adaptation. Still, these efforts have focused mainly on private CCCA to biophysical vulnerability, without generating insights on indirect climate change vulnerability, adaptive capacity, and adaptation that are salient to the firm's stakeholders. Research in the insurance industry, on the other hand, has generated some knowledge about CCCA to indirect exposure involving club and public adaptation, but the extent and effectiveness of CCCA in this context have yet to be examined. We would encourage scholars to address these gaps in other industry contexts, such as forestry, commercial fishing, and food and beverage production, which are embedded in global supply chains and transnational institutional fields. Such research could help illuminate what effective adaptation should generally look like, how private, club, and public adaptation are interrelated, and how firms might build comprehensive adaptive capacity to the multiple exposure pathways facing organizations.

We also believe that the area offers opportunities to develop novel and integrative applications of organizational theory. For example, Tashman and Rivera (Forthcoming) describe how resource dependence theory can be applied to the natural realm to explain biophysical CCCV, because it involves dependence on climate-sensitive resources and uncertainty generated by biophysical climate change exposure. Further, as suggested above, theories of ecological sensemaking and embeddedness (e.g. Whiteman and Cooper, 2000, 2011) may help explain the firm's willingness, capacity, and perceptions for the need for CCCA. We also believe that the natural-resource-based view of the firm (e.g. Hart, 1995) has broad applications for the firm's CCCAC to biophysical, industrial–economic, and institutional climate change exposure, as well as its ability to engage in effective private, club, or public adaptation. Finally, given the literature's emerging theme that institutions can enable or constrain the firm's ability to adapt to climate change, we believe there are opportunities to integrate logics from institutional theory with these other perspectives. We also urge more research into uncovering and explaining instances of institutional entrepreneurship by firms that build institutional support for CCCA.

Bibliography

Adger, W. (1999). Social vulnerability to climate change and extremes in coastal Vietnam. *World Development*, 27, 249–69.

Assadourian, E. (2012). The path to degrowth in overdeveloped countries. In Worldwatch Institute, *State of the World 2012* (pp. 22–37). Washington, DC: Island Press/Center for Resource Economics.

Belliveau, S., Smit, B., and Bradshaw, B. (2006). Multiple exposures and dynamic vulnerability: Evidence from the grape industry in the Okanagan Valley, Canada. *Global Environmental Change – Human and Policy Dimensions*, 16, 346–78.

Berkhout, F. (2012). Adaptation to climate change by organizations. *Wiley Interdisciplinary Reviews: Climate Change*, 3(1), 91–106.

Berkhout, F., Hertin, J., and Gann, D. M. (2006). Learning to adapt: Organisational adaptation to climate change impacts. *Climatic Change*, 78, 125–56.

Bleda, M., and Shackley, S. (2008). The dynamics of belief in climate change and its risks in the business organisation. *Ecological Economics*, 66, 517–32.

Brooks, N., Adger, N., and Kelly, P. (2005). The determinants of vulnerability and adaptive capacity at the national level and the implications for adaptation. *Global Environmental Change*, 15, 151–63.

Busch, T. (2011). Organizational adaptation to disruptions in the natural environment: The case of climate change. *Scandinavian Journal of Management*, 27(4), 389–404.

Das, T., and Teng, B. (1998). Between trust and control: Developing confidence in partner cooperation in alliances. *Academy of Management Review*, 23, 491–512.

Dyer, J., and Singh, H. (1998). The relational view: Cooperative strategy and sources of interorganizational competitive advantage. *Academy of Management Review*, 23, 660–79.

Füssel, H. (2007). Vulnerability: A generally applicable conceptual framework for climate change research. *Global Environmental Change*, 17, 155–67.

Grothmann, T., and Patt, A. (2005). Adaptive capacity and human cognition: The process of individual adaptation to climate change. *Global Environmental Change*, 15, 199–213.

Haigh, N., and Griffiths, A. (2012). Surprise as a catalyst for including climatic change in the strategic environment. *Business and Society*, 51, 89–120.

Hamel, G. (1991). Competition for competence and interpartner learning within international strategic alliances. *Strategic Management Journal*, 12, 83–103.

Handmer, J., and Dovers, S. (1996). A typology of resilience: Rethinking institutions for sustainable development. *Organization and Environment*, 9, 482–511.

Hart, S. (1995). A natural-resource-based view of the firm. *Academy of Management Review*, 20, 986–1014.

Hertin, J., Berkhout, F., Gann, D, and Barlow, J. (2003). Climate change and the UK house building sector: Perceptions, impacts and adaptive capacity. *Building Research and Information*, 31, 278–90.

Hoffman, A. (2006). *Getting ahead of the Curve: Corporate Strategies that Address Climate Change*. Arlington, VA: Pew Center on Global Climate Change.

Hoffman, A. J. (2011). Talking past each other? Cultural framing of skeptical and convinced logics in the climate change debate. *Organization and Environment*, 24, 3–33.

Hoffmann, V., Sprengel, D., Ziegler, A., Kolb, M., and Abegg, B. (2009). Determinants of corporate adaptation to climate change in winter tourism: An econometric analysis. *Global Environmental Change*, 19, 256–64.

Intergovernmental Panel on Climate Change (IPCC). (2001). *Third Assessment Report of the IPCC*. Cambridge: Cambridge University Press.

Ireland, R. D., Hitt, M. A., and Vaidyanath, D. (2002). Alliance management as a source of competitive advantage. *Journal of Management*, 28, 413–46.

Kuhn, K., Campbell-Lendrum, D., Haines, A., and Cox, M. (2005). *Using Climate to Predict Infectious Disease Epidemics*. Geneva: World Health Organization.

Linnenluecke, M., Griffiths, A., and Winn, M. (2012). Extreme weather events and the critical importance of anticipatory adaptation and organizational resilience in responding to impacts. *Business Strategy and the Environment*, 21, 17–32.

— (2013). Firm and industry adaptation to climate change: A review of climate adaptation studies in the business and management field. *Wiley Interdisciplinary Reviews: Climate Change*, 4(5), 397–416.

Maddison, D. (2001). In search of warmer climates? The impact of climate change on flows of British tourists. *Climatic Change*, 49(1–2), 193–208.

Meyer, A. (1982). Adapting to environmental jolts. *Administrative Science Quarterly*, 27, 515–37.

Mills, E. (2005). Insurance in climate of change. *Science*, 309, 1040–4.

— (2012). The greening of insurance. *Science*, 338, 1424–5.

Nitkin, D., Foster, R., and Medalye, R. (2009). *A Systematic Review of the Literature on Business Adaptation to Climate Change: Concepts and Theories*. London, ON: Network for Business Sustainability.

Oliver, C. (1991). Strategic responses to institutional processes. *Academy of Management Review*, 16, 145–79.

Pelling, M., High, C., Dearing, J., and Smith, D. (2008). Shadow spaces for social learning: A relational understanding of adaptive capacity to climate change within organisations. *Environment and Planning A*, 40, 867–84.

Pfeffer, J., and Salancik, G. R. (1978). *The External Control of Organizations: A Resource Dependence Approach*. New York: Harper and Row.

Pinkse, J., and Kolk, A. (2011). Addressing the climate change–sustainable development nexus: The role of multistakeholder partnerships. *Business and Society*, 51, 176–210.

Prakash, A., and Potoski, M. (2007). Collective action through voluntary environmental programs: A club theory perspective. *Policy Studies Journal*, 35, 773–92.

Schlenker, W., Hanemann, W. M., and Fischer, A. C. (2005). Will US agriculture really benefit from global warming? Accounting for irrigation in the hedonic approach. *American Economic Review*, 95, 395–406.

Schwartz, P. (2007). Risk: Investing in global security. *Harvard Business Review*, 85, 24.

Scott, D., and McBoyle, G. (2007). Climate change adaptation in the ski industry. *Mitigation and Adaptation Strategies to Global Change*, 12, 1411–31.

Scott, D., McBoyle, G., and Mills, B. (2003). Climate change and the skiing industry of southern Ontario: Exploring the importance of snowmaking as a technical decision. *Climate Research*, 23, 171–81.

Scott, W. R. (2008). *Institutions and Organizations: Ideas and Interests*. Thousand Oaks, CA: Sage.

Smit, B., and Skinner, M. W. (2002). Adaptation options in agriculture to climate change: a typology. *Mitigation and Adaptation Strategies for Global Change*, 7(1), 85–114.

Smit, B., McNabb, D., and Smithers, J. (1996). Agricultural adaptation to climatic variation. *Climatic Change*, 33, 7–29.

Spittlehouse, D., and Stewart, R. (2003). Adaptation to climate change in forest management. *British Columbia Journal of Ecosystems and Management*, 4, 1–11.

Starik, M., and Rands, G. (1995). Weaving an integrated web: Multilevel and multisystem perspectives of ecological sustainable organizations. *Academy of Management Review*, 20, 908–35.

Sussman, F., and Freed, J. (2008). *Adapting to Climate Change: A Business Approach*. Arlington, VA: Pew Center on Global Climate Change.

Tashman, P. (2011). Climate change and environmental performance: A longitudinal study in the US ski resort industry. *Best Paper Proceedings of the Academy of Management Annual Meeting*, 1, 1–6.

Tashman, P., and Rivera, J. (Forthcoming). Ecological uncertainty, adaptation, and mitigation in the US ski resort industry: Managing resource dependence and institutional pressures. *Strategic Management Journal*.

Thistlethwaite, J. (2012). The ClimateWise principles self-regulating climate change risks in the insurance sector. *Business and Society*, 51(1), 121–47.

Tushman, M., and Anderson, P. (1986). Technological discontinuities and organizational environments. *Administrative Science Quarterly*, 31, 439–65.

Whiteman, G., and Cooper, W. (2000). Ecological embeddedness. *Academy of Management Journal*, 43, 1265–82.

— (2011). Ecological sensemaking. *Academy of Management Journal*, 54, 889–911.

Winn, M., and Kirchgeorg, M. (2005). The siesta is over: A rude awakening from sustainability myopia. In S. Sharma and M. Starik (eds.), *Corporate Environmental Strategy and Competitive Sustainability*, Volume 3 (pp. 232–58). Northampton, MA: Edward Elgar.

Winn, M., and Pogutz, S. (2013). Business, ecosystems, and biodiversity: New horizons for management research. *Organization and Environment*, 26(2), 203–29.

Winn, M., Kirchgeorg, M., Griffiths, A., Linnenluecke, M., and Günther, E. (2011). Impacts from climate change on organizations: A conceptual foundation. *Business Strategy and the Environment*, 20(3), 157–73.

World Bank. (2011). *Vulnerability, Risk Reduction, and Adaptation to Climate Change: Philippines*. http://sdwebx.worldbank.org/climateportalb/doc/GFDRRCountryProfiles/wb_gfdrr_climate_change_country_profile_for_PHL.pdf (accessed June 13, 2013).

World Business Council on Sustainable Development (WBCSD). (2008). *Adaptation: An Issue Brief for Business*. www.wbcsdpublications.org/viewReport.php?repID=1 (accessed December 20, 2013).

Zollo, M., and Winter, S. (2002). Deliberate learning and dynamics capabilities evolution. *Organization Science*, 13, 3.

18

Stakeholder collaboration as a catalyst for development

Company–NPO partnerships in New Zealand

Gabriel Eweje and Nitha Palakshappa

In recent years there has been an escalation in both the number and variety of collaborative relationships formed between business and nonprofit organizations (NPOs). It has been argued that the resulting relationships – firmly based on the firm's core competencies and demonstrating clear objectives – are connected to the private sector's core values and responsiveness to moral pressures. In this sense, corporations are adopting these initiatives as a response to perceived pressures from the moral market place (Hess and Rogovsky, 2002), alongside the convergence of political, economic, environmental, and social pressures. Furthermore, such collaborations are emerging because firms are increasingly reexamining their traditional philanthropic practices and seeking new strategies of engagement with their communities that will result in greater corporate relevance and higher social impact (Austin, 2000a).

Whilst business and NPOs have long formed collaborative relationships within their own sectors as a strategy to address specific needs, increasingly they are turning to cross-sector partnerships that provide benefit to both parties, concurrently serving a common good (Sagawa, 2001). Collaborative processes, particularly those that involve corporate–community relations, and public–private partnerships have become a predominant means for addressing social issues and social problem-solving (Blockson, 2003). However, the perception of the role of the business sector in development has also changed significantly. For example, in the United States and Europe, distrust in corporations is at an all-time high (Berger, Cunningham, and Drumwright, 2004). In the past, a number of accounting scandals, exorbitant CEO compensation packages, and concerns about the role of globalization in contributing to income disparities meant that business was often seen as part of the problem, rather than as having a role in enhancing social development. Recent events, such as the financial downturn, have not improved the situation. Indeed, globalization has increased calls for corporations to use firms' resources to help alleviate a wide range of social problems, and calls for expanded responsibilities for business are intuitively appealing to those who see governments as unable or unwilling to deal with such problems (Hillman and Keim, 2001). Thus, we now see a new paradigm where business and the social sector work together while retaining the integrity of their core functions. These often disparate organizations are increasingly seen as key players in developing integrated solutions, resulting in an evolutionary change in institutional forms of governance (Austin, 2000a).

Evidence suggests that the recurring economic downturn has increased social problems. As these problems have grown in magnitude and complexity, NPOs have stepped up to address them. This new paradigm pairs visionary companies that recognize how the social context in which they operate influences their bottom line with NPOs who understand how business principles can enable them to fulfill their social missions more effectively (Sagawa and Segal, 2000). Together, they are "reshaping how communities tackle some of their most intractable social challenges" (Sagawa and Segal, 2000: 105). Thus, we argue that collaborations offer a form of engagement that can use the strengths of both partners to produce gains of value to many stakeholders (Covey and Brown, 2001).

While changes in their external environment have encouraged NPOs to extend beyond traditional sources and modes of funding, businesses have been motivated by the need for greater corporate social responsibility and the requirement to provide more input into the environments in which they operate. Historically, businesses have been more attracted to direct-impact partnerships, such as education, environmental sustainability, or job development, rather than those with indirect impact, such as social mobilization, advocacy, or good governance (Eweje and Palakshappa, 2009). That said, it is argued that the search for new resources and more effective organizational approaches is bringing together NPOs and corporations. In addition, it is argued in this chapter that collaboration between business and NPOs shows promise in solving societal problems and improving social development. Accordingly, this chapter examines some of the relationships that bring nonprofit organizations into the "focal orbit" (Abzug and Webb, 1999) of business (for-profit organizations) and examines how the relationship and initiated projects are improving the wellbeing of society, a group, or a community. More importantly, it endeavors to examine the impact of the projects initiated on agreed shared goals. The empirical domain is New Zealand.

This chapter is intended to contribute to the growing knowledge that is strengthening contemporary understanding of collaborative relationships between business and NPOs. We examine whether such relationships have developed in New Zealand. Specifically, we address the following two questions:

- What are the value and long-term benefits of such collaborations?
- Were the objectives of the stated goals achieved?

From formation through to ongoing nurturing of the relationship, some key aspects of social partnerships are identified, then placed within the New Zealand context.

Collaboration: defining and understanding key concepts

Defining social partnerships

It is pertinent at this juncture to mention that corporate social action (Marquis, Glynn, and Davis, 2007) or collaborations between business and NPOs are commonly referred to as "social alliances" (Berger, Cunningham, and Drumwright, 2004), "cross-sector collaborations" (Austin, 2000b), "strategic partnerships" (Eweje, 2007b), or "social partnerships" (Eweje and Palakshappa, 2009), to mention but a few. Corporate social action is defined as "behaviours and practices that extend beyond immediate profit maximisation goals and are intended to increase social benefits or mitigate social problems for constituencies external to the firm"

(Marquis, Glynn, and Davis, 2007: 926). Furthermore, corporate social action can focus on any number of diverse social needs or issues, including, but not limited to: arts, housing, the physical environment, education and schooling, human welfare, disease, wellness, and general improvement in the quality of life. According to Kapucu (2006: 207), partnership is defined as "any intentionally collaborative relationship between two or more organizations from multiple sectors [that is public, private, and non-profit] which joins resources to identify and subsequently pursue a joint approach to solving one or more common problems." He further asserts that partnership can also be perceived as a social exchange that involves commitment of knowledge, skills, and emotions by leaders and staff of participating organizations. Similarly, Gray (1985) argues that, from an organizational point of view, partnership entails the commitment of organizational resources to an initiative that involves two or more entities coming together to act in recognition of the fact that they cannot accomplish their missions and goals alone.

Roberts and Bradley (1991: 212) have defined collaboration as a "temporary social arrange-ment in which two or more social actors work towards a single common end requiring the transmutation of materials, ideas, and/or social relations to achieve that end." Similarly, Wood and Gray (1991: 139) describe collaboration as a situation wherein "a group of autonomous stakeholders of a problem domain engage in an interactive process, using shared rules, norms, and structures, to act or decide on issues related to that domain." As such, the collaboration process encompasses problem-setting, direction-setting, and implementation stages (Gray, 1989). Accordingly, the partners intend to retain organizational autonomy while joining forces with one or more other organizations to achieve shared goals (Parker and Selsky, 2004). In this chapter, we adopt Eweje and Palakshappa's (2009: 340) definition of social partnership as a "situation wherein business and nonprofits collaborate and work together to achieve a successful outcome of a collective project(s) initiated primarily to address specific needs that will improve the wellness of communities and society at large." This is achieved through various non-market strategies solely for the betterment of society.

Social partnership in the literature

The formation of collaborations (also termed social alliances, social partnerships, or relation-ships) among organizations is touted as a significant strategy that organizations can use to cope with the turbulence and complexity of the environment (Gray and Wood, 1991; Guo and Acar, 2005; Heath, 2007). It is further argued that social collaborations show promise for solving organizational and societal problems. In effect, the economics of globalization together with the importance of non-market environment and social issues are creating a convergence of relationships among NPOs, states, and multinational corporations (MNCs) (O'Riain, 2000; Prakash, 2002). The 1990s witnessed an explosion in business–NPO relationships with an "unprecedented surge in interest and activity between firms and non profits" (Crane, 2000: 163). At the time, collaborations involving the natural environment were often described, but the dynamics remained underexplored. All working partnerships involve complex mixtures of factors, demographics, tasks, processes, and cultures that each partner brings to the initial encounter (Parker and Selsky, 2004). One type of collaborative engagement is partnerships among business, government, and civil society that address social issues and causes (Austin, 2000a; Eweje and Palakshappa, 2009; Gray, 1989; Stone, 2000).

Scholars have identified different factors that facilitate a successful collaborative process, including having the right partners, partners' interdependence, coincidence of values, having a skilled convener, positive beliefs about expected outcomes, how decision-making is organized, behavioral learning, the size and configuration of the collaboration, the type and duration of interaction, and the fit with the environment (Butterfield, Reed, and Lemak, 2004; Chung, Singh, and Lee, 2000; Eweje and Palakshappa, 2009; Pasquero, 1991; Wood and Gray, 1991).

Faced with numerous complications, fierce competition, and the fear of failure, why do corporations continue to engage in social partnership or action (Berger, Cunningham, and Drumwright, 2004; Eweje and Palakshappa, 2009; Marquis, Glynn, and Davis, 2007)? Austin (1998) and Heath (2007) suggest that the imperative for collaboration stems from the rapid, structural, and probably irreversible changes being thrust upon us by powerful political, economic, and social forces. Austin (1998: 2; emphasis in original) argues further:

> The fundamental question is not what can nonprofits, businesses, and governments do, but rather how can society most effectively organize itself to deal with major social problems. If we are to think creatively and freshly about this question, we must escape from the mental prisons of our traditional institutional perspectives. We must look outward to each other and seek out *new forms of collaboration, interaction, and organization.*

Austin (1998: 3) further asserts that "going it alone is on the endangered strategy list. Only by combining vision, efforts, and resources creatively will nonprofits be able to confront effectively the magnitude of rising demands facing them." Therefore, organizations in different institutional sectors work collectively to achieve common goals (see Hood, Logsdon, and Thomson, 1993). On a more general level Ackoff (1974) suggests that many pressing issues are the result of sets of interconnected problems. The multifaceted nature of these complex problems makes them difficult to conceptualize and analyze, and thus immune to simple solutions. Drawing on Ackoff's suggestion, this complexity and interdependence often require extensive collaboration among different types and various levels of organizations. In short, the complex social and economic problems faced by society require "complex" non-market solutions. The messy nature of complex social problems pushes each organization into activities that are beyond its traditional areas of competence (Parker and Selsky, 2004).

Collaboration can offer new methods for organizations to acquire expertise and access to other resources (Berger, Cunningham, and Drumwright, 2004, 2007; Egels-Zandén and Wahlqvist, 2007; Faulkner and de Rond, 2000; Gomes-Casseres, 1996), to cope with increased turbulence in their environments (Emery and Trist, 1965; Gray 1985; Millar, Choi, and Chen, 2004), to anticipate potential problems, and to learn how to transform themselves for an uncertain future (Marquis, Glynn, and Davis, 2007; Roberts and Bradley, 1991). The idea is fundamental to the belief that a corporation that cultivates a more positive and distinctive reputation will attract consumers (Berger, Cunningham, and Drumwright, 2004; Creyer and Ross, 1997; Ellen, Mohr, and Webb, 2000; Egels-Zandén and Wahlqvist, 2007; Sen and Bhattacharya, 2001) and potential employees (Eweje and Bentley, 2007; Turban and Greening, 1997), thereby boosting profitability (Marquis, Glynn, and Davis, 2007; Parker and Selsky, 2004).

Further to the aforementioned arguments, development-oriented NPOs are facing increasing uncertainty and reduction in financial resource flows from national governments. In addition, NPOs are being called upon to serve more people, with better results, than they have in the past (Eweje, 2007b). But they do so with an uncertain resource base, as the number of NPOs has continued to increase and NPOs have come to understand that increases in personal income and a growing economy do not necessarily result in proportionate increases in private giving and government spending (Sagawa and Segal, 2000). Simultaneously, demand for services is growing as large numbers of people suffer from decreased government services and economic dislocations that are associated with global financial shifts (Ashman, 2001; Rangan, Samii, and Van Wassenhove, 2006). Similarly, Austin (2000a: 79) argues that social problems have grown in magnitude and complexity, and NPOs have proliferated to address these. However, traditional funding sources and institutional capacities have not kept pace. The search for "new resources and more effective organizational approaches is bringing nonprofits and corporations together."

Social partnerships, like their for-profit counterparts, can enable access to difficult markets and extra resources, or strengthen an organization's position in the market place. According to Kapucu (2006), social partnerships can provide an essential mechanism to ensure an effective community response to issues. Thus, it is no surprise that the core business strategies of many organizations increasingly incorporate social partnerships. Despite their initial concerns, many NPOs now view their partnerships with the business sector as a necessary tactic (Murphy and Bendell, 1999; Sagawa and Segal, 2000). Indeed, these partnerships are often regarded as fundamental components of an organization's corporate social responsibility.

Essentially, among the distinguishing facets of social partnerships are the types of objectives with which business and NPOs might enter into collaboration, effectively reflecting a combination of non-economic and economic objectives (Berger, Cunningham, and Drumwright, 2004). Social partnerships may begin with a host of objectives, but, as with other collaborative forms, these relationships also face a number of challenges. Issues associated with cultural differences between partners, differing goals and objectives, unequal learning, or partner asymmetries may complicate the final outcomes of social partnerships. Furthermore, the context of such partnerships and the firm-related goals of many NPOs complicate the benefits to be derived from collaborative arrangements.

Social partnership in the global arena

Globally, there is significant public support and high expectations for business–NPO collaboration. For example, the Environics International's millennium poll of over 25,000 people in twenty-three countries showed that in almost all of these countries, and particularly in the United States and Great Britain, the public believed corporations should go beyond simply making a profit and creating jobs to help build a better society for all (Hess and Rogovsky, 2002). Multinational corporations and NPOs, such as General Motors, McDonald's, Shell, the World Wide Fund for Nature, and Greenpeace, have all collaborated on social and environmental concerns (Elkington and Fennel, 2000).

In the international context, the declining legitimacy of government to provide basic services has resulted in increasing pressure on private actors in civil society and the market to address social demands. Global leaders in the development field are promoting collaboration between civil society and the market as a significant new strategy for promoting sustainable development and reducing poverty. Major actors such as the World Bank, the United Nations Development Program, and several bilateral donors are convening international forums, supporting innovative projects, and advocating strategies for collaboration between sectors (Ashman, 2001). For example, the former United Nations Secretary General Kofi Annan, in a speech to encourage business–civil society partnerships, observed:

> We now understand that both business and society stand to benefit from working together. And more and more we are realizing that it is only by mobilizing the corporate sector that we can make significant progress . . . The corporate sector has the finances,

the technology, and the management to make all this happen. The corporate sector need not wait for governments to take decisions for them to take initiatives.

(United Nations, 2002)

Methodology

The fieldwork for this study was undertaken in Auckland, Huntly, and Wellington between October 2010 and July 2011. Twenty organizations were surveyed (ten businesses and their ten non-profit partners). Interviews were conducted with senior managers and the CEOs of the corporations and their nonprofit partners. Transcripts were coded and analyzed to identify key themes. It should be emphasized that the managers interviewed were directly responsible for the collaboration and oversaw the interaction between their organizations and partners.

Theoretical framework

Legitimacy theory is used to guide the analysis and interpretation of empirical data in this study. This theory, which is explained briefly below, is useful for understanding corporate responsiveness to social issues.

Corporations, as one kind of social arrangement, require legitimacy to maintain functional, long-term relationships with the various communities on which they depend. This theory originated with Davis's (1973) iron law of responsibility. According to Davis, business is a social institution that must use its power responsibly; otherwise, society may revoke it. Davis (1973: 314) wrote: "Society grants legitimacy and power to business. In the long run, those who do not use power in a manner which society considers responsible will tend to lose it." He further suggested that the social power which businesspeople possessed would be unlikely to continue unless they were willing to assume more social responsibility for their actions.

Suchman (1995: 574) defined legitimacy as "a generalised perception or assumption that the actions of an entity are desirable, proper or appropriate within some socially constructed system of norms, values, beliefs and definitions." According to this argument: "*legitimacy affects not only how people act toward organizations, but how* they understand them. Thus, audiences perceive the legitimate organization not only as more worthy, but also as more meaningful, more predictable, and *more trustworthy*" (Suchman, 1995: 575; emphasis in original). Furthermore, according to Dowling and Pfeffer (1975), a corporation is said to be legitimate when it is judged to be just and worthy of support. Corporations that lose legitimacy face a number of problems, ranging from punitive legislation to difficulties in hiring qualified personnel. The benefits associated with legitimacy, combined with social pressures towards conformity, generally lead managers of corporations perceived as "illegitimate" to act to improve the legitimacy of their companies (Nasi, Nasi, Phillips, and Zyglidopoulos, 1997).

Consequently, legitimacy may be granted when either the goals being pursued by an organization conform to social morals, or procedures by which an organization pursues its goals are deemed proper. It is pertinent to stress at this point that society judges the legitimacy of a corporation based on the corporation's image. However, both the perceptions of a corporation and the expectations for that corporation can change over time (leading to changes in the legitimacy of the corporation) without there being any change in the actual activities of the corporation. The corporate image (how it is perceived) and societal expectations are the important factors that must be managed.

Sethi (1979) also held the view that if corporations ignore social expectations, they are likely to lose control over their internal decision-making and external dealings. He posits that legitimacy problems occur when societal expectations for corporate behavior differ from societal perceptions of a corporation's behavior, and suggests:

> At any given time, there is likely to be a gap between performance and societal expectations caused by business actions or changing expectations. A continuously widening gap would cause business to lose legitimacy and threaten its survival. Business must therefore strive to narrow this "legitimacy gap" to maintain maximum discretionary control over its internal decision-making and external dealings.
>
> *(Sethi, 1979: 64)*

We propose that the management of social issues in a corporation will be driven by the existence of legitimacy gaps. Management will adopt non-market strategies, such as partnership with NPOs, which will have the highest perceived possibility of success.

New Zealand context

This section provides key details of the ten cases (twenty organizations) that form the basis for this chapter (see Table 18.1). While only four cases will be fully described in this chapter, references will be made to the other cases. The quotes used in this section are comments made by respondents during interviews. To protect the identities of individuals, we do not give their names.

Selected case descriptions

Genesis Energy–HEET

The participants in this relationship are a major energy supplier and a nonprofit organization dedicated to the promotion of energy efficiency. Genesis Energy is acutely aware of the fact that population growth has resulted in power generation moving closer to communities. For this reason, it has strong environmental values that guide business operations within the community: "We have teams of people just managing community relations ... We have environmental values and policies that [dictate] how we want to operate ... Our aim is 100 percent compliance with our resource consent conditions."

Genesis Energy and Huntly Energy Efficiency Trust (HEET) have been working together loosely for a number of years to promote healthy homes and energy efficiency. In this new partnership the organizations came together to provide curtains to low-income families within the Waikato Region in an initiative termed the "Curtain Bank." This initiative functions in an area of high-level power-generation facilities. Genesis Energy has provided key marketing expertise in promoting the program and encouraging curtain donations. They also provided the marketing collateral, including an innovative advertising campaign, posters, and billboard installations. HEET has been responsible for ensuring that the donated curtains are suitable for use prior to their redistribution. HEET liaises with key social service agencies to identify candidates for the program.

Both organizations showed a long-term commitment to the relationship and highlighted the level of donations as a key objective. HEET showed a clear understanding of the fact that any partnership had to satisfy the needs of both partners. As our key interviewee in HEET

Table 18.1 Social partnerships investigated in New Zealand

Business partner	Not-for-profit partner	Partnership type
Genesis Energy	Huntly Energy Efficiency Trust (HEET)	Curtain Bank – Providing curtains to low-income families
Meridian Energy	Royal New Zealand Ballet	Funding and support; special events – TUTUs on Tour
ANZ National Bank	Cancer Society of New Zealand	Fundraising; marketing and sponsorship – Daffodil Day
Westpac Bank NZ	Auckland Rescue Helicopter Trust	Rescue helicopter/air ambulance services
Telecom NZ	IHC (Intellectual Handicapped Trust)	Art Awards – promoting arts for intellectually disabled and sponsorship
DHL NZ	Surf Life Saving NZ	Beach rescue and education enhancement
BP NZ	Surf Life Saving NZ	Beach rescue and education enhancement
The Warehouse	Starship Foundation	Providing support for a premier children's hospital in Auckland
Vodafone Foundation	Royal New Zealand Foundation for the Blind (RNFB)	Adaptive technology – mobile products and services that help a vision-impaired person access information more simply, and education
Nestlé NZ	Lifeline NZ	Counseling, education, and "life-saving"

indicated, an understanding of the corporate partner's objectives provides an important starting point for a successful relationship:

> I [have] worked in corporates so I think that is beneficial because it allows me to engage with a bit of an understanding about "What are they trying to get out of this?" because if I can't put something forward that is going to align with their objectives then there is no chance for me to get the money.

While cross-promotion and a willingness to support other programs were objectives of the nonprofit, the direct benefit of this program in particular was not discussed as an objective of the relationship for Genesis Energy. For the latter the main imperative in aligning with HEET was to further its objective to "act as a good corporate citizen [and] put investments back into the community." The recent focus on climate change has merely strengthened its resolve to support such programs. For HEET, the main impetus to collobrate was that this allowed the nonprofit to have an impact on the lives of people: "We make a difference in people's eyes. We make a difference in this community and the wider community of NZ. That's the best work I have ever done in my life and I feel privileged, really privileged to be part of it." Of note is the importance of a level of both organizational and individual commitment to the "cause."

Meridian Energy–Royal New Zealand Ballet

Meridian Energy, one of New Zealand's largest energy generators, and the Royal New Zealand Ballet (RNZB) have a relationship that dates back to 2000. Its association with the ballet provides Meridian with a new means of interacting with key stakeholders. For Meridian, its partnerships are all about "building relationships with the community that we interact with." This view is taken very seriously by both organizations. The RNZB recognizes the importance of providing their partner with suitable opportunities to interact with key clients. This is fulfilled through careful discussions regarding invitations to opening-night and post-performance functions. The RNZB interviewee stated, "Meridian has a strong understanding of our relationship with NZ audiences . . . Their involvement [in this regard] is based on knowledge of audience development." Such partnerships provide opportunities to interact with stakeholders – a key outcome that is used to assess the success of this partnership. This is an important aspect of partnership strategy for an organization relying on the natural resources of a community.

The agreement provides the RNZB with funding and support, and allows Meridian naming rights to three productions each year. But the collaboration functions well beyond these basic naming rights – each organization considers this to be an important partnership that requires constant support and interaction. It has been a "win–win" situation for both organizations, but by all accounts this success is hard to measure. However, in order to assess the success, Meridian conducts surveys regularly to try to measure net benefits of brand exposure and communication with key stakeholder groups.

Part of the success is attributable to the fact that both organizations interact from the outset of any joint project. This was clearly demonstrated in a 2008, exclusively New Zealand, production of *The Wedding*. Meridian worked with the ballet company in planning and marketing the show from day one. This ensured that both organizations met key objectives and started with a mutual understanding of what the partnership needed to achieve.

For the RNZB, key objectives in this partnership were working together, maintaining clear communication, showing generosity of spirit, and sharing knowledge. All of these outcomes were successfully achieved. The two organizations demonstrated an understanding and connection that extended beyond a mere working agreement to collaborate. As one interviewee said: "It is not just that we need to talk to Meridian; we actually like to talk to each other."

A key objective for Meridian was developing interaction with stakeholders, and this was also achieved through the partnership. Meridian had clear procedures in place to assess the uptake of special events designed within the scope of the partnership, and conducted regular reputation surveys with stakeholders. These indicated that the relationship had been a success:

> It's been a win–win thing. We have done lots of things together . . . You have got an organization that is basically engineers and [another that is] basically ballet dancers. You would have thought that the two wouldn't mix, but we asked them to do a little production in Twizel [an isolated community in the South Island], where we control our hydro dams . . . You can't get much amusement in Twizel but we asked them to send a troupe down there . . . So we used them to deliver a benefit to a community that is important to us . . . They got to understand our business a lot more.

ANZ National Bank–Cancer Society of New Zealand

At the time of these interviews, the partnership between ANZ National Bank and the Cancer Society had just finished its seventeenth year. The relationship is primarily designed around providing support for Daffodil Day – an iconic moment in the NZ fundraising calendar. Each year since 1990 the two organizations have planned and implemented programs designed to raise funds for cancer treatment through the sale of daffodils. This involves considerable administrative and resource input from the bank's head office and all of its branches. In addition, the bank undertakes advertising and program development, volunteer support, donation collection, and the counting of funds received through each branch.

The partnership was initiated after careful thought and consideration, with the bank investing considerable time and effort on a search for the right partner. Its eventual collaboration with the Cancer Society is now definitely seen as a "value fit":

> We have our values to give something back to our community . . . It's doing the right thing, it's making sure you get it right for the customers. We are looking after people and [have] a caring attitude . . . which the Cancer Society [also] has . . . so that is a good fit.

> We realize that it is a great relationship to have and we wouldn't want to lose it, just as they realize that we are a good partner to have as well . . . so it is mutual.

Key objectives that the bank uses to assess the success of the relationship include level of fundraising achieved, general "fit" of the relationship, and visibility that the alignment offers. All of these were cited as extremely important, and all have been achieved through the operation of the partnership. The nature of the Daffodil Day collection in particular ensures the visibility of the alignment as it is a highly visible and well-recognized fundraising event which invites donations during the purchase of daffodils.

The Cancer Society receives a sponsorship fee, marketing support, and considerable administrative support from the bank. It views this as a long-term relationship and in 2009 renegotiated the agreement. The Cancer Society measures the success of the partnership through annual surveys, the percentage increase in donations each year, and anecdotal evidence that Daffodil Day is the country's most successful appeal.

DHL NZ–Surf Life Saving New Zealand

The participants in this partnership are a leading international courier company and the foremost water safety organization in New Zealand. The partnership was formed in 2003 between DHL, owned by Deutsche Post World Net, an international organization specializing in the rapid delivery of documents and products by air, and Surf Life Saving New Zealand (SLSNZ), a national association that provides surf life-saving services to many New Zealand communities. In New Zealand, DHL has been in operation since 1973 and employs more than 500 people. The company cites its attention to the individual needs of customers and its ability to work as a partner in creating competitive edge as key reasons for its growth.

From DHL's perspective, the relationship with SLSNZ provided an opportunity to make a connection with a broader target audience, the general public, and the media: "We wanted something that would make us seem to be a local company, keep us in touch with our local audiences and with the community, so as not to become this big global company that only looks after certain [large] customers."

According to SLSNZ:

> DHL were looking to establish their new corporate brand around the values that they support. So they were looking for the whole concept of safety, security, and of convincing

people of their security. So swimming between the flags gives us that . . . You are safe if you swim between the flags. In terms of handing over the property, your goods to us, it is quite similar . . . so their corporate values were the important thing they wanted to achieve, but also they were trying to give their brands a bit of a jump start.

DHL's investment enabled SLSNZ to brand all of its clubhouses consistently and to update its facilities and equipment. In addition, the agreement provided for a reasonable level of funding towards the beach education program launched as a result of this social partnership. This program works with approximately 450 schools nationwide each year. DHL also uses the program to communicate internally with employees' children. Joint advertising efforts on radio, television, and billboards are also key aspects of the partnership. The level of collaboration has evolved to a point where both organizations have a degree of representation at the other's key events, providing additional opportunities for communicating with stakeholders. Opportunities to showcase the partnership brand are passed on freely: "I certainly work on it all year round in terms of internally and externally building awareness from a PR perspective with our customers" (DHL); "They understand that the main thing we were looking for was our brand, so the branding on Surf Life Saving uniforms was our number-one priority" (SLSNZ).

By all accounts, a high level of commitment and shared values were evident between the two organizations. This commitment and interaction were seen at various levels of the organizations, with senior executives managing the relationship: "We work together very closely. It's not sort of one-sided, that we expect you to deliver and we'll sit back" (DHL); "We have very clear communication channels . . . so we do not end up with any conflict" (SLSNZ).

There is evidence to suggest that the public perception of both brands is high, and that the relationship has not been detrimental to either party. Since the partnership began, an unexpected bonus has come to DHL in the form of a reality television program called *Piha Rescue*. Television New Zealand (the major state-funded television network) is now into its sixth season of the program about Piha, the busiest surf beach in the country. Further, the long-term nature of the partnership indicates that it is intended to be a strategic contribution to the development of both organizations.

Findings

Social partnerships between business and NPOs in New Zealand demonstrate that such collaborations have added value in terms of resources and, more importantly, benefit various stakeholders. Furthermore, these collaborations are emerging because the actors involved are exploiting their differences and searching for solutions that go beyond their own limited visions of what is possible (Gray, 1989). While the business partners made references to corporate social responsibility and license to operate as one of the few reasons why they are involved in social partnerships in New Zealand, the NPOs referred to the need to extend their resource base in order to tackle new challenges (Eweje and Palakshappa, 2009). Thus, the NPOs have welcomed corporate involvement as a source of additional funding. Based on the empirical data collected for the study, it could be argued that these collaborations have addressed some societal problems and achieved greater social impact. Essentially, they were established because the partners identified problems with finding a common definition, generating a variety of information, making a joint commitment to collaborate, and identifying initial resources (Waddell, 1999; Westley and Vredenburg, 1997).

Our evidence reveals that business participation is thought to increase efficiency and introduce new sources of finance, and helps to provide a better solution to pressing social problems. Companies enter into collaborations in the hope of improving societal perception of their activities and legitimacy to operate as well as to access resources, skills, or markets. As one of the managers stated:

> Our brand has been associated with it for thirty-nine years and we are very proud of that. It is quite very well recognized in terms of market research that people do associate the two together, and it fits with us in terms of committing, giving back to this country . . . We have a positive feeling about what we are doing for our community and various stakeholders.

Furthermore, during interviews with partner organizations, the existence of social partnerships connecting corporations and NPOs was seen as essential for increasing social benefits. Another manager stated: "There are those who think that the organization, because of its standing, because of its size, because of its importance to the country, because of all that . . . [has] some higher obligations to the community. I believe that."

The above assertions are supported by Berger, Cunningham, and Drumwright (2006), who assert that positive associations for an organization can be important sources of competitive advantage. They also suggest that corporate social initiative efforts can create positive associations among consumers that influence the ways in which they identify with companies, and such associations can translate into an array of benefits for both companies and NPOs.

We also found that partnerships bring new skills and human resources to NPOs and thereby strengthen them by making some services more efficient and more effective (Jørgensen, 2006). For example, the relationships between BP and SLSNZ (enduring over forty years) and DHL and SLSNZ have made it possible for the surf life-saving organization to continue to perform health and safety duties on all of New Zealand beaches. They have also enabled the organization to purchase the necessary equipment and to train its staff and volunteers, and to visit schools to teach water and beach health and safety. One of the business managers in the relationship stated:

> SLSNZ saved, I think, almost fourteen hundred lives last year [2007] and more than half of them are using our boats. Because of the money that we invest there are seven hundred people who got back to their families that wouldn't otherwise . . . That really means something, particularly to our staff. SLSNZ is a favourite with our staff. They really get behind it and they are very proud to talk about the company being associated with it.

> Our investment will enable them [SLSNZ] to have all of their seventy-five clubs branded consistently and provide them with new facilities, equipment, a good funding of resources for taking their next step with the organization. Also, a quite significant part of our funding goes into the beach education program.

SLSNZ's manager was similarly enthusiastic about the partnership:

> We are the community part of the fabric of society . . . we are something that two million people a year engaged with. We go to the beach, some of us patrol the beach . . . the whole family safety values, security type of things that we offer. So I think very much [through] the family values, rather than being a sports team or something, we are

an underlying part of New Zealand culture . . . There is goodwill among the corporates to do something right. We could see why they wanted the values that we offered . . . It was really important in terms of having a shared vision for a relationship.

Wood and Gray (1991) and Gray and Wood (1991) have argued that successful outcomes of collaborations include finding solutions to problems, learning from partners, distributing risks, a greater level of collective understanding, greater efficiency, and organizational survival. Based on the data collected for the present study, there was evidence to suggest that all of these key points were present. All twenty senior managers representing the ten relationships studied stressed the importance of these factors. For instance, one corporate manager stated:

We . . . committed to [them] a long time ago and have since benefited from building up our brand and linkage with them . . . We are planning to continue with them in the future. Our teams are doing team-building exercises, planting trees or cleaning up the beaches – all that sort of thing which is more around the community. And for a big corporate, we are more involved in making NZ a better place . . . from a social view point and also from an economic viewpoint.

Another senior manager asserted:

As much as a community investment, it is a brand-awareness campaign. We do other things like put roofs on swimming pools or build new swimming pools for councils, put a lot of money into stadiums and theatres . . . We also have projects which will have lasting impacts in many years to come: for example, we have got two or three Ph.D. students working on and researching a melanoma study at the moment.

We also found that partners intend to retain organizational autonomy while joining forces to tackle shared social problems (Parker and Selsky, 2004). In all of the organizations studied, partners find a "strategic fit" between their organizations to share skills and resources and work on community projects initiated in the collaboration without affecting their distinct identities and primary functions, and without crowding each other out. Our research also supports London, Rondinelli, and O'Neill's (2005) suggestion that firms facing a less coercive external environment and an internal context that supports relationships are more proactive in identifying opportunities to create new knowledge through collaborations. For instance, one NPO manager commented:

They belong to a different industry and we belong to another industry. They don't tell us what to do. They respect us as an organization and never ask us to do things differently for them, but having a relationship with them has improved us as an organization and our people like that.

Meanwhile, a senior corporate manager pointed out:

It is a true partnership . . . We did a lot of different things to improve energy efficiency and improve homes. We provided all the marketing, we did the advertising campaign, we did posters, and we did some very clever billboards of types of insulation in shopping malls . . . We developed a logo and brand for them. This is a good – really good – partnership.

Another corporate manager asserted: "One of our objectives obviously is under corporate social responsibility and to get more of our people out into the community, offering their skills and learning themselves, employee motivation, volunteering, job satisfaction – those kinds of things."

According to Bachman (2001), trust is one of the mechanisms for coordinating inter-organizational relationships, such as partnerships, as it carries positive and emotionally laden connotations. Therefore, dynamics around trust are a normative context of any partnership. It is a key aspect of the structural relationship between two social entities (Bachman, 2001; Das and Teng, 2001). During our interviews with them, many managers used such phrases as "they trust us," "we trust them," "they trust our judgment," and "we cannot have this relationship without trust." Hence, we argue that trust is the bedrock of a successful social partnership: without it, partnerships cannot function and key projects and initiatives cannot be executed.

Discussion and implications

The findings from this study suggest that legitimacy theory (discussed earlier in this chapter) is useful for understanding corporate responsiveness to social issues. In this section, we will explore how the theoretical perspective fits with the empirical findings.

This study found strong evidence in support of legitimacy theory. The drive for legitimacy motivated all of the companies to focus on "putting something back into the community," and some to assist in the development of socio-economically "underdeveloped" regions (Genesis and HEET). Interactions with key stakeholders ensured the "organization is just and worthy of support" (ANZ National Bank and Cancer Society of New Zealand; Telecom and IHC; Westpac Bank NZ and Auckland Rescue Helicopter Trust; DHL and SLSNZ; Nestlé and Lifeline NZ; Vodafone Foundation and RNFB). Indeed, all of the companies were striving to be considered "meaningful, predictable, and trustworthy." Further, they wanted to "localize" and create a meaningful local community perception.

Based on our empirical research, it could be argued that business partners enter into these relationships in order to achieve more focused results and truly make a difference in terms of corporate social responsibility. These businesses are reaching into the community through their relationships with NPOs to form significant and enduring relationships. The companies were clearly sensitive to their stakeholders and believed that having strong social relationships with NPOs improved their images and provided exposure for their social activities. For example, they all agreed that having relationships with NPOs gave them added visibility in the locations where they operate. For instance, one senior company manager asserted:

> We still believe that we need to act as a good corporate citizen in the sense that we put investments back into the community. As much as it is a community investment, it is a brand awareness campaign; it is a way of informing the public of what we do.

This was supported by a nonprofit partner, who stated: "Our business partner has a strong understanding of our relationship with NZ audiences . . . so I suggest that their involvement with us is based on knowledge of audience development." In addition, a senior energy company manager declared: "If we are making a difference, if we can see that we are impacting positively on people, if there are still homes there to benefit from our partnership, we will keep the program going." Another senior energy company manager reflected:

I don't think you can conduct business in this day and age without acknowledging the fact that you are part of a community. You have to behave as a responsible member of that community, a part of the community that makes a contribution . . . especially the kind of business we are in, where we do use a lot of localized resources to do a lot of national good.

Conclusion

This chapter has offered insights into the relationships between companies and NPOs in New Zealand, and has demonstrated that company managers are increasingly aware of the roles their businesses play in the wider social community in terms of using non-market strategy to improve society. Accordingly, they have formed social partnerships with NPOs in order to reach out to society and demonstrate their social responsibility and legitimacy. Our research demonstrates that social partnership is seen as an integral part of corporate strategy (non-market) and companies' social responsibility to society in New Zealand.

Based on the cases involved in this research, it appears that corporate social responsibility is employed as a significant strategy when corporations partner with NPOs in New Zealand. Thus, we argue that businesses enter into these relationships to improve societal perception of their activities and legitimacy to operate as well as to gain access to resources, skills, and markets. The companies involved do not normally use their partnerships with NPOs to publicize their own products and services, but they do draw attention to their social relationships.

Bibliography

Abzug, R. and Webb, N. (1999). Relationship between nonprofit and for-profit organizations: A stakeholder perspective. *Nonprofit and Voluntary Sector Quarterly*, 28(4), 416–31.

Ackoff, R. L. (1974). *Redesigning the future: A systems approach to societal problems.* New York: Wiley.

Ashman, D. (2001). Civil society collaboration with business: Bringing empowerment back in. *World Development*, 29(7), 1097–113.

Austin, J. (1998). *Partnering for progress.* Harvard Business School Working Papers, Social Enterprise Series No. 5. www.hbs.edu/socialenterprise/pdf/SE5PartneringforProgress.pdf (accessed November 17, 2014).

— (2000a). Strategic collaboration between nonprofits and businesses. *Nonprofit and Voluntary Sector Quarterly*, 19(1), 79–97.

— (2000b). *The collaborative challenge.* San Francisco, CA: Jossey-Bass.

Bachman, R. (2001). Trust, power, and control in trans–organizational relations. *Organizational Studies*, 22(2), 337–65.

Berger, I., Cunningham, P., and Drumwright, M. (2004). Social alliances: Company/nonprofit collaboration. *California Management Review*, 47(1), 58–90.

— (2006). Identity, identification, and relationship through social alliances. *Journal of the Academy of Marketing Science*, 34(2), 128–37.

— (2007). Mainstreaming corporate social responsibility: Developing markets for virtue. *California Management Review*, 49(4), 132–57.

Blockson, L. C. (2003). Multisector approaches to societal issues management. *Business and Society*, 42, 381–90.

Butterfield, K. D., Reed, R., and Lemak, D. J. (2004). An inductive model of collaboration from the stakeholder's perspective. *Business and Society*, 43(2), 162–95.

Chung, S., Singh, H., and Lee, K. (2000). Complementarity, status similarity, and social capital as drivers of alliance formation. *Strategic Management Journal*, 39, 1479–512.

Covey, J. and Brown, L. D. (2001). Critical cooperation: An alternative form of civil society–business engagement. *Institute for Development Research (IDR) Reports*, 17(1), 1–18.

Crane, A. (2000). Culture clash and mediation. In J. Bendell (ed.), *Terms of endearment* (pp. 163–77). Sheffield: Greenleaf.

Creyer, E. H. and Ross, W. T. (1997). The influence of firm behaviour on purchase intention: Do consumers really care about business ethics? *Journal of Consumer Marketing*, 14, 421–32.

Das, T. K. and Teng, B. S. (2001). Trust, control, and risk in strategic alliances: An integrated framework. *Organization Studies*, 22(2), 251–83.

Davis, K. (1973). The case for and against business assumption of social responsibilities. *Academy of Management Journal*, 16, 312–22.

Dowling, J. and Pfeffer, J. (1975). Organizational legitimacy: Social value and organizational behaviour. *Pacific Sociological Review*, 18, 122–38.

Egels-Zandén, N. and Wahlqvist, E. (2007). Post-partnership strategies for defining corporate social responsibility: The business social compliance strategy. *Journal of Business Ethics*, 70(2), 175–89.

Elkington, J. and Fennel, S. (2000). Partners for sustainability. In J. Bendell (ed.), *Terms of endearment* (pp. 150–62). Sheffield: Greenleaf.

Ellen, P., Mohr, L., and Webb, D. (2000). Charitable programs and retailer: Do they mix? *Journal of Retail*, 76, 393–406.

Emery, F. E. and Trist, E. L. (1965). The causal texture of organizational environments. *Human Relations*, 18, 21–32.

Eweje, G. (2007a). Multinational oil companies' CSR initiatives in Nigeria: The scepticism of stakeholders in host communities. *Managerial Law*, 49(5/6), 218–35.

— (2007b). Strategic partnerships between MNEs and civil society: The post-WSSD perspectives. *Sustainable Development Journal*, 15, 15–27.

Eweje, G. and Bentley, T. (2006). CSR and staff retention in New Zealand companies: Literature review. *Research Working Paper Series, Massey University, New Zealand*, 6, 1–16.

— (2007). CSR and staff retention in New Zealand companies: Literature review. *Research Woking Paper Series, Massey University, New Zealand*, 6, 1–16.

Eweje, G. and Palakshappa, N. (2009). Business partnerships with nonprofits: Working to solve mutual problems in New Zealand. *Corporate Social Responsibility and Environmental Management Journal*, 16(6), 337–51.

Faulkner, D. and de Rond, M. (2000). Perspectives on cooperative strategy. In D. Faulkner and M. de Rond (eds.), *Cooperative strategy: Economic, business and organizational issues* (pp. 3–39). Oxford: Oxford University Press.

Gomes-Casseres, B. (1996). *The alliance revolution: The new shape of business rivalry*. Cambridge, MA: Harvard University Press.

Gray, B. (1985). Conditions facilitating interorganizational collaboration. *Human Relations*, 38(10), 911–36.

— (1989). *Collaboration: Finding common ground for multiparty problems*. San Francisco, CA: Jossey-Bass.

Gray, B. and Wood, D. (1991). Collaborative alliances: Moving from practice to theory. *Journal of Applied Behavioural Science*, 27(1), 3–22.

Guo, C. and Acar, M. (2005). Understanding collaboration among nonprofit organizations: Combining resource dependency, institutional, and network perspectives, *Nonprofit and Voluntary Sector Quarterly*, 34(3), 340–61.

Hamann, R. (2006). Can business make decisive contributions to development? Towards a research agenda on corporate citizenship and beyond. *Development Southern Africa*, 23(2), 175–95.

Heath, R. G. (2007). Rethinking community through a dialogic lens: Creativity, democracy, and diversity in community organising. *Management Communication Quarterly*, 21(2), 145–71.

Hess, D. and Rogovsky, N. (2002). The next wave of corporate community involvement. *California Management Review*, 44(2), 110–25.

Hillman, A. J. and Keim, G. (2001). Shareholder value, stakeholder management, and social issues: What's the bottom line? *Strategic Management Journal*, 22, 126–39.

Hood, J. N., Logsdon, J. M., and Thomson, J. K. (1993). Collaborating for social problem solving: A process model. *Business and Society*, 32(1), 1–17.

Jørgensen, M. (2006). Evaluating cross-sector partnerships. Paper presented at the Public–Private Partnerships in the Post-WSSD Context Conference, Copenhagen Business School, Denmark, August 14.

Kapucu, N. (2006). Public–nonprofit partnerships for collective action in dynamic contexts of emergencies. *Public Administration*, 84(1), 205–20.

London, T., Rondinelli, D. A., and O'Neill, H. (2005). Strange bedfellows: Alliances between corporations and nonprofits. In O. Shenkar and J. Reur (eds.), *Handbook of strategic alliances* (pp. 353–66). Thousand Oaks, CA: Sage.

Marquis, C., Glynn, M. A., and Davis, F. D. (2007). Community isomorphism and corporate social action. *Academy of Management Review*, 32(3), 925–45.

Millar, C. C. J., Choi, C. J., and Chen, S. (2004). Global strategic partnerships between MNEs and NGOs: Drivers of change and ethical issues. *Business and Society Review*, 109(4), 395–414.

Murphy, D. F. and Bendell, J. (1999). *Partners in time? Business, NGOs and sustainable development.* UNRISD Discussion Paper No. 109. Geneva: UNRISD.

Nasi, J., Nasi, S., Phillips, N., and Zyglidopoulos, S. (1997). The evolution of corporate social responsiveness. *Business and Society*, 36(3), 296–321.

O'Riain, S. (2000). States and markets in an era of globalisation. *Annual Review Sociology*, 26, 187–213.

Parker, B. and Selsky, J. (2004). Interface dynamics in cause-based partnerships: An exploration of emergent culture. *Nonprofit and Voluntary Sector Quarterly*, 33(3), 458–88.

Pasquero, J. (1991). Supraorganizational collaboration: The Canadian environmental experiment. *Journal of Applied Behavioural Science*, 27, 38–64.

Prakash, A. (2002). Beyond Seattle: Globalisation, the nonmarket environment and corporate strategy. *Review of International Political Economy*, 9(3), 513–37.

Rangan, S., Samii, R., and Van Wassenhove, L. (2006). Constructive partnerships: When alliances between private firms and public actors enable creative strategies. *Academy of Management Review*, 31(3), 738–51.

Roberts, N. C. and Bradley, R. T. (1991). Stakeholder collaboration and innovation: A study of public initiation at the state level. *Journal of Behavioural Science*, 272(2), 209–27.

Sagawa, S. (2001). New value partnerships: The lessons of Denny's/Save the Children partnership for building high-yielding cross-sector alliances. *International Journal of Voluntary Sector Marketing*, 6(3), 199–214.

Sagawa, S. and Segal, E. (2000). Common interest, common good: Creating value through business and social sector partnerships. *California Management Review*, 42(2), 105–22.

Sen, S. and Bhattacharya, C. B. (2001). Does doing good always lead to doing better? Consumer reactions to corporate social responsibility. *Journal of Marketing*, 38, 225–43.

Sethi, S. P. (1979). A conceptual framework for environmental analysis of social issues and evaluation of business response patterns. *Academy of Management Review*, 4, 63–74.

Stone, M. (2000). Exploring the effects of collaboration on members' organizations: Washington County's welfare toward partnership. *Nonprofit and Voluntary Sector Quarterly*, 29(1), 98–119.

Suchman, M. (1995). Managing legitimacy: Strategic and institutional approaches. *Academy of Management Review*, 20, 571–610.

Turban, D. B. and Greening, D. W. (1997). Corporate social performance and organizations' attractiveness to prospective employees. *Academy of Management Journal*, 40, 658–72.

United Nations. (2002). Summit historic opportunity to further business role in sustainable development says Secretary-General in remarks to "business day" event. www.un.org/events/wssd/summaries/envdevj15.htm (accessed December 12, 2014).

Waddell, S. (1999). Business–government–nonprofit collaborations as agents for social innovation and learning. Paper presented at the Academy of Management, Chicago, August.

Westley, F. and Vredenburg, H. (1997). Strategic bridging: The collaboration between environmentalists and business in the marketing of green products. *Journal of Applied Behavioural Science*, 27, 65–90.

Wicks, A. and Berman, S. L. (2004). The effects of context on trust in firm–stakeholder relationships: The institutional environment, trust creation, and firm performance. *Business Ethics Quarterly*, 14(1), 142–60.

Wood, D. J. and Gray, B. (1991). Towards a comprehensive theory of collaboration. *Journal of Applied Behavioural Science*, 27, 139–162.

19

Regional trade agreements

Non-market strategy in the context of business regionalization

Gabriele Suder

A complex network of regional trade agreements (RTAs) spans our globalized world. For the most part, the scholarly literature refers to these as free trade agreements (FTAs), although they may potentially constitute a variety of market grouping and market integration constructs. Many of these RTAs emanate from the design of FTAs or customs unions, common markets, economic unions, currency unions, or other political or geo-economic constructs ruled under preferential trade agreements. The FTA is typically limited to the elimination of certain tariffs; the customs union also establishes a common customs duty; and each one of the above-cited constructs has its own politically negotiated variations. These variations, in essence, establish different types of level playing field for firms with distinctive variants of harmonization effects that influence internal and external trade and investment conditions.

The most advanced form of economic integration in the world remains, to date, the European Union (EU), with its long-established body of *acquis communautaire*: that is, a vast, far-reaching internal market harmonization through a complex, yet incomplete set of measures (Suder, 2011). It is far from being the only RTA, however. In 2013, the World Trade Organization (WTO) counted some 575 notifications of RTAs (counting goods, services, and accessions separately) (WTO, 2013a), and this number excludes unilateral preferential trade agreements. Such a high figure confirms the dynamics of RTA agreements negotiation and formalization amongst WTO members. Because it lists only those WTO members entering into regional integration arrangements through which they grant more favorable conditions to their trade with other parties to that arrangement than to other WTO members' trade (WTO, 2013a), we can legitimately believe that the overall number of such agreements is even higher. And the intentions of creating or joining RTAs can be considered to increase that number still further.

Advocates of globalization see their heyday as the 1990s and the turn of the millennium (Arestis et al., 2012). The aforementioned WTO data indicates that the regionalization phenomenon is not only worldwide in scope but also has gained momentum since the end of the Cold War. Even more so, RTAs with specific reciprocal trade liberalization provisions for trade in goods constitute the majority of agreements since 2002. Most recently, developing countries have surpassed developed countries in the formalization of trade liberalizing agreements (Crawford, 2012: 2).

The most prominent regional networks, in addition to the EU, include the North American Free Trade Agreement (NAFTA), the Southern Common Market (MERCOSUR), the Association of Southeast Asian Nations (ASEAN) Free Trade Area (AFTA), and the Common Market of Eastern and Southern Africa (COMESA). Many more illustrations of the ongoing trend towards a dense regionalization network around the world can be found in the negotiation of agreements between Switzerland and China, the EU and Japan, and Australia and the Gulf Cooperation Council (GCC), amongst many others.

Increasing regionalism enhances the dimension and impact of regionalization on non-market forces, specifically the complexity of political/regulatory arenas that senior-level management anticipates, pre-empts, responds to, and builds its strategy upon.

I will now turn to a literature review that sheds light on the scholarly understanding of RTA development as well as the distinctions between "the region," "regionalism," and "regionalization".

Theoretical context: the link between globalization, regionalization, and non-market strategy

Because of the complexity of RTA contexts and the resulting multi-polarity of stakeholders, non-market strategy locus, design, and implementation have become key elements when defining corporate dynamic capabilities, in that "the firm's ability to integrate, build, and reconfigure internal and external competences to address rapidly changing environment" (Teece et al., 1997: 516) is increasingly challenged. As Table 19.1 illustrates, "regionalism" refers to the general interpretation of a formalization of cooperation through a body of ideas and values on a geographically defined regional level. The term is used mainly in the political science literature. It is described in the *Dictionary of Trade Policy Terms* (Goode, 2007) as "actions by governments to liberalize or facilitate trade on a regional basis, sometimes through free-trade areas or customs unions."

The term "regionalization," which we see mainly in economics and business literature, is derived from "regionalism" and refers to the applied cooperation, convergence, coherence, and identity-seeking construct itself (Schulz et al., 2001).

From a political economy perspective, the economic and political world is intertwined in a complex network of trade agreements under the denomination of regionalization or regionalism, which is often synonymous with RTAs and regional economic cooperation. From a corporate perspective, the regional economic and political integration that results from RTAs enhances deliberate or coerced adaptation of market and non-market strategies of the firm that operates across borders.

While non-market strategy traditionally centered on national or local political decision-makers, the regionalization of governmental power agendas has added a venue in which a number of participating political decision-makers of different origins and with potentially varying agendas are influenced to reach a shared goal. For example, a German firm will strive to lobby not only Berlin but also Brussels, because decision-makers in both locations influence the regulatory environment in which it mainly operates. This is because member states have agreed to share specific sets of sovereignty and power, and not others. In the example of the EU, a firm that engages in a cross-border merger will talk to national and regionalized (EU) decision-makers that interact to permit or reject such mergers. The firm hence needs to adapt its non-market strategy to ensure effective interest representation in more than one venue, and to adapt its strategy choices to the agendas and options available in those various venues. Will the decision-makers in Brussels, who represent all twenty-eight

Table 19.1 Understanding overlapping concepts

Concept	Region	Regionalism	Regionalization	RTA
Definition	A grouping or locational proximity of countries that "sustain(s) a central and self-assuring pole of familiarity"	"Cooperation through a body of ideas and values"	"Applied cooperation, convergence, coherence and identity-seeking construct"; "spatial reorganization of foreign investments and regional economic integration"	Regional trade agreement; networks that grant more favorable conditions to its trade with certain parties (typically, members or associated economies) than to others
Scale	"Physical continuity and proximity"	Geographically defined regional level	Not necessarily subject to geographical limitations or proximity	A variety of market groupings and market integration constructs that represent forms of regionalization
Aim	Simplification of some of the complexities resulting from globalization	"Actions by governments to liberalize or facilitate trade on a regional basis"	Deliberate or coerced adaptation of political and by consequence economic strategies	Selective liberalization that induces by consequence inherent discrimination of non-members
Scholarly origin	Geography, geo-economics, geopolitics literature	Political science literature	Economics and business literature	Political economy; international business literature

EU member states, be attentive to the same argumentation used in one given member state? Which forces are in favor of or against the proposed action, and why? This is part of the multi-level, multi-venue analysis that regionalization of the regulatory environment for business enforces (van Schendelen, 2010; Suder, 2011). This is a crucial part of company strategy under the assumption that RTAs are, as Ravenhill (2011: 178) argues, undertaken mostly with political objectives in mind. Also, if the efficient allocation of resources and the spread of welfare are the main goals of RTA engagement, again, the negotiating power of transnational business secures opportunities at a regionalized level (Ravenhill, 2011: 180; see also Donas et al., 2014).

Many scholars acclaim regionalization not only as an addition to or extension of the nation state, but as a complement or alternative to globalization that helps counteract "the inherent discrimination that liberalization on a preferential basis entails" (Crawford, 2012: 25). RTAs vary in the scale and scope of integration, particularly in the:

- number of members;
- depth of their integration; and
- degree of linkage to non-members and to other similar constructs.

I contend that these forms of regionalization are not necessarily limited to a geographical definition of a region or a continent (Crawford, 2012; Suder, 2013), as defined by WTO. Yet, in the management literature, there is some disagreement about the geographical limitation of regionalization and its virtues. Arregle et al. (2009: 89), for example, defines regions as an alliance or grouping of countries with physical continuity and proximity. With this interpretation, scholars agree to the "crucial role of economic geography and raise questions about the spatial reorganization of foreign investments and regional economic integration" (Buckley and Ghauri, 2004: 82). This is of great importance to firms that engage in corporate political activity (CPA), which often constitutes the main part of non-market strategy. It encompasses their attempt to shape the development of integration in favorable terms, coherent with business objectives.

Since firms that engage in CPA have a variety of origins and agendas, scholars have also explored the threats that regionalization may represent for free trade (Borrmann and Koopmann, 1994). First, as a diversion from broad international negotiation (Collier et al., 2000: 104); second, in its latent exclusiveness that penalizes non-member economies and firms (Miller and Richards, 2002); and finally in the complexity that this may represent for internal networks (Rugman and Verbeke, 2007). Bhagwati et al. (1998: 1138–9) called this a "spaghetti bowl effect" that could impede diversified trade liberalization. They refer to a mixture of regulatory norms and clauses (such as those on rules of origin) that create complexity, not as a consequence of the number of RTAs, but due to their scale and scope.

Questions are raised as to how an internationalizing firm can possibly cope with the many variations of tariffs, standards, and rules that comprise national and international sets of conditions. How can the firm influence agendas and outcomes of these sets? Which firms can and influence them and which cannot?

The international firm is subject to a mix of market and non-market forces that define its degree of operability, and that the firm strives to influence.

In this context, the management literature explores interest group influence and lobbying success (Kluever, 2013) in securing favorable legislation or counteracting potentially damaging regulation, as well as the limits of business lobbying on multiple levels.

Krugman (1991) specifically analyzed the formation of the triad (EU, US/NAFTA, and Japan/Asian integration) as a challenge to broader economic development in which trade is at once created (internally) and diverted (externally). Again, the management literature argues that trade creation and diversion are influenced by the non-market strategies of firms that hope to shape the agenda of RTAs and integration, be it individually or in sector or geographic alliance with firms with similar objectives.

In the weakening of multilateral cooperation, Krugman found that regional cooperation could benefit welfare and increase the capabilities needed to enlarge and enhance such market integration mechanisms. In this context,

The CPA literature argues that regional integration provides more efficient lobbying arenas than vast quasi-global multilateral negotiations for deregulation.

Indeed, RTAs have the advantage of relatively few, selective numbers of candidates or members, which eases negotiations and CPA activity relative to those that are held on an international, multilateral level. This limited number of participants allows for better monitoring of internal rules than on a vast, multilateral (e.g., WTO) level. Krugman (1991: 73–5) argues that it also counteracts or equilibrates the "hegemonic stability," in which a very small number of world powers rule the international economy and inhibit broad multilateral efforts. Finally, it allows RTAs to deal better with institutional differences. The regionalization of power is therefore both a challenge and a benefit to the market- and non-market strategies of internationalizing firms, and to the interplay of business and political forces.

A great number of scholars assume that the progress of European integration (and its single market) has been central to the contemporary spur in the number of regionalized constructs. The difficulties of European integration, due to the complexity of its scale and scope, may well explain the preference of many countries to negotiate simpler, less engaging free trade agreements as opposed to more advanced integrations that require the pooling of national sovereignty.

Overall, the "region" in this sense is a construct that forms the basis of regionalization of political and corporate interaction. It allows economic actors to simplify some of the complexities resulting from globalization, with its compression of space and time (Harvey, 1990; Friedman, 2005) and to align resources accordingly. This is dependent on the (potential) member states' willingness to develop further from the Westphalian model of geopolitics when relinquishing a certain degree of national sovereignty in an effort to pool policies for the benefit of mutual and reciprocal objectives of cooperation. It expands the geographic term of the region to the extent that proximity is no longer a limiting factor and distance becomes an asset for diversification, market access, and resource- and knowledge-seeking objectives. It is also dependent on the sense-giving and sense-making of the bias for the economic world and its firms that use a privileged environment to perform (or enhance) business activity across borders.

While the term "region" holds a range of meanings in the political and economic literature, scholars agree that it reflects a need to provide or sustain a central and self-assuring pole of familiarity in the international world. RTAs' "common functional and institutional arrangements" (Kacowicz, 1998) are mainly (though not exclusively) state- or business-promoted (Rozman, 2004: 7), translating into political, economic or social integration, or they formalize identity- or security-driven formations. In any of these circumstances, they allow the firm to develop and align strategies with national- and regional-level impact.

> *What constitutes a "region" is contingent upon political and economic actors that form a construct of (mainly economic) integration; it may be geographically adjacent or dispersed.*

This creates opportunity; the phenomenon shapes a macro-environment that is constituted by "a range of heterogeneous units in multiple, interwoven, and overlapping layers of governance" (Kobrin, 2001: 220).

The WTO (2013b) warns that

> the proliferation of RTAs, especially as their scope broadens to include policy areas not regulated multilaterally, increases the risks of inconsistencies in the rules and procedures among RTAs themselves, and between RTAs and the multilateral framework. This is likely to give rise to regulatory confusion, distortion of regional markets, and severe implementation problems, especially where there are overlapping RTAs.

Non-market strategy therefore needs to align RTA development and the opportunities lying therein to remain effective in an international business environment.

Regional trade agreements (RTAs): the impact of regionalization on internationalization and non-market strategy

In theory, RTAs constitute non-market forces at a similar level as the state. For corporations and organizations that engage in public affairs management and CPA, the decision-making members and bodies of RTAs become key venues for interest intermediation. As soon as governments of member states settle – to the extent covered by the RTA and its provisions – on shared decision-making and implementation of policies that were traditionally under the auspices of the state, the firm can coordinate its lobbying activity accordingly.

The transfer of a state's sovereignty is more or less extensive (Wang, 2013). For example, it is less pronounced in East Asia than in Europe. This means that the RTA will have less influence on the business environment in Asia than in Europe, and the venue for non-market strategy remains on national and local (rather than regional) levels.

RTAs potentially serve to support the efficient and effective functioning of member states' organizations. By definition, regionalization leads to favorable conditions for trade and investment across members' borders, depending on the nature of the agreement. To some extent, firms that are located in states that benefit from preferential partnerships within an RTA will thus benefit from facilitated business conditions when doing business with the partner member state(s) and potentially with its linkages (markets linked in by association).

This RTA conception aims to deter market failure and malfunction, and aims indirectly to increase firms' internationalization capability and performance, which are considered favorable for overall economic welfare and thus directly benefit shared political objectives.

The formal agreement of an RTA forms part of its member states' international trade policies and foreign policies that broaden its political and economic reach to a polycentric political status (with a range of decision-makers), as opposed to mono-centric (state) constructs. In the management literature, we read this as a facilitator for a business environment that extends from the home market to the host market(s). For international business strategists, the main challenge in the negotiation and formalization of an RTA is hence to ensure that the design and implementation of RTAs, or their evolution, are business friendly.

However, business's impact on FTA constructs is limited to a "voice," not a vote or a decision-making right, and a firm's influence remains effectively indirect. A solid understanding and assessment of RTA rules and their impact on business in this increasingly interwoven, regionalized world is thus crucial and requires attention to non-market strategy options in direct adaptation to regulations and policies that shape the business environment in both national and integrated regional markets.

Consequently, international business strategy is increasingly dependent on non-market strategy in home and host countries, in home and host regions, and in their nexus (e.g., association agreements with other RTAs or countries). Regions have gained importance as non-market forces and firms need an increasingly multi-layered corporate knowledge, specifically about institutional regulatory contexts, appropriate corporate political activity (CPA), and how to handle fundamental issues.

The literature establishes that most enterprises are multinational and, specifically, regional in response to market and non-market forces. As a consequence of their resulting scale and scope, non-market strategy needs to be multi-layered and multi-venued: that is, national, regional, and international in scale and scope.

In the contemporary management and international business literature, multinational companies (MNCs) are viewed as organizations that depend on regional business (Rugman, 2000, 2005; Rugman and Verbeke, 2004, 2005; Collinson and Rugman, 2008), in particular with regards to sales and assets, comprising:

- Home-regional firms: more than 50 percent of sales in the home region.
- Bi-regional firms: less than 50 percent of sales in the home region and more than 20 percent in another region of the triad.
- Host-regional firms (a form of bi-regional firm; see Rugman, 2005: 11): more than 50 percent of sales in a triad region other than the home region.
- Global firms: less than 50 percent of sales in the home region and more than 20 percent in each of the other two triad regions (Rugman and Verbeke, 2004; Osegowitsch and Sammartino, 2008: 185).

MNC strategies as introduced by Enright (2005: 78) are based on bilateral and unilateral factors, evaluated typically on the basis of cultural, administrative, geographic, and economic (CAGE) distance (Ghemawat, 2001) that demonstrate commonalities on regional and sub-regional levels. With differences fading over time and due to regulatory arrangements, an increasing level of "semi-globalization" (Ghemawat, 2003) appears. There are variations in firms' focus on home-country, sub-region, home-region, bi-regional, or global strategy (Osegowitsch and Sammartino, 2008: 191), and a multi-regional, triangular strategy (as a subset of bi-regional strategy, yet not limited to the triad today) that follows the nexus of RTA relations.

For example, a firm that operated mainly in the EU and between EU member states may also, thanks to free trade negotiations, engage in new or enhanced trade with South Korea and Singapore, which also entertain preferential agreements with each other, and thus allow for potential advantages through norms and tariffs that reduce costs in multiple RTA-based constellations.

The international business literature therefore distinguishes between inter- and intra-regional business. In this manner, a firm which regionalizes and uses regional integration to its benefit in either of the two modes is able to yield advantage from increased economies of scale and scope, to use "competitive blindspots" (Ohmae, 1986), and the deployment of firm-specific advantages (FSA), for example brand awareness or internationalization capabilities. However, there is some debate about their transferability and acceptability (no matter if "embodied in exports, transferred to licensees, or transferred to subsidiaries"; Osegowitsch and Sammartino, 2008: 186) that may ultimately be embedded in the (home) region-boundedness of FSAs (Rugman and Verbeke, 2004: 13) or else become region-specific advances that can be transferred between regions, for example in the capability to yield advantage from economic integration and RTA business environments (Suder, 2013).

Limits are set by the inclusiveness of RTAs (which vary from case to case) and inherent protective measures that may hinder the deployment of firm-specific advantages in host regions and affiliated or associated markets. In this case, a liability of regional foreignness (LRF) – that is, the cost of doing business across regions – becomes a barrier to entry or performance (Qian et al., 2013: 640) through local government's discriminatory policies, local customers' bias, business networks, and privileged links with stakeholders. This liability adds to that of country foreignness and increases with the number of locations that a firm targets. Intuitively, one may assume that these costs may be higher when doing business on an inter-regional level – that is, between regions – compared with intra-regional business

– that is, within a single region of geographic or institutional proximity, or both. Yet, Ose-gowitsch and Sammartino (2008) posit that "the liability of interregional diversification is too small to discourage inter-regional diversification" (quoted in Qian et al. 2013: 636), while Qian et al. (2013) find that LRF is positively correlated with inter-regional diversification. Sethi and Judge (2009: 407) distinguish between two categories of liabilities of foreignness (LoF). Incidental LoF – the "non-discriminatory costs of learning and adaptation to cope with the unfamiliarity and lack of roots" in a host location – can be reduced relatively quicker than the second category, the more systemic discriminatory LoF, which includes costs stemming from, for instance, explicit regulations targeted at MNE subsidiaries to the benefit of domestic firms and implicit prejudices and nationalism. In any circumstances, liabilities are known to vary between locations and decline with time and knowledge.

Non-market strategy that targets a beneficial business environment across an RTA thus sets a crucial scene to reduce costs of adaptation. The institutional relationships that a firm constitutes in a region have the potential to increase its opportunity gains and to counteract loss and cost; yet the firm does not operate in a vacuum.

The vaster the scale and scope of the RTA and the transfer of sovereignty, the vaster the interests that firms and other influences attempt to exercise.

Kobrin (2009) contends that we may be approaching an uncharted phase of opportunities and challenges characterized by new types of participants (governments, firms, non-governmental organizations) that have more diverse and unaligned interests, purposes, and preferences than in previous eras. Recent modifications in power patterns and balancing acts (as analyzed in geopolitics) are increasingly acknowledged by academics and practitioners. Moreover, scholars concede that globalization has become a phenomenon accompanied by the loss of state governmental authority, to the benefit of multilateral, multinational forces and amongst them the multinational enterprise (MNE), as one key vector of a new phase of globalization. In this era, while economic benefits have spread ever more freely across the world, so have challenges, threats, and crises. As a consequence, globalization has become increasingly seconded by regionalization, from a political and economic perspective.

The positional analysis that determines strategy includes the analysis of "market forces, firm competencies and the non-market environment" upon which trade and investment choices are contingent (Aggarwal, 2001: 91).

The phenomenon of regionalization, formalized in the various forms of RTAs, demands appropriate adaptation and adaptability from firms that operate across borders, because RTAs alter the business environments in the home country, host country (or countries), and between them. Political economists define non-market forces as power-based correctives, a political "voice," or corporate political activity (CPA) that aims to mend the organization of economic, political, social, and cultural nature to assure survival (e.g., Hirschman, 1970; McGuire et al., 2012).

Firms gain advantage through regional institutional knowledge and networking position.

These advantages are encompassed in non-market strategy, associated with cognitive, nor-mative, and regulatory differences and similarities (Zaheer, 2002; Bell et al., 2012) and they constitute essential assets, because an important part of the liability of regional foreignness (in addition to that on the country level) that a foreign firm may suffer is based on government bias (Qian et al., 2013): that is, unfavorable government policies toward firms from other regions outside of the integrated construct.

This non-market dimension of regionalization has yet to receive sufficient attention from scholars (as is the case in Kaiser and Sofka, 2007; McGuire et al., 2012). Yet, practitioners face its impacts routinely in cross-border trade and investments. For example, the customs tariffs, duties, quotas, standards, and norms a business must respect are not only defined by national authorities. In many regions, the integration of markets and market authorities through RTAs determines those criteria for a number of member countries constituting a market grouping. In Europe, for instance, EU institutions determine them (with those institutions constituted in various forms by the member states).

Non-market strategy is thus a corporation's means to avoid the "spaghetti bowl effect" that McGuire et al. (2012) term regional liability of foreignness or un-familiarity, and Qian et al. (2013) call LRF complexities. Osegowitsch and Sammartino (2008: 192) explain that "Regionalisation theory and its concepts, such as the inter-regional LOF, are fundamentally dependent on intra-regional integration and enduring inter-regional differences." Therefore, the regulatory mix is dense when firms work across borders.

Regionalized non-market strategy is hence about intra- and inter-regional alignment of internationalized business interest to political and regulatory integration. The process of adjusting non-market strategy into a suitable, relative position is to counterbalance the cost of doing business in the home region and one or more host regions. An arrangement or positioning of players is a proactive or defensive alignment, seeking to create, improve, or defend a firm's interests in the location that becomes part of an RTA or is influenced by RTA alterations (internally or in its networks) (Houghton-Mifflin Company, 2009).

Firms can therefore also be considered active when they exercise political activity that directly drives or supports regionalization. For example, the US government explains that the role of the US auto industry in the negotiation of its free trade agreement with South Korea of 2012 was significant (www.ustr.gov/trade-agreements/free-trade-agreements/korus-fta). One example of corporate actors exercising CPA in this field is the firm Coeur, Inc (www.coeurinc.com). In Europe, a comprehensive example is BusinessEurope, an association of forty-one industrial and employers' federations from thirty-five countries, which provides detailed input about EU–India FTA negotiations and harmonization efforts in EU–China and EU–Russia relations (www.businesseurope.eu).

In economic terms, non-market forces are viewed as rule-of-the-game leverage exercised by a number of actors that strive to gain competitive advantage. Inter-regional forces also come into play in the context of the inter-regional negotiations between the EU and MERCOSUR (the Mercado Común del Sur) since 2000, the Trans-Pacific Partnership Agreement (TPP) in 2013, and the EU (as a whole) and US negotiations toward the Transatlantic Trade and Investment Partnership (TTIP), which is expected to allow EU firms to sell an additional €187 billion worth of goods and services annually once ratified: "80% of the benefits of an agreement would result from reducing this regulatory burden and bureaucracy, as well as from opening up services and public procurement markets" (http://ec.europa.eu/trade/policy/in-focus/ttip/, 11 December 2013); US exports are estimated to increase by 17 percent if the negotiations succeed (Erixon and Bauer, 2010).

Consequently, the implication of firms in the shaping of regionalization is based on the yielding of opportunity and performance. With their study of internalization theory, Banalieva and Dhanaraj (2013: 89) state, "technological advantage and institutional diversity determine firms' home-region orientation (HRO)," in which they find that "performance significantly reduces HRO, but HRO does not have a significant effect on performance." In other words, firms that excel in performance are more likely to operate outside their home region and are consequently more likely to engage in the ongoing regionalization in their international business arena than others, and to focus CPA on this level.

In this regionalized world, there is consensus that the "vitality, salience and legitimacy of the state" (Hall and Biersteker, 2002: 8) is thus insufficient as a locus for non-market strategy.

> *Given that the prevailing market-regulating authority in the modern world that impacts international business scale and scope is constituted of various regional layers in various locations, non-market strategy follows suit in the triangular trend of local, regional, and international interplay of market strategy.*

This is so because "Business firms need to manage their politico-social market as well as the business market" (Hadjikhani et al., 2008: 912).

The interplay of corporate political activity and regionalization knowledge advantage in corporate performance

Non-market strategy is a "factor of production" or a "firm resource" that can be seen as part of internationalization knowledge (IK) representing "higher-order" organizational capabilities (Fletcher et al., 2013). An increasing number of scholars recognize that "firms must manage in their international value-added chains" (Boddewyn and Brewer, 1994: 121) and that these are similarly complex through interwoven forms of regionalization. They are considered instrumental in the reduction of regulatory uncertainty in the international business environment (Kingsley et al., 2012). The adaptation and adaptability of firms and the dynamic capabilities of MNEs that learn from this corporate and economic–political environment are considered crucial by all streams of literature that explore the phenomena of international business and internationalization, including the institutional, the resources, and, specifically, the knowledge view (Barney, 1991).

Institutional theory teaches that an organization's field or arena is constituted by actors that directly or indirectly determine a firm's strategic actions from legitimate options, defined by actors and practices normalized by market (including customers, suppliers, etc.) and non-market forces (including formal and informal institutions) (DiMaggio and Powell, 1983; Scott, 2001; Deligonul et al., 2013). Knowledge of institutional contexts is subsequently an asset (Teece et al., 1997); the more multi-layered this knowledge is, the more visibility the firm has about regionalization benefits and can thus strategize the knowledge.

The non-market dimension of corporate strategy is part of the firm's IK that is "experiential knowledge about internationalization" (Blomstermo et al., 2004: 358) and has an inter- and intra-regional dimension through RTA-related knowledge. This knowledge of non-market forces of RTAs encompasses dimensions including tariff and customs harmonization, red-tape and transaction-cost reduction, standardized regulatory multi-country markets, bi- and multi-regional economic linkages etc., and how to yield benefits thereof. If this knowledge is rare, imperfectly imitable, and non-substitutable, it has the potential to serve as a strategic asset: the resource-based view (RBV) of international business (Barney, 1991) claims that this can result in considerable competitive advantage.

From an inter-linkage of the discussion of IK (Fletcher et al., 2013) and regionalization (Qian et al., 2013) we can conclude that region-centric internationalization knowledge (RIK) is path-dependent and contingent on firms' ability to transform learning from one regional construct "into responses to emerging international opportunities" (Cui et al., 2005: 36).

That is, on intra- and inter-regional levels, regionalization-benefit knowledge is a net contributor to gaining advantage over domestic or global competitors that lack such knowledge, and this counterbalances effects of liabilities of foreignness. In this context, "IK regarding the development, implementation, and operationalization of strategies in new territories is difficult to transfer or imitate because it comes from the systemization of accrued knowledge from other territories" (Fletcher et al., 2013: 50). This encompasses market and non-market knowledge that is embedded in processes and procedures and feeds into strategy development, deployment, and change. Here, CPA is central to firms' overall business strategies (Oberholzer-Gee et al., 2007). Barron (2011) states that firms use non-market strategy primarily, but not exclusively, to influence home/domestic institutional environments. Hillman and Keim (1995) notably affirmed the growing tendencies from the 1990s onwards to use CPA in other markets than at home, and Deligonul et al. (2013: 506) recently improved our understanding of non-market networks "outside of . . . indigenous institutional environments." The interplay of home and host country and regional dimensions is thus established for non-market strategy, as much as it is for market strategy. Through CPA, firms reduce potential dependence on socio-political actors' actions (cost, political risk, risk of passiveness or inertia, harm, coercion, lack of support) and seek to influence public policy and increase performance directly or indirectly. Mutual benefit may be maximized when interests are aligned. This results, it is anticipated, in "positive economics of regulations" (Stigler, 1975: 361).

Scholars argue that the attractiveness of "political markets" interaction for firms varies, depending on whether "new or to-maintain existing policies . . . affect their current business operations or future opportunities" (Bonardi et al., 2005: 399). As mentioned earlier, non-market strategy is multi-layered and multi-venued, but it is also multi-timed. CPA specifically varies between short–medium- and long-term action and objectives. In the short term, non-market strategy aims to create favorable conditions, and to deter unfavorable conditions. In the long term, it strives for institutionalization of relations that are beneficial for the firm, through mutual interdependency, direct or indirect, of political and corporate entities (Boddewyn, 1988; Hadjikhani et al., 2008). Hillman (2003), for example, argues from an institutional perspective that CPA may be corporatist (with long-standing networks) or pluralist (based on ad hoc action).

Its performance is typically measured on the basis of the firm's relative power or influence on public policy and the impact of this power on firm performance. Hadjikhani et al. (2008: 915) state, "the higher the influence, the more specific and heterogeneous is the impact of the government on different firms and the stronger is the firm's legitimate market position." Lux et al. (2012: 310) refer to this activity as influencing

> government officials – such as politicians or bureaucrats – to act on the business' behalf. Through CPA, businesses expect officials to help them with (1) appropriations, (2) policy maintenance, (3) policy change, and/or (4) policy creation, which in turn can help improve business performance.

Indeed, Lux et al. (2012) posit, through a meta-analysis of thirty years of CPA research, that there is a direct, strong, and positive link between CPA and business performance, despite the inherent risks that are entailed within it. They note that "businesses that do [engage in CPA] tend to outperform competitors" in overall business performance (Lux et al., 2012: 313).

The multiplicity-focused nature of regionalized non-market strategy improves the internationalization and business performance of the firm. It is contingent on the adaptation and convergence of strategy within competing or concurring national, regional, and international regulatory forces.

Current theory acknowledges that firms' overall performance (no matter if considered by shareholder or stakeholder theory) is embedded in dependencies on governments (Ozer and Lee, 2009), competition in various forms, and resources (Cook and Fox, 2000). Effective (adaptive) non-market strategy underpins market strategy (Baron, 1997; Aggarwal, 2001); non-market and market strategies are integrated in firms with the relevant antecedents, including managerial drivers (Hillman et al., 2004), and lead to various degrees of convergence (Heritier et al., 2001). The "logic of influence" of public policy (Richardson, 2012) is traditionally national, intensely regional, and somewhat global. Adaptation to these dynamic forces is therefore crucial for performance. It encompasses a variety of strategies that are not mutually exclusive and may focus on individual (based on firm-specific, thus heterogeneous, advantage), collective (based on industry-specific, country-specific, or other homogeneous advantage), and mixed approaches. In Europe, two-thirds of business-related regulations are made at the EU (that is, intra-regional) level.

Conclusion

This chapter has explored the regional nature of the world economy, and specifically the regionalization of the business environment for multinational firms. Its contribution to this book is a perspective on multi-level, multi-venued non-market strategy in RTAs as a lever for performance gains in corporate internationalization (Figure 19.1).

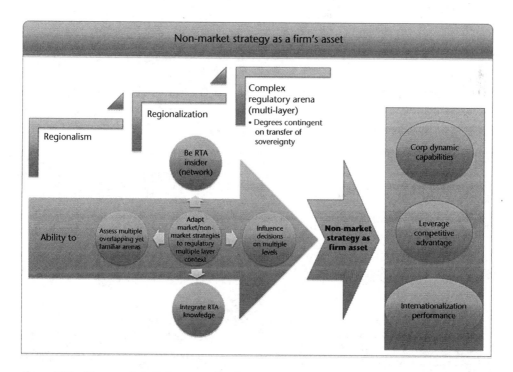

Figure 19.1 Non-market strategy as a firm's asset

The chapter sheds light on non-market strategy through a focus on the regulatory impacts of corporate lobbying in an increasingly regionalized business environment that is characterized by interwoven structures and process at both political and geographic levels. I argue that the focus an MNE gives to national, regional, and global non-market strategizing in non-market activity is dependent on its cross-border reach, and on the internationalization–regionalization knowledge that it creates, assesses, and utilizes. The corporate can be mastered despite its non-market complexities (Kobrin, 2001: 101) and its discriminatory nature through the relevant assessment and strategizing of regionalization. Indeed, as Kobrin (2009: 352) stated, MNEs "have become actors with significant political power and authority which should entail responsibility and liability."

On an RTA level, non-market power can be key to competitive advantage and an important lever for corporate internationalization performance through the strategic utilization of knowledge and influence and the political formalization of business regulation. This is contingent on the use of multi-level non-market forces as rule-of-the-game leverage at the national, regional, and international level.

Bibliography

Aggarwal, V. (2001) Corporate market and nonmarket strategies in Asia: a conceptual framework, *Business and Politics*, 3 (2): 89–108.

Arestis, P., Chortareas, G., Desli, E., and Pelagidis, T. (2012) Trade flows revisited: further evidence on globalisation, *Cambridge Journal of Economics*, 36 (2): 481–93.

Arregle, J.-L., Beamish, P., and Hebert, L. (2009) The regional dimension of MNEs' foreign subsidiary localization, *Journal of International Business Studies*, 40 (1): 86–107.

Banalieva, E. R. and Dhanaraj, C. (2013) Home-region orientation in international expansion strategies, *Journal of International Business Studies*, 44: 89–116.

Barney, J. (1991) Firm resources and sustained competitive advantage, *Journal of Management*, 17 (1): 99–120.

Baron, D. P. (1995) *Business and its Environment*, Upper Saddle River, NJ: Prentice-Hall.

— (1997) Integrated strategy, trade policy and global competition, *California Management Review*, 39 (2): 145–69.

Barron, A. (2011) Exploring national culture's consequences on international business, *Journal of World Business*, 46: 320–7.

Bell, R. G., Filatotchev, I., and Rasheed, A. (2012) The liability of foreignness in capital markets: sources and remedies, *Journal of International Business Studies*, 43 (2): 107–22.

Bhagwati, J., Greeaway, D., and Panagariya, A. (1998) Trading preferentialy: theory and practise, *Economic Journal*, 108 (449): 1128–48.

Blomstermo, A., Eriksson, K., Lindstrand, A., and Sharma, D. D. (2004) The perceived usefulness of network experiential knowledge in the internationalizing firm, *Journal of International Management*, 10 (3): 355–74.

Boddewyn, J. J. (1988) Political aspects of MNE theory, *Journal of International Business Studies*, 14 (3): 341–62.

Boddewyn, J. and Brewer, T. (1994) International-business political behavior: new theoretical directions, *Academy of Management Review*, 19 (1): 119–43.

Bonardi, J.-P., Hillman, A. J., and Keim, G. D. (2005) The attractiveness of political markets: implications for firm strategy, *Academy of Management Review*, 30 (2): 397–413.

Borrmann, A. and Koopmann, G. (1994) Regionalisation and regionalism in world trade, *Intereconomics*, 29 (4): 163–70.

Buckley, P. and Ghauri, P. (2004) Globalization, economic geography and the strategy of multinational enterprises, *Journal of International Business Studies*, 35 (2): 81–98.

Coen, D. (2007) Empirical and theoretical studies in EU lobbying, *Journal of European Public Policy*, 14 (3): 333–45.

Collier, P., Schiff, M., Venables, A., and Winters, L. (2000) *Trading Blocs*, New York: Oxford University Press for the World Bank.

Collinson, S. C. and Rugman, A. M. (2008) The regional nature of Japanese multinational business, *Journal of International Business Studies*, 39 (2): 215–30.

Cook, R. G. and Fox, D. (2000) Resources, frequency, and methods: an analysis of small and medium-sized firms' public policy activities, *Business and Society*, 39 (1): 94–113.

Crawford, J.-A. (2012) *Market Access Provisions on Trade in Goods in Regional Trade Agreements*, Staff Working Paper ERSD-2012-20, Geneva: World Trade Organization Economic Research and Statistics Division.

Cui, A. S., Griffith, D. A., and Cavusgil, S. T. (2005) The influence of competitive intensity and market dynamism on knowledge management capabilities of multinational corporation subsidiaries, *Journal of International Marketing*, 13 (3): 32–53.

Deligonul, S., Elg, U., Cavusgil, E., and Ghauri, P. N. (2013) Developing strategic supplier networks: an institutional perspective, *Journal of Business Research*, 66 (4): 506–15.

DiMaggio, P. J. and Powell, W. W. (1983) The iron cage revisited: institutional isomorphism and collective rationality in organizational fields, *American Sociological Review*, 48 (2): 147–60.

Donas, T., Fraussena, B., and Beyers, J. (2014) It's not all about the money: explaining varying policy portfolios of regional representations in Brussels, *Interest Groups and Advocacy*, 3: 79–98.

Duer, A., Bernhagen, P., and Marshall, D. (2013) Interest group success in the European Union: when (and why) does business lose?, paper presented at the General Conference of the European Conference for Political Research (ECPR), Bordeaux, September 4–7.

Enright, M. (2005) Regional management centers in the Asia-Pacific, *Management International Review*, 45 (Special Issue 1): 59–82.

Erixon, F. and Bauer, M. (2010) *A Transatlantic Zero Agreement: Estimating the Gains from Transatlantic Free Trade in Goods*, ECIPE Occasional Paper No. 4/2010, Brussels: European Centre for International Political Economy (ECIPE).

Fletcher, M., Harris, S., and Glenn Richey Jr., R. (2013) Internationalization knowledge: what, why, where, and when?, *Journal of International Marketing*, 21 (3): 47–71.

Friedman, T. (2005) *The World is Flat: A Brief History of the Twenty-first Century*, New York: Farrar, Straus, and Giroux.

Getz, K. A. (1993) Selecting corporate political tactics, in B. Mitnick (ed.), *Corporate Political Agency*, Newbury Park, CA: Sage Publications: 242–73.

Ghemawat, P. (2001) Distance still matters: the hard reality of global expansion, *Harvard Business Review*, 79 (8): 137–47.

— (2003) Semiglobalization and international business strategy, *Journal of International Business Studies*, 34 (2): 138–52.

Goode, W. (2007) *Dictionary of Trade Policy Terms*, Cambridge: Cambridge University Press.

Hadjikhani, A., Lee, J. W., and Ghauri, P. N. (2008) Network view of MNCs' socio-political behavior, *Journal of Business Research*, 61: 912–24.

Hall, R. and Biersteker, T. (2002) The emergency of private authority in the international system, in R. Hall and T. Biersteker (eds.), *The Emergency of Private Authority in Global Governance*, Cambridge: Cambridge Studies in International Relations: 3–22.

Harvey, D. (1990) *The Condition of Postmodernity: An Enquiry into the Origins of Cultural Change*, Cambridge, MA: Blackwell.

Heritier, A., Kerwer, D., Knill, C., Lehmkuhl, D., Teutsch, M., and Douillet, A.-C. (2001) *Differential Europe: The European Union Impact on National Policy Making*, Lanham, MD: Rowman and Littlefield.

Hillman, A. (2003) Determinants of political strategies in US multinationals, *Business and Society*, 42 (4): 455–84.

Hillman, A. and Keim, G. (1995) International variation in the business–government interface: institutional and organizational considerations, *Academy of Management Review*, 20 (1): 193–214.

Hillman, A., Keim, G., and Schuler, D. (2004) Corporate political activity: a review and research agenda, *Journal of Management*, 30 (6): 837–57.

Hirschman, A. O. (1970) *Exit, Voice and Loyalty: Responses to Decline in Firms, Organizations and States*, Cambridge, MA: Harvard University Press.

Houghton-Mifflin Company (2009) *The American Heritage Dictionary of the English Language*, 4th edition, New York: Houghton-Mifflin Company.

Kacowicz, A. (1998) *Regionalisation, Globalisation, and Nationalism: Convergent, Divergent, or Overlapping?*, Helen Kellogg Institute for International Studies. www.ciaonet.org/wps/kaa01/ (accessed November 17, 2014).

Kaiser, U. and Sofka, W. (2007) *The Pulse of Liability of Foreignness: Dynamic Legitimacy and Experience Effects in the German Car Market*, CIE Discussion Papers, Copenhagen: University of Copenhagen, Department of Economics, Centre for Industrial Economics.

Kingsley, A., Vanden Bergh, R., and Bonardi, J. P. (2012) Political markets and regulatory uncertainty: insights and implications for integrated strategy, *Academic Management Perspective*, 26 (3): 52–67.

Kluever, H. (2013) *Lobbying in the European Union: Interest Groups, Lobbying Coalitions, and Policy Change*, Oxford: Oxford University Press.

Kobrin, S. J. (1998) The MAI and the clash of globalizations, *Foreign Policy*, Fall, 97–109.

— (2001) Sovereignty@bay: globalization, multinational enterprise, and the international political system, in A. M. Rugman and T. L. Brewer (eds.), *The Oxford Handbook of International Business*, Oxford: Oxford University Press: 193–207.

— (2009) Private political authority and public responsibility: transnational politics, transnational firms and human rights, *Business Ethics Quarterly*, 19 (3): 349–74.

Krugman, P. (1991) Is bilateral bad?, in E. Helpman and A. Razin (eds.), *International Trade and Trade Policy*, Cambridge, MA: MIT Press: 97–109.

Lux, S., Russell Crook, T., and Leap, T. (2012) Corporate political activity: the good, the bad and the ugly, *Business Horizons*, 55 (3): 307–12.

McGuire, S (2012) What happened to the influence of business? Corporations and organized labour in the WTO, in A. Narlikar, M. Staunton, and R. Stern (eds.), *The Oxford Handbook on the World Trade Organization*, Oxford: Oxford University Press: 320–39.

McGuire, S., Lindeque, J., and Suder, G. (2012) Learning and lobbying: emerging market firms and corporate political activity in Europe, *European Journal of International Management*, 6 (3): 342–62.

Miller, S. and Richards, M. (2002) Liability of foreignness and membership in a regional economic group: analysis of the European Union, *Journal of International Management*, 8 (3): 323–37.

Oberholzer-Gee, F., Cantrill, L., and Wu, P. (2007) *Lobbying*, Boston, MA: Harvard Business School Publishing.

Oh, C. and Rugman, A. (2012) Regional integration and the international strategies of large European firms, *International Business Review*, 21 (3): 493–507.

Ohmae, K. (1986) Becoming a triad power: the new global corporation, *International Marketing Review*, 3 (3): 7–20.

Osegowitsch, T. and Sammartino, A. (2008) Reassessing (home-) regionalisation, *Journal of International Business Studies*, 39: 184–96.

Ozer, M. and Lee, S.-H. (2009) When do firms prefer individual action to collective action in the pursuit of corporate political strategy? A new perspective on industry concentration, *Business and Politics*, 11(1): 1–23.

Prakash, A. (2002) Beyond Seattle: globalization, the nonmarket environment and corporate strategy, *Review of International Political Economy*, 9: 513–37.

Qian, G., Li, L., and Rugman, A. (2013) Liability of country foreignness and liability of regional foreignness: their effects on geographic diversification and firm performance, research note, *Journal of International Business Studies*, 44: 635–47.

Ramamurti, R. (2001) The obsolescing "bargaining model"? MNC–host developing country relations revisited, *Journal of International Business Studies*, 32: 23–39.

Ravenhill, J. (2011) *Global Political Economy*, Oxford: Oxford University Press.

Richardson, J. (2012) New governance or old governance? A policy style perspective, in D. Levi-Faur (ed.), *Oxford Handbook of Governance*, Oxford: Oxford University Press: 311–24.

Rival, M. (2012) Are firms' lobbying strategies universal? Comparison of lobbying by French and UK firms, *Journal of Strategy and Management*, 5 (2): 211–30.

Rozman, G. (2004) *Northeast Asia's Stunted Regionalism: Bilateral Distrust in the Shadow of Globalization*, Cambridge: Cambridge University Press.

Rugman, A. (2000) *The End of Globalization*, London: Random House.

— (2005) *The Regional Multinationals: MNEs and "Global" Strategic Management*, Cambridge: Cambridge University Press.

Rugman, A. and Verbeke, A. (2004) A perspective on regional and global strategies of multinational enterprises, *Journal of International Business Studies*, 35 (1): 3–18.

— (2005) Towards a theory of regional multinationals: a transaction cost economics approach, *Management International Review*, 45 (Special Issue 1): 5–17.

— (2007) Liabilities of regional foreignness and the use of firm-level versus country-level data: a response to Dunning et al., *Journal of International Business Studies*, 38(1): 200–5.

Schulz, M., Söderbaum, F., and Öjendal, J. (2001) Introduction: a framework for understanding regionalization, in M. Schulz, F. Söderbaum, and J. Öjendal (eds.), *Regionalization in a Globalizing World: A Comparative Perspective on Forms, Actors and Processes*, London: Zed Books: 1–21.

Scott, W. R. (2001) *Institutions and Organizations*, Thousand Oaks, CA: Sage.

Sethi, P. and Judge, W. (2009) Reappraising liabilities of foreignness within an integrated perspective of the costs and benefits of doing business abroad, *International Business Review*, 18 (4): 404–16.

Shadrina, E. (2006) *Regionalization and Regionalism: Featuring Northeast Asia*, Niigata University. http://dspace.lib.niigata-u.ac.jp:8080/dspace/bitstream/10191/6383/1/01_0037.pdf (accessed November 17, 2014).

Stigler, G. (1975) *The Citizen and the State: Essays on Regulation*, Chicago: University of Chicago Press.

Suder, G. (2011) *Doing Business in Europe*, London: Sage Publications.

— (2013) *Regional Trade Agreements and Regionalisation: Motivations and Limits of a Global Phenomenon*, ANUCES Briefing Paper, Canberra: ANU Centre for European Studies.

Teece, D., Pisano, G., and Shuen, A. (1997) Dynamic capabilities and strategic management, *Strategic Management Journal*, 18 (7): 509–33.

Van Schendelen, R. (2010) *More Machiavelli in Brussels: The Art of Lobbying the EU*, Amsterdam: Amsterdam University Press.

Wang, H. (2013) Comparative regionalization: EU model and East Asia's practice for regional integration, *Journal of Global Policy and Governance*, 2 (2): 245–53.

Westney, E. (2006) Book review: *The regional multinationals: MNEs and "global" strategic management*, *Journal of International Business Studies*, 37 (3): 445–9.

World Trade Organization (WTO) (2013a) Regional trade agreements: RTA database. www.wto.org/english/tratop_e/region_e/region_e.htm (accessed November 17, 2014).

— (2013b) Regional trade agreements: scope of RTAs. www.wto.org/english/tratop_e/region_e/scope_rta_e.htm (accessed November 17, 2014).

Zaheer, S. (2002) The liability of foreignness, redux: a commentary, *Journal of International Management*, 8 (3): 351–8.

20

Wholly owned foreign subsidiary government relation-based strategies in the Philippines

Regulatory distance and performance implications

George O. White III and Thomas Hemphill

Volatile emerging market environments such as the Philippines represent a key source of operational uncertainty for wholly owned foreign subsidiaries (WOFSs). WOFS performance outcomes can be affected by operational uncertainty associated with unpredictable and elastic policy shifts (Wan and Hillman, 2006), thereby making the conduct of doing business in the Philippines exceptionally difficult (Chung and Beamish, 2005). Such uncertainty can have serious consequences for WOFS performance outcomes since regulations established by host governments will often dominate transactions within a specific market (Rodriguez, Uhlenbruck, and Eden, 2005).

Scholars have argued that the development of informal relationships with key host country actors, such as government authorities, will help to mitigate uncertainty and thereby enhance a subsidiary's performance (e.g., market benefits and financial outcomes) in volatile environments (Park and Luo, 2001; Peng and Luo, 2000), as commercial transactions in volatile environments such as the Philippines are often based on informal personal and implicit agreements (Li, 2005). However, research findings have been mixed regarding performance implications for organizations implementing informal relational ties with government authorities. These studies have also failed to account for the contingency effects that regulatory distance might have on relationships with key host country actors in a volatile environment such as the Philippines.

We wish to fill these gaps in the literature and add to the current theoretical discussion by proposing that WOFSs will establish deeply embedded informal relationships with key government actors through relation-based strategies (RBSs), a unique form of non-market strategy, proactively to create competitive advantages that will enhance organizational performance in a volatile environment. These strategic competencies will act as a legitimizing mechanism (Kostova and Zaheer, 1999; Rosenzweig and Singh, 1991), thereby aligning the WOFSs with their environment by deploying informal, relationally embedded networks that fill voids inherent in volatile structures (Miller, Lee, Chang, and Le Breton-Miller, 2009;

Peng, Lee, and Wang, 2005; Podolny and Page, 1998). We suggest that developing this non-market form of capital will enhance certain (but not all) types of performance by developing informal market structures that minimize the negative influence that regulatory distance will have on WOFSs operating in the Philippines. This leads us to ask the following two questions:

- What dimensions of satisfaction with performance will be enhanced through WOFS RBS deployment with government actors in a volatile environment?
- How will regulatory distance moderate the relationship between WOFS government RBS deployment and different dimensions of satisfaction with performance?

We depart from prior literature in at least four ways. First, by integrating social network, non-market strategy, and institutional theories, we set out to extend the theoretical boundaries of the extant literature. We accomplish this by exploring how WOFSs deploy RBSs with key government host country actors – as a unique form of non-market strategy – to fill institutional voids and create informal market structures that mitigate the negative effects of regulatory distance and enhance firm performance in a volatile environment. Second, to try to resolve a paradox in the literature, we perform a fine-grained analysis to determine how WOFS government RBS deployment will impact both qualitative and quantitative dimensions of performance. Third, we attempt to fill an existing gap in the literature by examining how regulatory distance will moderate the relationship between WOFS RBS deployment and different dimensions of performance. Fourth, we test our hypotheses by employing a unique dataset acquired through field research conducted in the Philippines. In this field research, senior executives and managers of WOFSs were asked about their organizations' relationships with host country government actors and their satisfaction with different dimensions of WOFS performance.

Theory and hypotheses

Government relation-based strategy deployment and performance

Social network theory regards the network as a distinct form of organization (Podolny and Page, 1998; Zuckerman, 2003). Network forms of organization are characterized by repetitive exchanges among semi-autonomous organizations that rely on trust and embedded social relationships to foster learning, gain legitimacy, and maintain status in a particular market (Anderson, Forsgren, and Holm, 2002; Peng and Heath, 1996; Podolny and Page, 1998). These relations emphasize the embeddedness of economic actions in social networks – to the extent that economic action is linked to or depends on action or institutions that are non-economic in content, such as goals or processes (Ouchi, 1980).

This line of research also suggests that enhanced operational efficiencies and potential strategic advantages may be achieved when enterprises pursue economic goals through non-economic institutions and practices (Granovetter, 2005). This notion is especially true in environments that are volatile in nature and susceptible to market failure (Boisot and Child, 1996; Ouchi, 1980; Uzzi, 1997). For instance, drawing on ethnographic fieldwork conducted at twenty-three entrepreneurial firms, Uzzi (1997) identified components of embedded social relationships and described the mechanisms by which embeddedness shapes enterprises and their economic outcomes. He also found that the positive effects of embeddedness promoted integrative agreements and complex adaptation of the enterprises.

Peng (2003) and Peng et al. (2005) suggested that relation-based social capital, a type of social network, is an important strategic device for enterprises operating in underdeveloped institutional environments. These embedded relationships are strategic networks that provide benefits in the form of social capital (Kostova and Roth, 2003; Nahapiet and Ghoshal, 1998) for the purpose of reducing uncertainty (Gulati, 1998).

We posit that government RBSs comprise a form of informal network tie that will act as a non-market strategic asset, attempting to align WOFSs with actors in non-market environments (Bonardi, 1999; Rosenzweig and Singh, 1991). While not all WOFSs deploy RBSs, those that do will recognize the ambiguities and unique features of the institutional environment (Luo, 2001; Park and Luo, 2001) and deploy non-market strategies in order to co-opt uncertainties by creating informal networks that will fill institutional voids through relational embeddedness (Peng and Heath, 1996). WOFSs deploying government RBSs will realize that the strategic advantages of informal network ties enhance performance through alignment with and embeddedness in the environment. They will deploy RBSs in order to develop critical relational connections with government actors.

Government RBSs that form relational connections with government authorities (such as regulatory officials, industrial authorities, tax bureaus, political leaders, and government-sponsored banks) will be characterized by extensive "deep-seated" ties that provide access to information and favors (in the form of quid pro quos) that can be called upon during times of unpredictability (Li and Zhang, 2007; Peng and Luo, 2000). These relationships allow WOFSs to position themselves strategically in the non-market (political and legal) spaces of a volatile environment where formal institutional rules of the game are made (Baron, 2010). Further, the deployment of government RBSs will fill institutional voids with informal market structures (Bonardi, 2008; Peng et al., 2005). The private and invisible nature of these informal structures renders the network undetectable, creating an inimitable strategic advantage for the WOFSs.

Various studies have empirically investigated how these types of relationship impact different dimensions of firm performance in emerging market environments. For example, Li and Zhang (2007) (using an aggregate performance variable made up of eight financial and strategic performance items) found that political networking had a positive and significant influence on high-technology new-venture performance. Acquaah (2007) (using an aggregate performance variable consisting of five financial and strategic performance items) found that social capital from managerial networking relationships with top managers at other firms, community leaders, and government officials enhanced organizational performance. Luo (1997) (using single-item measures) found that relational networks (*guanxi*) enhanced financial (i.e., profitability, return on investment (ROI), domestic sales growth, and asset turnover) performance. Park and Luo (2001) (using single-item measures) found that managerial relational networks with government authorities were positively and significantly associated with sales growth, but not profit growth. Peng and Luo (2000) (using single-item measures) found that managerial ties with government officials were positively and significantly associated with both strategic (market share) and financial (return on assets) performance. Luo (2001) (using single-item measures) found that relational networks had a positive and significant impact on strategic performance (market expansion), but no discernible influence on financial performance (financial returns).

Other studies, such as that of Li, Poppo, and Zhou (2008), argued that domestic and foreign firms exhibited similar levels of political tie utilization in China. Their research found that the utilization of these relationships had a positive effect on both domestic and foreign firm return on assets (ROA), and that the positive relationship between foreign firm managerial ties and ROA diminished over time, resulting in an inverted U-shaped relationship (suggesting a competitive disadvantage for foreign firms using relational networks). Their study also found that the effect of managerial tie utilization on firm ROA increased when structural uncertainty (industry instability) was high, rather than low.

Taken together, an unresolved question in the literature has emerged regarding whether the deployment of RBSs will have a positive or negative effect on different types of WOFS performance in a volatile emerging market environment.

We set out to try to resolve this question by taking a fine-grained approach investigating how government RBSs influence WOFS satisfaction with regard to different dimensions of qualitative and quantitative performance. We suggest that government RBSs will enhance cooperation through lobbying effects, creating reciprocal relationships with government authorities that act as an institutional lubricant affording the WOFSs greater market access and buffering effects against market competition. This is because government regulatory regimes in volatile environments have significant influence and power to approve projects and allocate resources (Hillman and Wan, 2005). These institutionally embedded non-market relational assets will not necessarily benefit a WOFS's financial performance, because deploying government RBSs, and ultimately maintaining non-market relational assets derived from these strategies, can entail high financial costs and produce operating inefficiencies associated with a WOFS's normal production of goods and services (White, Hemphill, Joplin, and Marsh, 2014). In essence, capital, both human and financial, will be diverted away from their intended use or normal operating processes. Consequently:

> *Hypotheses 1a and 1b: In a volatile emerging market environment, WOFS deployment of government RBSs as institutionally embedded non-market relational assets will be (a) positively related to satisfaction with qualitative performance, but (b) negatively related to satisfaction with quantitative performance,* ceteris paribus.

A regulatory distance contingency perspective

A regulatory environment consists of multiple factors, making up dimensions that determine the volatility of a country's regulatory structure, which vary from country to country (Brewer, 1993; Glendon, Gordon, and Osakwe, 1994; Hoskisson, Eden, Lau, and Wright, 2000; La Porta, Lopez-De-Silanes, Shleifer, and Vishny, 1997, 2000). The effectiveness of laws, enforcement of laws and legal instruments, impartiality in dispute settlement processes, safeguarding of business assets, and overall legal and political institutional stability are important factors to consider when addressing regulatory distance (Xu and Shenkar, 2002; Xu, Pan, and Beamish, 2004). For example, Luo (2005) argued that the completeness of a legal system and extent of enforcement of laws will play important roles in how firms operate outside their home country institutional environment. However, how regulatory distance (between a WOFS's home and host country) influences government RBSs and performance has yet to be investigated in the international non-market strategy research.

March and Olsen (1989) posited that inconsistencies in the regulatory environment can create room for strategic discretion. Different dimensions within the regulatory environment, being embedded in both a WOFS's home and host country, can impact the way in which the subsidiary implements strategies to enhance performance outcomes (Gaur, Delios, and Singh, 2007). This is because differences in the regulatory environment are codified into a WOFS's operating routines (Xu and Shenkar, 2002). When regulatory constraints are unfamiliar and constantly changing – such as labor restrictions and trade policies – they can undermine and create substantial inefficiencies in WOFS strategic processes. Further, Luo and Zhao (2013: 521) have argued, "In the presence of large regulatory distance, [foreign] subsidiaries will perceive greater deterrence and higher transaction costs escalated by administrative regulations enacted by host government authorities . . . [T]his deterrence elevates environmental impediments and increases information search costs." Thus, we suggest that WOFSs from distant regulatory environments will be more likely to utilize government RBSs to embed the firm socially in the environment in order to mitigate performance barriers associated with regulatory constraints and uncertainties. They will, in essence, rely more heavily on government actors as third-party intermediaries; these actions help management to navigate the unfamiliar regulatory structure and buffer the WOFS against environmental volatility. Out of necessity, such WOFSs will quickly adapt by implementing government RBSs that will bridge the regulatory distance gap, thereby having a positive impact on qualitative performance outcomes. Hence:

Hypothesis 2: The positive relationship between government RBS deployment and satisfaction with qualitative performance will be stronger when regulatory distance is high rather than low.

Methods

Sample and data

For our survey-based study, we collected primary data in the Philippines over a four-month period. Using the Philippines as the source of data seemed appropriate because it is an emerging market (United Nations, 2007) that is a primary foreign investment location choice for multinational enterprise (MNE) subsidiaries operating in Southeast Asia (Heinrich and Konan, 2001). The data for this study was collected from senior executives of WOFSs operating in the Philippines. These key informants were highly knowledgeable about their WOFSs' strategies and had access to hard data as points of reference.

The sample consisted of 540 WOFSs selected from the *Foreign Companies in the Philippines Yearbook* (2007), compiled and published by the Commercial Intelligence Service of Business Monitor International, London, UK. All of the WOFSs selected had been established for at least three years. We then proceeded to collect our data by administering a questionnaire through field visits rather than through the use of archival data or mail surveys, because the lack of reliable archival data and the inadequate postal system in the Philippines (as in many emerging markets) made the use of these latter methods extremely difficult and risky (Hoskisson et al., 2000). After several visits to WOFSs, we received responses from 194 subsidiaries. All but thirteen of the returned questionnaires were complete and usable, providing a final response rate of 33.5 percent (181/540).

In order to provide triangulation with some of the survey results, semi-structured interviews were conducted with fifteen key informants in order to check the accuracy of their answers (Krishnan, Martin, and Noorderhaven, 2006). Selected informants were interviewed and asked to identify, per the original survey instrument, specific aspects of their WOFS strategic behavior, satisfaction with WOFS performance, and characteristics of the Philippine regulatory environment. The results (Pearson correlations: $0.96 - 0.83$, $p < .001$; Guttman split-half Rs: $0.82 - 0.71$) displayed strong consistency between interview and survey answers. We also used the *Foreign Companies in the Philippines Yearbook* (2007) to check for non-response bias. From this source we were able to compare some attributes between responding and non-responding WOFSs identified from the code numbers written on each questionnaire. The mean difference between responding informants and non-responding informants with respect to the number of employees (size), years operating in the Philippines (experience), and business sector (manufacturing or service industry) was analyzed using an unpaired t-test. The results demonstrated that all t statistics were insignificant (p > 0.05 level), establishing that the two groups were not significantly different.

The WOFSs were involved in a diverse array of manufacturing and service industries, such as electronics and electrical equipment (10.48 percent), construction and engineering (8.29 percent), chemicals (7.86 percent), various consultancies (7.42 percent), trade (7.42 percent), pharmaceuticals and medical care (6.98 percent), machinery and heavy equipment (6.98 percent), and banking/finance/insurance (6.55 percent). WOFS regions of origin included the Americas (29.8 percent), Asia (33.1 percent), and Europe (36 percent).

Variables and measurement

Dependent variables

Similar to previous studies (e.g., Acquaah, 2007; Brouthers, Brouthers, and Werner, 2000; Li and Zhang, 2007; Luo, 2007; Peng and Luo, 2000), perceptual measures of firm performance were used in this study. Past studies have suggested that it is desirable to utilize subjective measures in emerging markets for the purpose of capturing specific aspects of performance largely unavailable in secondary data (Luo and Peng, 1999; Park and Luo, 2001).

"Distribution channels" was employed as a proxy for our qualitative performance metric. This item is defined as formal distribution networks of goods and services to customers (Brouthers, Brouthers, and Werner, 2000; Geringer and Hebert, 1991). Using the past three years as a reference point, respondents were asked to rate how satisfied they were on a seven-point Likert-type scale (1 = "very dissatisfied"; 7 = "very satisfied") with their WOFS's distribution channels. Net profit growth was employed as the proxy for our quantitative performance metric. "Net profit growth" came from Park and Luo (2001) and was defined as "growth of positive net cash flows." Again using the past three years as a reference point, respondents were asked to rate how satisfied they were on a seven-point Likert-type scale (1 = "very dissatisfied"; 7 = "very satisfied") with their WOFS's net profit growth.

Predictor variable

"Government RBS" was used as predictor variables in this study. Government RBS (Cronbach's alpha = .87; communality loadings = .84 – .78) was measured by five items adapted from Peng and Luo (2000). Using the past three years as a reference point, respondents were asked to rate their WOFS's informal personal ties and connections to (1) regulatory authorities, (2) political leaders in various levels of government, (3) industrial authorities, (4) commercial administration bureaus, and (5) tax bureaus on a seven-point Likert-type scale (1 = "very little"; 7 = "very much").

Contingency variable

"Regulatory distance" was used as contingency variable in this study. Regulatory distance (Xu et al., 2004) assessed the differences between the rules, laws, and legal institutions that exist in the WOFS's home and host country (the Philippines) regulative environments. The distance, or lack of distance, between these two regulatory environments can significantly shape WOFS strategic behavior and performance benchmarks (e.g., how familiar, and comfortable, will a WOFS abide by the rules of the game in a particular country?). This multi-item construct was adopted from Xu et al. (2004). Six items were averaged together by Xu et al. (2004) in order to create a country's score for its regulative dimension, including (1) how anti-trust or anti-monopoly policies effectively promote competition, (2) how effective is the legal system in enforcing commercial contracts, (3) can private businesses readily file suits at independent and impartial courts if there is a breach of trust on the part of the government, (4) can citizens willingly accept legal means to adjudicate disputes rather than depending on physical force or illegal means, (5) there is little chance that legal and political institutions will drastically change over the next five years, and (6), being an important business activity consideration, police are effective in safeguarding personal security. The regulatory distance between a particular home country and the Philippines was then measured as the absolute difference between the two countries' regulative scores (taken from Xu et al., 2004: 302).

Control variables

"Respondent experience," "WOFS experience," "WOFS size," "industry," "industry sales growth," "market orientation," and "cultural distance" were used as control variables. Respondent experience was taken from the survey instrument and referred to the number of years that a WOFS senior executive or senior manager had spent working in the Philippines. WOFS experience, referring to the number of years the subsidiary had been operating (from initial year of establishment) in the Philippines and taken from the *Foreign Companies in the Philippines Yearbook* (2007), was added in the analysis since the number of years a WOFS operates in a host country will play a major role in its learning, adapting (or not adapting) to, and strategically positioning itself in a volatile regulatory environment by cultivating informal relationships that will potentially enhance performance (Li and Zhang, 2007; Luo, 1999). We included WOFS size, based on the total number of full-time employees taken from the *Foreign Companies in the Philippines Yearbook* (2007), because larger WOFSs will normally have more resources (i.e., human capital) at their disposal, whereas smaller WOFSs will often have greater strategic flexibility to carry out government RBSs that will yield positive performance outcomes (e.g., Brouthers, 2002; Brouthers and Nakos, 2004; Erramilli and Rao, 1993).

The dummy variable market orientation (coded 1 = local market focused; 0 = otherwise – export-oriented) was taken from the *Foreign Companies in the Philippines Yearbook* (2007) (Luo, 2007). Industry growth was measured by the compound growth rate (percentage) of the respective industry's sales from 2005 to 2007, taken from the *Philippine Statistical Yearbook* (National Statistical Information Center, 2007). Lastly, cultural distance could play a role in how successful a WOFS will be in implementing government RBSs that enhance performance (Luo, 2001). Thus, we controlled for cultural distance by using Kogut and Singh's (1988) formula, which is based on Hofstede's (1980) four cultural dimensions (individualism, masculinity, power distance, and uncertainty avoidance), to compute the distance between the Philippines' national culture and the national culture of the country of origin of each WOFS.

Data analysis and results

Table 20.1 reports the means, standard deviations, and correlation coefficients among all variables in this study. The correlation matrix indicates consistently significant relationships between the variables of interest and dependent variables. There were also several other

Table 20.1 Descriptive statistics and correlations

Variables	Mean	S.D.	1	2	3	4	5	6	7	8	9	10	11
1 Distribution channels	4.58	1.40	—										
2 Net profit growth	4.09	1.81	-0.25	—									
3 Government RBS	4.31	2.13	0.33	-0.38	—								
4 Regulatory distance	1.51	0.33	-0.16	0.18	-0.19	—							
5 Cultural distance	29.22	26.53	0.07	-0.06	0.16	-0.42	—						
6 Industry growth	9.17	9.94	-0.15	0.19	-0.21	0.18	-0.11	—					
7 Industry	0.19	0.40	-0.04	-0.02	0.01	0.08	-0.13	0.18	—				
8 Market orientation	0.74	0.44	0.22	-0.02	0.25	0.06	-0.01	0.24	-0.08	—			
9 WOFS size	460.54	864.54	0.09	0.02	-0.01	-0.03	0.02	-0.04	0.01	-0.22	—		
10 WOFS experience	29.42	25.30	0.02	0.05	-0.15	0.17	-0.19	0.08	0.07	-0.01	0.23	—	
11 Respondent experience	14.54	8.04	-0.13	0.06	-0.09	0.10	-0.07	0.03	0.14	0.04	0.01	0.15	—

Notes: Number of observations = 175. Correlations with an absolute value of .14 and greater are significant at the .05 level (two-tailed significance tests).
Means and standard deviations reported here are for raw scores.
RBS = relation-based strategy; WOFS = wholly owned foreign subsidiary.

statistically significant relationships. However, no unreasonably high correlations were observed between any of the variables in the correlation matrix (Field, 2005; Tabachnick and Fidell, 2001). Also, the variance inflation factors (VIFs) for all variables were well below 10, indicating that multi-collinearity is not a serious problem (Hair, Anderson, Tatham, and Black, 1998).

In order to test our hypotheses and examine the relationships between WOFS government RBS implementation and performance, we performed a series of Ordinary Least Squares (OLS) moderated hierarchical multiple regression analyses (Tables 20.2 and 20.3). Hypothesis 1a predicted that WOFS government RBS implementation would be positively related to satisfaction with qualitative performance. The positive and significant coefficient (β = .38, p < .01) on the government RBS measure in Model 3 supports this hypothesis, indicating that government RBSs are positively related to WOFS satisfaction with qualitative performance (i.e., distribution channels). Hypothesis 1b predicted that WOFS government RBS implementation would be negatively related to satisfaction with quantitative performance. The negative and significant coefficient (β = −.54, p < .01) on the government RBS measure in Model 7 supports this hypothesis, indicating that government RBSs are negatively related to WOFS satisfaction with quantitative performance (i.e., net profit growth).

In Hypothesis 2 we predicted that the positive relationship between government RBS implementation and satisfaction with qualitative performance will be stronger when

Table 20.2 Results of OLS regression analysis

Variables	Satisfaction with qualitative performance			
	Model 1	Model 2	Model 3	Model 4
Control variables				
Informant experience	−0.14(−1.93)*	−0.13(−1.73)[†]	−0.11(−1.60)[†]	−0.12(−1.80)[†]
WOFS experience	0.13(1.58)[†]	0.15(1.84)[†]	0.17(2.33)*	0.20(2.64)**
WOFS size	0.01(0.07)	0.02(0.26)	0.05(0.66)	0.05(0.61)
Industry	−0.02(−0.24)	−0.02(−0.21)	−0.04(−0.53)	−0.04(−0.58)
Industry growth	−0.13(−1.61)[†]	−0.11(−1.32)	−0.03(−0.42)	−0.05(−0.60)
Market orientation	0.20(2.54)**	0.20(2.53)**	0.11(1.37)	0.09(1.13)
Cultural distance	0.09(1.11)	0.03(0.36)	0.01(0.04)	0.02(0.25)
Predictor variables				
Regulatory distance (RD)[a]		−0.17(2.13)*	−0.14(1.82)[†]	−0.13(1.65)[†]
Government RBSs (GRBSs)[a]			0.38(4.84)**	0.37(4.84)**
Interactions				
GRBSs × RD				0.18(2.54)**
R^2	0.12	0.14	0.24	0.27
Adjusted R^2	0.08	0.10	0.20	0.23
Change in R^2		0.02*	0.10**	0.03**
Change in F		4.54*	23.46**	6.45**
Model df	167	166	165	164

Notes: Number of Observations = 175. Values in this table represent standardized coefficients (βs).
RBS = relation-based strategy; WOFS = wholly owned foreign subsidiary.
The highest Variance Inflation Factor value in any of the models is 1.49.
[a]Standardized variables.
[†]p <.10; *p <.05; **p <.01 (two-tailed significance tests).

Table 20.3 Results of OLS regression analysis

Variables	Satisfaction with quantitative performance			
	Model 5	Model 6	Model 7	Model 8
Control variables				
Informant experience	−0.01(0.16)	−0.01(0.02)	−0.02(−0.38)	−0.03(−0.39)
WOFS experience	0.09(1.17)	0.08(0.96)	0.04(0.52)	0.03(0.48)
WOFS size	0.11(1.43)	0.10(1.28)	0.06(0.87)	0.06(0.83)
Industry	−0.05(−0.69)	−0.05(0.73)	−0.02(−0.36)	−0.02(−0.30)
Industry growth	0.20(2.55)**	0.18(2.29)*	0.08(1.11)	0.07(1.07)
Market orientation	0.20(2.49)**	0.19(2.48)**	0.06(0.87)	0.06(0.83)
Cultural distance	−0.03(−0.42)	0.02(0.19)	0.05(0.74)	0.05(0.70)
Predictor variables				
Regulatory distance (RD)[a]		0.14(1.82)[†]	0.01(0.10)	0.02(0.20)
Government RBSs (GRBSs)[a]			−0.54(−7.40)**	−0.54(−7.39)**
Interactions				
GRBSs × RD				−0.04(−0.53)
R^2	0.13	0.14	0.35	0.35
Adjusted R^2	0.09	0.10	0.31	0.31
Change in R^2		0.01[†]	0.21**	0.00
Change in F		3.30[†]	54.74**	0.27
Model df	167	166	165	164

Notes: N = 175. Values in this table represent standardized coefficients (βs).
RBS = relation-based strategy; WOFS = wholly owned foreign subsidiary.
The highest VIF value in any of the models is 1.42.
[a]Standardized variables.
[†]p <.10; *p <.05; **p <.01 (two-tailed significance tests).

regulatory distance is high rather than low. The interaction with government RBS and regulatory distance on qualitative performance was positive and significant (Model 4; β = .18, p < .01). Therefore, Hypothesis 2 was supported. These findings suggest that the greater the regulatory distance is between a WOFS's home and host country, the more likely it is to implement government RBSs that, in turn, will provide it with closer ties to local government actors, enhancing its logistical efficiencies by minimizing uncertainties associated with uncertainty due to differences in home and host country regulatory environments.

To validate further and gain insights into the nature of the moderation effects, we plotted the interactions where regulatory distance is treated as a contingency variable affecting government business RBS's influence on qualitative performance (Figure 20.1). The slopes of the regression lines vary significantly (grow positively steeper) when regulatory distance values change from low (mean − one standard deviation) to high (mean + one standard deviation) (Aiken and West, 1991; Cohen, Cohen, West, and Aiken, 2003), substantiating the moderated results in that government RBSs become stronger in relation to distribution channels.

Discussion

Four sets of findings, ideas, and methods distinguish this study from prior research, with this study making several contributions to the non-market strategy literature. First, we found that government RBSs (GRBSs) had a significant impact on qualitative performance. Also,

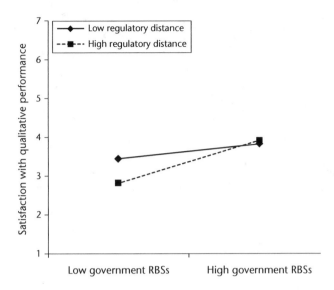

Figure 20.1 Regulatory distance moderates the relationship between government RBSs and WOFS satisfaction with qualitative performance

unlike Luo (1997), Peng and Luo (2000), and Park and Luo (2001), we found that GRBSs with government officials had a significant negative effect on quantitative performance. This finding also indicates that more recent studies (e.g., Acquaah, 2007; Li and Zhang, 2007) using a single aggregate performance variable, consisting of both qualitative and quantitative measures, may not have accurately captured the true nature of performance outcomes associated with non-market strategic practices. Nevertheless, our findings imply that GRBSs will enhance a WOFS's satisfaction regarding qualitative performance; but they will also have a negative influence on WOFS satisfaction with quantitative performance.

Second, this study fills an existing gap in the international non-market literature, as non-market strategy research has yet to focus on how regulatory distance influences the relationship between GRBSs and WOFS performance in the Philippines. Therefore, from a contingency perspective, we specifically considered how our results inform that, at high levels of regulatory distance, the positive relationship between GRBSs and qualitative performance strengthens, while the negative relationship between GRBSs and quantitative performance strengthens. Thus, the benefits of implementing and maintaining GRBSs, when unfamiliarity with the host country regulatory structure is high, are considerable for foreign subsidiaries operating in emerging markets. But the costs and inefficiencies associated with the implementation of GRBSs, due to redistribution of potential human and financial assets when carrying out such non-market strategies, may also be very high. By recognizing these tendencies, our study takes a substantial step toward determining how the implementation of GRBSs will influence manager satisfaction with WOFS performance, especially if the regulatory environment is considerably distant in nature.

Third, this study has geographic implications, as it focuses on a country context in a region of the world (Southeast Asia) that has received relatively little attention in the non-market strategy literature. MNEs often operate foreign subsidiaries in numerous countries; yet, most of the countries where foreign subsidiaries operate are not on non-market strategy research maps. Oddly enough, this observation comes several years after Hoskisson et al.'s (2000) call for a more diversified research agenda focusing on emerging markets other than China and regions other than Eastern Europe. Our study helps to begin the process of filling this gap in the non-market strategy literature.

Fourth, our findings have important and relevant practical implications. There have been numerous calls for research that is more relevant to practice. For example, editors of the *Academy of Management Journal* have argued that more interaction with, and close observation of, the business community is needed in order to bring practical relevance to scholarly research (Rynes, 2007). Rynes (2007: 745) stated: "A commitment to field research, built on a profound respect for practitioners ... [will create] academic respectability by combining rigor with relevance." In this study we performed field research based on theoretical ideas with practical significance. Our hope was that we would bridge this gap by performing field research over a period of several months. During this time our team interacted with managers and executives, asking questions to investigate serious issues facing organizations in the uncertain business environment of the Philippines. Practitioners (both local and foreign) in emerging markets have long understood that it is not "what you know" but "who you know" that counts. This study's results point to the fact that managers of certain foreign subsidiaries operating in the Philippines understand this notion and incorporate GRBSs into their organizations' strategic processes in order to enhance satisfaction with WOFS performance.

With this in mind, our study points to the fact that the deployment of GRBSs, for the purpose of cultivating institutionally embedded, non-market relational assets, are of tremendous importance for managers hoping to achieve greater returns concerning qualitative aspects of operations in an emerging market environment. For example, well-established, informal relations with government regulators will assist a foreign subsidiary in better understanding the rules of the game – and thus improve operational effectiveness – in an otherwise uncertain operating environment. This notion also holds true for aligning operations with norms and standards imposed by industrial authorities and commercial administrative bureaus via GRBSs. GRBSs with host country political leaderships will also potentially mitigate the uncertainty associated with political risk (i.e., expropriation of assets) in the host country. Moreover, for managers of WOFSs with parents from home countries having significantly different regulatory environments, GRBSs can be of great assistance by helping management learn the regulatory process and proactively engage non-market actors holding positions of regulatory influence. Finally, our results demonstrate that managers deploying GRBSs, as non-market strategic actions, can benefit from these institutionally embedded linkages, which may be helpful in enhancing qualitative performance outcomes, such as development of more effective distribution channels or increased access to new sources of energy for more efficient manufacturing production. However, deployment of GRBSs can also result in dissatisfaction with, for example, the level of net profit growth. These findings suggest that managers should be aware of how the deployment of GRBSs can influence resource allocations – whether financial or strategic in nature – within host country operations in emerging markets such as the Philippines.

In conclusion, we began this study by attempting to extend, fill a gap, and resolve a paradox in the literature by asking two questions: "What dimensions of satisfaction with performance will be enhanced through WOFS RBS deployment with government actors in a volatile environment?" and "How will regulatory distance moderate the relationship between WOFS government RBS deployment and different dimensions of satisfaction with performance?" We went on to hypothesize that GRBSs would be positively related to satisfaction with WOFS qualitative performance, but negatively or not related to satisfaction with quantitative performance. We also hypothesized that the relationship between GRBS implementation and performance would be contingent on the regulatory distance between a WOFS's home and host country. Institutional theory was employed in order to help explain this process.

We found empirical support for our hypotheses using primary data consisting of 181 WOFSs collected through extensive field research in the Philippines. Our results demonstrate that WOFS GRBSs are positively related to satisfaction with qualitative performance, but negatively to satisfaction with quantitative performance. They also show that these relationships will become stronger as regulatory distance reaches higher levels. These results extend the non-market strategy and institutions literature. This study also creates avenues for future research inquiry with regard to the link between GRBSs and performance outcomes, particularly in terms of investigating WOFS non-market strategic behavior in relation to regulatory distance in a Southeast Asian environmental context. Furthermore, by addressing these issues, scholars and practitioners may be able to provide better guidance to foreign subsidiaries as they attempt to enhance business opportunities in emerging markets.

Bibliography

Acquaah, M. 2007. Managerial social capital, strategic orientation, and organizational performance in an emerging economy. *Strategic Management Journal*, 28: 1235–55.

Aiken, L. S., and West, S. G. 1991. *Multiple regression: Testing and interpreting interactions*. Thousand Oaks, CA: Sage Publications.

Anderson, U., Forsgren, M., and Holm, U. 2002. The strategic impact of external networks: Subsidiary performance and competence development in the multinational corporation. *Strategic Management Journal*, 23: 979–96.

Asian Development Bank. 2007. Philippines: Critical development constraints. *Country Diagnostic Studies*. Manila: Asian Development Bank.

Bagozzi, R. P., and Phillips, L. W. 1982. Representing and testing organizational theories: A holistic construal. *Administrative Science Quarterly*, 27: 459–89.

Barden, J. Q., Steensma, H. K., and Lyles, M. A. 2005. The influence of parent control structure on parent conflict in Vietnamese international joint ventures: An organizational justice-based contingency approach. *Journal of International Business Studies*, 36: 156–74.

Barney, J. B., and Hesterly, W. S. 2006. *Strategic management and competitive advantage: Concepts and cases*. Upper Saddle River, NJ: Pearson Prentice-Hall.

Baron, D. P. 1995. Integrated strategy: Market and nonmarket components. *California Management Review*, 37: 47–65.

— 2010. *Business and its environment*. 6th edition. Upper Saddle River, NJ: Pearson Prentice-Hall.

Bevan, A., Estrin, S., and Meyer, K. 2004. Foreign investment location and institutional development in transition economies. *International Business Review*, 13: 43–64.

Boisot, M., and Child, J. 1996. From fiefs to clans and network capitalism: Explaining China's emerging economic order. *Administrative Science Quarterly*, 41: 600–28.

Bonardi, J. P. 1999. Market and nonmarket strategies during deregulation: The case of British Telecom. *Business and Politics*, 1: 203–31.

— 2008. The internal limits to firms' nonmarket activities. *European Management Review*, 5: 165–74.

Bonardi, J. P., Holburn, G. L. F., and Vanden Bergh, R. G. 2006. Nonmarket strategy performance: Evidence from US electric utilities. *Academy of Management Journal*, 49: 1209–28.

Bowman, C., and Ambrosini, V. 1997. Perceptions of strategic priorities, consensus, and firm performance. *Journal of Management Studies*, 34: 241–58.

Boyd, B. K., Dess, G. G., and Rasheed, A. M. A. 1993. Divergence between archival and perceptual measures of the environment: Causes and consequences. *Academy of Management Review*, 18: 204–26.

Brewer, T. L. 1993. Government policies, market imperfections, and foreign direct investment. *Journal of International Business Studies*, 24: 101–20.

Brouthers, K. D. 2002. Institutional, cultural and transaction cost influences on entry mode choice and performance. *Journal of International Business Studies*, 33: 203–21.

Brouthers, K. D., and Nakos, G. 2004. SME entry mode choice and performance: A transaction cost perspective. *Entrepreneurship Theory and Practice*, 28: 229–47.

Brouthers, L. E., Brouthers, K. D., and Werner, S. 2000. Perceived environmental uncertainty, entry mode choice and satisfaction with EC-MNC performance. *British Journal of Management*, 11: 183–95.

Carpenter, M. A., and Sanders, W. G. 2007. *Strategic management: A dynamic perspective*. Upper Saddle River, NJ: Pearson Prentice-Hall.

Chang, S. J., van Witteloostuijn, A., and Eden, L. 2010. From the editors: Common method variance in international business research. *Journal of International Business Studies*, 41: 178–84.

Child, J. 1997. Strategic choice in the analysis of action, structure, organizations and environment: Retrospect and prospect. *Organization Studies*, 18: 43–76.

Child, J., and Tsai, T. 2005. The dynamic between firms' environmental strategies and institutional constraints in emerging economies: Evidence from China and Taiwan. *Journal of Management Studies*, 42: 95–125.

Child, J., and Tse, D. K. 2001. China's transition and its implications for international business. *Journal of International Business Studies*, 32: 5–21.

Chowdhury, J. 1992. Performance of international joint ventures and wholly owned subsidiaries: A comparative perspective. *Management International Review*, 32: 115–33.

Chung, C. C., and Beamish, P. W. 2005. The impact of institutional reforms on characteristics and survival of foreign subsidiaries in emerging economies. *Journal of Management Studies*, 42: 35–62.

Cohen, J., Cohen, P., West, S. G., and Aiken, L. S. 2003. *Applied multiple regression/correlation analysis for the behavioral sciences*. 3rd edition. Mahwah, NJ: Lawrence Erlbaum Associates.

Contractor, F. J. 1990. Ownership patterns of US joint ventures abroad and the liberalization of foreign government regulations in the 1980s: Evidence from the benchmark surveys. *Journal of International Business Studies*, 21: 55–73.

David, D. A. 2005. *Strategic management: Concepts*. Upper Saddle River, NJ: Pearson Prentice-Hall.

Delios, A., and Henisz, W. J. 2003. Political hazards, experience, and sequential entry strategies: The international expansion of Japanese firms, 1980–98. *Strategic Management Journal*, 24: 1153–64.

Dess, G. D., and Beard, D. W. 1984. Dimensions of organizational task environments. *Administrative Science Quarterly*, 29: 52–73.

Dillman, D. A. 2000. *Mail and internet surveys: The tailored design method*. New York: Wiley.

Djankov, S., La Porta, R., Lopez-de-Silanes, F., and Shleifer, A. 2003. The regulation of entry. *Quarterly Journal of Economics*, 117: 1–37.

Dubini, P., and Aldrich, H. E. 1991. Personal and extended networks are central to the entrepreneurial process. *Journal of Business Venturing*, 6: 305–13.

Erramilli, M. K., and Rao, C. P. 1993. Service firms' international entry-mode choice: A modified transaction-cost analysis approach. *Journal of Marketing*, 57: 19–38.

Faccio, M. 2006. Politically connected firms. *American Economic Review*, 96: 369–86.

Fang, Y., Wade, M., Delios, A., and Beamish, P. W. 2007. International diversification, subsidiary performance, and the mobility of knowledge resources. *Strategic Management Journal*, 28: 1053–64.

Feinberg, S. E., and Gupta, A. K. 2009. MNC subsidiaries and country risk: Internalization as a safeguard against weak external institutions. *Academy of Management Journal*, 52: 381–99.

Field, A. 2005. *Discovering statistics using SPSS*. Thousand Oaks, CA: Sage Publications.

Foreign Companies in the Philippines Yearbook, 2007. 2007. London: Business Monitor International.

Fowler, F. J. 1995. *Improving survey questions: Design and evaluation*. Thousand Oaks, CA: Sage Publications.

Gaur, A. S., Delios, A., and Singh, K. 2007. Institutional environments, staffing strategies, and subsidiary performance. *Journal of Management*, 33: 611–36.

Geringer, J. M., and Hebert, L. 1991. Measuring performance of international joint ventures. *Journal of International Business Studies*, 21: 249–63.

Glendon, M. A., Gordon, M. W., and Osakwe, C. (eds.). 1994. *Comparative legal traditions: Text, materials and cases*. 2nd edition. St. Paul, MN: West Group.

Gong, Y., Shenkar, O., Luo, Y., and Nyaw, M. 2007. Do multiple parents help or hinder international joint venture performance? The mediating roles of contract completeness and partner cooperation. *Strategic Management Journal*, 28: 1021–34.

Granovetter, M. 1985. Economic action and social structure: The problem of embeddedness. *American Journal of Sociology*, 91: 481–510.

— 2005. The impact of social structure on economic outcomes. *Journal of Economic Perspectives*, 19: 33–50.

Grosse, R., and Trevino, L. J. 2005. New institutional economics and FDI location in Central and Eastern Europe. *Management International Review*, 45: 123–45.

Gulati, R. 1998. Alliances and networks. *Strategic Management Journal*, 19: 293–317.

Gulati, R., Nohria, N., and Zaheer, A. 2000. Strategic networks. *Strategic Management Journal*, 21: 203–15.

Hair, J. F., Anderson, R. E., Tatham, R. L., and Black, W. C. 1998. *Multivariate data analysis*. 5th edition. Delhi, India: Pearson Education.

Harman, H. H. 1967. *Modern factor analysis*. Chicago: University of Chicago Press.

Heinrich, J., and Konan, D. E. 2001. Prospects for FDI in AFTA. *ASEAN Economic Bulletin*, 18: 141–60.

Hillman, A. J., and Hitt, M. A. 1999. Corporate political strategy formulation: A model of approach, participation, and strategy decisions. *Academy of Management Review*, 24: 825–42.

Hillman, A. J., and Wan, W. P. 2005. The determinants of MNE subsidiaries' political strategies: Evidence of institutional duality. *Journal of International Business Studies*, 36: 322–40.

Hinkelman, E. G. (ed.). 1996. *Philippines business: The portable encyclopedia for doing business with the Philippines*. San Rafael, CA: World Trade Press.

Hofstede, G. 1980. *Culture's consequences: International differences in work-related values*. Beverly Hills, CA: Sage Publications.

Holburn, G. L. F., and Vanden Bergh, R. G. 2008. Making friends in hostile environments: Political strategy in regulated industries. *Academy of Management Review*, 33: 521–40.

Hoskisson, R. E., Eden, L., Lau, C. M., and Wright, M. 2000. Strategy in emerging economies. *Academy of Management Journal*, 43: 249–67.

Hult, G. T. M., Ketchen, D. J., and Arrfelt, M. 2007. Strategic supply chain management: Improving performance through a culture of competitiveness and knowledge development. *Strategic Management Journal*, 28: 1035–52.

Julian, S. D., and Ofori-Dankwa, J. C. 2008. Toward an integrative cartography of two strategic issue diagnosis frameworks. *Strategic Management Journal*, 29: 93–114.

Kale, P., Singh, H., and Perlmutter, H. 2000. Learning and protection of proprietary assets in strategic alliances: Building relational capital. *Strategic Management Journal*, 21: 217–37.

Kaufmann, D., Kraay, A., and Mastruzzi, M. 2007. *Governance matters VI: Aggregate and individual governance indicators 1996–2006*. World Bank Policy Research Working Paper WPS 4280. Washington, DC: World Bank.

Khanna, T., and Palepu, K. 1997. Why focused strategies may be wrong for emerging markets. *Harvard Business Review*, 75: 41–51.

— 1999. Policy shocks, market intermediaries, and corporate strategy: The evolution of business groups in Chile and India. *Journal of Economics and Management Strategy*, 8: 271–310.

Kogut, B., and Singh, H. 1988. The effect of national culture on the choice of entry mode. *Journal of International Business Studies*, 19: 411–32.

Kostova, T., and Roth, K. 2003. Social capital in multinational corporations and a micro–macro model of its formation. *Academy of Management Review*, 28: 297–317.

Kostova, T., and Zaheer, S. 1999. Organizational legitimacy under condition of complexity: The case of the multinational enterprise. *Academy of Management Review*, 24: 64–81.

Kotabe, M., Martin, X., and Domoto, H. 2003. Gaining from vertical partnerships: Knowledge transfer, relationship duration, and supplier performance improvement in the US and Japanese automotive industries. *Strategic Management Journal*, 24: 293–316.

Krishnan, R., Martin, X., and Noorderhaven, N. G. 2006. When does trust matter to alliance performance? *Academy of Management Journal*, 49: 894–917.

Krueger, A. O. 1974. The political economy of the rent-seeking society. *American Economic Review*, 64: 291–303.

La Porta, R., Lopez-De-Silanes, F., Shleifer, A., and Vishny, R. W. 1997. Legal determinants of external finance. *Journal of Finance*, 52: 1131–50.

— 2000. Agency problems and dividend policies around the world. *Journal of Finance*, 55: 1–33.

Lee, J., and Miller, D. 1999. People matter: Commitment to employees, strategy and performance in Korean firms. *Strategic Management Journal*, 20: 579–93.

Li, H., and Zhang, Y. 2007. The role of managers' political networking and functional experience in new venture performance: Evidence from China's transition economy. *Strategic Management Journal*, 28: 791–804.

Li, J., Yang, J. Y., and Yue, D. R. 2007. Identity, community, and audience: How wholly owned foreign subsidiaries gain legitimacy in China. *Academy of Management Journal*, 50: 175–90.

Li, J. J., Poppo, L., and Zhou, K. Z. 2008. Do managerial ties in China always produce value? Competition, uncertainty, and domestic vs. foreign firms. *Strategic Management Journal*, 29: 383–400.

Li, S. 2005. Why poor governance environment does not deter foreign direct investment: The case of China and its implications for investment protection. *Business Horizons*, 48: 297–302.

Li, S., and Filer, L. 2007. The effects of the governance environment on the choice of investment mode and strategic implications. *Journal of World Business*, 42: 80–98.

Li, S., Park, H. P., and Li, S. 2003. The great leap forward: The transition from relation-based governance to rule-based governance. *Organizational Dynamics*, 33: 63–78.

London, T., and Hart, S. L. 2004. Reinventing strategies for emerging markets: Beyond the transnational model. *Journal of International Business Studies*, 35: 350–70.

Luo, Y. 1997. Guanxi and performance of foreign-invested enterprises in China: An empirical inquiry. *Management International Review*, 37: 51–70.

— 1999. Time-based experience and international expansion: The case of an emerging economy. *Journal of Management Studies*, 36: 505–34.

— 2000. Dynamic capabilities in international expansion. *Journal of World Business*, 35: 355–78.

— 2001. Determinants of entry in an emerging economy: A multilevel approach. *Journal of Management Studies*, 38: 443–72.

— 2002a. Capability exploitation and building in a foreign market: Implications for multinational enterprises. *Organization Science*, 13: 48–63.

— 2002b. *Multinational enterprises in emerging markets*. Copenhagen: Copenhagen Business School Press.

— 2003. Market-seeking MNEs in an emerging market: How parent–subsidiary links shape overseas success. *Journal of International Business Studies*, 34: 290–309.

— 2004. Building a strong foothold in an emerging market: A link between resource commitment and environment conditions. *Journal of Management Studies*, 41: 749–73.

— 2005. Transactional characteristics, institutional environment and joint venture contracts. *Journal of International Business Studies*, 36: 209–30.

— 2007. Are joint venture partners more opportunistic in a more volatile environment? *Strategic Management Journal*, 28: 209–30.

Luo, Y., and Peng, M. W. 1999. Learning to compete in a transition economy: Experience, environment, and performance. *Journal of International Business Studies*, 30: 269–96.

Luo, Y., and Zhao, H. 2013. Doing business in a transitional society: Economic environment and relational political strategy for multinationals. *Business and Society*, 52: 515–49.

March, J., and Olsen, J. 1989. *Rediscovering institutions: The organizational basis of politics*. New York: The Free Press.

Mesquita, L. F., and Lazzarini, S. G. 2008. Horizontal and vertical relationships in developing economies: Implications for SMEs' access to global markets. *Academy of Management Journal*, 51: 359–80.

Meyer, K. 2001. Institutions, transaction costs, and entry mode choice in Eastern Europe. *Journal of International Business Studies*, 32: 357–67.

Miller, C. C., Cardinal, L. B., and Glick, W. H. 1997. Retrospective reports in organizational research: A reexamination of recent evidence. *Academy of Management Journal*, 40: 189–204.

Miller, D. 1987. The structural and environmental correlates of business strategy. *Strategic Management Journal*, 8: 55–76.

Miller, D., and Friesen, P. H. 1982. Innovation in conservative and entrepreneurial firms: Two models of strategic momentum. *Strategic Management Journal*, 3: 1–25.

Miller, D., Lee, J., Chang, S., and Le Breton-Miller, I. 2009. Filling the institutional void: The social behavior and performance of family vs. non-family technology firms in emerging markets. *Journal of International Business Studies*, 40: 802–17.

Murtha, T. P., and Lenway, S. A. 1994. Country capabilities and the strategic state: How national political institutions affect multinational corporations' strategies. *Strategic Management Journal*, 15: 113–29.

Nahapiet, J., and Ghoshal, S. 1998. Social capital, intellectual capital, and the organizational advantage. *Academy of Management Review*, 23: 242–66.

National Statistical Information Center. 2007. *Philippine Statistical Yearbook*. Makati City: National Statistical Information Center.

Neter, J., Kutner, M. H., Nachtsheim, C. J., and Wasserman, W. 1996. *Applied linear statistical models*. 4th edition. Boston, MA: WCB/McGraw-Hill.

North, D. C. 1990. *Institutions, institutional change, and economic performance*. Cambridge: Cambridge University Press.

Oliver, C. 1991. Strategic responses to institutional processes. *Academy of Management Review*, 18: 145–79.

Oliver, C., and Holzinger, I. 2008. The effectiveness of strategic political management: A dynamic capabilities framework. *Academy of Management Review*, 33: 496–520.

Ouchi, W. G. 1980. Markets, bureaucracies, and clans. *Administrative Science Quarterly*, 25: 129–41.

Park, S. H., and Luo, Y. 2001. Guanxi and organizational dynamics: Organizational networking in Chinese firms. *Strategic Management Journal*, 22: 455–77.

Peng, M. W. 2003. Institutional transitions and strategic choices. *Academy of Management Review*, 28: 275–96.

— 2009. *Global strategy*. 2nd edition. Cincinnati, OH: Thomson South-Western.

Peng, M. W., and Heath, P. S. 1996. The growth of the firm in planned economies in transition: Institutions, organizations, and strategic choice. *Academy of Management Review*, 21: 492–528.

Peng, M. W., and Luo, Y. 2000. Managerial ties and firm performance in a transition economy: The nature of a micro–macro link. *Academy of Management Journal*, 43: 486–501.

Peng, M. W., Lee, S. H., and Wang, D. Y. L. 2005. What determines the scope of the firm over time? A focus on institutional relatedness. *Academy of Management Review*, 30: 622–33.

Peteraf, M., and Reed, R. 2007. Managerial discretion and internal alignment under regulatory constraints and change. *Strategic Management Journal*, 28: 1089–112.

Podolny, J. M., and Page, K. L. 1998. Network forms of organization. *Annual Review of Sociology*, 24: 57–76.

Podsakoff, P. M., and Organ, D. W. 1986. Self-reports in organizational research: Problems and prospects. *Journal of Management*, 12: 531–44.

Podsakoff, P. M., MacKenzie, S. B., Lee, J. Y., and Podsakoff, N. P. 2003. Common method biases in behavioral research: A critical review of the literature and recommended remedies. *Journal of Applied Psychology*, 88: 879–903.

Ricart, J. E., Enright, M. J., Ghemawat, S. L. H., and Khanna, T. 2004. New frontiers in international strategy. *Journal of International Business Studies*, 35: 175–200.

Rodriguez, P., Uhlenbruck, K., and Eden, L. 2005. Government corruption and the entry strategies of multinationals. *Academy of Management Review*, 30: 383–96.

Rosenzweig, P. M., and Singh, J. V. 1991. Organizational environments and the multinational enterprise. *Academy of Management Review*, 16: 340–61.

Rynes, S. L. 2007. Editor's foreword: Carrying Sumantra Ghoshal's torch: Creating more positive, relevant, and ecologically valid research. *Academy of Management Journal*, 50: 745–7.

Sawyerr, O. O. 1993. Environmental uncertainty and environmental scanning activities of Nigerian manufacturing executives: A comparative analysis. *Strategic Management Journal*, 14: 287–99.

Tabachnick, B. G., and Fidell, L. S. 2001. *Using multivariate statistics*. 4th edition. Boston, MA: Allyn and Bacon.

Tan, J., and Peng, M. W. 2003. Organizational slack and firm performance during economic transitions: Two studies from an emerging economy. *Strategic Management Journal*, 24: 1249–63.

Tan, J. J., and Litschert, R. J. 1994. Environment–strategy relationship and its performance implications: An empirical study of the Chinese electronics industry. *Strategic Management Journal*, 15: 1–20.

Terpstra, V., Sarathy, R., and Russow, L. 2006. *Global business environment*. Garfield Heights, OH: Northcoast Publishers.

United Nations. 2007. *Millennium development indicators: World and regional groupings*. http://unstats.un.org (accessed March 21, 2008).

Uzzi, B. 1997. Social structure and competition in interfirm networks: The paradox of embeddedness. *Administrative Science Quarterly*, 42: 35–67.

Wan, W. P., and Hillman, A. J. 2006. One of these things is not like the others: What contributes to dissimilarity among MNE subsidiaries' political strategy? *Management International Review*, 46: 27–45.

Wan, W. P., and Hoskisson, R. E. 2003. Home country environments, corporate diversification strategies, and firm performance. *Academy of Management Journal*, 46: 27–45.

White, G. O., Hemphill, T. A., Joplin, J. R. W., and Marsh, L. A. 2014. Wholly owned foreign subsidiary relation-based strategies in volatile environments. *International Business Review*, 23: 303–12.

Xin, K. R., and Pearce, J. L. 1996. *Guanxi*: Connections as substitutes for formal institutional support. *Academy of Management Journal*, 39: 1641–58.

Xu, D., and Shenkar, O. 2002. Institutional distance and the multinational enterprise. *Academy of Management Review*, 27: 608–18.

Xu, D., Pan, Y., and Beamish, P. W. 2004. The effect of regulative and normative distances on MNE ownership and expatriate strategies. *Management International Review*, 44: 285–307.

Zaheer, A., and Bell, G. G. 2005. Benefiting from network position: Firm capabilities, structural holes, and performance. *Strategic Management Journal*, 26: 809–25.

Zahra, S. A., and Covin, J. G. 1993. Business strategy, technology policy and firm performance. *Strategic Management Journal*, 14: 451–78.

Zuckerman, E. W. 2003. On "Networks and markets" by Rauch and Casella, eds. *Journal of Economic Literature*, 41: 545–65.

21

Non-market strategy in Eastern Europe and Central Asia

Yusaf H. Akbar and Maciej Kisilowski[1]

As time passes since the collapse of the centrally planned political and economic systems of communist-controlled Eastern Europe and Central Asia (EECA), these countries tend to attract less and less research interest. This is particularly true in management studies and in the sub-field of non-market strategy. To the extent that EECA markets are mentioned at all, they often appear as parts of broader datasets of emerging and transitional economies (e.g. UNCTAD, 2013). This trend is only strengthened by the increasing importance of the resource-based and institutional approaches in the study of non-market strategy (see discussion in Section A of this *Companion*). Important as they are, these studies do not allow for a proper appreciation of managerial agency in the management of the non-market process (see, generally, Chapter 10). While institutions and resource constraints are important, non-market strategies can also be considered at the level of specific strategic options and individual managerial decisions.

Our focus on specific non-market strategic decisions and initiatives of managers reflects a broader academic interest in "pixels of managerial influence" within the processes of strategy formation and implementation (Jarzabkowski, 2008: 621). Scholars in this tradition have generally questioned the descriptive and prescriptive usefulness of the classic definition of strategy as a top-down "theory about how to gain competitive advantage" (Barney and Hesterly, 2010: 4) and emphasized instead the role of individual managerial decisions and middle-level managers in a reflexive process of strategic development (Floyd and Wooldridge, 2000). A key role in this perspective is played by the so-called "strategic initiatives," understood as "discrete, proactive undertakings [that] either reinforce the current strategy or alter it in order to realign the organization in accordance with changed environmental conditions" (Marx, 2004: 1). Strategic initiatives are blends of "analyses, behavioral techniques, and the use of power and organizational politics to bring about broadly conceived outcomes" (Workman, 2012: 23). They differ from tactics, which in this stream of research are defined as "managerial actions that enact a strategy" (Workman, 2012: 23) or, in other words, as individual acts of implementation of strategic initiatives.

This choice of the level of granularity of our analysis proves helpful in demonstrating some important characteristics of non-market strategies in the region under our consideration. These specificities are evident precisely when we look at non-market strategies through the prism of concrete decisions and types of initiative rather than broader strategy narratives. In the remainder of this chapter we will demonstrate, in particular, that the prevalence of each kind of initiative depends on the level of political–economic development (or, as we call it, "modernization") of a given EECA country. Non-market initiatives also vary based on whether they represent a proactive or reactive strategic posture. In addition, the level of non-market risk varies across different classes of non-market strategic initiatives.

Supplementary to the three above-mentioned sources of heterogeneity between types of non-market strategic initiatives we add a final one, related to the kind of business enterprises that tend to employ non-market initiatives of a given type. Unlike most studies in the field of international business that focus exclusively or predominantly on multinational enterprises (MNEs) (Wright et al., 2005), our survey discusses both foreign-owned and local businesses, as they operate side-by-side in the EECA context.

Our focus on specific managerial decisions and types of strategic initiatives is also reflected in the al choices that underlay this chapter. Among a number of sources that we use in our analysis, a particularly important role is played by a broad database of in-depth interviews that we conducted with middle-to-senior managers working in EECA. These interviews offer insights about actual decision-making processes in which EECA managers engage when confronting the turbulent non-market environments of their businesses.

The remainder of this chapter will proceed as follows. In the next section, we set the stage for our analysis by providing a brief overview of the political–economic context of the EECA region. Then we introduce the types of non-market strategic initiatives most often used in the region before analyzing the above-mentioned sources of heterogeneity between non-market strategies. We complete our mapping by juxtaposing the categories of initiatives and their underlying features. Finally, we offer a brief conclusion with main managerial implications.

Economic transition and transformation in EECA

Main EECA clusters

EECA is a broad region linked mainly by a shared history of central planning and communism. After 1991, all EECA countries began a transition from centrally planned economies toward varying forms of mixed economy. The term "transition economy" emerged in the early 1990s as academics and practitioners around the world confronted an unprecedented natural experiment in institutional and market-based reforms. Economic, political, legal, and social policies were constructed from scratch, and while significant ideas were imported from developed economies in North America and Western Europe, these approaches were adapted and revised to reflect new insights and regional specificities revealed by this unique experiment.

While the transition to a capitalist mixed economic system began with far-reaching changes to forms and levels of governance (especially changes in ownership of key sectors of the economy through privatization), the result – or, more precisely, the "present status" – of this transformation differs widely within the EECA region.

EECA markets are commonly divided into a number of geographically defined clusters. Starting from the west, there is the so-called Visegrad Group of Central European countries, including Czech Republic, Hungary, Poland, and Slovakia. To the northeast, there is the Baltic cluster, which includes Estonia, Latvia, and Lithuania. To the south, the Balkan cluster comprises Bulgaria, Romania, and the successor states of the former Yugoslavia. Importantly, all of the Visegrad and Baltic states, as well as Bulgaria, Romania, Slovenia, and Croatia from the Balkan cluster, are now full members of the European Union. They are sometimes referred to as "the EU11." The Russian Federation is obviously a discrete "cluster," but it is beyond the remit of this chapter. Geographically located between Russia and the EU11 are Belarus, Ukraine, and Moldova, whose economic and political orientation often alternates between the west (European Union) and the east (Russia). Beyond Europe, more former republics of the Soviet Union are concentrated in two regional clusters: Caucasus, consisting of Armenia, Azerbaijan, and Georgia; and Central Asia, including Kazakhstan, Turkmenistan, Tajikistan, and Uzbekistan.

The differences between these EECA countries are substantial. Yet, the experience of communism and of the post-communist transition has embedded in them a number of common vectors that impact non-market strategies. First, all EECA countries have experienced at least some level of foreign direct investment and thus some presence of multinational corporations (Akbar and McBride, 2004). Second, the EECA environment is characterized by significant improvements in the implementation and use of technology and capital and growing markets allowing companies to expand their activities. Third, in virtually all EECA countries the application and adoption of best managerial practices remain inconsistent, and the levels of professionalization of the managerial cadre in a range of industries remains low. (Horwitch and Kisilowski, 2014). A case in point is the observation of our interviewee from Armenia: "In general, the problem is that in Armenia we do not have enough people of entrepreneurial spirit, risk-takers, and there are so many things to change. And I would like them to change a.s.a.p., so we will have more breathing room."[2]

The EU11

With that said, the transformation that has occurred in the EECA countries that have been admitted to the EU – the EU11 – has been considerable. In 2009, two of these countries (Slovenia and Slovakia) adopted the euro as their currency, followed by Estonia (2013) and Latvia (2014). Most of these countries have liberalized both their trade and their investment rules, have independent central banks, and have near full currency convertibility, so early macroeconomic prescriptions for reform in them are all but complete.

On the meso level, pressures to converge regulatory systems toward EU standards and the adoption of the EU's *acquis communautaire* – the set of laws, regulations, and practices that comprises the EU's legal order – are less even. In those countries that have extensively adopted EU regulations, this has led to wholesale transformations in their regulatory environments. This process of integration and limited convergence has also encouraged, and been encouraged by, the growth in foreign direct investment (FDI) in the EU11 region. It has been further encouraged by strategic privatization of state enterprises – especially to foreign companies – throughout the region. The role of foreign multinational enterprises has been important in facilitating the adoption and implementation of the EU regulatory frameworks (Akbar, 2003a). Both companies and governments in the region have learned ways of managing their relationships (Peng and Luo, 2000).

Non-EU EECA markets

For countries that remain outside the EU, the extent of the transition has varied. Much of the reform has been piecemeal, partial, and subject to capture of vested interests (Arnold and

Quelch, 1998; Palepu and Khanna, 2010); and, despite inward-FDI flows, local idiosyncrasies remain regarding regulatory and legal processes. Institutional development has been weak, too (Gelbudaa et al., 2008). The EU has played an important role in forcing EU11 countries to introduce institutional reforms, whereas countries left outside the Union have been left to pursue different institutional trajectories. Very few of the EECA countries outside the EU are considered consolidated democracies (Freedom House, 2014). In particular, their judiciaries are only partially independent (Kühn, 2012). Many of the bedrock institutions of regulatory governance, such as antitrust authorities, are non-existent or extraordinarily opaque in their practices (World Bank, 2011). Intellectual property and other intangible asset protections are harder to find and court systems are unable to protect them effectively (Gelbudaa et al., 2008). Last but not least, numerous measures of corruption and bribery suggest that EECA countries outside the EU have systematically higher corruption, in part due to the absence of institutional safeguards and provisions (Transparency International, 2013).

Legacies of the past

In order to increase understanding of the nature of non-market strategies in the EECA region – and especially in the countries that remain outside the EU – it is germane to consider Bartlett and Ghoshal (1995: 472), who referred to the importance of administrative heritage in explaining the ways in which companies are managed and make strategy: "Each company is influenced by the path by which it developed – its organizational history and the values, norms and practices of its management." Factors that influence such heritage include both internal, idiosyncratic management styles and external factors, such as national cultures, histories, and established practices and norms of management.

Thus, while many of the institutions of communism, such as central planning ministries and state-owned monopolies, no longer exist because they have collapsed, been privatized, or been reformed or transformed, their residual values have been transferred to the managers and policy-makers who worked during communism. It is neither easy nor desirable to reform such practices based on several decades of experience. There can be little doubt that, even today, the influence of best-practice transfer from multinational corporations in the EECA region is at least partially offset by the impact of two generations of central planning on the mindsets of managers. While this residual impact on managerial practices is diminishing over time, the cultural and psychological transformation of people in the region remains far from complete.

Types of non-market strategic initiatives

Bribery

It is perhaps because of the strength of the legacies of the common past that, despite all the differences between EECA countries and their clusters, our empirical research has still revealed substantial similarities in the types of non-market strategic initiatives that managers tend to employ in the region. Figure 21.1 lists the most common initiatives.

Perhaps the first initiative to come to mind when thinking about emerging markets is bribery. In practice, money changes hands between businesses and government officials in two distinct ways. Managers can make a strategic decision to pursue desirable governmental actions by offering bribes to public officials. The "good" that they seek to acquire might be speeding up a governmental service, favorable treatment, or even a decision or an action that

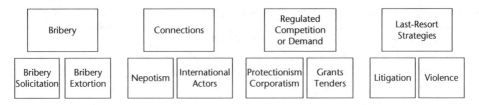

Figure 21.1   Popular non-market strategic initiatives in the EECA

would break the country's laws but benefit the business (Rose-Ackerman, 1999). Regardless of the "good" that the money is supposed to buy, we call this strategy of business-initiated corruption *bribery solicitation*. This non-market strategy initiative is so common that it is hard to open any newspaper dealing with EECA without finding examples. ExxonMobil, Texaco, Phillips Petroleum, and Amoco all paid bribes to obtain hydrocarbon rights in Kazakhstan in the 1990s. Their payments totaled an estimated $78 million (Stodghill, 2006). A UN study reports that, in the Balkan countries, the sector most affected by bribery is building and construction, followed closely by wholesale and retail trade (UNODC, 2013). Our Macedonian interviewee suggests that the reason why managers in these industries are particularly eager to offer bribes is that they heavily depend on public tenders (construction) or government permits (retail) for their operations: "Government tenders require you to offer something to win the tender in the form of payments to the government officials responsible for tendering."[3] Bribery solicitation is a common practice in the EU11 countries, too. In Hungary, the average amount of bribes paid to officials by businesses varied between 3000 and 10,000 euros each year (Index, 2014).

In EECA, an equally common scenario is for a public official to demand a bribe. For instance, a corrupt public official might "raid" a business, threatening the firm that he will look for legal infractions committed by the management. Managers must make a strategic decision on how best to deal with such instances of *bribery extortion*. In EECA, the default strategy is to negotiate with bureaucratic "raiders" and then pay up to be left alone. This is especially the case since vague laws and regulations in such areas as taxation and occupational safety make finding potential "crimes" extremely easy. When asked about the prevalence of such scenarios, our Azeri interviewee responded, "Oh, yes, it goes without saying,"[4] while one of our Tajik interviewees provided an especially ironic example:

> Among the most corrupt is the Anti-Corruption Agency. They come over and try to find evidence of corruption, which they will always find because everybody gives bribes. So they create a conclusion report, and if you pay the investigator, they can change this conclusion – so you pay an administrative fine and do not go to jail.[5]

As with bribery solicitation, available comparative studies corroborate the widespread nature of the business–government interactions reported by our interviewees (e.g. Transparency International, 2013; UNODC, 2013).

Connections – local and international

Another group of non-market strategies can be broadly characterized as using the social or relational capital of managers to support the strategic objectives of their businesses. If that social capital is mostly local, the resulting strategy often takes the form of *nepotism*.

This involves the use of close personal and familial bonds, including clan, tribal, or other such ties, in order to secure governmental decisions that are favorable to one's business or unfavorable to its competitors. As managers operating within EECA indicate, nepotism can be an effective substitute for securing governmental favors through bribery solicitation. An example is the nepotism in tobacco nationalization in Hungary, where the state-sponsored regulatory scheme will favor the ruling party's "friends and relatives" (Hungarian Spectrum, 2013; Politics.hu, 2013). In Romania, the situation is similar: the strategic importance of family and kinship clans is normal and the access of outsiders to management positions is barred by the elite (€FIN, 2013). A manager in Chechnya observes that "the whole state system is based on connections, on trust between each other. Families are strong and big – it's a clan system." This view corroborates previous analyses of the situation in Chechnya (Central Asia-Caucasus Institute, 2006; Prague Watchdog, 2009). The same interviewee goes as far as to suggest that nepotism is even more prevalent than bribery in his region: "Money is not so important; money does not solve problems that connections can solve."[6] This is confirmed by an interviewee from Ukraine: "The choice of payments or connections depends partly on how strongly you are related to a given official. If he is family, then of course [you do not need to pay]. Or if you studied together at a university; or did business together in the past."[7]

While some managers are in a position to use personal connections mostly at the local level, others try to employ the support of powerful *international actors*. These include embassies of foreign governments interested in the success of a given business, or international aid institutions, such as the European Bank for Reconstruction and Development (EBRD), the International Monetary Fund (IMF), and the World Bank. A case in Kosovo shows how MNEs use their embassies to lobby for their interests. Our interviewee reports that the Austrian ambassador vigorously supported Austrian construction firms.[8] Meanwhile, a manager from Moldova claims: "Our only tool is to put pressure through the IMF, the European Commission."[9] This manager, like a number of our interviewees, emphasizes that the support of international actors is helpful, since EECA governments seek foreign investment and try to project positive images of their countries to the world: "What the government wants from us is usually things like contacts in the West and [to portray a] positive public image of the country."[10] A similar comment is offered by our Armenian interviewee: "Government is very careful about adopting laws that affect investment. It's not only about the economy, but also about the image of the country."[11]

Regulated competition or demand

Since the objective of any business strategy (market and non-market alike) is to gain a sustainable stream of above-average industry returns, an important non-market strategic objective is to employ governmental power in order to artificially limit competition or increase demand for the company's products. For instance, a business may convince a government to introduce laws that would stifle competition within a given market, usually by limiting or even banning new market entrants. If such limitations are aimed solely at foreign businesses, they amount to strategic *protectionism*. Governmental action of a protectionist nature is difficult to pursue in the post-communist EU member states, since protectionism is inconsistent with the key principles and laws of the European Union. Nevertheless, some businesses and sectors are being protected in these countries. For example, Poland, the Czech Republic, and Hungary have all offered financial support to their loss-making national airlines (Akbar et al., 2014). In the case of Hungary, this support was later vetoed by the European Commission, which in turn led to the prompt bankruptcy of Malév, the Hungarian carrier (EC, 2010). But the subsidy offered to Czech Airlines was approved (EC, 2012b) and the restructuring aid to LOT Polish Airlines was also found to be in line with EU state aid rules (EC, 2013; EC, 2014). Historically, another sector that received significant EU protection was the automotive industry, through the Block Exemption on Automotive Distribution (Akbar, 2003b).

EU11 governments can also introduce protectionist policies by giving preferential treatment to local companies in public tenders. Yet, again, such support can occur only unofficially (EC, 2013a), since official preferences are banned by the procurement regulations that bind all EU member states. There is little doubt that states retain domestic control over banks, both to protect their economic models and to provide financial tools during times of crisis. For example, German and French banks have relied on their country-specific corporate governance rules to avoid foreign takeover (Epstein, 2013). In non-EU EECA countries, protectionist policies are much more widespread (Bohr, 2004).

Another option to constrain competition artificially is for businesses already active in a given market to claim some special feature of that market. Such features may include the sensitive or complex nature of a good or service provided, the general societal interest in maintaining a high level of quality of such goods or services, or a special level of public trust that a given industry should enjoy. The strategy initiatives aimed at attaining governmental monopoly protections through such arguments can be labeled *corporatism*. Unlike protectionism, corporatism does not involve targeting foreign businesses in particular, so it is more feasible in the common-market environment of the European Union. Within the Union, professional service providers such as lawyers, accountants, physicians, and real estate agents have managed to convince national governments to constrain competition in their respective industries. The most common model here is to introduce an elaborate process for admitting any new entrants into the profession. The professions themselves often administer these processes. Such a system gives businesses already operating in a given industry a final say about the entry of any potential competitors. The result, as a study in Bulgaria demonstrates, is that businesses in cartelized industries are able to charge prices significantly above free-market levels (Institute for Market Economics, 2009). In Romania, notaries and lawyers who (among other professionals) enjoy corporatist protections have come to the attention of the local Competition Council (Finantistii, 2012). In 2013, major taxi companies operating in Hungary's capital, Budapest, successfully lobbied the local municipal council to set fixed mandatory prices for all taxi services, with the result that the preceding free-market fares almost doubled. The move was also associated with increased entry restrictions to the industry (HVG, 2013).

Yet another strategy involves tapping into governmental demand for goods and services by bidding for public *tenders*. The reliability of statistics on public tenders is questionable, but based on a European report from 2012 there seems to be a persistent difference in the relative volumes of procurement advertised across Europe. This variation might reflect structural differences in the organization of procurement or in the provision of public services (EC, 2012a).

EECA firms also often link their business models to governmental demand for policy outcomes – or at least for the impression that such policy outcomes are being achieved – in cases when local or international institutions offer *grants* in the form of direct monetary gifts or preferential loans. The EU and the EBRD are particularly important grant donors in the EECA region. Between 2014 and 2020, the EU plans to distribute almost 80 billion euros in grants targeted at improving Europe's record in areas such as innovation and entrepreneurship (Horizon 2020, 2013). Even more money will be distributed as grants to businesses in the agricultural sector (Euractiv, 2013). In practice, applying for public grants and tenders is often not a distinct type of non-market strategy, but a "front" for extracting advantages arranged through bribery or connections (*Baltic Times*, 2014; BBC News Online, 2008; Oxford Analytica, 2014; Gawthorpe, 2010). Yet, as several of our interviewees point out, some EECA businesses do include participation in honest tenders and grant selection proceedings in their business models. In Romania, our interviewee cited numerous examples of businesses that won financial support from the European Union without recourse to any apparent bribes or political connections. For instance, a tourist resort built partly from EU funds "has thousands of visitors every year and manages to attract both individuals and companies."[12] Our Polish interviewee operates an educational business that offers a number of services to governmental agencies. It won all of its contracts in public tenders, again with no apparent corrupt dealings.[13] Our Kosovar interviewee pointed out that because his young state is still under the close watch of international aid institutions, many public tenders need to proceed in a fair and open way.[14]

Last-resort strategies

The final two types of strategic initiatives can be characterized as "last-resort strategies," since businesses tend to rely on them only when all other alternatives are unavailable. The first of these is *litigation*, either in local courts or through international arbitration. A typical scenario here might involve a business that becomes a subject of governmental harassment, such as a raid by officials who try to extort a bribe. Instead of paying the bribe, managers may choose to sue the agency that the officials represent, or defend themselves in court if the officials discover irregularities and bring criminal or civil charges. In general, data suggest that the direct success rate of this strategy is consistently low. EECA courts are often hesitant to decide against governmental agencies, especially since judges frequently have personal relations with major political power-holders. In the words of a Slovakian manager: "Personally, I don't believe in a working justice system in Slovakia. I have not personally seen one individual winning against the Slovak republic in court."[15] Such pessimism may be somewhat exaggerated, as winning in court is possible, especially if high political interests are not involved. "The Serbian Securities and Exchanges Commission asked me to pay a two-thousand-euro fee for closing a company I had owned," reports an entrepreneur from Serbia. "The fees were not specified in the schedule of fees, so I sued them and won the case."[16]

One way to improve one's chances against an EECA government is to pursue international arbitration as opposed to litigation in a local court. A number of Russian-owned companies have reportedly pursued this strategy in response to hostile behavior from the government of Uzbekistan (Uzmetronom, 2013). Another option is to try to sue in a court of another country, although this is mostly restricted to lawsuits brought against other businesses (which may have assets in the other country or be subject to that country's regulatory oversight), rather than governments. In London, the High Court has been dealing with what the local lawyers call "Russian super-cases," involving the richest members of Russia's business elite (Buckley, 2011).

Nevertheless, almost all of our interviewees felt that, whenever possible, any form of litigation should be avoided. Indeed, considerable fatalism surrounds the topic. For instance, our Chechen interviewee observes:

> You go to court because there is no other way! You think that maybe the judge will say something, maybe there will be an opportunity to negotiate with government during the court proceedings. You think: "Maybe I can get some justice." After all, it's written

in the law. And if you're not using this path, tomorrow people would ask you: "Why didn't you go?" In Russia, you never know.[17]

The second type of last-resort strategy is *violence*. While litigation constitutes the use of governmental power to achieve one's business objectives, violence involves managers deploying private and legally unsanctioned power. A typical scenario here would be physical intimidation of or credible threats toward a potential competitor or a debtor, usually with the help of a local organized-crime syndicate.

It is difficult to assess the scale of threats and physical coercion among EECA businesses, as very few systematic comparative studies of this issue have been conducted (Krkoska and Robeck, 2009). Nevertheless, our interviewees emphasize that such extreme measures are a real possibility in at least some EECA countries, and the available country-level studies and reports tend to confirm their opinions (e.g. Gounev, 2006; Hendley et al., 2000).

Main features of non-market strategic initiatives

Political–economic modernization

After outlining the eight types of non-market strategic initiatives, we now introduce four variables that help to describe and further categorize each type. We shall begin with the variable that accounts for differences in social, economic, and political environments within the EECA region. A thorough discussion of these differences was offered earlier. Now, we will simplify this and introduce a single index to categorize EECA market environments: the political–economic modernization index. This is calculated on the basis of thirteen indicators. It reflects the dual roles of economic liberalization and political democratization in understanding the terrain upon which firms build their non-market strategies. The core argument is that countries that have more transparent, rules-based economic institutions governing economies that are more open to international trade and investment will lead firms to develop different non-market strategies compared to countries that are more closed, less transparent and suffer from institutional dysfunction. By the same token, the non-market strategies adopted by firms in more democratic societies will tend to be different from those employed by firms in authoritarian societies. Put another way, differences in the degree of economic modernization and democratic development across countries in EECA explain variations in the type and intensity of non-market strategies pursued by firms.

Turning in more detail to the indicators, six of them are "transition indicators," as reported each year by the European Bank of Reconstruction and Development (EBRD). These can be used to chart an EECA country's progress in:

1   large-scale privatization;
2   small-scale privatization;
3   governance and enterprise restructuring;
4   price liberalization;
5   trade and foreign exchange system; and
6   competition policy.

(European Bank for Reconstruction and Development, 2013)

Based on a liberal economic paradigm, this is built on three related pillars: the removal of economically inefficient national barriers to trade and investment; limits on economic distortions caused by domestic policy intervention; and the creation of new economic institutions that are rules-based and more transparent than their predecessors. The EBRD's transition indicators thus deal with issues of economic policy that are central to institutional development and foster successful economic transition. On the one hand, the indicators focus on the removal of national barriers and controls on the flow of goods, services, and capital. On the other, they also consider institution-building and new national policy competencies, such as the development of competition policy.

Freedom House produces the remaining seven indicators annually. They relate to the development of political institutions that foster democracy. EECA countries are evaluated in respect of their:

7   electoral process;
8   civil society;
9   independent media;
10 national-level governance;
11 local-level governance;
12 judicial framework and independence; and
13 corruption.

(Freedom House, 2013)

Our political–economic modernization index is generated by calculating means of the EBRD and Freedom House indicators and then computing a weighted average of the two means (with the EBRD mean having double the weighting of the Freedom House mean). The weighting represents our understanding of the relatively greater importance of economic environment over political development, at least from a perspective of a manager operating in a given environment. The result is expressed in percentage terms.

Table 21.1 assembles all EECA countries into four discrete categories, based on their 2013 political–economic modernization index. These categories are: low modernization;

Table 21.1 Political–economic modernization index of EECA countries

	Low modernization (0–50)	Low–medium modernization (51–62)	Medium–high modernization (63–75)	High modernization (76–100)
Country	Turkmenistan (28)	Kosovo (53)	Georgia (65)	Slovenia (79)
	Belarus (35)	Russia (55)	Serbia (65)	Hungary (79)
	Uzbekistan (35)	Kyrgyz Republic (57)	Montenegro (66)	Slovak Republic (82)
	Azerbaijan (46)	Bosnia and	Albania (67)	Lithuania (83)
	Tajikistan (49)	Herzegovina (59)	Macedonia (68)	Latvia (84)
	Kazakhstan (49)	Ukraine (61)	Romania (73)	Poland (84)
		Armenia (61)	Croatia (74)	Estonia (86)
		Moldova (61)	Bulgaria (75)	Czech Republic*

Sources: EBRD data is available at: http://tr.ebrd.com/tr13/en/; Freedom House data is available at: www.freedomhouse.org/report-types/nations-transit.

Notes:
* The Czech Republic has "graduated" from EBRD transition programs and thus transition indicators have not been compiled for the country. The country was considered a "consolidated democracy" by Freedom House.
Numbers in brackets are weighted averages of means of 2013 EBRD transition indicators, expressed in percentage terms (weight of 2), and 2013 Freedom House democracy indices, expressed in percentage terms (weight of 1).

low–medium modernization; medium–high modernization; and high modernization. As can be readily observed from Table 21.1, political–economic modernization is implicitly tied to an EECA country's relationship with the EU. All of the highly modernized economies are full members of the EU. Moreover, no country rated low on modernization has formal associational relations with the EU. At best, they participate in the rather loose EU Neighborhood Policy; at worst, they have no meaningful relationship whatsoever.

Strategic posture

Traditionally, international business scholars have assumed that the key issue in analyzing non-market strategies in emerging, transitional, or developing countries is to understand the host country environment in which a business will be operating. This focus has been partial and has stemmed largely from the almost exclusive interest of international business scholars in the strategies of the MNEs operating in emerging countries. By ignoring the large majority of emerging countries' businesses that are local, rather than multinational, these scholars have essentially been looking at emerging economies through the lens of outsiders (Mathews, 2006; Meyer et al., 2009; Wright et al., 2005). Consequently, social and political systems in emerging economies have been treated mostly as sources of threats, known as "country risk" or "political risk." The role of managers in this framework was to minimize the threat/risk and, if necessary, defend the business if the anticipated attack occurred.

The limitations of this approach were first highlighted in two seminal papers by Boddewyn (1988) and Boddewyn and Brewer (1994). These authors criticized the traditional approach for its somewhat "passive or reactive" view of MNEs' political behavior (Boddewyn, 1988: 345) that considers "political factors . . . only as constraints" (Boddewyn and Brewer, 1994: 126). Instead, they emphasized the importance of proactive political activity as an attractive option for managers of MNEs and presented an array of tactics through which such political strategy could be implemented.

This shift toward proactive non-market strategies has continued in a number of more recent studies (Hillman and Hitt, 1999; Hillman and Wan, 2005; Puck et al., 2013). Our research in EECA confirms that proactive non-market strategies play an important role in everyday business activity in the region. Yet, we also recognize that not all non-market strategies are proactive. Hostile governmental actions do occur in the EECA region and managers need to be skillful when responding to such attacks. That is why, instead of determining by assumption whether non-market strategies are – or should be – mostly reactive or proactive, we have tried to learn about the actual managerial practices in EECA by introducing an explicit feature of a non-market strategic initiative that we call *strategic posture*.

A non-market strategic posture is proactive if a business initiates non-market actions in order to improve its strategic position or harm the position of a competitor. By contrast, a reactive non-market strategy is about responding to a government's or business competitor's hostile non-market action. Some strategic initiatives introduced in the previous section are inherently proactive or reactive. For instance, bribery solicitation is a proactive non-market strategy, as it is by definition initiated by the business. The same goes for applying for tenders or grants. Nepotism is almost always proactive, too, since developing local connections takes time that a business may not have if it is already under threat or attack. The same goes for pursuing corporatist or protectionist arrangements – the whole point of these tactics is to close entry to a given industry before dangerous competition arrives. Yielding to bribery extortion is, by contrast, inherently reactive.

Other strategies can, in principle, be either reactive or proactive, but in the actual EECA context most often they are practiced with only one kind of posture. Litigation, for instance, is rarely used as a proactive strategy. Perhaps because of the particularly low chance of success, EECA businesses go to court mostly only when government or well-connected competitors harass them. By contrast, violence is almost always used proactively in EECA. Very few managers *defend* their businesses by resorting to violence, although an exception may be when a business is itself under violent attack from a competitor; in this case, violence might breed violence.[18] One strategy that is regularly used in both proactive and reactive fashion in the EECA is the appeal to international support. International organizations and foreign embassies can both help if a business is under governmental harassment and, for instance, if it lobbies the local government in order to win a tender or obtain favorable legislation.

Non-market risk

As we mentioned earlier, the traditional international-business literature has tended to focus on potential threats that businesses (mostly, MNEs) may face in an emerging market, and as a result this literature has developed a complex understanding of the notion of "political risk" (Brewer, 1985; Diamonte et al., 1996; Fitzpatrick, 1983; Kobrin, 1979, 1982, 1987; Kotzian, 2007; McDermott, 1998; Sethi and Luther, 1986; Simon, 1984). Al Khattab, Anchor, and Davies (2007) identify six types of governmental action in emerging countries that can create such political risk: taxation; expropriation; contract repudiation; industrial espionage; currency inconvertibility; and restrictions on ownership, personnel, or import–export.

Yet, the literature has some significant limitations. Most importantly, it limits its understanding of political risk to "the risk that a sovereign host government will unexpectedly change the rules of the game under which business operates" (Butler and Joaquin, 1998: 599). An exclusive focus on the arbitrary action of the government changing the "rules of the game" assumes that businesses operating in emerging markets are always passive followers of the rules that are in place. However, as we have discussed above, businesses often engage proactively in the non-market environment. In such cases, the political risk may be a direct consequence of this involvement. For instance, using connections to influence governmental tenders bears an inherent risk of exposure in the press. If backroom lobbying comes to the public's attention, the government may deflect the ensuing political embarrassment by deciding against the interests of whichever business was involved. While this situation could hardly be called "changing the rules of the game," it is an example of the realization of a clear political risk.

Moreover, many non-market strategies involve breaking laws of the EECA countries. They thus involve the risk of criminal sanctions for managers and heavy penalties for the company involved. Here, a definition focused solely on changing the rules of the game makes even less sense. In fact, when acting in such cases, the EECA government is *enforcing* the rules that are in place. Indeed, it is even peculiar to call the risk of being caught while breaking the law a *political* risk. That is why, to describe the risk faced by EECA managers engaging in non-market strategies, we use the broader term *non-market* risk. As we know from the risk management literature, risk is a feature associated with every managerial decision (Clark, 1996; Snider, 1991). And while investors are often able to diversify away so-called systematic risk through a properly constructed asset portfolio (Grinold, 2010), these risks may still be relevant to the manager of an individual business operating in an emerging market. Thereby, it seems justified to include in the definition of the non-market risk any risk of adverse consequences for the business and its managers that is associated with a given non-market strategy. The notion of non-market risk mirrors the term "non-market strategy": as firms exercise agency in their non-market strategy, they create non-market risk as a function of the kind of strategy they choose to pursue.

It is important to emphasize that levels of non-market risk depend heavily on context. It is thereby impossible to ascribe a certain level of risk to a particular type of non-market strategy. Consequently, what we offer here is only a broad generalization that should be viewed as a first approximation. With that caveat in mind, we can conclude, for instance, that violence is most often associated with much higher levels of non-market risk than, say, bidding in governmental tenders. In general, our research in the region convinces us that even in the least modernized EECA countries, non-market strategies that involve illegal behavior carry more non-market risk than those that do not. Even engaging in bribery – a practice that is prevalent in the region – can lead to criminal prosecution. In the words of a Kazakh manager:

> [Bribery] is still happening. It's a big problem. But there is now a real risk of being caught if you give bribes. Partly because the government is organizing a constant fight against corruption, there is a hotline to report harassment, and every case needs to be opened. If you are caught . . . you are in big trouble.[19]

Furthermore, because crimes can be prosecuted many years after they have been committed, a manager engaging in any illegal activity runs the risk that a future toughening of a country's policies on certain crimes will affect him or her retroactively. For instance, in Poland, the 2005 general election was won by the conservative Law and Justice Party, which promptly established a new anti-corruption agency with broad powers and highly paid employees. Between 2006 and 2012, this agency brought criminal charges against more than 6000 individuals (Central Anticorruption Bureau, 2013). In the Balkan countries, UN research found that about 2 percent of corruption cases were reported (UNODC, 2013). That may sound like a small fraction, but to assess the risk level one needs to consider both the probability and the severity of the uncertain event (Skipper, 2007). Finally, managers of a foreign-owned company may also be criminally prosecuted in the company's country of origin. For instance, the US Foreign Corrupt Practices Act makes it illegal for American companies to pay bribes to foreign officials.

All in all, one can expect strategies that do not involve illegal behavior to generate lower levels of non-market risk. That applies to litigation, participating in honest public tenders, calling on the support of international actors, or seeking corporatist or protectionist regulations. By contrast, developing connections or nepotism may bring a manager close to illegal corruption. Even if no law is broken, a public disclosure over such influence peddling may harm the company's reputation or provoke an adverse action from a government responding to the pressure of public opinion.

Types of market actor

The final factor salient to our analysis is the organizational form under which an EECA business operates. While most research into non-market strategy has traditionally focused on MNEs, such a focus is insufficient to explain the true nature of non-market strategy in the EECA region. First, in all EECA countries, the majority of firms are both owned and managed locally. Indeed, the internal diversity among local EECA market actors is so sub-stantial that distinguishing further sub-categories is necessary. In particular, we have found an important difference between firms that are either formally owned or effectively controlled by the state and companies that function more or less independently from the state. We term the former *state-influenced enterprises* (SIEs) and the latter *independent local enterprises* (ILEs).

In many EECA countries, SIEs are generally larger and more prominent than ILEs (Iwasaki and Suzuki, 2007). This is a legacy of the communist past and the economic transition that followed. While under communism all enterprises – large and small – were owned by the state; after the introduction of the market economy many EECA governments were hesitant to sell their largest, most strategically important enterprises to foreign investors. Meanwhile, smaller enterprises were often privatized through management buyouts, and entrepreneurs created numerous new enterprises. While some of these new enterprises have succeeded in building substantial scale, many remain either small or medium-sized.

Turning to MNEs, it is important to point out that the line distinguishing a multinational from a local enterprise is not always as clear as it may seem. MNEs frequently invest in the EECA region through joint ventures with local enterprises. The relative balance between "foreign" and "local" in such ventures' ownership and management can vary substantially from case to case. The deeper involvement of an MNE may include establishing a local incorporated subsidiary. While, in the past, the literature rarely mentioned these subsidiaries, more recently their organizational importance has been recognized (Blumentritt and Nigh, 2002). This is logical since these local affiliates are often the actual locus of non-market strategy execution and at times even its formulation (White et al., 2014). Because of that, understanding the management structure of these subsidiaries, and especially the role of local managers, is important for understanding their market and non-market behavior.

Mapping non-market strategies

Putting it all together

We can now integrate what we have learned from our prior analysis by linking the various types of non-market initiatives with the four descriptive variables. Table 21.2 presents the resulting matrix. In the first column, all types of non-market strategic initiatives are listed. Column 2 tabulates levels of modernization of EECA countries where respective strategic initiatives are most often used. Column 3 presents types of strategic posture that given cate-gories of initiatives often represent. Column 4 identifies the level of non-market risk nor-mally associated with a specific class of initiatives. Finally, Column 5 catalogues the most frequent users of each group of strategic initiatives.

The matrix indicates that in EECA countries characterized by low levels of political–economic modernization, local market actors may be more inclined to pursue strategies associated with higher levels of non-market risk. Violence initiated by either SIEs or ILEs is not uncommon, while bribery solicitation is widespread. ILEs, in addition, are quite likely to be subjected to bribery extortion attempts. MNEs, by contrast, tend to stick to low-risk, reactive strategies in the poorly modernized EECA markets. If harassed, they may respond by going to court, pursuing international arbitration, or – most often – seeking support from the embassies of their home countries or from local offices of international aid organizations.

As discussed earlier, as the degree of economic modernization grows, the strategic menu of all groups of market players changes substantially. Most strikingly, in a highly modernized EECA country, *all* categories of market actors prefer to engage in proactive, rather than

Table 21.2 EECA non-market strategies and their features

Type of initiative	Conducive level of modernization	Strategic posture represented	Associated level of non-market risk	Most frequent users
Violence	Low	Proactive	High	SIEs/ILEs
Bribery solicitation	Generally Low	Proactive	High	SIEs/ILEs
Bribery extortion	Low	Reactive	Medium–High	ILEs
Litigation	Generally Low	Reactive	Low–Medium	MNEs
Involving international actors (e.g. international organizations)	Low High	Reactive Proactive	Low	MNEs
Nepotism	Generally High	Proactive	Medium–High	SIEs
Grants and tenders	High	Proactive	Low	MNEs/SIEs/ILEs
Corporatism and protectionism	High	Proactive	Low	MNEs/SIEs/ILEs

reactive, strategies. Boddewyn and Brewer (1994: 131) point out that a company follows proactive strategies when it has "sufficient power to affect the uncertain outcomes" of its actions. Accordingly, it seems that the more transparent and institutionally stable environment of highly modernized EECA countries makes businesses more empowered to pursue a more active role in a non-market environment. In addition, the riskiness of the strategies pursued decreases substantially, especially among local players. For MNEs, as they radically transform their reactive strategies typical of a poorly modernized EECA market into highly proactive ones, the level of non-market risk may not fall substantially – or, in some cases, it may actually rise.

While the scope of this chapter does not allow us to offer an exhaustive discussion of each strategy in each category of EECA markets, the next two sub-sections present a sample of our empirical findings. This sample should give the reader a sense of how EECA managers choose between the different strategies available to them, taking into account numerous environmental and strategic factors.

Poorly modernized EECA countries

In poorly modernized EECA countries, one of the most important contextual factors determining non-market behavior is corruption. Available data confirm far-reaching differences in the intensity of corruption between different groups of countries classified by our political–economic modernization index. As a part of its annual survey, Transparency International asked a representative sample of citizens from most EECA countries whether they had given at least one bribe over the preceding twelve months. The average rate of affirmative responses for countries in our low and low–medium modernization groups was 29 percent, compared to only 16 percent for countries in our medium–high and high groups (Transparency International, 2013).

Our interviews with local managers confirm this quantitative data. "Everyone pays bribes here," explains a manager from the Kyrgyz Republic. "It's part of everyday life. Petty bribes from all levels of administration are commonplace. Court prosecutors are especially prone to this. Bribery is crazy."[20] A Chechen interviewee adds a level of nuance to this conclusion, suggesting that governmental officials encourage businesspeople to give bribes or otherwise break the law not only to benefit immediately but also to increase their power to harass the business later: "It is the whole system. Officials give businesses freedom not to follow the rules. Even more, they want the culture of not following the rules to be created, so that they have more power to harass businesses when they want."[21] This opinion is corroborated by corruption research in Russia: "Once the company has paid a bribe, bureaucratic 'raiders' can use this violation of the law for their own purposes: they may threaten the company to bring this information to the relevant authorities if the company . . . refuse[s] to give them [more] bribes" (Gans-Morse, 2012a: 6; see also Gans-Morse, 2012b).

The level of such bureaucratic harassment is substantial. The aforementioned Transparency International report asked EECA citizens whether they had ever been asked to pay a bribe by a governmental official. In countries in the low and low–medium modernization groups, the average percentage of affirmative responses was 43 percent, compared to only 23 percent in medium–high and high groups (Transparency International, 2013). Our interviewees were in full agreement that the major targets of such bribery extortion are ILEs: "Raiding companies by tax auditors is more the case with [ILEs] because it is more likely to get a bribe from them";[22] "I have heard of *no case* where an unconnected business won against the illegal action of government."[23]

SIEs, by contrast, are too powerful and too well connected to be approached by ordinary bureaucrats who intend to extort a bribe. Instead, they use bribery and nepotism much more proactively. "The country is run by oligarchs who have excellent connections with the government," reports a manager from Ukraine.[24] "Local firms use influence peddling with connections in governments and, of course, bribes," concurs a Kosovar interviewee.[25] "Big local companies are better situated to initiate and lobby for favorable laws. Local companies also, in general, take more risk in their relations with governments," concludes our source in Armenia.[26]

This environment, characterized by extremely well-connected SIEs and ILEs struggling to survive in the face of frequent governmental abuse, poses challenges for the managers of MNEs operating in low and low–medium modernization EECA markets. Our interviewees suggest that MNEs rarely try to compete for influence with SIEs. "Since large local companies are often state owned, they do not fear MNEs. They can defend their interests well," observes a manager from Russia.[27] Instead, MNEs try to leverage their strengths and international legitimacy to avoid the harassment often suffered by ILEs. Going to court, or to international arbitration, may be an important part of this harassment-prevention strategy. Even if the company loses its case against the government in a politically influenced court, the lengthy proceedings and the corresponding negative publicity for the country may deter bureaucrats from "raiding" the MNE in the future. "Preventing precedents is important for MNEs. If you do not sue, the appetite of the [corrupt] officials will grow," argues an MNE manager from Moldova.[28] The MNEs may also defend themselves by garnering support from international actors. "If their interests are endangered, MNEs may use the power of the international community," observes our Armenian interviewee.[29] The aforementioned Moldovan manager revealed that his company frequently seeks support from international organizations "so that the laws that the parliament is considering will not destroy our business."[30]

Even if their reactive, harassment-preventing strategies are somewhat effective, MNE managers in poorly modernized EECA countries recognize their competitive disadvantages in non-market areas. "For my multinational law firm, local law firms are a threat," observes a senior professional from Azerbaijan. "They are dangerous because they use administrative connections and, through deals, corruption. We cannot do that."[31] Many MNEs simply decide not to enter, which further reduces the number (and concomitant political influence) of MNEs in a country. "Our law firm has made a conscious decision not to open a Kiev office," admits a partner in an international law firm.[32] "We have very few multinational companies," points out a manager from Tajikistan.[33]

Highly modernized EECA countries

One of the most important changes to take place as an EECA economy develops and modernizes is the erosion of the previously dominant position of SIEs. These large companies are often privatized and acquired by multinational investors. Such acquisitions often bring profound cultural changes to the former SIEs, but they can also affect the strategic approaches of the acquiring MNEs. This latter change may be encouraged by two factors. First, a modernizing market also grows, and thus its attractiveness for MNEs increases. If a market is large enough, an MNE may devote the resources and managerial attention needed to design more proactive market and non-market strategies.[34] Second, as a market develops, the availability of qualified human capital rises. Instead of relying solely on Western managers sent to EECA on short-term assignments, the MNE now has the option of hiring capable local managers (Giroud and Scott-Kennel, 2009). Our interviewee from Moldova explains, "These local managers stay in their positions for years – they do not come and go every two to three years. And thus they can build local contacts, a network."[35] "In the 1990s, there were a lot of 'paratroopers' from the US or Britain," recalls a manager from Poland. "Later, however, management [of many MNEs] was taken over by Poles. And their cultural background is different."[36] "MNEs I have worked with employ many Macedonians and are much less centralized in their management than local companies," observes our interviewee in Skopje.[37]

Host country managers are more able to pursue proactive non-market strategies. A telling example is an energy utility company in an EU11 country, where our interviewee is a manager. The firm hired this manager when it was still state-owned and worked there during its acquisition by a major multinational. After the acquisition, the parent company retained half of the local management board members; the other half now consists of foreign managers with extensive EECA experience. The company lobbies local regulators and engages key political constituencies. It also leverages the influence of its parent company to lobby host country governments through "European politics."[38]

In Poland, as local oligarchs like Ryszard Krauze and Aleksander Gudzowaty were tainted by political and financial scandals (Brzostek, 2013; Trębski and Piński, 2007), their influential positions in the social and business hierarchy was captured by CEOs of host country affiliates of MNEs. Among them is the former Prime Minister Jan Bielecki, who, after leaving politics, was the long-time CEO of Unicredit in Poland (*Wprost*, 2011). Another example is Henryka Bochniarz – the chairwoman of a major business lobby and the CEO of Boeing in Eastern Europe (Stanek, 2013). "Multinationals are no longer afraid to be actively engaged in Poland. We are more or less Europe now," concludes a local management consultant.[39] "There is no huge difference between local and foreign companies today. If, as an MNE, you have good local connections, it helps to act as a lobbyist to influence legislation," concurs a manager from Slovakia.[40] "When MNEs come to Georgia, they leverage already existing connections with the government. I have worked with lots of MNE directors and they prepare the ground."[41]

The growth in the economic and political significance of MNEs influences the remaining SIEs. "Since the EU integration process began, MNEs are perceived to be more powerful than local firms. In the past, local firms felt confident because they had local political connections. This has changed," observes a manager from Serbia.[42] In response to the new standards brought in by MNEs, and the generally changing political culture, local firms must abandon blatant bribery and turn to more risk-averse tactics to influence public administrators. Using politically popular arguments in support of protectionist of corporatist policies is clearly one such tactic. For instance, in Croatia, a retail chain owned by a local conglomerate successfully lobbied the government to launch a "Let's Buy Croatian" campaign.[43] Similarly, in Slovakia, "the activities of the Association of Automotive Industry, the umbrella organization defending the interests of the sector, have been said to influence a whole range of policies . . . including taxation, education and state-supported applied research" (Haughton and Malová, 2007: 3; see also Rybář, 2011). In Slovenia, powerful labor unions succeeded in their lobbying for far-reaching wage regulations, which benefited a number of private firms in addition to the public sector (Frane et al., 2009). In Latvia in 2011, the self-governing association of attorneys decided to strengthen the admissions rules for new lawyers.[44] While this strengthening was rationalized in terms of policies designed to foster increased professionalization in the legal profession, another obvious goal was to limit the entry of new lawyers, since the number of qualified, practicing attorneys "has been steadily increasing since the 1990s."[45]

Implications for managers

Our conclusions suggest that economic and political modernization has exerted an important impact on the evolution of non-market strategies in the EECA region in two ways. First, as economic and political modernization proceeds, both MNEs and their local counterparts (SIEs and ILEs) moderate the degree of risk they take in their non-market strategies. This impact appears to be greatest on SIEs and ILEs who begin to formalize their non-market strategies through a greater emphasis on lobbying, participation in tendering processes, and eschewing bribery, nepotism, and violence. Of course, the EU integration process that has brought in sixteen new member states and built varying degrees of association with other EECA countries is the primary driving force for this evolution. It may also help MNEs in their non-market strategies in the region since formalized non-market strategies, such as lobbying and corporatism, play into the hands of these types of firms, given their good connections and considerable resources at the EU level. For those EECA countries remote from the EU integration process and with low modernization, our research suggests that riskier non-market strategies are continuing – especially among local firms.

The second impact that modernization has exerted is the increasingly proactive non-market strategy posture displayed by MNEs, SIEs, and ILEs alike. Of note is that the bigger impact here is on the MNE which in low-modernization contexts will tend to use international organizations (World Bank, IMF, EU) as a means of exerting influence over EECA governments or use litigation through the court systems at national and international levels to sway decisions in its favor. Once a country becomes more modernized, the MNE is able to take a more proactive posture through more transparent participation in public tenders, corporatism, and lobbying through industry associations.

The implications for management are reasonably clear. First, MNEs need to become more proactive in their non-market strategies as economic modernization proceeds. Moreover, the active support for EU integration in the EECA region would appear to strengthen their hand in those countries. One country of note that remains outside the formal EU integration process yet has embarked upon significant economic and political modernization is Georgia.

Here, our research suggests that, even without EU integration, modernization has strengthened the hands of MNEs.

Second, SIEs will maintain their relatively strong position in countries that do not modernize. It is therefore in SIEs' interest to resist economic modernization and it should be expected that they will also resist pressures to integrate with the EU. MNEs are forced to adopt reactive postures in these environments, weakening their sources of competitive advantage.

Third, the position of ILEs is not as clear as those of MNEs and SIEs since they lack the financial and competitive resources of MNEs and the domestic political connections of SIEs. As a country modernizes, the ILE needs to adjust its non-market strategies more in line with those of MNEs through professionalization of its non-market strategy. This could be enhanced by forming alliances with MNEs in the local market, leveraging local market knowledge in exchange for opportunities to develop greater professionalization as well as building networks abroad.

Notes

1 The research on which this chapter is based would not have been possible were it not for extremely generous help from alumni of the Central European University Business School, Adema Yeshmagambetova, Oana Jajae, Umida Khusankhodjaeva, Károly Konkoly, Anna Zubitskaya, as well as from Anna Osińska, Maja Munivrana Vajda, Leszek Stypułkowski, and Dominika Sypniewska. Outstanding research assistance from Esztella Fazekas and generous financial assistance from the Central European University Business School are also gratefully acknowledged. Mel Horwitch provided valuable comments on earlier drafts.

2 Telephone interview conducted by M. Kisilowski with an anonymous management consultant in Yerewan, Armenia. December 7, 2013. Transcript on file with the authors.

3 Telephone interview conducted by Y. Akbar with an anonymous managing director of a local consulting firm in Skopje, Macedonia. December 21, 2013. Transcript on file with the authors.

4 Telephone interview conducted by M. Kisilowski with an anonymous employee of an international organization in Baku, Azerbaijan. December 12, 2013. Transcript on file with the authors.

5 Telephone interview conducted by M. Kisilowski with an anonymous corporate lawyer in Dushanbe. December 19, 2013. Transcript on file with the authors.

6 Telephone interview conducted by M. Kisilowski with an anonymous leader of a nonprofit organization in Grozny, Chechnya. December 3, 2013. Transcript on file with the authors.

7 Telephone interview conducted by M. Kisilowski with an anonymous middle manager of a large local production company in Kiev, Ukraine. December 12, 2013. Transcript on file with the authors.

8 Telephone interview conducted by Y. Akbar with an anonymous academic in Prisztina, Kosovo. December 10, 2013. Transcript on file with the authors.

9 Telephone interview conducted by M. Kisilowski with an anonymous country manager of a multinational company in Chisinau, Moldova. December 18, 2013. Transcript on file with the authors.

10 Telephone interview conducted by M. Kisilowski with an anonymous country manager of a multinational company in Chisinau, Moldova. December 18, 2013. Transcript on file with the authors.

11 Telephone interview conducted by M. Kisilowski with an anonymous management consultant in Yerewan, Armenia. December 7, 2013. Transcript on file with the authors.

12 Personal communication to M. Kisilowski from an anonymous management consultant in Bucharest, Romania. November 11, 2013. On file with the authors.

13 Interview conducted by M. Kisilowski with an anonymous general manager of a small privately held business in the education sector in Warsaw, Poland. November 11, 2013. Transcript on file with the authors.

14 Telephone interview conducted by Y. Akbar with an anonymous academic in Prisztina, Kosovo. December 10, 2013. Transcript on file with the authors.

15 Telephone interview conducted by M. Kisilowski with an anonymous freelance management consultant in Bratislava, Slovakia. December 13, 2013. Transcript on file with the authors.

16 Interview conducted by Y. Akbar with an anonymous middle manager in a foreign-owned financial institution in Belgrade, Serbia. December 12, 2013. Transcript on file with the authors.

17 Telephone interview conducted by M. Kisilowski with an anonymous leader of a nonprofit organization in Grozny, Chechnya. December 3, 2013. Transcript on file with the authors.

18 In the 1990s, two legitimate Polish entrepreneurs were harassed aggressively by a member of an organized-crime group. Having received no help from the authorities, they killed the harasser, and were later sentenced to twenty-five years in prison (Wróblewski, 2001).

19 Telephone interview conducted by M. Kisilowski with an anonymous manager in an international aid organization in Kazakhstan. November 20, 2013. Transcript on file with the authors.

20 Telephone interview conducted by Y. Akbar with an anonymous local employee of a foreign diplomatic mission in Bishkek, Kyrgyz Republic. December 17, 2013. Transcript on file with the authors.

21 Telephone interview conducted by M. Kisilowski with an anonymous leader of a nonprofit organization in Grozny, Chechnya. December 3, 2013. Transcript on file with the authors.

22 Telephone interview conducted by M. Kisilowski with an anonymous corporate lawyer in an international law firm in Baku, Azerbaijan. December 18, 2013. Transcript on file with the authors.

23 Telephone interview conducted by M. Kisilowski with an anonymous leader of a nonprofit organization in Grozny, Chechnya. December 3, 2013. Transcript on file with the authors. (The emphasis was clear in the conversation.)

24 Telephone interview conducted by M. Kisilowski with an anonymous partner of a multinational law firm active in Ukraine. December 13, 2013. Transcript on file with the authors.

25 Telephone interview conducted by Y. Akbar with an anonymous academic in Prisztina, Kosovo. December 10, 2013. Transcript on file with the authors.

26 Telephone interview conducted by M. Kisilowski with an anonymous management consultant in Yerewan, Armenia. December 7, 2013. Transcript on file with the authors.

27 Telephone interview conducted by Y. Akbar with an anonymous finance director of a company in the healthcare sector in Moscow, Russia. December 13, 2013. Transcript on file with the authors.

28 Telephone interview conducted by M. Kisilowski with an anonymous country manager of a multinational company in Chisinau, Moldova. December 18, 2013. Transcript on file with the authors.

29 Telephone interview conducted by M. Kisilowski with an anonymous management consultant in Yerewan, Armenia. December 7, 2013. Transcript on file with the authors.

30 Telephone interview conducted by M. Kisilowski with an anonymous country manager of a multinational company in Chisinau, Moldova. December 18, 2013. Transcript on file with the authors.

31 Telephone interview conducted by M. Kisilowski with an anonymous corporate lawyer in an international law firm in Baku, Azerbaijan. December 18, 2013. Transcript on file with the authors.

32 Telephone interview conducted by M. Kisilowski with an anonymous partner of a multinational law firm active in Ukraine. December 13, 2013. Transcript on file with the authors.

33 Telephone interview conducted by M. Kisilowski with an anonymous legal expert in Dushanbe, Tajikistan. December 19, 2013. Transcript on file with the authors.

34 Interview conducted by M. Kisilowski with an anonymous marketing manager of an international company in a highly regulated industry in Warsaw, Poland. December 3, 2013. Transcript on file with the authors.

35 Telephone interview conducted by M. Kisilowski with an anonymous country manager of a multinational company in Chisinau, Moldova. December 18, 2013. Transcript on file with the authors.

36 Telephone interview conducted by M. Kisilowski with an anonymous senior associate at an international law firm in Warsaw, Poland. December 27, 2013. Transcript on file with the authors.

37 Telephone interview conducted by Y. Akbar with an anonymous managing director of a local consulting firm in Skopje, Macedonia. December 21, 2013. Transcript on file with the authors.

38 Telephone interview conducted by M. Kisilowski with an anonymous middle manager of a multinational company in a highly regulated market in Central Europe. December 19, 2013. Transcript on file with the authors.

39 Interview conducted by M. Kisilowski with an anonymous associate in a multinational management consulting firm in Warsaw, Poland. November 23, 2013. Transcript on file with the authors.

40 Interview conducted by Y. Akbar with an anonymous country manager in a foreign-owned Slovakian real estate firm in Vienna, Austria. November 21, 2013. Transcript on file with the authors.

41 Telephone interview conducted by Y. Akbar with an anonymous middle manager in a foreign-owned financial institution in Tbilisi, Georgia. December 10, 2013. Transcript on file with the authors.

42 Interview conducted by Y. Akbar with an anonymous middle manager in a foreign-owned financial institution in Belgrade, Serbia. December 12, 2013. Transcript on file with the authors.

43 Personal communication to M. Kisilowski from an anonymous academic in Zagreb, Croatia. November 3, 2013. On file with the authors.

44 Personal communication to M. Kisilowski from Elina Kaminska, Secretary General of the Latvian Council of Sworn Advocates. October 29, 2013. On file with the authors.

45 Telephone interview conducted by M. Kisilowski with an anonymous partner in a local law firm in Riga, Latvia. December 17, 2013. Transcript on file with the authors.

Bibliography

€FIN. (2013). "Tineret, nepotism si performanta economica." Available at: www.efin.ro/articole_financiare/tineret_nepotism_si_performanta_economica.html (accessed November 18, 2014).

Akbar, Y. H. (2003a). *The Multinational Enterprise, EU Enlargement and Central Europe: The Effects of Regulatory Convergence*. New York: Palgrave Macmillan.

— (2003b). "Slip Sliding away? The Changing Politics of European Car Distribution." *Business and Politics*, 5(2), 175–92.

Akbar, Y. H., and McBride, J. B. (2004). "Multinational Enterprise Strategy, Foreign Direct Investment and Economic Development: The Case of the Hungarian Banking Industry." *Journal of World Business*, 39(1), 89–105.

Akbar, Y., Nemeth, A., and Niemeier, H.-M. (2014). "Here We Go Again: The Permanently Failing Organization: An Application to the Airline Industry in Central and East Europe." *Journal of Air Transport Management*, 35(1), 1–11.

Al Khattab, A., Anchor, J., and Davies, E. (2007). "Managerial Perceptions of Political Risk in International Projects." *International Journal of Project Management*, 25(7), 734–43.

Arnold, D. J., and Quelch, J. A. (1998). "New Strategies in Emerging Markets." *Sloan Management Review*, 40(1), 7–20.

Baltic Times. (2014). "Estonia Needs to Address Corruption Issues, Says Report." February 4. Available at: www.baltictimes.com/news/articles/34333/#.U1o-rl5dqfM (accessed April 26, 2014).

Barney, J. B., and Hesterly, W. S. (2010). *Strategic Management and Competitive Advantage: Concepts and Cases*. 3rd edition. Boston, MA: Prentice-Hall.

Bartlett, C. A., and Ghoshal, S. (1995). *Transnational Management: Text, Cases, and Readings in Cross-Border Management*. 2nd edition. Chicago: Irwin.

BBC News Online (2008). "EU Suspends Funding for Bulgaria." July 23. Available at: http://news.bbc.co.uk/2/hi/europe/7520736.stm (accessed April 26, 2014).

Blumentritt, T. P., and Nigh, D. (2002). "The Integration of Subsidiary Political Activities in Multinational Corporations." *Journal of International Business Studies*, 33(1), 57–77.

Boddewyn, J. J. (1988). "Political Aspects of MNE Theory." *Journal of International Business Studies*, 19(3), 341–63.

Boddewyn, J. J., and Brewer, T. L. (1994). "International-Business Political Behavior: New Theoretical Directions." *Academy of Management Review*, 19(1), 119–43.

Bohr, A. (2004). "Regionalism in Central Asia: New Geopolitics, Old Regional Order." *International Affairs*, 80(3), 485–502.

Brewer, T. L. (1985). *Political Risks in International Business: New Directions for Research, Management, and Public Policy*. London: Praeger.

Brzostek, A. (2013). "Ryszard Krauze: Kiedyś oligarcha zwany cesarzem, dziś zadłużony wyprzedaje aktywa i sprzęt domowy." Available at: http://twarzebiznesu.pl/artykuly/732992,ryszard-krauze-prokom-oligarcha-afera-gruntowa.html (accessed November 18, 2014).

Buckley, N. (2011). "Russians in London: Super Rich in Court." Available at: www.ft.com/cms/s/0/6c2ee702-f0d5-11e0-aec8-00144feab49a.html-axzz2qpfk6Dp6 (accessed November 18, 2014).

Butler, K. C., and Joaquin, D. C. (1998). "A Note on Political Risk and the Required Return on Foreign Direct Investment." *Journal of International Business Studies*, 29(3), 599–607.

Central Anticorruption Bureau. (2013). "Report on Activities of Central Anticorruption Bureau in 2011." Available at: www.antykorupcja.gov.pl/ak/analizy-i-raporty/raporty-cba/8706,Raport-z-dzialalnosci-CBA-za-2011-rok.html (accessed November 18, 2014).

Central Asia–Caucasus Institute. (2006). "Confronting Corruption in Chechnya." Available at: http://old.cacianalyst.org/?q=node/3801 (accessed April 26, 2014).

Clark, E. (1996). *Managing Risk in International Business: Techniques and Applications.* New York: Thomson Business Press.

— (1997). "Valuing Political Risk." *Journal of International Money and Finance,* 16(3), 477.

Diamonte, R. L., Liew, J. M., and Stevens, R. J. (1996). "Political Risk in Emerging and Developed Markets." *Financial Analysts Journal,* 52(3), 71–6.

EC. (2010). "State Aid: Commission Opens In-depth Investigation into Hungarian Support Measures for National Airline Malév." Available at: http://europa.eu/rapid/press-release_IP-10-1753_en.htm (accessed November 18, 2014).

— (2012a). "Public Procurement Indicators 2011." Available at: http://ec.europa.eu/internal_market/publicprocurement/docs/modernising_rules/public-procurement-indicators-2011_en.pdf (accessed November 18, 2014).

— (2012b). "State Aid: Commission Approves Restructuring Aid for Czech Airlines." Available at: http://europa.eu/rapid/press-release_IP-12-981_en.htm (accessed November 18, 2014).

— (2013a). "EU Report: Trade Protectionism Still on Rise across the World." Available at: http://europa.eu/rapid/press-release_IP-13-807_en.htm (accessed November 18, 2014).

— (2013b). "State Aid: Commission Opens In-depth Inquiry into €200 Million Restructuring Aid for LOT Polish Airlines." Available at: http://europa.eu/rapid/press-release_IP-13-1045_en.htm (accessed November 18, 2014).

— (2014). State Aid Weekly e-News, No. 29/14, 5 September 2014. Available at http://ec.europa.eu/competition/state_aid/newsletter/05092014.pdf (accessed March 14, 2015).

Epstein, R. A. (2013). "Central and East European Bank Responses to the Financial 'Crisis': Do Domestic Banks Perform Better in a Crisis than their Foreign-Owned Counterparts?" *Journal of European Public Policy,* 65(2), 528.

Euractiv. (2013). "CAP 2014–20: A Long Road to Reform." Available at: www.euractiv.com/cap/cap-reform-2014-2020-linksdossier-508393 (accessed November 18, 2014).

European Bank for Reconstruction and Development. (2013). "Stuck in Transition?" Available at: http://tr.ebrd.com/tr13/en (accessed November 18, 2014).

Finantistii. (2012). "Notarii, executorii si avocatii in atentia Consiliului Concurentei pentru practicarea de onorarii minime, restrictionarea numarului de birouri si a publicitatii." Available at: www.finantistii.ro/actualitate/notarii-executorii-si-avocatii-in-atentia-consiliului-concurentei-pentru-practicarea-de-onorarii-minime-restrictionarea-numarului-de-birouri-si-a-publicitatii-75244 (accessed November 18, 2014).

Fitzpatrick, M. (1983). "The Definition and Assessment of Political Risk in International Business: A Review of the Literature." *Academy of Management Review,* 8(2), 249–54.

Floyd, S. W., and Wooldridge, B. (2000). *Building Strategy from the Middle: Reconceptualizing Strategy Process.* Thousand Oaks, CA: Sage.

Frane, A., Primož, K., and Matevž, T. (2009). "Varieties of Capitalism in Eastern Europe (with Special Emphasis on Estonia and Slovenia)." *Communist and Post-Communist Studies,* 42(1), 65–81.

Freedom House. (2013). "Nations in Transit." Available at: www.freedomhouse.org/report-types/nations-transit (accessed November 18, 2014).

— (2014). *Freedom in the World.* 41st Edition. New York: Freedom House.

Gans-Morse, J. (2012a). "Delat' biznes v Rossii: novye ugrozy, novye otvety." Working paper, Northwestern University.

— (2012b). "The End of a Violent Era: The Role of Force in Russian Business Conflicts." Working paper, Northwestern University.

Gawthorpe, S. (2010). "Unstable Membership: Bulgaria, Corruption, and Policy of the European Union." *New Voices in Public Policy,* 4, 1–14.

Gelbudaa, M., Meyerb, K. M., and Deliosc, A. (2008). "International Business and Institutional Development in Central and Eastern Europe." *Journal of International Management,* 14(1), 1–11.

Giroud, A., and Scott-Kennel, J. (2009). "MNE Linkages in International Business: A Framework for Analysis." *International Business Review,* 18(6), 555–66.

Gounev, P. (2006). "Bulgaria's Security Industry." In A. Bryden and M. Caparini (eds.), *Private Actors in Security Governance.* Berlin: Verlag, pp. 109–28.

Grinold, R. C. (2010). *Active Portfolio Management: A Quantitative Approach for Providing Superior Returns and Controlling Risk.* New York: McGraw-Hill.

Haughton, T., and Malová, D. (2007). "Open for Business: Slovakia as a New Member State." *International Issues and Slovak Foreign Policy Affairs*, 16(2), 3.

Hendley, K., Murrell, P., and Ryterman, R. (2000). "Law, Relationships and Private Enforcement: Transactional Strategies of Russian Enterprises." *Europe–Asia Studies*, 52(4), 627–56.

Hillman, A. J., and Hitt, M. A. (1999). "Corporate Political Strategy Formulation: A Model of Approach, Participation, and Strategy Decisions." *Academy of Management Review*, 24(4), 825–42.

Hillman, A. J., and Wan, W. P. (2005). "The Determinants of MNE Subsidiaries' Political Strategies: Evidence of Institutional Duality." *Journal of International Business Studies*, 36(3), 322–40.

Horizon 2020. (2013). "EU Offers EUR 15 Billion to Fund Research in 2014, 2015." Available at: http://horizon-magazine.eu/article/eu-offers-eur-15-billion-fund-research-2014-2015_en.html (accessed November 18, 2014).

Horwitch, M., and Kisilowski, M. (2014). "Joining the Twenty-first Century and the Need for Creative Managerial Professionalism." In M. Kisilowski (ed.), *Free Market in its Twenties: Modern Business Decision Making in Central and Eastern Europe*. Budapest: CEU Press.

Hungarian Spectrum. (2013) "The Troubled Tobacco Shop Concessions." Available at: http://hungarianspectrum.wordpress.com/2013/09/16/the-troubled-tobacco-shop-concessions/ (accessed April 26, 2014).

HVG. (2013). "Megtizedeli a pesti taxisokat az új rendszer." Available at: http://hvg.hu/kkv/20131016_Megtizedeli_a_pesti_taxisokat_az_uj_rends (accessed November 18, 2014).

Index. (2014). "Ennyivel fizetjük le, akit le kell." Availabe at: http://index.hu/chart/2014/01/10/ennyivel_fizetjuk_le_akit_le_kell (accessed November 18, 2014).

Institute for Market Economics. (2009). "Effects of Regulation of Selected Free Professions in Bulgaria: Auditors, Architects, Engineers, Pharmacists." Sofia: Institute for Market Economics.

Iwasaki, I., and Suzuki, T. (2007). "Transition Strategy, Corporate Exploitation, and State Capture: An Empirical Analysis of the Former Soviet States." *Communist and Post-Communist Studies*, 40(4), 393–422.

Jarzabkowski, P. (2008). "Shaping Strategy as a Structuration Process." *Academy of Management Journal*, 51(4), 621–50.

King, Ch. (2010). *Extreme Politics: Nationalism, Violence, and the End of Eastern Europe*. Oxford: Oxford University Press.

Kobrin, S. J. (1979). "Political Risk: A Review and Reconsideration." *Journal of International Business Studies*, 10(1), 67–80.

— (1982). *Managing Political Risk Assessment: Strategic Response to Environmental Change*. Berkeley: University of California Press.

— (1987). "Testing the Bargaining Hypothesis in the Manufacturing Sector in Developing Countries." *International Organization*, 41(4), 609–38.

Kotzian, P. (2007). "Arguing and Bargaining in International Negotiations: On the Application of the Frame-Selection Model and its Implications." *International Political Science Review*, 28(1), 79–99.

Krkoska, L., and Robeck, K. (2009). "Crime, Business Conduct and Investment Decisions: Enterprise Survey Evidence from 34 Countries in Europe and Asia." *Review of Law and Economics*, 5(1), 493–516.

Kühn, Z. (2012). *Judicial Administration Reforms in Central-Eastern Europe: Lessons to be Learned*. Berlin: Springer.

Marx, K. (2004). *The Role of the Social Context for Strategy-making: Examining the Impact of Embeddedness on the Performance of Strategic Initiatives*. Wiesbaden: Deutscher Universitätsverlag.

Mathews, J. (2006). "Dragon Multinationals: New Players in 21st Century Globalization." *Asia Pacific Journal of Management*, 23(1), 5–27.

McDermott, R. (1998). *Risk-taking in International Politics: Prospect Theory in American Foreign Policy*. Ann Arbor: University of Michigan Press.

Meyer, K. E., Estrin, S., Bhaumik, S. K., and Peng, M. W. (2009). "Institutions, Resources, and Entry Strategies in Emerging Economies." *Strategic Management Journal*, 30(1), 61–80.

Oxford Analytica. (2014). "Corruption Will Cost Romania and Bulgaria EU Funds." February 7. Available at: www.oxan.com/display.aspx?ItemID=DB188621 (accessed April 26, 2014).

Palepu, K. G., and Khanna, T. (2010). *Winning in Emerging Markets: A Road Map for Strategy and Execution*. Cambridge, MA: Harvard Business School Press.

Peng, M. W., and Luo, Y. (2000). "Managerial Ties and Firm Performance in a Transition Economy: The Nature of a Micro–Macro Link." *Academy of Management Journal*, 43(3), 486–501.

Politics.hu. (2013). "Socialists Accuse Fidesz of Nepotism in Tobacco Nationalization Scheme." Available at: www.politics.hu/20130425/socialists-accuse-fidesz-of-nepotism-in-tobacco-nationalization-scheme/ (accessed November 18, 2014).

Porter, M. E. (1980). *Competitive Strategy: Techniques for Analyzing Industries and Competitors*. New York: Free Press.

Prague Watchdog. (2009). "Corruption in Chechnya – Interview with Jonathan Little." Available at: www.watchdog.cz/?show=000000-000024-000007-000001andlang=1 (accessed April 26, 2014).

Puck, J. F., Rogers, H., and Mohr, A. T. (2013). "Flying under the Radar: Foreign Firm Visibility and the Efficacy of Political Strategies in Emerging Economies." *International Business Review*, 22(6), 1021–33.

Rose-Ackerman, S. (1999). *Corruption and Government: Causes, Consequences, and Reform*. New York: Cambridge University Press.

Rybář, M. (2011). "National Determinants of International Preferences in Post-Communist Europe: The Case of Slovakia in the European Union." *Communist and Post-Communist Studies*, 44(3), 161–71.

Sethi, S. P., and Luther, K. A. N. (1986). "Political Risk Analysis and Direct Foreign Investment: Some Problems of Definition and Measurement." *California Management Review*, 28(2), 57.

Simon, J. D. (1984). "A Theoretical Perspective on Political Risk." *Journal of International Business Studies*, 15(3), 123–43.

Skipper, H. D. (2007). *Risk Management and Insurance: Perspectives in a Global Economy*. London: Blackwell.

Snider, H. W. (1991). "Risk Management: A Retrospective View." *Risk Management*, 38(4), 47–54.

Stanek, A. (2013). "Polak potrafi, czyli jak menedżerowie znad Wisły robią karierę w globalnych koncernach." Available at: www.biztok.pl/galeria/polak-potrafi-czyli-jak-menedzerowie-znad-wisly-robia-kariere-w-globalnych-koncernach_s9243/slide_3 (accessed November 18, 2014).

Stodghill, R. (2006). "Oil, Cash and Corruption." *New York Times*, November 5, 1.

Transparency International. (2013). "Corruption Perception Survey." Available at: www.transparency.org/research/cpi/overview (accessed November 18, 2014).

Trębski, C., and Piński, J. (2007). "Nowe taśmy Gudzowatego." Available at: www.wprost.pl/ar/100642/Nowe-tasmy-Gudzowatego (accessed November 18, 2014).

UNCTAD. (2013). "World Investment Report 2013." Available at http://unctad.org/en/Publications Library/wir2013_en.pdf (accessed November 18, 2014).

UNODC. (2013). "Business, Corruption and Crime in the Western Balkans." Available at: www.unodc.org/documents/data-and-analysis/statistics/corruption/Western_balkans_business_corruption_web.pdf (accessed November 18, 2014).

Uzmetronom. (2013). "Turki Namereny Sudit'sja." Available at: www.uzmetronom.com/2013/09/18/turki_namereny_suditsja.html (accessed November 18, 2014).

White, G. O., Hemphill, T. A., Joplin, J. R. W., and Marsh, L. A. (2014). "Wholly Owned Foreign Subsidiary Relation-Based Strategies in Volatile Environments." *International Business Review*, 23(1), 303–12.

Workman, M. (2012). "Bias in Strategic Initiative Continuance Decisions: Framing Interactions and HRD Practices." *Management Decision*, 50(1), 21–42.

World Bank. (2011). "Trends in Corruption and Regulatory Burden in Eastern Europe and Central Asia." Available at: http://siteresources.worldbank.org/ECAEXT/Resources/2011_report_fullreport.pdf (accessed November 18, 2014).

Wprost. (2011). "100 Najbardziej Wpływowych Polaków." November 7, 4.

Wright, M., Filatotchev, I., Hoskisson, R. E., and Peng, M. W. (2005). "Strategy Research in Emerging Economies: Challenging the Conventional Wisdom." *Journal of Management Studies*, 42(1), 1–33.

Wróblewski, B. (2001). "To Nie Był Dług." *Gazeta Wyborcza*, October 11.

22

Jeitinho Brasileiro

Adopting non-market strategies in Brazil

Susan Perkins and Ishva Minefee

Introduction

> "For my friends, anything – for my enemies, the law."
>
> *(Getulio Vargas, quoted in Plummer 2005)*

This quote, coined over fifty years ago by the former Brazilian president Getulio Vargas, describes how Brazil has historically valued personal loyalty over other societal responsibilities as dictated by the law. Though his regime has since passed, this sentiment remains true in Brazil's business environment, with familial and social ties influencing all too powerfully the manner in which business is conducted. The lingering habits from this historical context are still seen throughout Brazilian institutions and society, and they continue to be typified by two sets of rules – a set for insiders and a set for outsiders. Some obvious examples include dual class shares with and without voting rights, with the locals owning most of the former. Even more obvious are the different corporate governance regulations for Bolsa de Valores de São Paulo (BOVESPA) stock exchange listed firms (i.e., Novo Mercado versus classic BOVESPA), which require transparency of audited financials for some firms but not for others. These inconsistencies in the functioning of market-based rules, which are often usurped by the "rule of man," make it imperative for the naive foreign investment manager, unfamiliar with navigating this business context, to develop an astute non-market strategy. Otherwise, they will more likely than not fall prey to the expropriation traps set for foreign managers and investors.

This chapter on non-market strategy in Brazil provides both a context for market dynamics in Brazil and case examples of the institutional voids that require the most navigation. We expose the expropriation risks present in this complex corporate, legal, social, and political environment (Musacchio 2008; Perkins, Morck and Yeung 2014; Perkins and Zajac 2013; Schneider 2008) and show how foreign firms could benefit by developing a *jeitinho Brasileiro*, a Portuguese term that we use throughout this chapter which translates as "the Brazilian way of doing things." With the implementation of appropriate non-market strategies, a foreign investor can successfully navigate the tendentious institutional environment for which Brazil has become infamous.

First, we discuss the institutional context in Brazil to show why non-market strategies are needed in this host country context. We provide specific examples of mistakes foreign firms have made when entering Brazil and show how entering the market with a non-market strategy in place could have mitigated such risks. Next, we compare effective and ineffective strategies employed by foreign firms operating in Brazil. Finally, the chapter concludes with practical managerial implications and good *jeitinho* strategic moves for foreign investors seeking business opportunities in Brazil.

The Brazilian institutional context

As the largest economy in Latin America and the sixth-largest economy in the world (IMF 2013), Brazil is an attractive location for foreign direct investment (FDI). The success of the *Plano Real*, implemented in 1994, which tamed decades of hyperinflation, made Brazil's market rise relative to other global financial opportunities for FDI. However, institutional changes and market reforms have not kept pace with the country's swift economic expansion from eleventh-largest to sixth-largest economy. Much of the evolution toward a more market-based system is still unresolved and incomplete, leaving several institutional voids in this developing economy. For example, Brazil ranks 130th (out of 185) among countries listed on the World Bank's Ease of Doing Business Index (World Bank 2013). A high ranking on this index typically signals that the regulatory environment is conducive to entering a foreign market and operating a firm. Brazil's low ranking stems largely from the weak protections afforded to minority investors as well as the difficulties associated with enforcing contracts. It highlights the challenges foreign firms face when attempting to establish partnerships, whether through private equity, as joint venture partners or as minority shareholders in publicly listed firms. Moreover, the corporate governance and ownership structures in Brazil, which are far more complex for outsiders, comprise a unique set of hurdles for foreign firms trying to navigate local partnerships. Further exacerbating these problems is the fact that disputes are extremely difficult to resolve because of the lack of regulatory oversight and poor enforcement of institutional laws and rules. These core issues create a set of unique challenges germane to the institutional context in Brazil. Foreign firms must proceed with caution as a lack of understanding of Brazil's institutional environment can lead to business failure.

Corporate governance and ownership in Brazil

A common thread in the institutional environment of Brazil and other Latin American countries is the commonality in corporate governance and ownership structures of firms. It is estimated that approximately 80 percent of firms in Latin America are affiliated with pyramidal business groups (Perkins and Zajac 2013; Schneider 2008, 2009), more commonly called *grupos* or simply pyramidal groups. Scholars have consistently demonstrated that pyramidal groups are the dominant form of ownership structure in Brazil (Musacchio and Read 2007; Perkins and Zajac 2013). As defined by Khanna and Yafeh (2007: 331), this form of business group, with vertical chains of control, is a set of "legally independent firms, operating in multiple (often unrelated) industries, which are bound together by persistent formal (e.g., equity) and informal (e.g., family) ties." In addition, Perkins, McDonnell and Zajac (2012) show that these pyramidal groups are typically tied together through a detailed series of *acordo de acionistas* (shareholder agreements), which contractually specify governance clauses to maintain control and direct wealth flows to the dominant shareholders. Pyramidal business groups differ from widely held standalone firms, primarily found in the US, the UK, and Australia, in three fundamental ways:

- the top-tier firm, also known as the apex firm, both directly and indirectly controls all of the lower-tiered firms;
- intercorporate controlling equity blocks are commonly used to leverage and maintain ultimate control of the entire pyramid; and
- the apex firm's board members and owners (acting as both principals and agents) appoint the top management teams (e.g., family and friends) of every other firm in the group.

(Perkins, Morck and Yeung 2014)

In Brazil, nine of the ten largest firms are affiliated with family-owned groups (Fogel 2006). For example, Banco Itua, one of Brazil's largest banks, is owned by the Villela and Setubal families, within which ownership rights are secured by a series of shareholder agreements to maintain their controlling stakes in the pyramid. In a pyramidal ownership structure, the apex firm's managers delegate ownership among lower-tiered firms through both equity stakes and voting rights. On average, the main shareholder of a listed BOVESPA firm holds approximately 50 percent ownership of the firm, with higher averages of 80 percent ownership among the top three shareholders (Perkins and Zajac 2013: 6). To illustrate this point further, Table 22.1 shows that the ten largest private groups in Brazil are controlled, on average, by four shareholders owning 72 percent of the voting stakes of the firm.

A classic example is Grupo Pão de Açúcar, the oldest and one of the most successful supermarket chains in Brazil, which is owned by the Valentim do Santos Diniz family. The *grupo* was dominantly controlled by the Diniz family until 2005, when the ownership structure was reorganized to give control to their French retail partner Groupe Casino at the apex of the pyramid (see Figure 22.1).

This system is so ubiquitous in Brazil that it is rare to find a firm with a dispersed ownership structure. Even when dispersed ownership has been adopted, it rarely parallels the level of dispersion seen on the US, UK, and Australian stock exchanges. For example, the ten largest US-listed firms (including Procter & Gamble, AT&T, Disney, and McDonald's) on average have 190,000 shareholders (owners) and only rarely does any individual shareholder own more than 5 percent of shares.[1] In contrast, even the most diffusely owned Brazilian listed firm, Lojas Renner, one of Brazil's largest retailers, has only about 7000 shareholders,[2] and they all have parity voting and equity stakes. In this famous exception to typical Brazilian ownership, even managers found the company "difficult to run because the shareholders were so unaccustomed to the absence of a controlling blockholder" (Schneider 2008: 382). This points to the institutional emphasis placed on pyramidal group firms that are analogous to having a dominant controlling owner.

In many cases, Brazilian ownership structures also include some equity ownership, at least initially, for the government through either the Brazilian National Development Bank (BNDES) or the government employee pension fund, Previ (Musacchio and Lazzarini 2014). This government involvement often signifies a form of capitalism that aligns political interests with the economic interests of Brazil's elite families. Lazzarini (2010) termed this unique form of Brazilian capitalism *capitalismo de laços* ("capitalism of ties").

Table 22.1 Ten largest private Brazilian groups, 2006

Rank	Private Groups	Revenue (US$ billion)	Core Business	# of Main Shareholders	% Voting Shares	% Non-Voting Shares	% Total Shares
1	Bradesco	17,5	Banking	5	73	6	39
2	Itaúsa	16,8	Banking	6	49	17	29
3	Vale do Rio Doce	15,1	Mining	3	61	0.1	37
4	Ambev	12,3	Beverages	4	89	40	65
5	Ipiranga	12,0	Fuel distribution	5	31	41	37
6	Gerdau/Indac	10,9	Metallurgy	3	76	29	45
7	Telemar Norte Leste	10,1	Telecommunications	2	98	70	82
8	Odebrecht	10,0	Petrochemicals	3	60	2	31
9	Votorantim	9,5	Cement	5	100	18	60
10	Telefonica/Telesp	8,7	Telecommunications	2	85	89	89
	Means			**4**	**72**	**31**	**51**

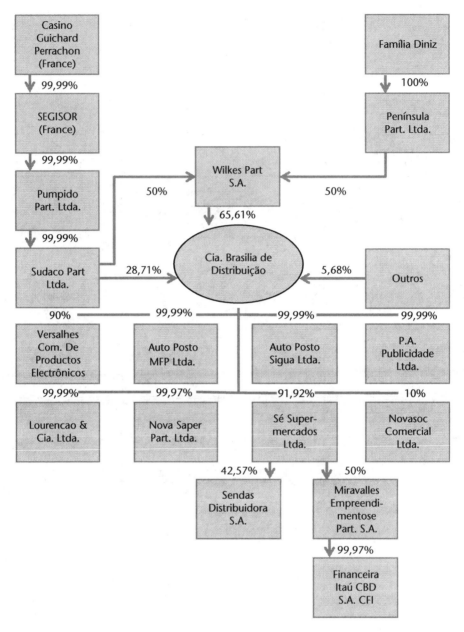

Figure 22.1   Grupo Pão de Açúcar

Source: www.revistavalor.com.br/home.aspx?pub=19&edicao=9 (accessed December 15, 2014).

The mystery of the pyramid

Pyramidal group owners also use small amounts of equity and large amounts of voting shares to control corporate assets through multiple tiers in the pyramid (Perkins, Morck and Yeung 2014; Schneider 2009). This disproportion of low-equity stakes and high levels of voting rights creates leverage in the pyramidal structure to gain control of far greater wealth than was invested. Let us expound here to illustrate this point clearly in Figure 22.2. Take, for example, this generic pyramidal group structure to think about how leverage is created through chains of control originating from the apex firm, where the voting stakes and equity stakes are usually 100 percent owned and controlled by the family. At the apex, the principals (owners) and agents (managers) of the firm are one and the same.

The key advantage of a pyramidal group is the leverage it provides for gaining control of the governance of the firm and the wealth creation of its legally tied lower-tiered firms. Leverage is critical to building pyramids because it allows a firm to subvert the wealth of outsiders (i.e., public shareholders or joint venture partners) tied to the pyramidal structure. Assuming a pyramidal group has $1 million to invest, so long as it maintains control at each tier level either directly or indirectly with more than 50 percent voting rights, the firm can split that equity into two lower-tiered companies by investing $0.5 million in each and gains control of more wealth by dispersing ownership across other shareholders. As a result, in the second tier, the family has control of $2 million in equity ($1 million invested by the family plus $1 million invested by outsiders) through a direct line of control. Two additional splits of these two second-tier firms create four firms worth $1 million each using the same direct and indirect control scheme. By the time the pyramidal structure has been split apart across

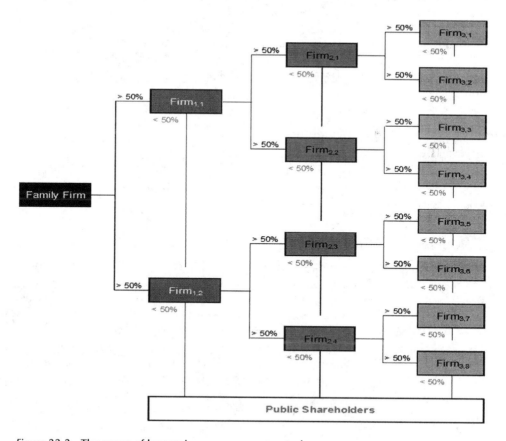

Figure 22.2 The game of leveraging governance control

four tiers in the control chain, the ultimate owner is able to manage $8 million of equity with only a $1 million investment.

This simplified example shows how a sophisticated pyramid could generate an 8:1 ratio of leverage with an unassuming outsider who might be accustomed to a 1:1 corporate govern-ance ratio between equity stakes and voting rights (i.e., the one vote, one share norms of US stock exchanges). The strategies most frequently used by pyramidal groups to connect these tiered structures are creating holding companies, super voting rights shares, and small equity investments at the lowest tiers in the pyramid. When transparency rules are weak in Brazil (we address this point more extensively in the next section), these strategic behaviors may be indications of exploitative expropriation schemes.

The leverage created through these vertical[3] control chains shifts the corporate govern-ance incentives for wealth maximization of the lower-tiered firms, which are usually the listed firms or joint ventures with outsiders, to the dominant shareholder of the apex firm to maximize their "private benefits of control" (Bebchuk, Kraakman and Triantis 2000), which can range from indirect financial benefits, such as on-the-job consumption and pur-chase of social status using corporate resources, to direct financial benefits, such as transfer-ring corporate funds across units of the control pyramid. Higher-tier firms in the pyramidal group, closer to the apex, are rarely listed on the BOVESPA stock exchange, which makes the ultimate owner more difficult to identify. Thus, transparency of the ultimate owners at the apex is often obfuscated when the disproportion between the leverage of voting rights and equity stakes is high. If the ambition of the ultimate owner is to control the firm in order to extract private benefits, exposing this expropriation risk to shareholders unfamiliar with such ownership schemes could deter even the least prudent investors.

The most severe expropriation risks in this scenario involve "tunneling," when the con-trolling owner siphons off the profits, and "asset shifting," moving the rights to assets from one part of the ownership structure to another that is directly or indirectly controlled by the apex owner. Such expropriation risks have led Khanna and Yafeh (2007) to liken pyramidal groups to "parasites" who benefit at the expense of minority shareholders. There is anecdotal evidence of tunneling schemes in other regions of the globe where pyramidal groups are ubiquitous (France, Belgium, and Italy – Johnson, La Porta, Lopez-de-Silanes and Shleifer 2000; India – Bertrand, Mehta and Mullainathan 2002; and South Korea – Bae, Kang and Kim 2002), and it is commonplace in Brazil.

The case of Brasil Telecom and Citigroup

One clear example of this parasitic behavior of pyramidal groups and how the expropriation schemes play out is Citigroup's joint venture in the Brazilian telecommunications industry. Brasil Telecom, a Brazilian telecom service provider and BOVESPA listed firm, was owned by a nexus of holding companies arranged in six tiers, which made the ownership structure quite complex. The known joint venture partner investors were Citigroup's CVC Fund (45 percent equity stake), Grupo Opportunity (10 percent) and an onshore private equity fund, II-FIA (with the remaining 45 percent). Citigroup was clear about its participation in the holding company Zain, the second-tier firm (see Figure 22.3), which was owned by the three joint venture partners. However, investors were less certain about the entire chain of control, especially the implications of Citigroup's ownership ties to firms in the lower tiers. Though not a deal breaker from the outset, this issue of control became critical because it determined which partner ultimately had rights to the profits and assets of the joint venture. Citigroup's assumption that its 45 percent equity stakes translated into 45 percent rights to the distribution of the profits and assets turned out to be fatal. The following was revealed in subsequent court proceedings:

> [Within the control chain Zain] holds 68.28 percent of the voting shares in Invitel S.A., which in turn holds 99.99 percent of the voting shares in Techold, which owns 61.98 percent of the equity stakes in Solpart. Of the remaining shares in Solpart, 38 percent are held by Telecom Italia and 0.02 percent by Timepart. Solpart holds 51 percent of the voting shares in Brasil Telecom Participações (BTP) and BTP, the preferred and common shares of which are traded publicly in Brazil, holds 99.07 percent of the voting shares in Brasil Telecom.[4]

The emergent reality revealed that Citigroup's invested equity stakes were disproportionate to the voting stakes, specifically within the lower tiers of the joint venture's ownership structure (see Figure 22.3). The voting stakes structure deviated dramatically from the shareholder agreement's original terms, which stipulated shares proportionate to invested capital. Although lack of disclosure is common practice in Brazil, even Citigroup was uncertain of the ownership structure in which it resided. Previous Brasil Telecom annual reports revealed shareholder configurations that were constantly evolving and ambiguous with regard to the ultimate parents and/or the presence of poorly identified holding companies. Anatel, the telecom regulatory agency, ordered Brasil Telecom to divulge the shareholder ownership structure of Timepart Holdings (a fourth-tier firm) because it suspected that this holding company was indirectly controlled by Grupo Opportunity rather than the Citigroup (CVC Fund).[5] Given the great disproportion between equity stakes and voting stakes, this firm planted in the middle of the pyramidal ownership structure of Grupo Opportunity acted as a fulcrum to counterbalance even the smallest of equity investments at the top.

At the time of the initial investment in 1998 it appeared, from Citigroup's point of view, that Timepart was not part of the control chain reflected in the ownership structure of Zain

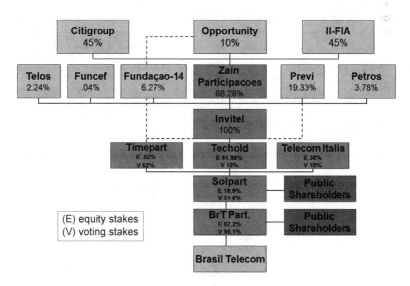

Figure 22.3 Brasil Telecom and Citigroup/Zain ownership structure

Source: Perkins (2007).

Participações because of its minuscule equity stakes (0.02 percent). If the owner of the voting stakes were subsequently revealed to be the Dantas – the family that owned Grupo Opportunity – the family would effectively have 100 percent control of the equity in Brasil Telecom through the indirect control chain with Timepart's 62 percent voting rights. As would later be discovered, this masterful scheme of creating leverage did place Grupo Opportunity in control of Brasil Telecom even though it had only 10 percent equity stakes at the apex of the pyramidal group. Unbeknownst to Citigroup and the other joint venture partner, II-FIA, Opportunity had control of Brasil Telecom through familial ties and business associates linked directly from Timepart to Grupo Opportunity's pyramidal ownership structure. "None of us knew that our partner [Opportunity] had additional control through another route. The people running Brasil Telecom are not the people that invested money in it,"[6] stated a senior manager from the other joint venture partner.

So, one of the largest banks in the world, Citigroup, fell prey to an expropriation scheme set up by its pyramidal group joint venture partner. The implications of the true ownership structure of Brasil Telecom masked the inevitable shareholder conflicts to come. Citigroup, in this case, lacked the ability to foresee where the ownership structure might have been subject to leverage creation indirectly in the six-tiered ownership chain (the dashed-lined relationships in Figure 22.3). Instead, it unknowingly walked right into the trap, blindsided by the expropriation that ensued. This granular example shows how lacking *jeitinho Brasileiro* can lead to blind spots in managerial strategic decision-making.

The regulatory environment in Brazil

Ownership manipulation designed to obfuscate the indirect chains of control in the pyramid is an expropriation risk that could cripple not only an otherwise successful foreign investor like Citigroup but also the market at the macroeconomic level. Such a series of exploitations of foreigners is obviously not sustainable if FDI inflows are to be maintained. Shleifer and Wolfenzon (2002) systematically show that widespread minority shareholder expropriation leads to unfeasible capital market formations. As the market eventually learns of such risks, foreign investors will flee or select less volatile host countries. This risk amplified across minority shareholders of public firms threatens the liquidity of the stock market. Stock exchanges in Latin American countries, from 1970 to 2000, experienced twice as much volatility in capital flows than those of "developed" nations (Schneider 2008). The implications of this volatility are dichotomous for local versus foreign investment. On the one hand, volatility serves as an antecedent to business group formation (Schneider 2009). The lack of access to capital through the stock market provides stronger incentives for pyramidal groups to diversify in unrelated industries and businesses. On the other hand, volatility leads to uncertainty for foreign investors, who are subjected to unexpected institutional changes.

The decline of the BOVESPA – the "new rules of the game"

Such was the case in the late 1990s when the BOVESPA stock exchange plummeted and became practically illiquid because "over $2 billion in foreign investment in the form of portfolio funds left Brazil . . . [L]iquidity of the BOVESPA relies mostly on non-voting preferred shares from the foreign market."[7] In parallel, the BOVESPA's liquidity plummeted by more than 75 percent in value from 1997 to the end of 1999 (see Figure 22.4). The lack of regulation or enforcement of "good" corporate governance practices is a key driver of the volatility of many emerging market stock exchanges. Dominant owners of pyramidal group firms could

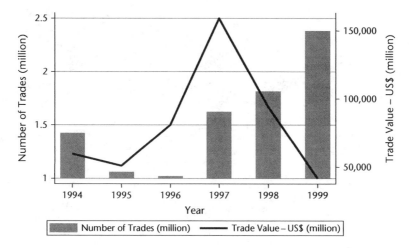

Figure 22.4   BOVESPA trade value and number of trades, 1994–9

Source: Perkins and Zajac (2013: 6).

effectively govern and determine the strategic decisions of their firms, with minority share-holders having little to no voting rights, similar to the experience of Citigroup. In this scenario, controlling insiders would be privy to consuming private benefits of control. Dyck and Zingales (2004) show that the most extreme case of private benefits of control found among thirty-nine global capital markets sampled was Brazil, with a 65-plus percent premium on the value of control. When the minority shareholder has greater institutional protection, the private benefits of control can potentially be curbed (Dyck and Zingales 2004).

In late 2000, the BOVESPA regulators took action in this direction. The Brazilian government reformed the "rules of the game" of the BOVESPA to institutionalize improvements toward greater transparency and protection of minority shareholder rights. Effectively, firms could voluntarily opt into four listing categories (Novo Mercado, Level 1, Level 2, and the classic BOVESPA) with varying degrees of regulatory stringency, such as owner and board member transparency, US GAAP accounting standards, audited financials, and one-vote/one-share stocks. The specific differences between regulations in each listing category are detailed in Table 22.2. Also important to note is the fact that these corporate governance practices are not mandated by law for all firms, which creates a dichotomy between firms that opt to signal stronger corporate governance versus firms that choose to operate in an institutional environment with ambiguity of information and weak protection for minority shareholders and other outside investors. Lojas Renner, for example, restructured its bylaws and share class offerings to migrate from the classic BOVESPA to the Novo Mercado in 2005. This change provided all shareholders with equal voting stakes to equity stakes, board independence, 100 percent tag-along rights, and US Generally Accepted Accounting Principles (GAAP) audited financials. Though progress has been made in providing a market signal to separate the firms by governance rules, Perkins and Zajac (2013) found that many firms' strategic responses to this non-market institutional change were more symbolic than substantive. Their study revealed that it is more difficult to detect whether firms adopted the new governance incentives to maximize the wealth of the listed firm in lieu of the dominant shareholder of the group. We elaborate on this problem in the next section by providing specific examples.

Table 22.2 BOVESPA institutional change – corporate governance reforms

Corporate governance regulations	BOVESPA classic	Level 1	Level 2	Novo Mercado
Stock class allocations	1/3 voting shares = ON; 2/3 non-voting shares = PN	1/3 voting shares = ON; 2/3 non-voting shares = PN; maintain 25% free-float of outstanding share	50% voting shares = ON; 50% non-voting shares = PN; maintain 25% free-float of outstanding share	Only voting shares; 25% minimum free-float; promote shareholder dispersion
Voting rights for minority stakeholders	No rights	No rights	Tag along rights at ≥ 70% of value/conditions; PN shareholders vote in special circumstances (i.e., related party transactions)	1 vote = 1 share; Max. 10% of votes; 100% tag-along rights
Management decision-making/board participation	PN stock = No board participation	PN stock = No board participation	Min. 5 members w/1-year term; PN stock = board meeting notification and attendance	Min. 5 members w/2-year term; 20% outside independent professional managers
Enforcement	CVM/judicial system; average dispute resolved in 8–10 years	CVM/judicial system; average dispute resolved in 8–10 years	BOVESPA arbitration guaranteed in 6 months	BOVESPA arbitration guaranteed in 6 months
Transparency/disclosure	No requirements	Brazilian GAAP reporting; lacks standardization	US GAAP or IFRS reporting standards	US GAAP reporting standards
Delistings	Tender offer; no regulation of fair market value to minority shareholders		Tender offer based on economic value criteria	Tender offer at fair market value to minority shareholders

Source: Perkins and Zajac (2013: 9).

ON: Ordinary Share (e.g. voting); PN: Preferred Shares (e.g. non-voting); CVM: Comissão de Valores Mobiliários; GAAP: Generally Accepted Accounting Principles; IFRS: International Financial Reporting Standards.

The legal environment in Brazil

Both legal and political economy scholars have noted that Latin American countries lack strong legal institutions that protect minority shareholders (Gorga 2006; La Porta, Lopez-de-Silanes, Shleifer and Vishny 2000; Musacchio 2008). Specifically, the Brazilian legal system is known for weak laws regarding property rights and shareholder protection (Musacchio 2008). Though the fundamental economic proposition of markets suggests that security of property and enforcement of contracts are essential to investment and trade (Smith 1776), Brazil's legal environment remains challenged by core institutional issues, such as the lack of dispute resolution capabilities, weak contract enforcement and a lack of judicial specialization in courts. "In 1997, the federal government managed to put through a law abolishing equal treatment to minority shareholders in the case of transfer of control" (Aldrighi and Postali 2010: 362). A 2001 reform in Brazilian Corporate Law[8] sought to remedy this concern by providing stronger investor protection. However, many of these reforms were merely palliative, because controlling shareholders were still able to manage the legislative constraints symbolically, and the new regulatory framework lacked enforcement mechanisms (Aldrighi and Postali 2010; Gorga 2006; Perkins and Zajac 2013).

In addition to these challenges, Brazil, like many other emerging markets, is laden with legal procedural formalities, which are strongly associated with having extraordinarily long lead times before a case is ever heard by a judge or a dispute is resolved (Djankov, La Porta, Lopez-de-Silanes and Shleifer 2003). These two factors of high procedural formalities and long duration of dispute resolution are primarily synonymous with countries based on civil law versus common law. In their cross-national study of legal institutions, Djankov et al. (2003) show that, on average, civil law countries, like Brazil, have higher than expected time durations to court proceedings, less consistency, less honesty, less fairness in judicial decision-making, and more corruption. Out of the 109 countries they examined, Brazil was in the lowest quartile for enforcement of the law through independent procedural actions (Djankov et al. 2003: 481, Table IIa).

This results in another form of duplicity in which the wealthy elites, such as pyramidal business group owners, with more economic and political power, can use the system to "encourage the supposedly impartial judge to favor [them], using either bribes or threats" (Djankov et al. 2003: 458). In a country like Brazil, where there are no limits on political campaign contributions, this is seen as a legitimate and legal mechanism of persuasion (Lazzarini 2010). Campaign contributions, such as those presented in Table 22.3, are a classic example of *jeitinho Brasileiro*. They are used to navigate the legal hurdles that may otherwise stop politically unconnected firms in their tracks. Gorga (2006: 889–90) presents a clear example of this type of behavior in the story of how megabroker Naji Nahas brought Rio's stock exchange to a halt:

> Nahas artificially inflated share prices in Rio de Janeiro's Stock Exchange (BOVERJ) in 1989. His scheme was supposed to be the cause of the crash of BOVERJ. Nahas has already been charged by American regulators and fined $250,000 for his speculative actions in the silver market. In Brazil, he was convicted but was granted an injunction against his incarceration so that he can enjoy his liberty while he awaits his appeal. Ultimately, in 1998 (almost 10 years later) his convictions for white collar crime and crime against the public economy were annulled by the Superior Court of Justice. Curiously, the appeals court refused to permit evidence from employees of the CVM (Comissão de Valores Mobiliários), Brazil's Securities Exchange Commission, because the CVM had brought a separate civil suit against Nahas . . . This example also shows how decisions can be manipulated to hinder the enforcement of laws. Usually persons who are well connected are able to skirt the law and avoid sanctions.

Table 22.3 The top twenty corporate donors for Lula's presidential campaign, 2006

Donor	Amount $(R)
Vale	4,050,000
Cutrale	4,000,000
Camargo Corrêa	3,504,000
Banco Itaú	3,500,000
Gerdau	3,100,000
JBS-Friboi	2,502,000
Bradesco	2,500,000
CSN/Vicunha	2,266,000
FSTP Brasil	2,000,000
Votorantim	1,700,000
OAS	1,700,000
Andrade Gutierrez	1,520,000
Banco ABN AMRO Real	1,500,000
Ambev	1,500,000
Unibanco	1,300,000
Embraer	1,300,000
Coopersucar	1,286,000
UTV Engenharia	1,000,000
Unigel/Acrinor	2,000,000
Instituto Brasileiro de Siderurgia (IBS)	1,000,000

Source: Translated from Lazzarini (2010: 69).

Note: Values officially declared by the Superior Electoral Court.

Problems for foreigners

This poor dispute resolution and weak contract enforcement climate in Brazil is problematic and has negative effects on partnering firms, particularly foreigners, in three primary ways. First, foreigners seeking dispute resolution with a local joint venture partner or controlling shareholder of a public firm are disadvantaged by the duplicity in applying procedural hurdles to some firms, but not all. This can result in endless complaints filed in the judicial system with no court remediation ever occurring. Time to trial delays are common in the Brazilian court system, like the example of Nahas, and in some cases it can take up to ten years to have the case heard in a court of law (Perkins and Zajac 2013).

Example 1: Lack of dispute resolution

For example, Telesystem International Wireless (TIW), a Canadian telecommunications firm, also created a joint venture with Grupo Opportunity in Brazil in 1998 as part of the privatization of the telecommunications industry. Despite TIW originally being the largest shareholder in the joint venture, with a 49 percent equity stake, within weeks Grupo Opportunity had created a holding company to consolidate its control over the joint venture via both direct and indirect control chains. This expropriation scheme was similar to the one used against Citigroup. TIW attempted to resolve its contractual dispute by taking Opportunity to court in Brazil repeatedly, but to no avail. The *Toronto Star* reported that "as many as 20 lawsuits in and outside of Brazil were launched."[9] TIW's efforts were futile because its inability to get through the formal procedural steps and have the case heard by a judge in the Brazilian court system led to the joint venture's failure. After losing veto power rights through shifts in the ownership structure, TIW's management was astounded to learn that the Brazilian courts were not willing to enforce shareholder rights. Due to its naivety, TIW ended up selling its ownership stakes to Opportunity two years later for less than one-fifth of its original investment.

Second, poor legal protection of minority shareholders allows wealthy owners to reap private benefits of control at the expense of minority shareholders (Bebchuk et al. 2000; Dyck and Zingales 2004). Large (controlling) owners can expropriate resources from minority shareholders via outright theft if the legal system is not in place to prevent or punish such behavior (Dyck and Zingales 2004). Wealth extraction from private benefits of control is easily achieved when minority shareholder protection is weak (Shleifer and Vishny 1997); conveniently, for the beneficiaries, markets such as Brazil's, where family-controlled pyramidal groups thrive (Fogel 2006), are ripe for such schemes.

Example 2: Private benefits of control

The Citigroup and TIW examples illustrate another common challenge faced when navigating ownership structures in Brazil: entrenchment. Many pyramidal groups place family members and friends in top management positions in firms, which is a blatant display of the entrenchment problem of the manager and owner being one and the same person. Therefore, outsiders, whether minority shareholders on the stock market or joint venture partners, can suffer from the corporate veil of silence that allows insiders to maximize the private benefits of control. This managerial positioning to gain access to decision rights allows for wealth to remain concentrated within the pyramidal group, as the top management team or board of directors is generally geared toward the interests of the group rather than the individual firm.

In the case of Citigroup, they fired Daniel Dantas, the fund manager of the CVC/Opportunity Fund, on the basis of confirmed reports of shareholder wrangling and misappropriation of joint venture funds, along with allegations of arbitrage. Citigroup stated: "Mr. Dantas and Opportunity engaged in self-dealing and wrongful conduct in order to misappropriate CVC/Opportunity Fund assets and enrich themselves at IEII's [Citigroup's subsidiary] expense."[10] Citigroup also filed a $300 million suit against Opportunity for siphoning funds from the Brasil Telecom joint venture to Opportunity entities and affiliates.[11] In this example, Citigroup did not cultivate an effective *jeitinho Brasileiro* and paid the price (upwards of $300 million) in expropriated funds and legal expenses to reclaim the assets in question.

Gorga (2006) suggests that Brazil also lacks strong social norms to support effective sanctioning because society does not condemn self-dealing. So any attempts to brand such behavior as illegal are largely futile.

Third, controlling shareholders and the managers they appoint typically cannot be dislodged within pyramidal structures as the controlling shareholder votes a control block in each firm of the pyramid (Morck, Shleifer and Vishny 1988). In extreme cases, the entrenched managers are locked into coveted control positions through umbrella agreements, which serve to regulate future contractual clauses. Thus, without political or legal pressures from outside of the host country's jurisdiction, controlling shareholders remain immune to challenges from minority shareholders. Perkins, Morck and Yeung (2014) provide systematic evidence that demonstrates that joint ventures between pyramidal group firms and freestanding firms (typically foreign minority shareholders) result in the highest failure rates over time (27 percent) because of unintended post-formation terminations associated with misaligned governance incentives. This high failure rate is also associated with the formation of a joint venture at the wrong tier level in a pyramidal scheme, where leverage creation and thus expropriation risks are highest.

Example 3: Challenges of dislodging entrenched JV partners

In the Citigroup and TIW cases, Daniel Dantas appointed family members and friends to senior positions in various holding companies. In the Citigroup case, four of the six BTP board members were associated with Dantas's family: his sister, brother-in-law, former brother-in-law and family attorney (Perkins 2007). The Brazilian legal system did not enforce the formal removal of Dantas from his role as fund manager, so Citigroup resorted to the US courts for remediation and a stay order to remove him from this complex ownership structure. After months of fighting, Citigroup finally won the right to remove Dantas's board of directors from the joint venture and install a new board. However, this decision was overturned by the Brazilian courts, where Dantas had more political influence.

Unwilling to depart without a fight, Dantas had previously written an umbrella agreement stating, "If either the CVC Fund [Citigroup] or the onshore fund [II-FIA] removes Opportunity as general partner or manager, that fund will lose its voting rights in Zain."[12] Immediately after the announcement of his removal, Dantas – through Opportunity – began to pursue transactions that would maximize his wealth at the expense of Citigroup's investment.

In order to develop a *jeitinho Brasileiro*, foreign firms must recognize the likelihood of family members serving on the boards of firms, see that their interests are tailored toward that group, and act accordingly.

Is using market-based strategies effective in non-market environments?

Even if a dispute were to receive a public hearing, the lack of specialization within the Brazilian court system would be a disadvantage to minority shareholders enacting legal cases of fiduciary responsibility. Judges in the civil courts lack specialization on corporate law matters, which creates an institutional void for common-law-oriented contracting deals. Gorga's (2006) study underscores this point that Brazilian judges do not have the experience to understand complex business transactions. Usually their decision power is circumscribed by the formalities of the law. This problem is exacerbated by the fact that there is a shortage of specialized prosecutors with the skill to bring complex securities cases to justice. Consequently, Citigroup used a market-based strategy because, much like TIW, it was unable to gain remediation in the local Brazilian justice system. Citigroup responded strategically by moving the jurisdiction to the US, where it sought corporate dispute resolution from the clearer laws regarding fiduciary responsibility. Specifically, it turned to the Southern District Court in New York City, where many cases of this kind are adjudicated by judges who specialize in corporate law.

Citigroup appealed to this court to stop Dantas from stripping more assets from the joint venture on March 10, 2005, just one day after Dantas had been removed as manager of the CVC Fund, by filing an injunction against him. On March 17, Judge Kaplan granted a preliminary injunction to stop Dantas from "taking any action that would impair the value of the CVC Fund or its assets or interfere with [Citigroup's] control over the assets."[13] He also issued a restraining order to prevent Dantas from engaging in further wrangling of the board's decision-making related to Brasil Telecom.

However, this did not stop Dantas from taking further action, as insiders face little risk of criminal liability for self-dealing or disclosure violations in Brazil. Moreover, criminal cases for such white-collar crimes are even rarer than civil liability cases in Brazil (Gorga 2006). For example, even in the case of scandals involving bankers that are widely reported by the press, the accused are usually not condemned (Gorga 2006).

Despite the US injunction, just six weeks later, on April 28, Dantas signed an agreement with Telecom Italia to sell off Opportunity's stake for $529 million – a price the court found excessive, as the current market value of the shares on April 27 was only approximately $100 million.[14] Just a year earlier, Opportunity had been willing to sell Telecom Italia its interest in Zain for $80 million. In effect, this agreement would have "transferred Brasil Telecom's cellular assets to Telecom Italia for low consideration and given Opportunity a windfall of hundreds of millions of dollars."[15]

On June 7, 2005, the New York court granted Citigroup a modified injunction to stop transactions related to the asset selling and shareholder shifting that Opportunity had orchestrated prior to Dantas's removal. Judge Kaplan stated, "It strongly appears that Opportunity is attempting to use advantages that it enjoys purely because of the former fiduciary responsibility to reap enormous gains for itself at the expense of those whom it owes fiduciary duties."[16]

The dispute over control and ownership between Citigroup and Opportunity had turned into a protracted battle, with Dantas resisting at every step. Because of his political and economic influence in his home country, an intermediate appellate court of Brazil overturned its prior decision to nullify the umbrella agreement, thus reestablishing Opportunity's right to manage Brasil Telecom. This effectively muted the US court ruling that Citigroup had fought so hard to win. The battle continued through to 2010 and was eventually resolved only by Citigroup selling off its assets in Brazil.

The key lesson from this case is that market-based strategies do not solve non-market problems effectively. As Citigroup managers would surely agree, fighting Dantas in the US and Brazilian courts was expensive, time-consuming and relatively futile. This was not an effective *jeitinho* to navigate Brazil. A higher level of non-market sophistication was needed. Moreover, Perkins's (2014b) research on multinational enterprise organization learning shows that when firms deploy the wrong type of institutional knowledge, the learning penalties are six times more damaging for them than for those firms that deploy institutional knowledge in the right contexts. So how can firms avoid these costly mistakes?

Navigating institutional challenges with *jeitinho Brasileiro*

It is crucial to understand and address the institutional gaps in corporate ownership, regulations and the legal functioning of the courts to develop an effective non-market strategy. Good *jeitinho Brasileiro* strategies occur in the form of redirecting thwarted governance incentives, specifying shareholder rights and creating enforcement mechanisms through commitment intensity in lieu of the market mechanisms that are present in developed economies. To illustrate these strategies, we provide some examples of firms with more sophisticated *jeitinho Brasileiro* that have been successful in navigating the Brazilian institutional voids.

Avoiding corporate governance expropriation risks of misaligned incentives

Portugal Telecom and Telefonica, two government-owned pyramids from Portugal and Spain, collectively created eight joint venture subsidiaries in Brazil in the telecommunications industry under the umbrella of the Vivo brand. In total, these firms have a 60 percent market share. As each joint venture was formed, both pyramidal firms provided equity to preserve a 50/50 ownership split. To align the incentives toward wealth maximization of the joint ventures and not the apex firms, each pyramidal group's parent firm acquired and held equity blocks in the other's apex firm. For example, Telefonica increased its stake in Portugal Telecom to 10 percent and Portugal Telecom increased its stake in Telefonica to a total of 1.5 percent of the overall shares. In each case, control of the governing board was split, so neither partner could dominate the decision-making of the joint venture: for example, their 2001 joint venture, Brasilcel, had a Portugal Telecom-appointed CEO and a Telefonica-appointed chair of the board. These *jeitinho* strategies create multiple points of contact between the two pyramidal groups and provide each with abundant ammunition to retaliate if the other breaks faith on the direction of wealth maximization.

Wrestling control from a dominant Brazilian family

During the same period as the Citigroup investments, Casino Groupe, a French retail business group, invested in the largest Brazilian grocery chain, Pão de Açúcar, as a minority shareholder, assuming 24 percent of the voting stakes and 25 percent of the equity stakes: effectively one vote, one share. During this six-year relationship as a minority shareholder, the group was able to observe whether its voting rights would be honored by the dominant controlling owner, the Diniz family, with Abilio dos Santos Diniz at the apex. Alive to the expropriation risks of minority shareholders in joint ventures with dominant owners, Casino Groupe insisted upon anti-tunneling and anti-freeze-out rights in its shareholder agreement by exercising its voting power as a block with the five Diniz family members. For example, "[both parties] hereby commit themselves irrevocably always to vote together with the Holding Company" was the legally binding clause used in their agreement.[17]

In 2005, Casino Groupe invested an additional $900 million in Pão de Açúcar and became an equal equity and voting stakes joint venture partner (50/50), using a savvy *jeitinho* strategy. Recognizing the risk of misaligned incentives, tunneling and self-dealing, Casino, along with the Diniz family, created a holding company, Wilkes Participacoes, which legally bound this joint venture with a shareholders' agreement in accordance with Article 118 of the Corporations Law of Brazil. Casino preemptively blocked expropriation by locking itself into both pyramidal structures with both lines of direct and indirect control (see Figure 22.2). In addition to indirect interest held by Casino in Companhia Brasileira de Distribuição (CBD) by Wilkes, Segisor, a Casino pyramidal group firm, held 1000 shares in CBD directly.[18] Effectively, this holding company, Wilkes, married the two pyramidal groups at the apex levels of their pyramidal ownership structures to form another tier of ownership that directly controlled Pão de Açúcar. To solidify this joint commitment between the two parents, the Diniz family and Casino also guaranteed that the newly created holding company, Wilkes, voted their control together as a voting block with the combined 50 percent stakes of each Casino *groupe* and the Diniz family.[19] Additionally, these parents strategized through the well-recognized legal weaknesses of the Brazilian courts by specifying that any and all disputes would be resolved by the jurisdictional rules of the International Chamber of Commerce (ICC) in France. This removed the risk of either partner being held hostage to the inefficiencies of the Brazilian legal system.

In both of these examples, the partners used contract specificity to create and enforce ownership incentives through *acordo de acionistas* to fill the institutional voids of corporate law. Many foreigners fail to realize the necessary legal protection needed when forming joint ventures in Brazil. Given the prevalence of decoupling "good" corporate governance practices (Perkins and Zajac 2013) and the lack of strong enforcement mechanisms, firms have an obligation to protect their investments with legally binding agreements that specify the governance incentives between the parties. In the case of TIW, part of the fault of the failure was TIW's alone. The company secured the equity deal with a weak contract, a memorandum of understanding (MOU), which had little chance of enforcement in Brazil. In these complex ownership environments, *acordo de acionistas* provide firms with far greater normative liberties to specify the governance terms (board selection, voting rights, limitations of voting blocks, anti-tunneling clauses, etc.) than a typical MOU or joint venture agreement, which are often used in common law countries where the courts have more experience in corporate dispute resolution and both civil and criminal recourse can be pursued against the self-interested managers.

In a recent study conducted by Perkins et al. (2012) into the contractual clauses in over 300 shareholder agreements, the authors found that Brazilian pyramidal group firms routinely protect their interests beyond the provisions of Brazilian corporate law with contractual strategies that include: maintaining control; protecting minority shareholders against tunneling; anti-freeze-out provisions; and dispute resolution jurisdiction specification and regulatory governing rules.

Others, who are not as savvy in foreseeing such hazards, have used more forceful *jeitinho* strategies that have proven to be effective, albeit costly. For example, Telecom Italia, a minority shareholder in a dispute with its Brazilian partner, which it accused of expropriations against the joint venture, resorted to multiple-point competition against the partner in other markets in order to retaliate against the self-interested behavior. Bernheim and Whinston (1990) reason that multiple simultaneous games heighten the incentives to cooperate by raising both the punishment for cheating and the reward for cooperation.

Managerial implications: developing non-market strategies in Brazil

While many of the above examples relate to firms that have struggled in the non-market environment, others have been more successful at developing and using an effective *jeitinho Brasileiro*. Here we share some practical managerial implications for foreign firms that wish to develop an effective *jeitinho Brasileiro* to navigate the non-market environment strategically.

Utilizing prior experience

The non-market issues raised in this chapter should not by any means deter companies from investing in Brazil. These cautionary tales are designed to help new foreign entrants build bridges of relatedness to their prior investment experience. An initial point of consideration is leveraging prior experience both within the host country and from other home and host country experiences to improve the odds of survival. Foreign direct investment scholars (Li 1995; Shaver, Mitchell and Yeung 1997) have shown that prior investments in the same host country context benefit the firm by increasing market-specific knowledge acquired in subsequent investments. These experienced firms have been shown to survive at significantly higher rates than firms with no market-specific (i.e., new entrants) or industry-specific experience. However, this does not need to be a deterrent for those firms with no experience in Brazil, as Perkins (2014b) found that new entrants to the Brazilian non-market environment can also be successful if they leverage related institutional experiences, particularly similarities in industry regulatory codes. Prior experience prolongs the survival of the investments when a firm operates in institutional environments that are similar to its host country regulatory environment. As a caution, dissimilar experiences, when applied in inappropriate non-market contexts, can increase the risks of failure sixfold because managers grossly overstate performance outcomes and inflate expectations.

The TIW case is an example of misusing prior experience from the home country. Canada's business sector features a mixture of freestanding, widely held firms and business groups, as four out of the top ten firms are group affiliated (Fogel 2006). Despite the operation of a number of business groups in the home environment, firms in Canada must disclose ownership stakes of shareholders and voting stakes. Furthermore, the top management teams or boards of group member firms have an unambiguous duty to the individual firm, not to the entire group or controlling shareholder. Although business groups are present, Canadian firms like TIW may expect formal checks and balances during business group transactions, particularly if they have interacted with group firms in Canada. Yet, in stark contrast, these formalities are rare in Brazil, suggesting that Canadian firms entering that market are forced to adjust their strategies when dealing with business groups. TIW failed to adjust its strategy, and this resulted in business failure.

To improve a firm's chances of more immediate success, managers should first choose countries with similar institutional environments to that of the home country where they have adaptable competencies. When relevant market knowledge is limited, partnership is an option to overcome the "liabilities of foreignness" (Zaheer 1995), but this comes with the considerable expropriation risks mentioned above. One alternative revealed by Perkins, Morck and Yeung (2014) is to enter Brazil alone (i.e., wholly owned subsidiaries), which is a significantly more successful strategy than navigating the hazards of joint venture partnership.

This strategy may be more easily identifiable in industries that have formal codifiable "rules of the game" that are likely to vary across countries. For example, in industries that have a high level of dependence and interaction with government goods and services, such as licenses issued or shared assets, having a non-market strategy becomes more imperative. The industries that are likely to have the most interdependencies with the government are oil and gas, mining, and utilities, such as electricity and telecommunications. These industries are all constrained by government industry interventions of licensure, pricing regulation and geographic expansion constraints. Firms competing in these sectors are more exposed to the non-market risks this chapter raises than firms in more consumer-driven markets, such as durable goods.

Prudent partner selection

For those firms where partnership is inevitable, selecting the right partner at the formation of the joint venture is paramount to success. Pyramidal groups are first and foremost about subjecting a huge constellation of seemingly distinct firms to the control of a single ultimate controlling shareholder. In Brazil, pyramidal groups are representative of the typical pool of available partners from which selections may be made. The controlling shareholder is thus highly savvy at strategically seizing and locking in control. Therefore, the onus is on the foreign firm to select a partner that is explicit regarding control rights. Positioning the firm with the wealth maximization incentives of the joint venture (or in some instances minority shareholder position) is the key to success. If a majority of the voting stakes cannot be secured, a 50/50 split, as seen in the Pão de Açúcar and Vivo examples, can work. Accepting a minority voting interest is risky unless the local partner's incentives to make the joint venture a success are unambiguous. If commitments relating to control with the potential partner are obfuscated, this raises a potential red flag of an ownership scheme that may be intended to be kept hidden.

Unrelenting due diligence

Given the multi-tiered structure of pyramidal partnerships, it remains imperative to know who owns whom. First, foreign firms must learn the identity of the *real* partner – the *dono ultimo*, or ultimate owner – when entering a joint venture. If a firm is unable to do this, there is a high chance that the partner is obfuscating its identity. Cautionary indicators that partnering firms may have governance motives that are not aligned with maximizing shareholder value are: great disproportions in the equity stakes to voting rights ratio; diversifications in the pyramidal group's portfolio that are indirectly controlling potential partnership investments; and common boards of other non-related BOVESPA listed firms on the stock exchange. Khanna and Thomas (2009) also found synchronicity in business group firms in the Chilean stock market, which suggests that monitoring co-movements of the partnering firm's portfolio can point to its governance motives. One indicator of when self-dealing might be occurring is when the profits/losses of non-related companies in a business group show synchronous patterns across industries (Bertrand et al. 2002). When this occurs, the inference is that the dominant controlling owner could be manipulating profits indirectly at other tier levels in the pyramidal structure away from the joint venture partnership. The adoption of American Depository Receipts (ADRs), which call for mandatory transparency of accounting practices, provides an opportunity for Brazilian listed firms to cross-list on multiple exchanges (Schneider 2008), which may also serve as a signal to foreign investors that this set of potential partners has more stringent corporate governance standards.

Additionally, as it is common for business groups to make ownership changes in their favor post-formation, it is imperative that foreign investors maintain routine due diligence checks to monitor their partners' motives and property rights changes over time.

Specifying terms and jurisdiction for dispute resolution

Given the average wait time for a court decision and the lack of specialization in Brazil, firms should be explicit with partners regarding the jurisdiction in which shareholder disputes will be resolved and the rules that will govern those decisions (e.g., the ICC). Not having this plan in place can lead to costly and ultimately unresolved legal battles and/or forced exits from unintended failures.

Conclusion

This chapter has highlighted why non-market strategies in Brazil are critical. Due to the complexities and ambiguities associated with the legal institutions, regulatory institutions and pyramidal ownership structures, firms unfamiliar with the institutional environment will be easy targets for wealth expropriation. Even though there have been many positive reforms in the Brazilian economy, the notion that the non-market features of the market will be synonymous with those of the US, the UK or elsewhere is simply a fallacy. It is more likely that institutions are path dependent. Therefore, investing wisely requires an effective *jeitinho Brasileiro*, something inexperienced firms need to learn.

In comparing Brazil to other BRIC (Brazil, Russia, India, and China) emerging-market economies, there may be some synergies that can be applied across institutional environments. For example, in India, business groups, referred to as "business houses," are dominated by families from the upper echelon of society. Fogel (2006) reports that over 96 percent of the top businesses in India are family-owned pyramidal groups. Given the parallels between the family-owned business groups of Brazil and India, the lessons gleaned and non-market strategies identified for Brazil may apply equally well in the Indian business context. However, this may not be the case in either Russia or China, as the business groups in those countries are dominated by government-controlled SOEs (state-owned enterprises), not family groups. Other countries that might be prime candidates for applying *jeitinho* non-market strategies are those whose Portuguese colonial ties are similar to those of Brazil. Mozambique, Angola, Cape Verde, Guinea-Bissau, and São Tomé, for example, all have similar patterns of market regulation to those that are prevalent in Brazil (Perkins 2014a).

Notes

1 The Securities and Exchange Commission requires US-listed firms to file a Schedule D when a shareholder owns more than 5 percent equity stakes in a company. These anomalies exist among US companies such as Walmart, which is about 41 percent collectively owned by the Walton family, or the Ford Motor Company, with the limited familial investments of the Ford family.
2 Lojas Renner's annual report, 2008: 17.
3 Note, the illustration in Figure 22.2 is a pyramid rotated 45 degres counterclockwise.
4 US Dist. Ct., S.D.N.Y., 407 F. Supp. 2d 483, 2005 US Dist. Lexis 10468, 4, decided June 2, 2005.
5 "Regulator Seeks Clarification on BrT Shareholding," *Business News Americas*, March 9, 2004.
6 J. Wheatley, "Funds Enter Ownership Dispute," *Financial Times*, March 8, 2004.
7 Interview with Luiz Oscario, former head of the Comissão de Valores Mobiliários (CVM).
8 This law, No. 10303, enacted on October 31, 2001, amends Corporation Law No. 6404/76 in many important ways to reduce the amount of leverage created in control schemes. For example, for all new corporations created after this reform, the issuance of stocks could not exceed more than 50 percent without voting rights. Under the previous law, firms could issue up to two-thirds of their stock as non-voting shares.
9 T. Hamilton, "Retreat from Brazil," *Toronto Star*, April 5, 2003.
10 J. Wheatley, "Citigroup in $300M Brazilian Lawsuit," *Financial Times*, April 13, 2005.
11 Ibid.
12 Ibid.
13 US Dist. Ct., S.D.N.Y., 441 F. Supp. 2d 552, 2006 US Dist. Lexis 28298, decided July 26, 2006, 3.
14 US Dist. Ct., S.D.N.Y., 407 F. Supp. 2d 483, 2005 US Dist. Lexis 10468, decided June 2, 2005, 12.
15 US Dist. Ct., S.D.N.Y., 441 F. Supp. 2d 552, 2006 US Dist. Lexis 28298, decided July 26, 2006, 3.
16 C. DeJuana, "US Judge Favors Citigroup in Opportunity Dispute," *Reuters News*, June 2, 2005.
17 *Acordo de Acionistas da Companhia Brasileira de Distribuição*, 2005: 8.
18 *Acordo de Acionistas da Companhia Brasileira de Distribuição*, 2006: 3.
19 *Acordo de Acionistas da Companhia Brasileira de Distribuição*, 2006: 9.

References

D. Aldrighi and F. Postali, Business groups in Brazil, in A. Colpan, T. Hikino and J. Lincoln (eds.), *The Oxford Handbook of Business Groups*, Oxford University Press, New York, 2010, 353–86.
K. Bae, J. Kang and J. Kim, Tunneling or value added? Evidence from mergers by Korean business groups, *Journal of Finance* 57, 2002, 2695–740.
L. Bebchuk, R. Kraakman and G. Triantis, Stock pyramids, cross ownership and dual class equity: The mechanisms and agency costs of separating control from cash flow rights, in R. Morck (ed.), *Concentrated Corporate Ownership*, University of Chicago Press, Chicago, 2000, 295–315.
B. Bernheim and M. Whinston, Multimarket contact and collusion behavior, *Rand Journal of Economics* 21, 1990, 1–26.
M. Bertrand, P. Mehta and S. Mullainathan, Ferreting out tunneling: An application to Indian business groups, *Quarterly Journal of Economics* 117, 2002, 121–48.
S. Djankov, R. La Porta, F. Lopez-de-Silanes and A. Shleifer, Courts, *Quarterly Journal of Economics* 118(2), 2003, 453–517.
A. Dyck and L. Zingales, Private benefits of control: An international comparison, *Journal of Finance* 59, 2004, 537–60.

K. Fogel, Oligarchic family control, social economic outcomes, and the quality of government, *Journal of International Business Studies* 37, 2006, 603–22.

E. Gorga, Culture and corporate law reform: A case study of Brazil, *University of Pennsylvania Journal of International Economic Law* 27, 2006, 803–905.

International Monetary Fund, *Data and Statistics*, 2013, www.imf.org/external/data.htm/ (accessed November 19, 2014).

S. Johnson, R. La Porta, F. Lopez-de-Silanes and A. Shleifer, Tunneling, *American Economic Review* 90, 2000, 22–7.

T. Khanna and C. Thomas, Synchronicity and firm interlocks in an emerging market, *Journal of Financial Economics* 92, 2009, 182–204.

T. Khanna and Y. Yafeh, Business groups in emerging markets: Paragons or parasites?, *Journal of Economic Literature* 45, 2007, 331–72.

R. La Porta, F. Lopez-de-Silanes, A. Shleifer and R. Vishny, Investor protection and corporate governance, *Journal of Financial Economics* 58(3), 2000, 3–27.

S. Lazzarini, *Capitalismo de Laços*, Elsevier, Rio de Janeiro, 2010.

J. Li, Foreign entry and survival: Effects of strategic choice on performance in international markets, *Strategic Management Journal* 16, 1995, 333–51.

R. Morck, A. Shleifer and R. Vishny, Management ownership and market valuation – an empirical analysis, *Journal of Financial Economics* 20, 1988, 293–315.

A. Musacchio, Laws vs. contracts: Shareholder protections and ownership concentration in Brazil, 1890–1950, *Business History Review* 82, 2008, 445–73.

A. Musacchio and S. Lazzarini, *Reinventing State Capitalism: Leviathan in Business, Brazil and beyond*, Harvard University Press, Cambridge, MA, 2014.

A. Musacchio and I. Read, Bankers, industrialists, and their cliques: Elite networks in Mexico and Brazil during early industrialization, *Enterprise and Society* 8, 2007, 842–80.

S. Perkins, Citigroup's shareholder tango in Brazil (A), Case 5-307-502(A) (KEL328), Kellogg School of Management, Northwestern University, 2007.

— Cross-national variations in industry regulation: A factor analytic approach with an application to telecommunications, *Regulation and Governance* 8(1), 2014a, 149–63.

— When does prior experience pay? Institutional experience and the case of the multinational corporation, *Administrative Science Quarterly* 59(1), 2014b, 145–81.

S. Perkins and E. Zajac, Signal or symbol? Interpreting firms' strategic responses to institutional change in the Brazilian stock market, working paper, 2013.

S. Perkins, M. McDonnell and E. Zajac, Fit to be tied: Using contracts strategically to ensure partner performance, working paper, 2012.

S. Perkins, R. Morck and B. Yeung, Innocents abroad: The hazards of international joint ventures with pyramidal groups, *Global Strategy Journal* 4, 2014, 310–30.

R. Plummer, Ruses that spring from Brazil's woes, BBC News, 2005, http://news.bbc.co.uk/2/hi/business/4468042.stm (accessed November 19, 2014).

B. Schneider, Economic liberalization and corporate governance: The resilience of business groups in Latin America, *Comparative Politics* 40, 2008, 379–97.

— A comparative political economy of diversified business groups, or how states organize big business, *Review of International Political Economy* 16, 2009, 178–201.

M. Shaver, W. Mitchell and B. Yeung, The effect of own-firm and other-firm experience on the foreign direct investment survival in the United States, 1987–92, *Strategic Management Journal* 18, 1997, 811–24.

A. Shleifer and R. Vishny, A survey of corporate governance, *Journal of Finance* 52, 1997, 737–83.

A. Shleifer and D. Wolfenzon, Investor protection and equity markets, *Journal of Financial Economics* 66, 2002, 3–27.

A. Smith, *Wealth of Nations*, W. Strahan and T. Cadell, London, 1776.

World Bank, *Doing Business 2013*, 10th edition, 2013, www.doingbusiness.org (accessed November 19, 2014).

S. Zaheer, Overcoming the liability of foreignness, *Academy of Management Review* 38(2), 1995, 341–63.

23

Conclusion

Where next for non-market strategy?

Thomas C. Lawton and Tazeeb S. Rajwani

As David Baron noted in his Foreword to this book, non-market strategies serve one or more of five purposes:

- *rent seeking* (e.g. the continuation of government subsidies);
- *unlocking opportunities* (such as pushing for industry deregulation);
- *defense* (against rivals, non-governmental organization (NGO) criticism, community activism, or government directives);
- *attracting customers* (those who place a premium on environmental protection, social justice, or the protection of rights); and
- *strengthening reputation, building trust, and enhancing legitimacy.*

Throughout this *Companion*, contributors have provided examples of these purposes in principle and practice. Chapters from established and emerging scholars from around the world have provided insights into a wide array of non-market strategy ideas and issues. In this final chapter, we identify and categorize key emergent research opportunities for non-market scholars. In doing so we emphasize four distinct thematics:

- *knowledge;*
- *mechanisms;*
- *context;* and
- *methodologies.*

These emerge from the collective enterprise of the preceding chapters and will be used as sub-headings in this final chapter. We will explore these four subjects so as to shed light on the way ahead for non-market strategy research.

Knowledge

Some of the contributors to this *Companion* have explored non-market knowledge in great depth. For instance, Jean-Philippe Bonardi and Richard Vanden Bergh focus on the role of organizational knowledge about the political environment in explaining firm-level differences in political engagement. They raise the importance of trade associations' non-market knowledge, third-party non-market knowledge, and in-house non-market knowledge. Future research needs to explicate the tacit and implicit aspects of these non-market knowledge types in navigating the different institutional arenas and contexts.

In Chapter 8, Anna John, Tazeeb Rajwani, and Thomas Lawton indirectly highlight the importance of different types of knowledge architectures using political network types – influential and less influential networks or dense or less dense networks – and political information types – research and data roles embedded in task structures using non-market knowledge: that is, policy- versus communication-based roles and responsibilities. Future research needs to look at the balance between policy knowledge and communication knowledge to understand corporate influence on political and social actors in the non-market environment. Studies may want to explore the different combinations and task designs used by firms in roles and responsibilities and how these impact on knowledge utilization.

We find a number of knowledge-based studies already established in the non-market field (Capron and Chatain, 2008; Oliver and Holzinger, 2008). Therefore, we believe that knowledge-based studies broadly using resource-based view (RBV) theory with emphasis on political resources need more attention from scholars in this field. The resource-based view and organizational capability theory have important implications for understanding how political knowledge is integrated, reconfigured, and deployed in the context of non-markets that are fragmented between countries (Lawton et al., 2013). This book complements earlier research on resource and capability views (Bonardi et al., 2006; Oliver and Holzinger, 2008). Implicitly, building on these important studies, future studies may look at political knowledge (tangible and intangible) configurations within different countries that are directly involved in market and non-market simultaneously.

Mechanisms

The contributors to this volume have explored different types of non-market mechanisms. In Chapter 6, Steven McGuire highlighted the importance of power mechanisms and he considered the *primes inter pares* among interest groups for their capacity to mobilize resources in support of policy preferences. Future research in the non-market field could draw on the discipline of international relations (IR), as it provides an alternative perspective for understanding the context of cross-border mechanisms leveraged by firms. IR can help us to understand the growth of private regulatory regimes and the impact of commercial mechanisms on states and societies.

Conversely, David Bach (Chapter 5) investigates the political and public policy mechanisms in helping to understand non-market strategy. He explores how, in the presence of market failures, normal business operations connect the firm's market and non-market environments. Building on his chapter, future studies might want to explore unsuccessful firms or negative market growth – Lehman Brothers, Enron, and Blackberry, amongst others. Studies here may want to explore the failure mechanisms and accountability aspects of these non-market and market forces, as this may shed light on corporate non-market failures, and specifically on the choices made at the top management team level in influencing – or defending the firm from – the public policy process. Moreover, future studies may want to explore how executives adopt responsible socio-political activities in order to avoid failure, as these strategic decisions have positive or negative socio-political impacts.

In Chapter 7, Jonathan Doh and Benjamin Littell trace the growth and development of corporate social responsibility (CSR) mechanisms as a concept in practice and scholarship, noting differing perspectives on the antecedents and objectives of CSR in corporations. They focus especially on strategic views of CSR and the connection to non-market strategy. Drawing on their chapter, future work may need to explore the company-specific and collective approaches to understand impact: for example, how companies leverage partnerships with non-profit organizations to enhance socio-political behaviors (see also Chapter 18, by Eweje and Palakshappa, for similar ideas). Researching collective approaches will ensure we understand how firms create positive non-market impacts through enhancing reputation and instilling trust.

From reputation and trust to relationships, Howard Viney and Paul Baines (Chapter 11) investigate relationship mechanisms based upon the non-market strategic options available to organizations. They find several options simultaneously or systematically can help to exploit opportunities or reduce threats from decisions taken by governments or regulators. Similarly, George White and Thomas Hemphill (Chapter 20) use empirical research on foreign subsidiaries in the Philippines to show that relationships with government actors impact on firm performance. Drawing on these chapters, future studies looking at government relation-based strategies need to explore the regulatory distance and context specificity of performance (Peng and Zhou, 2005). In particular, looking at temporal, context, and the type of relationships should help scholars to understand relational liabilities and relational assets in the non-market, as relationships have costs and benefits in the long run.

Context

The institutional context is open to criticism, as is seen in Chapter 3, by Feinberg, Hill, and Darendeli. Some chapters in this *Companion* provide strong conceptualizations of the different institutional forms offered by management studies and political science (see Chapters 19 and 22). Feinberg, Hill, and Darendeli attempt to address these institutional factors by using different ideas to showcase the various institutional factors. They raise the importance of looking at the institutional conditions to determine their boundaries and causes of institutional voids.

Expanding on various chapters (see Chapter 7), an up-and-coming challenge for non-market scholars is to understand socio-political activity in emerging economies, thus moving beyond the institutional voids perspective outlined by Khanna and Palepu (2005). As developing economies grow and assume greater importance for international business, it is natural to assume that their multi-level institutional arrangements will become more elaborate. This may be due to domestic pressure or derive from the international economy, but it is often a combination of both. Scherer and Palazzo (2011) use the term "political CSR" to describe what they view as the new, activist role of the firm in global governance. However, this role is not new – at least not for Western multinationals (Lawton et al., 2013). The emerging research agenda in non-market governance is to understand how emerging market firms come to act politically and socially. As emerging markets develop greater stakes in the international economy, it seems plausible to suggest that their firms will, like their Western counterparts, come to see socio-political activities as necessary complements to their market strategies. Firms in emerging markets have significant market shares in areas as diverse as mining, construction, solar energy and banking. They will therefore be affected by global governance initiatives. Thus, new work needs to understand how this development leads to new patterns of non-market strategy. Due to context risks in the non-market, future non-market research must not overstate the degree of convergence that emerging markets might achieve with developed economies.

As discussed above, institutional conditions are important considerations for future non-market research. Therefore, institutional uncertainty and risk attributes are important determinants for context boundaries. Jennifer Oetzel and Chang Hoon Oh (Chapter 15) focus on "discontinuous non-market uncertainty." These authors review what major non-market discontinuities are, how they can be characterized, and what factors influence the likelihood that they will affect businesses. They then explore the range of strategic responses available to managers. Rather than emphasizing risk avoidance strategies, they raise the importance of strategies that fit with situations and host country and of using specific contextual conditions in which it might be appropriate for firms to engage either directly or indirectly. Future non-market research might want to explore risk mitigation ideas around "resilience building" in firms and the communities and regions in which they operate.

Still on this subject of context uncertainty, we find uncertainty in political, social, and legal contexts is essential to an understanding of non-market conditions. See here the chapters by Kingsley and Vanden Bergh; Bach; Doh and Littell; Casarin; Tashman, Winn and Rivera; and White and Hemphill (Chapters 4, 5, 7, 9, 17 and 20). For instance, the Philippines, Libya, and Brazil all have political contexts characterized by high political uncertainty, where firms in such industries as mining, oil and gas, and banking use different combinations of non-market strategies to deal with that political risk. Building on those chapters, further non-market research needs to better understand the multilevel regulatory structures, or lack thereof, and non-market contexts to appreciate risk variance in order to explain performance. Furthermore, future studies may explore substitute effects on self-reporting and self-regulation used by firms to maintain their competitive positions in countries with low regulatory or legal compliance and enforcement structures.

While politics plays a large role in judicial contexts, in Chapter 9 Casarin focuses on the firm's non-market strategic behavior in legal arenas to draw attention primarily to judges and policy-makers. Future non-market research may want to explore further the influence of judges and industry policy-makers on firms, as their impact can be positive or negative due to their direct and indirect influence. However, we might also consider diplomats, both national and international. These actors have not been discussed in this book. Exploring this profession may increase understanding of dispute resolutions at the supranational level and how trade missions may facilitate corporate foreign market entry strategies.

Rodrigo Bandeira-de-Mello (Chapter 10) raises the importance of cultural context when exploring the internationalization of multinationals. Indeed, culture and the distance between home and host markets have implications for performance. George White and Thomas Hemphill (Chapter 20) use empirical research into foreign subsidiaries in the Philippines to show how regulatory distance and context specificity impact performance. Future research may want to explore why some firms that underperform at home do well abroad. What home and host country cultural aspects determine the sustainability of performance in different markets? As seen in Chapter 21, where Yusuf Akbar and Maciej Kisilowski explore Central Asia and Eastern Europe, we need to consider the importance of "initiatives." Future research may want to explore proactive and reactive non-market initiatives at the firm level, team level, and individual level to see how firms adapt to different contexts in developed or emerging economies.

From culture to regions, Gabriele Suder (Chapter 19) explores regionalization and its influence on corporate internationalization strategy. The author highlights that political and regulatory actors drive the form of regionalization in close proximity to firms' home markets or through extending those markets. They shape business context and in turn are shaped by these contexts. Hence, the regional nature of the world economy – determined in part by, or overlapping with, regional trade agreements (RTAs) – necessitates a regional strategy that includes non-market action. This non-market strategy used by firms is increasingly multi-layered, multi-venued (national, regional, and international), and multi-networked in scale and scope, and alters the internationalization knowledge available to the firm. With this in mind, future research could explore and map the connectivity between non-market strategy in RTAs and performance gains in corporate internationalization.

Sinziana Dorobantu and Bennet Zelner explore the industry contextual factors of the global electric power supply industry in Chapter 16. They raise the importance of certain strategic industries and their impact on climate change. Peter Tashman, Monika Winn, and Jorge Rivera (Chapter 17) focus on the important aspects of climate change as another contextual condition. They explain that climate change requires more scholars to explore biophysical, industrial–economic, and institutional environments together, especially in relation to the political, social, and technological forces related to climate change. Similarly, Thomas Graf and Carl Kock (Chapter 12) look at environmental management to understand how firms use proactive non-market strategies to manage different stakeholders. Future research might explore the strategic responses to extreme climate change in different parts of the world. Currently, research on environmental factors is growing slowly, so scholars need to find optimal structures and best practices to inform business policies on managing potential high costs emerging from climate change.

Methodologies

This *Companion* has provided numerous novel methodological choices and designs through the various contributions. We also find that there is a need for different qualitative and quantitative methods when exploring non-market strategies, especially in emerging markets. We are aware of the difficulties of obtaining robust and reliable data, particularly in Asia, Africa, the Middle East, and Latin America. Therefore, we believe that more mixed-methods studies need to be conducted in the future. These could be contextualized within different countries to understand the balance between positive and negative non-market activities. This may also help academics to find greater validity and to provide more insight into how firms behave in these contexts.

We suggest that scholars use more single continuous variables to capture responsible and irresponsible non-market action, wherein balance is modeled with a quadratic function that reaches maximum value at an intermediate point. Future research may contrast and evaluate the results obtained when alternative operationalizations of balance are employed.

Conclusion

This chapter highlights the significant progress that has been made in non-market research. *The Routledge Companion to Non-Market Strategy* has been structured around the interrelated concepts identified as themes for understanding the non-market perspective. We found that the body of knowledge on the non-market continues to grow, and that this reflects increasingly uncertain and volatile aspects of the business environment, particularly internationally. At the same time, non-market practices continue to expand in different countries but in more nuanced ways than might be expected. As data processing and power increase, those goods and services cross ever more borders, which in turn means more socio-political actors are involved. The challenge for academics is to keep these shifts in sight as we continue to develop our understanding of non-market strategy. This, in turn, will permit increased integration of market and non-market concepts and processes in management practice.

Bibliography

Bonardi, J. P., Holburn, G. L. F., and Vanden Bergh, R. G. 2006. Non-market strategy performance: evidence from US electric utilities. *Academy of Management Journal* 38: 288–303.

Capron, L. and Chatain, O. 2008. Competitors' resource-oriented strategies: acting on competitors' resources through interventions in factor markets and political markets. *Academy of Management Review* 33: 97–121.

Hillman, A. J. and Hitt, M. A. 1999. Corporate political strategy formulation: a model of approach, participation, and strategy decisions. *Academy of Management Review* 24(4): 825–42.

Khanna, T. and Palepu, K. 2005. Spotting institutional voids in emerging markets. Harvard Business School Background Note 9, 106–114. Cambridge, MA: Harvard Business School.

Lawton, T., McGuire, S., and Rajwani, T. 2013. Corporate political activity in firms: a literature review and research agenda. *International Journal of Management Reviews* 15(1): 86–105.

Oliver, C. and Holzinger, I. 2008. The effectiveness of strategic political management: a dynamic capabilities framework. *Academy of Management Review* 33(2): 496–520.

Peng, M. W. and Zhou, J. Q. 2005. How network strategies and institutional transitions evolve in Asia. *Asia Pacific Journal of Management* 22(4): 321–36.

Scherer, A. G. and Palazzo, G. 2011. The new political role of business in a globalised world: a review of a new perspective on CSR and its implications for the firm, governance and democracy. *Journal of Management Studies* 48: 899–931.

Index

Figures are shown by a reference in *italics* and a table is referenced in **bold**.